D1032095

Theory
and
Research
in
Abnormal
Psychology

edited by

David Rosenhan
Swarthmore College

Perry London
University of
Southern California

Theory

and

Research

in

Abnormal

Psychology

HOLT, RINEHART AND WINSTON, INC.
NEW YORK   CHICAGO   SAN FRANCISCO   ATLANTA   DALLAS
MONTREAL   TORONTO   LONDON   SYDNEY

Library
I.U P.
Indiana, Pa.
157 R725t
c.1

Copyright © 1969 by Holt, Rinehart and Winston, Inc.
All rights reserved
Library of Congress Catalog Card Number: 69–13558
03–074560–8
Printed in the United States of America
1 2 3 4 5 6 7 8 9

Preface

How shall we represent Abnormal Psychology?

By its works, you say?

But by which works, we ask?

For this question, there is no easy answer. Ours is not the first book of papers that has been assembled on abnormal psychology, nor is it likely to be the last. All have been, and will be, useful, not only because they are convenient and because they reduce pressure on libraries, but also because, as collections, they tacitly express a point of view, a philosophy if you will, about psychology in general and abnormal psychology in particular. Perhaps the most direct way to answer the question is to state directly our point of view, the guidelines we used in selecting papers for this book.

We perceive man as a unity and all of psychological science as potentially relevant to the study of man. Such a straightforward, even prettied, statement should not be objectionable to anyone. Yet, in fact, it is a much neglected view.

Students who are especially interested in abnormal psychology, for example, often find little of interest in research that emerges from experimental psychology, genetics, or even personality and social psychology. Psychoanalytic thinkers have more than occasionally suggested that the experimental method is irrelevant to a true understanding of man. And, by the same token, experimental psychologists have often expressed difficulty, indeed disinterest, in relating their ideas and concerns to the domains of abnormal phenomena.

We have little patience with these views, but we do not desire to vigorously refute them here since, in these matters, even the most competent refutation perpetuates difference and artificial division. It seems to us that much benefit can be accrued by broadening the horizon and by seeking to enlarge our comprehension of abnormal phenomena. We have therefore sought to bring together writings from a variety of viewpoints: both psychoanalytic theory and experimental psychology were included if they met our criteria of stimulating rich hypotheses and amplifying understanding of abnormal phenomena.

If normal man is complex, and our understanding of him primitive, abnormal man is neither less complex nor better understood. One should not plunge directly into the study of abnormal psychology without first examining some critical processes and phenomena in the general psychology of learning and emotion and in chemical and genetic processes. Regardless of the way they are categorized or diagnosed people are more alike than different, and the processes that power all of us are more likely to be similar than not. We have therefore devoted a full section to the *dynamics and development of human behavior,* which, we hope, will form a relevant basis for the understanding of abnormal behavior.

We have presented only a fraction of the solid thinking that is emerging in general psychology and in abnormal psychology today because we have had to select works that seemed central and could be fairly presented in this kind of book. But selection was not easy. For example, some of Freud's work is included, but much that we would consider seminal was omitted in favor of material that would increase the scope of the book. The works of Dollard and Miller and their colleagues who attempted to integrate psychoanalytic and learning theories are only minimally represented, and then only in the work of their intellectual heirs, Campbell, Kagan, and Jaynes.

In its short history, psychology has accumulated an impressive array of facts and documentable theories. We could have shown that tremendous accomplishment by simply assembling an array of papers that describe scientific findings of merit. But in addition to what is known

about abnormal phenomena, we also wanted to include the kind of theorizing, observation, and speculation that seems to isolate central problems even though they have not been fully understood. Freud, for example, speculated on a variety of processes which might have accounted for aspects of human behavior. Tomkins' consideration of emotion and commitment and Maddi's compelling description of the existential neurosis are similar speculations. These essays have not the status of fact, but they illuminate critical problems that beg for direct solution or alternative conceptualization. We consider such essays part of the excitement of psychology, and we urge the reader to savor them and to judge for himself whether the steps they take are in promising directions.

Speculation and theory, however exciting and compelling, are not substitutes for evidence. We have tried to include papers that demonstrate that what can be imagined can also be tested and known, and that testing and knowing extend and amplify theory in rich and compelling ways. It had been observed from patients' retrospective reports, for example, that infantile trauma breeds psychological disorder in adulthood. The observation seemed to make sense, but since retrospective reports are often unreliable, one could not be sure. Certainly one could not directly inflict trauma in young children and then observe their adult behaviors. But one could examine the problem with animals, as Campbell and Jaynes did. Their researchers found that infantile trauma (in rats) did in fact directly promote inordinate anxiety in adulthood, but only among rats for whom the trauma had been partially repeated during development. Infantile trauma alone, without subsequent partial repetition, had no effects in adulthood. Their observations are important not only for themselves, but for the way in which they demonstrate the intimate connections between theory and data, how each amplifies the other.

If there has been a further principle of selection, it has been to favor papers that have lively roots in the past, that seem to be part of a forest, over those that seem single trees, even if large and substantial ones. Thus we have included a series of papers on psychotherapy, beginning with a critique of the ordinary insight therapies and ending with a brilliant integrative analysis of insight and behavior therapies. Similarly, sustained attention is given in several papers to the meanings of abnormality and to the various roads by which it can be approached and understood.

The terms "abnormal psychology" and "abnormality" have long been equated with psychopathology and mental illness in the minds of scientists and the public alike. There are good historical reasons for this equation, and as will be seen in several of the papers, it was once thought that there was good scientific reason as well. Recent thinking on the nature of normality and abnormality has broadened our conceptions considerably. There is now genuine reason to believe that a definition of abnormality which includes both positive and negative deviations from the norm may be more descriptive of the phenomena of our concern, more economical and scientifically heuristic. We take up these matters at length in *Foundations of Abnormal Psychology* (New York: Holt, Rinehart and Winston, 1968, Chapters 1 and 5) mainly because our view departs markedly from the traditional ones. This volume reflects again that broadened conception. An entire section is therefore devoted to the positive abnormalities, including such matters as genius, creativity, and moral and altruistic behavior, and another section is concerned with the traditional matters of psychopathology.

We are indebted to the authors, publishers, and scientific organizations who granted permission to reprint these papers. Specific acknowledgments are offered with each paper.

To the extent that there is merit and utility in this volume, much of it is due to the patient efforts of Patricia Warren. Her concern and gentle humor contributed enormously to the pleasure of the undertaking, and her administrative skills, in large matters and the many small ones, to its quality. Our debt to her is great.

Much of the work on this volume was completed when the first author was a member of the Center for Psychological Studies, Educational Testing Service. In addition to acknowledging our debt to the Center for the use of its facilities, we want to particularly thank Joyce Crossland, Ann King, Katherine Mulligan, Betty Clausen, Donna Lembeck, and Lee Sierra for their editorial assistance and for typing both the correspondence necessary to such a volume and the manuscript itself.

David L. Rosenhan
Perry London

December 1968

Contents

Preface   *v*

**Texts in Abnormal Psychology Cross-Referenced
to *Theory and Research in Abnormal Psychology***   *xiv*

Section I   The Development and Dynamics of Human Behavior   *1*

1   Identification and Internalization   *3*

Introduction   *3*

Excerpts from *Group Psychology and the Analysis of the Ego*   *4*
SIGMUND FREUD

The Concept of Identification   *9*
JEROME KAGAN

Effects of Aggressive Cartoons
    on Children's Aggressive Play   *18*
PAUL MUSSEN AND ELDRED RUTHERFORD

2   Affect and Emotion   *23*

Introduction   *23*

The Constructive Role of Violence and Suffering
  for the Individual and for His Society   24
SILVAN S. TOMKINS

Cognitive, Emotional, and Physiological Determinants
  of Emotional State   44
STANLEY SCHACHTER AND JEROME E. SINGER

3   Fear, Anxiety, and Punishment   66

Introduction   66

Anxiety, Pain, and the Inhibition of Distress   67
WILLIAM KESSEN AND GEORGE MANDLER

Punishment   75
RICHARD L. SOLOMON

Reinstatement   92
BYRON A. CAMPBELL AND JULIAN JAYNES

The Origin of Self-criticism   95
JUSTIN ARONFREED

4   The Family and Social Milieu   120

Introduction   120

Some Psychosexual Differences
  between Kibbutz and Nonkibbutz Israeli Boys   121
ALBERT I. RABIN

Parent Discipline and the Child's Moral Development   126
MARTIN L. HOFFMAN AND HERBERT D. SALTZSTEIN

5   The Chemistry and Genetics of Behavior   141

Introduction   141

Biochemical Theories of Schizophrenia: Part I   142
SEYMOUR S. KETY

Biochemical Theories of Schizophrenia: Part II   151
SEYMOUR S. KETY

Of Flies and Men   165
THEODOSIUS DOBZHANSKY

Section II   Personality Dysfunction   177

6   Values: The Meanings of Mental Health and Illness   179

Introduction   *179*

"Sin," the Lesser of Two Evils   *181*
O. HOBART MOWRER

The Myth of Mental Illness   *186*
THOMAS S. SZASZ

Personality Disorder is Disease   *194*
DAVID P. AUSUBEL

"Mental Health" Reconsidered: A Special Case
   of the Problem of Values in Psychology   *201*
M. BREWSTER SMITH

Toward a Modern Approach to Values:
   The Valuing Process in the Mature Person   *211*
CARL R. ROGERS

7   Psychopathology   *221*

Introduction   *221*

The Existential Neurosis   222
SALVATORE R. MADDI

Psychological Deficit in Schizophrenia:
   Affect, Reinforcement, and Concept Attainment   *239*
ARNOLD H. BUSS AND PETER J. LANG

Psychological Deficit in Schizophrenia:
   Interference and Activation   *263*
PETER J. LANG AND ARNOLD H. BUSS

Schizophrenic Patients in the Psychiatric Interview:
   An Experimental Study of Their Effectiveness
   at Manipulation   292
BENJAMIN M. BRAGINSKY AND DOROTHEA D. BRAGINSKY

8   The Nature of Psychotherapy   *299*

Introduction   *299*

The Secrets of the Heart: Insight Therapy   *300*
PERRY LONDON

Critique and Reformulation of "Learning Theory"
   Approaches to Psychotherapy and Neurosis   *316*
LOUIS BREGER AND JAMES L. MCGAUGH

Reply to a "Critique and Reformulation"
   of Behavior Therapy   *339*
S. RACHMAN AND H. J. EYSENCK

Learning Theory and Behavior Therapy:
A Reply to Rachman and Eysenck   344
LOUIS BREGER AND JAMES L. MCGAUGH

Behavior Therapy and Psychotherapy   347
BERNARD WEITZMAN

9   The Effects of Psychotherapy   365

Introduction   365

The Elimination of Children's Fears   367
MARY C. JONES

Fear Reduction Following Observation of a Model   373
JAMES H. GEER AND ALAN TURTELTAUB

Insight versus Desensitization in Psychotherapy
Two Years after Termination   379
GORDON L. PAUL

Desensitization, Suggestibility, and Pseudotherapy   397
PETER J. LANG, A. DAVID LAZOVIK, AND DAVID J. REYNOLDS

Section III   Positive Social Behaviors   407

10   Genius and Creativity   409

Introduction   409

Classification of Men According to Their Reputation   411
FRANCIS GALTON

Classification of Men According to Their Natural Gifts   415
FRANCIS GALTON

Comparison of the Two Classifications   427
FRANCIS GALTON

The Logic of Laughter   434
ARTHUR KOESTLER

The Disposition toward Originality   451
FRANK BARRON

Personality and the Realization of Creative Potential   461
DONALD W. MACKINNON

11   Socially Constructive Character Traits   473

Introduction   473

Generality of Honesty Reconsidered   474
ROGER V. BURTON

Some Origins of Concern for Others   491
DAVID L. ROSENHAN

References Cited   *509*

Name Index   *537*

Subject Index   *545*

Texts in Abnormal Psychology Cross-referenced to *Theory and Research in Abnormal Psychology*

While *Theory and Research in Abnormal Psychology* can itself be used as a text, it is likely to serve primarily as a companion volume of readings for another text. On the following pages, this volume is correlated by author of reading to chapters in the major textbooks in abnormal psychology. Where the author's name is italicized, his article is referred to directly in the textbook. Those authors' names that are not italicized are relevant to the materials in the chapter, even though they have not been directly cited.

BUSS, A. H. *Psychopathology.*
New York: Wiley, 1966.

CHAPTER 1: *Szasz*; Smith; Rogers
CHAPTER 2: Szasz; *Ausubel*; Rogers
CHAPTER 4: Tomkins; Schachter and Singer
CHAPTER 5: Kessen and Mandler
CHAPTER 6: Freud; Kagan; Mussen and Rutherford; Kessen and Mandler; Solomon; Campbell; Mowrer; *Szasz*
CHAPTER 7: Freud; Kagan; Mussen and Rutherford; Aronfreed; Hoffman and Saltzstein; London; Breger and McGaugh (p. 316); Rachman and Eysenck; Breger and McGaugh (p. 344); Weitzman
CHAPTER 8: London; Breger and McGaugh (p. 316); *Rachman and Eysenck*; Breger and McGaugh (p. 344); Weitzman; Jones; Geer; Paul; Lang, Lazovik, and Reynolds
CHAPTER 11: Tomkins; Schachter and Singer; *Lang and Buss*
CHAPTER 12: *Buss and Lang*; Lang and Buss

CHAPTER 13: Buss and Lang; *Lang and Buss*; Braginsky and Braginsky
CHAPTER 14: *Kety*; Dobzhansky
CHAPTER 15: Rabin; Hoffman and Saltzstein
CHAPTER 16: Kety; Dobzhansky

COLEMAN, J. C. *Abnormal psychology and modern life.*
Third Edition. Chicago:
Scott, Foresman, 1964.

CHAPTER 1: *Szasz*; Ausubel; *Smith*; *Rogers*; MacKinnon
CHAPTER 2: Mowrer; Szasz
CHAPTER 3: Freud; Kagan; Tomkins; Schachter and Singer; Kessen and Mandler; Solomon; Campbell and Jaynes
CHAPTER 4: Mussen and Rutherford; Schachter and Singer; Kessen and Mandler; Solomon; Campbell and Jaynes; Rabin; Hoffman and Saltzstein; *Dobzhansky*; *Mowrer*; *Szasz*; Maddi
CHAPTER 6: *Kessen and Mandler*; Solomon; Campbell and Jaynes; Aronfreed; *Mowrer*; *Szasz*; *Rogers*; Maddi
CHAPTER 7: Tomkins; Schachter and Singer
CHAPTER 8: Rabin; Hoffman and Saltzstein; *Kety*; Buss and Lang; Lang and Buss; Braginsky and Braginsky
CHAPTER 9: Rabin; Hoffman and Saltzstein
CHAPTER 12: Galton
CHAPTER 14: London; Breger and McGaugh (p. 316); *Rachman and Eysenck*; Breger and McGaugh (p. 344); Weitzman; Jones; Geer and Turteltaub; Paul; Lang, Lazovik and Reynolds

CHAPTER 15: Rabin; Hoffman and Saltzstein; Dobzhansky; Rosenhan

LONDON, P. AND ROSENHAN, D.
Foundations of abnormal psychology.
New York: Holt, Rinehart and
Winston, 1968.

CHAPTER 1: Mowrer; *Szasz*; Ausubel
CHAPTER 2: Dobzhansky
CHAPTER 3: *Kessen and Mandler*; Solomon; Campbell and Jaynes; Aronfreed
CHAPTER 4: *Freud*; *Kagan*; Mussen and Rutherford; *Tomkins*; *Schachter and Singer*; Kessen and Mandler; *Aronfreed*
CHAPTER 5: Szasz; Smith; Rogers
CHAPTER 6: *Galton*
CHAPTER 7: *Koestler*; *Barron*; *MacKinnon*
CHAPTER 8: *Freud*; Hoffman and Saltzstein; Rogers; Burton; Rosenhan
CHAPTER 9: Mussen and Rutherford; Tomkins; Schachter and Singer; Rabin; Hoffman and Saltzstein; Szasz; Ausubel
CHAPTER 10: Kagan; Kessen and Mandler; Rabin; Hoffman and Saltzstein; Maddi
CHAPTER 11: *Kety*; Maddi; Buss and Lang; Lang and Buss; Braginsky and Braginsky
CHAPTER 12: Hoffman and Saltzstein
CHAPTER 15: Maddi; Buss and Lang; Lang and Buss; Braginsky and Braginsky; *London*; *Breger and McGaugh* (p. 316); *Rachman and Eysenck*; *Breger and McGaugh* (p. 344); Jones; *Paul*; *Lang, Lazovik and Reynolds*
CHAPTER 16: Freud; Kagan; Mussen and Rutherford; Mowrer; Szasz; Ausubel; Smith; Rogers

MAHER, B. A. *Principles of*
psychopathology: An experimental
approach. New York:
McGraw-Hill, 1966.

CHAPTER 2: *Mowrer*; *Szasz*; Ausubel
CHAPTER 3: Solomon; Campbell and Jaynes; Aronfreed
CHAPTER 4: Tomkins; Schachter and Singer; Kessen and Mandler; Kety; Dobzhansky
CHAPTER 5: Kety; Dobzhansky
CHAPTER 6: Solomon
CHAPTER 7: *Kessen and Mandler*
CHAPTER 8: *Aronfreed*
CHAPTER 10: Kety; Dobzhansky

CHAPTER 12: Maddi; Buss and Lang; Lang and Buss; Braginsky and Braginsky
CHAPTER 13: *Kety*; Dobzhansky; *Lang and Buss*
CHAPTER 14: *Buss and Lang*; *Lang and Buss*
CHAPTER 15: Buss and Lang; Lang and Buss
CHAPTER 16: Breger and McGaugh (p. 316); Rachman and Eysenck; Breger and McGaugh (p. 344); Weitzman; Geer and Turteltaub; Lang, Lazovik and Reynolds

KISKER, G. W. *The disorganized*
personality. New York:
McGraw-Hill, 1964.

CHAPTER 1: Szasz; Ausubel; Smith
CHAPTER 2: Mowrer; Szasz
CHAPTER 3: Kety; Dobzhansky; Galton
CHAPTER 4: *Freud*; Mussen and Rutherford; Kessen and Mandler; Solomon; Campbell and Jaynes; Aronfreed
CHAPTER 5: Rabin; Hoffman
CHAPTER 8: Maddi
CHAPTER 9: Kety; Dobzhansky; Buss and Lang; Lang and Buss; Braginsky and Braginsky
CHAPTER 10: Tomkins; Schachter and Singer; *Kety*; Dobzhansky
CHAPTER 15: London; Breger and McGaugh (p. 316); Rachman and Eysenck; Breger and McGaugh (p. 344); Weitzman
CHAPTER 16: Solomon; Maddi; Buss and Lang; Lang and Buss; Braginsky and Braginsky

WHITE, R. W. *The abnormal*
personality. Third Edition.
New York: Ronald Press, 1964.

CHAPTER 1: Freud; Szasz; Ausubel
CHAPTER 3: *Freud*; Kagan; Mussen and Rutherford; Tomkins; Schachter and Singer; Hoffman and Saltzstein
CHAPTER 4: Tomkins; Aronfreed; Hoffman and Saltzstein; Rogers; Burton; Rosenhan
CHAPTER 5: Kessen and Mandler; Solomon; Campbell and Jaynes; Aronfreed
CHAPTER 6: Kessen and Mandler; Solomon; Campbell and Jaynes; Aronfreed
CHAPTER 7: Maddi
CHAPTER 8: London
CHAPTER 9: Breger and McGaugh (p. 316); Rachman and Eysenck; Breger and Mc-

Gaugh (p. 344); Weitzman; Jones; Geer and Turteltaub; Paul; Lang, Lazovik and Reynolds

CHAPTER 11: Tomkins; Schachter and Singer; Kety; Dobzhansky

CHAPTER 12: Kety; Dobzhansky

CHAPTER 13: Kety; Dobzhansky

CHAPTER 15: *Kety*; Dobzhansky; Buss and Lang; Lang and Buss; Braginsky and Braginsky

Theory
and
Research
in
Abnormal
Psychology

The Development and Dynamics of Human Behavior

I

Identification and Internalization

We often fail to appreciate how well socialized even the most antisocial adult is, how responsive all of us are to the demands of the culture we have grown up in. To recognize the extent of everyone's socialization requires sensitivity to the multitude of great and small details that we have learned and that make up the flow of everyday life.

Consider the psychotic. He strikes you as odd, mad if you will, because in some ways his behavior and thinking deviate grossly from those of his fellows. But only a small segment of his total behavior actually deviates very grossly from our own, and it is that segment to which we are sensitive. In most respects he usually remains very much intact. He may, for example, speak sensibly much of the time, eat his meals as others do, partake of common cultural courtesies, and delight in common joys. He may recognize and respond to many of his responsibilities, pay his bills, observe regularities of meals, bath, shaving, and bedtime. It is probably fair to say that,

over a twenty-four-hour period, his behavior is overtly disturbed no more than 10 percent of the time. (If he seems more disturbed than this, we may, knowing that he is troubled during some of his life, be "reading trouble" into the rest of it.) During 90 percent of the time, his acculturation may be indistinguishable from ours. So great is the impact of socialization that even under enormous personal stress, much of it remains intact.

The example of psychosis is relevant here because it serves to underscore the degree to which all of us, regardless of our special status, share a common cultural stamp, which results from the enormous amount of learning that must occur before a man can function effectively in society.

It is not certain whether each of the elements in this immense behavioral-cognitive repertoire is separately acquired through continuous shaping and conditioning or whether more global processes are involved, but an analysis of man's social repertoire suggests that learning is acquired in large chunks. Certainly Sigmund Freud believed this. For him, much learning proceeded from the global process of *identification*, that is, the incorporation of aspects of another's personality into the self. To believe that "I am he" and to act accordingly is to acquire quickly much of the repertoire of another person. As we shall see, the various concepts of identification played major roles in Freud's views, accounting for such diverse matters as his theories of clinical depression, of successful resolution of the Oedipal complex, and of sex role acquisition.

Freud was not very specific about his meaning, and while many theorists could "identify" with the notion of identification, they could not easily stipulate its components. Some found the notion too fuzzy for their scientific tastes. Others responded to Freud's observations, extended them, and sought to examine the concept of identification more precisely. Jerome Kagan's essay follows the latter course. He examines the conditions under which identification occurs and then speculates about what identifi-

cation might be. His views are not uniformly shared by other theorists, but his paper is an important effort at careful delineation of the processes of identification.

So much for theory. How shall we know whether theories of identification are meaningful, in any sense of the word? One aspect of identification theory requires that the child's exposure to a model will eventuate in his imitation of the model. And while in the ordinary course of development, the models in a child's life are his parents, they need not necessarily be. In theory, any person who displays a particular behavior to an attending other might be expected to have some influence on that other, however momentary. In the final paper in this section, Mussen and Rutherford take up this matter with regard to the disinhibition of aggressive behavior. The models they use are cartoon figures, so distant from the kinds of models referred to in earlier papers that one would not expect them to yield substantive findings. Nevertheless, they do, and the evidence constitutes one significant documentation of identification theory.

Group Psychology and the Analysis of the Ego

Sigmund Freud

Identification is known to psycho-analysis as the earliest expression of an emotional

Reprinted from *Group Psychology and the Analysis of the Ego*, Chap. 7, Vol. 23, in *The Complete Psychological Works of Sigmund Freud*, with the permission of Sigmund Freud Copyrights Ltd., The Institute of Psycho-Analysis and Mrs. Alix Strachey, and the Hogarth Press Ltd., and Liveright Publishing Corporation.

tie with another person. It plays a part in the early history of the Oedipus complex. A little boy will exhibit a special interest in his father; he would like to grow like him and be like him, and take his place everywhere. We may say simply that he takes his father as his ideal. This behaviour has nothing to do with a passive or feminine attitude towards his father (and towards males in general); it is on the contrary typically masculine. It fits in very well with the Oedipus complex, for which it helps to prepare the way.

At the same time as this identification with his father, or a little later, the boy has begun to develop a true object-cathexis towards his mother according to the attachment [anaclitic] type.[1] He then exhibits, therefore, two psychologically distinct ties: a straightforward sexual object-cathexis towards his mother and an identification with his father which takes him as his model. The two subsist side by side for a time without any mutual influence or interference. In consequence of the irresistible advance towards a unification of mental life, they come together at last; and the normal Oedipus complex originates from their confluence. The little boy notices that his father stands in his way with his mother. His identification with his father then takes on a hostile colouring and becomes identical with the wish to replace his father in regard to his mother as well. Identification, in fact, is ambivalent from the very first; it can turn into an expression of tenderness as easily as into a wish for someone's removal. It behaves like a derivative of the first, *oral* phase of the organization of the libido, in which the object that we long for and prize is assimilated by eating and is in that way annihilated as such. The cannibal, as we know, has remained at this standpoint; he has a devouring affection for his enemies and only devours people of whom he is fond.[2]

The subsequent history of this identification with the father may easily be lost sight of. It may happen that the Oedipus complex becomes inverted, and that the father is taken as the object of a feminine attitude, an object from which the directly sexual instincts look for satisfaction; in that event the identification with the father has become the precursor of an object-tie with the father. The same holds good, with the necessary substitutions, of the baby daughter as well.[3]

It is easy to state in a formula the distinction between an identification with the father and the choice of the father as an object. In the first case one's father is what one would like to *be*, and in the second he is what one would like to *have*. The distinction, that is, depends upon whether the tie attaches to the subject or to the object of the ego. The former kind of tie is therefore already possible before any sexual object-choice has been made. It is much more difficult to give a clear metapsychological representation of the distinction. We can only see that identification endeavours to mould a person's own ego after the fashion of the one that has been taken as a model.

Let us disentangle identification as it occurs in the structure of a neurotic symptom from its rather complicated connections. Supposing that a little girl (and we will keep to her for the present) develops the same painful symptom as her mother—for instance, the same tormenting cough. This may come about in various ways. The identification may come from the Oedipus complex; in that case it signifies a hostile desire on the girl's part to take her mother's place, and the symptom expresses her object-love towards her father, and brings about a realization, under the influence of a sense of guilt, of her desire to take her mother's place: 'You wanted to be your mother, and now you *are*—anyhow so far as your sufferings are concerned.' This is the complete mechanism of the structure

---

[1] [See Section II of Freud's paper on narcissism (1914c).]
[2] See my *Three Essays* (1905d) [*Standard Ed.*, 7, 198] and Abraham (1916).

[3] [The 'complete' Oedipus complex, comprising both its 'positive' and its 'negative' forms, is discussed by Freud in Chapter III of *The Ego and the Id* (1923b).]

of a hysterical symptom. Or, on the other hand, the symptom may be the same as that of the person who is loved; so, for instance, Dora[4] imitated her father's cough. In that case we can only describe the state of things by saying *that identification has appeared instead of object-choice, and that object-choice has regressed to identification*. We have heard that identification is the earliest and original form of emotional tie; it often happens that under the conditions in which symptoms are constructed, that is, where there is repression and where the mechanisms of the unconscious are dominant, object-choice is turned back into identification—the ego assumes the characteristics of the object. It is noticeable that in these identifications the ego sometimes copies the person who is not loved and sometimes the one who is loved. It must also strike us that in both cases the identification is a partial and extremely limited one and only borrows a single trait from the person who is its object.

There is a third particularly frequent and important case of symptom formation, in which the identification leaves entirely out of account any object-relation to the person who is being copied. Supposing, for instance, that one of the girls in a boarding school has had a letter from someone with whom she is secretly in love which arouses her jealousy, and that she reacts to it with a fit of hysterics; then some of her friends who know about it will catch the fit, as we say, by mental infection. The mechanism is that of identification based upon the possibility or desire of putting oneself in the same situation. The other girls would like to have a secret love affair too, and under the influence of a sense of guilt they also accept the suffering involved in it. It would be wrong to suppose that

they take on the symptom out of sympathy. On the contrary, the sympathy only arises out of the identification, and this is proved by the fact that infection or imitation of this kind takes place in circumstances where even less pre-existing sympathy is to be assumed than usually exists between friends in a girls' school. One ego has perceived a significant analogy with another upon one point—in our example upon openness to a similar emotion; an identification is thereupon constructed on this point, and, under the influence of the pathogenic situation, is displaced on to the symptom which the one ego has produced. The identification by means of the symptom has thus become the mark of a point of coincidence between the two egos which has to be kept repressed.

What we have learned from these three sources may be summarized as follows. First, identification is the original form of emotional tie with an object; secondly, in a regressive way it becomes a substitute for a libidinal object-tie, as it were by means of introjection of the object into the ego; and thirdly, it may arise with any new perception of a common quality shared with some other person who is not an object of the sexual instinct. The more important this common quality is, the more successful may this partial identification become, and it may thus represent the beginning of a new tie.

We already begin to divine that the mutual tie between members of a group is in the nature of an identification of this kind, based upon an important emotional common quality; and we may suspect that this common quality lies in the nature of the tie with the leader. Another suspicion may tell us that we are far from having exhausted the problem of identification, and that we are faced by the process which psychology calls 'empathy [*Einfühlung*]' and which plays

4 In my 'Fragment of an Analysis of a Case of Hysteria' (1905e) [*Standard Ed.*, 7, 82–3].

the largest part in our understanding of what is inherently foreign to our ego in other people. But we shall here limit ourselves to the immediate emotional effects of identification, and shall leave on one side its significance for our intellectual life.

Psycho-analytic research, which has already occasionally attacked the more difficult problems of the psychoses, has also been able to exhibit identification to us in some other cases which are not immediately comprehensible. I shall treat two of these cases in detail as material for our further consideration.

The genesis of male homosexuality in a large class of cases is as follows.[5] A young man has been unusually long and intensely fixated upon his mother in the sense of the Oedipus complex. But at last, after the end of puberty, the time comes for exchanging his mother for some other sexual object. Things take a sudden turn: the young man does not abandon his mother, but identifies himself with her; he transforms himself into her, and now looks about for objects which can replace his ego for him, and on which he can bestow such love and care as he has experienced from his mother. This is a frequent process, which can be confirmed as often as one likes, and which is naturally quite independent of any hypothesis that may be made as to the organic driving force and the motives of the sudden transformation. A striking thing about this identification is its ample scale; it remoulds the ego in one of its important features—in its sexual character—upon the model of what has hitherto been the object. In this process the object itself is renounced —whether entirely or in the sense of being preserved only in the unconscious is a question outside the present discussion.

Identification with an object that is renounced or lost, as a substitute for that object—introjection of it into the ego— is indeed no longer a novelty to us. A process of the kind may sometimes be directly observed in small children. A short time ago an observation of this sort was published in the *Internationale Zeitschrift für Psychoanalyse*. A child who was unhappy over the loss of a kitten declared straight out that now he himself was the kitten, and accordingly crawled about on all fours, would not eat at table, etc.[6]

Another such instance of introjection of the object has been provided by the analysis of melancholia,[7] an affection which counts among the most notable of its exciting causes the real or emotional loss of a loved object. A leading characteristic of these cases is a cruel self-depreciation of the ego combined with relentless self-criticism and bitter self-reproaches. Analyses have shown that this disparagement and these reproaches apply at bottom to the object and represent the ego's revenge upon it. The shadow of the object has fallen upon the ego, as I have said elsewhere.[8] The introjection of the object is here unmistakably clear.

But these melancholias also show us something else, which may be of importance for our later discussions. They show us the ego divided, fallen apart into two pieces, one of which rages against the second. This second piece is the one which has been altered by introjection and which contains the lost object. But the piece which behaves so cruelly is not unknown to us either. It comprises the conscience, a critical agency within the ego, which even in normal times takes

---

[5] [See Chapter III of Freud's study on Leonardo (1910c). For other mechanisms of the genesis of homosexuality see pp. 158 f. and 231 f.]

[6] Marcuszewicz (1920).

[7] [Freud habitually uses the term 'melancholia' for conditions which would now be described as 'depression'.]

[8] See 'Mourning and Melancholia' (1917e).

up a critical attitude towards the ego, though never so relentlessly and so unjustifiably. On previous occasions[9] we have been driven to the hypothesis that some such agency develops in our ego which may cut itself off from the rest of the ego and come into conflict with it. We have called it the 'ego ideal', and by way of functions we have ascribed to it self-observation, the moral conscience, the censorship of dreams, and the chief influence in repression. We have said that it is the heir to the original narcissism in which the childish ego enjoyed self-sufficiency; it gradually gathers up from the influences of the environment the demands which that environment makes upon the ego and which the ego cannot always rise to; so that a man, when he cannot be satisfied with his ego itself, may nevertheless be able to find satisfaction in the ego ideal which has been differentiated out of the ego. In delusions of observation, as we have further shown, the disintegration of this agency has become patent, and has thus revealed its origin in the influence of superior powers, and above all of parents.[10] But we have not forgotten to add that the amount of distance between this ego ideal and the real ego is very variable from one individual to another, and that with many people this differentiation within the ego does not go further than with children.

It is now easy to define the difference between identification and such extreme developments of being in love as may be described as "fascination" or "bondage".[11] In the former case the ego has enriched itself with the properties of the object, it has 'introjected' the object into itself, as Ferenczi [1909] expresses it. In the second case it is impoverished, it has surrendered itself to the object, it has substituted the object for its own most important constituent. Closer consideration soon makes it plain, however, that this kind of account creates an illusion of contradistinctions that have no real existence. Economically there is no question of impoverishment or enrichment; it is even possible to describe an extreme case of being in love as a state in which the ego has introjected the object into itself. Another distinction is perhaps better calculated to meet the essence of the matter. In the case of identification the object has been lost or given up; it is then set up again inside the ego, and the ego makes a partial alteration in itself after the model of the lost object. In the other case the object is retained, and there is a hypercathexis of it by the ego and at the ego's expense. But here again a difficulty presents itself. Is it quite certain that identification presupposes that object-cathexis has been given up? Can there be no identification while the object is retained? And before we embark upon a discussion of this delicate question, the perception may already be beginning to dawn on us that yet another alternative embraces the real essence of the matter, namely, *whether the object is put in the place of the ego or of the ego ideal.*

[9] In my paper on narcissim (1914c) and in 'Mourning and Melancholia' (1917e).
[10] Section III of my paper on narcissism.

[11] [The 'bondage' of love had been discussed by Freud in the early part of his paper on 'The Taboo of Virginity' (1918a).]

The Concept of Identification[1]

Jerome Kagan

Several years ago Sanford (1955) presented an analysis of the concept of identification. In brief, Sanford suggested that the term be applied to situations in which "an individual may be observed to respond to the behavior of other people or objects by initiating in fantasy or reality the same behavior himself . . . the individual strives to behave in a way that is exactly like that of the object" (1955, p. 109). Sanford further suggested that the motive for this imitative behavior was a threat to the person's self esteem. By limiting the term "identification" to those imitative behavioral sequences in which the motivation for the act was anxiety over self esteem, Sanford emphasized two points: (*a*) mere similarity in overt behavior between a subject and a model was not necessarily a measure of identification, and (*b*) the motive for the imitative behavior was one of the defining characteristics of an indentificatory response.

The various behavioral phenomena which have been labeled "identification"

Reprinted from *Psychological Review*, 1958, vol. 65, pp. 296–305 with the permission of the American Psychological Association and the author.

[1] This research was supported, in part, by a research grant (M-1260) from the National Institute of Mental Health of the National Institute of Health, United States Public Health Service. The views of Wesley Allinsmith, Vaughn J. Crandall, Leonard M. Lansky, and Howard A. Moss are especially acknowledged. A major stimulus for the present essay was a workshop in parent-child relations supported by USPHS Grant 1649 and held at the Merrill-Palmer School, Detroit, Michigan, July 14–27, 1957.

differ in their manifest properties and motivations. The following four classes of behavior have been described as related to the process of identification because they all can lead to similarities in behavior between a subject and a model.

Imitation Learning

This term refers to the initiation and practice of certain responses (gestures, attitudes, speech patterns, dress, etc.) which are not subject to prohibition by the social environment and which are assumed to be the result of an attempt to imitate a model. The behavior has been labeled either "matched-dependent behavior" or "copying" by Miller and Dollard (1941). Miller and Dollard posit that initially the imitative act occurs by chance and the act can only be reinforced if some drive is reduced following the execution of the response. According to this view only direct reward from the social environment, like praise or affection, can strengthen the person's tendency to imitate a model. Mowrer (1950) distinguishes between developmental and defensive identification. In the former process, the person imitates or reproduces the behavior of a model in order to "reproduce bits of the beloved and longed-for parent" (1950, p. 615). Mowrer suggests that most imitation of a model is the result of the desire to reproduce responses which have acquired secondary reward value through association with a nurturant and affectionate model. Thus, Mowrer emphasizes the self-rewarding aspect of certain imitative acts as opposed to Miller and Dollard's emphasis on direct reward from the social environment.

Prohibition Learning

This term refers to the adoption and practice of the prohibitions of the parents and parent substitutes. The acquisition of these prohibitions bears some relation to the process of superego development as described by psychoanalytic theory (A. Freud, 1937; S. Freud, 1933, 1935; Knight, 1940). Several investigators have suggested that a major motivation for the acquisition of some prohibition is anxiety over anticipated loss of love (Kagan, 1958; Knight, 1940; Mowrer, 1950; Sanford, 1955; Sears, Maccoby, & Levin, 1957). Sanford labeled this process "introjection" and suggested that the learning and maintenance of this class of behavior might be explained without use of the concept of identification.

Identification with the Aggressor

This phrase refers to the adoption of behaviors which are similar to those of an aggressive or threatening model. The motivation for this "imitation" is assumed to be anxiety over anticipated aggression or domination by the threatening model. It is difficult to explain this behavior as a product of either prohibition or imitation learning, since the motive and reinforcement do not seem related to anxiety over anticipated loss of love or desire for a direct, social reward like praise or affection. Anna Freud (1937) has labeled this phenomenon "identification with the aggressor," Mowrer has called this process "defensive identification" (as distinct from developmental identification), and Sanford has suggested that the term "identification proper" be restricted to this class of behavior.

Vicarious Affective Experience

This phrase refers to the experience of positive or negative affect on the part of a person as a result of an event which has occurred to a model. Salient examples of this phenomenon are (a) a child's elation or depression at learning that his parent is a success or failure, or (b) a mother's elation following the success of her child in school. This phenomenon of vicarious, affective experience has been attributed to a person's identification with a model, but this affective response has been difficult to explain and often neglected by psychologists investigating the identification process. These four phenomena (imitation learning, prohibition learning, identification with the aggressor, and vicarious, affective experience) appear to be mediated by different motives and rewards, and an analysis of each of them is one purpose of this paper.[2]

In different contexts, social scientists have used the term "identification" to refer to three different sets of variables: (a) the process of identification; (b) individual differences in the content of the behaviors, motives, and attitudes acquired as a result of the identification process; and (c) the differential effect of various models that are used during the identification process (S. Freud, 1933, 1935, 1949; Gray & Klaus, 1956; Kagan, 1956; Knight, 1940; Lazowick, 1955; Maccoby & Wilson, 1957; Martin, 1954; Seward, 1954; Stoke, 1950). This paper recognizes the relevance of the model and content dimensions but is primarily concerned with the process of

[2] In an unpublished paper presented at a symposium at Harvard University in 1957, Bronfrenbrenner described three types of identification: (a) anaclitic identification, (b) identification with a source of power, and (c) identification through reinforcement of a role model. These three terms are similar in meaning to the present phrases of prohibition learning, identification with the aggressor, and imitation learning, respectively.

identification, and will attempt to analyze this process in behavioral terms. It is suggested that the process remains the same regardless of the models used or the specific behavioral content that is acquired as a result of an identification.

Definitions of Identification

The concept of identification originated in psychoanalytic theory, and Freud made a distinction between primary and secondary identification (S. Freud, 1933, 1935, 1949). Primary identification referred to the initial, undifferentiated perception of the infant in which an external object was perceived as part of the self, while secondary identification began after the child had discriminated a world of objects separate from the self. Freud implied in his later writings that the process of secondary identification was motivated primarily by the motives and anxieties created by the oedipal situation. In order to reduce the anxiety over anticipated aggression or rejection from the same-sex parent and obtain vicariously the affection of the opposite-sex parent, the child identified with the former. Identification was described by Freud as "the endeavor to mould a person's own ego after the fashion of one that has been taken as a model (S. Freud, 1949, p. 63).

Mowrer's concept of "defensive identification," Sanford's definition of "identification proper," and Anna Freud's description of "identification with the aggressor" are all related to the earlier psychoanalytic hypothesis that the threat value of the same-sex parent motivated the child to identify with him in order to reduce the anxiety associated with this threat. However, it is suggested that an individual may identify with a model not only to reduce anxiety over anticipated aggression from a model but also to experience or obtain positive goal states which he perceives that the model

commands. The thesis of this paper is that the motivation to command or experience desired goal states of a model is salient in the development and maintenance of an identification.[3] It will be suggested later that two major goal states involved in identification behavior are (*a*) mastery of the environment and (*b*) love and affection. However, it is not implied that these are the only goals which an individual desires to command.

Definition

Identification is defined as an acquired, cognitive response within a person (S). The content of this response is that some of the attributes, motives, characteristics, and affective states of a model (M) are part of S's psychological organization. The major implication of this definition is that the S may react to events occurring to M as if they occurred to him.

The Acquisition and Maintenance of an Identification

Although identification has been defined as a cognitive response, it is not implied that the content of the response is available to consciousness or easily verbalized. Thus the terms "cognitive response," "belief," "wish," or "assumption" will be used in this text to include cognitive processes not always available through verbal report. Identification is not viewed as an all-or-none process. Identification is a response that can vary in strength and there will be differences in the degree to which an S believes that the characteristics of a model,

---

[3] It is assumed that anticipation of a positive goal state is associated with the anticipation of a change in affect, and thus the phrase "experience goal states of the model" will be used synonymously with the phrase "experience affective states of the model." This assumption agrees with McClelland's definition of a motive as an "anticipation of a change in affective state" (1951, p. 466).

whether assets or liabilities, belong to him. In addition, the S may become identified, to differing degrees, with a variety of models. The motives and reinforcements that are involved in the acquisition and maintenance of this cognitive response are elaborated in the following assumptions.

Assumption 1

Initially the S perceives that the M possesses or commands goals and satisfactions that the S desires. This perception leads to a wish to possess these desired goal states.

Assumption 2

The wish to command the goal states of the M leads to the desire to possess the characteristics of the M because S believes that if he were similar to the M he would command the desired goals. That is, the S assumes that the more similarity there is between the S and M the more likely S is to possess or command the desired goal states of the M.

To illustrate, let the S be a child and the M a mother, although S and M could be an adolescent boy and the leader of a group, or a girl and her older sister. The child perceives that the mother can feed the child, restrict the child, obtain articles out of the child's reach, punish the child, etc. Thus, to the S, the M appears to command desired skills and goal states. The discrepancy between the child's perception of his inability to obtain these desired goals and his perception of the more adequate adult elicits the wish to possess or control those goals which he perceives that M commands. The perceptions of the child are subject to distortion, and the child may exaggerate the degree to which M commands desired goals. It was assumed (Assumption 2) that the

wish to command these goal states led to the expectation that if S possessed M's characteristics he would also command these desired goals. There often is direct reinforcement of the belief that to "be similar to" a model is equivalent to possessing his positive attributes. Often, the social environment tells the child directly that he is similar to a parent in certain characteristics, and this communication may be contiguous in time with statements related to some of the model's desired goal states. For example, parents and relatives may tell the child "You have your father's eyes," and often add, "You'll grow up to be big and strong just like Daddy." It is suggested that these statements which associate similarities in external attributes with command of desired goal states have an important effect on the child's learning about himself, and lead the child to the expectation that to be similar to the model is equivalent to possessing his positive and desirable attributes.

Assumption 3

The identification response (i.e., "some of the characteristics of the model are mine") is reinforced each time S perceives or is told that he is similar to the M. One type of reinforcement for the identification response occurs when an S is told directly that he and the M are similar in temperament or appearance. It is suggested that a second type of reinforcement for this cognitive response is S's own perception of similarity to the M. Once again, consider the case of the small child and his parent. Although the child may perceive marked differences in size, strength, and skills between himself and the M, he may perceive a similarity in affective states, such as joy, anger, or sadness. The importance of the perception of similarities in affective states between the S and M is stressed because a major motive for identification is a desire to experience positive affective states of the model. Thus, perception of similarity in affect is assumed to have saliency as a reinforcement. If the parent becomes angry, sad, or happy and communicates these affects to the child, the child has the opportunity to perceive that he and the M experience similar feelings. This perception reinforces the belief that there is similarity between the S and M. In addition to similarity in affective states, perception of similarities in external characteristics will reinforce the identification response. With specific reference to the child-parent relation, it is assumed that perception of similarities in sexual anatomy, dress, amount and distribution of hair, and other external attributes are potential reinforcements of the identification. Thus, while the identification response is being learned, the major reinforcements for the response are perceptions of similarity between the S and M.[4] Freud suggested that perceptions of similarity strengthen an identification, for he wrote,

> Identification . . . may arise with every new perception of a common quality shared with some other person who is not an object of the sexual instinct. The more important this common quality is, the more successful may this partial identification become, and it may thus represent the beginning of a new tie (1949, p. 65).

[4] It is suggested that the concept of identification has not yielded to a behavioral analysis because the notion of social reinforcement has been viewed as a specific action directed at an individual by a reinforcing agent. There has been a tendency to overlook the possibility that a perception, fantasy, or thought may be a potential reinforcement of a response. A recent experimental finding by Estes and Johns (1958) supports the hypothesis that a person's perception of a situation, even though objectively inaccurate, can reinforce his subsequent behavior.

Assumption 4

In order for the identification belief to be maintained, the S must not only perceive similarity between the S and M but he also must experience some of the desired, affective goal states of the M. Thus, if the M were successful or happy and S believed that M was experiencing positive affect, the S would also feel positive affect appropriate to the success, and this experience would reinforce his identification. The S also may experience affect appropriate to events occurring to M as a result of the expectation that the social environment will respond to him the same way it responds to the M. That is, when the S has developed some degree of identification with the M he may anticipate that when the social environment praises or rewards the M, it will behave similarly to him. If, on the other hand, the M were sad or criticized, S might experience negative affect because of the identification belief that he and the M were similar and the expectation that the environment might react to him as it did to M. However, if no vicarious command of desired goals or positive affect were experienced as a result of the identification, then the response should extinguish just as any other habit does in the absence of positive reinforcement.[5] That is, some degree of identification should be maintained as long as S perceives that the M commands desired goals. When the S no longer perceives the M in this fashion, then both the motivation for the identification and

[5] This view of identification suggests a measurement operation which differs from the usual practice of assessing similarities in behavior between an S and an M. One measure of degree of identification would be the degree to which an S's affective state or behavior was influenced as a result of events that occurred to an M. That is, praise or criticism of an M in S's presence should lead to corresponding changes in the affective state of an S who was identified with the M.

the intensity of the positive reinforcement should decrease.

The Acquisition of Behavior Similar to a Model: The Motives for Imitation, Identification, and Prohibition Learning

Since perceptions of similarity between the S and M reinforce the identification response, the S may imitate the M during the acquisition phase of an identification in order to increase the degree of similarity. It is acknowledged that the social environment rewards imitative behaviors with affection and praise, and these direct, social reinforcements may strengthen the tendency to imitate adults independently of any identification motives. However, it is suggested, along with Sears *et al.* (1957), that direct, social reinforcement of imitative behavior cannot account for all of the imitative responses that the S initiates. A four-year-old child may simulate adult behaviors when the child is alone or in situations where the parents discourage or punish the imitative response. However, despite the punishment or absence of social reward for some imitative behaviors, the behavior continues to be practiced. Sears *et al.* call this behavior "role practice" and assume that it is motivated by the "desire to reproduce pleasant experiences" (1957, p. 370). Consider the three-year-old girl who plays the role of mother alone in her room. It is hypothesized that a potential reinforcement for this behavior is the creation, in fantasy, of perceptual similarity between the behaviors of the S and M. This perception strengthens S's identification with the M and allows S to share vicariously some of the positive goal states which M commands.

A somewhat different phenomenon is the behavior called "identification with the aggressor" by A. Freud or "defensive identifications" by Mowrer. Anna Freud describes a girl who was afraid of ghosts and suddenly began to make peculiar gestures as she ran in the dark. She told her brother, "there is no need to be afraid, you just have to pretend that you're the ghost who might meet you" (1937, p. 119). The present theory assumes that the child desired the threatening power of the feared object and this motive elicited the imitative behavior. The fantasied perception of similarity to the feared model gave S a vicarious feeling of power and reduced her anxiety over attack. It is suggested that "identification with the aggressor" does not differ from other identification responses with respect to the basic mechanism of acquisition but does involve a specific motive and goal state. Identification with the aggressor involves a specific relationship between the S and M in which S fears the M. Thus, S desires the aggressive power or threat value of the M in order to reduce his own anxiety over anticipated attack. It may be misleading to classify "identification with the aggressor" as qualitatively different from other identificatory behavior merely because the motive and goal differ from those involved in other identifications.

A third motive which can lead to behavioral similarity between an S and M is anxiety over anticipated loss of love or nurturance. It is suggested that many social prohibitions which the M practices are learned by the S in situations in which this anxiety motivates the acquisition and maintenance of the response. The reinforcement for the learned prohibition is continued acceptance and a consequent reduction in anxiety over rejection. The research of Sears *et al.* (1957) suggests a relationship between "high conscience" in a child and a pattern in which the mother is nurturant and uses withdrawal of love as a disciplinary technique. In summary, any one response which is imitative of a model may be mediated by three different motive-reinforcement sequences, and in many instances all three may be involved in producing behavioral similarity between an S and M.[6] Thus, "eating neatly," "getting good grades," or "being nonaggressive" could be motivated by the desire for praise as in imitation learning, by anxiety over loss of love as in prohibition learning, or by the desire to create perceptual similarity between the S and M as in identification. Thus, mere similarity in overt behavior between an S and M may not be the most sensitive measure of degree of identification.

At a more speculative level, it is suggested that the behaviors which have been called "self actualizing" (1939) could be motivated and reinforced by a desire for perceptual similarity to an M and be an indication of early identification tendencies. Even the most orthodox supporters of the importance of simple imitation learning find it difficult to explain the child's initial imitations of a model. Once the child has begun to imitate a model it is likely that praise and recognition from adults could maintain this behavior. However, why does the child suddenly want to dress himself, sit on the toilet alone, or put on Daddy's shoes? It is difficult to account for the initial display of this imitative behavior, and the term "self actualization" implies that the child has some biological drive to use his potentialities. This hypothesis seems no more parsimonious than the suggestion that the initiation of these "self actualizing" behaviors is motivated by S's desire to create perceptual similarity between himself and a model.

[6] In a manuscript being prepared for publication, H. Kelman suggests that the response of conformity to the attitudes of another person can be mediated by three different motives. His analysis of conformity parallels the present discussion of imitative behavior.

Two Goals Motivating Identification: Mastery and Love

It has been assumed that S's desire to command certain goal states motivates his identification with a model. It is suggested, for the child especially, that two important goal states that the S desires to command are (a) a feeling of power or mastery over the environment and (b) love and affection. Attainment of these goals should lead to diminution in anxiety over helplessness or loneliness. The young child perceives that he is not able to gratify all of his needs while the parental model is perceived as more capable of dealing with the environment. This discrepancy between the S's perception of his own relative helplessness and the power that he perceives M to possess motivates the wish to have M's power and the search for perceptions of similarity between himself and the M.

Unfortunately, there are no empirical studies which directly test these hypotheses because most of the research on identification has used similarities in behavior between an S and M as the measure of identification. However, there are some results which are at least consistent with the view that the child identifies with the more powerful parent and the one who is perceived to command important sources of gratification. Payne and Mussen (1956) reported that adolescent boys who perceived the father as rewarding on projective tests were more highly identified with the father (based on similar answers to a personality inventory) than boys who pictured their fathers as nonrewarding. In addition, boys with dominant and "masculine" mothers tended to be poorly identified with the father. P. S. Sears (1953) reported a finding that is more difficult to explain without use of the concept of identification. She found, in a doll-play situation, that kindergarten girls used the mother doll as agent significantly more often than the father doll, while boys used both mother and father dolls with more nearly equal frequency. Since the mother is initially the major controller of gratifications for both sexes, one might expect an initial identification with her for both boys and girls. P. S. Sears (1953) also reports that the kindergarten boys who used the mother doll most often had mothers who were (a) more nurturant than the father, (b) more critical of the father, and (c) more restrictive of the child's mobility outside the home. This result is consistent with the hypothesis that the child is predisposed to identify with the parental model who is perceived as controlling important goal states.

A study of Maccoby and Wilson (1957) furnishes more direct support for the present hypotheses. The authors showed movies to seventh grade boys and girls and then determined the protagonist with whom the child identified. The most significant result was that a "boy's choice of screen character (the one with whom he was presumed to identify) is more closely related to the social class level *to which he aspires* than to the level his family currently occupies" (1957, p. 79). This result suggests that the child identified with models who commanded desired goals.

A second goal state which may motivate identification is the desire for nurturance and affection. In addition to Freud's classical hypothesis that the child identified with the same-sex parent in order to receive vicariously the affection of the opposite-sex parent, there are situations in which nonparental models command sources of affection. The relation between siblings is such a situation, and the younger child may identify with an older sibling if the former perceives that the latter commands parental affection. The research of Helen Koch (1956) indirectly supports this hypothesis. She

reported that school-age boys with older sisters tended to develop more feminine attributes than boys with older brothers. On the other hand, girls with older brothers tend to be more masculine than girls with older sisters. In the experiment of Maccoby and Wilson, described earlier, the authors reported that girls were more likely than boys to recall movie content involving boy-girl interaction while boys were superior on recall of aggressive acts by the hero. If one assumes that the need for affection is stronger for girls than for boys, and that the recalled content is influenced by the model chosen for identification, then these results suggest that the specific goal states desired by the S determine the models chosen for identification.

Factors Influencing the Strength of Identification

The strength of the identification habit, following a basic behavioral law, should be a function of the strength of the motive and the quality and frequency of the reinforcement (1943). It would be predicted, therefore, that the most intense identification would occur when the S had strong needs for love and power, felt incapable of gratifying these motives through his own skills, and perceived similarity between himself and an M who commanded these goals. Utilizing this hypothesis, two generalized predictions can be made concerning the strength of identification for different ages and models.

1. The strength of identification tendencies should decrease with age because, in general, the individual's ability to gratify his needs for mastery and love through his own behavior, rather than through a vicarious mechanism, should increase with development. Thus, the identifications of a young child should be more intense than the identifications of older individuals.

2. An identification with an M with whom S was in direct contact should be stronger than with an M with whom S was not in contact, assuming that the motivation for identification was constant and the models were perceived as equally potent. This statement is based on the assumption that the reinforcements of perceived similarity are stronger when S perceives the affects and attributes of the M directly as opposed to instances in which he is merely told that he is similar to the M. Thus, degree of identification with a father with whom S was in contact should be greater than with an imagined fantasy father whom S had never seen. Only very indirect evidence is available to support this prediction. However, reports by P. S. Sears (1951) and R. R. Sears, Pintler, & P. S. Sears, (1946) suggest that absence of the father from the home tends to decrease the degree of "masculine" doll play in preschool boys while this experience has little effect on the doll play of girls. The results are open to alternative interpretations but are not inconsistent with the present hypothesis.

SUMMARY

This paper has attempted to analyze the concept of identification and place the concept within a learning-theory framework. Identification was defined as an acquired, cognitive response. The content of this response was that some of the characteristics of a model belonged to the individual and the individual behaved as if some of the characteristics and affective states of the model belonged to him. Identification was not viewed as an all-or-none process. An identification can vary in strength and the individual can identify, to differing degrees, with a variety of models. The motive for the acquisition and maintenance of the identification response was a desire for the positive goal states commanded by the model, and mastery of the environment and love-nurturance were suggested as two important goals. The reinforcement for the acquisition of the identification was perceived similarity in attributes between the person and the model. Thus, the person may strive to imitate aspects of the model's behavior in order to create perceptual similarity between himself and the model. Once the identification was established, the individual behaved as if the goal states of the model belonged to him and the positive affect derived from this vicarious sharing of desired goal states helped to maintain the identification.

It was suggested that the usual emphasis on similarities in overt behavior between an individual and a model is not the best measure of identification, since the motives and reinforcements involved in imitation and prohibition learning could also explain similarities in behavior between two people. A differentiation of imitative behavior based on imitation learning, prohibition learning, and identification was attempted.

Effects of Aggressive Cartoons on Children's Aggressive Play

Paul Mussen and Eldred Rutherford[1]

Despite widespread concern about the possible harmful consequences of exposure to the violence and aggression prominently portrayed in movies, television, and comic books, there has been relatively little systematic research on the problem. Two diametrically opposed hypotheses about the effects have been proposed: one emphasizing the possible beneficial results, the other stressing the possible deleterious effects. According to the often-invoked catharsis hypothesis, involvement in fantasy aggression may serve as a "displacement," providing a harmless "release" for children's hostile impulses, and thus reducing the instigation to overt acts of aggression (Dollard, Doob, Miller, Mowrer, & Sears, 1939). On the other hand, a number of popular reports, based on the experiences of criminologists and psychiatrists who have worked with criminals and delinquents (e.g., Wertham, 1953), maintain that the portrayal of violence in the mass media stimulates hostile impulses and increases antisocial behavior.

Experimental confirmation of the catharsis hypothesis applied to fantasy aggression was obtained by Feshbach who found that "self-initiated verbal responses" (italics ours), writing aggressive TAT stories following the arousal of ag-

Reprinted from the *Journal of Abnormal and Social Psychology*, 1961, Vol. 62, pp. 461–464 with the permission of the American Psychological Association and the authors.

[1] The authors gratefully acknowledge the assistance of Maryly Blew, a first grade teacher in the Berkeley elementary school system, in conducting this study.

gression, led to a reduction in the amount of subsequent interpersonal aggression manifested (Feshbach, 1955). The results of other studies of children's reactions in play situations, however, are clearly inconsistent with this finding (Feshbach, 1956; Siegel, 1956). For example, in a later study, Feshbach (1956) found that second and third grade children who played with aggressive toys displayed significantly *more* inappropriate aggression (aggression not directly determined by the type of play object, e.g., striking or insulting another child) than those who played with neutral playthings. Similarly, Siegel (1956) found that preschool subjects tended to be more aggressive in social interactions with peers after viewing an aggressive animated cartoon than they were after viewing a neutral one, although the difference was not statistically significant.

On the basis of these findings, it may be hypothesized that under permissive conditions, indulgence in aggressive fantasy may result in increased aggressive play. Such an increase may be the consequence of identification with aggressive fantasy characters, or, under these conditions, fantasy-produced reduction of inhibition against the expression of aggression, or both.

The present research was designed to test the specific prediction, derived from this hypothesis, that exposure to violence in an animated cartoon may intensify the aggression that children manifest in their play activities. The possible effects of two other variables were also investigated: experimentally-induced frustration, since both Feshbach and Siegel suggest that this may strongly influence reactions to aggressive fantasy; and sex of subject, since boys and girls may react differently to this kind of stimulus.

PROCEDURE

A $3 \times 2 \times 2$ factorial design was employed in this investigation. The subjects, 36 lower middle class first grade pupils between the ages of 6 and 7, were randomly assigned to one of six groups, each group consisting of three boys and three girls. Three groups, the *frustration groups*, were assigned a task which, according to their teacher, was both tedious and frustrating to the children. It was similar to the frustration experience used by Yarrow (1948) and consisted of copying numbers repeatedly while the teacher criticized their work frequently. Immediately following the frustration session, one group viewed an aggressive cartoon, another viewed a nonaggressive cartoon, and the third, no cartoon. Similarly, each of the other three groups was assigned to one of the three treatment conditions—viewing an aggressive cartoon, a nonaggressive cartoon, or no cartoon—but none of these groups were experimentally frustrated beforehand.

The cartoons. The aggressive cartoon showed a continuous sequence of aggressive activity in which an animated weed attempted to choke a flower, and a panda bear struggled to destroy the weed. The theme of the nonaggressive cartoon was the fun of playing cooperatively, a frog and duck being the central characters portrayed. Each cartoon was exactly 8-minutes long.

Immediately after seeing the cartoons, the children were taken individually to a room where the test of aggressive drive was administered by one of the six young women who acted as testers. The two groups of children who did not see a cartoon were taken directly from their classroom to the testing room.

The test of aggression. The strength of aggressive drive must, of course, be inferred from behavior. Siegel's indices were based on overt aggression in an interpersonal situation with peers (Siegel, 1956). The measure used in the present study was the verbal expression of desire to destroy an inanimate object, a balloon. The test used, adapted from Stone's (1956) balloon-breaking procedures, consisted of eight questions, asked orally in fixed sequence, about an inflated balloon held by the tester. Five of the questions concerned the child's desire to "pop" the balloon himself or to see the tester do it (e.g., "Do you think it would be fun to see me 'pop' this balloon?"; "If I gave one to you, would you take it home and 'pop' it, or would you just play with it?"). Subjects were not actually given an opportunity to break the balloon, however. The child's aggression score was simply the number of times he chose the "popping" response. Although the possible range of scores was 0–5, the actual range was 0–2.

The testers, who did not know anything about the experimental treatments the children had experienced prior to the test, were also asked to check any of the following adjectives that they felt described the subject's behavior during the testing period: angry, excited, tense, relaxed, cooperative. At the conclusion of the experiment, all children who had been frustrated were given balloons to take home and permitted to see another, nonaggressive cartoon as rewards for their cooperation.

RESULTS

The results of analysis of variance of the aggression test data, summarized in Table 1, indicate that the only significant effect was the main effect for the cartoon variable. Table 2, which gives the mean aggression scores of the six groups, shows that subjects who saw the aggressive cartoon were more willing to express aggressive impulses in this setting than those who saw the nonaggressive cartoon or no cartoon at all. This finding supports the hypothesis that viewing violence in a cartoon may actually stimulate or intensify the child's aggression in a subsequent permissive situation. There was no evidence in these data that the sexes differed from each other in their reactions to the cartoon.

Table 1

Analysis of Variance for Aggression-Test Data

Source	df	SS	MS	F	P
Cartoon	2	11.05	5.51	15.31	<.01
Frustration	1	.44	.44	1.22	NS
Sex	1	1.00	1.00	2.78	NS
Frustration × Sex	1	0	0		
Frustration × Cartoon	2	.08	.04		
Sex × Cartoon	2	.52	.26		
Frustration × Sex × Cartoon	2	.11	.06		
Within cells	24	8.69	.36		

Table 2

Group Means for Aggression-Test Data

Cartoon Treatment	Frustrated	Nonfrustrated
Aggressive Cartoon	1.67	2.00
Nonaggressive Cartoon	.67	.83
No Cartoon	.50	.67

It is interesting to note that, contrary to what would be predicted on the basis of the frustration-aggression hypothesis,

the frustrated and nonfrustrated groups experiencing the same cartoon treatments did not differ significantly with respect to aggressive expression as measured here. The data from the adjective check lists, filled in by the testers, indicated, however, that feelings of anxiety and tension were more likely to occur subsequent to seeing an aggressive cartoon than after the other treatments. Eight of the 12 subjects (67%) who saw the aggressive cartoon were described as "tense" while among the 24 other subjects, only 8 (33%), 4 who had seen the nonaggressive cartoon and 4 who had not seen any cartoon, were rated in this way ($\chi^2 = 3.94$, $p < .05$).

These findings may be interpreted as evidence that reaction to frustration did not increase overt aggression but rather heightened feelings of tension—i.e., that the frustration-aggression hypothesis did not hold in this situation. On the other hand, it is also possible that, in spite of the rationale underlying the use of this frustration procedure, the task assigned to the "frustration" group was not actually frustrating. In view of these considerations, it is difficult to make any generalizations about the possible effects of experimentally induced frustration or subsequent aggression.

DISCUSSION

The experimental results provide evidence supporting the basic hypothesis of the study which stated that film-mediated fantasy aggression may intensify aggressive expression in permissive play. Since the present findings may be directly applicable only to the restricted situation of permissible aggressive play, it is difficult to evaluate their implications, if any, for the validity of the catharsis hypothesis. This hypothesis is generally interpreted, as it was in the Feshbach and Siegel studies, to refer to *interpersonal* aggression subsequent to other aggressive activities, such as a fantasy aggression. There is no evidence in the data to suggest that, in an unselected group of subjects, those who increase in the measure of aggression used here become more hostile toward other children, although pretests show that this measure differentiated at the .02 level the children rated high and low in aggression by their nursery school teachers. Nevertheless, it should be noted that our findings are entirely consistent with the results of Feshbach's second experiment in which children's "inappropriate aggression" increased during play with aggressive toys. If, as is generally assumed, a child's aggression is largely a function of the strength of his aggressive drive and his internalized inhibitions against aggression, then increases in aggression must be due to either temporary intensification of drive or reduction of inhibitions, or both. In the present study, intensification of instigation to aggression may have resulted directly from identification with aggressive cartoon characters with accompanying assumption of their motives. In Feshbach's study, the aggressive toys may have provided cues eliciting associations with real or fictional aggressive identificands, and consequently, increased aggressive motivation.

The second possible, perhaps more parsimonious, explanation is that the permissive "fun" context of animated cartoons or play with aggressive toys leads to a reduction of inhibitions against aggressive expression, particularly in situations where aggressive play is not likely to be punished. It has frequently been observed that aggression in doll play increases from session to session, presumably because "the deliberate permissiveness of the experimental procedure progressively acts to reduce the inhibitions about aggression the child has heretofore

acquired" (Levin & Sears, 1956, p. 149). Moreover, Feshbach (1956) found that, particularly among boys initially low in aggression, aggressive behavior increased following permissive free play experiences. The child may regard these situations as "permission-giving," with respect to aggression (Siegel & Kohn, 1959); i.e., he may infer that aggression is distinctly permissible and appropriate in these situations. The response of behaving aggressively may then generalize to other relatively permissive situations, e.g., doll play or a balloon-breaking test.

These considerations may also help to explain the discrepancy between the findings of the present study and those of Siegel who found that children did not display significantly more aggression toward peers after watching an aggressive cartoon than they did after watching a control cartoon. The two studies appear to differ most importantly in the indices of aggression employed.[2] In the test used in the present study, a relaxed tester asked questions phrased in a way that permitted, or even encouraged, the free expression of aggressive feeling, not overt aggression. The test setting contained no apparent threat of counteraggression and there were no strong cues evoking internalized inhibitions against aggression. Increased aggressive feelings, stimulated by the aggressive cartoon, were therefore likely to be generalized and expressed in a permissive test situation.

Siegel's measure of aggression, on the other hand, was based on overt aggres-

[2] While Siegel's subjects were somewhat younger than ours, this age difference could hardly explain the discrepancy in the results. It is also possible that differences in the cartoon stimuli account, at least partially, for the differences in the findings. For example, compared with those used by Siegel, the aggressive cartoons of the present study may have provided better (i.e., more immediate or intimate) identification models or a more "permission-giving" context for aggression. There is no evidence to support such an explanation, however.

sion in social play in the absence of adults. This is a situation in which strong inhibitions against aggression are likely to be evoked (Siegel & Kohn, 1959). Siegel and Kohn (1959) have pointed out that "lacking any adults to define the social situation and to express expectations of his behavior in it, the child will . . . rely . . . on his own learned standards of conduct . . . which, in the middle-class child, will typically be that aggression is unacceptable in social play" (p. 134). It may be reasonably hypothesized that there was a reduction of inhibition against aggression among Siegel's subjects, as among ours, after they viewed an aggressive cartoon, but this effect was not apparent in a test situation that contained cues that elicit powerful inhibitory responses.

SUMMARY

The purpose of this study was to test the hypothesis that exposure to aggressive fantasy in an animated cartoon may intensify children's impulses to aggression. Subjects were 36 first grade children, 18 girls and 18 boys, of middle class origin. The intensity of the child's aggressive impulses was inferred from his responses to questions concerning desire to "play with" or "pop" a large yellow balloon held by a tester.

The experimental findings clearly supported the major prediction that exposure to aggressive fantasy in an animated cartoon would stimulate children's aggressive behavior in play. Two possible explanations for these results were discussed: that intensification of instigation to aggression may have resulted from the child's identification with the aggressive cartoon characters, with accompanying assumption of their motives; that the relaxed, "fun" context of animated cartoons may lead to a reduction of inhibitions against aggressive expression in a permissive play situation.

2

Affect and Emotion

That feelings or affects are significant elements in human functioning needs little documentation. They provide the color for our lives, the pleasures and pains of existence, and they influence our descriptions of the past and our expectations of the future. Thinking, memory, social functioning, goal-directed behavior, perception, and even the uses we make of our native intelligence are deeply influenced by the course of emotion.

It is reasonable therefore that the nature of affect should be a central concern to theoretical psychology, and that the study of normal and abnormal phenomena should require its description and understanding. That is why there has always been much debate regarding the origin, nature, and dynamics of affect.

Two quite disparate contemporary views are presented here. Tomkins argues that there are eight primary affects, and that they are innate, which is to say that affects themselves are not learned but simply elicited by certain conditions (which may themselves be learned). Moreover, affects are enormously plastic; negative ones can, on occasion, take on positive values, while positive feelings can acquire negative tones. The vicissitudes of affect are taken up in detail in Tomkins' *Affect, Imagery and Consciousness*, Volumes I and II (New York: Springer, 1962 and 1963).

In this essay, Tomkins reviews briefly his theory of affect and goes on to explicate its relationship to commitment (sustained activity) on behalf of the abolition of slavery. The essay is of interest for its relevance to persistent altruism, a positive abnormality, as well as for its delineation of the course of affect.

The course of affect is as much Tomkins' concern as are its origins. One affect leads to the next, sustaining or weakening it according to fixed patterns of internal dynamics. This is particularly true for *high-density* or intense affects, and Tomkins is as careful to distinguish weak, transient feelings from intense ones, as positive from negative feelings.

An understanding of affects, however, depends somewhat on a view of their origins. Unlike Tomkins, Schachter and Singer do not consider them innate. To describe how an affect develops is therefore important for them, as it was for James and Cannon before them. Schachter and Singer consider that a feeling arises from the faint activity of two systems: cognition and arousal. The systems must interact in such a way that neither one is powerful enough to suppress the other. Moreover, cognition must not be a mere byproduct of the arousal; it must arise from an evaluation of the circumstances. Knowing that my heart beats faster because I have consumed a drug does not necessarily produce an emotion in me. But if my heart beats faster and I ascribe it to some exciting cause in my environment, then emotion is produced.

Both theories leave much to be examined, and both are likely to stimulate further research. It has not been proved that the eight primary affects in Tomkins' scheme are, in fact, innate, and the dynamics of affect described so compellingly in the selection have not been verified. At the same time, the apparently simpler theory proposed by Schachter and Singer may require extension to account for the phenomena to which Tomkin's theory is addressed: sustained high-intensity emotion, and continuous maintenance and alteration of emotional states over time and circumstances.

The Psychology of Commitment
Part I: The Constructive Role of Violence and Suffering for the Individual and for his Society

Silvan S. Tomkins

We have argued that the primary motives of man are his eight innate affects, or feelings. These are the positive affects of excitement, enjoyment and surprise, and the negative affects of distress, anger, fear, shame and contempt. These are innate. One does not learn to smile in enjoyment nor to cry in distress. However, the objects of each affect are *both* innate and learned. A baby does not

Reprinted from Silvan S. Tomkins and Carroll E. Izard (Eds.), *Affect, Cognition and Personality*, New York: Springer Publishing Co., 1965, Chap. 6, pp. 148–171 with the permission of Springer Publishing Co., Tavistock Publications, Ltd., London, and the authors.

learn the birth cry. It is an innate response to the excessive stimulation attendant upon being born. He will later cry when he is hungry or tired or exposed to too loud sounds. None of these are learned responses. But eventually he *will* learn to cry about many things about which he was initially unconcerned. He may learn to cry in sympathy when others are in distress, and cry. But if the crying of others may be learned to evoke one's own distress cry, so may it also be learned to evoke contempt or shame rather than sympathy. There is thus nothing under the sun which some

Library
I.U.P.
Indiana, Pa.

157 R725t
c.1

human beings have not learned to enjoy, to fear, or to hate, to be ashamed of, or to respond to with excitement or contempt or anger. It is the innate plasticity of the affect mechanism which permits the investment of any type of affect in any type of activity or object which makes possible the great varieties of human personalities and societies. Cultural diversity rests upon the biological plasticity of the affect system in man. Puritanism, or negative affect about pleasure, and masochism, or positive affect about pain, are extreme examples of the plasticity of affect investment. The theoretical possibilities of the variety of profiles of activation, maintenance and decay of each affect are without limit. I may be very happy as a child and very sad as an adult, or conversely. I may be angry for a moment, for an hour, for a day, or always, or never. I may be frightened only occasionally or I may be anxious all my life. I may feel mildly ashamed for myself or deeply humiliated. I may feel ashamed because I have shown my feelings too publicly or because I was unable to show my feelings toward someone who needed my sympathy. In short, the object, the duration, the frequency, and the intensity of affect arousal and investment are without limit. It is this capacity of the individual to feel strongly or weakly, for a moment or for all his life, about anything under the sun and to govern himself by such motives that constitutes his essential freedom.

IDEO-AFFECTIVE DENSITY

It is to a closer examination of the phenomenon of density of affect investment that we now turn. We have defined affect density as the product of its intensity times its duration. We will now introduce a derivative concept: ideo-perceptual-memorial-action-affect density. By this we mean the product of the intensity times the duration of all the capacities for involvement which the individual possesses. At one time his involvement may be primary ideational, at another time, primarily affective, or primarily overtly behavioral, or primarily perceptual or memorial, or any combination of these. For purposes of brevity we will henceforth refer to this as *ideo-affective density* and use the term *ideation* to refer to the variety of non-affective cognitions as well as to action. We do not mean by this to imply in any way that we regard action as a type of thinking, or in any way to blur the differences between perception, memory and thinking. We will use the term simply as a convenient abbreviation for the density of involvement of all of the critical sub-systems which together constitute a human being. Bearing in mind this special usage of the words ideo- and ideation, we will now define ideo-affective density as the product of the intensity and duration of affect and the concurrent ideation about the object of the affect. Low ideo-affective density refers to those experiences which generate little or no affect, and little or no ideation, or if the affect and ideation are intense they do not last long. High density occurs whenever the individual has both intense feelings and ideation which continue at a high level over long periods of time. In such a case there is a monopolistic capture of the individual's awareness and concern. Low and high densities represent two ends of a continuum of organizations of motive, thought and behavior which are critical for the understanding of commitment.

We wish to distinguish two gross segments of an ideo-affect density continuum—the low and high density segments. Further, we will examine some characteristic examples of each end of this continuum, so that commitment may be seen in its larger context.

LOW DENSITY END
OF CONTINUUM

Let us first consider the low end of the continuum. We distinguish two different kinds of organization both of which are characteristically low density organizations. Further, each type of organization may be primarily positive or negative in affect. One organization is *transient, casual* and the other is *recurrent, habitual.*

Consider first a transitory positive, low density ideo-affective organization. Such would be the laughter in response to a joke. The experience might be extremely enjoyable but nonetheless of very low density, because it recruited no continuing ideation or affect beyond the momentary experience. An example of a transitory negative low density ideo-affective organization would be a cut while shaving which occasioned a brief stab of pain and distress, but no further thought or feeling beyond this isolated experience. Each individual's lifetime contains thousands of such relatively casual, transient encounters. Collectively they may sum to a not inconsiderable segment of the life span. Nonetheless they constitute an aggregate of isolated components without substantial impact on the personality of the individual.

The recurrent, habitual types of low density ideo-affective organizations characteristically begin with considerable intensity of affect and ideation but end with minimal involvement. Consider first the negative recurrent habitual case. Everyone learns to cross streets with minimal ideation and affect. We learn to act as if we were afraid, but we do not in fact experience any fear once we have learned how to cope successfully with such contingencies. Despite the fact that we know that there is real danger involved daily in walking across intersections and that many pedestrians are in fact killed, we exercise normal caution with minimal attention and no fear. It remains a low density ideo-affective organization, despite daily repetition over a lifetime. Successful avoidance strategies remain low density organizations because they do not generalize or spread. They do not spread just because they are successful. It should be noted that these organizations, though we have called them recurrent habitual, are far from being simple motor habits. They are small programs for processing information with relatively simple strategies, but one may nonetheless never repeat precisely the same avoidance behaviors twice in crossing the street. These simple programs generate appropriate avoidant strategies of dealing with a variety of such situations, and caution is nicely matched to the varying demands of this class of situations, with a minimum of attention and affect. Every individual, including the psychotic, possesses hundreds such avoidance and escape low density organizations. (It is a great surprise on first exposure to psychotic patients to discover as my friend Edward Engel confided to me one day, that a schizophrenic when eating soup for lunch does not put the soup into his eye!) This is not to say that crossing the street was always a low density ideo-affective organization. The earliest such experiences may well have been high adventures for the daring child, or they may have been the occasion of severe punishment at the hands of an anxious parent terrified at the sight of his toddler walking in front of a speeding automobile. Both the excitement and the pain or distress or fear which might have been suffered at the hands of a parent do not long continue. Quickly all children learn some caution in this matter and it ceases to claim either much ideation or feeling. Such attenuation of feeling and thought necessarily depend upon the success of problem solutions. Paradoxically human beings are least involved in what they can do best, when problems once solved, remain solved. Man as a successful problem solver ceases to think and to feel about successful performance and turns ideation and affect to the continuing or new, unsolved challenges.

This is so whether the original affect which powered problem solving was positive or negative. Just as we experience no terror in confronting traffic at the curb, so too with positive, low density ideo-affective organizations we experience no positive enjoyment or excitement in the daily recurrent performance which once delighted. As I finish my daily shaving I rarely puff with pride and think, "There I've done it again." I act in this case, as in crossing the street, *as if* I experienced an affect, and had a wish to achieve this goal. I do indeed achieve my intention—to shave—but the positive affect behind this ritual has long ceased to be emitted concurrently with the action. Like the low density avoidance strategy of crossing the street, it may be done daily—repeated several thousand times during a lifetime—with little or no effect on other action, or affect, or memory or perception.

HIGH DENSITY END OF CONTINUUM—NEGATIVE MONOPOLISM

What then of the high density ideo-affective organizations? By definition they can be neither transitory nor recurrent but must be enduring. Whether predominantly positive or negative in tone, they must seize the individual's feelings and thoughts and actions to the exclusion of almost all else. Consider first negative monopolism of thought and feeling. If successful and continuing problem solution is the necessary condition of the low density organization, *temporary* problem solution is the neces-

sary condition of the negative high density organization. Consider our man on the curb. He is normally cautious but not overly concerned because his solution to the problem has always worked. But suppose that one day a passing motorist loses control of his car and seriously injures our hero. After his return from the hospital he is a bit more apprehensive than before, and now stands back a little farther from the edge of the curb than he used to. He may continue his somewhat excessive caution for some time, and, as he notes a car approaching with what appears a little too much speed, may even begin to wonder with occasional fear, whether such an accident might ever happen again. But if all goes well this increase in density of ideation and affect will pass and before long he will be indistinguishable from any other casual pedestrian. But in our tragedy all does not go well. Uncannily a drunken driver pursues our hero and he is hit again. This time it is more serious and we see the beginnings of a phobia. Our hero stations himself inside a building, peering up and down the street, before he will venture out to dare negotiate the crossing. By now his preoccupation with and fear of the deadly vehicle has grown to invade his consciousness even when he is far from the scene of potential danger. In the last act of this drama it is a bulldozer which penetrates his apparent fortress. What next? Will he be safe in the hospital? His ideation and affect have now reached a point of no return. He will henceforth generate possibilities which no reasonable man would entertain and these phantasies will evoke affects proportional to their extremity.

He will now begin negative ideo-affective creativity. Such a high density ideo-affective organization is capable of providing a lifetime of suffering and of resisting reduction through new evidence. This happens if, and only if, there has occurred a sequence of events of this type: threat, successful defense, breakdown of defense and re-emergence of threat, second successful new defense, second breakdown of defense and re-emergence of threat, third successful new defense, third breakdown of defense and re-emergence of threat, and so on, until an expectation is generated that no matter how successful a defense against a dread contingency may seem, it will prove unavailing and require yet another new defense, ad infinitum. Not only is there generated the conviction that successful defense can be successful only temporarily, but also as new and more effective defenses are generated the magnitude of the danger is inflated in the imagination of the harried one. We have defined this dynamic as a circular incremental magnification. It is circular and incremental since each new threat requires a more desperate defense and the successive breakdown of each newly improved defense generates a magnification of the nature of the threat and the concurrent affect which it evokes. We have defined such a circular incremental magnification series as a set of —+— triads in which negative affect is defended against and replaced by positive affect, but then breaks down and again produces negative affect. In comparison with the analogous low-density organization, it is the continuing uncertainty of permanent problem solution which is critical in monopolizing the individual's ideation and affect. Paradoxically it is just the fact that the individual is *not* entirely helpless in dealing with a given situation which continually magnifies both the apparent nature of the threat and his skill in coping with it. In this respect the individual may be likened to a tennis player who is first defeated by a poor opponent and who then practices sufficiently to defeat that opponent. But his triumph proves short-lived since his opponent now also improves and in turn defeats him. This then leads our hero to improve his skill so that once again he defeats his adversary, but this leads to yet another defeat when the latter improves his skill, and so on and on.

POSITIVE HIGH DENSITY IDEO-AFFECTIVE ORGANIZATION

Let us now examine the structure of the positive, high density ideo-affective organization. Instead of a series of —+— triads, here it is a series of +—+ triads which is responsible for the circular incremental magnification. Instead of increasing concern with warding off a threat, it is rather the magnification of a positive affect and the ideation about its object which is involved. Although there is negative affect sandwiched in between two positive affects in this type of triad, the individual is primarily concerned with attaining the object of positive affect. Let us consider two types of such positive ideo-affective organizations.

Psychological Addiction

First, consider what we will define as the psychological addiction. The addicted cigarette smoker will serve as an example. Individual A enjoys smoking a cigar or a cigarette after dinner. This is an unadulterated reward. At other times of the day he is unaware both of the enjoyments of smoking and of any suffering because he is not smoking. Individual B does not enjoy smoking per se, but rather uses cigarettes as a pacifier or sedative whenever he becomes distressed or anxious. Smoking at such times reduces his suffering and makes him feel better. It is not only that the function of smoking is here limited to the reduction of negative affect, but also that such negative affect arises from some source other than smoking. He is *not* disturbed simply because he is not smoking, but rather is disturbed because something else went wrong in his life. So, when everything goes well for B, he does not miss smoking, because the only function which smoking serves is to reduce other kinds of suffering. B does not think of smoking when he is not smoking—except for those occasions when he is disturbed. If he is not disturbed he has concerns other than smoking. Individual C is an addicted smoker. Like A he too enjoys smoking and like B he uses smoking to reduce all types of suffering. But here the resemblances end. C first of all is *always* aware of not smoking whenever this occurs. Second, he always responds to this awareness with negative affect which continues to increase in intensity until he can smoke. Third, he will always drop all competitors for his attention and try to get a cigarette and fourth, upon getting a cigarette and beginning to smoke he will respond with intense enjoyment at the reduction of his suffering of negative affect. Like A he enjoys smoking, and like B he also reduces his suffering by smoking, but the suffering which he *must* reduce is the suffering he experiences (and has created) just because he is not smoking. No matter how well his life goes, he is unable to be unaware of not smoking, whenever this occurs. Contrary to B he may be able to tolerate many other types of suffering without resort to sedation by smoking. So long as he has a cigarette in hand he may be quite courageous in confronting innumerable problems other than that of not smoking. B in similar circumstances might have had resort to smoking to leave the field, to sedate himself into comfort rather than to confront his problem. In addiction, too, there is circular incremental magnification produced by an ever accelerating suffering in the absence of a cigarette and an ever increasing rewarding experience of positive affect

upon the reduction of the suffering of negative affect.

The hold of cigarette smoking or any other high density addiction arises from the intolerability of the ever mounting negative affect which is experienced whenever the addict attempts to break his addiction. As his suffering mounts he becomes more and more unable to tolerate the absence of smoking and extrapolates into the future a vision of an increasingly intolerable suffering, till in panic at this prospect he succumbs to his longing. It is a series of painful longings reduced by smoking which increases both the suffering of negative affect and the intensity of positive affect while smoking, in an accelerating circular incremental magnification.

Psychologically this process is similar to the mourning experience of the bereaved. The lost love object is magnified in value because of the conjoint suffering and longing which makes vivid to the bereaved his hitherto not entirely appreciated dependence on the lost love object. It is the barrier to ever again enjoying the presence of the beloved which reveals and *creates* a new appreciation. Although addiction is thereby heightened in mourning and though longing and suffering may be intensified to the point of intolerability, the mourner ultimately is freed from his heightened dependence because he is forced to endure the abstinence suffering until it no longer increases in intensity and then begins slowly to decline in intensity, until finally there is minimal suffering and no *awareness* that the lost love object has been lost. In this respect the mourner is returned to the state of someone who has been able to overcome his addiction to smoking. The addicted cigarette smoker will not willingly suffer through such abstinence suffering, because it seems to him, as to the bereaved, that he will never be able to tolerate the loss of the love object. In addiction, it should be noted, we are dealing with the lure of the familiar and the positive affect which is involved is enjoyment. It is the return to the familiar, heightened in value by the suffering of separation which creates the magic of reunion, be that reunion with an old friend, an old place or an old activity such as smoking. In contrast to commitment, as we will presently see, there is here much less involvement of exploration and of novelty and of created challenge.

Commitment

In commitment the positive high density ideo-affective organization also involves the reward of the positive affect of enjoyment, but in addition the positive affect of excitement becomes more prominent. Let us consider two examples of commitment, one characteristically abortive commitment which ends either by transformation into an addiction at somewhat less than maximal density, or ends in disenchantment; the other a high density commitment which for some extends over the entire life span. We refer in the first instance to romantic love and in the second to the committed scientist.

Consider first the *romantic lover* who intends to commit himself for life to his beloved. As we distinguished cigarette smokers, A, B, and C, we may distinguish A in this domain as one who very much enjoys his contacts with his lady friend, but who does not miss her when he is otherwise occupied. B has a lady friend he does not miss when all goes well. But he always turns to her for comfort when he becomes disturbed. She does in fact always bring him tranquility, and having been mothered back into peace of mind he is prepared again to pick up his life, and to forget his benefactress with gratitude but no regret, for the time being. Not so with C, the romantic lover. He is forever aware of the absence of his be-

loved, and of their enforced separation, to which he responds with intense suffering and longing. Every time he is separated he dies a little and thereby, like the true mourner, comes to appreciate more and more his dependence upon the beloved who grows increasingly desirable in her absence. Upon reunion with the beloved the intensity of his enjoyment and excitement is proportional to his prior suffering, and there is begun a circular incremental magnification. If the beloved becomes more valuable when she brings to an end the intolerable suffering and longing which preceded reunion, so much the greater will the next suffering of separation become since the beloved has by now become even more wonderful than before. Just as the nature of the threat is magnified in the negative high density series of $-+-$ triads, so here is the nature of the positive object magnified in the series of $+-+$ triads. In contrast to the ever increasing negative threat, the beloved does not necessarily continue to support indefinite magnification of her magical qualities. Romantic love imposes separation and uncertainty which increases the period of time over which longing for the love object can occur, but with the transition to the honeymoon and marriage, the prolonged intimacy and mutual exploration eventually produces a sufficient reduction in novelty and uncertainty so that excitement can no longer be indefinitely maintained. When under these conditions of continuing contact the beloved will no longer support the indefinite magnification of wonder and excitement, there may appear disenchantment or boredom, or an ideo-affective organization of reduced intensity and duration with excitement replaced by the enjoyment of the familiar and deepening relationship. But the husband will no longer miss his wife throughout the working day even though he deeply enjoys his daily reunion with her at each day's end. We have traced this potential high density ideo-affective organization, which may be short circuited by marriage, to better illuminate the nature of enduring high density commitment.

Consider next the varieties of *committed scientists* and those who are interested but not committed. Scientist A enjoys tremendously both the discovery of truth and the search for truth. He likes to putter around the laboratory. He likes to run experiments. He enjoys it when they succeed. But he is a nine-to-five scientist. When he goes home it is to another world. He does not take his scientific troubles home with him. Indeed he experiences a minimum of suffering in his role as scientist. He is in this respect like the person who loves to smoke after dinner, and like the person who enjoys the company of his lady friend, but who do not miss their enjoyment or suffer in the interim periods. Individual B, on the other hand, uses science as a sedative. Whenever he becomes depressed he turns to reading science or watching TV programs concerning the latest advances in science. However, as soon as his life becomes more rewarding, his interest in science flags, like the person who smoked to comfort himself, and like the individual who sought out his lady friend to ease his suffering, but once mothered back into peace of mind forgot his benefactress. Consider now scientist C who is committed for a lifetime to the pursuit of truth. Like the addicted smoker he is always aware of the absence of his longed-for ideal object—ultimate, permanent, truth. Like individual A, he enjoys the scientific way of life. He enjoys puttering with laboratory equipment, and with running experiments. But underlying all his enjoyment is a continuing unrest and suffering over the possibilities of error, and over the possibility of missing the main chance. When everything works as planned he is deeply excited and enjoys briefly the fruits of his labor. But his contact with truth is ordinarily as brief as it is sweet. Truth is a mistress who never gives herself completely or permanently. She must be wooed and won arduously and painfully in each encounter. With each encounter she deepens both the scientist's suffering and then his reward. It is a love affair which is never entirely and deeply consummated. Immediately following each conquest, the victory is always discovered to have been less than it appeared and the investigation must now be pursued with more skill and more energy than before.

The set of triads $+-+$ is in some respects similar to the negative set of triads $-+-$. In both cases skill must constantly be improved and in both cases the effectiveness of achieved skill is only temporary. The difference is that in the negative high density ideo-affective organization the individual is pursued by a threat, whereas in positive commitment he pursues an object of ever increasing attractiveness. In both cases circular incremental magnification is responsible for the *creation* of an idealized object. The magic of truth exists in such a magnified form only in the mind of one who will pursue truth despite increasing suffering so that each encounter becomes both more bitter and more sweet. There is minimal uncertainty in the familiar object of addiction, and there is a finite uncertainty in the romantic love affair which is almost entirely explored during the honeymoon. In the scientific commitment, however, there is sufficient continuing uncertainty so that endless circular incremental magnification of the $+-+$ triad can be sustained indefinitely if the individual has become committed. Thus a scientist who has made a major discovery and thereafter elects to rest on his laurels has ceased to be a committed scientist with high density of ideation and affect about science. It is a critical feature of high density commitment that there can be no *enduring* positive affect in having attained the pursued finite object. Rather the object is continually redefined so that a newer version of the quest can be mounted. The same dynamic appears in the pursuit of money or power. These are also capable of committing the individual to an endless insatiable quest for an object which is put out of reach almost immediately after it is attained.

COMMITTED REFORMERS

Let us turn now to yet another group of the committed—the reformer and those he reforms. Why and how do individuals and societies become committed to ideologies and to social movements? We will examine four abolitionists, Garrison, Phillips, Weld and Birney, as committed reformers. Why and how did each of these become committed to abolitionism? How did they influence others to become committed to abolitionism, or at the least to oppose the extension of slavery? It is our thesis that the same psychological dynamic underlies the commitment of the individual and the group. More particularly, we will argue that violence and suffering are critical in a democratic society, in heightening antipathy for violations of democratic values and in heightening sympathy for the victims of such violations. A radical magnification of negative feeling toward the oppressors and of positive feeling toward the oppressed is the major dynamic which powers the commitment first of the individual reformer and then of increasing numbers who are influenced by him.

Let us turn to the interpretation of abolitionism in the light of our theory of the nature of both negative and posi-

tive high density ideo-affective organizations. We will now also examine more closely just how such high density organizations are formed as well as the numerous ways in which they may fail to be sustained.

The commitment of Garrison, Phillips, Weld and Birney to abolitionism proceeded in a series of steps consistent with our general theory of commitment. The critical role of adult experience in the spiral stepwise triads of $+-+$ affects which gradually deepen commitment is underlined by the early resonance of each of these leaders to ways of life quite diverse from each other and from their future way of life. No one could have predicted with any confidence that these four young men would eventually provide the leadership for the abolitionist movement. Garrison was first attracted to writing and to politics as a way of life. Phillips led the life typical of the Boston Brahmin of his time: attendance at Harvard College, Harvard Law School and then the opening of a law practice. Weld first gave a series of lectures on mnemonics, the art of improving the memory. Birney was twice suspended from Princeton for drinking, though he was each time readmitted and graduated with honors. He, like Phillips, became a gentleman lawyer, priming himself for a political career. After an early failure in politics he became a planter and lived the life of the young Southern aristocrat, drinking and gambling to excess. Paradoxically, of the four he was the earliest to interest himself in the slaves, but the last to commit himself to their emancipation as his way of life.

One cannot account for the abolitionist reformer on the assumption that his was a commitment such as "falling in love at first sight." None of these men knew at first that they were to commit their lives to the emancipation of the slave. Three of the four were first attracted to a career in politics. But if there is a perennial danger of exaggerating the continuity of human development, and especially the influence of the early years on the adult personality, there is also the opposite danger of exaggerating the impact of adult experience on crucial adult choices and overlooking the contribution of the early years to choices which on the surface appear to represent novelty in the experience of the adult. Our argument will stress both the continuity and the discontinuity in the development of Garrison, Phillips, Weld and Birney in their growing commitment to abolitionism.

All were early prepared and destined for leadership of a special kind, for saving the self through saving others. Each might have become a crusading politician, writer or orator or preacher. Indeed, Birney did later run as a crusading candidate for the Presidency of the United States. Weld later, because of his failing speech, did become a writer for abolitionism instead of an orator. Phillips, after the Civil War, did continue crusading for labor, for temperance, for Ireland against England, for the American Indians, and for the abolition of capital punishment. Garrison, too, after the Civil War, maintained his interest in women's rights and in temperance reform, though with much less zeal than Phillips. Therefore we must neither exaggerate the novelty of their commitment to abolitionism nor the continuity of their interest in salvation. It is to some extent a historical accident that they became abolitionists but it is not an accident that they became deeply committed to leadership for the salvation of others.

The stages in the development of their commitment to abolitionism can now be summarized. First, a resonance to the general idea of the salvation of others; second, risk is ventured on behalf of those who need to be saved; third, as a consequence of the risk which has been taken, there is punishment and suffering; fourth, as a consequence of such suffering, resonance to the original idea of the necessity of salvation is deepened and identification with the oppressed is increased as is hostility toward the oppressor; fifth, as a result of increased density of affect and ideation, there will be an increased willingness to take even greater risks and more possible punishment and more suffering; sixth, increased risk taking does evoke more punishment and more suffering; seventh, there is an increasing willingness to tolerate suffering which follows risk taking, concomitant with a proportionately increasing intensity and duration of positive affect and ideation in identification with the oppressed and with fellow abolitionists, and an increasing negative affect toward the enemy whose apparent power and undesirability is magnified as the density of affect and ideation increases. The $+-+$ triad alternates between resonance and risk taking ($+$), punishment and suffering ($-$), increased density of positive affect and ideation ($+$), resulting in increased risk taking ($+$), so that the entire triad is endlessly repeated. This cumulatively deepens commitment until it reaches a point of no return— when no other way of life seems possible to the committed reformer. The spiral, composed of $+-+$ triads, is therefore a $+-+$, $+-+$ set rather than a $+-+-+$ sequence. The increased density of positive affect and ideation at the end of the $+-+$ results in an increased positive affect invested in the more *risk*, the $+$ in the next $+-+$ triad.

It should be noted that the pathway from early resonance to final commitment is not necessarily without internal conflict. Some of the suffering comes from within as well as from the enemy. Each of these men was to suffer doubt at some point whether to give himself completely to abolitionism as a way of life.

The Original Resonance

Let us now examine the original resonance that first attracted these and other men to abolitionism. By resonance we mean the engagement of feeling and thought by any organized ideology or social movement. The fit between the individual's own loosely organized ideas and feelings, that we have called his ideo-affective posture, and the more tightly organized ideology, or social movement, need not be a very close one to induce resonance. Some men resonated to abolitionism because slavery violated their Christian faith; others because of a general sympathy for the underdog; others because of belief in the perfectibility of man; others because of a belief in the democratic assertion of the equal rights of all men, or in individualism; some were originally attracted because their own salvation required that they save others; and there were those who were attracted because they hated oppression and oppressors and some because they could not tolerate humiliation, even vicariously. The plight of the slave induced resonance for these and many other reasons.

The bases for the original resonance of Garrison, Phillips, Weld and Birney to abolitionism contained common elements and also differences. First, all four were deeply Christian. Three of the four had conversion experiences. For Garrison, Phillips and Weld, their Christianity required that they save others if they would save themselves. Each of the three had been impressed by strong, pious Christian mothers that to be good meant to do good. The fourth, Birney, had been left motherless at the age of three, and his strongest relationship was with his father who believed not only in Christian

good works, but, more specifically, had along with *his* father fought to make Kentucky a free state; though they lost this fight they continued to be active against slavery. In all four families, moral and Christian zeal for the salvation of their children (and other sinners) was combined with great affection for their children. The parents provided the appropriate models for future reformers. The children were taught how to combine concern and contempt for the sinner with love for those sinners who would reform.

Second, the parents of the four had also shown a pervasive concern with public service. Garrison's mother, who was the sole provider, nursed the sick. Birney's father was politically active in favor of emancipation. Phillips' father was mayor of Boston. Weld's father was a minister. All were concerned with service to others and provided a model which predisposed their sons to resonate to any movement based on public service.

Third, all four appear to have been physically active and extroverted as children. They had abundant energy which they translated into vigorous play and into fighting with their peers. This, too, contributed to their resonance to a movement which called for direct action and face to face confrontation before large groups.

Fourth, all were exposed to, influenced by, and modeled themselves after, the great orators of their day. As Perry Miller (1961) has noted, one of the salient features of the puritans' reformation was the substitution of the sermon for the Mass. All four men were early exposed to the magic of the great orators of the day, both Christian and political. All four as young men were fluent and articulate and gave evidence of being able to hold audiences by their speaking powers. The combination of great energy, extroversion, and the power to influence others by oratorical ability predisposed them to resonate to a movement which required those who could influence others in just such ways.

Fifth, all of them were physically courageous. They had all experienced and mastered the art of fighting with their peers, so that they had a zest for combat rather than a dread of it. No one who too much feared physical combat could afford to resonate to the defense of those held in bondage by the ever present threat of force. The overly timid cannot entertain a rescue phantasy.

These are some of the characteristics which these four shared and which attracted them to abolitionism. But there were also important differences. Phillips was first attracted to the defense of abolitionism by the murder of the abolitionist Lovejoy. He was outraged, as a patrician, at the tyranny of the mob and its violation of civil liberties. He was in no sense an abolitionist at the time. He was also outraged that "gentlemen" of his own class from his own beloved Boston should form a mob and threaten the life of Garrison. He was attracted at first more by disgust at mob violence than by sympathy for the slaves. In contrast, Garrison, Birney and Weld were first attracted to the problem of slavery out of sympathy for the slave. Each resonated first not to abolitionism but to the program of the American Colonization Society of gradual emancipation with transportation of free American Negroes to Africa. Nor was even this interest salient from the outset. Although slavery interested Weld increasingly, temperance and manual labor education were his primary concerns for some time, following his initial speaking tour on the art of saving one's memory. Birney, due to his exposure to his father's and grandfather's political activity on behalf of emancipation, was earliest interested in the problem of slavery, but it was some

time before he committed himself wholeheartedly to even the program of the American Colonization Society. It was to be several more years, when he was over forty, that he committed himself to abolitionism.

Garrison and Weld were soon to change the nature of their relationship to the problem of slavery. Garrison led the way with a frontal attack on the slaveholder and those who trafficked in slavery and with a denunciation of the American Colonization Society. In this he was radically to influence the entire movement, including Weld, Phillips and finally Birney. Added to sympathy for the slave was now contempt and anger both for the Southern sinners and for those Northerners who either cooperated with or were indifferent to Southern tyranny. Birney held back because he was not yet convinced that the Southern slaveholder could not be reached by reason, because he was temperamentally allergic to enthusiasm, and because he was at that time more interested in improving and preserving his beloved South than in destroying the slaveholder. Only painfully and reluctantly was he forced to leave the South and become an abolitionist.

Garrison, in contrast, had the greatest enthusiasm for nailing the sinner to the cross, while Phillips, disgusted more with his own class than with the Southern slaveholder and responsive to the perfectibility of the lower classes, also resonated to somewhat different aspects of abolitionism. Weld, in contrast both to Phillips and Garrison, was a shy "backwoodsman" as he described himself. He was indifferent to the political action which Birney espoused, disliked politicians and all sophisticates, was suspicious of too great a reliance on "reason," was greatly troubled by exhibitionism (in contrast to Garrison who thrived on it) and was much concerned about the general problem of sin, in himself and in others, and tried to "test" himself. The resonance to abolitionism on the part of these four was prompted by both the communalities and the differences we have here examined.

The Second Stage:
Risk is Ventured

So much for the first stages in the development of commitment, the resonance by which the individual is initially attracted to the new ideology. The second stage occurs when risk is first ventured following this initial resonance. Not all who are attracted will venture any risk on behalf of the ideology. Garrison was perhaps the boldest risk taker, in part because he wanted so much "to be heard" as he said. But to be heard he had not only to write but to speak in public. Early in his career he had been invited by the Congregational Societies in Boston to give the Fourth of July address at the Park Street Church. Garrison, in a letter to Jacob Horton, tells of his knees shaking in anticipation of the lecture, and a newspaper account reported that at first his voice was almost too faint to be heard, but eventually he overcame his stage fright and made a strong plea for the gradual emancipation of the slaves. Soon after this speech, however, he decided that immediate emancipation was required. He became more bold and accused a northern ship captain and ship owner of trafficking in slaves. For this he spent seven weeks in jail. It cannot be said that this was altogether painful to Garrison. He appeared to enjoy both his martyrdom and the notoriety he gained, writing to everyone and conducting interviews from his cell. Although Garrison suffered least of the four abolitionists and indeed appeared to enjoy combat, it would be a mistake to overlook the fear he experienced on numerous occasions when his life was in jeopardy from angry mobs. Indeed mob violence was a constant danger for all the abolitionists.

The Third Stage: Suffering in Consequence of Risk Taking

Garrison, Birney, Weld and Phillips continually exposed themselves to violent opposition. Each reacted somewhat differently. Garrison, though sometimes frightened, was more often delighted to be the center of attention and to respond with a crushing retort. Phillips responded primarily with patrician contempt. Birney became depressed at the unreasonableness of his opposition. Weld regarded his trials as tests by God of his mettle and worthiness. Each man was troubled in different ways. Phillips risked and lost his status and former friends in Boston upper class society. Weld was severely reprimanded by the Trustees and President of the Lane (theological) Seminary for his "monomania" in stirring the students to debate over slavery. This debate had extended 18 days and ended with a declaration in favor of immediate emancipation. After joining the American Anti-Slavery Society he toured Ohio, converting thousands to the cause, but always facing angry mobs intent on attacking him and breaking up his meetings. He was hurt on numerous occasions. He considered these riots to be a test not only of his own mettle but of all his converts. Birney's reaction to the violence his pro-Negro activity evoked was disappointment at the intransigency of the South, depression at the turning away of former friends and his loss of status, chagrin and surprise at the impotence of "reason" to influence reasonable men, considerable regret at having to leave his homeland and settle in the North and, not least, depression over the increasing alienation between his father and himself. Garrison clearly had least to lose and most to gain from assuming the risks of abolitionism. He too risked his life on more than one occasion and was badly frightened despite his zest for the fight and his love of being the center of attention.

The Fourth Stage: Deepened Romances, Increased Commitment

Identification with the oppressed Negro increased as did the hostility toward the oppressor and those who were uncommitted. It should be noted that the same characteristics which prompted the initial resonance were also critical in creating the ability to tolerate opposition and such negative affect as this ordinarily provokes. It was the combination of the general wish to save and reform coupled with energetic, articulate and courageous extroversion which diminished the sting of fear, of disappointment, and of depression at the loss of status, the loss of friends and the threat of physical injury and possible loss of life.

All four responded to initial opposition by increased commitment. Phillips now began to see the nobility and generosity of the Negro and of the lower classes in general. He began to compare their nobility invidiously with the smugness and corruption of upper class society. Here he found for the first time, he insisted, real and true friends. "Who are we that we should presume to rank ourselves with those that are marshalled in such a host? What have *we* done? Where is the sacrifice *we* have made? Where the luxury *we* have surrendered?" (Bartlett, 1961, p. 57).

Weld also regarded the violence of the opposition as a test of the true believer (for himself and for others): "Poor outside whitewash! The tempest will batter it off the first stroke, and masks and veils, and sheep clothing gone, gone at the first blast of fire. God gird us to do all valiantly for the helpless and innocent.

Blessed are they who die in the harness and are buried on the field or bleach there" (Thomas, 1950, p. 116).

Birney's initial response to the violence of the opposition was loneliness and depression. In 1834 he wrote to Weld: "I have not one helper—not one from whom I can draw sympathy, or impart joy, on this topic! . . . My nearest friends . . . think it is very silly in me to run against the world in a matter that cannot in any way do me any good . . . Even my own children . . . appear careless and indifferent—if anything rather disposed to look upon my views as chimerical and visionary . . . My nearest friends here are of the sort that are always crying out: take care of yourself—don't meddle with other people's affairs—do nothing, say nothing, get along quietly—make money" (Fladeland, 1955, p. 90). However, this did not deter Birney from again and again confronting both censure and the threat of physical violence against himself, "believing that if ever there was a time, it is now come, when our republic, and with her the cause of universal freedom is in a strait, where everything that ought to be periled by the patriot should be freely hazarded for her relief." Men must "themselves die freemen [rather] than slaves, or our Country, glorious as has been her hope, is gone forever." (Fladeland, 1955, p. 90).

Garrison too responded to opposition with increased defiance and with an increased identification with the Negro. In the first issue of *The Liberator* (*see* Ruchames, 1963) he flung his defiance in the face of the enemy:

Assenting to the "self-evident truth" maintained in the American Declaration of Independence, "that all men are created equal, and endowed by their Creator with certain inalienable rights— among which are life, liberty, and the pursuit of happiness," I shall strenuously contend for the immediate enfranchisement of our slave population. In Park Street Church, on the Fourth of July, 1829, in an address on slavery, I unreflectingly assented to the popular but pernicious doctrine of gradual abolition. I seize this opportunity to make a full and unequivocal recantation, and thus publicly to ask pardon of my God, of my country, and of my brethren, the poor slaves, for having uttered a sentiment so full of timidity, injustice and absurdity. A similar recantation, from my pen, was published in the *Genius of Universal Emancipation*, at Baltimore, in September, 1829. My conscience is now satisfied.

I am aware, that many object to the severity of my language; but is there not cause for severity? I will be as harsh as truth, and as uncompromising as justice. On this subject, I do not wish to think, or speak, or write, with moderation. No! no! Tell a man, whose house is on fire, to give a moderate alarm; tell him to moderately rescue his wife from the hands of the ravisher; tell the mother to gradually extricate her babe from the fire into which it has fallen; but urge me not to use moderation in a cause like the present! I am in earnest. I will not equivocate—I will not excuse—I will not retreat a single inch—AND I WILL BE HEARD. The apathy of the people is enough to make every statue leap from its pedestal, and to hasten the resurrection of the dead.

It is pretended that I am retarding the cause of emancipation by the coarseness of my invective, and the precipitancy of my measures. The charge is not true. On this question, my influence, humble as it is, is felt at this moment to a considerable extent, and shall be felt in coming years—not perniciously, but beneficially—not as a curse, but as a blessing; and POSTERITY WILL BEAR TESTIMONY THAT I WAS RIGHT. I desire to thank God, that he enables me to disregard "the fear of man which bringeth a snare" and to speak his truth in its simplicity and power. And here I close with this fresh dedication:

Oppression! I have seen thee, face to face,
And met thy cruel eye and cloudy brow;

But thy soul-withering glance I fear not now—
For dread to prouder feelings doth give place,
Of deep abhorrence! Scorning the disgrace
Of slavish knees that at thy footstool bow,
I also kneel—but with far other vow
Do hail thee and thy herd of hirelings base:
I swear, while life-blood warms my throbbing veins,
Still to oppose and thwart, with heart and hand,
Thy brutalizing sway—till Afric's chains
Are burst, and Freedom rules the rescued land,
Trampling Oppression and his iron rod:
Such is the vow I take—so help me God.

In an address to an audience of Negroes he said: "It is the lowness of your estate, in the estimation of the world, which exalts you in my eyes. It is the distance that separates you from the blessings and privileges of society, which brings you so closely to my affections. It is the unmerited scorn, reproach and persecution of your persons, by those whose complexion is colored like my own, which command for you my sympathy and respect. It is the fewness of your friends—the multitude of your enemies—that induces me to stand forth in your defense" (Ruchames, 1963).

The defiance and the disgust and the disappointment with the opposition deepened early commitment, but it also raised doubts and conflicts about the wisdom of such a commitment. Phillips and Birney, who had most to lose in social position and privilege, had the most serious and prolonged reservations. Phillips, almost thirty, travelled through Europe with his invalid wife. He knew that his mother and family expected that he would return from his year abroad cleansed of his youthful enthusiasm for the radical movement. By the end of the year he had made a firm decision. He wrote to Garrison: "I recognize in some degree the truth of the assertion that associations tend to destroy individual dependence; and I have found difficulty in answering others, however clear my own mind might be, when charged with taking steps which the sober judgement of age would regret . . . with being hurried recklessly forward by the enthusiasm of the moment and the excitement of heated meetings. I am glad, therefore, to have the opportunity of holding up the cause, with all its incidents and bearings calmly before my own mind; . . . of being able to look back, cleared of all excitement, though not I hope of all enthusiasm . . . upon the course we have taken for the last few years; and . . . I am rejoiced to say that every hour of such thought convinces me more and more of the overwhelming claims our cause has in the life-long devotion of each of us" (Bartlett, 1961, pp. 73, 74).

Birney's period of doubt and indecision as we have seen was prolonged. In 1828 he had written "It (is) hard to tell what one's duty (is) toward the poor creatures; but I have made up my mind to one thing . . . I will not allow them to be treated brutally" (Birney, Times, p. 12). He was always concerned lest he be seduced by feeling. "Fearing the reality as well as the imputation of enthusiasm . . . each ascent that my mind made to a higher and purer moral and intellectual region, I used as a standpoint to survey very deliberately all the tract that I had left. When I remember how calmly and dispassionately my mind has proceeded from truth to truth connected with this subject (i.e., slavery) to another still higher, I feel satisfied that my conclusions are not the fruits of enthusiasm" (Birney, Letter on Colonization, p. 45).

Even after Birney had apparently firmly committed himself to abolitionism

he wrote to Gerrit Smith: "I am at times greatly perplexed. To have alienated from us those with whom we [went] up from Sabbath to Sabbath to the house of God—many of our near connections and relations estranged from us, and the whole community with but here and there an exception, looking upon you as an enemy to its peace, is no small trial" (Fladeland, 1955, p. 114).

In 1837, he accepted the nomination of Secretary of the American Anti-Slavery Society. Just before his departure to New York he wrote to Lewis Tappan: "I know my own powers, I think, better than anyone else, and I fear their insufficiency for what is before me. My health is not generally so good as it was two or three years since. I am not capable of such continuous mental or physical effort as I used to be. Add to this, I have a large family of children and a sickly and dispirited wife, who is unable to control and educate them. Besides these circumstances embarrassing to myself—I apprehend, and I did from the first, that the salary I am to receive, will create some jealousy and jarring. Notwithstanding I hope for the best. Should my hope not be met I shall most cheerfully yield to circumstances that may point out to me an humbler sphere" (Fladeland, 1955, p. 160).

Nor was Birney ever to be entirely free of doubts—of his own competence—or of the effectiveness of the struggle against slavery. Six years before the end of his life, in 1851, he wrote: "I have heretofore been very earnest in my wishes and somewhat sanguine in my hopes that the North or free states would so array themselves against slavery, that it would before long be abolished; that the system would never be any stronger, and that whatever changes happened to it, would be to weaken it. I yet think, under the operation of various principles it will ultimately go out— as slavery has in Europe.

But when or how it will expire, I must say I see not. It appears to me far off, that any exertion that I can make by writing or by showing it to be wrong is unnecessary and futile" (Fladeland, 1955, p. 274). Here we see the corrosion of commitment which can result from enduring and unrelenting opposition. Birney had by this time essentially withdrawn from the struggle.

For Weld the only doubts which ever assailed him were doubts about his own worthiness, his ability to control himself and to tolerate trial by fire. To his beloved Angelina Grimke he had confessed: "You know something of my structure of mind—that I am *constitutionally*, as far as emotions are concerned, a quivering mass of intensities kept in subjection only by the *rod of iron* in the strong hand of conscience and reason and never laid aside for a moment with safety" (Thomas, 1950, p. 154).

Slavery, like sex, was primarily a moral issue to Weld. "As a question of politics and national economy, I have passed it with scarce a look or a word, believing that the business of abolitionists is with the heart of the nation, rather than with its purse strings" (Thomas, 1950, p. 102). It was against conscience, to which he brought to bear "the accumulated pressure of myriad wrongs and woes and hoarded guilt." Weld was concerned not only about the control of sex, but also about the control of fear: "Let every abolitionist debate the matter once and for all, and settle it for himself . . . whether he can lie upon the rack—and clasp the faggot—and tread with steady step the scaffold—whether he can stand at the post of duty and having done all and suffered all, stand—and if cloven down, fall and die a martyr 'not accepting deliverance'" (Thomas, 1950, p. 116). Whereas Phillips had been concerned with the wisdom of his choice and Birney with the nature and consequences

of his choice, Weld was concerned with his ability to tolerate the inevitable consequences of the morally necessary choice.

Only Garrison suffered no serious doubts once he had embarked on his voyage "against wind and tide." As he had written in an editorial on his twenty-fifth birthday, "I am now sailing up a mighty bay with a fresh breeze and a pleasant hope—the waves are rippling merrily, and the heavens are serenely bright. I have encountered many a storm of adversity—rough, and cruel, and sudden—but not a sail has been lost nor a single leak sprung" (Merril, 1963, p. 34). Later that year after he spent seven weeks in jail he wrote: "How do I bear up under my adversities? I answer—like the oak—like the Alps—unshaken, stormproof. Opposition, and abuse, and slander, and prejudice, and judicial tyranny, are like oil to the flame of my zeal. I am not dismayed, but bolder and more confident than ever. I say to my persecutors, 'I bid you defiance! Let the courts condemn me to fine and imprisonment for denouncing oppression: Am I to be frightened by dungeons and chains? can they humble my spirit? do I not remember that I am an American citizen? and, as a citizen, a freeman, and what is more, a being accountable to God? I will not hold my peace on the subject of African oppression. If need be, who would not die a martyr to such a cause?" (Merril, 1963, p. 39).

Engaging the Commitment of Society

Let us consider now the collective influence of the four men on their society. The same dynamic of violence and suffering which gradually deepened the commitment of the four was also responsible for engaging the commitment of others to abolitionism or at least to resistance against the extension of slavery to free soil. The violence inflicted on the early abolitionists and the suffering they endured led others to take up their cause.

The murder of the abolitionist Lovejoy and the mob action against Garrison, which had drawn Phillips into the struggle, also excited the sympathies and indignation of others. Dr. Henry Ingersoll Bowditch, a prominent physician, became an abolitionist in response to the Garrison mob: "Then it has come to this that a man cannot speak on slavery within sight of Faneuil Hall." Seeing Samuel A. Eliot, a member of the city government, he offered to help him suppress the rioters. "Instead of sustaining the idea of free speech . . . he rather intimated that the authorities, while not wishing for a mob, rather sympathized with its object which was to forcibly suppress the abolitionists. I was completely disgusted and I vowed in my heart as I left him with utter loathing, 'I am an abolitionist from this very moment'" (Lader, 1961, pp. 22–23).

Because the abolitionists were fearless, and again and again exposed themselves to the danger of physical violence they evoked widespread sympathy and respect and simultaneous indignation against those who hurt and threatened them.

After the mob destroyed Birney's press in Cincinnati and threatened his life, Salmon Chase stood openly with the abolitionists. He was to become the congressional representative of abolitionism. Chase later wrote that he "became an opponent of slavery and the slave Power while witnessing Birney's display of conviction and intelligence as he confronted the mobocrats" (Hart, 1899, p. 51).

William T. Allan's indecision between preaching Christianity or becoming an abolitionist was resolved by the same mob. Birney's own son, William, was converted to the movement by virtue of having faced the mob when it came after his father. From all over the country came letters of encouragement. Not the least of these was from the influential and widely respected New England minister, Dr. William Ellery Channing, who had previously denounced the abolitionist movement:

> I earnestly desire, my dear Sir that you and your associates will hold fast the right of free discussion by speech and the press, and, at the same time, that you will exercise it as Christians, and as friends of your race. That you, Sir, will not fail in these duties, I rejoice to believe. Accept my humble tribute of respect and admiration for your disinterestedness, for your faithfulness to your convictions, under the peculiar sacrifices to which you have been called . . . I look with scorn on the selfish greatness of this world, and with pity on the most gifted and prosperous in the struggle for office and power, but I look with reverence on the obscurest man, who suffers for the right, who is true to a good but persecuted cause. (Fladeland, 1955, p. 144)

Lewis Tappan expressed confidence that Birney would again publish the *Philanthropist*. Daniel Henshaw, a Lynn, Massachusetts, editor, called Birney "one of the noblest sons of the West" who had "dared to lift up his voice in favor of liberty when all around him seemed given over to corruption, to slavery, to moral destruction" (Fladeland, 1955, p. 145). Even Alva Woods, whom Birney had once hired as president of the University of Alabama, in his baccalaureate address expressed his deep indignation at this action by the mob.

But it was not only Garrison, Phillips, Weld and Birney who evoked violence, sympathy and indignation. There were hundreds of agents who were stoned, tarred and feathered, whipped, beaten up and in some cases killed. In addition to physical violence there was continual verbal abuse and threat of violence heaped publicly on every abolitionist. In

Garrison's case a price was actually placed on his head in the South. Indeed it seems clear that without the exaggeration of Garrison's reputation by the South, his influence could never have been as great as it was.

VIOLENCE AND SUFFERING

We have argued that violence and suffering played a central role in the commitment first of the abolitionists and then in influencing general public opinion. What do we mean by violence and suffering? We refer by violence to any negative affect inflicted by someone on another, with intent to hurt; it may be an aggressive threat of physical violence, or a verbal insult. By suffering we refer to any negative affect which is instigated in the victim as a result of violence whether this be a feeling of humiliation, helpless rage, terror or distress. It is our argument that in a democratic society the impact of such violence and suffering on the observer is to arouse equally intense affect and to arouse vicarious distress, shame, fear or sympathy for the victim and anger and contempt for the aggressor. Because of this identification with the victim his ideas will tend to become more influential than before such an attack. In hierarchically organized societies, identification with the upper classes and castes will radically attenuate empathy with the victims of oppression.

Since most men in a democratic society share its values to some extent, even those who identify with the aggressor will feel a certain amount of guilt at the challenge to democratic values. Thus in the North, some of those who had identified with slaveholders and been most hostile to the abolitionists joined in lionizing them after the Civil War had ended—as if they were atoning for having identified with the "anti-democratic" position.

We would argue that guilt over slavery was experienced in the South, too. There is some indirect evidence for this from the great increase in popularity of Garrison and Phillips after the Civil War. We assume that guilt over slavery was experienced in the South but that it was defended against by only half-believed exaggeration of the villainy of the victims and by exaggeration of the evils of wage "slavery" in the North.

The grounds for identification with the victim are numerous. First, the tendency to identify with any human being is quite general. Second, in a democratic society there is a taboo on inflicting hurt on anyone since it denies his equal right to life, liberty and the pursuit of happiness. Third, to the extent to which there is a tendency to identify with the aggressor, vicarious guilt is experienced, and, as a secondary reaction, sympathy for the victim is increased. Insofar as the victim is defending others (including oneself) there is, fourth, anger against the aggressor because the self is being vicariously attacked and, fifth, guilt and sympathy for the victim who is selflessly fighting the battles of others (including one's own battles).

Because of heightened identification with the victim, polarization between aggressor and victim increases; this magnifies the conflict and draws into the struggle, on both sides, thousands who would otherwise not have become involved. One half of the battle for radical social change is to increase the density of affect and ideation about the change. To look steadily at a social condition that violates the shared basic values of a society produces suffering for the society as a whole just as does the condition itself for a segment of the society. Contrary to the $+-+$ and $--+-$ triads, the Northern American citizen of the mid-nineteenth century was essentially ambivalent about slavery. He neither could approve it nor steadily disapprove it. He would have preferred to forget it. They were responsible for forcing confrontation and thereby radically increased the density of affect and ideation about the issue. This is precisely what the abolitionists made more and more difficult. Not all Americans became committed with maximum density of ideation and affect, but it is certain that the abolitionists greatly magnified the awareness and level of feeling of enemy and sympathizer alike and thereby exerted an amplified influence. The abolitionists did not permit them to look away from the ugly violation of the democratic ethos. In part they achieved this by provoking opposition and by offering themselves as victims. Thereby they evoked sympathy for themselves and their cause, and provoked anger and contempt for those who supported slavery.

The influence of the abolitionists was amplified by the growing polarization between the North and the South in their competition for the expanding frontier to the West. Again and again sectional conflict amplified the relevance and influence of their doctrine. The abolitionists converted what might have remained political issues into moral issues and thereby radically increased their influence.

As early as 1834 the American Antislavery Society encouraged all efforts to petition Congress to abolish slavery. In 1837, Congress was deluged with petitions signed by over 200,000 people. Southern congressmen, aided by Northern sympathizers, invoked a gag rule prohibiting the reception or discussion of these petitions. John Quincy Adams, unsympathetic as he had been to abolitionism, was deeply disturbed by this threat to constitutional rights and used every device to put antislavery petitions before Congress. Abolition at last had a national forum. Adams ultimately became a one-

man symbol of the struggle against slavery and was indicted to be censured. Day after day "old man eloquent" held the floor in his own defense. Petitions against his censure began to pour into the House. He had suddenly, late in his life, captured the imagination of the North and become its hero. He defeated his enemies decisively. As Weld described it to his wife: "The triumph of Mr. Adams is complete. This is the first victory over the slaveholders in a body ever yet achieved since the foundation of the government and from this time their downfall takes its date" (Lader, 1961, p. 98).

The abolitionists also succeeded in converting the Fugitive Slave Law, the visit of Hoar to South Carolina, the burning of the mail in Charleston, the Dred Scott Decision, and the war with Mexico into footnotes to the abolitionist struggle. The Fugitive Slave Law of 1850 produced a very strong reaction in the North. Free Northern Negroes began an exodus to Canada. Everyone was under a potential obligation to be a slave catcher. By the 1850's, it appeared to many, for the first time, that perhaps the abolitionists had not really exaggerated the moral iniquity of the South. Many who at one time had regarded the abolitionists as the lunatic fringe were to have second thoughts when in 1854 a former slave had to be taken by force from Boston and shipped back to slavery as, ashamed and helpless, thousands were forced to look on, as their own militia guarded the prisoner against rescue. Gradually more and more Northerners came to experience the suffering of violence, at first vicariously and then more directly, until the firing on Fort Sumter suddenly galvanized all to respond in kind. War is a special case of commitment, and we would defend the position that a democratic society can commit itself to war only if it feels it has suffered violence upon itself, directly or vicariously.

The epilogue to our theory of commitment would account for the ironic necessity, one hundred years later, to repeat the struggle initiated by the abolitionists. Our history can be understood as a series of identifications with suffering against the violence which provoked it. It was widely said, before the attack on Fort Sumter, that the North could not possibly enter into war with the South. That attack produced an immediate identification with the nation which had suffered such violence. As war weariness grew, however, many in the North were prepared to relent toward the South and even to forget the issue of slavery. But the assassination of Lincoln stiffened the posture of the North once again and the North supported a severe Reconstruction against the South. Then, seeing how the South suffered violence at its hands, the North, identifying vicariously with its own victim, relented, and gave tacit consent to the reestablishment of a caste society. Now, again, we have become aware of the suffering of the Negro and are increasingly committed to rescue him.

Cognitive, Social, and Physiological Determinants of Emotional State[1]

Stanley Schachter
Jerome E. Singer

The problem of which cues, internal or external, permit a person to label and identify his own emotional state has been with us since the days that James (1890) first tendered his doctrine that "the bodily changes follow directly the perception of the exciting fact, and that our feeling of the same changes as they occur *is* the emotion" (p. 449). Since we are aware of a variety of feeling and emotion states, it should follow from James' proposition that the various emotions will be accompanied by a variety of differentiable bodily states. Following James' pronouncement, a formidable number of studies were undertaken in search of the physiological differentiators of the emotions. The results, in these early days, were almost uniformly negative. All of the emotional states experimentally manipulated were characterized by a general pattern of excitation of the sympathetic nervous system but there appeared to be no clear-cut physiological discriminators of the various emo-

Reprinted from *Psychological Review*, 1962, Vol. 69, pp. 379–399 with the permission of the American Psychological Association and the authors.

[1] This experiment is part of a program of research on cognitive and physiological determinants of emotional state which is being conducted at the Department of Social Psychology at Columbia University under PHS Research Grant M-2584 from the National Institute of Mental Health, United States Public Health Service. This experiment was conducted at the Laboratory for Research in Social Relations at the University of Minnesota.

The authors wish to thank Jean Carlin and Ruth Hase, the physicians in the study, and Bibb Latané and Leonard Weller who were the paid participants.

tions. This pattern of results was so consistent from experiment to experiment that Cannon (1929) offered, as one of the crucial criticisms of the James-Lange theory, the fact that "the same visceral changes occur in very different emotional states and in non-emotional states" (p. 351).

More recent work, however, has given some indication that there may be differentiators. Ax (1953) and Schachter (1957) studied fear and anger. On a large number of indices both of these states were characterized by a similarly high level of autonomic activation but on several indices they did differ in the degree of activiation. Wolf and Wolff (1947) studied a subject with a gastric fistula and were able to distinguish two patterns in the physiological responses of the stomach wall. It should be noted, though, that for many months they studied their subject during and following a great variety of moods and emotions and were able to distinguish only two patterns.

Whether or not there are physiological distinctions among the various emotional states must be considered an open question. Recent work might be taken to indicate that such differences are at best rather subtle and that the variety of emotion, mood, and feeling states are by no means matched by an equal variety of visceral patterns.

This rather ambiguous situation has led Ruckmick (1936), Hunt, Cole, and Reis (1958), Schachter (1959) and others to suggest that cognitive factors may be major determinants of emotional states. Granted a general pattern of sympathetic excitation as characteristic of emotional states, granted that there may be some differences in pattern from state to state, it is suggested that one labels, interprets, and identifies this stirred-up state in terms of the characteristics of the precipitating situation and one's apper-

ceptive mass. This suggests, then, that an emotional state may be considered a function of a state of physiological arousal[2] and of a cognition appropriate to this state of arousal. The cognition, in a sense, exerts a steering function. Cognitions arising from the immediate situation as interpreted by past experience provide the framework within which one understands and labels his feelings. It is the cognition which determines whether the state of physiological arousal will be labeled as "anger," "joy," "fear," or whatever.

In order to examine the implications of this formulation let us consider the fashion in which these two elements, a state of physiological arousal and cognitive factors, would interact in a variety of situations. In most emotion inducing situations, of course, the two factors are completely interrelated. Imagine a man walking alone down a dark alley, a figure with a gun suddenly appears. The perception-cognition "figure with a gun" in some fashion initiates a state of physiological arousal; this state of arousal is interpreted in terms of knowledge about dark alleys and guns and the state of arousal is labeled "fear." Similarly a student who unexpectedly learns that he has made Phi Beta Kappa may experience a state of arousal which he will label "joy."

Let us now consider circumstances in which these two elements, the physiological and the cognitive, are, to some extent, independent. First, is the state of physiological arousal alone sufficient to induce an emotion? Best evidence

[2] Though our experiments are concerned exclusively with the physiological changes produced by the injection of adrenalin, which appear to be primarily the result of sympathetic excitation, the term physiological arousal is used in preference to the more specific "excitation of the sympathetic nervous system" because there are indications, to be discussed later, that this formulation is applicable to a variety of bodily states.

indicates that it is not. Marañon[3] (1924), in a fascinating study, (which was replicated by Cantril & Hunt, 1932, and Landis & Hunt, 1932) injected 210 of his patients with the sympathomimetic agent adrenalin and then simply asked them to introspect. Seventy-one percent of his subjects simply reported their physical symptoms with no emotional overtone; 29% of the subjects responded in an apparently emotional fashion. Of these the great majority described their feelings in a fashion that Marañon labeled "cold" or "as if" emotions, that is, they made statements such as "I feel *as if* I were afraid" or "*as if* I were awaiting a great happiness." This is a sort of emotional "déjà vu" experience; these subjects are neither happy nor afraid, they feel "as if" they were. Finally a very few cases apparently reported a genuine emotional experience. However, in order to produce this reaction in most of these few cases, Marañon (1924) points out:

> One must suggest a memory with strong affective force but not so strong as to produce an emotion in the normal state. For example, in several cases we spoke to our patients before the injection of their sick children or dead parents and they responded calmly to this topic. The same topic presented later, during the adrenal commotion, was sufficient to trigger emotion. This adrenal commotion places the subject in a situation of 'affective imminence' (pp. 307–308).

Apparently, then, to produce a genuinely emotional reaction to adrenalin, Marañon was forced to provide such subjects with an appropriate cognition.

Though Marañon (1924) is not explicit on his procedure, it is clear that his subjects knew that they were receiving an injection and in all likelihood knew that

[3] Translated copies of Marañon's (1924) paper may be obtained by writing to the senior author.

they were receiving adrenalin and probably had some order of familiarity with its effects. In short, though they underwent the pattern of sympathetic discharge common to strong emotional states, at the same time they had a completely appropriate cognition or explanation as to why they felt this way. This, we would suggest, is the reason so few of Marañon's subjects reported any emotional experience.

Consider now a person in a state of physiological arousal for which no immediately explanatory or appropriate cognitions are available. Such a state could result were one covertly to inject a subject with adrenalin or, unknown to him, feed the subject a sympathomimetic drug such as ephedrine. Under such conditions a subject would be aware of palpitations, tremor, face flushing, and most of the battery of symptoms associated with a discharge of the sympathetic nervous system. In contrast to Marañon's (1924) subjects he would, at the same time, be utterly unaware of why he felt this way. What would be the consequence of such a state?

Schachter (1959) has suggested that precisely such a state would lead to the arousal of "evaluative needs" (Festinger, 1954), that is, pressures would act on an individual in such a state to understand and label his bodily feelings. His bodily state grossly resembles the condition in which it has been at times of emotional excitement. How would he label his present feelings? It is suggested, of course, that he will label his feelings in terms of his knowledge of the immediate situation.[4] Should he at the time

[4] This suggestion is not new for several psychologists have suggested that situational factors should be considered the chief differentiators of the emotions. Hunt, Cole, and Reis (1958) probably make this point most explicitly in their study distinguishing among fear, anger, and sorrow in terms of situational characteristics.

be with a beautiful woman he might decide that he was wildly in love or sexually excited. Should he be at a gay party, he might, by comparing himself to others, decide that he was extremely happy and euphoric. Should he be arguing with his wife, he might explode in fury and hatred. Or, should the situation be completely inappropriate he could decide that he was excited about something that had recently happened to him or, simply, that he was sick. In any case, it is our basic assumption that emotional states are a function of the interaction of such cognitive factors with a state of physiological arousal.

This line of thought, then, leads to the following propositions:

1. Given a state of physiological arousal for which an individual has no immediate explanation, he will "label" this state and describe his feelings in terms of the cognitions available to him. To the extent that cognitive factors are potent determiners of emotional states, it could be anticipated that precisely the same state of physiological arousal could be labeled "joy" or "fury" or "jealousy" or any of a great diversity of emotional labels depending on the cognitive aspects of the situation.

2. Given a state of physiological arousal for which an individual has a completely appropriate explanation (e.g., "I feel this way because I have just received an injection of adrenalin") no evaluative needs will arise and the individual is unlikely to label his feelings in terms of the alternative cognitions available.

Finally, consider a condition in which emotion inducing cognitions are present but there is no state of physiological arousal. For example, an individual might be completely aware that he is in great danger but for some reason (drug or surgical) remain in a state of physiological

quiescence. Does he experience the emotion "fear"? Our formulation of emotion as a joint function of a state of physiological arousal and an appropriate cognition, would, of course, suggest that he does not, which leads to our final proposition.

3. Given the same cognitive circumstances, the individual will react emotionally or describe his feelings as emotions only to the extent that he experiences a state of physiological arousal.[5]

PROCEDURE

The experimental test of these propositions require (*a*) the experimental manipulation of a state of physiological arousal, (*b*) the manipulation of the extent to which the subject has an appropriate or proper explanation of his bodily state, and (*c*) the creation of situations from which explanatory cognitions may be derived.

In order to satisfy the first two experimental requirements, the experiment was cast in the framework of a study of the effects of vitamin supplements on vision. As soon as a subject arrived, he was taken to a private room and told by the experimenter:

> In this experiment we would like to make various tests of your vision. We are particularly interested in how certain vitamin compounds and vitamin supplements affect the visual skills. In particular, we want to find out how the vitamin compound called 'Suproxin' affects your vision.
>
> What we would like to do, then, if we

---

[5] In his critique of the James-Lange theory of emotion, Cannon (1929) also makes the point that sympathectomized animals and patients do seem to manifest emotional behavior. This criticism is, of course, as applicable to the above proposition as it was to the James-Lange formulation. We shall discuss the issues involved in later papers.

can get your permission, is to give you a small injection of Suproxin. The injection itself is mild and harmless; however, since some people do object to being injected we don't want to talk you into anything. Would you mind receiving a Suproxin injection?

If the subject agrees to the injection (and all but 1 of 185 subjects did) the experimenter continues with instructions we shall describe shortly, then leaves the room. In a few minutes a physician enters the room, briefly repeats the experimenter's instructions, takes the subject's pulse and then injects him with Suproxin.

Depending upon condition, the subject receives one of two forms of Suproxin— epinephrine or a placebo.

Epinephrine or adrenalin is a sympathomimetic drug whose effects, with minor exceptions, are almost a perfect mimicry of a discharge of the sympathetic nervous systems. Shortly after injection systolic blood pressure increases markedly, heart rate increases somewhat, cutaneous blood flow decreases, while muscle and cerebral blood flow increase, blood sugar and lactic acid concentration increase, and respiration rate increases slightly. As far as the subject is concerned the major subjective symptoms are palpitation, tremor, and sometimes a feeling of flushing and accelerated breathing. With a subcutaneous injection (in the dosage administered to our subjects), such effects usually begin within 3–5 minutes of injection and last anywhere from 10 minutes to an hour. For most subjects these effects are dissipated within 15–20 minutes after injection.

Subjects receiving epinephrine received a subcutaneous injection of ½ cubic centimeter of a 1 : 1000 solution of Winthrop Laboratory's Suprarenin, a saline solution of epinephrine bitartrate.

Subjects in the placebo condition received a subcutaneous injection of ½ cubic centimeter of saline solution. This is, of course, completely neutral material with no side effects at all.

Manipulating an Appropriate Explanation

By "appropriate" we refer to the extent to which the subject has an authoritative, unequivocal explanation of his bodily condition. Thus, a subject who had been informed by the physician that as a direct consequence of the injection he would feel palpitations, tremor, etc. would be considered to have a completely appropriate explanation. A subject who had been informed only that the injection would have no side effects would have no appropriate explanation of his state. This dimension of appropriateness was manipulated in three experimental conditions which shall be called: Epinephrine Informed (Epi Inf), Epinephine Ignorant (Epi Ign), and Epinephrine Misinformed (Epi Mis).

Immediately after the subject had agreed to the injection and before the physician entered the room, the experimenter's spiel in each of these conditions went as follows:

Epinephrine informed. I should also tell you that some of our subjects have experienced side effects from the Suproxin. These side effects are transitory, that is, they will only last for about 15 or 20 minutes. What will probably happen is that your hand will start to shake, your heart will start to pound, and your face may get warm and flushed. Again these are side effects lasting about 15 or 20 minutes.

While the physician was giving the injection, she told the subject that the injection was mild and harmless and repeated this description of the symptoms that the subject could expect as a consequence of the shot. In this condition, then, subjects have a completely appropriate explanation of their bodily state. They know precisely what they will feel and why.

Epinephrine ignorant. In this condition, when the subject agreed to the injection, the experimenter said nothing more relevant to side effects and simply left the room. While the physician was giving the injection, she told the subject that the injection was mild and harmless and would have no side effects. In this condition, then, the subject has no experimentally provided explanation for his bodily state.

> *Epinephrine misinformed.* I should also tell you that some of our subjects have experienced side effects from the Suproxin. These side effects are transitory, that is, they will only last for about 15 or 20 minutes. What will probably happen is that your feet will feel numb, you will have an itching sensation over parts of your body, and you may get a slight headache. Again these are side effects lasting 15 or 20 minutes.

And again, the physician repeated these symptoms while injecting the subject.

None of these symptoms, of course, are consequences of an injection of epinephrine and, in effect, these instructions provide the subject with a completely inappropriate explanation of his bodily feelings. This condition was introduced as a control condition of sorts. It seemed possible that the description of side effects in the Epi Inf condition might turn the subject introspective, self-examining, possibly slightly troubled. Differences on the dependent variable between the Epi Inf and Epi Ign conditions might, then, be due to such factors rather than to differences in appropriateness. The false symptoms in the Epi Mis condition should similarly turn the subject introspective, etc., but the instructions in this condition do not provide an appropriate explanation of the subject's state.

Subjects in all of the above conditions were injected with epinephrine. Finally, there was a placebo condition in which subjects, who were injected with saline solution, were given precisely the same treatment as subjects in the Epi Ign condition.

Producing an Emotion
Inducing Cognition

Our initial hypothesis has suggested that given a state of physiological arousal for which the individual has no adequate explanation, cognitive factors can lead the individual to describe his feelings with any of a diversity of emotional labels. In order to test this hypothesis, it was decided to manipulate emotional states which can be considered quite different—euphoria and anger.

There are, of course, many ways to induce such states. In our own program of research, we have concentrated on social determinants of emotional states and have been able to demonstrate in other studies that people do evaluate their own feelings by comparing themselves with others around them (Schachter 1959; Wrightsman 1960). In this experiment we have attempted again to manipulate emotional state by social means. In one set of conditions, the subject is placed together with a stooge who has been trained to act euphorically. In a second set of conditions the subject is with a stooge trained to act in an angry fashion.

Euphoria

Immediately[6] after the subject had been injected, the physician left the room

[6] It was, of course, imperative that the sequence with the stooge begin before the subject felt his first symptoms for otherwise the subject would be virtually forced to interpret his feelings in terms of events preceding the stooge's entrance. Pretests had indicated that, for most subjects, epinephrine-caused symptoms began within 3–5 minutes after injection. A deliberate attempt was made then to bring in the stooge within 1 minute after the subject's injection.

and the experimenter returned with a stooge whom he introduced as another subject, then said:

Both of you have had the Suproxin shot and you'll both be taking the same tests of vision. What I ask you to do now is just wait for 20 minutes. The reason for this is simply that we have to allow 20 minutes for the Suproxin to get from the injection site into the bloodstream. At the end of 20 minutes when we are certain that most of the Suproxin has been absorbed into the bloodstream, we'll begin the tests of vision.

The room in which this was said had been deliberately put into a state of mild disarray. As he was leaving, the experimenter apologetically added:

The only other thing I should do is to apologize for the condition of the room. I just didn't have time to clean it up. So, if you need any scratch paper or rubber bands or pencils, help yourself. I'll be back in 20 minutes to begin the vision tests.

As soon as the experimenter had left, the stooge introduced himself again, made a series of standard icebreaker comments, and then launched into his routine. For observation purposes, the stooge's act was broken into a series of standard units, demarcated by a change in activity or a standard comment. In sequence, the units of the stooge's routine were the following:

1. Stooge reaches for a piece of paper and starts doodling saying, "They said we could use this for scratch, didn't they?" He doodles a fish for some 30 seconds, then says:
2. "This scrap paper isn't even much good for doodling" and crumples paper and attempts to throw it into wastebasket in far corner of the room. He misses but this leads him into a "basketball game." He crumples up other sheets of paper, shoots a few baskets, says "Two

points" occasionally. He gets up and does a jump shot saying, "The old jump shot is really on today."
3. If the subject has not joined in, the stooge throws a paper basketball to the subject saying, "Here, you try it."
4. Stooge continues his game saying, "The trouble with paper basketballs is that you don't really have any control."
5. Stooge continues basketball, then gives it up saying, "This is one of my good days. I feel like a kid again. I think I'll make a plane." He makes a paper airplane saying, "I guess I'll make one of the longer ones."
6. Stooge flies plane. Gets up and retrieves plane. Flies again, etc.
7. Stooge throws plane at subject.
8. Stooge, flying plane, says, "Even when I was a kid, I was never much good at this."
9. Stooge tears off part of plane saying, "Maybe this plane can't fly but at least it's good for something." He wads up paper and making a slingshot of a rubber band begins to shoot the paper.
10. Shooting, the stooge says, "They [paper ammunition] really go better if you make them long. They don't work right if you wad them up."
11. While shooting, stooge notices a sloppy pile of manila folders on a table. He builds a tower of these folders, then goes to the opposite end of the room to shoot at the tower.
12. He misses several times, then hits and sheers as the tower falls. He goes over to pick up the folders.
13. While picking up, he notices, behind a portable blackboard, a pair of hula hoops which have been covered with black tape with a few wires sticking out of the tape. He reaches for these, taking one for himself and putting the other aside but within reaching distance of the subject. The stooge tries the hula hoop, saying, "This isn't as easy as it looks."
14. Stooge twirls hoop wildly on arm, saying, "Hey, look at this—this is great."
15. Stooge replaces the hula hoop and sits down with his feet on the table. Shortly thereafter the experimenter returns to the room.

This routine was completely standard, though its pace, of course, varied depending upon the subject's reaction, the extent to which he entered into this bedlam and the extent to which he initiated activities of his own. The only variations from this standard routine were those forced by the subject. Should the subject originate some nonsense of his own and request the stooge to join in, he would do so. And, he would, of course, respond to any comments initiated by the subject.

Subjects in each of the three "appropriateness" conditions and in the placebo condition were submitted to this setup. The stooge, of course, never knew in which condition any particular subject fell.

Anger

Immediately after the injection, the experimenter brought a stooge into the subject's room, introduced the two and after explaining the necessity for a 20 minute delay for "the Suproxin to get from the injection site into the bloodstream" he continued, "We would like you to use these 20 minutes to answer these questionnaires." Then handing out the questionnaires, he concludes with, "I'll be back in 20 minutes to pick up the questionnaires and begin the tests of vision."

Before looking at the questionnaire, the stooge says to the subject,

> I really wanted to come for an experiment today, but I think it's unfair for them to give you shots. At least, they should have told us about the shots when they called us; you hate to refuse, once you're here already.

The questionnaires, five pages long, start off innocently requesting face sheet information and then grow increasingly personal and insulting. The stooge, sitting directly opposite the subject, paces his own answers so that at all times subject and stooge are working on the same question. At regular points in the question-

naire, the stooge makes a series of standardized comments about the questions. His comments start off innocently enough, grow increasingly querulous, and finally he ends up in a rage. In sequence, he makes the following comments.

1. Before answering any items, he leafs quickly through the questionnaire saying, "Boy, this is a long one."
2. Question 7 on the questionnaire requests, "List the foods that you would eat in a typical day." The stooge comments, "Oh for Pete's sake, what did I have for breakfast this morning?"
3. Question 9 asks, "Do you ever hear bells? ————. How often? ————." The stooge remarks, "Look at Question 9. How ridiculous can you get? I hear bells every time I change classes."
4. Question 13 requests, "List the childhood diseases you have had and the age at which you had them" to which the stooge remarks, "I get annoyed at this childhood disease question. I can't remember what childhood diseases I had, and especially at what age. Can you?"
5. Question 17 asks "What is your father's average annual income?" and the stooge says, "This really irritates me. It's none of their business what my father makes. I'm leaving that blank."
6. Question 25 presents a long series of items such as "Does not bathe or wash regularly," "Seems to need psychiatric care," etc. and requests the respondent to write down for which member of his immediate family each item seems most applicable. The question specifically prohibits the answer "None" and each item must be answered. The stooge says, "I'll be damned if I'll fill out Number 25. 'Does not bathe or wash regularly'— that's a real insult." He then angrily crosses out the entire item.
7. Question 28 reads:
"How many times each week do you have sexual intercourse?" 0–1 ————
2–3 ———— 4–6 ———— 7 and over ————. The stooge bites out, "The hell with it! I don't have to tell them all this."
8. The stooge sits sullenly for a few moments then he rips up his questionnaire, crumples the pieces and hurls them to the floor, saying, "I'm not wasting

any more time. I'm getting my books and leaving" and he stamps out of the room.

9. The questionnaire continues for eight more questions ending with: "With how many men (other than your father) has your mother had extramarital relationships?" 4 and under ———: 5–9 ———: 10 and over ———.

Subjects in the Epi Ign, Epi Inf and Placebo conditions were run through this "anger" inducing sequence. The stooge, again, did not know to which condition the subject had been assigned.

In summary, this is a seven condition experiment which, for two different emotional states, allows us (a) to evaluate the effects of "appropriateness" on emotional inducibility and (b) to begin to evaluate the effects of sympathetic activation on emotional inducibility. In schematic form the conditions are the following:

Euphoria	Anger
Epi Inf	Epi Inf
Epi Ign	Epi Ign
Epi Mis	Placebo
Placebo	

The Epi Mis condition was not run in the Anger sequence. This was originally conceived as a control condition and it was felt that its inclusion in the Euphoria conditions alone would suffice as a means of evaluating the possible artifactual effect of the Epi Inf instructions.

Measurement

Two types of measures of emotional state were obtained. Standardized observation through a one-way mirror was the technique used to assess the subject's behavior. To what extent did he act euphoric or angry? Such behavior can be considered in a way as a "semiprivate"

index of mood for as far as the subject was concerned, his emotional behavior could be known only to the other person in the room—presumably another student. The second type of measure was self-report in which, on a variety of scales, the subject indicated his mood of the moment. Such measures can be considered "public" indices of mood for they would, of course, be available to the experimenter and his associates.

Observation

Euphoria

For each of the first 14 units of the stooge's standardized routine an observer kept a running chronicle of what the subject did and said. For each unit the observer coded the subject's behavior in one or more of the following categories:

Category 1. Joins in activity. If the subject entered into the stooge's activities, e.g., if he made or flew airplanes, threw paper basketballs, hula hooped, etc., his behavior was coded in this category.

Category 2. Initiates new activity. A subject was so coded if he gave indications of creative euphoria, that is, if, on his own, he initiated behavior outside of the stooge's routine. Instances of such behavior would be the subject who threw open the window and, laughing, hurled paper basketballs at passersby; or, the subject who jumped on a table and spun one hula hoop on his leg and the other on his neck.

Categories 3 and 4. Ignores or watches stooge. Subjects who paid flatly no attention to the stooge or who, with or without comment, simply watched the stooge without joining in his activity were coded in these categories.

For any particular unit of behavior, the subject's behavior was coded in one or more of these categories. To test reliability of coding two observers independently coded two experimental sessions. The observers agreed completely on the coding of 88% of the units.

Anger

For each of the units of stooge behavior, an observer recorded the subject's responses and coded them according to the following category scheme:

Category 1. Agrees. In response to the stooge the subject makes a comment indicating that he agrees with the stooge's standardized comment or that he, too, is irked by a particular item on the questionnaire. For example, a subject who responded to the stooge's comment on the "father's income" question by saying, "I don't like that kind of personal question either" would be so coded (scored +2).

Category 2. Disagrees. In response to the stooge's comment, the subject makes a comment which indicates that he disagrees with the stooge's meaning or mood; e.g., in response to the stooge's comment on the "father's income" question, such a subject might say, "Take it easy, they probably have a good reason for wanting the information" (scored −2).

Category 3. Neutral. A noncommittal or irrelevant response to the stooge's remark (scored 0).

Category 4. Initiates agreement or disagreement. With no instigation by the stooge, a subject, so coded, would have volunteered a remark indicating that he felt the same way or, alternatively, quite differently than the stooge. Examples would be "Boy I hate this kind of thing" or "I'm enjoying this" (scored +2 or −2).

Category 5. Watches. The subject makes no verbal response to the stooge's comment but simply looks directly at him (scored 0).

Category 6. Ignores. The subject makes no verbal response to the stooge's comment nor does he look at him; the subject, paying no attention at all to the stooge, simply works at his own questionnaire (scored −1).

A subject was scored in one or more of these categories for each unit of stooge behavior. To test reliability, two observers independently coded three experimental sessions. In order to get a behavioral index of anger, observation protocol was scored according to the values presented in parentheses after each of the above definitions of categories. In a unit-by-unit comparison, the two observers agreed completely on the scoring of 71% of the units jointly observed. The scores of the two observers differed by a value of 1 or less for 88% of the units coded and in not a single case did the two observers differ in the direction of their scoring of a unit.

Self Report of Mood and Physical Condition

When the subject's session with the stooge was completed, the experimenter returned to the room, took pulses and said:

Before we proceed with the vision tests, there is one other kind of information which we must have. We have found, as you can probably imagine, that there are many things beside Suproxin that affect how well you see in our tests. How hungry you are, how tired you are, and even the mood you're in at the time —whether you feel happy or irritated at the time of testing will affect how well you see. To understand the data we collect on you, then, we must be able to figure out which effects are due to causes such as these and which are caused by Suproxin.

The only way we can get such information about your physical and emotional state is to have you tell us. I'll hand out these questionnaires and ask you to answer them as accurately as possible. Obviously, our data on the vision tests will only be as accurate as your description of your mental and physical state.

In keeping with this spiel, the questionnaire that the experimenter passed out contained a number of mock questions about hunger, fatigue, etc., as well as questions of more immediate relevance to the experiment. To measure mood or emotional state the following two were the crucial questions:

1. How irritated, angry or annoyed would you say you feel at present?

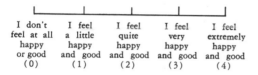

| I don't feel at all irritated or angry (0) | I feel a little irritated and angry (1) | I feel quite irritated and angry (2) | I feel very irritated and angry (3) | I feel extremely irritated and angry (4) |

2. How good or happy would you say you feel at present?

| I don't feel at all happy or good (0) | I feel a little happy and good (1) | I feel quite happy and good (2) | I feel very happy and good (3) | I feel extremely happy and good (4) |

To measure the physical effects of epinephrine and determine whether or not the injection had been successful in producing the necessary bodily state, the following questions were asked:

1. Have you experienced any palpitation (consciousness of your own heart beat)?

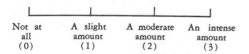

| Not at all (0) | A slight amount (1) | A moderate amount (2) | An intense amount (3) |

2. Did you feel any tremor (involuntary shaking of the hands, arms or legs)?

| Not at all (0) | A slight amount (1) | A moderate amount (2) | An intense amount (3) |

To measure possible effects of the instructions in the Epi Mis condition, the following questions were asked:

1. Did you feel any numbness in your feet?
2. Did you feel any itching sensation?
3. Did you experience any feeling of headache?

To all three of these questions was attached a four-point scale running from "Not at all" to "An intense amount."

In addition to these scales, the subjects were asked to answer two open-end questions on other physical or emotional sensations they may have experienced during the experimental session. A final measure of bodily state was pulse rate which was taken by the physician or the experimenter at two times—immediately before the injection and immediately after the session with the stooge.

When the subjects had completed these questionnaires, the experimenter announced that the experiment was over, explained the deception and its necessity in detail, answered any questions and swore the subjects to secrecy. Finally, the subjects answered a brief questionnaire about their experiences, if any, with adrenalin and their previous knowledge or suspicion of the experimental setup. There was no indication that any of the subjects had known about the experiment beforehand but 11 subjects were so extremely suspicious of some crucial feature of the experiment that their data were automatically discarded.

Subjects

The subjects were all male, college students taking classes in introductory psychology at the University of Minnesota. Some 90% of the students in these classes volunteer for a subject pool for which they receive two extra points on their final exam for every hour that they serve as experimental subjects. For this study the records of all potential subjects were cleared with the Student Health Service in order to insure that no harmful effects would result from the injections.

Evaluation of the Experimental Design

The ideal test of our propositions would require circumstances which our experiment is far from realizing. First, the proposition that: "A state of physiological arousal for which an individual has no immediate explanation will lead him to label this state in terms of the cognitions available to him" obviously requires conditions under which the subject does not and cannot have a proper explanation of his bodily state. Though we toyed with such fantasies as ventilating the experimental room with vaporized adrenalin, reality forced us to rely on the disguised injection of Suproxin—a technique which was far from ideal for no matter what the experimenter told them, some subjects would inevitably attribute their feeling to the injection. To the extent that subjects did so, differences between the several appropriateness conditions should be attenuated.

Second, the proposition that: "Given the same cognitive circumstances the individual will react emotionally only to the extent that he experiences a state of physiological arousal" requires for its ideal test the manipulation of states of physiological arousal and of physiological quiescence. Though there is no question that epinephine effectively produces a state of arousal, there is also no question that a placebo does not prevent physiological arousal. To the extent that the experimental situation effectively produces sympathetic stimulation in placebo subjects, the proposition is difficult to test, for such a factor would attenuate differences between epinephrine and placebo subjects.

Both of these factors, then, can be expected to interfere with the test of our several propositions. In presenting the results of this study, we shall first present condition by condition results and then evaluate the effect of these two factors on experimental differences.

RESULTS

Effects of the Injections on Bodily State

Let us examine first the success of the injections at producing the bodily state required to examine the propositions at test. Does the injection of epinephrine produce symptoms of sympathetic discharge as compared with the placebo injection? Relevant data are presented in Table 1 where it can be immediately seen that on all items subjects who were in epinephrine conditions show considerably more evidence of sympathetic activation than do subjects in placebo conditions. In all epinephrine conditions pulse rate increases significantly when compared with the decrease characteristic of the placebo conditions. On the scales it is clear that epinephrine subjects experience considerably more palpitation and tremor than do placebo subjects. In all possible comparisons on these symptoms, the mean scores of subjects in any of the epinephrine conditions are greater than the corresponding scores in the placebo conditions at better than the .001 level of significance. Examination of the absolute values of these scores makes it quite clear that subjects in epinephrine conditions were, indeed, in a state of physiological arousal, while most subjects in placebo conditions were in a relative state of physiological quiescence.

The epinephrine injection, of course, did not work with equal effectiveness for all subjects; indeed for a few subjects it

Table 1
The Effects of the Injections on Bodily State

Condition	N	Pulse		Self-rating of				
		Pre	Post	Palpitation	Tremor	Numbness	Itching	Headache
Euphoria								
Epi Inf	27	85.7	88.6	1.20	1.43	0	0.16	0.32
Epi Ign	26	84.6	85.6	1.83	1.76	0.15	0	0.55
Epi Mis	26	82.9	86.0	1.27	2.00	0.06	0.08	0.23
Placebo	26	80.4	77.1	0.29	0.21	0.09	0	0.27
Anger								
Epi Inf	23	85.9	92.4	1.26	1.41	0.17	0	0.11
Epi Ign	23	85.0	96.8	1.44	1.78	0	0.06	0.21
Placebo	23	84.5	79.6	0.59	0.24	0.14	0.06	0.06

did not work at all. Such subjects reported almost no palpitation or tremor, showed no increase in pulse and described no other relevant physical symptoms. Since for such subjects the necessary experimental conditions were not established, they were automatically excluded from the data and all further tabular presentations will not include such subjects. Table 1, however, does include the data of these subjects. There were four such subjects in euphoria conditions and one of them in anger conditions.

In order to evaluate further data on Epi Mis subjects it is necessary to note the results of the "numbness," "itching," and "headache" scales also presented in Table 1. Clearly the subjects in the Epi Mis condition do not differ on these scales from subjects in any of the other experimental conditions.

Effects of the Manipulations on Emotional State

Euphoria: self-report. The effects of the several manipulations on emotional state in the euphoria conditions are presented in Table 2. The scores recorded in this table are derived, for each subject, by subtracting the value of the point he

Table 2
Self-Report of Emotional State in the Euphoria Conditions

Condition	N	Self-Report scales	Comparison	p^a
Epi Inf	25	0.98	Epi Inf vs. Epi Mis	<.01
Epi Ign	25	1.78	Epi Inf vs. Epi Ign	.02
Epi Mis	25	1.90	Placebo vs. Epi Mis. Ign or Inf	ns
Placebo	26	1.61		

^{a} All p values reported throughout paper are two-tailed.

checks on the irritation scale from the value of the point he checks on the happiness scale. Thus, if a subject were to check the point "I feel a little irritated and angry" on the irritation scale and the point "I feel very happy and good" on the happiness scale, his score would be $+2$. The higher the positive value, the happier and better the subject reports himself as feeling. Though we employ an index for expositional simplicity, it should be noted that the two components of the index each yield results completely consistent with those obtained by use of this index.

Let us examine first the effects of the appropriateness instructions. Comparison of the scores for the Epi Mis and Epi Inf conditions makes it immediately clear that the experimental differences are not due to artifacts resulting from the informed instructions. In both conditions the subject was warned to expect a variety of symptoms as a consequence of the injection. In the Epi Mis condition, where the symptoms were inappropriate to the subject's bodily state the self-report score is almost twice that in the Epi Inf condition where the symptoms were completely appropriate to the subject's bodily state. It is reasonable, then, to attribute differences between informed subjects and those in other conditions to differences in manipulated appropriateness rather than to artifacts such as introspectiveness or self-examination.

It is clear that, consistent with expectations, subjects were more susceptible to the stooge's mood and consequently more euphoric when they had no explanation of their own bodily states than when they did. The means of both the Epi Ign and Epi Mis conditions are considerably greater than the mean of the Epi Inf condition.

It is of interest to note that Epi Mis subjects are somewhat more euphoric than are Epi Ign subjects. This pattern repeats itself in other data shortly to be presented. We would attribute this difference to differences in the appropriateness dimension. Though, as in the Epi Ign condition, a subject is not provided with an explanation of his bodily state, it is, of course, possible that he will provide one for himself which is not derived from his interaction with the stooge. Most reasonably he could decide for himself that he feels this way because of the injection. To the extent that he does so he should be less susceptible to the stooge. It seems probable that he would

be less likely to hit on such an explanation in the Epi Mis condition than in the Epi Ign condition for in the Epi Mis condition both the experimenter and the doctor have told him that the effects of the injection would be quite different from what he actually feels. The effect of such instructions is probably to make it more difficult for the subject himself to hit on the alternative explanation described above. There is some evidence to support this analysis. In open-end questions in which subjects described their own mood and state, 28% of the subjects in the Epi Ign condition made some connection between the injection and their bodily state compared with the 16% of subjects in the Epi Mis condition who did so. It could be considered, then, that these three conditions fall along a dimension of appropriateness, with the Epi Inf condition at one extreme and the Epi Mis condition at the other.

Comparing the placebo to the epinephrine conditions, we note a pattern which will repeat itself throughout the data. Placebo subjects are less euphoric than either Epi Mis or Epi Ign subjects but somewhat more euphoric than Epi Inf subjects. These differences are not, however, statistically significant. We shall consider the epinephrine-placebo comparisons in detail in a later section of this paper following the presentation of additional relevant data. For the moment, it is clear that, by self-report manipulating appropriateness has had a very strong effect on euphoria.

Behavior. Let us next examine the extent to which the subject's behavior was affected by the experimental manipulations. To the extent that his mood has been affected, one should expect that the subject will join in the stooge's whirl of manic activity and initiate similar activities of his own. The relevant data are presented in Table 3. The column labeled

Table 3
Behavioral Indications of Emotional State in the Euphoria Conditions

Condition	N	Activity index	Mean number of acts initiated
Epi Inf	25	12.72	.20
Epi Ign	25	18.28	.56
Epi Mis	25	22.56	.84
Placebo	26	16.00	.54

	p value[a]	
Comparison	Activity index	Initiates
Epi Inf vs. Epi Mis	.05	.03
Epi Inf vs. Epi Ign	ns	.03
Plac vs. Epi Mis, Ign, or Inf	ns	ns

[a] Tested by X^2 comparison of the proportion of subjects in each condition initiating new acts.

"Activity index" presents summary figures on the extent to which the subject joined in the stooge's activity. This is a weighted index which reflects both the nature of the activities in which the subject engaged and the amount of time he was active. The index was devised by assigning the following weights to the subject's activities: 5—hula hooping; 4—shooting with slingshot; 3—paper airplanes; 2—paper basketballs; 1—doodling; 0—does nothing. Pretest scaling on 15 college students ordered these activities with respect to the degree of euphoria they represented. Arbitrary weights were assigned so that the wilder the activity, the heavier the weight. These weights are multiplied by an estimate of the amount of time the subject spent in each activity and the summed products make up the activity index for each subject. This index may be considered a measure of behavioral euphoria. It should be noted that the same between-condition relationships hold for the two com-

ponents of this index as for the index itself.

The column labeled "Mean number of acts initiated" presents the data on the extent to which the subject deviates from the stooge's routine and initiates euphoric activities of his own.

On both behavioral indices, we find precisely the same pattern of relationships as those obtained with self-reports. Epi Mis subjects behave somewhat more euphorically than do Epi Ign subjects who in turn behave more euphorically than do Epi Inf subjects. On all measures, then, there is consistent evidence that a subject will take over the stooge's euphoric mood to the extent that he has no other explanation of his bodily state.

Again it should be noted that on these behavioral indices, Epi Ign and Epi Mis subjects are somewhat more euphoric than placebo subjects but not significantly so.

Anger: Self-report. Before presenting data for the anger conditions, one point must be made about the anger manipulation. In the situation devised, anger, if manifested, is most likely to be directed at the experimenter and his annoyingly personal questionnaire. As we subsequently discovered, this was rather unfortunate, for the subjects, who had volunteered for the experiment for extra points on their final exam, simply refused to endanger these points by publicly blowing up, admitting their irritation to the experimenter's face or spoiling the questionnaire. Though as the reader will see, the subjects were quite willing to manifest anger when they were alone with the stooge, they hesitated to do so on material (self-ratings of mood and questionnaire) that the experimenter might see and only after the purposes of the experiment had been revealed were many of these subjects willing to admit to the experimenter that they had been irked or irritated.

This experimentally unfortunate situation pretty much forces us to rely on the behavioral indices derived from observation of the subject's presumably private interaction with the stooge. We do, however, present data on the self-report scales in Table 4. These figures are derived in the same way as the figures presented in Table 2 for the euphoria conditions, that is, the value checked on the irritation

Table 4
Self-Report of Emotional State in the Anger Conditions

Condition	N	Self-Report scales	Comparison	p
Epi Inf.	22	1.91	Epi Inf vs. Epi Ign	.08
Epi Ign	23	1.39	Placebo vs. Epi Ign or Inf	ns
Placebo	23	1.63		

scale is subtracted from the value checked on the happiness scale. Though, for the reasons stated above, the absolute magnitude of these figures (all positive) is relatively meaningless, we can, of course, compare condition means within the set of anger conditions. With the happiness-irritation index employed, we should, of course, anticipate precisely the reverse results from those obtained in the euphoria conditions; that is, the Epi Inf subjects in the anger conditions should again be less susceptible to the stooge's mood and should, therefore, describe themselves as in a somewhat happier frame of mind than subjects in the Epi Ign condition. This is the case; the Epi Inf subjects average 1.91 on the self-report scales while the Epi Ign subjects average 1.39.

Evaluating the effects of the injections, we note again that, as anticipated, Epi Ign subjects are somewhat less happy than Placebo subjects but, once more, this is not a significant difference.

Behavior. The subject's responses to the stooge, during the period when both were filling out their questionnaires, were systematically coded to provide a behavioral index of anger. The coding scheme and the numerical values attached to each of the categories have been described in the methodology section. To arrive at an "Anger index" the numerical value assigned to a subject's responses to the stooge is summed together for the several units of stooge behavior. In the coding scheme used, a positive value to this index indicates that the subject agrees with the stooge's comment and is growing angry. A negative value indicates that the subject either disagrees with the stooge or ignores him.

The relevant data are presented in Table 5. For this analysis, the stooge's

Table 5
Behavioral Indications of Emotional State in the Anger Conditions

Condition	N	Neutral units	Anger units
Epi Inf	22	+0.07	−0.18
Epi Ign	23	+0.30	+2.28
Placebo	22[a]	−0.09	+0.79

Comparison for anger units	p
Epi Inf vs. Epi Ign	<.01
Epi Ign vs. Placebo	<.05
Placebo vs. Epi Inf	ns

[a] For one subject in this condition the sound system went dead and the observer could not, of course, code his reactions.

routine has been divided into two phases —the first two units of his behavior (the "long" questionnaire and "What did I have for breakfast?") are considered essentially neutral revealing nothing of the stooge's mood; all of the following units are considered "angry" units for they begin with an irritated remark about the "bells" question and end with the stooge's fury as he rips up his questionnaire and stomps out of the room. For the neutral units, agreement or disagreement with the stooge's remarks is, of course, meaningless as an index of mood and we should anticipate no difference between conditions. As can be seen in Table 5, this is the case.

For the angry units, we must, of course, anticipate that subjects in the Epi Ign condition will be angrier than subjects in the Epi Inf condition. This is indeed the case. The Anger index for the Epi Ign condition is positive and large, indicating that these subjects have become angry, while in the Epi Inf condition the Anger index is slightly negative in value indicating that these subjects have failed to catch the stooge's mood at all. It seems clear that providing the subject with an appropriate explanation of his bodily state greatly reduces his tendency to interpret his state in terms of the cognitions provided by the stooge's angry behavior.

Finally, on this behavioral index, it can be seen that subjects in the Epi Ign condition are significantly angrier than subjects in the Placebo condition. Behaviorally, at least, the injection of epinephrine appears to have led subjects to an angrier state than comparable subjects who received placebo shots.

Conformation of Data to Theoretical Expectations

Now that the basic data of this study have been presented, let us examine closely the extent to which they conform to theoretical expectations. If our hypotheses are correct and if this experimental design provided a perfect test for these hypotheses, it should be anticipated that in the euphoria conditions the degree of experimentally produced euphoria should vary in the following fashion:

$$\text{Epi Miss} \gtrsim \text{Epi Ign} > \text{Epi Inf} = \text{Placebo}$$

And in the anger conditions, anger should conform to the following pattern:

$$\text{Epi Ign} > \text{Epi Inf} = \text{Placebo}$$

In both sets of conditions, it is the case that emotional level in the Epi Mis and Epi Ign conditions is considerably greater than that achieved in the corresponding Epi Inf conditions. The results for the Placebo condition, however, are ambiguous for consistently the Placebo subjects fall between the Epi Ign and the Epi Inf subjects. This is a particularly troubling pattern for it makes it impossible to evaluate unequivocally the effects of the state of physiological arousal and indeed raises serious questions about our entire theoretical structure. Though the emotional level is consistently greater in the Epi Mis and Epi Ign conditions than in the Placebo condition, this difference is significant at acceptable probability levels only in the anger conditions.

In order to explore the problem further, let us examine the experimental factors identified earlier, which might have acted to restrain the emotional level in the Epi Ign and Epi Mis conditions. As was pointed out earlier, the ideal test of our first two hypotheses requires an experimental setup in which the subject has flatly no way of evaluating his state of physiological arousal other than by means of the experimentally provided cognitions. Had it been possible to physiologically produce a state of sympathetic activation by means other than injection, one could have approached this experimental ideal more closely than in the present setup. As it stands, however, there is always a reasonable alternative cognition available to the aroused subject—he feels the way he does because of the injection. To the extent that the subject seizes on such an explanation of his bodily state, we should expect that he will be uninfluenced by the stooge. Evidence presented in Table 6 for the anger condition and in Table 7 for the euphoria conditions indicates that this is, indeed, the case.

Table 6
The Effects of Attributing Bodily State to the Injection on Anger in the Anger Epi Ign Condition

	N	Anger index
Self-informed Ss	3	−1.67
Others	20	+2.88
Self-informed vs. Others		$p = .05$

Table 7
The Effects of Attributing Bodily State to the Injection on Euphoria in the Euphoria Epi Ign and Epi Mis Conditions

Epi Ign		
	N	Activity index
Self-informed Ss	8	11.63
Others	17	21.14
Self-informed vs. Others		$p = .05$

Epi Mis		
	N	Activity index
Self-informed Ss	5	12.40
Others	20	25.10
Self-informed vs. Others		$p = .10$

As mentioned earlier, some of the Epi Ign and Epi Mis subjects in their answers to the open-end questions clearly attributed their physical state to the injection, e.g., "the shot gave me the shivers." In Tables 6 and 7 such subjects are labeled "Self-informed." In Table 6 it can be seen that the self-informed subjects are considerably less angry than are the remaining subjects; indeed, they are not angry at all. With these self-informed subjects eliminated the difference between the Epi Ign and the Placebo conditions is significant at the .01 level of significance.

Precisely the same pattern is evident in Table 7 for the euphoria conditions. In both the Epi Mis and the Epi Ign conditions, the self-informed subjects have considerably lower activity indices than do the remaining subjects. Eliminating self-informed subjects, comparison of both of these conditions with the Placebo condition yields a difference significant at the .03 level of significance. It should be noted, too, that the self-informed subjects have much the same score on the activity index as do the experimental Epi Inf subjects (Table 3).

It would appear, then, that the experimental procedure of injecting the subjects, by providing an alternative cognition, has, to some extent, obscured the effects of epinephrine. When account is taken of this artifact, the evidence is good that the state of physiological arousal is a necessary component of an emotional experience for when self-informed subjects are removed, epinephrine subjects give consistent indications of greater emotionality than do placebo subjects.

Let us examine next the fact that consistently the emotional level, both reported and behavioral, in Placebo conditions is greater than that in the Epi Inf conditions. Theoretically, of course, it should be expected that the two conditions will be equally low, for by assuming that emotional state is a joint function of a state of physiological arousal and of the appropriateness of a cognition we are, in effect, assuming a multiplicative function, so that if either component is at zero, emotional level is at zero. As noted earlier this expectation should hold if we can be sure that there is no sympathetic activation in the Placebo conditions. This assumption, of course, is completely unrealistic for the injection of placebo does not prevent sympathetic activation. The experimental situations were fairly dramatic and certainly some of the placebo subjects gave indications of physiological arousal. If our general line of reasoning is correct, it should be anticipated that the emotional level of subjects who give indications of sympathetic activity will be greater than that of subjects who do not. The relevant evidence is presented in Tables 8 and 9.

Table 8
Sympathetic Activation and Euphoria in the Euphoria Placebo Condition

Subjects whose:	N	Activity index
Pulse decreased	14	10.67
Pulse increased or remained same	12	23.17
Pulse decreasers vs. pulse increasers or same	5	$p = .02$

Table 9
Sympathetic Activation and Anger in Anger Placebo Condition

Subjects whose:	N^a	Activity index
Pulse decreased	13	+0.15
Pulse increased or remained same	8	+1.69
Pulse decreasers vs. pulse increasers or same		$p = .01$

[a] N reduced by two cases owing to failure of sound system in one case and experimenter's failure to take pulse in another.

As an index of sympathetic activation we shall use the most direct and unequivocal measure available—change in pulse rate. It can be seen in Table 1 that the predominant pattern in the Placebo condition is a decrease in pulse rate. We shall assume, therefore, that those subjects whose pulse increases or remains the same give indications of sympathetic activity while those subjects whose pulse decreases do not. In Table 8, for the euphoria condition, it is immediately clear that subjects who give indications of sympathetic activity are considerably more euphoric than are subjects who show no sympathetic activity. This relationship is, of course, confounded by the fact that euphoric subjects are considerably more active than noneuphoric subjects—a factor which independent of mood could elevate pulse rate. However, no such factor operates in the anger condition where angry subjects are neither more active nor talkative than calm subjects. It can be seen in Table 9 that Placebo subjects who show signs of sympathetic activation give indications of considerably more anger than do subjects who show no such signs. Conforming to expectations, sympathetic activiation accompanies an increase in emotional level.

It should be noted, too, that the emotional levels of subjects showing no signs of sympathetic activity are quite comparable to the emotional level of subjects in the parallel Epi Inf conditions (see Tables 3 and 5). The similarity of these sets of scores and their uniformly low level of indicated emotionality would certainly make it appear that both factors are essential to an emotional state. When either the level of sympathetic arousal is low or a completely appropriate cognition is available, the level of emotionality is low.

DISCUSSION

Let us summarize the major findings of this experiment and examine the extent to which they support the propositions offered in the introduction of this paper. It has been suggested, first, that given a state of physiological arousal for which an individual has no explanation, he will label this state in terms of the cognitions available to him. This implies, of course, that by manipulating the cognitions of an individual in such a state we can manipulate his feelings in diverse directions. Experimental results support this proposition for following the injection of epinephrine, those subjects who had no explanation for the bodily state thus produced, gave behavioral and self-report indications that they had been readily manipulable into the disparate feeling states of euphoria and anger.

From this first proposition, it must follow that given a state of physiological arousal for which the individual has a completely satisfactory explanation, he will not label this state in terms of the alternative cognitions available. Experimental evidence strongly supports this expectation. In those conditions in which subjects were injected with epinephrine and told precisely what they would feel and why, they proved relatively immune to any effects of the manipulated cognitions. In the anger condition, such subjects did not report or show anger; in the euphoria condition, such subjects reported themselves as far less happy than subjects with an identical bodily state but no adequate knowledge of why they felt the way they did.

Finally, it has been suggested that given constant cognitive circumstances, an individual will react emotionally only to the extent that he experiences a state of physiological arousal. Without taking account of experimental artifacts, the evidence in support of this proposition is consistent but tentative. When the effects of "self-informing" tendencies in epinephrine subjects and of "self-arousing" tendencies in placebo subjects

are partialed out, the evidence strongly supports the proposition.

The pattern of data, then, falls neatly in line with theoretical expectations. However, the fact that we were forced, to some extent, to rely on internal analyses in order to partial out the effects of experimental artifacts inevitably makes our conclusions somewhat tentative. In order to further test these propositions on the interaction of cognitive and physiological determinants of emotional state, a series of additional experiments, published elsewhere, was designed to rule out or overcome the operation of these artifacts. In the first of these, Schachter and Wheeler (1962) extended the range of manipulated sympathetic activation by employing three experimental groups—epinephrine, placebo, and a group injected with the sympatholytic agent, chlorpromazine. Laughter at a slapstick movie was the dependent variable and the evidence is good that amusement is a direct function of manipulated sympathetic activation.

In order to make the epinephrine-placebo comparison under conditions which would rule out the operation of any self-informing tendency, two experiments were conducted on rats. In one of these Singer (1961) demonstrated that under fear inducing conditions, manipulated by the simultaneous presentation of a loud bell, a buzzer, and a bright flashing light, rats injected with epinephrine were considerably more frightened than rats injected with a placebo. Epinephrine-injected rats defecated, urinated, and trembled more than did placebo-injected rats. In nonfear control conditions, there were no differences between epinephrine and placebo groups, neither group giving any indication of fear. In another study, Latané and Schachter (1962) demonstrated that rats injected with epinephrine were notably more capable of avoidance learning than were rats injected with a placebo. Using a modified Miller-Mowrer shuttlebox, these investigators found that during an experimental period involving 200 massed trials, 15 rats injected with epinephrine avoided shock an average of 101.2 trials while 15 placebo-injected rats averaged only 37.3 avoidances.

Taken together, this body of studies does give strong support to the propositions which generated these experimental tests. Given a state of sympathetic activation, for which no immediately appropriate explanation is available, human subjects can be readily manipulated into states of euphoria, anger, and amusement. Varying the intensity of sympathetic activation serves to vary the intensity of a variety of emotional states in both rats and human subjects.

Let us examine the implications of these findings and of this line of thought for problems in the general area of the physiology of the emotions. We have noted in the introduction that the numerous studies on physiological differentiators of emotional states have, viewed en masse, yielded quite inconclusive results. Most, though not all, of these studies have indicated no differences among the various emotional states. Since as human beings, rather than as scientists, we have no difficulty identifying, labeling, and distinguishing among our feelings, the results of these studies have long seemed rather puzzling and paradoxical. Perhaps because of this, there has been a persistent tendency to discount such results as due to ignorance or methodological inadequacy and to pay far more attention to the very few studies which demonstrate *some* sort of physiological differences among emotional states than to the very many studies which indicate no differences at all. It is conceivable, however, that these results should be taken at face value and that emotional states may, indeed, be gen-

erally characterized by a high level of sympathetic activation with few if any physiological distinguishers among the many emotional states. If this is correct, the findings of the present study may help to resolve the problem. Obviously this study does *not* rule out the possibility of physiological differences among the emotional states. It is the case, however, that given precisely the same state of epinephrine-induced sympathetic activation, we have, by means of cognitive manipulations, been able to produce in our subjects the very disparate states of euphoria and anger. It may indeed be the case that cognitive factors are major determiners of the emotional labels we apply to a common state of sympathetic arousal.

Let us ask next whether our results are specific to the state of sympathetic activation or if they are generalizable to other states of physiological arousal. It is clear that from our experiments proper, it is impossible to answer the question for our studies have been concerned largely with the effects of an epinephrine created state of sympathetic arousal. We would suggest, however, that our conclusions are generalizable to almost any pronounced internal state for which no appropriate explanation is available. This suggestion receives some support from the experiences of Nowlis and Nowlis (1956) in their program of research on the effects of drugs on mood. In their work the Nowlises typically administer a drug to groups of four subjects who are physically in one another's presence and free to interact. The Nowlises describe some of their results with these groups as follows:

> At first we used the same drug for all 4 men. In those sessions seconal, when compared with placebo, increased the checking of such words as expansive, forceful, courageous, daring, elated, and impulsive. In our first statistical analysis

we were confronted with the stubborn fact that when the same drug is given to all 4 men in a group, the N that has to be entered into the analysis is 1, not 4. This increases the cost of an already expensive experiment by a considerable factor, but it cannot be denied that the effects of these drugs may be and often are quite contagious. Our first attempted solution was to run tests on groups in which each man had a different drug during the same session, such as 1 on seconal, 1 on benzedrine, 1 on dramamine, and 1 on placebo. What does seconal do? Cooped up with, say, the egotistical benzedrine partner, the withdrawn, indifferent dramamine partner, and the slightly bored lactose man, the seconal subject reports that he is distractible, dizzy, drifting, glum, defiant, languid, sluggish, discouraged, dull, gloomy, lazy, and slow! This is not the report of mood that we got when all 4 men were on seconal. It thus appears that the moods of the partners do definitely influence the effect of seconal (p. 350).

It is not completely clear from this description whether this "contagion" of mood is more marked in drug than in placebo groups, but should this be the case, these results would certainly support the suggestion that our findings are generalizable to internal states other than that produced by an injection of epinephrine.

Finally, let us consider the implications of our formulation and data for alternative conceptualizations of emotion. Perhaps the most popular current conception of emotion is in terms of "activation theory" in the sense employed by Lindsley (1951) and Woodworth and Schlosberg (1958). As we understand this theory, it suggests that emotional states should be considered as at one end of a continuum of activation which is defined in terms of degree of autonomic arousal and of electroencephalographic measures of activation. The results of the experiment described in this paper do, of course, suggest that such a formulation is not completely adequate. It is possible to have very high degrees of activation without a subject either appearing to be or describing himself as "emotional." Cognitive factors appear to be indispensable elements in any formulation of emotion.

SUMMARY

It is suggested that emotional states may be considered a function of a state of physiological arousal and of a cognition appropriate to this state of arousal. From this follows these propositions:

1. Given a state of physiological arousal for which an individual has no immediate explanation, he will label this state and describe his feelings in terms of the cognitions available to him. To the extent that cognitive factors are potent determiners of emotional states, it should be anticipated that precisely the same state of physiological arousal could be labeled "joy" or "fury" or "jealousy" or any of a great diversity of emotional labels depending on the cognitive aspects of the situation.
2. Given a state of physiological arousal for which an individual has a completely appropriate explanation, no evaluative needs will arise and the individual is unlikely to label his feelings in terms of the alternative cognitions available.
3. Given the same cognitive circumstances, the individual will react emotionally or describe his feelings as emotions only to the extent that he experiences a state of physiological arousal.

An experiment is described which, together with the results of other studies, supports these propositions.

3

Fear, Anxiety, and Punishment

Most theoretical positions, including psychoanalysis and the modern learning theories, consider anxiety a central problem, especially in neurotic and psychotic behavior. This is one of the few matters on which such diverse thinkers as Sigmund Freud, Ivan Pavlov, and O. Hobart Mowrer have agreed. Although each differs in his view of the dynamics of anxiety, there is substantial agreement among them on its effects.

A majority of theorists believe that *all* anxiety is primitively rooted in pain. William Kessen and George Mandler, in the selection presented here, urge a reexamination of this position. Are those who are congenitally unable to experience pain also unable to experience anxiety? Kessen and Mandler argue for a theory that extends the traditional formulation of anxiety and incorporates in it nontraumatic as well as traumatic origins. Moreover, they suggest that escaping from and avoiding danger are not the only routes to reducing anxiety,

but that such behavior as nonnutritive sucking, which is neither avoidance nor escape, can reduce anxiety in the newborn baby.

Freud's view of the neurosis-producing effects of punishment is partly responsible for the common belief that punishment can have only adverse effects on the organism. In his selection, Richard Solomon describes how, for many years, people simply ignored studies that demonstrated positive effects from punishment. Solomon also indicates that studying punishment has been remarkably rewarding in the development of learning theories.

One of the ideas explicit in Freudian theory is that traumatic punishment in infancy often has an enduring impact. This is not a matter that can be studied directly in humans, for it would involve exposing infants to the high probability of permanent psychological damage. It can, however, be examined in animals, and in the paper entitled "Reinstatement," Byron Campbell and Julian Jaynes find the Freudian theory of infantile trauma, as stated, deficient. Their correction of it has important implications for the development of psychopathology.

The final selection in this section is concerned with how one learns self-criticism. Justin Aronfreed combines the analyses presented in the previous papers and indicates their relevance to self-critical behavior. Self-criticism, of course, can be both adaptive and maladaptive. It is useful for adopting and internalizing standards of conduct, an important part of the socialization process. Aronfreed shows how both anxiety and punishment are powerful instruments in acquiring self-critical responses, and how these responses are related to such matters as guilt and cognition.

Anxiety, Pain, and the Inhibition of Distress [1]

William Kessen
George Mandler

Theories of anxiety have been developed from evidence as diverse as the avoidance behavior of animals and the symptomatic behavior of human neurotics; the language of these theories ranges from existentialism to learning theory. For all the differences in detail, however, there is remarkable similarity in the approach of different theorists to the problem of anxiety.[2]

We will, in the present paper, examine the proposition that these theoretical communalities do not fully encompass available data about human and animal distress and then go on to present several theoretical propositions supplementary to current theories of anxiety.

Briefly and without extenuation, the following shared characteristics of contemporary theories of anxiety can be noted. First, there exists an archetypical event or class of events which evokes anxiety primitively or innately or congenitally. For Freud (1936), this original inciter was overstimulation; for Mowrer (1939), it is pain; for Miller (1951), the

Reprinted from *Psychological Review*, 1961, vol. 68, pp. 396–404 with the permission of the American Psychological Association and the authors.

[1] Parts of this paper were read at the 1960 meetings of the Western Psychological Association at San Jose, California; it was written during the author's stay at the Center for Advanced Study in the Behavioral Sciences, Stanford, California, and was prepared in relation to USPHS Research Grants M–1787 and M–2442.

[2] "Anxiety" has come to be one of psychology's umbrella constructs; it covers so wide an area of research and speculation that no precise specification of its usages is possible. Nonetheless, as in the case of "learning" or "perception," "anxiety" is a useful summary expression for a set of different but related observations (see Mandler & Kessen, 1959, for a discussion of problems in the definition of theoretical terms). The theoretical differentiations which are proposed here are held to be relevant to the study of avoidance behavior, of physiological indicators of visceral disturbance, and of reported phenomenal distress.

"innate fear reaction"; for Rank (1929), birth trauma; for Selye (1956), stress; for the existentialists, it is the very fact of being human and alive. The second communality in theories about anxiety is the postulation that, somehow, the response to the archetypical event is transferred to previously innocuous events, events either in the external environment or in the action of the organism. The typical assumption has been that this association takes place with contiguous occurrence of trauma and neutral event, although the students of human learning have been more detailed than this in discussing the conditioning of fear (see, for example, Dollard & Miller, 1950). Finally, it is assumed that the events terminating or reducing anxiety are closely related to the events which evoke it. Thus, the primitive danger of overstimulation is controlled by a reduction in level of stimulation; similarly, the "fear" of electric shock is reduced by moving away from events associated with shock, presumably in inverse analog to the model of hunger and thirst, where a deficit of some substance (deprivation) is repaired by its replacement (eating or drinking).

These common elements of present day conceptions of anxiety—the archetypical evoker, the mechanism for association to previously neutral events, and the parallelarity of the elicitation and the reduction of anxiety—have produced discernible biases in contemporary psychology. In theory, in research, and apparently in therapy, the problem of anxiety has come to be, on one hand, largely a problem of trauma—that is, what events set off the anxiety—and on the other hand, largely a problem of flight—that is, what responses will lead away from the inciting event. In what follows, we will examine the place of the "trauma" or "archetype" notion by examining in detail the best candidate for

primary primitive evoker of anxiety—pain—and then we will go on to a consideration of a position that is alternative to, but not necessarily incompatible with, the common elements of anxiety theory sketched out here.[3]

DEATH OF PAIN

We will defend the position—coming to be widely held in American psychology—that a theory of anxiety based solely on pain as an archetypical precondition is untenable. The evidence at hand suggests two conclusions: first, that pain is not a necessary condition for the development of anxiety and avoidance behavior; and second, that when pain is apparently a sufficient condition for the development of anxiety, there is at work a variety of factors rather than a single innate link.

There are three areas of evidence that support the conclusion that anxiety can occur even when pain does not occur. First, there are external events other than pain which arouse, without prior experience of association with pain, behavior which bears the marks of distress or anxiety. Of particular interest to our argument in the next section are the startle and distress responses of the newborn human infant to loud noise or to loss of support (Peiper, 1956; Watson, 1919). Among animals, escape, avoidance, and species-appropriate signs of distress to nonpainful events have been reported in abundance by ethologists; the mobbing of chaffinches at the appearance of an owl reported by Hinde (1954) is an example in point. Unless a severe twist is given to the behavioral

---

[3] No attention will be given to the problem of individual differences in anxiety (Mandler & Sarason, 1952; Taylor, 1953); presumably they can be represented, at least theoretically, as parametric variations of the general theoretical formulations which we are considering in this paper.

interpretation of "anxiety," these cases, among others, stand against the Original Pain principle.

More striking as a demonstration of the separability of pain and anxiety is the behavior of human beings afflicted with congenital analgesia. This apparently inherited syndrome consists typically of a complete' absence of pain sensitivity despite otherwise normal registration of the environment. A review of 30-odd cases reported in the literature (Fanconi & Ferrazzini, 1957) shows the severely debilitating effects accompanying the absence of pain mechanisms. The patients are usually discovered to be mutilated during childhood; undiscovered fractures, scarred tongues and limbs, are among the injuries found. Despite the fact that these patients fail to develop specific adaptive avoidance behavior in the face of many injurious and noxious situations, anxiety toward other —nonpainful—events always seems to develop normally. The conclusion applied to one such case by West and Farber (1960) can be generalized to all observed cases of congenital analgesia: "anxiety plays a motivating role in determining certain aspects of the patient's behavior." In brief, the development of anxiety and avoidance behavior is not halted by the absence of pain sensitivity, even though the avoidance of normally painful events is absent.

The foregoing two points have shown that distress will develop in the absence of pain. A third collection of evidence supports the assertion of the disjunction without conclusively demonstrating the absence of an association with pain, but the data, when seen all in a row, strongly indict an exclusive commitment to a pain-traumatic theory of anxiety. We refer here to the occurrence of anxiety or discomfort when highly practiced and well organized responses are interrupted. The early research of Lewin and his stu-

dents and that of more recent workers (for example, Lewin, 1935; Marquis, 1943) suggests that the interruption of highly motivated, well-integrated behavior arouses emotional responses much like anxiety. To these data can be added the research on emotional responses of animals to frustration (for example, Marx, 1956). Similar and perhaps more revealing phenomena can be observed in young infants where, usually after and rarely before the sixth month of life, both the appearance of a stranger and the disappearance of the mother can give rise to signs of extreme distress. The fear shown by chimpanzees when confronted with the severed heads of other chim-·panzees (Hebb, 1946) is another case which falls into this category of distress consequent on extreme perceptual discrepancy. It is at least difficult to fit these cases to a theory of anxiety which depends primitively on pain or any other archetypical trauma.

If it can be agreed that pain is not a necessary condition for the development of anxiety, another question comes to the fore. To what degree or in what fashion is pain a sufficient antecedent condition for the development of anxiety? The skeptical answer that appears to be warranted by the evidence is that the relation between pain and anxiety is rarely simple or obvious, and further that attention to the distinction between pain as a sensory event and the distress reaction which usually but does not always accompany pain may clarify the complexity somewhat. The presentation of this line of discourse is made easier by the recent appearance of a stimulating review by Barber (1959) of problems associated with pain. We will, therefore, only summarize what seem to be legitimate supports for the two-or-more-factor theory of pain and then move on to a more extended treatment of the nature of distress.

There is some, though admittedly very little, evidence that the appearance of discomfort with painful stimulation requires early experience of as-yet-unknown character. Puppies raised by Melzack and Scott (1957) in a restricted environment showed indifference to stimulation painful to normal dogs and great difficulty in learning to avoid objects associated with pain. These observations are of crucial importance to speculations about anxiety and warrant replication and extension. In human infants, there is a striking temporal difference between the first "defensive" response to painful stimulation (withdrawal or startle) and the second "distressful" response (crying, increased motility, and so on). Peiper (1956) reports that the first response has a latency of 0.2 second while the second response has a latency as high as 5–7 seconds.

A similar separability of what might be called cognitive pain and distress occurs in some cases of prefrontal surgical interference to deal with intractable pain. Barber (1959), in reviewing the evidence, concludes:

> When prefrontal leucotomy alleviates intractable pain it does not necessarily elevate the pain threshold or alter "the sensation of pain." . . . [Further,] with few, if any, exceptions, investigators report that the "sensation" or "perception" of pain is practically unaltered by any of these procedures (p. 438).

Finally, Barber suggests that noxious painful stimulation has wide cortical effects and argues against a neurology of pain based exclusively on specific pain pathways or pain areas. The discomfort-pain association seems to depend on extensive cortical organization—in the words of the present argument, on experience of pain and discomfort.

The death of pain as original in all anxiety does not rule out alternative formulations of the traumatic or archetypical variety. Solomon and Brush (1956), for example, have taken students of aversive behavior to task for neglecting the investigation of noxious stimuli other than electric shock. When they ask, "Are all aversive anticipatory states alike?" they point to one alternative suggested by the elimination of pain as the sole antecedent of anxiety. Another alternative, which will be explored here, is to examine a postulation of anxiety which is independent not only of pain, but of any archetypical traumatic event.

NATURE OF FUNDAMENTAL DISTRESS

It is our contention that a nontraumatic theory of the sources of anxiety can be defended and, further, that anxiety may be reduced or terminated by devices other than escape from and avoidance of threat. These alternative formulations are proposed as supplements to, rather than as substitutes for, the archetypical theories of anxiety.

The schematic model suggested here for the occurrence of anxiety—in distinction from the classical model of the organism fleeing the associations of pain—is the cyclical distress of the human newborn. There may be antecedent events which could account for the crying and increased activity we recognize as distressful in the young infant—for example, food privation, shifts in temperature, and so on—but *it is not necessary to specify or even to assume such a specific antecedent event*. It is a defensible proposition that the strong bent of the archetypical formulations to study those conditions of distress for which a specific evoker could be discerned seriously limits the range of proper investigation. The distress of the human newborn, as obviously "anxious" as a rat in a shuttlebox, can be taken as an example of human anxiety and as a starting point for changes in speculations about human emotion, regardless of the absence of known or well-guessed "unconditioned" archetypical evokers. More than that, this modification suggests that there are cases in which the old and respected saw about anxiety as the conditioned form of the stimulus-specific fear reaction may be misleading; that is, there may be interesting cases in which a stimulus-specific fear (as indicated by flight or avoidance) may be better understood as a conditioned form of primitive anxiety or *fundamental distress*.[4]

To see anxiety as fundamental distress raises the ghosts of an old dispute in psychology—that between James and Cannon on the nature of emotion. Let us take a further theoretical step and suggest that the crucial event in fundamental distress is the perception or afferent effect of variable and intense autonomic, visceral activity. This is a rough restatement of James' position that emotions are the result of the perception of visceral events or are those perceptions themselves (James, 1890). Most of Cannon's counterarguments to such a position are not relevant to the postulation of such an effect during early infancy, since his position depends to a large extent on the identification of external threatening stimuli—a feat beyond the powers of the newborn (Cannon, 1927). But Cannon's major argument that emotional reactions take place with a latency far shorter than the latency of autonomic reactions deserves particular attention here. The delayed emotional response of the infant cited earlier, as well as the variable, badly organized reactions of infants, suggests just such a delayed emotional mechanism as Cannon ascribes to James. If we assume further (cf. Mandler

& Kremen, 1958) that these visceral reactions are eventually represented centrally (in other words, that "central" anxiety shortcircuits visceral events), then ascription of a developmental shift from a Jamesian to a Cannonic mechanism becomes plausible.[5] A closely related point was recently made by Schneirla (1959):

> although the James-Lange type of theory provides a useful basis for studying the early ontogeny of mammals, . . . a Cannon-type theory of higher-center control is *indispensable* for later stages of perceptual and motivational development. If ontogeny progresses well, specialized patterns of [approach] and [withdrawal] . . ., or their combinations, perceptually controlled, often short-circuit or modify the early viscerally dominated versions (p. 26).

One final comment on the nature of distress is warranted. It is not assumed that the distress reaction is usually terminated suddenly by the occurrence of an escape or of an avoidance response. Rather, we assume that, except for a few laboratory situations, the distress reaction is reverberatory in character. Particular events or responses do not terminate the anxiety immediately; moreover, the distress reaction will serve as a signal for further distress. Depending on partially understood environmental and organismic conditions, these reverberations will augment the initial anxiety (see Mednick, 1958) or gradually damp out and disappear.

---

[4] Auersperg (1958) has presented a treatment of "fundamental anxiety" (*Fundamentalangst*) which bears on the present discussion.

[5] The argument that visceral discomfort may become centrally represented does not necessarily imply that the visceral response will not thereafter occur; the postulation of central representation is required to explain the quick and efficient reaction of the adult to threatening events. However, given the possibility of rapid removal from the situation of threat, the "post-threat" visceral response may in fact not occur. Recent research by Solomon and Wynne (1954) supports a similar interpretation.

In short, fundamental distress is held to be a state of discomfort, unease, or anxiety which bears no clear or necessary relation to a specific antecedent event (archetypical evoker). The model or "ideal case" of fundamental distress is held to be the recurrent distress of the human newborn. Examination of the notion of anxiety in the light of these propositions is compatible with a resolution of the conflict between James' and Cannon's views on the nature of emotion. What remains for consideration is an examination of the occasions of reduction or termination of anxiety and the relation of such occasions to fundamental distress.

INHIBITION OF ANXIETY

The second departure from conventional views of anxiety has to do with techniques for the reduction or termination of anxiety. It is proposed that, in addition to the classical mechanisms of escape and avoidance of danger, anxiety is brought under control (that is, diminished or removed) by the operation of *specific inhibitors*. Before moving on to a discussion of the inhibitory mechanism, however, we must emphasize a point that is implicit in the foregoing treatment. The undifferentiated discomfort of the infant which we have taken as an example of fundamental distress may accompany particular conditions of need or drive; that is, the newborn may be hungry *and* distressed, thirsty *and* distressed, cold *and* distressed, and so on. With the removal of the privation or drive, the distress may disappear, but this reduction by the repair of a deficit—which is formally equivalent with escape from danger—is not of primary interest in the present discussion. Rather, our concern is with those responses of the organism and events in the environment which inhibit distress, *regardless of their*

relation to a specifiable need, drive, or privation.

Anecdotal evidence of the operation of congenital inhibitors of anxiety in infants abounds, but there has been relatively little systematic exploration of these inhibitors in the newly born, human or animal. However, two recent empirical studies will serve to illustrate the character of the inhibitory mechanism; one of them is based on a response of the infant, the other on a particular pattern in the environment. Research by Kessen and his associates has shown that infant distress, as indicated by crying and hyperactivity, is dramatically reduced by the occurrence of empty—that is, nonnutritive—sucking as early as the fourth day of life. The performance of the congenital sucking response on a rubber nipple stuffed with cloth brings the newborn to a condition of motor and vocal quiescence. Thus, sucking appears to fit the pattern of the congenital inhibitor of distress, or, more broadly, of anxiety. Systematic observation of the effects of sucking on motility in the period immediately after birth will be necessary to demonstrate that the inhibition is not "secondary" to the experience of food. There can be cited the incidental observation that the hungry infant during the first days of life, with little or no experience of feeding, will quiet when given breast or bottle, even though it is unlikely that his hunger has been reduced during the first several sucking responses.

The second instance of distress-inhibition derives from Harlow's (1958) research with infant monkeys. These animals when distressed, whether by a frightful artificial Monster Rhesus or in the routine cyclicity of discomfort, seek out a situation—the experimental "mother"—which inhibits the distress. Harlow has made some provocative assumptions about the characteristics of the model which serve to reduce the infant monkey's distress and he has established an empirical procedure for testing them. What seems beyond doubt are the facts that a complex environmental event serves to terminate a condition of the animal that meets our usual criteria for the presence of anxiety and that this event bears no obvious relation to physiological privation or deficit.

There are undoubtedly several congenital or early developed inhibitors of distress which have not received adequate empirical examination; the quieting effects of rocking and the response of the 2-month-old infant to the adult face come to mind. A strong presumptive case can be made for the operation of a class of such distress terminators which do not depend for their effects on escape from or avoidance of an archetypical or traumatic evoker of distress.[6]

There is a further aspect of the problem of distress-inhibition which will illustrate the relation of fundamental distress and its inhibitions to anxiety of the archetypical variety. If distress is under control by the operation of an, inhibitor, what is the effect of withdrawing the inhibitor? What, in other words, are the consequences of disinhibition of distress? For some occurrences of some inhibitors—for example, rocking the hungry and distressful infant—it seems that disinhibition "releases" or "reinstates" the distress. For others—for example, sucking on the hands until asleep

—the withdrawal of the inhibitor does not result in the recurrence of distress.

The following proposals can be made to deal with this kind of disjunction. Archetypical evokers (for example, pain, hunger) are accompanied by or lead to distress. This distress can usually be reduced in two quite distinct ways: by action of a specific inhibitor which reduces distress but does not necessarily affect the primitive evoker; or by changes acting directly on the level of the primitive evokers. The best example of how these mechanisms work together in nonlaboratory settings is nutritive sucking. The infant's *sucking* inhibits the fundamental distress accompanying hunger; at a slower rate, the *ingestion of food* "shuts off" the source of distress. It is maintained here that these two mechanisms for the reduction of distress or anxiety are profitably kept separate in psychological theory.[7]

The separation of distress reduction by specific inhibition and distress reduction by changes in archetypical evokers can be defended on other grounds as well. As noted earlier, much infantile (and later) distress is of a periodic variety without obvious relation to specific environmental evokers. Specific inhibitors may serve to tide the organism over the peaks of these distress cycles, whatever their source, until some other occurrence (for example, the onset of sleep) results in a more stable reduction of the level of organismic disturbance.

It is reasonable to assume that the inhibitory mechanism under discussion is not limited to the operation of primitive inhibitors early in development. Rather, events associated with inhibitors may, under appropriate circumstances, acquire learned or secondary inhibitory

[6] One group of inhibitors of distress appears to be characterized by rhythmic periodicity: regular sounds, rocking, the nodding head of the adult, and so on. Investigation of the relation of this class of events to visceral rhythms would lead to increased precision in speculations about fundamental distress. It is interesting to speculate in this connection about the relation between distress-inhibition on one side and sympathetic-parasympathetic incompatibility on the other.

[7] These postulations are formally equivalent to the theory Deutsch (1960) has proposed to account for behavioral phenomena associated with hunger and thirst.

properties. Under this proposal, it can be maintained that the immediate "satisfying" effects of food may be ascribable to its association with the inhibition of distress by eating, rather than the other way round. F. D. Sheffield (unpublished) has proposed a mechanism for reinforcement which is closely akin to this argument.

With the foregoing reservations in view, we would argue finally that among the earliest differentiations the child makes are those that have to do with the handling of distress. Whether in regard to what we have called fundamental distress or in regard to distress set off by specific environmental events, much of early infant behavior can be related to the management of discomfort or unease. Furthermore, it is probably in these connections that the infant first learns about the consequences of interruption of organized response sequences or expectations. Just as it has been assumed that secondary inhibitors of distress can be developed, so it is assumed that learned signals of disinhibition—that is, the reinstatment of distress at the withdrawal of an inhibitor—can be developed over the course of infancy. Thus, the phenomenon of separation anxiety seen in the young child can be understood as the interruption of well-established inhibitory sequences. The failure of the mother to appear, that is, the omission of an important inhibitor, leads to the rearousal of distress.[8]

[8] It is tempting to speculate that tendencies in the older organism to be active (Bühler's *Funktionslust*, 1930, or White's "competence motivation," 1959) may be related to the repeated arousal of distress as a consequence of the withdrawal or omission of a well-entrenched inhibitor of anxiety. In other words, the interruption of well-established behavior sequences may lead to anxiety and their continuation may ward it off. Such a position would suggest that in psychotherapy it may be as profitable for the patient to be able to complete interrupted behavior sequences as it is for him to avoid traumatic events.

In short, anxiety is not only the trace of a trauma which must be fled, but is as well a condition of distress which can be met by the action of specific inhibitors. The model of fundamental distress and its inhibition which is proposed here may serve to provide a testable alternative to the current metaphysics of anxiety (May, Angel, & Ellenberger, 1958).

SUMMARY

Contemporary theories of anxiety, while showing divergency in the statement of specific antecedents for and indicators of anxiety, have shared a dual emphasis. They have called on an archetypical evoker of anxiety (or trauma) to explain the first occurrences of anxiety and on the association of neutral events with the archetypical evoker in order to account for learned, symptomatic, or secondary anxiety. The second communality has been an emphasis on flight (escape or avoidance) from trauma or its signals as the basic mechanism for the control of anxiety.

We have presented evidence to suggest that the "flight from trauma" view of anxiety is incomplete. Specifically, the conception of pain as the sole source of later anxiety has been shown to be untenable.

Two supplements to the traumatic theory of anxiety were proposed. The burden of one was to point out the occurrence of anxiety or distress in the absence of any clearly discernible antecedent trauma. The periodic distress of the human newborn was taken as an example of this phenomenon. The second modification suggested that anxiety may be controlled not only by flight from trauma and its signals but may be reduced by the action of specific inhibitors. These inhibitors may be responses of the organism (for example, the sucking response of the newborn) or external environmental events (for example, Harlow's experimental "mother").

The implications of these supplementary proposals for a theory of anxiety were explored.

Punishment [1]

Richard L. Solomon

First, an introduction: I will attempt to achieve three goals today. (*a*) I will summarize some *empirical generalizations and problems* concerning the effects of punishment on behavior; (*b*) I will give some demonstrations of the *advantages of a two-process learning theory* for suggesting new procedures to be tried out in punishment experiments; and (*c*) finally, I shall take this opportunity today to *decry some unscientific legends* about punishment, and to do a little pontificating—a privilege that I might be denied in a journal such as the *Psychological Review*, which I edit!

Now, for a working definition of punishment: The definition of a punishment is not operationally simple, but some of its attributes are clear. A punishment is a noxious stimulus, one which will support, by its termination or omission, the growth of new escape or avoidance responses. It is one which the subject will reject, if given a choice between the punishment and no stimulus at all. Whether the data on the behavioral effects of such noxious stimuli will substan-

Reprinted from *American Psychologist*, 1964, vol. 19, pp. 239–253 with the permission of the American Psychological Association and the author.

[1] This is a slightly revised text of the author's Presidential Address to the Eastern Psychological Association, New York City, April 1963. The research associated with this address was supported by Grant No. M–4202 from the United States Public Health Service.

tiate our commonsense view of what constitutes an effective punishment, depends on a wide variety of conditions that I shall survey. Needless to say, most of these experimental conditions have been studied with infrahuman subjects rather than with human subjects.

SAMPLE EXPERIMENTS

Let us first consider two sample experiments. Imagine a traditional alley runway, 6 feet long, with its delineated goal box and start box, and an electrifiable grid floor. In our first experiment, a rat is shocked in the start box and alley, but there is no shock in the goal box. We can quickly train the rat to run down the alley, if the shock commences as the start-box gate is raised and persists until the rat enters the goal box. This is *escape* training. If, however, we give the rat 5 seconds to reach the goal box after the start-box gate is raised, and only then do we apply the shock, the rat will usually learn to run quickly enough to avoid the shock entirely. This procedure is called *avoidance* training, and the resultant behavior change is called *active* avoidance learning. Note that the response required, either to terminate the shock or to remove the rat from the presence of the dangerous start box and alley, is well specified, while the behavior leading to the onset of these noxious stimulus conditions is left vague. It could be any item of behavior coming *before* the opening of the gate, and it would depend on what the rat happened to be doing when the experimenter raised the gate.

In our second sample experiment, we train a hungry rat to run to the goal box in order to obtain food. After performance appears to be asymptotic, we introduce a shock, both in the alley and goal box, and eliminate the food. The rat quickly stops running and spends its time in the start box. This procedure is called the *punishment procedure*, and the resulant learning-to-stay-in-the-start-box is called *passive* avoidance learning. Note that, while the behavior *producing* the punishment is well specified, the particular behavior *terminating* the punishment if left vague. It could be composed of any behavior that keeps the rat in the start box and out of the alley.

In the first experiment, we were teaching the rat *what to do*, while in the second experiment we were teaching him exactly *what not to do*; yet in each case, the criterion of learning was correlated with the rat's receiving *no* shocks, in contrast to its previous experience of receiving several shocks in the same experimental setting. One cannot think adequately about punishment without considering what is known about the outcomes of both procedures. Yet most reviews of the aversive control of behavior emphasize active avoidance learning and ignore passive avoidance learning. I shall, in this talk, emphasize the similarities, rather than the differences between active and passive avoidance learning. I shall point out that there is a rich store of knowledge of active avoidance learning which, when applied to the punishment procedure, increases our understanding of some of the puzzling and sometimes chaotic results obtained in punishment experiments.

But first, I would like to review some of the empirical generalities which appear to describe the outcomes of experiments on *punishment* and passive avoidance learning. For this purpose, I divide the evidence into 5 classes: (*a*) the effects of punishment on behavior previously established by *rewards* or positive reinforcement, (*b*) the effects of punishment on *consummatory* responses, (*c*) the effects of punishment on complex, sequential patterns of *innate* responses, (*d*) the effects of punishment on discrete reflexes, (*e*) the effects of punishment on responses previously established by punishment—or, if you will, the effects of punishment on active escape and avoidance responses. The effectiveness of punishment will be seen to differ greatly across these five classes of experiments. For convenience, I mean by *effectiveness* the degree to which a punishment procedure produces *suppression* of, or facilitates the *extinction* of, existing response patterns.

Now, let us look at punishment for *instrumental responses* or *habits previously established by reward or positive reinforcers*. First, the outcomes of punishment procedures applied to previously rewarded habits are strongly related to the *intensity* of the punishing agent. Sometimes intensity is independently defined and measured, as in the case of electric shock. Sometimes we have qualitative evaluations, as in the case of Maier's (1949) rat bumping his nose on a locked door, or Masserman's (Masserman & Pechtel, 1953) spider monkey being presented with a toy snake, or Skinner's (1938) rat receiving a slap on the paw from a lever, or my dog receiving a swat from a rolled-up newspaper. As the intensity of shock applied to rats, cats, and dogs is increased from about .1 milliampere to 4 milliamperes, these orderly results can be obtained: (*a*) *detection* and *arousal*, wherein the punisher can be used as a cue, discriminative stimulus, response intensifier, or even as a secondary reinforcer; (b) *temporary suppression*, wherein punishment results in suppression of the punished response, followed by complete recovery, such that the subject later appears unaltered from his pre-punished state; (c) *partial suppression*, wherein the subject always displays some lasting suppression of the punished response, without total recovery; and (d) finally, there is *complete suppression*, with no observable recovery. Any of these outcomes can be produced, other things being equal, by merely varying the intensity of the noxious stimulus used (Azrin & Holz, 1961), when we punish responses previously established by reward or positive reinforcement. No wonder different experimenters report incomparable outcomes. Azrin (1959) has produced a response-rate *increase* while operants are punished. Storms, Boroczi, and Broen (1962) have produced long-lasting suppression of operants in rats.[2] Were punishment intensities different? Were punishment durations different? (Storms, Boroczi & Broen, 1963, have shown albino rats to be more resistant to punishment than are hooded rats, and this is another source of discrepancy between experiments.)

But other variables are possibly as important as punishment intensity, and their operation can make it unnecessary to use *intense* punishers in order to produce the effective suppression of a response previously established by positive reinforcement. Here are some selected examples:

1. *Proximity* in time and space to the punished response determines to some extent the effectiveness of a punishment. There is a response-suppression gradient.

This has been demonstrated in the runway (Brown, 1948; Karsh, 1962), in the lever box (Arzin, 1956), and in the shuttle box (Kamin, 1959). This phenomenon has been labeled the gradient of temporal delay of punishment.

2. The conceptualized *strength* of a response, as measured by its resistance to extinction after omission of positive reinforcement, predicts the effect of a punishment contingent upon the response. Strong responses, so defined, are more resistant to the suppressive effects of punishment. Thus, for example, the overtraining of a response, which often decreases ordinary resistance to experimental extinction, also increases the effectiveness of punishment (Karsh, 1962; Miller, 1960) as a response suppressor.

3. *Adaptation* to punishment can occur, and this *decreases* its effectiveness. New, intense punishers are better than old, intense punishers (Miller, 1960). Punishment intensity, if slowly increased, tends not to be as effective as in the case where it is introduced initially at its high-intensity value.

4. In general, resistance to extinction is decreased whenever a previously reinforced response is punished. However, if the subject is habituated to receiving shock together with positive reinforcement during reward training, the relationship can be reversed, and punishment during extinction can actually increase resistance to extinction (Holz & Azrin, 1961). Evidently, punishment, so employed, can functionally operate as a *secondary reinforcer*, or as a cue for a reward, or as an arouser.

5. Punishments become extremely effective when the response-suppression period is tactically used as an aid to the reinforcement of new responses that are topographically *incompatible* with the punished one. When new instrumental acts are established which lead to the old goal (a new *means* to an old *end*),

[2] Since the delivery of this address, several articles have appeared concerning the punishment intensity problem. See especially Karsh (1963), Appel (1963), and Walters and Rogers (1963). All these studies support the conclusion that shock intensity is a crucial variable, and high intensities produce lasting suppression effects.

a punishment of very low intensity can have very long-lasting suppression effects. Whiting and Mowrer (1943) demonstrated this clearly. They first rewarded one route to food, then punished it. When the subjects ceased taking the punished route, they provided a new rewarded route. The old route was not traversed again. This reliable suppression effect also seems to be true of temporal, discriminative restraints on behavior. The suppression of urination in dogs, under the control of *indoor stimuli*, is extremely effective in housebreaking the dog, as long as urination is allowed to go unpunished under the control of *outdoor stimuli*. There is a valuable lesson here in the effective use of punishments in producing *impulse control*. A *rewarded alternative*, under discriminative control, makes passive avoidance training a potent behavioral influence. It can produce a highly reliable dog or child. In some preliminary observations of puppy training, we have noted that puppies raised in the lab, if punished by the swat of a newspaper for eating horsemeat, and rewarded for eating pellets, will starve themselves to death when only given the opportunity to eat the taboo horsemeat. They eagerly eat the pellets when they are available.

It is at this point that we should look at the experiments wherein punishment appears to have only a temporary suppression effect. Most of these experiments offered the subject *no* rewarded alternative to the punished response in attaining his goal. In many such experiments, it was a case of take a chance or go hungry. Hunger-drive strength, under such no-alternative conditions, together with punishment intensity, are the crucial variables in predicting recovery from the suppression effects of punishment. Here, an interesting, yet hard-to-understand phenomenon frequently occurs, akin to Freudian "reaction formation." If a subject has been punished for touching some

manipulandum which yields food, he may stay nearer to the manipulandum under low hunger drive and move farther away from it under high hunger drive, even though the probability of finally touching the manipulandum increases as hunger drive increases. This phenomenon is complex and needs to be studied in some detail. Our knowledge of it now is fragmentary. It was observed by Hunt and Schlosberg (1950) when the water supply of rats was electrified, and we have seen it occur in approach-avoidance conflict experiments in our laboratory, but we do not know the precise conditions for its occurrence.

Finally, I should point out that the attributes of effective punishments vary *across species* and *across stages in maturational development* within species. A toy snake can frighten monkeys. It does not faze a rat. A loud noise terrified Watson's little Albert. To us it is merely a Chinese gong.

I have sketchily reviewed some effects of punishment on *instrumental* acts established by *positive reinforcers*. We have seen that any result one might desire, from response enhancement and little or no suppression, to relatively complete suppression, can be obtained with our current knowledge of appropriate experimental conditions. Now let us look at the effects of punishment on *consummatory acts*. Here, the data are, to me, surprising. One would think that consummatory acts, often being of biological significance for the survival of the individual and the species, would be highly resistant to suppression by punishment. The *contrary* appears to be so. Male sexual behavior may be seriously suppressed by weak punishment (Beach, Conovitz, Steinberg, & Goldstein, 1956; Gantt, 1944). Eating in dogs and cats can be permanently suppressed by a moderate shock delivered through the feet or through the food dish itself (Lichtenstein, 1950; Masserman,

1943). Such suppression effects can lead to fatal self-starvation. A toy snake presented to a spider monkey while he is eating can result in self-starvation (Masserman & Pechtel, 1953).

The interference with consummatory responses by punishment needs a great deal of investigation. Punishment seems to be especially effective in breaking up this class of responses, and one can ask *why*, with some profit. Perhaps the intimate temporal connection between drive, incentive, and punishment results in drive or incentive becoming conditioned-stimulus (CS) patterns for aversive emotional reactions when consummatory acts are punished. Perhaps this interferes with vegetative activity: i.e., does it "kill the appetite" in a hungry subject? But, one may ask why the same punisher might not appear to be as effective when made contingent on an *instrumental* act as contrasted with a consummatory act. Perhaps the nature of operants is such that they are separated in time and space and response topography from consummatory behavior and positive incentive stimuli, so that appetitive reactions are not clearly present during punishment for operants. We do not know enough yet about such matters, and speculation about it is still fun.

Perhaps the most interesting parametric variation one can study, in experiments on the effects of punishment on consummatory acts, is the *temporal order* of rewards and punishments. If we hold hunger drive constant, shock-punishment intensity constant, and food-reward amounts constant, a huge differential effect can be obtained when we reverse the order of reward and punishment. If we train a cat to approach a food cup, its behavior in the experimental setting will become quite stereotyped. Then, if we introduce shock to the cat's feet while it is eating, the cat will vocalize, retreat, and show fear reactions. It will be slow

to recover its eating behavior in this situation. Indeed, as Masserman (1943) has shown, such a procedure is likely, if repeated a few times, to lead to self-starvation. Lichtenstein (1950) showed the same phenomenon in dogs. Contrast this outcome with that found when the temporal order of food and shock is *reversed*. We now use shock as a discriminative stimulus to signalize the availability of food. When the cat is performing well, the shock may produce eating with a latency of less than 5 seconds. The subject's appetite does not seem to be disturbed. One cannot imagine a more dramatic difference than that induced by reversing the temporal order of reward and punishment (Holz & Azrin, 1962; Masserman, 1943).

Thus, the effects of punishment are partly determined by those events that directly precede it and those that directly follow it. A punishment is not just a punishment. It is an event in a temporal and spatial flow of stimulation and behavior, and its effects will be produced by its temporal and spatial point of insertion in that flow.

I have hastily surveyed some of the effects of punishment when it has been made contingent either on rewarded *operants* and instrumental acts or on *consummatory* acts. A third class of behaviors, closely related to consummatory acts, but yet a little different, are *instinctive act sequences*: the kinds of complex, innately governed behaviors which the ethologists study, such as nest building in birds. There has been little adequate experimentation, to my knowledge, on the effects of punishment on such innate behavior sequences. There are, however, some hints of interesting things to come. For example, sometimes frightening events will produce what the ethologists call displacement reactions—the expression of an inappropriate behavior pattern of an innate sort. We need to experiment with such phenomena in a systematic fashion. The best example I could find of this phenomenon is the imprinting of birds on moving objects, using the locomotor following response as an index. Moltz, Rosenblum, and Halikas (1959), in one experiment, and Kovach and Hess (1963; see also Hess, 1959a, 1959b) in another, have shown that the punishment of such imprinted behavior sometimes depresses its occurrence. However, if birds are punished prior to the presentation of an imprinted object, often the following response will be energized. It is hard to understand what this finding means, except that punishment can either arouse or inhibit such behavior, depending on the manner of presentation of punishment. The suggestion is that imprinting is partially a function of fear or distress. The effectiveness of punishment also is found to be related to the critical period for imprinting (Kovach & Hess, 1963).

However, the systematic study of known punishment parameters as they affect a wide variety of complex sequences of innate behaviors is yet to be carried out. It would appear to be a worthwhile enterprise, for it is the type of work which would enable us to make a new attack on the effects of experience on innate behavior patterns. Ultimately the outcomes of such experiments *could* affect psychoanalytic conceptions of the effects of trauma on impulses of an innate sort.[3]

A fourth class of behavior upon which

[3] Since the delivery of this address, an article has appeared on this specific problem. See Adler and Hogan (1963). The authors showed that the gill-extension response of *Betta splendens* could be conditioned to a previously neutral stimulus by a Pavlovian technique, and it could also be suppressed by electric-shock punishment. This is an important finding, because there are very few known cases where the same response can be both conditioned and trained. Here, the gill-extension response is typically elicited by a rival fish, and is usually interpreted to be aggressive or hostile in nature.

punishment can be made contingent, is the simple, discrete reflex. For example, what might happen if a conditioned or an unconditioned knee jerk were punished? We are completely lacking in information on this point. Can subjects be trained to inhibit reflexes under aversive motivation? Or does such motivation sensitize and enhance reflexes? Some simple experiments are appropriate, but I was unable to find them in the published work I read.

A fifth class of behavior, upon which punishment can be made contingent, is behavior *previously established by punishment procedures*: in other words, the effect of passive avoidance training on existing, active avoidance learned responses. This use of punishment produces an unexpected outcome. In general, if the same noxious stimulus is used to punish a response as was used to establish it in the first place, the response becomes strengthened during initial applications of punishment. After several such events, however, the response may weaken, but not always. The similarity of the noxious stimulus used for active avoidance training to that used for punishment of the established avoidance response can be of great importance. For example, Carlsmith (1961) has shown that one can increase resistance to extinction by using the same noxious stimuli for both purposes and yet decrease resistance to extinction by using equally noxious, but discriminatively different, punishments. He trained some rats to run in order to avoid shock, then punished them during extinction by blowing a loud horn. He trained other rats to run in order to avoid the loud horn, then during extinction he punished them by shocking them for running. In two control groups, the punisher stimulus and training stimulus were the same. The groups which were trained and then punished by different noxious stimuli extinguished more rapidly during punishment than did the groups in which the active avoidance training unconditioned stimulus (US) was the same as the passive avoidance training US. Thus, punishment for responses established originally by punishment may be ineffective in eliminating the avoidance responses they are supposed to eliminate. Indeed, the punishment may strengthen the responses. We need to know more about this puzzling phenomenon. It is interesting to me that in Japan, Imada (1959) has been systematically exploring shock intensity as it affects this phenomenon.

Our quick survey of the effects of punishment on five classes of responses revealed a wide variety of discrepant phenomena. Thus, to predict in even the grossest way the action of punishment on a response, one has to know *how* that particular response was originally inserted in the subject's response repertoire. Is the response an instrumental one which was strengthened by reward? Is it instead a consummatory response? Is it an innate sequential response pattern? Is it a discrete reflex? Was it originally established by means of punishment? *Where*, temporarily, in a behavior sequence, was the punishment used? How *intense* was it? These are but a few of the relevant, critical questions, the answers to which are necessary in order for us to make reasonable predictions about the effects of punishment. Thus, to conclude, as some psychologists have, that the punishment procedure is typically either effective or ineffective, typically either a temporary suppressor or a permanent one, is to oversimplify irresponsibly a complex area of scientific knowledge, one still containing a myriad of intriguing problems for experimental attack.

Yet, the complexities involved in ascertaining the effects of punishment on behavior *need not* be a bar to useful speculation ultimately leading to experimentation of a fruitful sort. The complexities should, however, dictate a great deal of caution in making dogmatic statements about whether punishment is effective or ineffective as a behavioral influence, or whether it is good or bad. I do *not* wish to do that. I would like now to speculate about the data-oriented theories, rather than support or derogate the dogmas and the social philosophies dealing with punishment. I will get to the dogmas later.

THEORY

Here is a theoretical approach that, for me, has high pragmatic value in stimulating new lines of experimentation. Many psychologists today consider the punishment procedure to be a special case of avoidance training, and the resulant learning processes to be theoretically identical in nature. Woodworth and Schlosberg (1954) distinguish the two training procedures, *"punishment for action"* from *"punishment for inaction,"* but assume that the same theoretical motive, a "positive incentive value of safety" can explain the learning produced by both procedures. Dinsmoor (1955) argues that the facts related to both procedures are well explained by simple stimulus-response (S-R) principles of avoidance learning. He says:

If we punish the subject for making a given response or sequence of responses —that is, apply aversive stimulation, like shock—the cues or discriminative stimuli for this response will correspond to the warning signals that are typically used in more direct studies of avoidance training. By his own response to these stimuli, the subject himself produces the punishing stimulus and pairs or correlates it with these signals. As a result, they too become aversive. In the meantime, any variations in the subject's behavior that interfere or conflict with the chain of reactions leading to the punishment delay the occurrence of the final response and the receipt of the stimulation that follows it. These variations in behavior disrupt the discriminative stimulus pattern for the continuation of the punished chain, changing the current stimulation from an aversive to a nonaversive compound; they are conditioned, differentiated, and maintained by the reinforcing effects of the change in stimulation [p. 96].

The foci of the Dinsmoor analysis are the processes whereby: (a) discriminative stimuli become aversive, and (b) instrumental acts are reinforced. He stays at the quasi-descriptive level. He uses a peripheralistic, S-R analysis, in which response-produced proprioceptive stimuli and exteroceptive stimuli serve to hold behavior chains together. He rejects, as unnecessary, concepts such as fear or anxiety, in explaining the effectiveness of punishment.

Mowrer (1960) also argues that the facts related to the two training procedures are explained by a common set of principles, but Mowrer's principles are somewhat different than those of either Woodworth and Schlosberg, or Dinsmoor, cited above. Mowrer says:

> In both instances, there is fear conditioning; and in both instances a way of behaving is found which eliminates or controls the fear. The only important distinction, it seems is that the stimuli to which the fear gets connected are different. In so-called punishment, these stimuli are produced by (correlated with) the behavior, or response, which we wish to block; whereas, in so-called avoidance learning, the fear-arousing stimuli are not response-produced—they are, so to say, extrinsic rather than intrinsic, independent rather than response-dependent. But in both cases there is avoidance and in both cases there is its antithesis, punishment; hence the impropriety of referring to the one as "punishment" and to the others as "avoidance learning." Obviously precision and clarity of understanding are better served by the alternative terms here suggested, namely, passive avoidance learning and active avoid-

ance learning, respectively. . . . But, as we have seen, the two phenomena involve exactly the same basic principles of fear conditioning and of the reinforcement of whatever action (or inaction) eliminates the fear [pp. 31–32].

I like the simple beauty of each of the three unifying positions; what holds for punishment and its action on behavior should hold also for escape and avoidance training, and vice versa. Generalizations about one process should tell us something about the other. New experimental relationships discovered in the one experimental setting should tell us how to predict a new empirical event in the other experimental setting. A brief discussion of a few selected examples can illustrate this possibility.

APPLICATIONS OF THEORY

I use a case in point stemming from work done in our own laboratory. It gives us new hints about some hidden sources of effectiveness of punishment. Remember, for the sake of argument, that we are assuming many important similarities to exist between active and passive avoidance-learning processes. Therefore, we can look at active avoidance learning as a theoretical device to suggest to us new, unstudied variables pertaining to the effectiveness of punishment.

Turner and I have recently published an extensive monograph (1962) on human traumatic avoidance learning. Our experiments showed that when a very reflexive, short-latency, skeletal response, such as a toe twitch, was used as an escape and avoidance response, grave difficulties in active avoidance learning were experienced by the subject. Experimental variations which tended to render the escape responses more emitted, more deliberate, more voluntary, more operant, or less reflexive, tended also to render the avoidance responses easier to learn. Thus, when a subject was required to move a knob in a slot in order to avoid shock, learning was rapid, in contrast to the many failures to learn with a toe-flexion avoidance response.

There are descriptions of this phenomenon already available in several published experiments on active avoidance learning, but their implications have not previously been noted. When Schlosberg (1934) used for the avoidance response a highly reflexive, short-latency, paw-flexion response in the rat, he found active avoidance learning to be unreliable, unstable, and quick to extinguish. Whenever the rats made active avoidance flexions, a decrement in response strength ensued. When the rats were shocked on several escape trials, the avoidance response tended to reappear for a few trials. Thus, learning to avoid was a tortuous, cyclical process, never exceeding 30% success. Contrast these results with the active avoidance training of nonreflexive, long-latency operants, such as rats running in Hunter's (1935) circular maze. Hunter found that the occurrence of avoidance responses tended to produce more avoidance responses. Omission of shock seemed to reinforce the avoidance running response. Omission of shock seemed to extinguish the avoidance paw flexion. Clearly the operant-respondent distinction has predictive value in active avoidance learning.

The same trend can be detected in experiments using dogs as subjects. For example, Brogden (1949), using the forepaw-flexion response, found that meeting a 20/20 criterion of avoidance learning was quite difficult. He found that 30 dogs took from approximately 200–600 trials to reach the avoidance criterion. The response used was, in our language, highly reflexive—it was totally elicited by the shock on escape trials with a very short latency, approximately .3 second. Compare, if you will, the learning of active avoidance by dogs in the shuttle box with that found in the forelimb-flexion experiment. In the shuttle box, a large number of dogs were able to embark on their criterion trials after 5–15 active avoidance-training trials. Early escape response latencies were long. Resistance to extinction is, across these two types of avoidance responses, inversely related to trials needed for a subject to achieve criterion. Conditions leading to quick acquisition are, in this case, those conducive to slow extinction. Our conclusion, then, is that high-probability, short-latency, *respondents* are not as good as medium-probability, long-latency operants when they are required experimentally to function as active avoidance responses. This generalization seems to hold for rats, dogs, and college students.

How can we make the inferential leap from such findings in active avoidance training to possible variations in punishment experiments? It is relatively simple to generalize across the two kinds of experiments in the case of CS-US interval, US intensity, and CS duration. But the inferential steps are not as obvious in the case of the operant-respondent distinction. So I will trace out the logic in some detail. If one of the major effects of punishment is to motivate or elicit new behaviors, and reinforce them through removal of punishment, and thus, as Dinsmoor describes, establish avoidance responses incompatible with a punished response, how does the operant-respondent distinction logically enter? Here, Mowrer's two-process avoidance-learning theory can suggest a possible answer. Suppose, for example, that a hungry rat has been trained to lever press for food and is performing at a stable rate. Now we make a short-duration, high-intensity pulse of shock contingent upon the bar press. The pulse elicits a startle pattern that produces a release of the lever in .2 second, and the shock is gone. The rat freezes for a few seconds, breathing heavily, and he urinates and defecates. It is our supposition that a conditioned emotional reaction (CER) is thereby established, with its major stimulus control coming from the sight of the bar, the touch of the bar, and proprioceptive stimuli aroused by the lever-press movements themselves. This is, as Dinsmoor describes it, the development of acquired aversiveness of stimuli; or, as Mowrer describes it, the acquisition of conditioned fear reactions. Therefore, Pavlovian conditioning variables should be the important ones in the development of this process. The reappearance of lever pressing in this punished rat would thus depend on the extinction of the CER and skeletal freezing. If no further shocks are administered, then the CER should extinguish according to the laws of Pavlovian extinction, and reappearance of the lever press should not take long, even if the shock-intensity level were high enough to have been able to produce active avoidance learning in another apparatus.

Two-process avoidance theory tells us that something very important for successful and durable response suppression was missing in the punishment procedure we just described. What was lacking in this punishment procedure was a good operant to allow us to reinforce a reliable avoidance response. Because the reaction to shock was a respondent, was highly *reflexive*, and was quick to occur, I am led to argue that the termination of shock will *not* reinforce it, nor will it lead to stable avoidance responses. This conclusion follows directly from our experiments on human avoidance learning. If the termination of shock is made contingent on the occurrence of an operant, especially an operant topographically incompatible with the lever press, an active avoidance learning process should then

ensue. So I will now propose that we shock the rat until he huddles in a corner of the box. The rat will have learned to *do* something arbitrary whenever the controlling CSs reappear. Thus, the rat in the latter procedure, if he is to press the lever again, must undergo *two* extinction processes. The CER, established by the pairing of CS patterns and shock, must become weaker. Second the learned huddling response must extinguish. This combination of requirements should make the effect of punishment more lasting, if my inferences are correct. Two problems must be solved by the subject, not one. The experiments needed to test these speculations are, it would appear, easy to design, and there is no reason why one should not be able to gather the requisite information in the near future. I feel that there is much to be gained in carrying on theoretical games like this, with the major assumptions being (a) that active and passive avoidance learning are similar processes, ones in which the same variables have analogous effects, and (b) that two processes, the conditioning of fear reactions, and the reinforcement of operants incompatible with the punished response, may operate in punishment experiments.

There is another gain in playing theoretical games of this sort. One can use them to question the usual significance imputed to past findings. Take, for example, the extensive studies of Neal Miller (1959) and his students, and Brown (1948) and his students, on gradients of approach and avoidance in conflict situations. Our foregoing analysis of the role of the operant-respondent distinction puts to question one of their central assumptions—that the avoidance gradient is unconditionally steeper than is the approach gradient in approach-avoidance conflicts. In such experiments, the subject is typically trained while hungry to run down a short alley to obtain food. After the running is reliable, the subject is shocked, usually near the goal, in such a way that entering the goal box is discouraged temporarily. The subsequent behavior of the typical subject consists of remaining in the start box, making abortive approaches to the food box, showing hesitancy, oscillation, and various displacement activities, like grooming. Eventually, if shock is eliminated by the experimenter, the subject resumes running to food. The avoidance tendency is therefore thought to have extinguished sufficiently so that the magnitude of the conceptualized approach gradient exceeds that of the avoidance gradient at the goal box. The steepness of the avoidance gradient as a function of distance from the goal box is inferred from the behavior of the subject *prior* to the extinction of the avoidance tendencies. If the subject stays as far away from the goal box as possible, the avoidance gradient may be inferred to be either displaced upward, or if the subject slowly creeps up on the goal box from trial to trial, it may be inferred to be less steep than the approach gradient. Which alternative is more plausible? Miller and his collaborators very cleverly have shown that the latter alternative is a better interpretation.

The differential-steepness assumption appears to be substantiated by several studies by Miller and his collaborators (Miller & Murray, 1952; Murray & Berkun, 1955). They studied the displacement of conflicted approach responses along both spatial and color dimensions, and clearly showed that the approach responses generalized more readily than did the avoidance responses. Rats whose running in an alley had been completely suppressed by shock punishment showed recovery of running in a similar alley. Thus the inference made was that the avoidance gradient is steeper than is the approach gradient; avoidance

tendencies weaken more rapidly with changes in the external environmental setting than do approach tendencies. On the basis of the analysis I made of the action of punishment, both as a US for the establishment of a Pavlovian CER and as a potent event for the reinforcement of instrumental escape and avoidance responses, it seems to me very likely that the approach-avoidance conflict experiments have been carried out in such a way as to produce inevitably the steeper avoidance gradients. In other words, these experiments from my particular viewpoint have been inadvertently biased, and they were not appropriate for testing hypotheses about the gradient slopes.

My argument is as follows: Typically, the subject in an approach-avoidance experiment is trained to perform a specific sequence of responses under reward incentive and appetitive drive conditions. He runs to food when hungry. In contrast, when the shock is introduced into the runway, it is usually placed near the goal, and no specific, long sequence of instrumental responses is required of the subject before the shock is terminated. Thus, the initial strengths of the approach and avoidance instrumental responses (which are in conflict) are not equated by analogous or symmetrical procedures. Miller has thoroughly and carefully discussed this, and has suggested that the avoidance gradient would not have as steep a slope if the shock were encountered by the rat early in the runway in the case where the whole runway is electrified. While this comment is probably correct, it does not go far enough, and I would like to elaborate on it. I would argue that if one wants to study the relative steepnesses of approach and avoidance responses in an unbiased way, the competing instrumental responses should be established in a *symmetrical* fashion. After learning to run down an alley to food, the subject should be shocked near the goal box or in it, and the shock should not be terminated until the subject has escaped all the way into the start box. Then one can argue that two conflicting instrumental responses have been established. First, the subject runs one way for food; now he runs the same distance in the opposite direction in order to escape shock. When he stays in the start box, he avoids shock entirely. Then the generalization or displacement of the approach and avoidance responses can be fairly studied.

I am arguing that we need *instrumental*-response balancing, as well as *Pavlovian*-conditioning balancing, in such conflict experiments, if the slopes of gradients are to be determined for a test of the differential-steepness assumption. Two-process avoidance-learning theory requires such a symmetrical test. In previous experiments, an aversive CER and its respondent motor pattern, not a well-reinforced avoidance response, has been pitted against a well-reinforced instrumental-approach response. Since the instrumental behavior of the subject is being used subsequently to test for the slope of the gradients, the usual asymmetrical procedure is, I think, not appropriate. My guess is that, if the symmetrical procedure I described is actually used, the slopes of the two gradients will be essentially the same, and the recovery of the subject from the effects of punishment will be seen to be nearly all-or-none. That is, the avoidance gradient, as extinction of the CER proceeds in time, will drop below the approach gradient, and this will hold all along the runway if the slopes of the two gradients are indeed the same. Using the test of displacement, subjects should stay in the starting area of a similar alley on initial tests and when they finally move forward they should go all the way to the goal box.

The outcomes of such experiments would be a matter of great interest to me, for, as you will read in a moment, I feel that the suppressive power of punishment over instrumental acts has been understated. The approach-avoidance conflict experiment is *but one* example among many wherein the outcome *may have been* inadvertently biased in the direction of showing reward-training influences to be superior, in some particular way, to punishment-training procedures. Now let us look more closely at this matter of bias.

LEGENDS

Skinner, in 1938, described the effect of a short-duration slap on the paw on the extinction of lever pressing in the rat. Temporary suppression of lever-pressing rate was obtained. When the rate increased, it exceeded the usual extinction performance. The total number of responses before extinction occurred was not affected by the punishment for lever pressing. Estes (1944) obtained similar results, and attributed the temporary suppression to the establishment of a CER (anxiety) which dissipated rapidly. Tolman, Hall, and Bretnall (1932) had shown earlier that punishment could enhance maze learning by serving as a cue for correct, rewarded behavior. Skinner made these observations (on the seemingly ineffective nature of punishment as a response weakener) the basis for his advocacy of a positive reinforcement regime in his utopia, *Walden Two*. In *Walden Two*, Skinner (1948) speaking through the words of Frazier, wrote: "We are now discovering at an untold cost in human suffering—that in the long run punishment doesn't reduce the probability that an act will occur [p. 260.]" No punishments would be used there, because they would produce poor behavioral control, he claimed.

During the decade following the publication of *Walden Two*, Skinner (1953) maintained his position concerning the effects of punishment on instrumental responses: Response suppression is but temporary, and the side effects, such as fear and neurotic and psychotic disturbances, are not worth the temporary advantages of the use of punishment. He said:

> In the long run, punishment, unlike reinforcement works to the disadvantage of both the punished organism and the punishing agency [p. 183].

> The fact that punishment does not permanently reduce a tendency to respond is in agreement with Freud's discovery of the surviving activity of what he called repressed wishes [p. 184].

> Punishment, as we have seen, does not create a negative probability that a response will be made but rather a positive probability that incompatible behavior will occur [p. 222].

It must be said, in Skinner's defense, that in 1953 he devoted about 12 pages to the topic of punishment in his introductory textbook. Other texts had devoted but a few words to this topic.

In Bugelski's (1956) words about the early work on punishment: "The purport of the experiments mentioned above appears to be to demonstrate that punishment is ineffective in eliminating behavior. This conclusion appears to win favor with various sentimentalists [p. 275]." Skinner (1961) summarized his position most recently in this way:

> Ultimate advantages seem to be particularly easy to overlook in the control of behavior, where a quick though slight advantage may have undue weight. Thus, although we boast that the birch rod has been abandoned, most school children are still under aversive control—not because punishment is more effective in the long run, but because it yields immediate results. It is easier for the teacher to control the student by threatening punishment than by using positive reinforcement with its *deferred, though more powerful,* effects [p. 36.08, italics mine].

Skinner's conclusions were drawn over a span of time when, just as is the case *now*, there was no conclusive evidence about the supposedly more powerful and long-lasting effects of positive reinforcement. I admire the humanitarian and kindly dispositions contained in such writings. But the scientific basis for the conclusions therein was shabby, because, even in 1938, there were conflicting data which demonstrated the great effectiveness of punishment in controlling instrumental behavior. For example, the widely cited experiments of Warden and Aylesworth (1927) showed that discrimination learning in the rat was more rapid and more stable when incorrect responses were punished with shock than when reward alone for the correct response was used. Later on, avoidance-training experiments in the 1940s and 1950s added impressive data on the long-lasting behavioral control exerted by noxious stimuli (Solomon & Brush, 1956). In spite of this empirical development, many writers of books in the field of learning now devote but a few lines to the problem of punishment, perhaps a reflection of the undesirability of trying to bring satisfying order out of seeming chaos. In this category are the recent books of Spence, Hull, and Kimble. An exception is Bugelski (1956) who devotes several pages to the complexities of this topic. Most contemporary *introductory psychology* texts devote but a paragraph or two to punishment as a scientific problem. Conspicuously, George Miller's new book, *Psychology, the Science of Mental Life,* has no discussion of punishment in it.

The most exhaustive textbook treatment today is that of Deese (1958), and it is a thoughtful and objective evaluation, a singular event in this area of our science. The most exhaustive journal article is that by Church (1963), who has thoroughly summarized our knowledge of punishment. I am indebted to Church for letting me borrow freely from his fine essay in prepublication form. Without this assistance, the organization of this paper would have been much more difficult, indeed.

Perhaps one reason for the usual textbook relegation of the topic of punishment to the fringe of experimental psychology is the widespread belief that punishment is unimportant because *it does not really weaken habits*; that it pragmatically is a *poor controller* of behavior; that it is extremely *cruel* and unnecessary; and that it is a technique leading to *neurosis* and worse. This legend, and it is a legend without sufficient empirical basis, probably arose with Thorndike (1931). Punishment, in the time of Thorndike, used to be called punishment, not passive avoidance training. The term referred to the use of noxious stimuli for the avowed purpose of discouraging some selected kind of behavior. Thorndike (1931) came to the conclusion that punishment did not really accomplish its major purpose, the destruction or extinction of habits. In his book, *Human Learning*, he said:

> Annoyers do not act on learning in general by weakening whatever connection they follow. If they do anything in learning, they do it indirectly, by informing the learner that such and such a response in such and such a situation brings distress, or by making the learner feel fear of a certain object, or by making him jump back from a certain place, or by some other definite and specific change which they produce in him [p. 46].

This argument is similar to that of Guthrie (1935), and of Wendt (1936),

in explaining the extinction of instrumental acts and conditioned reflexes. They maintained that extinction was not the weakening of a habit, but the replacement of a habit by a new one, even though the new one might only be sitting still and doing very little.

When Thorndike claimed that the effects of punishment were indirect, he was emphasizing the power of punishment to evoke behavior other than that which produced the punishment; in much the same manner, Guthrie emphasized the extinction procedure as one arousing competing responses. The competing-response theory of extinction today cannot yet be empirically chosen over other theories such as Pavlovian and Hullian inhibition theory, or the frustration theories of Amsel or Spence. The Thorndikian position on punishment is limited in the same way. It is difficult to designate the empirical criteria which would enable us to know, on those occasions when punishment for a response results in a weakening of performance of that response, whether a habit was indeed weakened or not. How can one tell whether competing responses have displaced the punished response, or whether the punished habit is itself weakened by punishment? Thorndike could not tell, and neither could Guthrie. Yet a legend was perpetuated. Perhaps the acceptance of the legend had something to do with the lack of concerted research on punishment from 1930–1955. For example, psychologists were not then particularly adventuresome in their search for experimentally effective punishments.

Or, in addition to the legend, perhaps a bit of softheartedness is partly responsible for limiting our inventiveness. (The Inquisitors, the Barbarians, and the Puritans could have given us some good hints! They did not have electric shock, but they had a variety of interesting ideas, which, regrettably, they often put to practice.) We clearly need to study new kinds of punishments in the laboratory. For most psychologists, a punishment in the laboratory means electric shock. A few enterprising experimenters have used air blasts, the presentation of an innate fear releaser, or a signal for the coming omission of reinforcement, as punishments. But we still do not know enough about using these stimuli in a controlled fashion to produce either behavior suppression, or a CER effect, or the facilitation of extinction. Many aversive states have gone unstudied. For example, conditioned nausea and vomiting is easy to produce, but it has not been used in the role of punishment. Even the brain stimulators, though they have since 1954 tickled brain areas that will instigate active escape learning, have not used this knowledge to study systematically the punishing effects of such stimulation on existing responses.

While the more humanitarian ones of us were bent on the discovery of new positive reinforcers, there was no such concerted effort on the part of the more brutal ones of us. Thus, for reasons that now completely escape me, some of us in the past were thrilled by the discovery that, under some limited conditions, either a light onset or a light termination could raise lever-pressing rate significantly, though trivially, above operant level. If one is looking for agents to help in the task of getting strong predictive power, and strong control of behavior, such discoveries seem not too exciting. Yet, in contrast, discoveries *already have* been made of the powerful aversive control of behavior. Clearly, we have been afraid of their implications. Humanitarian guilt and normal kindness are undoubtedly involved, as they should be. But I believe that one reason for our fear has been the widespread implication of the *neurotic syndrome* as a *necessary* outcome of all severe punishment proce-

dures. A second reason has been the general acceptance of the behavioral phenomena of rigidity, inflexibility, or narrowed cognitive map, as *necessary* outcomes of experiments in which noxious stimuli have been used. I shall question *both* of these conclusions.

If one should feel that the Skinnerian generalizations about the inadequate effects of punishment on instrumental responses are tinged with a laudable, though thoroughly incorrect and unscientific, sentimentalism and softness, then, in contrast, one can find more than a lurid tinge in discussions of the effects of punishment on the *emotional* balance of the individual. When punishments are asserted to be ineffective controllers of instrumental behavior, they are, in contrast, often asserted to be devastating controllers of emotional reactions, leading to neurotic and psychotic symptoms, and to general pessimism, depressiveness, constriction of thinking, horrible psychosomatic diseases, and even death! This is somewhat of a paradox, I think. The convincing part of such generalizations is only their face validity. There *are* experiments, many of them carefully done, in which these neurotic outcomes were clearly observed. Gantt's (1944) work on neurotic dogs, Masserman's (1943) work on neurotic cats and monkeys, Brady's (1958) recent work on ulcerous monkeys, Maier's (1949) work on fixated rats, show some of the devastating consequences of the utilization of punishment to control behavior. The side effects are frightening, indeed, and should *not* be ignored! But there *must be* some rules, some principles, governing the appearance of such side effects, for they *do not* appear in all experiments involving the use of strong punishment or the elicitation of terror. In Yates' (1962) new book, *Frustration and Conflict*, we find a thorough discussion of punishment as a creator of conflict. Major attention is paid to the instrumental-response outcomes of conflict due to punishment. Phenomena such as rigidity, fixation, regression, aggression, displacement, and primitivization are discussed. Yates accepts the definition of neurosis developed by Maier and by Mowrer: self-defeating behavior oriented toward no goal, yet compulsive in quality. The behavioral phenomena that reveal neuroses are said to be fixations, regressions, aggressions, or resignations. But we are not told the necessary or sufficient experimental conditions under which these dramatic phenomena emerge.

Anyone who has tried to train a rat in a T maze, using food reward for a correct response, and shock to the feet for an incorrect response, knows that there *is* a period of emotionality during early training, but that, thereafter, the rat, when the percentage of correct responses is high, looks like a hungry, well-motivated, happy rat, eager to get from his cage to the experimenter's hand, and thence to the start box. Evidently, merely going through conflict is not a condition for neurosis. The rat is reliable, unswerving in his choices. Is he neurotic? Should this be called subservient resignation? Or a happy adjustment to an inevitable event? Is the behavior constricted? Is it a fixation, an evidence of behavioral rigidity? The criteria for answering such questions are vague today. Even if we should suggest some specific tests for rigidity, they lack face validity. For example, we might examine *discrimination reversal* as a test of *rigidity*. Do subjects who have received reward for the correct response, and punishment for the incorrect response, find it harder to reverse when the contingencies are reversed, as compared with subjects trained with reward alone? Or, we might try a *transfer test*, introducing our subject to a new maze, or to a new jumping stand. Would the previously punished subject general-ize more readily than one not so punished? And if he did, would he then be *less discriminating* and thus neurotic? Or, would the previously punished subject generalize poorly and hesitantly, thus being *too discriminating*, and thus neurotic, too? What are the criteria for behavioral *malfunction* as a consequence of the use of punishment? When instrumental responses are used as the indicator, we are, alas, left in doubt!

The most convincing demonstrations of neurotic disturbances stemming from the use of punishment are seen in Masserman's (Masserman & Pechtel, 1953) work with monkeys. But here the criterion for neurosis is *not* based on instrumental responding. Instead, it is based on emotionality expressed in consummatory acts and innate impulses. Masserman's monkeys were frightened by a toy snake while they were eating. Feeding inhibition, shifts in food preferences, odd sexual behavior, tics, long periods of crying, were observed. Here, the criteria have a face validity that is hard to reject. Clearly, punishment was a dangerous and disruptive behavioral influence in Masserman's experiments. Such findings are consonant with the Freudian position postulating the pervasive influences of traumatic experiences, permeating all phases of the affective existence of the individual, and persisting for long time periods.

To harmonize all of the considerations I have raised concerning the conditions leading to neurosis due to punishment is a formidable task. My guess at the moment is that neurotic disturbances arise often in those cases where *consummatory* behavior or *instinctive* behavior is punished, and punished under *nondiscriminatory* control. But this is merely a guess, and in order for it to be adequately tested, Masserman's interesting procedures would have to be repeated, using discriminative stimuli to signalize when it is safe and not safe for the monkey. Such experiments should be carried out if we are to explore adequately the possible effects of punishment on emotionality. Another possibility is that the number of rewarded behavior alternatives in an otherwise punishing situation will determine the emotional aftereffects of punishments. We have seen that Whiting and Mowrer (1943) gave their rats a rewarding alternative, and the resulting behavior was highly reliable. Their rats remained easy to handle and eager to enter the experimental situation. One guess is that increasing the number of behavioral alternatives leading to a consummatory response will, in a situation where only one behavior alternative is being punished, result in reliable behavior and the absence of neurotic emotional manifestations. However, I suspect that matters cannot be that simple. If our animal subject is punished for Response A, and the punishment quickly elicits Response B, and then Response B is quickly rewarded, we have the stimulus contingencies for the establishment of a masochistic habit. Reward follows punishment quickly. Perhaps the subject would then persist in performing the punished Response A? Such questions need to be worked out empirically, and the important parameters must be identified. We are certainly in no position today to specify the necessary or sufficient conditions for experimental neurosis.

I have, in this talk, decried the stultifying effects of legends concerning punishment. To some extent, my tone was reflective of bias, and so I overstated some conclusions. Perhaps now it would be prudent to soften my claims.[4] I must

admit that all is not lost! Recently, I have noted a definite increase in good parametric studies of the effects of punishment on several kinds of behavior. For example, the pages of the *Journal of the Experimental Analysis of Behavior* have, in the last 5 years, become liberally sprinkled with reports of punishment experiments. This is a heartening development, and though it comes 20 years delayed, it is welcome.

SUMMARY

I have covered a great deal of ground here, perhaps too much for the creation of a clear picture. The major points I have made are as follows: *First, the effectiveness of punishment as a controller of instrumental behavior varies with a wide variety of known parameters.* Some of these are: (*a*) intensity of the punishment stimulus, (*b*) whether the response being punished is an instrumental one or a consummatory one, (*c*) whether the response is instinctive or reflexive, (*d*) whether it was established originally by reward or by punishment, (*e*) whether or not the punishment is closely associated in time with the punished response, (*f*) the temporal arrangements of reward and punishment, (*g*) the strength of the response to be punished, (*h*) the familiarity of the subject with the punishment being used, (*i*) whether or not a reward alternative is offered during the behavior-suppression period induced by punishment, (*j*) whether a distinctive, incompatible avoidance response is strengthened by omission of punishment, (*k*) the age of the subject,

---

[4] Presidential addresses sometimes produce statements that may be plausible at the moment, but on second thought may seem inappropriate. In contrast to my complaints about inadequate research on punishment and the nature of active and passive avoidance learning are Hebb's (1960) recent remarks in his APA Presidential

Address. He said: "The choice is whether to prosecute the attack, or to go on with the endless and trivial elaboration of the same set of basic experiments (on pain avoidance for example); trivial because they have added nothing to knowledge for some time, though the early work was of great value [p. 740]."

and (*l*) the strain and species of the subject.

Second, I have tried to show the theoretical virtues of considering active and passive avoidance learning to be similar processes, and have shown the utility of a two-process learning theory. I have described some examples of the application of findings in active avoidance-learning experiments to the creation of new punishment experiments and to the reanalysis of approach-avoidance conflict experiments.

Third, I have questioned persisting legends concerning both the ineffectiveness of punishment as an agent for behavioral change as well as the inevitability of the neurotic outcome as a legacy of all punishment procedures.

Finally, I have indicated where new experimentation might be especially interesting or useful in furthering our understanding of the effects of punishment.

If there is one idea I would have you retain, it is this: Our laboratory knowledge of the effects of punishment on instrumental and emotional behavior is still rudimentary—much too rudimentary to make an intelligent choice among conflicting ideas about it. The polarized doctrines are probably inadequate and in error. The popularized Skinnerian position concerning the inadequacy of punishment in suppressing *instrumental* behavior is, if correct at all, only conditionally correct. The Freudian position, pointing to pain or trauma as an agent for the pervasive and long-lasting distortion of *affective* behavior is equally questionable, and only conditionally correct.

Happily, there is now growing attention being paid to the effects of punishment on behavior, and this new development will undoubtedly accelerate, because the complexity of our current knowledge, and the preplexity it engenders, are, I think, exciting and challenging.

Reinstatement[1]

Byron A. Campbell and Julian Jaynes

In most of the phyla from anthropods to man early experience exerts a multiplicity of effects on adult behavior (Beach & Jaynes, 1954; Scott, 1962). Sometimes such effects are the simple persistence in adult behavior of habits formed early in life. In other instances it may be that early experience influences later behavior

Reprinted from *Psychological Review*, 1966, vol. 73, pp. 478–480 with the permission of the American Psychological Association and the author.

[1] This research was supported in part by Public Health Service Grant M-1562 from the National Institutes of Mental Health and by National Science Foundation Grant GB 2814.

by structuring the individual's perceptual or response capacities. And in still others, there is a critical period of development during which some aspect of behavior, on which later behaviors depend, is learned and molded for life.

In this paper we suggest yet another mechanism. Although obvious and disarmingly simple, it yet seems to the authors of such neglected importance as to warrant this note and the coining of a term for it. By *reinstatement* we denote a small amount of partial practice or repetition of an experience over the development period which is enough to maintain an early learned response at a high level, but is not enough to produce any effect in animals which have not had the early experience. The following experiment is meant as a demonstration of this phenomenon in a commonly studied instance of learning.

METHOD

The subjects were 30 albino rats of the Wistar strain born and raised in the Princeton colony. They were divided into three groups of 10 each, with an equal number of males and females in each. The apparatus used was one commonly used in fear experiments (Campbell & Campbell, 1961). It consisted of two compartments separated by a door, a black one with a grid floor, and a white compartment with a solid metal floor. Shock could be administered to the grid of the black compartment. To two of the three groups an early fear-arousing experience was given in the black compartment. This consisted of placing the rat just after weaning, when approximately 25 days old, on the grid side of the apparatus with the door fixed so that the rat could not escape, then giving the rat 15 2-second 170-volt shocks on a 20-second variable interval schedule, taking approximately 5 minutes, then removing the animal and placing him on the non-shock side for 5 minutes, and then repeating this entire procedure once. Thus each animal received a total of 30 shocks. At the end of this period the rat was removed and placed in a home cage. A third control group was run through this procedure without any shock being administered to the grid. During the next month a total of three shocks—the reinstatements—were given to one of the early experience groups and to the control group. These shocks were administered 7, 14, and 21 days after the original training session. The procedure was

to administer, at some random number of seconds up to a minute after the animal was placed on the grid side of the apparatus, a single 2-second shock of the same intensity as before. The rat was then placed in the white compartment for an identical period of time and then returned to its home cage. On alternate weeks the animal was placed first on the nonshock side of the cage and then on the shock side, with half of the animals being placed on the shock side for the first reinstatement procedure and half on the safe side. Otherwise this procedure was precisely the same as the training procedure except that only 1 instead of 30 shocks was administered. The second pretrained group was given the same procedure except that no shock was administered. One week after the third reinstatement procedure, when the animals were 53 days of age, they were all tested for the effects of their early experience. This was done by placing them individually in the black compartment (where all of them had been shocked at one time or another) with the door removed so that the animal could run freely into the white compartment. The time spent in the white compartment over the ensuing hour was then recorded.

RESULTS AND DISCUSSION

The results were unequivocal. As seen in Figure 1, the group that had received the early fearful experience followed by three 2-second shocks administered at weekly intervals, spent an increasing percentage of its time in the white compartment during the 1-hour test period, thus showing the effects of the early fearful experience with the black compartment. In contrast, the group that had had a similar early experience just after weaning, but no reinstatement of it in the intervening month, failed to show any significant fear of the black compartment, spending on the average all but about 10 minutes of the hour on that side. Similarly the group which had not had any early traumatic experience, but had received the three brief shocks over the month, failed to acquire any significant fear of the black compartment. The difference between the first group and the other two groups is, as it appears on the graph, highly reliable statistically ($p < .01$, Mann-Whitney U test).

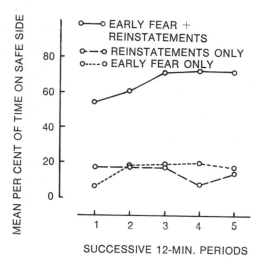

Figure 1 The effect of reinstatement of early fear on later behavior.

There is nothing dramatically surprising about this finding. It is indeed what anyone thinking carefully about learning and practice would expect, namely, that there is some small amount of practice over certain time intervals which could maintain a previously learned response and yet not be enough to train naïve animals to perform that response. The possibility that this mechanism of reinstatement has wide and important applicability in the ontogeny of behavior in many vertebrate species seems beyond question.

In theoretical analyses of human growth and development traumatic

events in infancy and childhood have long occupied a central, if controversial, role. In Freud's early analyses, traumatic events in childhood were considered a major cause of adult behavior disorders. With time, this view was gradually modified such that White writing in 1956 summed up current opinion by stating:

> Undoubtedly it is true that some adult neuroses have their origin in violently frightening events. . . . The theory has long since been abandoned, however, that all neuroses, or even a majority of neuroses, take their start from traumatic events [1956, p. 238].

The early trauma theory has inconsistencies with certain facts of memory and learning as well. First, on a mere phenomenological level, we know that memory becomes more and more dim the further back into our childhood we try to remember. Second, in rats, the earlier in life that a fearful experience is given the animal, the more likely it is to be forgotten in adulthood (Campbell & Campbell, 1962). Third, in chickens, the earlier in the critical period that the chick is imprinted, the more likely it is to be forgotten when the animal reaches the juvenile stages (Jaynes, 1957). This evidence seems to indicate that the organism is constantly forgetting, time or neurological maturation or perhaps other processes constantly changing the mnemonic traces of events and feelings. And all the evidence suggests that the earlier the experience has occurred, the more profound and the faster the forgetting.

In this context reinstatement is proposed as a major mechanism by which the effects of early experiences can be perpetuated and incorporated into adult personality. Following an early experience, either pleasant or unpleasant, three developments may occur. First, the experience may be gradually forgotten as described above. Second, it may be remembered and persist indefinitely if it is occasionally reinstated. The language-based cultures of human societies are particularly rich in methods of such re-instatement, including ones so simple as occasionally reminding a child of a previous event or feeling. Even the child may occasionally reinstate the experience himself under the prompting of his ethical value system. A third possibility is the active repression of the experience, and we suggest here that the repression itself—as well as the experience—may undergo either forgetting or maintenance by reinstatement in exactly the same way. Again, the language based cultures of man contain many reinstatement-of-repression mechanisms such as parental conversational taboos, etc., which determine what repressions are maintained into adult life. In a general sense, we propose that any learned response,

whether acquired in infancy or adult-hood, conscious or unconscious, instrumental or autonomic, joyful or traumatic, can be maintained at a high level by an occasional reinstatement.

Moreover, reinstatement as a principle has considerable adaptive significance, particularly in the learning of fear. Young organisms, at least after a short initial period of apparent fearlessness in some species, become highly vulnerable to the acquisition of fears. These fears have, of course, great survival value in keeping the young organism away from danger. But if they all persisted and could not be forgotten, they would imprison the animal in his own prior experience, making adult adaptive behavior impossible. It is thus essential to adult activity that most early experiences be forgotten, and that only those experiences which are periodically reinstated by a particular habitat or culture be retained.

The Origin of Self-Criticism[1]

Justin Aronfreed

The reproduction of the punitive reactions of socializing agents is a readily observable phenomenon in the behavior of young children. Children often show punitive responses to their own actions, and they sometimes recreate their par-

Reprinted from *Psychological Review*, 1964, vol. 71, pp. 193–218 with the permission of the American Psychological Association and the author.

[1] The author is indebted to two of his colleagues, F. W. Irwin and R. L. Solomon, for their kind readings of an earlier version of this paper. He also wishes to thank Selma Roseman for her capable research assistance in collecting the experimental data.

ents' disciplinary actions in exact motor detail. As language and cognition increasingly take the place of action, social punishment becomes most extensively and persistently reproduced in the form of verbal and evaluative responses. It is very common, for example, to see a young child react to its misdemeanors by saying aloud to itself: "You're a bad boy!" or "That was bad!" Such responses become more covert as the child's symbolic equipment expands. But people do continue beyond childhood to frequently direct toward themselves (and toward others) various components of the social punishment to which they have been previously exposed. These self-punitive reactions belong to a class of behavior whose social learning represents one important type of imitation or identification. They are also of considerable interest because they seem rather paradoxical when approached in terms of our conventional concepts of motivation and reinforcement.

My purpose in this paper is to examine the origin of self-criticism as an illustrative case of the learning and motivational processes which more broadly underlie the adoption of a model's punitive responses. The conditions of aversive learning under which children acquire the use of the label "blue" to refer to their own actions, when the label has been repeatedly used as a component of punishment by a socializing agent, will be demonstrated with a series of experimental socialization paradigms. Evidence bearing upon the resistance to extinction of the self-critical response will also be presented. The results of the paradigms will be used, together with an analysis of naturalistic socialization, to advance the view that self-criticism is acquired because it actually reduces anxiety, and that it does so precisely because evaluative labels were originally subsumed under or contiguous with external punishment. The acquisition of self-punitive responses in general will be described as having only a very limited and indirect relationship to the rewarding characteristics of a model. Finally, it will be argued that self-criticism reveals the essential motivational antecedents and consequences of any internalized evaluative response to a socially defined transgression, regardless of the nature or extent of the cognitive substance of the response.

The evaluative judgment of one's own actions has been traditionally regarded as the foundation of internalized conduct (Freud, 1936, Ch. 8; Hartshorne & May, 1928; Piaget, 1948; Sears, Maccoby, & Levin, 1957, Ch. 10). Many self-evaluative responses must be derived, of course, from social learning based on reward. But the tendency of children to independently replicate the punitive and prohibitive functions of socialization makes a distinct contribution, and one that is at least comparable with the effects of social reward, to the distant relationship that human behavior often bears to what would seem like more inherently preferred responses. This replicative effect of social punishment is clearly displayed in the internalized dispositions which lead people to impose upon themselves both restraint and unpleasant consequences of their own actions. In many contemporary psychological conceptions of internalization (Miller et al., 1960, Ch. 5; Sears et al., 1957, Ch. 10; Whiting & Child, 1953, Ch. 11), self-criticism is viewed as the mediator of other reactions to transgression, and also of control over the occurrence of transgression, when such responses can be elicited in the absence of direct external surveillance. It is, in fact, commonly assumed that the internalized consequences of social punishment require the operation of explicit standards or values which have been adopted from those of a model.

There is actually considerable evidence to question the assumption that the adoption of a model's values or standards is requisite to internalization. The casual observation of the first appearance of internalization in preverbal children makes it particularly obvious that internalized reactions to socially punished acts do not necessarily imply the presence of self-critical cognition. Even when they do not yet have the equipment for social evaluation, young children frequently show signs of anxiety and anxiety-reducing maneuvers following a transgression that has not been apparently open to external observation. Some recent work with dogs (reported by R. L. Solomon in Mowrer, 1960b, pp. 399–404) also suggests that internalization does not require a highly developed cognitive base. Moreover, numerous studies have indicated that internalized responses to transgression show great variability, among both children and adults, in the nature and extent of the cognitive mediating processes on which they rest (Allinsmith, 1960; Aronfreed, 1960; Kohlberg, 1963; Whiting, 1959). Even self-corrective responses, such as confession or reparation, have been found to occur frequently without evaluative standards being applied to a transgression (Aronfreed, 1961). Nevertheless, self-criticism surely deserves special attention among the internalized consequences of social punishment. In addition to its significance for the phenomenon of identification, it also provides verbal and cognitive signals through which other social responses can be mediated with a persistence and generalization that would be impossible if they were forced to depend only on the immediate stimuli of the transgression itself and of its external context.

ACQUISITION

Actions (and, sometimes, intentions or other intrinsic precursors of action) may be defined as transgressions to the extent that they have been followed, in the child's experience, by any form of social punishment. Social punishment includes, of course, not only the application of concrete noxious stimuli, as in physical punishment, but also withdrawal of affection and a wide variety of other kinds of aversive events. When an action is defined as a transgression, through its aversive social consequences for the child, its response-produced cues become

signals for a conditioned drive state that can be given the general designation of anxiety. The anxiety may have, however, qualitative variations which reflect its cognitive context and possibly the nature of the original punishment. It is the invariant motivational source of the child's suppression of transgression, and also of a number of different responses to the occurrence of transgression, all of which share in common their instrumental value for reducing the anxiety. The instrumental status of these responses is derived from the attachment of anxiety attenuation to their discriminant stimulus properties, as a result of certain significant reinforcement contingencies which are present in the socialization process. The responses may be said to be internalized to the extent that the anxiety which motivates them has come to be directly elicited by transgression and independent of either external punishment or social cues which portend punishment.[2] Such instrumental responses are quite variable with respect to the precise patterns of learning through which they become self-reinforcing for the child. Recent studies in the experimental induction of self-criticism and reparation suggest, for example, that these two reactions to transgression are different in the specific contingencies required for their acquisition and in their dependence on evaluative cognition

[2] In defining internalization, one might make a more subtle distinction between whether the anxiety occurs merely in the absence of punishment of whether it occurs in the absence of other external aspects of the original punishment situation (such as perceived observation by others). While the latter condition is a more stringent criterion of internalization, there are significant advantages in providing a broader base of definition. It is very difficult to know whether a person's *perceived* environment includes the possibility of external observation. And once reactions to transgression become independent of punishment, they may take much the same form regardless of the actual presence or absence of observers.

(Aronfreed, 1963; Aronfreed, Cutick, & Fagen, 1963). They cannot be regarded as alternative expressions of a unitary evaluative and punitive agency such as "conscience" or "superego."

The anxiety-reducing value of some internalized responses to transgression, such as confession or reparation, may be acquired because the responses themselves originally received direct external reinforcement through the prevention or arrest of punishment (or through the removal of social cues which portended punishment). But other responses can produce cues to which anxiety reduction has become attached even when the responses have not occurred during the initial socialization process. The most prevalent instances of such responses are those in which the child reproduces components of its previous punishments. Under the ordinary circumstances of child rearing, many components of relatively brief social punishments are sufficiently close to the anxiety termination that follows them to take on substantial power as cues for the reduction of the anticipatory anxiety that has already become directly associated with transgression. The anxiety-reducing function of these components of punishment is central to an understanding of self-criticism. Quite aside from its cognitive requirements, self-criticism is a replication of the verbal medium of punishment. When a child's punishment incorporates verbal criticism—the application of verbal labels or standards to its behavior—the criticism, like any component of punishment, may attain the significance of a cue signaling the attenuation of the antecedent anxiety that occurs in the interval between transgression and punishment. Following subsequent transgressions, the child itself can make the critical response and thus provide itself with anxiety-reducing cues. The cue aspects of the self-critical re-

sponse, initially presented in the punitive behavior of a model, thus acquire reinforcement value through their conjunction with anxiety reduction, without the response having to be first overtly emitted by the child and then externally reinforced. A component of punishment becomes preferred to the experience of anticipatory anxiety.[3]

This description of the learning of self-criticism specifies that it is established as the consequence rather than the source of the negative affect that we experience following a transgression. The anxiety-reducing function of reproduced punishment is sometimes compellingly visible in young children who, even though they are unaware of being observed, may show evidence of acute discomfort when they misbehave and then apparent relief after they have criticized or punished themselves. The introspective perception that the self-critical response sometimes precedes unpleasant feelings may be phenomenologically misleading if it is used to judge the validity of the mechanism of acquisition set forth here. The response, once firmly acquired on an instrumental basis, may begin to occur directly to the cues of transgression with a latency shorter than that with which anxiety reaches substantial intensity. Its maintenance would continue to be dependent on anxiety reduction, however, since the response would tend to be repeated once the anxiety had attained sufficient strength. Recent studies (Brady, Schreiner, Geller, & Kling, 1954; Brush, Brush, & Solomon,

[3] The anxiety-reducing cue value of punishment may also be useful in understanding why some individuals rely primarily on punitive external events to define the consequences of transgression (Aronfreed, 1961; Kohlberg, 1963). Such individuals may be those who have been given sparse verbal and cognitive equipment or who have not found it reinforcing to use their own behavioral resources in response to transgression (for example, young children or members of lower status groups).

1955) emphasize the importance of distinguishing the position of anxiety in the acquisition of an aversive response from its position in the maintenance of the response, and Solomon and Wynne (1954) have analyzed this problem specifically in terms of latencies.[4]

The learning of self-criticism embraces, then, two processes: (a) the attachment of anxiety to the response-produced cues of transgression through their repeated association with punishment; (b) an accrual of the intrinsic reinforcement value of the self-critical response through the inclusion of its cue properties within external punishment in such a way as to make them contiguous with the attenuation of anxiety. The use of two distinct processes to account for the establishment of aversive responses is not uncommon (Mowrer, 1960a, Ch. 3–7; Solomon & Brush, 1956). But the second process described here has certain features which are not ordinarily found in the experimental literature on aversive learning. The learning of an aversive response is typically effected by having the response first occur and then receive direct external reinforcement through avoidance of, or escape from, punishment. In contrast, self-criticism is representative of a class of responses whose acquisition of functional value does not require either that they occur overtly

or that they have discriminable effects upon external reinforcing events. Instead, their value is accumulated as their cue properties are repeatedly presented independently, through the external social behavior of a model, in a temporal position that permits them to serve as signals for the reduction of an anticipatory state of anxiety. The child's subsequent emission of these responses therefore becomes immediately self-reinforcing upon their first occurrence. Support for such a conception is found in demonstrations that neutral stimuli may acquire either motivating or reinforcing properties, according to their temporal association with aversive states, while relevant instrumental responses are not being made by the organism (Gleitman, 1955; Montgomery & Galton, 1955; Solomon & Turner, 1962).

There are some convincing indications that direct instrumental learning can bring an organism to make responses which correspond to those of a model (Church, 1957; Darby & Riopelle, 1959; Miller & Dollard, 1941). And Hill (1960) has recently specifically attempted to describe the learning of self-criticism by using punishment avoidance or escape as the external reinforcement of an initially overt response. But one would expect behavior that is established through direct social reinforcement, even when it happens to be similar to the behavior of a model, to have the kind of latitude usually permitted to responses whose instrumental consequences are originally externally defined. Social reinforcement is not ordinarily so selective as to be contingent on an extremely restricted form of response. Self-criticism, however, has the earmarks of the truly imitative response. It reproduces fairly precisely the stimulus properties of a model, and thus allows a strong presumption that its reinforcement is rather narrowly bound to those properties.

[4] The child's repeated or sustained emission of self-criticism following a transgression may be attributable to the persistence of the anxiety response. Its extension in time is very probably a function of the marked variability in the duration of punishment used by socializing agents and in the temporal position of their critical labels with respect to onset and termination of both transgression and punishment. It should also be noted that verbal criticism is often used as a warning signal that punishment will follow if an incipient transgression is carried out or if an ongoing transgression is not corrected. Consequently, the self-critical response, though motivated by antecedent anxiety, may not be sufficiently anxiety-reducing unless it is accompanied by inhibition or corrections of deviance.

It also seems implausible for other reasons that direct external reinforcement makes any substantial contribution to the initial emergence of self-criticism. Of course, the overt verbalization of the response by young children, once it has been established, might result in the withholding of punishment or even in reward by their parents. But socializing agents can hardly consistently reinforce a response that is generally not apparent in behavior (indeed, they must often be administering punishment following self-criticism, whether it be implicit or overt). In view of the very limited opportunity for such a contingency that one sees in naturalistic child rearing, it would certainly seem a cumbersome and lengthy process to externally reinforce a tendency in the child to reconstruct a component of its previous punishment in order to avoid the delivery of punishment that is externally imminent.

Anyone who has observed the vigor and suddenness with which self-criticism characteristically becomes observable in young children cannot escape the inference that the response already has considerable strength at its first verbalization. This prepotency makes it necessary to go beyond the assertion that the stimulus properties of the response attain anxiety-reducing value without its overt occurrence. We must also assume that the critical label is implicitly emitted by the child during the original punishment learning. The response would then, before it became overt, have already been strengthened through the reinforcement value gradually attached to its intrinsic cue aspects. Given the cognitive capacity of children, the presence of the label in their response repertoire, and the possibly close connection between the receptive and productive functions of language, we might well expect their covert repetition of any label used by a socializing agent.

Finally, it should be noted that this conception of the learning of self-criticism touches upon an issue of more general significance. There are currently a number of inconsistent experimental findings on the question of whether stimuli can become positive reinforcers through their association with the termination of aversive states. The phenomenon has apparently been observed in some animal studies, under the appropriate conditions (Buchanan, 1958; Goodson & Brownstein, 1955; Montgomery & Galton, 1955), but other studies indicate primarily the difficulty of its demonstration in the laboratory (Littman & Wade, 1955; Mowrer & Aiken, 1954; Nefzger, 1957). Some of these experiments, however, do not really duplicate the conditions of social learning under which we could expect to observe such an effect. As Beck (1961) has recently pointed out, attempts to test the reinforcing properties of stimuli which have been contiguous with termination of anxiety or punishment may not be successful if they are carried out in situations in which neither anxiety nor pain is present. The acquisition of self-punitive responses does depend, of course, on the presence of anxiety during both socialization and subsequent occasions when the child itself can reproduce the components of punishment.

Naturalistic and Experimental Socialization

The view that self-criticism is acquired because it attenuates an aversive state does not require that the external criticism of socializing agents occur at a particular point in the course of punishment. What is crucial to the child's reproduction of punishment is the temporal position of its components with respect to onset and termination of anxiety, and not their position with respect to onset and termination of the punishment itself. The usual duration and intensity of social punishment is such that even a component at its onset might acquire some anxiety-reducing significance, provided only that there is sufficient time after the transgression for the arousal of anxiety. When children are quite young and under close parental control, punishment often follows fairly quickly upon transgression. But it does not follow so quickly as to prevent an interval of anticipatory anxiety, particularly since the anxiety comes to be elicited by the incipient precursors of transgression and not merely by its commitment. And, as children become older and more mobile, the interval between transgression and punishment tends to lengthen. Consequently, despite the great variability of parents in their timing and ordering of components of punishment, any component could assume some anxiety-reducing value.

To the extent, then, that parental punishment induces internalized anxiety and is administered in a verbal and cognitive medium, some acquisition of self-criticism by the child would seem inevitable. A close examination of the learning of self-criticism therefore requires artificial conditions under which the verbal components of social punishment are varied in their anxiety-reducing significance. The critical labels would presumably not become anxiety-reducing, for example, if they were to follow immediately upon the intrinsic cues of transgression (so that anticipatory anxiety would be negligible) and were consistently the first element in a punitive reaction of some duration. Conversely, one would expect the labels to have maximal anxiety-reducing value if they were always to occur at the termination of punishment. The acquisition of self-criticism under experimental conditions

might also be facilitated if the onset of punishment (but not the critical labels) were close to the completion of transgression. Such a temporal contingency probably occurs quite often in the early phases of socialization, when the young child's behavioral limitations make it subject to fairly immediate punishment following forbidden behavior, and it may make a potent contribution to the anxiety that motivates self-punitive responses. Animal studies (Davitz, Mason, Mowrer, & Viek, 1957; Kamin, 1959) have indicated that short intervals between response-produced cues and the occurrence of punishment facilitate the acquisition of anxiety-reducing responses. These temporal variations do not occur with any consistency, of course, in the behavior of parents. But they can be brought under control in experimental situations.

An experimental induction of self-criticism ought further to be enhanced if the model's critical labels coincide with the termination of the response-produced cues associated with the transgression. In a naturalistic setting, parental punishment and criticism often interfere with an ongoing transgression, and thus eliminate its intrinsic cues and the anticipatory anxiety already attached to them. The child's reproduction of cue components of punishment might well be supported by this effect, since responses have been shown to have an advantage in learning when their stimulus properties coincide with the termination of a conditioned aversive stimulus (Brush et al., 1955; Church, Brush, & Solomon, 1956; Mowrer & Lamoreaux, 1942). A rapid acquisition of value by the critical labels of a socializing agent, when they coincide with termination of transgression, might also reflect the absence of any delay of the reinforcement represented in anxiety reduction. When the anxiety-reducing significance of a component of punishment becomes discriminable to a child, there is no delay between the parent's use of that component and the occurrence of anxiety reduction. Neutral stimuli have been shown to attain more powerful secondary reinforcing properties when there is a short interval between their presentation and the original reinforcement (Jenkins, 1950; Schoenfeld, Antonitis, & Bersh, 1950).

There is one other feature of naturalistic socialization whose effect upon the internalized consequences of punishment is difficult to assess, because it is relatively restricted in variation and inseparable from the total parent-child relationship. It is the parental nurturance and affection that serves as the background for punishment learning. Many psychologists have felt that the gratifications and rewards provided by parents are an essential ingredient of the child's adoption of their behavior and values in any form. Freud (1936, Ch. 8), for example, regarded the motivation to reproduce a loving and rewarding parental model as one of the major sources of identification. And other theorists (Bronfenbrenner, 1960; Miller *et al.*, 1960, Ch. 10; Whiting & Child, 1953, Ch. 11) have attempted to extend this motivation to the internalization of social punishment.

The most detailed rationale for the generalized effects of nurturance upon internalization is found in the work of Sears *et al.* (1957, Ch. 10) and of Whiting and Child (1953, Ch. 11). The child is presumed to be broadly motivated to identify with its parents in order to reproduce the pleasurable experience associated with the stimulus aspects of their behavior. In making responses like those of the parents, particularly when they are absent or have withdrawn affection, the child provides itself with stimuli which have become powerful secondary reinforcers through their conjunction

with parental rewards and gratifications. Thus, the child's application of the parents' critical evaluative responses to its own actions represents, according to this view, an instance of a more general tendency to reproduce many kinds of parental behavior. And when the child critically evaluates its own behavior, it experiences unpleasant feelings, just as when it was previously exposed to external criticism; that is, self-criticism is regarded as the original internalized source, rather than the consequence, of the anxiety that follows a transgression.

The use of experimental paradigms affords an opportunity to compare the contribution of a socializing agent's nurturance to the induction of self-criticism with that of the anxiety reducing value of cue components of punishment. If the internalization of social punishment were a function of the model's nurturance, or of the withdrawal of affection conveyed in the model's punishment, one would expect that the child would be likely to adopt the criticism of an otherwise nurturant model in a punishment learning situation. Its adoption of the model's criticism would presumably reflect a more general motivation to reproduce the stimulus aspects of the model, and should accordingly not be contingent on the timing of the criticism with respect to onset and termination of anxiety.

Four Socialization Paradigms

In order to examine the origin of self-criticism at close range and under controlled conditions, four experimental paradigms were devised, in each of which the experimenter repeatedly used the label "blue" to refer to a specific response whenever it was made by the child in the course of 10 training trials. The label "red" was used to refer to alternative responses. A contrived task made it possible to control the frequency of the blue response and to use an artificial external signal to indicate its occurrence. In three of the paradigms, the blue response was defined as a transgression by punishment that consisted of the experimenter's sharp disapproval and removal of a candy that had been given to the child. The punishment and the external signal were given a common onset and termination. In the fourth paradigm, the blue response was not associated with punishment. None of the training paradigms offered the child an opportunity to overtly verbalize the evaluative labels used by the experimenter. However, all of the paradigms were uniformly followed by three test trials designed to observe whether the child would use the labels to refer to its own actions when the socializing agent's role was temporarily eliminated.

The external signal and the punitive reaction of the experimenter were initiated, during the three punishment paradigms, immediately upon occurrence of the blue response. Since the punishment had a number of components and some extension in time, the label "blue" could be placed in different positions so as to produce extreme variations in its timing with respect to onset and termination of both the punishment and the external signal of the forbidden response. In the first punishment paradigm, the experimenter placed the label at termination of signal and punishment, the position at which it was expected to assume maximal anxiety-reducing value. In a second paradigm, the label was used at the very onset of signal and punishment, where there was virtually no time for anticipatory anxiety to develop. The experimenter's general (nonpunitive) demeanor, in both of these first two paradigms, was neutral and somewhat distant.

In the third punishment paradigm, the experimenter displayed considerable warmth and approval toward the child, except when administering punishment, and expressed both physical and verbal affection. This procedure was designed to create a nurturant context for socialization and an experience of nurturance withdrawal when the child was punished. The label "blue" was placed at the onset of punishment and signal, so that the effects of the nurturance itself could be compared with the effects, in the first paradigm, of maximizing the anxiety-reducing value of the label. The fourth paradigm was devised as a control to support the interpretation of the role of punishment in establishing the anxiety-reducing function of the label. No punishment was used, but the label occurred at the same point, the termination of the external response-signal, as it did in the first paradigm.

The basic design of these paradigms, and some of their other operational features, were arrived at on the basis of three central tactical considerations which emerged from preliminary studies:

1. Parents ordinarily get a number of "trials" in which to induce an internalized reaction to transgression, because young children commit the transgression on many occasions before internal controls are effective. But if the already socialized children who must be used in an experiment had their own intrinsic response cues to identify a punished act, they might inhibit the act well before a new self-critical response had been learned. Furthermore, their incipient response cues would make it impossible to have an experimental condition in which anticipatory anxiety was negligible. Accordingly, the blue response was designed to be intrinsically indistinguishable from other available responses. Its occurrence was signaled by a fairly loud buzzer, whose onset was immediately coincident with the response. This signal was, then, an externalized response-produced cue.

2. The punishment paradigms would be poor replicates of naturalistic socialization, and might arouse irrelevant competing responses, if the child were punished for transgression on every trial. Children do not always make the socially disapproved response. Blue responses were therefore interspersed with red responses which were not punished and were actually rewarded in the nurturance paradigm. This procedure made the label "blue" a more discriminative stimulus, and also permitted a comparison of the child's adoption of two different kinds of labels.

3. Since self-criticism had to be observable on the test trials, a stimulus was required to elicit it in a verbal form. Moreover, the experimenter had to remain in the situation, in order to observe the response. At the same time, the experimenter's punitive presence had to be somehow perceived as temporarily absent or deferred, if the child were to have occasion and motivation to reproduce the experimenter's evaluative responses. These requirements for the test trials were met by having the experimenter: (a) appear to be absorbed in other matters and temporarily discontinue the socializing role, and (b) casually provide brief nondirective verbal-eliciting stimuli, so as to make the situation appropriate for a wide variety of verbal responses from the child.

Subjects

The subjects for the acquisition phase of the study were 89 girls drawn from the fourth- and fifth-grade populations of two public schools.[5] The number of subjects assigned to each of the four socialization paradigms was as follows: Labeling at Termination of Punishment: 27;

Labeling at Onset of Punishment: 24; Nurturance (with labeling at onset of punishment): 26; Control: 12.

Procedure

Each child was taken by the experimenter (E), who was a female, from her classroom to the experimental room. The child sat in front of a small table, upon which was a piece of apparatus referred to as "the machine" and also a small box containing 15 Tootsie Rolls. The machine was simply an enclosed, black, metal cabinet, roughly 15 inches wide, 10 inches high, and 8 inches deep. In addition to a buzzer located within the machine, the following items were embedded in its inclined face: an a.c. voltmeter, an electrical counter (with display), four small lights (two red and two green) ordered vertically along the left edge, and four locking lever switches running horizontally along the bottom edge and spaced about 3 inches apart. The primary purpose of these units was to convey to the child that the machine was a formidable device. Under each unit was a decal purporting to refer to a complex instrument within the cabinet, such as "ACO Narrow Band Monitor," etc.

In order to generate the operation of the machine on each trial, the child was given the task of pushing down the number of levers that indicated her guess as to how many of four hidden dolls were looking in her direction. The nature of the blue response was vaguely defined for the child as having to do with the way in which the levers were pushed. However, the actual occurrence of transgression was controlled by E through a hidden silent mercury switch that monitored the activation of the units in the machine. The children tended to push first the lever on their far left. This lever was therefore made inactive, so that the blue response would not always occur at

[5] The author is grateful to a number of administrators and teachers in the Philadelphia school system, whose cooperation made this study possible.

the beginning of a guessing sequence. The other three levers were equivalent in that any one of them could activate the buzzer and the other units. When activated, the indicator on the voltmeter would swing, the counter would click and turn over once, and one, two, or three of the four lights would go on (according to which of the levers had been pushed). The child was told that there would always be at least two dolls looking toward her, in order to guarantee the occurrence of the blue response on appropriate trials.

Approximately 6 feet behind the child, E sat at a second table, upon which was a high black cardboard screen. Behind the screen were the four identical small dolls and the mercury switch. After E and S were seated, E used one of four paradigms, each of which consisted of initial instructions and a sequence of training trials designed to make it difficult for S to anticipate events on any given trial. Blue responses occurred on Trials 2, 5, 6, 8, and 9, and red responses on Trials 1, 3, 4, 7, and 10. Each trial began at roughly 8 to 10 seconds after the previous one ended.

Labeling at Termination of Punishment (LTP). The E's initial instructions were as follows:

Here's what we're going to do today. Back here, I have four dolls (E held up dolls, then replaced them behind screen). I'm going to place some of them looking at you from behind here and some looking away (E appeared to handle dolls behind screen). You're supposed to guess how many are looking at you. There are always at least two looking at you, but sometimes there might be more. Sometimes three of them might be looking at you, and sometimes all of them. Each time, you guess, and then I change them, and then you guess again.

The E then walked over to S's table and said:

Now what I really want to see is how you work with a machine. The way you guess is: you tell the machine what you think is the answer. The machine is automatic. When I set the dolls, the machine is set, too, with the right answer. Here's the way the machine knows whether you've guessed how many dolls are looking at you: you push down as many levers as you think there are dolls. If you think there are two dolls looking at you, push two levers (E pushed down first two levers from the left. The mercury switch was open at this point, so that none of the levers were activated). If you think there are three dolls looking at you, push three levers (E pushed down third lever). And if you think there are four, push four (E pushed down last lever). Remember that you always push at least two, and leave them down. Don't push them back up. The machine doesn't show you whether you guessed right, but it tells my instruments, so I know. And when we're all done, I'll tell you how many times you guessed right. Do you understand?

After S's indication of understanding, E reset all levers, returned to her own table, and, while appearing to handle the dolls, closed the mercury switch. Then E returned to S's table and continued:

Now the most important thing is the way you use the machine, the way you push down the levers. I've done this with a lot of girls, and I've found out that there are two different kinds of girls who use the machine in two different ways. I don't know what to call them, so I just call one kind the girls who do it the *red* way and the others who do it the *blue* way.

Over here is a pile of Tootsie Rolls for you (E removed Tootsie Rolls from box and placed them in front of S). When you use the machine the *red* way, it just tells my instruments over there what you've guessed (E pointed to her own table). You push the lever down with your finger from the top (E demonstrated, carefully pushing down the inactive lever). Now the machine has a buzzer that sometimes goes on (here E ostensibly adjusted something at the back of the machine)—it sounds like this (*E* pushed down the second lever, activating the buzzer and the other units in the cabinet). You can hear the buzzer and you can see what's happening (*E* indicated voltmeter and lights). When that happens, you lose some of your Tootsie Rolls. I take them away and put them in this empty box here, because you did it the *blue* way (as *E* said the word "blue," she reset the levers, thus terminating the buzzer and the activation of the other units).

The *E* then returned to her seat behind *S*, and the training trials began. To begin the first trial, *E* said: "All right, guess how many dolls are facing you. Just push down the number of levers you think is right." To begin subsequent trials, *E* simply said: "All right, you can guess now." On a nontransgression trial, the mercury switch was open. *E* merely rose from her seat and said: "Uh-huh, you did it the *red* way." She then walked over to *S*'s table, reset the levers, and returned to her own table to begin the next trial. On a transgression trial, the mercury switch was closed, and the buzzer and other units were activated. *E* rose immediately, as the buzzer went on, and said: "No!" (fairly sharply). After walking quickly over to *S*'s table and looking with concern at the machine, *E* added: "You lose some of your Tootsie Rolls." The *E* then emphatically removed two Tootsie Rolls from *S*'s pile, put them in the box from which they came, and finally added: "Because you did it the *blue* way." Just as *E* spoke the word "blue," she simultaneously reset all of the levers that had been pushed down, so that the label was contiguous with the termination of both punishment and buzzer. Then *E* returned to her own table and began the next trial.

Labeling at Onset of Punishment (LOP). The procedure for this paradigm was identical, in most respects, to that de-

scribed for the LTP paradigm above, except that the label "blue" was used at onset of punishment during the training trials and occupied a corresponding position in the demonstration that accompanied instructions. The modification of instructions began at the point at which the Tootsie Rolls were introduced:

Over here is a pile of Tootsie Rolls for you. When you use the machine the *red* way, it just tells my instruments over there what you've guessed. You push the lever down with your finger from the top (*E* demonstrated on inactive lever). When you use it the *blue* way, the machine has a buzzer that goes on—it sounds like this (*E* pushed down the second, active lever). You can hear the buzzer and you can see what's happening. When that happens, you lose some of your Tootsie Rolls. I take them away and put them in this empty box here (then *E* reset the levers and terminated the buzzer, but without using the label "blue" at this point).

Nontransgression training trials were treated in the same way as in the LTP paradigm. On transgression trials, however, *E* rose and said, immediately at the onset of buzzer and punishment: "You did it the *blue* way—No!" Then *E* walked over to *S*'s table and added, while looking at the machine: "You lose some of your Tootsie Rolls." *E* removed two Tootsie Rolls from *S*'s pile, put them into the box, and terminated buzzer and punishment by resetting all levers. The label "blue" was not used, of course, at this termination point.

Nurturance (with labeling at onset of punishment). The procedure in this paradigm was basically the same as that used in the LOP paradigm. Here, however, *E*'s manner and voice conveyed considerable warmth and approval of *S* (except on transgression trials), in contrast to her generally neutral demeanor in all of the other paradigms. The modifications of procedure entailed intersticed expressions of verbal and physical affection during the instructions and the nontransgression trials. Thus, after the initial distinction between the two kinds of girls who used the machine the red way or the blue way, and just before introducing the Tootsie Rolls, E interjected the following comment (in a smiling, relaxed fashion):

Most of the girls in my own special machine class (E had been originally introduced to all Ss as a "special teacher") are girls who do it the red way. As a matter of fact, you look something like one of them. I think I'm going to like you as much as I like my own girls (and E gently patted S on the head or shoulder).

On transgression trials, E's behavior was identical to that described above for the LOP paradigm. On nontransgression trials, E rose and said, with maximal warmth and enthusiasm: "Good!—you did it the red way." The E then walked over to S's table, reset the levers, and smilingly patted S on the head or shoulder before returning to her own table.

Control (labeling without punishment). The procedure for the control paradigm was similar in most respects to the procedure used in the LTP paradigms. There was, however, no punishment. The last brief section of the instructions was modified to inform the child of the possibility of punishment, so that this paradigm would be equated to others in having the general threat of punitive sanctions. The informational role of the buzzer was also emphasized somewhat more than it had been in other paradigms, in order to eliminate any punitive connotation in the association between the buzzer and the label "blue." After the initial introduction to the task, the modified section of the instructions continued as follows:

Over here is a pile of Tootsie Rolls for you. I might take a couple of them away sometimes, depending on how you use the machine. The machine and I need to know whether it's the red way or the blue way. So we have a buzzer in the machine. When you use the machine the red way, it just tells my instruments over there what you've guessed (E pushed down the inactive lever). When you use the machine the blue way, we can tell that, too, because the buzzer goes on—it sounds liks this (E pushed down second lever). You can hear the buzzer and you can see what's happening —because you did it the blue way (as E said the word blue, she reset the levers, terminating the buzzer).

On trials in which the blue response occurred, E rose, walked over to S's table and said: "Uh-huh, you did it the blue way." As E said the word "blue," she terminated the buzzer. The E's reaction to red responses was the same as in the LTP and LOP paradigms.

Test trials. Trials 11, 12, and 13 were test trials uniformly employed immediately after all of the socialization paradigms. The S's lever choices on Trials 11 and 12 were followed by the buzzer, in order to test S's use of the label "blue" in reference to her action. To test for S's use of the label "red," S's lever choices on Trial 13 were not followed by the buzzer. The S's verbal responses on all test trials were recorded verbatim.

The E remained seated behind S on Trial 11, and appeared oblivious to the buzzer, having intentionally preoccupied herself with her recording sheets. If the child made no comment within 10 seconds after buzzer onset, E casually asked: "What happened this time?" This stimulus was used to elicit a verbal response from S. If S applied the label "blue" to her own behavior in any way, either spontaneously or in response to the eliciting stimulus, E then terminated the test trial in the same way that she terminated trials in the preceding training series (including the labeling and punishment, where the latter was appropriate). If S made a verbal response that did not include the use of the label "blue," E asked: "What do you mean?" After this last question, E terminated the test trial regardless of S's response. The punishment used in training was continued, in closing the test trial, so that the label "blue," if used by the child, would not receive a direct external reinforcement through punishment avoidance, since it was also to be tested on the subsequent trial (12).

The procedure for Trial 12 was the same as that for Trial 11, but was preceded by a statement intended to facilitate spontaneous responses. Before Trial 12 began, E said: "My eyes are getting tired from looking at these instruments. After you've guessed this time, you can tell me what happened yourself." The same procedure was also used on Trial 13, but the introductory statement used on Trial 12 was not repeated. After testing for S's use of the label "red," E concluded Trial 13 in the way appropriate to red responses on the preceding training series.

Closing Procedure. A closing procedure was used to assure S of the adequacy of her performance, to relieve any anxiety about the loss of Tootsie Rolls, and to invoke S's cooperation in not discussing the experiment with other children.

Results and Discussion

Certain features of the children's behavior during the training paradigms were strikingly apparent. They uniformly exercised great care in pushing the levers and showed obvious signs of discomfort upon the occurrence of transgression. Their pleased smiles in the nurturance paradigm also affirmed the experimenter's success in conveying affection. The power acquired by the buzzer was clearly visible on Test Trial 11 and 12 (except in the case of the control paradigm). The children were restless and tense, and most of them looked back expectantly at the now preoccupied experimenter. Although some children in the LTP paradigm made spontaneous labeling responses, the children generally verbalized the labels only in response to the experimenter's eliciting stimuli. This was true even on Trial 12, despite the initial statement that the children themselves could report on what happened, and was very possibly attributable to the effective functioning of the labels at an implicit level.

Numerous responses were given to the experimenter's verbal stimuli. Many children simply offered reportorial statements such as: "the buzzer went on," "I pushed the levers," "the lights went on," "I don't know," "you'll have to get up again," "I lose some Tootsie Rolls," etc. But only the relevant labeling responses, applied by the children to their behavior or to themselves, were used as evidence of self-evaluation. These generally took the form of: "I did it the blue (red) way!" or, less commonly, "I was blue (red)!" Table 1 shows, for each of the test trials, the relative frequencies of the appropriate labeling responses among the four paradigms. Chi-square values for comparisons of the frequencies are presented in Table 2. The observations on Test Trial 12 add only an indication of the stability of the responses seen on Trial 11.

The paradigm that is singularly effective in the induction of self-criticism is the one in which the socializing model uses the critical label at the termination of both the punishment and the externalized response-contingent signal of

Table 1
Frequency of Labeling and Nonlabeling Responses on Three Test Trials

Response	LTP[a] (N = 27)	LOP[b] (N = 24)	Nurturance (LOP)[b] (N = 26)	Control[c] (N = 12)
Trial 11				
Blue label used	19	5	5	3
Blue label not used	8	19	21	9
Trial 12				
Blue label used	19	6	6	3
Blue label not used	8	18	20	9
Trial 13				
Red label used	9	6	7	3
Red label not used	18	18	18	9

[a] LTP = Labeling at termination of punishment.
[b] LOP = Labeling at onset of punishment.
[c] Control = Labeling without punishment.

transgression. This finding strongly confirms the view that the child's reproduction of a component of social punishment rests on its original external position with respect to the onset and attenuation of anxiety. The fact that the blue label clearly attains functional value only in the temporal setting of the LTP paradigm, despite its not having been overtly verbalized during training, also points to the acquisition of self-criticism as an instrumental response that does not require direct external reinforcement. The infrequent use of the label among children exposed to a model who used it at onset of punishment and transgression signal, including those socialized in a nurturant context, makes it apparent that the reinforcing properties of the label are not to be assigned to any generalized effect of punishment. There is also no support for the view that self-criticism represents a broader tendency to reproduce the behavior of a model who is nurturant but withdraws nurturance in order to deliver punishment. The results of the experiment indicate that self-criticism is acquired as a specific response through aversive learning. Its high probability of occurrence, when its

Table 2
Chi-square Values for Comparisons among Four Experimental Socialization Paradigms of the Frequency of Labeling and Nonlabeling Responses

Comparison	Trial 11 (Blue label)	Trial 12 (Blue label)	Trial 13 (Red label)
LTP versus LOP	10.61**	8.73**	0.12
LTP versus nurturance (LOP)	11.99**	10.07**	0.01
LTP versus control	5.23*	5.23*	0.02
LOP versus nurturance (LOP)	0.05	0.03	0.01
LOP versus control	0.02	0.16	0.16
Nurturance (LOP) versus control	0.00	0.10	0.04

Note—Chi-square values for 2×2 contingency tables (employing correction for continuity) based on frequencies in Table 1.
* $p < .05$ (one-tailed test).
** $p < .01$ (one-tailed test).

stimulus properties have been independently presented as the terminal component of punishment, cannot be understood without reference to the mediation of anxiety and anxiety reduction.

The control paradigm eliminates interpretation of these findings in terms of associative processes not contingent on punishment—such as recency or stimulus impact (salience) effects stemming from the conjunction of the label with the termination of the buzzer at the end of each trial. It cannot be said, for example, that all children would be generally predisposed to imitate the experimenter's labels, for reasons unrelated to their anxiety-reducing value, unless the labels had been made aversive stimuli through their association with onset of punishment. Few children in the control paradigm used the label "blue," even though it occurred at the termination of buzzer and training trial. Embedding the label in a punitive context is clearly a prerequisite of its adoption by the children.[6]

A comparison of the frequencies of occurrence of the blue and red labels, following the LTP paradigm, also indicates no general tendency of the children to imitate the experimenter's verbalization, and again points to the specific anxiety-reducing function of the blue label. Of course, the red label would not have been expected to acquire much value from its association with relatively neutral events. Its restricted use following nurturant socialization might be regarded as more surprising, however, since there it occurs in the context of warm verbal approval and physical affection. It may be that the reinforcing effects of the kind of nurturance given are not as discrete and well defined as the effects of anxiety reduction. But perhaps a more plausible explanation is that the motivation to produce an evaluative label associated with reward is difficult to establish in a learning situation so largely defined by punishment. In any case, the findings suggest that positive self-evaluation requires its own distinct reinforcing consequences.

MAINTENANCE

One of the remarkable characteristics of the internalized derivatives of social learning is their persistent maintenance in the absence of external surveillance and reinforcement. Aversive responses, in particular, can often be quite resistant to extinction (Miller, 1959; Solomon & Brush, 1956), and one would expect that self-criticism, a response that is even initially intrinsically reinforced, might easily become independent of its original conditions of learning. As has already been pointed out, the punishment and criticism of parents sometimes follow fairly rapidly upon occurrence of a response to which internalized anxiety is to be attached. Yet once the child's anxiety comes to precede its punishment, certain cue components of the punishment become associated with anxiety reduction. Correspondingly, in the experimental paradigm with labeling at termination of punishment, onset of punishment was immediately coincident with onset of the transgression signal, but the (external) presentation of the critical label directly coincided with the signal's termination. Such temporal re-

---

[6] The buzzer, though used as a cue, undoubtedly had some inherent aversive properties, the termination of which may have been sufficient in itself, for a few children, to lend anxiety-reducing value to the blue label in the control paradigm. The occasional use of the blue label by children exposed to the paradigms where it appeared directly upon transgression may be attributable to covert situational cues or irregularities of timing which permitted too much anticipatory anxiety before its occurrence.

lationships among the cues to which anxiety is attached, the occurrence of punishment, and the stimulus properties of aversive responses, appear to contribute as much to the maintenance of these responses as to their acquisition (Brush *et al.*, 1955; Church *et al.*, 1956).

Part of the relative insensitivity that self-criticism can show to changes in external conditions may be a function of the resistance to extinction of the intense anxiety attached to some transgressions (Bitterman & Holtzman, 1952; Solomon & Wynne, 1954). The actions around which parents hope to inculcate the most permanent and generalized internalization are those which they are likely to punish most severely. The failure of anxiety to disappear, when apparently deprived of its original support in the form of explicit punishment, may also follow from a kind of inconsistent reinforcement related to generalization of perceived punitive events. Children may perceive punitive implications even where punishment is not intended, because they can so easily assimilate both social and impersonal events to their experience of the wide spectrum of punitive capacities previously represented in the behavior of socializing agents. In the ecology of interaction between parents and children, inconsistency of perceived punishment would be inevitable. And even beyond childhood, the most infrequent application of real or perceived punishment would be sufficient to interfere with the extinction of internalized anxiety.

While internalized reactions to transgression do persist in the absence of predictable external punishment, their endurance when followed by punishment perhaps even more effectively shows that their reinforcement is not tied to external consequences. Children are often punished for their actions despite the intervening implicit or overt presence of self-criticism. The cue properties of their self-critical responses would, under these circumstances, precede external punishment. They would therefore no longer have quite the same signal value, with respect to onset and termination of anxiety, which they initially had as a component of punishment. The anxiety-reducing status of self-criticism could not be sustained under such conditions, if it actually remained dependent on the temporal relationship of the critical labels to the external events which originally marked anxiety reduction. Moreover, the continued experience of social punishment affords children many opportunities to observe that internalized anxiety can be terminated without their criticizing or punishing themselves, though not in a way that is equally under their control. It is possible, of course, that the irregular presence of punishment serves primarily to strengthen the anxiety that motivates self-criticism. A number of studies with animals have indicated that punishment of aversive responses heightens their resistance to extinction (Gwinn, 1949; Sidman, Herrnstein, & Conrad, 1957; Solomon & Wynne, 1954). But whatever the effects of external punishment upon the self-critical response, once it is established, it seems necessary to attribute its persistent maintenance to the anxiety-reduction attached to its intrinsically produced cues.

In order to assess the durability of the tendency to reproduce a verbal component of punishment, three distinct attempts were made to eliminate the use of the blue label among additional groups of children, after they had acquired it through exposure to the socialization paradigm with labeling at termination of punishment. The three procedures may be designated as extinction paradigms, even though the original reinforcement (anxiety reduction) for the self-critical response cannot really be withdrawn by changes in external conditions. One group was taken through a procedure intended to diminish the anxiety-reducing properties of the blue label by changing its temporal relationship to both punishment and anxiety. The procedure used with the second group was directed to the question of whether the label would retain its value over a period during which punishment and anxiety reduction occurred without its being verbalized by either child or socializing agent. The third paradigm, which made the most direct attack upon the autonomy of self-criticism, removed punishments as well as verbalization of the critical label, in an attempt to extinguish the anxiety attached to the transgression.

Three Extinction Paradigms

Subjects

Thirty-seven additional subjects, drawn from the same population used in the original four socialization paradigms, were exposed to the LTP paradigm. Thirty of these new subjects met the previously employed acquisition criterion, and 10 were assigned to each of the three extinction series.

Procedure

In an effort to eliminate the self-critical response before it was given repeated overt verbalization, all of the extinction procedures were begun as soon as S verbalized the label "blue" on either of the two acquisition test trials (11 or 12), and all subsequent trials were run as the extinction series. The procedures were run so that each two transgression (buzzer) trials were followed by a nontransgression trial, in order to avoid uninter-

rupted punishment in the first two extinction paradigms. Thus, beginning with the first acquisition test trial, the sequence of transgression trials during extinction was: 11, 12, 14, 15, 17, 18, etc.[7]

Extinction Paradigm 1. In this series, E continued to use, on transgression trials, the same verbal eliciting stimuli used on acquisition test trials. As soon as S gave the self-critical response on either Trial 11 or 12, and regardless of S's response on subsequent transgression trials, E rose and said, while walking to S's table: "Well, you lose some of your Tootsie Rolls."[8] The E then removed two Tootsie Rolls from S's supply and terminated the buzzer, but no longer used the label blue. On nontransgression trials, E simply rose and reset the levers on the machine (without using the label "red"). The effect of this procedure was that the label "blue," when now "presented" by S during transgression trials, was consistently followed by punishment and temporary continuation of the buzzer that signaled transgression. Extinction trials were run until there were four consecutive transgression trials without verbalization of the blue label, or until 10 transgression trials had occurred, although additional trials were permitted if S showed signs of extinguishing.

Extinction Paradigm 2. The blue label was eliminated from punishment during

---

[7] Children to be taken through the two extinction paradigms in which punishment was continued were provided, before training began, with 20 Tootsie Rolls (instead of the 15 provided in the original socialization paradigms), so that they could continue to be deprived of them during the entire sequence of transgression trials throughout the acquisition and extinction procedures.

[8] The expletive, "No!," used as a component of punishment during training trials, was removed in this first extinction paradigm. Its continued use, once the child began to verbalize the blue label, might have led to elimination of the label for reasons unrelated to the change in its temporal relationship to anxiety and punishment.

this procedure, and *E* also discontinued the verbal stimuli used to elicit *S*'s overt expression of the label. The *S* was consequently exposed to termination of both punishment and buzzer without verbalization of the label. Following *S*'s self-critical response on Trial 11 or 12, *E* rose, administered the usual punishment without using the blue label, and terminated the buzzer. On all subsequent transgression trials, *E* carried out the same procedure, beginning immediately upon onset of the buzzer. On nontransgression trials, *E* reset the levers without comment. The extinction series was run through Trial 25. Trials 26 and 27 were extinction test trials, and restored the verbal eliciting stimuli used by *E* on acquisition test trials. If *S* verbalized the blue label on neither of the two test trials, the self-critical response was considered to be extinguished.

RESULTS

The effective induction of self-criticism, in the socialization paradigm with labeling at termination of punishment, was again confirmed by the fact that 30 of the 37 children taken through the paradigm met the acquisition criterion. Table 3 shows that, in each of the three extinction groups, only two of the ten children used met the extinction criterion. None of the children in whom the response failed to extinguish gave any indication of relinquishing their use of the critical label. Under the first extinction procedure, children who did not meet the extinction criterion used the label uniformly throughout the extinction trials. And in the second and third paradigms, children who retained the response invariably gave it on both of the extinction test trials.

Table 3
Frequency of Extinction and Nonextinction of the Self-Critical Response under Each of Three Extinction Paradigms

Response	Extinction 1 (N = 10)	Extinction 2 (N = 10)	Extinction 3 (N = 10)
Did not extinguish	2	2	2
Extinguished	8	8	8

Extinction Paradigm 3. In this paradigm, both punishment and verbalization of the label "blue" were entirely removed. When *S* gave the self-critical response on Trial 11 or 12, *E* merely rose, walked over to *S*'s table, and terminated the buzzer. On subsequent extinction trials, both transgression and nontransgression, *E* continued to simply walk over and reset the levers without comment. The extinction criterion was *S*'s failure to use the self-critical label on either of the two extinction test trials (26 and 27), when *E*'s eliciting stimuli were restored.

The three extinction paradigms do not go to the limit of effort that could be made to eliminate the self-critical response. Other methods which have been used to facilitate extinction of aversive responses, such as pairing the anxiety-inducing stimulus with positive reinforcement (Hall, 1955) or rewarding an incompatible response (Solomon & Wynne, 1954), are not represented here. It seems apparent, however, that the experimentally socialized labeling response has some of the tenacity that we might expect of internalized self-evaluation.

SOME FURTHER THEORETICAL IMPLICATIONS

Reproduction of Punishment

The experimental literature on punishment learning typically centers on the conditioning of anxiety (or "aversiveness") to the organism's own response cues, and the consequences of punishment are indexed in the suppression of the punished behavior (Dinsmoor, 1954; Estes, 1944; Miller, 1959; Mowrer & Viek, 1948). The inhibition of transgressions would be, of course, one of the derivatives of their definition through social punishment. But self-criticism provides a response for reducing the anxiety that follows the commission of a transgression. The response does not require reinforcement by avoidance or termination of external punishment, and it actually reproduces stimulus events which have been previously part of that punishment. We are confronted, then, with an anxiety-reducing response whose acquisition is contingent on the prior association of its stimulus properties with the presence rather than with the absence of punishment.

It is not really paradoxical that self-criticism can be acquired, and often permanently maintained, despite the fact that it reproduces punishment. Aversive responses have frequently been shown to be at least as sensitive to anxiety reduction as they are to punishment avoidance, when these two outcomes are partially separated, and sometimes they seem relatively impervious to their punitive consequences (Gwinn, 1949; Sidman & Boren, 1957; Solomon & Wynne, 1954). It is possible, in fact, to interpret certain studies of both human and animal subjects (D'Amato & Gumenik, 1960; Farber, 1948; Maier, 1949) as indicating that, under high anticipatory anxiety and with no easily available avoidance response, subjects will move in the direction of external punishment because of its anxiety-attenuating significance. In a similar way, the anxiety that motivates self-criticism is initially dependent on the motivating properties of punishment, while the reinforcement of the response is dependent on its replication of the anxiety-reducing signal properties of punishment. Self-punitive responses are, therefore, clearly not to be regarded as having been originally learned as avoidance responses. Their self-reinforcing character is acquired on the basis of anxiety-reduction as the "primary reinforcement."

It is interesting to note that Freud (1936, Ch. 8) saw anxiety reduction as the function of children's adoption of the punitive or threatening behavior of a model, and that its role has also been previously suggested in concepts such as "identification with the aggressor" (A. Freud, 1946, Ch. 9) and "defensive identification" (Mowrer, 1950, Ch. 21). Certainly it is not difficult to perceive that the mechanism of reinforcement in the learning of self-criticism may serve as the general mechanism for what may be called identification through aversive learning—that is, for the acquisition of any response in which, without the benefit of external reinforcement, the individual directs toward himself the socially punitive behavior that he has previously experienced from without.[9]

Further research on the anxiety-reduc-

[9] Children also often react to the transgressions of others by reproducing the same punitive responses to which they have been previously subjected. A tentative beginning toward accounting for this phenomenon might be offered by noting that stimulus generalization may operate to cause the transgressions of others to arouse the child's anxiety, and to elicit its reproduction of punishment, if they are similar to those for which the child itself has been previously punished. One must also account, however, for the change in the target of the punishment.

ing properties of social punishment, and on their imitative reproduction, might well give attention to the intensity of punishment. There is no reason to assume that the punishment to be reproduced must be less "painful" than the antecedent anxiety. Nevertheless, when punishment is very severe, whatever decrement of anticipatory anxiety attaches to its cue properties could be overshadowed by the increment of aversive stimulation from its drive properties. Experimental socialization paradigms might be used to compare the conditions required for the learning of self-criticism with those required for the self-directed replication of nonverbal components of punishment, some of which would be more inherently unpleasant than a verbal label. Such paradigms might also be devised so as to suggest the theoretical extensions necessary to account for the child's learning to direct its reproduction of punishment toward others. They could further be used to examine other relationships of timing and magnitude among components of punishment. Presumably, any component of punishment could assume anxiety-reducing value, provided that it follows some minimal internalized anxiety. But the breadth of the phenomenon may be limited by the duration and relative severity of the remaining punishment that follows a given component. Verbal social responses which already have become mildly punitive to the child are often used by socializing agents as cues to signal more severe punishment if a transgression is completed or continued. It would be interesting to know whether such cues attain some anxiety-reducing value, despite their position as warning signals, because of their mediation of inhibitory responses which avoid the punishment. Finally, perhaps the most intriguing experimental translations of naturalistic

socialization would be in the area of inconsistent punishment. Studies of the discriminative events within which punishment is inconsistent, and of the extent to which socializing agents provide consequences of transgression other than direct punishment, might reveal that inhibition, self-punishment, and other internalized reactions to transgression have common elements other than the anxiety that motivates them and the anxiety reduction that serves as their reinforcement.

Nurturance and the Internalized Consequences of Punishment

A comparison of the effects of the various socialization paradigms described earlier indicates that the internalization of punishment does not rest on a broader predisposition to reproduce the behavior of an otherwise nurturant or affectionate model. Nor does it appear, as some theorists have suggested (Kagan, 1958; Maccoby, 1959; Whiting, 1960), that self-criticism represents a generalized tendency to exercise control over the threatening punitive resources at the disposal of a socializing agent. While the duration and intensity of nurturant treatment are more extended in a parent-child relationship, the warm approval and physical affection given to the children in the nurturance paradigm would certainly have been expected to attach some positive value to the model's role and to cause punishment to be experienced as a withdrawal of affection. And, in view of the effectiveness of the paradigm with labeling at termination of punishment, the failure of the nurturance paradigm to induce many self-critical responses cannot be attributed simply to an insufficiency of nurturance. The reproduction of social punishment appears to be acquired only when the relevant components of punishment have a circumscribed temporal relationship to an anticipatory aversive state.

The contributions of punishment and anxiety to the learning of self-criticism should not be extrapolated, of course, to other kinds of imitative social learning, in which children do appear to provide their own reinforcement by reproducing those stimulus aspects of a model which have been directly associated with nurturance or reward. Persuasive theoretical cases have been made for the place of a reinforcement mechanism derived from reward in much of imitative behavior (Mowrer, 1950, Ch. 21; Mowrer, 1960b, Ch. 3; Sears et al., 1957, Ch. 10; Whiting & Child, 1953, Ch. 11); and there are empirical findings (Bandura & Huston, 1961; Mussen & Distler, 1959; Sears, 1953) which support the common observation that the warmth and affection of socializing agents foster the child's tendency to adopt a great variety of their responses. We can hardly be surprised, however, to find that the reproduction of social punishment cannot be subsumed under the consequences of a model's rewarding characteristics. Children sometimes reproduce behavioral pieces of the most entirely frightening figures which they encounter in both reality and fantasy. Similar phenomena in adults are described in Bettelheim's (1943) well-known report of life in a concentration camp, and are also seen by the sensitive observer under ordinary social circumstances. Conversely, there is no reason to expect the child's motivation to reproduce the behavior of a nurturant model to be so powerfully indiscriminate, even under the duress of withdrawal of affection, as to encompass the model's punishment. An account of the diversity of modeling responses usually taken as evidence of identification requires, then, an extension of learning processes derived

from punishment as well as of those derived from reward.[10]

The internalized consequences of social punishment would, nevertheless, not be totally indifferent to the nurturance and affection of socializing agents. Numerous descriptive surveys of internalized responses to transgression, whose rough indices of internalization have given much attention to self-criticism, indicate the absence of any consistently direct relationship between extent of internalization in the child and the amount of nurturance given by parents (Bronfenbrenner, 1961; Heinecke, 1953; Sears et al., 1957, Ch. 10; Whiting & Child, 1953, Ch. 11). There is evidence, however, that the usual effects of punishment upon internalization require a minimally nurturant context. The children of extreme parental groups, who are highly rejecting or punitive toward their offspring, appear to show poor internalization in their social behavior (Bandura & Walters, 1959; Nye, 1958; Sears et al., 1957, Ch. 10; Whiting & Child, 1953, Ch. 11). Loss of affection is probably a major element in the effectiveness of any form of social punishment administered by parents to their children. This element could be negligible, if parents have been so generally cold or punitive as to adapt the child to a high level of aversive stimulation in their presence. Their specific punishments might then not produce an increment of anxiety sufficient to independently attach itself to the child's own response cues, so that it could motivate

[10] Even if the effects of the parents' nurturance were so powerful as to generalize and attach some value to their punitive presence, a gradient of generalization would yield the hardly credible prediction that, if the child transgressed and consequently felt deprived of their affection, it would then be more likely to apply their rewarding actions to itself than it would any component of their punishment.

self-criticism or other reactions to transgression even in the absence of external control. It seems even more probable that parents who are generally lacking in nurturance use unusually severe punishments. The intensity of ordinary social punishment permits its components to have some significance for attenuating anxiety and is not likely to disrupt the child's attention to this significance. Severe punishment, in contrast, may evoke competing responses, such as withdrawal or escape, which are more closely associated with anxiety reduction than is any aspect of the punishment itself.

The key role that has been assigned to self-criticism in many surveys of internalization also affords an opportunity to inferentially confirm the importance of the temporal relationships so vividly illustrated in the experimental paradigms. A number of investigators (Allinsmith, 1960; Aronfreed, 1961; MacKinnon, 1938; Sears et al., 1957, Ch. 10; Whiting & Child, 1953, Ch. 11) have found a rather limited positive association between the extent of children's internalization of responses to transgression and their parents' use of methods of punishment variously referred to as "love oriented," "psychological," or "induction" techniques. Withdrawal of affection has always been included among such techniques, and it often has been presumed to be their dominant common element. But the experimental findings reported here do not support the view that an explicit withdrawal of affection by a nurturant model induces a state of deprivation which is singularly effective in motivating a child's reproduction of the model's critical evaluative responses. The apparent discrepancy may be resolved by observing that, while loss of affection would enter into the child's experience of any form of punishment employed by its parents, their use of

withdrawal of affection as the focus of their punishment might well incorporate certain features of administration and timing which are much less characteristic of other disciplinary techniques. These features are precisely those which have been artificially removed in the experimental nurturance paradigm, where the socializing agent's critical labels acquire little or no anxiety-reducing value because they are presented immediately upon the child's awareness of transgression, before substantial anxiety can be evoked.

Parents who focus on withdrawal of affection in their discipline may be those who are also most oriented toward inducing an internal governor of conduct in their children, in contrast to other parents who are more oriented toward sensitizing their children to the punitive external consequences of transgressions with which they are visibly confronted (Aronfreed, 1961; Bronfenbrenner, 1958). Accordingly, parents who emphasize withdrawal of affection may be more disposed to punish transgressions well beyond the point of their occurrence. And they may tend to maintain the cognitive and affective salience of their children's transgressions by reinstating affection only after some time has elapsed. It is the manner in which they use withdrawal of affection, then, that would induce in their children internalized anxiety of greater and more uncertain duration than that induced by other more direct and quickly terminated punishments. This more variable and prolonged period of anxiety would sustain a greater probability that the child would reproduce components of parental criticism, or otherwise make its own anxiety-reducing responses, rather than wait upon external events. The fact that deprivation of affection does not require the physical presence of the parents (and is often effected by their absence) is also useful in understanding why it makes the child prone to produce anxiety-reducing stimuli through its own resources.[11]

Cognitive Processes in Self-Evaluation

The critical label "blue," used in the experimental socialization paradigms, was primarily a color designation in the children's previous experience. It was applied to a transgression that was not really within their volitional control and not clearly related to evaluative standards with which they were already familiar. The presence and absence of the label during training were not even respectively associated with responses which could be intrinsically identified by the children. Yet, under the appropriate temporal conditions, they adopted the blue label to refer to their own actions— a behavioral change that appears to demonstrate that the motivational prerequisites for the learning of self-criticism may be present in the most limited cognitive surroundings. The infrequent application of the red label to nonpunished actions, even among children who did use the blue label and who would surely have some cognition of the blue-red distinction, suggests further that these motivational precursors are essential to the acquisition of self-evaluative responses.

That the cognitive context of a labeling response is insufficient to fully define

its evaluative properties, without taking into account the affective conditions under which it is acquired, is also made clear by more general considerations. The discrepancies which individuals may perceive between their behavior and their standards, particularly in areas of performance or achievement, are subjected to evaluative cognition and sometimes result in subsequently rewarded modifications of behavior. But their evaluative processes would not require that they reproduce, and apply to their own behavior, a verbal component of the punishment to which they have been previously exposed. Nor do the rewarding consequences of their behavioral corrections reveal the motivation or the reinforcement for their self-critical responses. When self-criticism does occur, its reinforcement cannot be understood without reference to its aversive motivational antecedents, which are in turn dependent on the affective correlates of evaluative processes. We seem to be in the habit of regarding self-evaluation as being the instrumental verbal responses which are motivated by these affective correlates. But evaluative processes might better be conceived of as cognitive and affective phenomena which do not in themselves require verbal praise or censure.

The treatment of self-criticism as an instrumental labeling response does not circumvent the importance of understanding the complex cognitive processes upon which self-evaluation is often based. We might consider, for example, whether reproducing the verbal components of social punishment is to be regarded as a moral response—or, to put it another way, whether it is to be taken as evidence of guilt. In the normative framework of our society, the term *moral* is commonly restricted to actions which follow from some degree of judgment exercised by the actor. The evaluative dimensions of such judgment are pre-

---

[11] The survey findings are often ambiguous because highly verbal parental behaviors, such as reasoning, explanation, and appeals to the child's already established standards, are commonly grouped together with actual withdrawal of affection within the class of disciplinary techniques which seem to have some association with greater evidence of internalization in the child. The findings could therefore indicate that it is the verbal and cognitive context of punishment, rather than the specific properties of deprivation of affection as a method of punishment, that fosters the internalization of self-criticism.

sumed to be ethical in nature, in the sense that they make articulate distinctions between right and wrong or good and bad. But many of the internalized derivatives of social reinforcement, including the application of either punitive or rewarding labels to one's own actions, may require only very rudimentary and tenuous cognitive support. Many other internalized responses reflect socially derived cognitive processes which are highly developed along evaluative dimensions which are not necessarily moral. This would surely be the case with the self-evaluation that attaches to success or failure in certain kinds of performance or control.

There are formidable problems associated with any attempt to define moral cognition in a way that escapes cultural relativism. It might be possible, however, to assign invariant properties to moral evaluation by reference to particular kinds of cognitive processes. Certainly the moral properties of an evaluative response would be determined by its cognitive dimensions. In Western society at least, moral cognition appears to be characterized by reference to the consequences of an act for others, and, to a less definitive extent, by reference to the intention of the act. The labeling responses induced by the socialization paradigms reported here cannot be regarded as moral responses, since they would rest in only the most primitive

way on cognitive mediating processes. But the experimental phenomenon does demonstrate learning and motivational mechanisms which are fundamental to self-criticism, regardless of its moral status. With appropriate cognitive buffering across a sufficient variety of situations, the label "blue" could be endowed with an unmistakable moral connotation.[12]

These suggested limitations on the boundaries of morality also imply that the concept of guilt is too liberally employed when it is used to describe either the arousal of anxiety in the absence of external punishment or the presence of a self-critical labeling response that reduces the anxiety. The concept might be reserved more appropriately for an affective state with certain distinctive cognitive features. Both introspection and common usage suggest that the experience of guilt is compounded of the anxiety aroused by transgression and the evaluative perceptions which come through the filter of moral cognition. While this cognition can be normatively circumscribed for a given society and operationalized in verbal behavior, guilt must be viewed as an essentially phenomenological construct of variable substance.

[12] An excellent discussion of the place of moral cognition within the larger realm of internalized responses can be found in some of Kohlberg's (1963) recent work.

4

The Family and Social Milieu

The existence of societal variation often allows a reasonable test of the effects of particular social structures. Consider the Oedipus complex (the child's desire to possess the opposite-sexed parent), which Freud viewed as a particularly critical universal drama in parent-child relations. Upon the outcome of that drama depends the child's capacity to identify with the same-sexed parent, the child's identification, and a host of other matters. Freud held that ordinarily the same-sexed parent is opposed to the child's sexual imperialism and, gently or firmly, requires the child to abandon it. As a consequence, the child represses his desire and begins to identify with the same-sexed parent.

The extent to which the Oedipus conflict is as universal as Freud thought it has been a matter of some dispute. Freud's observations were, of course, limited to the narrow range of family life observable in Vienna at the turn of the century. But what of other family structures? Would the Oedipus complex be as evident and as intense if the family structure were more diffuse than it was for the families of Freud's experience? Is the quality of the conflict rooted in the special character of parent-child relations? Albert Rabin's paper is addressed to these questions. Examining the children of a kibbutz, a cooperative settlement where all children are raised together and rather apart from their natural parents, he compares indices of their Oedipus conflict to those observed in children reared in more traditional environments. The differences turn out to be illuminating both for psychoanalytic theory and for the impact of societal structure on personality development.

If the structures of society are important for child rearing, so also are the techniques that its agents employ within those structures. Martin Hoffman and Herbert Saltzstein examine the impact of three kinds of parental discipline on moral development: 1) assertion of power, 2) withdrawal of love, and 3) reasoning with the child. If you expect relations between parent and child to be complex, you will not be surprised that lower-class children respond to parental discipline quite differently from middle-class children and that girls and boys, regardless of class, differ in their responses and in their moral development. The results of this study shed considerable light on the dynamics of family discipline and on the acquisition of moral standards.

Some Psychosexual Differences between Kibbutz and Nonkibbutz Israeli Boys

Albert I. Rabin

INTRODUCTION

Psychoanalysis and psychoanalytic theory have served for a number of years as an unfailing source of ideas and hypotheses for investigation. Many a psychoanalytic notion has been brought into the laboratory for close scrutiny. Then, certain artificial conditions have been produced and, presumably, psychoanalytic phenomena were either confirmed or rejected. These attempts met with varying degrees of success (Sears, 1943). The conclusions of a number of these studies may also be rightfully questioned on the grounds that they employed certain methodologies which, by their very use, already deny in part the phenomena under investigation (Blum, 1949). The present study differs in two important aspects from many hitherto reported. In the first place, the conditions of the experiment are not set up or varied in the laboratory, but were found to exist in life itself and are admirably suited for the investigation of certain psycho-

Reprinted from the *Journal of Projective Techniques*, 1958, vol. 22, pp. 328–332 with the permission of the *Journal of Projective Techniques* and the author.

analytic contentions. Secondly, the method of study employed is one particularly designed for the purpose.

SOME PSYCHOANALYTIC CONCEPTS

A cardinal, but much discussed and much disputed, tenet of psychoanalytic theory, is the Oedipus complex. It is one of the most crucial stages of psychosexual development. It essentially refers to the erotic attachment of the child to the parent of the opposite sex, which eventually becomes repressed, and the solution via identification with the same sex parent is ordinarily found. There has been much questioning regarding the universality of the Oedipus complex. Even such expositors of orthodox psychoanalytic theory as Fenichel consider the form of the Oedipus complex as dependent on the type of family structure in which the child is reared (Fenichel, 1945). He states that ". . . the Oedipus complex is undoubtedly a product of family influence. If the institution of the family were to change, the problem of the Oedipus complex would necessarily change (p. 97)." Thus, the admission that intrafamilial relationships in a non-patriarchal type of family setting, much different from the one from which Freud himself emerged, may differ from the classical Oedipus situation is made by Fenichel. However, *how* different those relationships are apt to be, neither Fenichel nor other theorists of physo-analysis were ready to say. Since psycho-analysis was mainly a product of observations and reflections upon the family relationships in Western society of the late 19th and early 20th century, its concepts and, perhaps, its constructs are fairly strictly limited by them. This, despite the considerable anthropological sophistication and scholarly knowledge of different societies reflected in the works of the founder of psychoanalysis.

Considering the preceding discussion, and particularly the quotation from Fenichel, it would be of some theoretical interest to examine some psychoanalytically inferred relationships in families whose structure differs markedly from those which served as a source for early and later psychoanalytic practice and speculation. One source of such families is the Israeli Kibbutz (collective settlement) in which it was the author's good fortune to have studied some of these and related issues in considerable detail.

THE KIBBUTZ

It is not the present intention to give a detailed description of Kibbutz society, economy, infant rearing practices, etc. This was done previously by several authors (Irvine, 1952; Rabin, 1957; Spiro, 1956). We will attempt to deal only with those aspects of family relationships in the Kibbutz society which are most relevant to our inquiry.

The experiences of the Kibbutz-reared child differ from those of the child reared in the conventional family in a number of significant ways—

1. Shortly after the child arrives in the world he is placed in the "children's house" with two or three of his peers, close to his own age. He shares his daily life with them, hereafter, until late adolescence. Thus, he grows up with a group of "siblings" from the very beginning and is constantly encouraged to cooperate with them in activities and share with them in supplies.

2. Since, unlike the child in the ordinary family, the Kibbutz child does not live at "home" with his biological parents, his care and early training are placed in the hands of a parent surrogate—a nurse ("metapeleth"). The biological mother feeds the infant during the first several months of life, but the nurse is the one who feeds him later, teaches him how to eat by himself, trains him in habits of cleanliness, supervises his interaction with his peers, etc. Thus, it would seem that the biological mother is not the sole first "object"; she shares the position with the nurse.

3. After breast and/or bottle feeding ceases, contacts of the child with his biological parents are limited to daily visits of one or two hours, and longer visits on holidays. During those visits the parents are exclusively "at the child's service." They are very permissive and minimally frustrating to the child. This function is left to the nurse who is charged with most of the "socializing" functions. Thus, neither parent is a source of great frustration to the child. They are both, geographically speaking, somewhat distant for a great deal of jealousy to develop and to be directed (consciously or unconsciously) toward the parent of the opposite sex.

HYPOTHESES

Considering the different life conditions of the Kibbutz-reared child in relation to his parents and family, a number of predictions or hypotheses as to how he would compare with the child reared in the ordinary family may be made. Some of the basic differences in the family structure would dictate the following hypotheses:

1. Fewer Kibbutz-reared children will exhibit strong "Oedipal intensity" when compared with children reared in the ordinary family setting.

2. More boys, reared in the conventional family, will identify with the father figure, as compared with Kibbutz-reared boys whose identification objects will be more diffuse.

3. There will be evidence of greater frequency of sibling rivalry in the control group than in the experimental group of boys (Kibbutz-reared).

SAMPLES

The experimental group consists of 27 Kibbutz-reared boys. They represent a random selection of fourth grade children from five different villages. The control group of 27 fourth graders was similarly obtained from four non-Kibbutz Israeli agricultural villages. These children were reared in the traditional patriarchal family setting. The structure of these families differs little from usual agricultural families in Western society.

The age means for each group were 10 years and two months. The age range: from 9–3 to 11–3. There were no significant differences between the ages of the two groups.

PROCEDURE

All 54 children were examined individually by means of the Blacky Test (Blum, 1950), a projective technique especially devised for assessing psychosexual development, within the psychoanalytic framework. The test consists of a series of cartoons depicting a family of dogs—papa, mama, Blacky the son, and a brother named Tippy. The subjects told stories about each cartoon which were followed up by a more structured inquiry.

Since not all cartoons, and the responses which they evoked, are relevant to our hypotheses, only the ones which have a direct bearing on the present investigation will be dealt with at some length.

Cartoon IV (Oedipal intensity) portrays papa and mama making love to each other, whereas Blacky stands on the side watching them.

Cartoon VII (positive identification) shows Blacky in a threatening attitude toward a much smaller toy dog.

Cartoon VIII (sibling rivalry) represents papa and mama showering their affection upon Tippy who is standing between them while Blacky is watching.

The inquiry questions for these cartoons follows the form suggested for children (Appendix B), of the Manual of Instructions (2) devised for the Blacky.

The questions about Cartoon IV are as follows:

1. How does Blacky feel about seeing Mama and Papa make love?
3. What will Papa do if he sees Blacky peeking?
4. What will Mama do if she sees Blacky peeking?
5. Which would be better—Mama here and Blacky with Papa . . . or Papa here and Blacky with Mama?

The following are the questions to Cartoon VII:

1. Who talks like that to Blacky—Mama or Papa or Tippy?
2. Whom is Blacky most likely to obey—Mama or Papa or Tippy?
3. Whom is Blacky acting like here—Mama or Papa, etc.?
4. Which one would Blacky rather be like—Mama or etc.?

Finally, Cartoon VIII questions are:

1. What does Blacky feel like doing now?
2. Does Blacky think Tippy deserves the praise?
5. If Blacky is angry, whom is he most angry at—Mama, or Papa or Tippy?

It may be noted that questions 2 to Cartoon IV, 5 to Cartoon VII, and 3 and 4 to Cartoon VIII were omitted. They refer to frequency of occurrence ("how often"), or other issues which are practically impossible to classify and treat statistically.

Specific predictions concerning responses to each of the questions were made, consistent with the more general

Papa and Mama make love (express anger, aggression, etc.), will expect greater punitiveness from the parents for "peeking" and would think that Blacky would prefer to be with mother rather than father. In responding to questions on Cartoon VII (positive identification), more controls would expect that Papa "talks that way," would most likely to be obeyed or would likely be the model

Table 1
Responses to Questions concerning Cartoon IV (Oedipal Intensity) by the Experimental (E) and Control (C) Groups

Questions Groups	1			3		4			5	
	E	C		E	C	E	C		E	C
Fear-Jealousy	10	11	Rejection	19	19	14	15	With Mama	10	17
No concern-positive	17	16	Acceptance	8	8	13	12	Papa or other	17	10
Chi square	N.S.			N.S.		N.S.			3.64	
p (one-tailed test)									< .03	

Table 2
Responses to Cartoon VII (Positive Identification)

Questions Groups	1		2		3		4	
	E	C	E	C	E	C	E	C
Papa	17	19	15	21	18	15	15	22
Mama and Tippy	10	8	12	6	9	12	12	5
Chi square	N.S.		3.00		N.S.		4.21	
p (one-tailed test)			< .045				< .02	

Table 3
Responses to Cartoon VIII (Sibling Rivalry)

Questions Groups	1			2			5	
	E	C		E	C		E	C
Aggression-attack	4	10	Yes	4	6	Parent	14	8
Passive-positive	23	17	No	23	21	Tippy	13	19
Chi square	3.48			N.S.			2.76	
p (one-tailed test)	< .035						< .05	

hypotheses stated above. With respect to "Oedipal intensity" (Cartoon IV), it was predicted that more control children will say that Blacky is disturbed by seeing

for identification. As to Cartoon VIII (sibling rivalry), more controls would be expected to say that Blacky will react aggressively, will think that Tippy does not deserve the praise, and that Blacky will be angry at Tippy rather than at his parents.

RESULTS

The responses to questions on Cartoon IV are classified and summarized in Table 1. About 60 percent in each group show no special concern about the scene depicted in the cartoon. Both groups are about equal with respect to the incidence of these responses. Similarly, no differences were obtained on items 3 and 4. However, on the last item, more control subjects think it best for Blacky to be "with Mama" whereas the experimental group divides its affiliation more equally between both parents. These results are significant statistically and are consonant with the first hypothesis stated above.

In Table 2 the frequencies of categorized responses to questions relating to Cartoon VII (positive identification) are presented. Statistically significant differences in the predicted direction were obtained for two of the four items. More control subjects say that Blacky is most likely to obey the father rather than mother or Tippy, and more of them believe that Blacky would rather be like father than mother or Tippy. Again, the frequency of subjects in each group responding to two of these four items clearly support the second hypothesis which predicted clearer like-sex identification for the control group as compared with the experimental one.

Responses to three of the questions related to sibling rivalry (Cartoon VIII) were most readily classifiable, and their incidence in the two groups appears in Table 3. The answers to the first question (What does Blacky feel like doing now?) indicate statistically significant differences between the groups. A larger number of controls, as compared with experimental

subjects, attribute aggressive and hostile behavior to Blacky, whereas fewer controls see positive, constructive or non-aggressive behavior. This finding would tend to support the prediction of greater frequency or sibling rivalry in the control group. No differences are noted on question 2, but question 5 again yields responses in the predicted direction. The vast majority of the controls believe that Blacky's anger is directed most at Tippy (the sibling) rather than at the parents. The experimental group is about equally divided, with respect to the attributed anger, between the parents and Tippy. Here, too, two of the three items considered produce findings in support of the third hypothesis stated above.

In all calculations of the levels of significance, from the Chi square values obtained, one-tailed tests were used. The restrictions for small samples suggested by Edwards (1948) were followed. Values of p were mainly obtained from Wilcoxon (1949).

DISCUSSION

The results which we have presented show that whatever statistically significant differences were obtained were in the predicted direction. To be sure, not all of the items considered showed such differences. With none of the items did we obtain significant differences in the direction opposite to our predictions. Moreover, it is quite possible that some individual items are more powerful tests of the several general hypotheses than are some of the others.

The first question on Cartoon IV does not yield any significant differences between the groups, although it is probably one of the two most direct questions dealing with Oedipal intensity. However, question 5, which is the second one of such a direct nature, reveals important differences between the groups. The remaining two questions are of lesser importance since they are more indirect. It is fair to say that the first hypothesis is at least confirmed in part—more controls, when forced to make a choice, select mother and reject father.

Again, in response to questions on Cartoon VII, the crucial question (that of identification), question 4, is consonant with our predictions. Although the remaining three items are more indirectly related to the issue of identification, one of them also shows differences in the hypothesized direction.

Finally, although both groups feel that Blacky thinks that Tippy does not "deserve the praise" (item 2), when it comes to actual expression of hostility and aggression (items 1 and 5), the control group more frequently clearly attributes such reactions to Blacky. This reaction is consistent with the notion of greater sibling rivalry (hypothesis 3), which is probably due to greater attachment to the parents and less experience in an "original" sibship situation in the

controls as compared with the experimental Kibbutz-reared group.

It appears that the hypotheses, which stem from a psychoanalytic theoretical framework, are to some degree supported by our findings. The results indicate that the type of family structure has considerable influence on the nature of the identification process, relationship to parents and attitude to siblings.

SUMMARY

A group of 27 ten-year-old boys from patriarchal-type families were compared with a group of 27 boys who were reared in the Kibbutz (collective settlement) with respect to three psychosexual dimensions: Oedipal intensity, positive identification, and sibling rivalry. The structured response items of the Blacky Test inquiry were used as a basis for comparison. Consistent with the stated hypotheses, the experimental group gave evidence of lesser Oedipal intensity, more diffuse positive identification, and less intense sibling rivalry.

Parent Discipline and the Child's Moral Development[1]

Martin L. Hoffman and Herbert D. Saltzstein

Recent years have seen the accumulation of a body of findings relating moral de-

Reprinted from the *Journal of Personality and Social Psychology*, 1967, vol. 5, pp. 45–57 with the permission of the American Psychological Association and the authors.

[1] This study was supported by Public Health Service Research Grant M-02333 from the National Institute of Mental Health. It was carried

velopment, especially internalization of moral values and the capacity for guilt, to parental practices. In a recent review of this research (Hoffman, 1963a) the following propositions received support:

out while both authors were at the Merrill-Palmer Institute.

The authors wish to thank Lois W. Hoffman for her many helpful comments and suggestions.

(a) A moral orientation based on the fear of external detection and punishment is associated with the relatively frequent use of discipline techniques involving physical punishment and mental deprivation, here called power assertive discipline; (b) a moral orientation characterized by independence of external sanctions and high guilt is associated with relatively frequent use of nonpower assertive discipline—sometimes called psychological, indirect, or love-oriented discipline.

Several explanations of these findings have been advanced, each focusing on a different aspect of the parent's discipline. Thus, Allinsmith and Greening (1955) suggest that the significant variable may be the difference in the model presented by the parent during the disciplinary encounter (i.e., parent openly expresses anger versus parent controls anger). The importance of this factor may lie in the model it provides the child for channeling his own aggression. Where the parent himself expresses his anger openly, he thereby encourages the child to express his anger openly; where the parent controls his anger, he discourages the child from openly expressing anger and therefore may promote a turning of the anger inward which according to psychoanalytic theory is the process by which the guilt capacity is developed.

Another explanation of the difference between power assertive and nonpower assertive techniques is in terms of the duration of the punishment; that is, whereas nonpower assertive discipline may last a long time, the application of force usually dissipates the parent's anger and thus may relieve the child of his anxiety or guilt rather quickly. A third possibility, suggested by Sears, Maccoby, and Levin (1957), is that punishing the child by withholding love, which is frequently involved in nonpower assertive discipline, has the effect of intensifying the child's efforts to identify with the parent in order to assure himself of the parent's love.

A still different formulation has recently been suggested by Hill (1960). According to this view, the crucial underlying factor is the timing of the punishment. Love-withdrawal punishment is believed more often to terminate when the child engages in a corrective act (e.g., confession, reparation, overt admission of guilt, etc.), whereas physical punishment is more likely to occur and terminate at the time of the deviant act and prior to any corrective act.

Finally, the important variable may be the information often communicated by nonpower assertive techniques regarding the implications of the child's deviant behavior. For example, Aronfreed's (1961) view is that such information can provide the cognitive and behavioral resources necessary for the child to examine his actions independently and accept responsibility for them.

Though varied, all but the last of these explanations assume the key ingredient for nonpower assertive discipline to be its punitive—more specifically, its love-withdrawing—quality. This hypothesis stems from psychoanalytic and learning theories that emphasize anxiety over loss of love as the necessary motivational basis for moral development.

In examining instances of nonpower assertive discipline it became apparent that the amount of love withdrawal, real or threatened, varied considerably. In some cases, the love-withdrawal aspect of the discipline seemed to predominate. In others it seemed totally absent, and in still others it seemed to be a minor part of a technique primarily focused on the harmful consequences of the child's behavior for others. This suggested that the effectiveness of these techniques might lie in their empathy-arousing capacity rather than, or in addition to, their love-with-drawing property. In the present study we accordingly made the distinction between two kinds of nonpower assertive discipline. One, called *induction*, refers to techniques in which the parent points out the painful consequences of the child's act for the parent or for others. In the second, called *love withdrawal*, the parent simply gives direct but nonphysical expression to his anger or disapproval of the child for engaging in the behavior. In a sense by these latter techniques the parent points out the painful psychological consequences of the act for the child himself, that is, the withdrawal of love by the parent.

It is probable, of course, that the child experiences both these types of nonpower assertive techniques as involving a loss of love. However, as indicated above, the love-withdrawing component of the induction techniques is more subdued, and in addition they provide him with the knowledge that his actions have caused pain to others. By doing this the technique capitalizes on the child's capacity for empathy. In our view (see Hoffman, 1963b; Hoffman, in press; Hoffman & Saltzstein, 1960) it is this capacity for empathy which provides a powerful emotional and cognitive support for development of moral controls and which has been overlooked in other psychological theories of moral development. For this reason it was expected that *induction, and not love withdrawal, would relate most strongly to the various indexes of moral development.*

Affection has often been supposed to be a necessary condition for moral development. Measures of the parent's affection were therefore included for completeness. We expected, following the pattern of the previous research, that power assertion would relate negatively, and affection positively, to the moral indexes.

METHOD

Sample

The children studied were all seventh graders in the Detroit metropolitan area. The test battery was administered to groups of children in the schools during three sessions spaced about a week apart. Sometimes an individual class was tested in the homeroom, and sometimes several groups were tested together in the gymnasium or auditorium.

Data bearing on the various dimensions of moral development were obtained from over 800 children broadly representative of the population in the area. Because of the apprehension of some of the school officials, however, we were unable to obtain reports of parental discipline from about a fourth of these children, the loss being greater among the lower-class sample. In addition, children identified as behavior problems and those from nonintact families were screened from the sample. Further shrinkage due to absences, incomplete background information, and unintelligible or incomplete responses resulted in a final sample of 444 children. Included were 146 middle-class boys, 124 middle-class girls, 91 lower-class boys, and 83 lower-class girls.

Subsequently, interviews were conducted with a subsample consisting of 129 middle-class mothers (66 boys and 63 girls) and 75 middle-class fathers (37 boys and 38 girls). No interviews were conducted with parents of the children from the lower class.

Child Morality Indexes

Several different moral indexes were used—each tapping a different aspect of conscience.[2] The two major indexes per-

[2] These dimensions were used because they clearly bear on morality and because they represent different levels (affective, cognitive, overt) and directions for behavior (proscriptions, pre-

tain to the degree to which the child's moral orientation is internalized. These are (*a*) the intensity of guilt experienced following his own transgressions, and (*b*) the use of moral judgments about others which are based on internal rather than external considerations. The other indexes pertain to whether the child confesses and accepts responsibility for his misdeeds and the extent to which he shows consideration for others. Identification, though not a direct moral index, was also included because of its relationship to moral development, as hypothesized by psychoanalytic theory and by recent researchers (e.g., Sears *et al.*, 1957).

Guilt. Two semiprojective story-completion items were used to assess the intensity of the child's guilt reaction to transgression. The technique presents the child with a story beginning which focuses on a basically sympathetic child of the same sex and age who has committed a transgression. The subject's instructions are to complete the story and tell what the protagonist thinks and feels and "what happens afterwards." The assumption made is that the child identifies with the protagonist and therefore reveals his own internal reactions (although not necessarily his overt reactions) through his completion of the story.

The first story used here was concerned with a child who through negligence contributed to the death of a younger child. The story beginning was constructed so as to provide several other characters on whom to transfer blame. The second story was about a child who cheats in a swimming race and wins. In both stories detection was made to appear unlikely. In rating the intensity of the guilt from the subject's completion of the story, care was taken to assess first that the subject identified with the central character. If such identification was dubious, the story was not coded for guilt, nor were stories involving only external detection or concern with detection coded for guilt. All other stories were coded for guilt. For a story to receive a guilt score higher than zero there had to be evidence of a conscious self-initiated and self-critical reaction. Given evidence for such a reaction, the intensity of guilt was rated on a scale ranging from 1 to 6. At the extreme high end of the scale were stories involving personality change in the hero, suicide, etc. In coding the stories the attempt was made to ignore differences in sheer style of writing and to infer the feeling of the subject as he completed the story.

A departure from the usual practice was to assign two guilt scores to each story—one for the maximum guilt experienced by the hero, usually occurring early in the story, and the other for terminal guilt. In relating discipline to this and other facets of morality extreme groups were chosen. In choosing the high- and low-guilt groups, attention was paid to both scores. That is, the high-guilt group included those who sustained a high level of guilt throughout the stories. The low-guilt group included children who manifested little or no guilt throughout the stories. Children who initially manifested intense guilt which was dissipated through confession, reparation, defenses, etc., were not included in the guilt analysis.

Internalized moral judgments. The moral judgment items consisted of several hypothetical transgressions which the children were asked to judge. These situations

---

scriptions). Each dimension has its advantages and disadvantages, and since a strong case for including one and not the others could not be made we included them all. In doing this our intention was not to treat them as indexes of a single underlying "moral development." Doing this would seem premature, since, although the different aspects of morality presumably increase with age (empirical data on age progression are available only for moral judgments), they very likely begin to develop—and reach full development—at different ages and progress at different rates.

were of the general type used by Piaget, including moral judgments about persons committing various crimes, for example, stealing; choosing which of two crimes was worse, for example, one involving simple theft and the other a breach of trust; and judgments of crimes with extenuating circumstances, for example, a man who steals in order to procure a drug which he cannot afford and which is needed to save his wife's life.[3] In each case the child's response was coded as external (e.g., "you can get put in jail for that"), internal (e.g., "that's not right, the man trusted you"), or indeterminate. The individual internal scores were then summed for all items, and the sum constituted the child's internalization score on moral judgments.

Overt reactions to transgression. Two measures were used to assess the child's overt reactions to transgression. The first was the teacher's report of how the child typically reacts when "caught doing something wrong." The categories included: "denies he did it"; "looks for someone else to blame"; "makes excuses"; "cries, looks sad, seems to feel bad"; "accepts responsibility for what he has done"; and "where possible tries on own initiative to rectify situation."

The second measure was a questionnaire item asked of the child's mother, similar to the item used by Sears *et al.* (1957). The question was: "when . . . . has done something that (he) (she) knows you would not approve of, and you haven't found out about it yet, how often does (he) (she) come and tell you about it without your asking?" The mother was asked to check one of five alternatives, the extremes of which were "all the time" and "never."

Neither of these measures is ideal. The first has the disadvantage of asking for the child's reaction in the presence of an

authority figure after detection. The second has the defect of being based on a report by the parent, who is the same person providing much of the discipline data and who is more likely to be influenced by "social desirability" than the teacher. Yet, the parent may well be the only person with enough background information and close contact with the child to make a knowledgeable estimate of how he acts before detection.

Consideration for other children. This measure was obtained from sociometric ratings by the children in the same classroom. Each child made three nominations for the child first, second, and third most "likely to care about the other children's feelings" and "to defend a child being made fun of by the group." The usual weights were used and the two scores summed.

Identification. Our major measure of identification was based on the child's responses to several items bearing on his orientation toward the parent: (*a*) admiration: "Which person do you admire or look up to the most?"; (*b*) desire to emulate: "Which person do you want to be like when you grow up?"; (*c*) perceived similarity: "Which person do you take after mostly?" Responses which mention the parent were coded as parent-identification responses and summed to obtain an overall identification score. It should be noted that this measure is designed to assess the child's conscious identification with the parents and not necessarily the unconscious identification of which Freud wrote.

Coding procedure. The story completion and moral judgment coding were done by one of the authors (HDS). To avoid contamination, the procedure was to go through all 444 records and code one item at a time. Especially difficult responses were coded independently by both authors, and discrepancies were resolved in conference.

---

[3] This item was an adaptation of one used by Kohlberg (1963).

Before the final coding was begun, coding reliabilities of 82% for maximum guilt, 73% for terminal guilt, and 91% for internal moral judgment were attained by the authors. These figures represent the percentage of agreement in giving high (top quartile), low (bottom quartile), and middle ratings. There were no extreme disagreements, that is, no instances in which a child received a high rating by one judge and a low rating by the other.

Measures of Parent Practices

Two reports of each parent's typical disciplinary practices were available—one from the children who reported the disciplinary practices of both parents, another from the mothers and fathers who each reported their own typical disciplinary practices. The reports from the children were collected during the third testing session in the schools. The parents were interviewed separately by trained female interviewers. The interview typically lasted about an hour.

Assessment of parental discipline was made in the following way. Each respondent (the child or parent) was asked to imagine four concrete situations: one in which the child delayed complying with a parental request to do something, a second in which the child was careless and destroyed something of value, a third in which he talked back to the parent, a fourth situation in which he had not done well in school. Following each situation was a list of from 10 to 14 practices. The respondent was asked to look over the list, then rate the absolute frequency of each and finally to indicate the first, second, and third practice most frequently used.[4] These three choices were weighted, and the scores summed across the four situations. The practices listed

[4] Ratings of the absolute frequency were included primarily to make sure the respondent thought about all the items in the list before ranking them.

represented our three main categories. The first category, *power assertion*, included physical punishment, deprivation of material objects or privileges, the direct application of force, or threat of any of these. The term "power assertion" is used to highlight the fact that in using these techniques the parent seeks to control the child by capitalizing on his physical power or control over material resources (Hoffman, 1960). The second category, *love withdrawal*, included techniques whereby the parent more or less openly withdraws love by ignoring the child, turning his back on the child, refusing to speak to him, explicitly stating that he dislikes the child, or isolating him. The third category, *induction regarding parents*, includes appeals to the child's guilt potential by referring to the consequences of the child's action for the parent. Included are such specifics as telling the child that his action has hurt the parent, that an object he damaged was valued by the parent, that the parent is disappointed, etc.

These lists were administered to each parent twice, once with instructions to select the techniques which he used at present, and next to select those he remembers using when the child was about 5 years old. Reports of past discipline were not asked of the children because it was unlikely that they could remember parent practices used several years before.

The above measure of induction is a limited one in that it only included instances where the parent made references to the consequences of a transgression for the parent himself. To supplement this, an additional measure of induction was constructed. This dealt with the parent's reaction to two situations in which the child's transgression had harmful consequences for another child. In the first situation the child, aged 5, aggresses against another child and destroys something the other child has built, causing the other child to cry. In the second situation the parent sees his child aged 6–10 making fun of another child. The parent was asked what he would have done or said in such a situation, and his reaction was coded along a 3-point scale for the degree to which he (the parent) makes reference to and shows concern for the *other* child's feelings. The scores were summed to arrive at a measure of the parent's use of *induction regarding peers*.

Assessment of the parent's affection for the child was also obtained from the child and from the parent. The child was given a list of 19 behaviors indicating affection, approval, criticism, advice giving, and participation in child-centered activities and asked to indicate along a 4-point scale how often the parent engaged in such behaviors. The affection score was a simple weighted sum for the affection and approval items.

A slightly different measure was used to obtain affection data from the parents. They were given a list of eight behaviors indicating affection, approval, qualified approval, and material reward and asked to indicate along a 4-point scale how often they engaged in such behaviors when the child "did something good." The affection score was a weighted sum for the affection items.

Background information. The family's social class was determined from the child's responses to questions about the father's occupation and education. The distinction was basically between white collar and blue collar. In a few cases, families initially classified as middle class were later recategorized as lower class as a result of more accurate and specific information from the parent about the father's actual occupation and education.

Data analysis. The data were analyzed separately for middle-class boys, middle-class girls, lower-class boys, and lower-class girls. The procedure for each of these subsamples was to form two groups—one

scoring high and one scoring low on each moral development index—and then to compare these groups on the child-rearing-practice scores obtained in the child reports and (in the case of the middle class only) the parent interviews. In forming the comparison groups, the cutoff points were made as close as possible to the upper and lower quartile points within each subsample.

The test of significance used throughout was the median test.

Control on IQ. An important feature of this study, which was not true in the previous moral development research, was the control on intellectual ability which was instituted. Scores on either the California Test of Mental Maturity or the Iowa Tests of Basic Skills were found—with social class controlled—to relate positively to internalized moral judgments and consideration for others, negatively to confession, and negatively to parent identification. This suggested that some of the findings previously reported in the literature might be the artifactual results of a lack of IQ control. In forming the high and low quartile groups for these variables we therefore controlled IQ—to the point of making the high-low differences in IQ negligible. Since IQ did not relate to guilt, there was no need to control IQ in the guilt analysis.

RESULTS AND DISCUSSION

To facilitate presentation of the results, the significant findings relating moral development indexes and parental discipline are summarized in Tables 1 and 2 for the middle-class sample and Tables 4 and 5 for the lower-class sample.[5]

[5] Seven pages of tables giving medians for each of the high and low quartile groups have been deposited with the American Documentation Institute. Order Document No. 9079 from the ADI Auxiliary Publications Project, Library of Congress, Washington, D. C. 20540. Remit in advance $1.25 for microfilm or $1.35 for photocopies and make checks payable to: Chief, Photoduplication Service, Library of Congress.

Table 1
Statistically Significant Relations between Child's Morality Indexes and Mother's Discipline Techniques: Middle Class

Morality index	Power assertion			Love withdrawal			Induction re parent			Induction re peers[a]		
	Boys	Girls	Sum	Boys	Girls	Sum	Boys	Girls	Sum	Boys	Girls	Sum
Guilt (child's response)		−p*	−c* −n* −p*				+c*	+p*	+c* +n* +p*	+p*		+p**
Internal moral judgment (child's response)		−n*	−c*		−c*	−c*			+c*			
Confession (mother's report)	−p**		−p**				+n*		+c*			
Accepts responsibility (teacher's report)	−c*	−c* −n*	−c** −n**		+n*		+c* +n* +p*		+c**			
Consideration for other children (peers' ratings)	+n*	−p*		−p*				+n* +p*	+c*		+p**	+p**
Identification (child's response)	−c*	−c*	−c**		−n*		+p*	+c*	+c*			

Note.—The data sources of the significant findings summarized in Tables 1, 2, and 4–6 are indicated as follows: c (child report), n (parent report of current practices), p (parent report of past practices).
[a] Data on induction regarding peers are incomplete since these data were obtained only from the parent reports of past practices.
* $p < .05$.
** $p < .01$.

Table 2
Statistically Significant Relations between Child's Morality Indexes and Father's Discipline Techniques: Middle Class

Morality index	Power assertion			Love withdrawal			Induction re parent			Induction re peers		
	Boys	Girls	Sum	Boys	Girls	Sum	Boys	Girls	Sum	Boys	Girls	Sum
Guilt (child's response)												
Internal moral judgment (child's response)		−c*						+c*				
Confession (mother's report)	+p*		+p*	+c*			−p*		−p*			
Accepts responsibility (teacher's report)	−c**		−c*			+c*						
Consideration for other children (peers' ratings)	+n*		+p*		−c*			+c**	+c**			
Identification (child's response)												

* $p < .05$.
** $p < .01$.

Included in each table are relationships between each of the six indexes of moral development and each of the four measures of parental discipline: power assertion, love withdrawal, induction regarding parents, and induction regarding peers. Tables 1 and 2 are based on present discipline as reported by the child and present and past discipline as reported by the parent. Since the parent's report was not available for the lower-class sample, Tables 4 and 5 are based solely on the child's report of present parental discipline.

Middle-class discipline. The overall pattern of the findings in the middle class provides considerable support for our expectations, at least with respect to the mother's practices. Thus the frequent use of power assertion by the mother is consistently associated with weak moral development. The use of induction, on the other hand, is consistently associated with advanced moral development. This is true for both induction regarding parents and induction regarding peers. In all, there are a large number of significant findings especially for the major moral indexes—guilt and internalized moral judgments.

In contrast to the mothers, few significant findings were obtained for fathers —for boys as well as girls—and those that were obtained did not fit any apparent pattern.

A further step in the analysis of induction was to combine all indexes of this category into a composite index. The results, presented in Table 3, were quite striking in the case of mothers for all the moral indexes. Significant findings, all in the expected direction, were obtained for boys on guilt, internal moral judgments, confession, and acceptance of responsibility; and for girls on guilt, internal moral judgments, and consideration for others. When both sexes are combined, the findings are significant for all the

Table 3
Statistically Significant Relations between Child's Morality Indexes and Parent's Composite Induction Score: Middle Class

Morality index	Mother's induction			Father's induction		
	Boys	Girls	Sum	Boys	Girls	Sum
Guilt (child's response)	+*	+*	+*			
Internal moral judgment (child's response)	+*	+*	+**			
Confession (mother's report)	+**			+***		
Accepts responsibility (teacher's report)	+*			+*		
Consideration for other children (peers' ratings)		+**	+*		··	
Identification (child's response)	+*					

   * $p < .05$.
  ** $p < .01$.
 *** $p < .005$.

moral indexes. The findings on identification are significant only for boys, however.

In contrast to induction, love with-drawal relates infrequently to the moral indexes (see Table 1). Further, in most cases in which significant relations between love withdrawal and moral development do occur, they prove to be negative. Taken as a whole, the importance of the distinction between love withdrawal and induction has been clearly demonstrated by these findings.

In sum it is a pattern of infrequent use of power assertion and frequent use of induction by middle-class mothers which generally appears to facilitate the facets of morality included in this study.[6]

There is, however, one major exception to this pattern. The peers' reports of the boy's consideration for other children is positively related to the mother's report of their present use of power assertion (Table 1). A possible explanation of this finding is that our measure of consideration is a poor one especially for the boys. In particular, there is no built-in provision to assure that the behavior is based on internal motivation. The motive behind such behavior in the case of boys might instead often be a need for approval by peers. Why this should be the case for boys and not for girls remains unclear. It should be noted, however, that consideration is a more deviant value for boys than girls. Evidence for this is provided from a measure of values administered to the children. The largest

[6] The question might be raised here as to the extent to which these findings should be interpreted as independent. Do induction and power assertion exert independent influence on morality, or are they but two aspects of the same influence; for example, do the measures used require that someone high on induction is necessarily low on power assertion? The findings in Table 1 suggest the influences are largely independent. That is, there are only a few instances in which negative power assertion findings and positive induction findings for the same subsample were obtained with the same measure. In most cases the findings for the two types of discipline were obtained with different measures, and in some instances a finding was obtained for one but not the other (e.g., guilt in boys relates to induction, but not to power assertion).

sex difference found was on the consideration item ("goes out of his way to help others"). The girls valued this trait more than the boys ($p < .001$). Thus consideration does appear to have a different meaning for the two sexes.

Lower-class discipline. In discussing the lower-class findings the lack of parent between the child's moral development and his report of parental discipline. This is especially striking in the case of the mother's discipline. Furthermore, of those significant relationships that emerge, two are inconsistent with our expectations. First, as with the middle-class sample, the boy's consideration is related positively to

Table 4
Statistically Significant Relations between Child's Morality Indexes and Mother's Discipline: Lower Class

Morality index	Power assertion			Love withdrawal			Induction re parent		
	Boys	Girls	Sum	Boys	Girls	Sum	Boys	Girls	Sum
Guilt (child's response)				+c*					
Internal moral judgment (child's response)							+c*		
Accepts responsibility (teacher's report)									
Consideration for other children (peers' ratings)	+c*						+c*		
Identification (child's response)				−c*	−c*				

Note.—Interview data were not obtained from the lower-class parents. Thus all entries in Tables 3 and 4 are based on child reports. For the same reason lower-class data on confession and on induction regarding peers were unavailable.
* $p < .05$.

Table 5
Statistically Significant Relations between Child's Morality Indexes and Father's Discipline: Lower Class

Morality index	Power assertion			Love withdrawal			Induction re parent		
	Boys	Girls	Sum	Boys	Girls	Sum	Boys	Girls	Sum
Guilt (child's response)	−c*			+c*					
Internal moral judgment (child's response)									
Accepts responsibility (teacher's report)									
Consideration for other children (peers' ratings)									
Identification (child's response)	−c*			−c*				+c*	+c*

* $p < .05$.

interview data must be kept in mind. Nevertheless, there are several very apparent contrasts with the middle-class sample. Foremost among these is the general paucity of significant relationships the mother's use of power assertion. Second, in contrast with the findings for the middle-class boys, guilt is positively associated with the mother's use of love withdrawal, but unrelated to the mother's use of power assertion or induction. In summary, our expectations were not confirmed for the lower-class sample, and no general conclusion may be drawn.

The infrequent relationships between the child's moral development and the mother's discipline, compared to the middle-class sample, suggest that the lower-class mother's discipline may be less crucial and singular a variable. This in turn may be due to several factors. First, the mothers more often work full time in the lower than in the middle class. Second, the combination of large families and less space may result in the parent and child interacting with many other people besides each other. Third, according to the more traditional family structure usually found in the lower class (e.g., Bronfenbrenner, 1958), the father is more often the ultimate disciplining agent. In our sample, for example, boys more often reported that their mothers had the fathers do the disciplining ("says she'll tell your father") in the lower class than in the middle class ($p < .01$). Fourth, lower-class children are encouraged to spend more time outside the home than middle-class children. For all these reasons the socializing process may be more diffuse in the lower class; that is, it may be more equally shared by the mother with the father, with siblings, members of the extended family, the child's peers, and others.[7]

Further research comparing the two

classes needs to be performed. One might conjecture that because of the more diffuse socialization process in the lower class the basis of internalization may be quite different for children in the two classes, with consequent differences in the kind of morality that develops.

Affection. The relations between affection and the six moral indexes are presented in Table 6. The most notable features of this table are first, as expected, the relationships are positive; second, most of the findings, as with the discipline data, were obtained for middle-class mothers. It should also be noted that most of the findings are based on the child's report.

Role of the father. Several studies of delinquency (e.g., Glueck & Glueck, 1950; McCord & McCord, 1958; Miller, 1958) suggest that the father is important in the development of internal controls. Our findings, especially in the middle class, seem to suggest that this is not so. Relatively few significant relationships were obtained between paternal discipline and the child's morality, and several were in a direction opposite to that expected.

Of course, it is possible that the role of the father is more important than indicated in this study. For example, the father might provide the cognitive content of the standards by direct instruction rather than by his discipline techniques. Lacking data on direct instruction, we could not test this possibility. Another possibility is that the role of the father is a less direct one. That is, he may affect the moral development of the child by his relationship to the mother and his influence on the discipline techniques chosen by the mother. This is indicated in a study of preschool children where evidence was found suggesting that women who are treated power assertively by their husbands tend to react by using power assertive discipline on their chil-

[7] Another possible explanation for the paucity of findings in the lower class is that the lower-class children are very low on morality. Thus if the upper quartile of the lower class on morality were like the lower quartile of the middle class, there would be no reason to expect similar associations for the two classes. This possibility can be discounted since there was no overlap between the lower-class upper quartile and the middle-class lower quartile. And although there was a general tendency for the lower class to be lower on morality than the middle class, the difference was significant only for internal moral judgment and consideration for others, and only for girls.

dren (Hoffman, 1963c). It may also be that the father's role is ordinarily latent in its effects and only becomes manifest under exceptional circumstances such as those often associated with delinquency. That is, under normal conditions with the father away working most of the time and the mother handling most of the disciplining, as in our middle-class sample, the father's importance may lie mainly in providing an adequate role model that operates in the background as a necessary supporting factor. Under these conditions, the specific lines along which the child's moral development proceeds may be determined primarily by the mother's discipline. An adequate role model is lacking, however, in extreme cases as when there is no father, when the father is a criminal, or when the father is at home but unemployed, and this may account for the findings obtained in the delinquency research.

Methodological issues. Any study of child rearing and moral development that relies on indexes of discipline and morality from the same source is open to the criticism that the relationships that emerge are due to the lack of independence of the sources. If that source is the child himself, the suspicion might be held that the child's report of parental discipline is simply another projective measure of the child's personality. It should be noted that in the present study the relationships between the child's morality and the parent's report of discipline were generally in the same direction as those involving the child's report of discipline. (We refer here to the middle-class-mother findings.) In addition, over half the significant findings for each sex involve relations between measures obtained from different respondents.

Further support for our findings comes from a recent review in which our threefold discipline classification was applied to the previous research (Hoffman, in press). Since most studies used a power assertive-nonpower assertive dichotomy, as indicated earlier, the raw data were examined (and recoded where necessary) to determine whether love withdrawal, induction, or some other form of nonpower assertion was responsible for the findings. The results were clearly consistent with ours. Since a wide range of theoretical and methodological approaches were involved in the studies reviewed, our confidence in the findings reported here is considerably strengthened.

A common problem also relevant to the present design is that no definitive conclusion may be drawn about causal

Table 6
Statistically Significant Relations between Child's Morality Indexes and Parent's Affection

Morality index	Middle class						Lower class					
	Mothers			Fathers			Mothers			Fathers		
	Boys	Girls	Sum	Boys	Girls	Sum	Boys	Girls	Sum	Boys	Girls	Sum
Guilt (child's response)	+c*		+c*									
Internal moral judgment (child's response)		+c*	+n*			+n*						
Confession (mother's report)	+c*		+c*			+p*						
Accepts responsibility (teacher's report)		+n*		+n*								
Consideration for other children (peers' ratings)	+p*	+c**	+c* +n*				+c*				+c*	
Identification (child's response)	+c**	+c**	+c**				+c*					

* $p < .05$.
** $p < .01$.

direction of the relationships obtained. Any solution to this will have to wait upon application of the experimental method or longitudinal studies. Nevertheless, some support for the proposition that discipline affects moral development, rather than the reverse, may be derived from the fact that several findings bear on the use of discipline in the past. If these reports are assumed to be reasonably valid, to argue that the child's moral development elicits different discipline patterns (rather than the reverse) necessitates the further assumption that the child's morality has not changed basically from early childhood. This is an unlikely assumption in view of common observations (e.g., about the child's changing acceptance of responsibility for transgression) and the findings about the developmental course of moral judgments obtained by Piaget (1948), Kohlberg (1963), and others.

Theoretical discussion. In this section we will analyze the disciplinary encounter into what we believe to be some of its most basic cognitive and emotional factors.

First, any disciplinary encounter generates a certain amount of anger in the child by preventing him from completing or repeating a motivated act. Power assertion is probably most likely to arouse intense anger in the child because it frustrates not only the act but also the child's need for autonomy. It dramatically underscores the extent to which the child's freedom is circumscribed by the superior power and resources of the adult world. This is no doubt exacerbated by the fact that power assertion is likely to be applied abruptly with few explanations or compensations offered to the child. (The empirical evidence for a positive relation between power assertion and anger has been summarized by Becker, 1964.)

Second, a disciplinary technique also provides the child with (a) a model for discharging that anger, and may provide him with (b) an object against which to discharge his anger. The disciplinary act itself constitutes the model for discharging the anger which the child may imitate.

Third, as much animal and human learning research has now shown, what is learned will depend on the stimuli to which the organism is compelled to attend. Disciplinary techniques explicitly or implicitly provide such a focus. Both love withdrawal and power assertion direct the child to the consequences of his behavior for the actor, that is, for the child himself, and to the external agent producing these consequences. Induction, on the other hand, is more apt to focus the child's attention on the consequences of his actions for others, the parent, or some third party. This factor should be especially important in determining the content of the child's standards. That is, if transgressions are followed by induction, the child will learn that the important part of transgressions consists of the harm done to others.

Fourth, to be effective the technique must enlist already existing emotional and motivational tendencies within the child. One such resource is the child's need for love. This factor depends on the general affective state of the parent-child relationship, the importance of which may be seen in the consistent relationship obtained between affection and the moral indexes (Table 6). Given this affective relationship, some arousal of the need for love may be both necessary for and capable of motivating the child to give up his needs of the moment and attend to (and thus be influenced by) the parent's discipline technique. Too much arousal, however, may produce intense feelings of anxiety over loss of love which may disrupt the child's response especially to the cognitive elements of the technique. All three types of discipline communicate some parental disapproval and are thus capable of arousing the child's need for love. But it is possible that only inductions can arouse this need to an optimal degree because the threat of love withdrawal implicit in inductions is relatively mild. Also, it is embedded in the context of a technique which explicitly or implicitly suggests a means of reparation. Inductions are thus likely to disrupt the child's response—as well as his general affective relationship with the parent— than either love withdrawal which may arouse undue anxiety, or power assertion which arouses anger and other disruptive affects.

The second emotional resource, empathy, has long been overlooked by psychologists as a possibly important factor in socialization. Empathy has been observed in children to occur much before the child's moral controls are firmly established (e.g., Murphy, 1937). We believe that it is a potentially important emotional resource because it adds to the aroused need for love the pain which the child vicariously experiences from having harmed another, thus intensifying his motivation to learn moral rules and control his impulses. Of the three types of discipline under consideration, induction seems most capable of enlisting the child's natural proclivities for empathy in the struggle to control his impulses. As indicated in greater detail elsewhere (Hoffman, 1963b; Hoffman, in press; Hoffman & Saltzstein, 1960), we view induction as both directing the child's attention to the other person's pain, which should elicit an empathic response, and communicating to the child that he caused that pain. Without the latter, the child might respond empathically but dissociate himself from the causal act. The coalescence of empathy and the awareness of being the causal agent should produce a response having the necessary cognitive

(self-critical) and affective properties of guilt.

It follows from this analysis that power assertion is least effective in promoting development of moral standards and internalization of controls because it elicits intense hostility in the child and simultaneously provides him with a model for expressing that hostility outwardly and a relatively legitimate object against which to express it. It furthermore makes the child's need for love less salient and functions as an obstacle to the arousal of empathy. Finally, it sensitizes the child to the punitive responses of adult authorities, thus contributing to an externally focused moral orientation.

Induction not only avoids these deleterious effects of power assertion, but also is the technique most likely to optimally motivate the child to focus his attention on the harm done others as the salient aspect of his transgressions, and thus to help integrate his capacity for empathy with the knowledge of the human consequences of his own behavior. Repeated experiences of this kind should help sensitize the child to the human consequences of his behavior which may then come to stand out among the welter of emotional and other stimuli in the situation. The child is thus gradually enabled to pick out on his own, without help from others, the effects of his behavior, and to react with an internally based sense of guilt. Induction in sum should be the most facilitative form of discipline for building long-term controls which are independent of external sanctions, and the findings would seem to support this view.

Love withdrawal stands midway between the other two techniques in promoting internalization. It provides a more controlled form of aggression by the parent than power assertion, but less than induction. It employs the affectionate relationship between child and parent perhaps to a greater degree than the other two techniques, but in a way more likely than they to produce a disruptive anxiety response in the child. However, it falls short of induction in effectiveness by not including the cognitive material needed to heighten the child's awareness of wrong-doing and facilitate his learning to generalize accurately to other relevant situations, and by failing to capitalize on his capacity for empathy.

The weak and inconsistent findings for love withdrawal suggest that anxiety over loss of love may be a less important factor in the child's internalization than formerly thought to be the case. Before drawing this conclusion, however, the possibility that love withdrawal is only effective when the parent also freely expresses affection, as suggested by Sears et al. (1957), should be considered. We were able to test this hypothesis by examining the relation between love withdrawal and the moral indexes within the group of subjects who were above and below the median on affection, and also within the the upper and lower quartile groups. The results do not corroborate the hypothesis: the relations between love withdrawal and the moral indexes do not differ for the high- and low-affection groups.

In an earlier study with preschool children, however, love withdrawal was found to relate negatively to the expression of overt hostility in the nursery school (Hoffman, 1963b). It was possible to make a similar test in the present study since teacher ratings of overt hostility were available. Here, too, love withdrawal related negatively to hostility outside the home ($p < .05$).[8] We also found that

love withdrawal is used more when the child expresses hostility toward the parent than in other types of discipline situations. These findings suggest that the contribution of love withdrawal to moral development may be to attach anxiety directly to the child's hostile impulses, thus motivating him to keep them under control. Psychoanalytic theory may thus be correct after all in the importance assigned love withdrawal in the socialization of the child's impulses. Our data, however, do not support the psychoanalytic view that identification is a necessary mediating process. That is, we found no relation between love withdrawal and identification (Tables 1–4). It remains possible, of course, that a form of unconscious identification which may not be tapped by our more consciously focused measure serves to mediate between the parent's love withdrawal and the child's inhibition of hostile impulses—as suggested in psychoanalytic theory.

In any case, our data do tend to show that love withdrawal alone is an insufficient basis for the development of those capacities—especially for guilt and moral judgment—which are critical characteristics of a fully developed conscience.[9]

---

[8] Power assertion related positively to hostility ($p < .05$), and induction showed a slight non-significant negative relation.

Some relevant experimental evidence is also available. Gordon and Cohn (1963) found that

doll-play aggression expressed by children in response to frustration decreased after exposure to a story in which the central figure, a dog, searches unsuccessfully for friends with whom to play. Assuming the story arouses feelings of loneliness and anxiety over separation in the child—feelings akin to the emotional response to love-withdrawal techniques—these findings may be taken as further support for the notion that love withdrawal may contribute to the inhibition of hostility.

[9] It should be noted that love withdrawal might relate positively to guilt as defined in psychoanalytic terms, that is, as an irrational response to one's own impulses. Clearly our concept of guilt is quite different from the psychoanalytic, pertaining as it does to the real human consequences of one's actions.

5

The Chemistry
and Genetics
of Behavior

The previous sections, with few exceptions, have dealt with the processes and contents of learning. But not all things teach all men equally; there are differences in learning even when the teaching agent is constant. These differences depend not only on prior learning histories, as was once believed, but also on genetic and chemical variation within the species. We now turn to the implications of these individual differences for human development and for abnormal psychology.

Man and fruitfly have some things in common, and the dependence of behavioral traits on genetic structures may be one of them. Theodosius Dobzhansky's thesis, as presented here, concerns the relationship between what the genetic constitution offers and what the environment yields and the degree to which a constant environment may be influential when genes have already been determined.

Nowhere have psychological theories of psychopathology proved weaker than in their analysis of severe psychiatric disorders, the schizophrenias in particular. It has become commonplace to read that since psychological theory and psychological therapy do not seem to apply, the essential problems must be genetic and biochemical. The logic is less than compelling: obviously, the failure to adduce proof for one view has no direct implications for any other. Nevertheless, enormous effort has gone into the search for biochemical antecedents and correlates of psychiatric disorders, the discovery of which would obviously have implications for the well-ordered, as well as the disordered, mind. Seymour S. Kety, in the two papers presented here, summarizes the evidence: the needle, if it is there at all, has proved enormously elusive in the big haystack.

Biochemical Theories of Schizophrenia: Part I[1]

Seymour S. Kety

The concept of a chemical etiology in schizophrenia is not new. The Hippocratic school attributed certain mental aberrations to changes in the composition of the blood and disturbances in the humors of the brain, but it was Thudichum (1), the founder of modern neurochemistry, who in 1884 expressed the concept most cogently: "Many forms of insanity are unquestionably the external manifestations of the effects upon the brain substance of poisons fermented within the body, just as mental aberrations accompanying chronic alcoholic intoxication are the accumulated effects of a relatively simple poison fermented out of the body. These poisons we shall, I have no doubt, be able to isolate after we know the normal chemistry to its uttermost detail. And then will come in their turn the crowning discoveries to which our efforts must ultimately be directed, namely, the discoveries of the antidotes to the poisons and to the fermenting causes and processes which produce them." In these few words were anticipated and encompassed most of the current chemical formulations regarding schizophrenia.

It may be of value to pause in the

Reprinted from *Science*, vol. 129, pp. 1528–1532, June 5, 1959 with the permission of the American Association for the Advancement of Science and the author.

[1] The author is chief of the Laboratory of Clinical Science, National Institute of Mental Health, National Institutes of Health, Bethesda, Md. This article is based on the Eastman Memorial Lecture, delivered at the University of Rochester, December 1957, and on a paper presented at the third International Neurochemical Symposium, Strasbourg, August 1958.

midst of the present era of psychochemical activity to ask how far we have advanced along the course plotted by Thudichum. Have we merely substituted "enzymes" for "ferments" and the names of specific agents for "poisons" without altering the completely theoretical nature of the concept? Or, on the other hand, are there some well-substantiated findings to support the prevalent belief that this old and stubborn disorder which has resisted all previous attempts to expose its etiology is about to yield its secrets to the biochemist?

An examination of the experience of another and older discipline may be of help in the design, interpretation, and evaluation of biochemical studies. The concepts of the pathology of schizophrenia have been well reviewed recently (2). As a result of findings of definite histological changes in the cerebral cortex of patients with schizophrenia which were described by Alzheimer at the beginning of the present century and confirmed by a number of others, an uncritical enthusiasm for the theory of a pathological lesion in this disease developed, and this enthusiasm penetrated the thinking of Kraepelin and Bleuler and persisted for 25 years. This was followed by a period of questioning which led to the design and execution of more critically controlled studies and, eventually, to the present consensus that a pathological lesion characteristic of schizophrenia or any of its subgroups remains to be demonstrated.

Earlier biochemical theories and findings related to schizophrenia have been reviewed by a number of authors, of whom McFarland and Goldstein (3), Keup (4), and Richter (5) may be mentioned (6). Horwitt and others (7–9) have pointed out some of the difficulties of crucial research in this area. It is the purpose of this review to describe the biochemical trends in schizophrenia research of the past few years, to discuss current theories, and to examine the evidence which has been used to support them.

Sources of Error

Because of the chronicity of the disease, the prolonged periods of institutionalization associated with its management, and the comparatively few objective criteria available for its diagnosis and the evaluation of its progress, schizophrenia presents to the investigator a large number of variables and sources of error which he must recognize and attempt to control before he may attribute to any of his findings a primary or characteristic significance.

Despite the phenomenological similarities which permitted the concept of schizophrenia as a fairly well defined symptom complex to emerge, there is little evidence that all of its forms have a common etiology or pathogenesis. The likelihood that one is dealing with a number of different disorders with a common symptomatology must be recognized and included in one's experimental design (8, 10, 11). Errors involved in sampling from heterogeneous populations may help to explain the high frequency with which findings of one group fail to be confirmed by those of another. Recognition that any sample of schizophrenics is probably a heterogeneous one would seem to indicate the importance of analyzing data not only for mean values but also for significant deviations of individual values from group values. The biochemical characteristics of phenylketonuria would hardly have been detected in an average value for phenylalanine levels in blood in a large group of mentally retarded patients.

Most biochemical research in schizophrenia has been carried out in patients with a long history of hospitalization in institutions where overcrowding is difficult to avoid and where hygienic standards cannot always be maintained. It is easy to imagine how chronic infections, especially of the digestive tract, might spread among such patients. The presence of amebiasis in a majority of the patients at one large institution has been reported (12), and one wonders how often this condition or a former infectious hepatitis has caused the various disturbances in hepatic function found in schizophrenia. Even in the absence of previous or current infection, the development of a characteristic pattern of intestinal flora in a population of schizophrenic patients living together for long periods and fed from the same kitchen is a possibility which cannot be dismissed in interpreting what appear to be deviant metabolic pathways.

In variety and quality the diet of the institutionalized schizophrenic is rarely comparable to that of the nonhospitalized normal control. Whatever homeostatic function the process of free dietary selection may serve is often lost between the rigors of the kitchen or the budget and the overriding emotional or obsessive features of the disease. In the case of the "acute" schizophrenic, the weeks and months of emotional turmoil which precede recognition and diagnosis of the disease are hardly conducive to a normal dietary intake. Kelsey, Gullock, and Kelsey (13) confirmed findings of certain abnormalities in thyroid function previously reported in schizophrenia and showed that in their patients these abnormalities resulted from a dietary deficiency of iodine, correctable by the introduction of iodized salt into the hospital diet. It is not surprising that a dietary vitamin deficiency has been found to explain at least two of the biochemical abnormalities recently attributed to schizophrenia (9, 14–16). It is more surprising that the vitamins and other dietary constituents, whose role in metabolism has become so clearly established, should so often be relegated to a position of unimportance in consideration of the intermediary metabolism of schizophrenics. Horwitt (17) has found signs of liver dysfunction during ingestion of a diet containing borderline levels of protein, while nonspecific vitamin therapy accompanied by a high protein and carbohydrate diet has been reported to reverse the impairment of hepatic function in schizophrenic patients (18).

Another incidental factor which sets the schizophrenic apart from the normal control is the long list of therapies to which he may have been exposed. Hypnotic and ataractic drugs and their metabolic products or effects produce changes which have sometimes been attributed to the disease. Less obvious is the possibility of residual electrophysiological or biochemical changes resulting from repeated electroshock or insulin coma.

Emotional stress is known to cause profound changes in man—in adrenocortical and thyroid function (19), in the excretion of epinephrine and norepinephrine (20), and in the excretion of water, electrolytes, or creatinine (21), to mention only a few recently reported findings. Schizophrenic illness is often characterized by marked emotional disturbance even in what is called the basal state and by frequently exaggerated anxiety in response to routine and research procedures. The disturbances in behavior and activity which

mark the schizophrenic process would also be expected to cause deviations from the normal in many biochemical and metabolic measures—in volume and concentration of urine, in energy and nitrogen metabolism, in the size and function of numerous organic systems. The physiological and biochemical changes which are secondary to the psychological and behavioral state of the patient are of interest in themselves, and understanding of them contributes to total understanding of the schizophrenic process; it is important, however, not to attribute to them a primary or etiological role.

An additional source of error which must be recognized is one which is common to all of science and which it is the very purpose of scientific method, tradition, and training to minimize— the subjective bias. There are reasons why this bias should operate to a greater extent in this field than in many others. Not only is the motivation heightened by the tragedy of this problem and the social implications of findings which may contribute to its solution, but the measurements themselves, especially of the changes in mental state or behavior, are so highly subjective, and the symptoms are so variable and so responsive to nonspecific factors in the milieu, that only the most scrupulous attention to controlled design will permit the conclusion that a drug, or a diet, or a protein fraction of the blood, or an extract of the brain is capable of causing or ameliorating some of the manifestations of the disease. This is not to suggest that the results of purely chemical determinations are immune to subjective bias; the same vigilance is required there to prevent the hypothesis from contaminating the data. In a field with as many variables as this one, it is difficult to avoid the subconscious tendency to reject for good reason data which weaken a hypothesis while uncritically accepting those data which strengthen it. Carefully controlled and "double blind" experimental designs which are becoming more widely utilized in this area help to minimize this bias.

Obvious as many of these sources of error are, it is expensive and difficult, if not impossible, to prevent some of them from affecting results obtained in this field, especially in the preliminary testing of interesting hypotheses. It is in the interpretation of these results, however, and in the formulating of conclusions, that the investigator has the opportunity, and indeed the responsibility, to recognize and evaluate his uncontrolled variables rather than to ignore them, for no one knows better than the investigator himself the possible sources of error in his particular experiment. There are enough unknowns in our guessing game with nature to make it unnecessary for us to indulge in such a sport with one another.

Schizophrenia Program of the Laboratory of Clinical Science

Since 1956, the Laboratory of Clinical Science of the National Institute of Mental Health has been developing and pursuing a program of biological research in schizophrenia designed to minimize many of the sources of error discussed above while increasing the opportunity to detect, and to correlate with psychiatric and behavioral information, true biological characteristics if they exist. One of the wards houses a group of approximately 14 clearly diagnosed schizophrenic patients, representative of as many clinical subgroups as possible, chosen from a patient population of 14,000. In selecting these patients an attempt was made to minimize the variables of age, sex, race, and physical illness and, on the basis of careful family surveys, to maximize the likeli-

hood of including within the group individuals representative of whatever genetic subgroups of the disease may exist (10). These patients are maintained for an indefinite period of time on a good diet, receiving excellent hygienic, nursing, medical, and psychiatric care. Each patient receives a careful and sophisticated psychiatric and genealogical characterization, and detailed daily records are kept on his psychiatric and behavioral status; these, it is hoped, will be of value in a more complete interpretation of biological findings. No specific therapy is employed or even found to be necessary, and drugs or dietary changes are introduced only for research purposes and for short periods of time. The other ward houses a comparable number of normal controls, who volunteer to remain for protracted periods of time on the same diet and in a reasonably similar milieu. We recognize, of course, that only a few of the variables are thus controlled and that any positive difference which emerges in this preliminary experiment between some or all of the schizophrenics and the normal population will have to be subjected to much more rigorous examination before its significance can be evaluated. Such reexamination has rarely been necessary, since our schizophrenic patients, individually or as a group, have shown little abnormality in the biological studies which have thus far been completed (9, 14, 22–24).

Oxygen, Carbohydrate, and Energetics

A decrease in basal metabolism was found in schizophrenia by earlier workers, although more recent work has not confirmed this (5), and theories attributing the disease to disturbances in the fundamental mechanisms of energy supply or conversion in the brain have enjoyed some popularity, but on the basis of extremely inadequate evidence, such as spectroscopic oximetry of the ear lobe or nail bed (25). Our finding of a normal rate of cerebral circulation and oxygen consumption in schizophrenic patients (26) was confirmed by Wilson, Schieve, and Scheinberg (27) and, more recently, in our laboratory by Sokoloff and his associates (28), who also found a normal rate of cerebral glucose consumption in this condition. These studies make it appear unlikely that the moderate decrease in these functions reported by Gordan and his associates (29); but only in patients with long-standing disease, is fundamental to the disease process. These studies do not, of course, rule out a highly localized change in energy metabolism somewhere in the brain, but cogent evidence for such a hypothesis has yet to be presented.

Richter (5) has pointed out the uncontrolled factors in earlier work which indicated that a defect in carbohydrate metabolism was characteristic of the schizophrenic disease process. The finding in schizophrenia of an abnormal glucose tolerance in conjunction with considerable other evidence of hepatic dysfunction (30), or evidence of an abnormally slow metabolism of lactate in the schizophrenic (31), do not completely exclude incidental hepatic disease or nutritional deficiencies as possible sources of error. Horwitt and his associates (32) were able to demonstrate and correct similar abnormalities by altering the dietary intake of the B group of vitamins.

Evidence for greater than normal anti-insulin or hyperglycemic activity in the blood or urine of a significant segment of schizophrenic patients was reported in 1942 by Meduna, Gerty, and Urse (33) and as recently as 1958 by Moya and his associates (34). Some progress has been made in concentrating or characterizing such factors in normal (35) urine as well as in urine from schizophrenics (36). Harris (37) has thrown some doubt on the importance of such anti-insulin mechanisms in the pathogenesis of schizophrenia, and it is hoped that further investigation may clarify the nature of the substance or substances involved and their relevance to schizophrenia.

Defects in oxidative phosphorylation have been thought to occur in this disease. Reports of alterations in the phosphorus metabolism of the erythrocyte (38) await further definition and independent confirmation.

Two recent reports of a more normal pattern of carbohydrate metabolism and of clinical improvement following the infusion of glutathione (39) in psychotic patients, some of whom were schizophrenic, are perhaps of interest. There is little verifiable evidence for a reduction in the blood glutathione index in schizophrenia (9); one group which has repeatedly postulated this reduction has done so on the basis of decreasingly convincing data (16, 40), while our laboratory has failed to find it at all (14), and a very recent report publishes identical figures for the schizophrenic and normal groups (41). Clinical and biochemical improvement in a variety of psychoses following glutathione infusion, even if it is accepted without the necessary controls, suggests at best that glutathione is of secondary and nonspecific import.

It is difficult for some to believe that a generalized defect in energy metabolism—a process so fundamental to every cell in the body—could be responsible for the highly specialized features of schizophrenia. On the other hand, a moderate lack of oxygen, an essential requirement of practically every tissue, produces highly selective manifestations involving especially the higher mental functions and as suggestive of schizophrenia as manifestations produced by many of the more popular hallucinogens. It may not, therefore, be completely appropriate that, in a search for biochemical factors etiologically related to schizophrenic psychoses, the center of interest today appears to have shifted to other, more specialized aspects of metabolism.

Amino Acids and Amines

The well-controlled studies of the Gjessings (42) on nitrogen metabolism in periodic catatonia arouse considerable interest in that they suggest the possibility of a relationship between intermediary protein metabolism and schizophrenia, although earlier workers had postulated defects in amino acid metabolism in this disease (43). The hallucinogenic properties of some compounds related directly or indirectly to biological amines reawakened this interest, and the techniques of paper chromatography offered new and almost unlimited opportunity for studying the subject.

The first group to report chromatographic studies of the urine of schizophrenic and control groups found certain differences in the amino acid pattern and, in addition, the presence of certain unidentified imidazoles in the urine of schizophrenics (44). Although a normal group of comparable age was used for comparison, there is no indication of the extent to which dietary and other variables were controlled, and the authors were properly cautious in their conclusions. In a more extensive series of studies, another group has reported a significantly higher than normal concentration of aromatic compounds in the urine of schizophrenic patients (45), and has suggested that there are certain qualitative differences in the excretion of such compounds

(46). Others have reported the abnormal presence of unidentified amines (47) or indoles (48), and one group has reported the absence of a normally occurring indole (49) in the urine of schizophrenic patients. In some of these studies there appears to have been no control relative to possible drug therapy or to volume or concentration of urine, and in few of them was there control of diet. There are numerous mechanisms whereby vitamin deficiencies may cause substantial changes in the complex patterns of the intermediary metabolism of amino acids. In addition, the fact that a large number of aromatic compounds in the urine have recently been shown to be of dietary origin (50) suggests the need for considerably more caution than has usually been employed in drawing conclusions with regard to this variable. Another point which has not been emphasized sufficiently is that chromatographic procedures which make possible the simultaneous determination of scores of substances, many of them unknown, require statistical analyses somewhat different from those which were developed for the testing of single, well-defined hypotheses. It is merely a restatement of statistical theory to point out that in a determination of 100 different compounds carried out simultaneously in two samples of the *same* population, five would be expected to show a difference significant at the 0.05 level! It is interesting to note that a more recent study was able to demonstrate considerably fewer differences between the urines of normal and schizophrenic populations and drew very limited and guarded conclusions (51). In our own laboratory, Mann and LaBrosse (24) undertook a search for urinary phenolic acids, in terms of quantity excreted in a standard time interval rather than in terms of concentration, which disclosed significantly higher levels of four compounds in the urine of schizophrenics than in that of the normal test subjects. These compounds were found to be known metabolites of substances in coffee, and their presence in the urine was, in fact, better correlated with the ingestion of this beverage than with schizophrenia.

The hypothesis that a disordered amino acid metabolism is a fundamental component of some forms of schizophrenia remains an attractive though fairly general one, chromatography as a means of searching for supporting evidence is convenient and valuable, and preliminary indications of differences are certainly provocative. Proof that any of these differences are characteristic of even a segment of the disease rather than artifactual or incidental has not yet been obtained.

The Epinephrine Hypothesis

The theory which relates the pathogenesis of schizophrenia to faulty metabolism of epinephrine (52–54) is imaginative, ingenious, and plausible. It postulates that the symptoms of this disease are caused by the action of abnormal, hallucinogenic derivatives of epinephrine, presumably adrenochrome or adrenolutin. By including the concept of an enzymatic, possibly genetic, defect with another factor, epinephrine release, which may be activated by stressful life situations (22), it encompasses the evidence for sociological as well as constitutional factors in the etiology of the schizophrenias.

The possibility that some of the oxidation products of epinephrine are psychotomimetic received support from anecdotal reports of psychological disturbances associated with the therapeutic use of the compound, especially when it was discolored (52), and from some early experiments in which the administration of adrenochrome or adrenolutin in appreciable dosage was fol-

lowed by certain unusual mental manifestations (54). A number of investigators failed to demonstrate any hallucinogenic properties in adrenochrome (55), and the original authors were not always able to confirm their earlier results.

Meanwhile, reports were emerging from the group at Tulane University, suggesting a gross disturbance in epinephrine metabolism in schizophrenic patients. Five years previously, Holmberg and Laurell (56) had demonstrated a more rapid oxidation of epinephrine in vitro in the presence of pregnancy serum than with serum from the umbilical cord and had suggested that this was due to higher concentrations of ceruloplasmin in the former. There had also been a few reports of an increase in levels of this protein in the blood of schizophrenics. Leach and Heath (57) reported a striking acceleration in the in vitro oxidation of epinephrine in the presence of plasma from schizophrenic patients as compared with that from normal subjects and shortly thereafter implicated ceruloplasmin or some variant of ceruloplasmin as the oxidizing substance (58). Hoffer and Kenyon (59) promptly reported evidence that the substance formed from epinephrine by blood serum in vitro was adrenolutin and pointed out how this strengthened the epinephrine hypothesis.

All of the evidence does not, however, support the epinephrine theory. In the past few years the major metabolites of epinephrine have been identified: 3-methoxy-4-hydroxymandelic acid, by Armstrong and his associates (60), and its precursor, metanephrine, by Axelrod and his coworkers of this laboratory (61), where, in addition, the principal pathways of epinephrine metabolism in animals (62) and man (63) have been demonstrated. The metabolites of C^{14}-labeled epinephrine in the urine of schizophrenic patients (64) and in normal man (65) have been studied independently by others. No evidence has been found for the oxidation of epinephrine via adrenochrome and adrenolutin in any of these populations. Although it has been reported that there are appreciable amounts of adrenochrome in the blood of normal subjects and that these amounts increase considerably following administration of lysergic acid diethylamide (66), Szara, Axelrod, and Perlin, using techniques of high sensitivity, have been unable to detect adrenochrome in the blood of normal test subjects or in that of acute or chronic schizophrenic patients (22). In a recent ingenious study of the rate of destruction of epinephrine in vivo, no difference between normal subjects and schizophrenic patients was found in this regard (67). Finally, it has been shown by McDonald (9) in our laboratory and by members of the Tulane group themselves (16), that the low level of ascorbic acid in the blood is an important and uncontrolled variable in the rapid in vitro oxidation of epinephrine by plasma from schizophrenic patients. The fact that McDonald has been able to produce wide fluctuations in the epinephrine oxidation phenomenon, from normal to highly abnormal rates, in both normal subjects and schizophrenics merely by altering the level of ascorbic acid in the blood by dietary means, and that this has had no effect on the mental processes of either group, is quite convincing evidence of the dietary and secondary nature of the phenomenon.

It should be pointed out that none of this negative evidence invalidates the theory that some abnormal product of epinephrine metabolism, existing somewhere in the body, produces the major symptoms of schizophrenia; it does, however, considerably weaken the evidence which has been used to support the theory. In addition, there is the bothersome observation of numerous workers (68) that the administration of epinephrine to schizophrenics, which, according to the theory, should aggravate the psychotic symptoms, is not accompanied by appreciably greater mental disturbances than occurs in normal subjects.

Quite recently a new report on inconstant psychotomimetic effects of epinephrine oxidation products in a small number of subjects has appeared (69), with evidence suggesting that the psychotoxic substance is neither adrenochrome nor adrenolutin, that it is active in microgram quantities, and that it is highly labile. This report, like the previous ones which described the phychotomimetic effects of epinephrine products, is highly subjective and incompletely controlled. Even if these conclusions are accepted, the relevance of such hallucinogens to, or their presence in, schizophrenia remains to be demonstrated.

REFERENCES AND NOTES

1. J. W. L. Thudichum, *A Treatise on the Chemical Constitution of the Brain* (Balliere, Tindall, and Cox, London, 1884).
2. G. Peters, "Dementia praecox," in *Handbuch der Speziellen Pathologischen Anatomie und Histologie*, Lubarsch, Henke, and Rössle, Eds. (Springer, Berlin, 1956), vol. 13, pt. 4, pp. 1–52; G. B. David, "The pathological anatomy of the schizophrenias," in *Schizophrenia: Somatic Aspects* (Pergamon, London, 1957), pp. 93–130; D. K. Dastur, A.M.A. *Arch. Neurol. Psychiat.* 81, 601 (1959).
3. R. A. McFarland and H. Goldstein, *Am. J. Psychiat.* 95, 509 (1938).
4. W. Keup, *Monatsschr. Psychiat. Neurol.* 128, 56 (1954).
5. D. Richter, "Biochemical aspects of schizophrenia," in *Schizophrenia: Somatic Aspects* (Pergamon, London, 1957), pp. 53–75.
6. For the most recent review see J. D. Benjamin, *Psychosom. Med.* 20, 427 (1958).

7. M. K. Horwitt, *Science* 124, 429 (1956).
8. E. V. Evarts, *Psychiat. Research Repts.* 9, 52 (1958).
9. R. K. McDonald, *J. Chronic Diseases* 8, 366 (1958).
10. S. Perlin and A. R. Lee, *Am. J. Psychiat.*, in press.
11. D. A. Freedman, *Diseases of Nervous System* 19, 108 (1958).
12. P. Vestergaard, M. T. Abbott, N. S. Kline, A. M. Stanley, *J. Clin. Exptl. Psychopathol.* 19, 44 (1958).
13. F. O. Kelsey, A. H. Gullock, F. E. Kelsey, *A.M.A. Arch. Neurol. Psychiat.* 77, 543 (1957).
14. R. K. McDonald, "Plasma ceruloplasmin and ascorbic acid levels in schizophrenia," paper presented at the annual meeting of the American Psychiatric Association, Chicago, Ill., 1957.
15. M. H. Aprison and H. J. Grosz, *A.M.A. Arch. Neurol. Psychiat.* 79, 575 (1958).
16. C. Angel, B. E. Leach, S. Martens, M. Cohen, R. G. Heath, *ibid.* 78, 500 (1957).
17. M. K. Horwitt, "Report of Elgin Project No. 3 with Emphasis on Liver Dysfunction," *Nutrition Symposium Ser. No. 7* (National Vitamin Foundation, New York, 1953), pp. 67–83.
18. R. Fischer, F. Georgi, R. Weber, R. M. Piaget, *Schweiz. med. Wochschr.* 80, 129 (1950).
19. F. Board, H. Persky, D. A. Hamburg, *Psychosom. Med.* 18, 324 (1956).
20. R. Elmadjian, J. M. Hope, E. T. Lamson, *J. Clin. Endocrinol. and Metabolism* 17, 608 (1957).
21. W. W. Schottstaedt, W. J. Grace, H. G. Wolff, *J. Psychosom. Research* 1, 147 (1956); *ibid.* 1, 292 (1956).
22. S. Szara, J. Axelrod, S. Perlin, *Am. J. Psychiat.* 115, 162 (1958).
23. I. J. Kopin, *Science* 129, 835 (1959); C. Kornetsky, personal communication.
24. J. D. Mann and E. H. Labrosse, *A.M.A. Arch. Genl. Psychiat.*, in press.
25. J. W. Lovett Doust, *J. Mental Sci.* 98, 143 (1952).
26. S. S. Kety, R. B. Woodford, M. H. Harmel, F. A. Freyhan, K. E. Appel, C. F. Schmidt, *Am. J. Psychiat.* 104, 765 (1948).
27. W. P. Wilson, J. F. Schieve, P. Schein-

berg, *A.M.A. Arch. Neurol. Psychiat.* 68, 651 (1952).
28. L. Sokoloff, S. Perlin, C. Kornetsky, S. S. Kety, *Ann. N.Y. Acad. Sci.* 66, 468 (1957).
29. G. S. Gordan, F. M. Estes, J. E. Adams, K. M. Bowman, A. Simon, *A.M.A. Arch. Neurol. Psychiat.* 73, 544 (1955).
30. V. Longo, G. A. Buscaino, F. D'Andrea, A. Uras, E. Ferrari, F. Rinaldi, F. Pasolini, *Acta Neurol.* (Naples) Quad. III, 21 (1953).
31. M. D. Altschule, D. H. Henneman, P. Holliday, R. M. Goncz, *A.M.A. Arch. Internal Med.* 98, 35 (1956).
32. M. K. Horwitt, E. Liebert, O. Kreisler, P. Wittman, *Bull. Natl. Research Council (U.S.) No. 116* (1948).
33. L. J. Meduna, F. J. Gerty, V. G. Urse, *A.M.A. Arch. Neurol. Psychiat.* 47, 38 (1942).
34. F. Moya, J. Dewar, M. MacIntosh, S. Hirsch, R. Townsend, *Can. J. Biochem. and Physiol.* 36, 505 (1958).
35. F. Moya, J. C. Szerb, M. MacIntosh, *ibid.* 34, 563 (1956).
36. M. S. Morgan and F. J. Pilgrim, *Proc. Soc. Exptl. Biol. Med.* 79, 106 (1952).
37. M. M. Harris, *A.M.A. Arch. Neurol. Psychiat.* 48, 761 (1942).
38. I. Boszormenyi-Nagy, F. J. Gerty, J. Kueber, *J. Nervous Mental Disease* 124, 413 (1956); I. Bosbormenyi-Nagy and F. J. Gerty, *ibid.* 121, 53 (1955).
39. M. D. Altschule, D. H. Henneman, P. D. Holliday, R. M. Goncz, *A.M.A. Arch. Internal Med.* 99, 22 (1957); M. P. Surikow, G. K. Ushakov, B. N. Il'ina, A. A. Verbliunskaia, L. K. Khokhlov, *Zhur. Neuropatol.* 57, 237 (1957).
40. S. Martens, B. E. Leach, R. G. Heath, M. Cohen, *A.M.A. Arch. Neurol. Psychiat.* 76, 630 (1956).
41. A. J. Barak, F. L. Humoller, J. D. Stevens, *ibid.* 80, 237 (1958).
42. R. Gjessing, *J. Mental Sci.* 84, 608 (1938); ———, *Arch. Psychiat. Nervenkrankh.* 108, 525 (1939); L. Gjessing, A. Bernhardsen, H. Freshaug, *J. Mental Sci.* 104, 188 (1958).
43. V. M. Buscaino, *Acta Neurol.* (Naples) 13, 1 (1958).
44. H. K. Young, H. K. Berry, E. Beerstecher, *Univ. Texas Publ. No. 5109* (1951), pp. 189–197.
45. P. L. McGeer, F. E. McNair, E. G.

McGeer, W. C. Gibson, *J. Nervous Mental Diseases* 125, 166 (1957).

46. E. G. McGeer, W. T. Brown, P. L. McGeer, *ibid.* 125, 176 (1957).
47. F. Georgi, C. G. Honegger, D. Jordan, H. P. Rieder, M. Rottenberg, *Klin. Wochschr.* 34, 799 (1956).
48. L. M. Riegelhaupt, *J. Nervous Mental Disease* 123, 383 (1956).
49. E. J. Cafruny and E. F. Domino, *A.M.A. Arch. Neurol. Psychiat.* 79, 336 (1958).
50. M. D. Armstrong and K. N. F. Shaw, *J. Biol. Chem.* 225, 269 (1956); ———, M. J. Gortatowski, H. Singer, *ibid.* 232, 17 (1958); M. D. Armstrong, P. E. Wall, V. J. Parker, *ibid.* 218, 921 (1956); A. N. Booth, O. H. Emerson, F. T. Jones, F. Deeds, *ibid.* 229, 51 (1957); T. P. Waalkes, A. Sjoerdsma, C. R. Creveling, H. Weissbach, S. Udenfriend, *Science* 127, 648 (1958).
51. R. M. Acheson, R. M. Paul, R. V. Tomlinson, *Can. J. Biochem. Physiol.* 36, 295 (1958).
52. H. Osmond, *Diseases of Nervous System* 16, 101 (1955).
53. ——— and J. Smythies, *J. Mental Sci.* 98, 309 (1952); A. Hoffer, *J. Clin. Exptl. Psychopathol.* 18, 27 (1957).
54. A. Hoffer, H. Osmond, J. Smythies, *J. Mental Sci.* 100, 29 (1954).
55. M. Rinkel and H. C. Solomon, *J. Clin. Exptl. Psychopathol.* 18, 323 (1957).
56. C. G. Holmberg and C. B. Laurell,

Scand. J. Clin. & Lab. Invest. 3, 103 (1951).
57. B. E. Leach and R. G. Heath, *A.M.A. Arch. Neurol. Psychiat.* 76, 444 (1956).
58. B. E. Leach, M. Cohen, R. G. Heath, S. Martens, *ibid.* 76, 635 (1956).
59. A. Hoffer and M. Kenyon, *ibid.* 77, 437 (1957).
60. M. D. Armstrong, A. McMillan, K. N. F. Shaw, *Biochem. et Biophys. Acta* 25, 422 (1957).
61. J. Axelrod and R. Tomchick, *J. Biol. Chem.* 233, 702 (1958).
62. J. Axelrod, S. Senoh, B. Witkop, *ibid.* 233, 697 (1958).
63. E. H. Labrosse, J. Axelrod, S. S. Kety, *Science* 128, 593 (1958).
64. O. Resnick, J. M. Wolfe, H. Freeman, F. Elmadjian, *ibid.* 127, 1116 (1958).
65. N. Kirshner, McC. Goodall, L. Rosen, *Proc. Soc. Exptl. Biol. Med.* 98, 627 (1958).
66. A. Hoffer, *Am. J. Psychiat.* 114, 752 (1958).
67. B. Holland, G. Cohen, M. Goldenberg, J. Sha, L. Leifer, *Federation Proc.* 17, 378 (1958).
68. E. Lindemann, *Am. J. Psychiat.* 91, 983 (1935); R. G. Heath, B. E. Leach, L. W. Byers, S. Martens, C. A. Feigley, *ibid.* 114, 683 (1958); J. B. Dynes and H. Tod, *J. Neurol. Psychiat.* 3, 1 (1940); and workers in this laboratory.
69. G. Taubmann and H. Jantz, *Nervenarzt* 28, 485 (1957).

Biochemical Theories of Schizophrenia: Part II[1]

Seymour S. Kety

In part I of this article, an attempt was made to discuss the possible sources of error peculiar to biological research in

Reprinted from *Science*, vol. 129, pp. 1590–1596, June 12, 1959 with the permission of *Science* and the author.

[1] The author is chief of the Laboratory of Clinical Science, National Institute of Mental Health, National Institutes of Health, Bethesda, Md. This article is based on the Eastman Me-

schizophrenia, including the possible heterogeneity of that symptom complex and the presence of certain biological features—such as adventitious disease, nutritional deficiencies, disturbances associated with abnormal motor or emo-

morial Lecture, delivered at the University of Rochester, December 1957, and on a paper presented at the Third International Neurochemical Symposium, Strasbourg, August 1958.

tional states, and changes brought about by treatment, all of which may be said to result from the disease or from its current management rather than to be factors in its genesis. The difficulty of avoiding subjective bias was emphasized. Some of the hypotheses relating to oxygen, carbohydrate, and energy metabolism, to amino acid metabolism, and to epinephrine were presented, and the existing evidence relevant to them was discussed. Among the recent or current concepts there remain to be discussed those concerned with ceruloplasmin, with serotonin, and with the general genetic aspects of schizophrenic disorders.

Ceruloplasmin and Taraxein

The rise and fall of interest in ceruloplasmin as a biochemical factor significantly related to schizophrenia is one of the briefest, if not one of the most enlightening, chapters in the history of biological psychiatry. The upsurge of interest can be ascribed to a report that a young Swedish biochemist had discovered a new test for schizophrenia. The test depended upon the oxidation of N,N-dimethyl-p-phenylenediamine by ceruloplasmin (1, 2). It is difficult to understand the exaggerated interest which this report aroused, since Holmberg and Laurell (3) had demonstrated previously that ceruloplasmin was capable of oxidizing a number of substances, including phenylenediamine and epinephrine, and Leach and Heath (4) had already published a procedure based on epinephrine oxidation which was equally valid as a means of distinguishing schizophrenics from normal subjects and had identified the oxidizing substance as ceruloplasmin (5). All of these observations were compatible with earlier reports in the German literature (6) of an increase in serum copper in schizophrenia and with the demonstration that

practically all of the serum copper was in the form of ceruloplasmin and that the levels of this compound in blood were elevated during pregnancy and in a large number of diseases (7, 8). There had even been preliminary observations of an increase in blood ceruloplasmin in schizophrenia (8). Following the announcement of the Akerfeldt test, however, interest in copper and ceruloplasmin rose, and very soon a number of investigators reported this reaction, or some modification of it, to be positive in a high percentage of schizophrenics (2, 9), although as a diagnostic test the Akerfeldt procedure was discredited because of the large number of diseases, besides schizophrenia, in which the results were positive. Both Akerfeldt and Heath recognized that ascorbic acid could inhibit the oxidation of phenylenediamine and of epinephrine, respectively, but neither felt that this was crucial to his findings, since each had satisfied himself that the feeding of large doses of ascorbic acid to the patients had not influenced the respective reactions (2). In addition, Abood (9), who used a modification of the Akerfeldt procedure which was not affected by ascorbic acid, was able to obtain a positive reaction indicating abnormally high ceruloplasmin levels in two-thirds of the more than 250 schizophrenics he had examined.

In the past 18 months there has been a remarkable decline in the interest in, and the reported levels of, ceruloplasmin in schizophrenia. In May of 1957, McDonald (10) reported his findings on three groups of schizophrenics, one group from the wards of the National Institute of Mental Health, where the patients had been maintained on a more than adequate diet, and two groups from state hospitals. He performed the Akerfeldt test and the Abood modification of it, as well as independent tests to measure ascorbic acid and copper, on these groups and on three groups of controls. In none of the schizophrenic groups was there an increase in serum copper or other evidence of increase in ceruloplasmin. In the state-hospital patients and one group of controls, however, ascorbic acid levels were low and the results of Akerfeldt tests were positive, whereas in schizophrenic patients from the National Institute of Mental Health, levels of ascorbic acid were normal and the results of Akerfeldt tests were negative. It was clear that a high ceruloplasmin level was not characteristic of schizophrenia and that a positive response to the Akerfeldt test, where it occurred, could be completely explained by a dietary insufficiency of ascorbic acid.

In findings of the Tulane group, the mean values for serum copper in schizophrenia have decreased from a high of 216 micrograms per 100 milliliters in 1956 (5) to 145 micrograms per 100 milliliters at the end of 1957 (4), mean normal values having remained at 122 and 124 micrograms per 100 milliliters during the same period. Other groups have found slight differences or no differences at all with respect to blood levels of ceruloplasmin or copper between schizophrenic and normal subjects (11) and no support for the theory that the Akerfeldt test is a means of distinguishing between schizophrenic and non-schizophrenic patients (12). It is not clear why some schizophrenics apparently show an elevated level of ceruloplasmin in the blood; among suggested explanations are dietary factors, hepatic damage, chronic infection, or the possibility that excitement tends to raise the level of ceruloplasmin in the blood, as preliminary experiments appear to indicate (13).

Quite early in their studies, members of the Tulane group recognized that the potent oxidant effects of the serum of schizophrenics on epinephrine in vitro could not be satisfactorily explained by the ceruloplasmin levels alone (5). Before they recognized the importance to this reaction of ascorbic acid deficiency (14), they had postulated the presence in the blood of schizophrenics of a qualitatively different form of ceruloplasmin (5), which they proceeded to isolate and to test in monkey and man, and to which they have given the name taraxein (from the Greek root tarassein, meaning "to disturb"). They have reported that when certain batches of this material were tested in monkeys, marked behavioral and electroencephalographic changes occurred. When samples of these active batches were injected intravenously at a rapid rate into carefully selected prisoner volunteers, all of the subjects developed symptoms which have been described as characteristic of schizophrenia—disorganization and fragmentation of thought, autism, feelings of depersonalization, paranoid ideas, auditory hallucinations, and catatonic behavior (15–17).

Demonstration of toxic materials in the blood and in the body fluids of schizophrenic patients is not new. The voluminous and inconclusive work of earlier investigators was well reviewed by Keup in 1954 (6). Since that time, many new reports have appeared, although there has been no extensive substantiation of any of them. The results of one, on the toxicity of serum and urine of schizophrenic patients for the larvae of Xenopus laevis (18), were disputed by the laboratory in which the work was done (19). Edisen (20), was unable to demonstrate toxicity of such serum for the species of tadpole previously used, or for other species and other genera. A report that serum from schizophrenic patients is toxic to cells in tissue culture (21) lost some of its significance when 1 year later the same laboratory reported that the sera of surgical patients (22) was of comparable toxicity. Reports that injection of certain extracts of the urine of schizophrenic patients induces electroencephalographic and behavioral changes in rats (23) or disturbances in web construction in spiders (24) have not yet received confirmation in the scientific literature. Such urine, however, has been reported to have no effect on the Siamese fighting fish, which is remarkably sensitive to certain hallucinogens (25). Contrary to earlier findings, a recent attempt to demonstrate behavioral changes in rats following the injection of cerebrospinal fluid from catatonic patients was unsuccessful (26). A highly significant decrease in rope-climbing speed in rats injected with sera from psychotic patients as opposed to sera from nonpsychotic controls has been reported by Winter and Flataker (27). Their later finding (28) that the phenomenon occurs with sera of patients with a wide variety of mental disorders, including mental retardation and alcoholism, and that there is a considerable variation in this index between similar groups at different hospitals, coupled with the inability of at least one other investigator (29) to demonstrate this phenomenon in the small group of schizophrenic patients under investigation in this laboratory, suggests that the quite real and statistically significant phenomenon originally observed may be related to variables other than those specific for, or fundamental to, schizophrenia. More recently, Ghent and Freedman (29) have reported their inability to confirm the observations of Winter and Flataker.

It has been reported that rabbits pretreated with serum from schizophrenics do not exhibit a pressor response following the local application of an epinephrine solution to the cerebral cortex (30). No difference between the action of sera from normal subjects and that from

schizophrenics was demonstrated by means of this procedure in tests of sera from a small number of individuals on our wards.

The significance of all of these studies in animals, whether the studies are successful or unsuccessful in demonstrating a toxic factor in schizophrenia, is quite irrelevant to, and considerably dwarfed by, the implications of the taraxein studies. It is because of the tremendous implications which these results could have in the etiology and rational therapy of this important disorder that a reviewer must evaluate them with even more than the usual care.

In the first place, the important biochemical phenomena originally reported in schizophrenia—lowered blood levels of glutathione and rapid oxidation of epinephrine in vitro—which prompted the search for taraxein and directed work on its isolation toward the ceruloplasmin fraction of serum (15, 16, 17), have since been controverted by data reported by the same group, as well as by others and have been regarded by most workers as spurious or at least unrelated in any direct way to the schizophrenic process (14, 31). This, in itself, does not preclude the possible validity of the taraxein phenomenon, since bona fide discoveries have occasionally been made on the basis of erroneous leads; it does, however, reduce the probability of its occurrence from that involved in a logical interrelationship of sequential proven steps to the extremely small chance of selecting this particular and heretofore unknown substance from the thousands of substances which occur in blood and which might have been chosen.

One attempt by Robins, Smith, and Lowe (32) to confirm the Tulane findings, in tests in which they used comparable numbers and types of subjects and at least equally rigorous controls, was quite unsuccessful. In 20 subjects who at different times received saline or extracts of blood from normal or schizophrenic donors, prepared according to the method for preparing taraxein, there were only five instances of mental or behavioral disturbances, resembling those cited in the original report on taraxein, and these occurred with equal frequency following the administration of saline, extracts of normal plasma, or taraxein. It is easy to dismiss the negative findings with taraxein on the basis of the difficulty of reproducing exactly the 29 steps described in its preparation; it is considerably more difficult to dismiss the observation that a few subjects who received only saline or normal blood extract developed psychotic manifestations similar to those reported with taraxein.

During the preliminary investigations it was stated, on the basis of unpublished studies (5), that taraxein was qualitatively different from ceruloplasmin. A physicochemical or other objective characterization of taraxein would do much to dispel some of the confusion regarding its nature. Is it possible, for example, that taraxein is, in fact, ceruloplasmin but ceruloplasmin that derives its special properties from the psychosocial characteristics of the situation in which it has been tested? This question was raised more than a year ago (33), and since then additional evidence has become available which tends to support it. This is a detailed report from a psychoanalyst at Tulane of the experience of one of his patients who received taraxein (34). Even though a "double blind" procedure was said to have been used, there are enough possibilities for the operation of unconscious bias in this one case, if it is at all typical of the means used to demonstrate the psychotomimetic properties of taraxein, to raise some doubts concerning the validity of these properties. The subject, a psychiatric resident, knew before the in-

jection that he was to get either saline or a potent sample of taraxein which had made a monkey catatonic for several hours. Immediately following the injection he noted venous distension, tachycardia, a swollen feeling of the head, and flushing of the head and face, which, a footnote explains, was probably a reaction to the ammonium sulfate in the taraxein solution. Following these symptoms, which the subject could hardly have attributed to saline, there ensued a period of introspective cogitation, with occasional mild mental disturbances quite compatible with the anxiety-producing nature of the situation, with the preparation and cues which the subject had received, and with his anticipation of marked psychotic reactions and not necessarily symptomatic of a chemical toxin at all. The changes were not qualitatively dissimilar to those which Robins and his associates had on a few occasions obtained with their control solutions (32). The report of the observer who injected the material was longer and mentioned more numerous and more bizarre subjective feelings than the subject himself reported. The observer's summary of the subject's reactions as blocking of thought processes, autism, bodily estrangement, and suspiciousness seems incompletely supported by the subject's retrospective report.

The possibility, remote as it may be, that the reported effects of taraxein are the result of a combination of suggestion, nonspecific toxic reactions from ammonium sulfate or other contaminants, and reinforcement of these cues by the unconscious biases of subject and observer through the device of an unstructured interview, is one which has not been ruled out. Hypotheses related to the mechanism of action of this material have moved from concern with abnormalities in the blood to concern with abnormalities in the blood-brain barrier; but the question of whether taraxein acts as a biological cause or as a mediator of some of the symptoms of schizophrenia is by no means resolved. I have already mentioned the only attempt of which I am aware on the part of an independent group to confirm the original results in a controlled series of significant size, and that attempt was unsuccessful.

Serotonin

Serotonin, an important derivative of tryptophan, was first shown to exist in the brain in high concentration by Amin, Crawford, and Gaddum (35). Interest in its possible function in the central nervous system and speculation that it might even be related to schizophrenia were inspired by the findings that certain hallucinogens, notably lysergic acid diethylamide, could, in extremely low concentration, block the effects of serotonin on smooth muscle. Thus, Woolley and Shaw in 1954 (36) wrote: "The demonstrated ability of such agents to antagonize the action of serotonin in smooth muscle and the finding of serotonin in the brain suggest that the mental changes caused by the drugs are the result of a serotonin-deficiency which they induce in the brain. If this be true, then the naturally occurring mental disorders— for example, schizophrenia—which are mimicked by these drugs, may be pictured as being the result of a cerebral serotonin deficiency arising from a metabolic failure. . . ." Simultaneously, in England, Gaddum (37) was speculating, "it is possible that the HT in our brains plays an essential part in keeping us sane and that the effect of LSD is due to its inhibitory action on the HT in the brain." Since that time additional evidence has appeared to strengthen these hypotheses.

Levels of serotonin have been found to be considerably higher in the limbic system and other areas of the brain which appear to be associated with emotional states (38) than elsewhere. Bufotenin, or dimethyl serotonin, extracted from a hallucinogenic snuff of West Indian tribes, was found to have some properties similar to those of lysergic acid diethylamide (39). A major discovery was the finding that the ataractic agent, reserpine, causes a profound and persistent fall in the level of serotonin in the brain (40), a process which more closely parallels the mental effects of reserpine than does its own concentration in the brain. By administration of the precursor, 5-hydroxytryptophan, the levels of serotonin can be markedly elevated in the brain, with behavioral effects described as resembling those of lysergic acid diethylamide (41)—a finding quite at odds with the original hypotheses. On the other hand, administration of this precursor to mental patients, along with a benzyl analog of serotonin to block the peripheral effects of the amine, has been reported, in preliminary trials, to suppress the disease (42), while confusion is compounded by the report that the benzyl analog alone is an effective tranquilizing drug in chronically psychotic patients (43).

Still another bit of evidence supporting the hypotheses of a central function for serotonin was the accidental discovery of toxic psychoses in a certain fraction of tuberculous patients treated with iproniazid (44, 45), which has led to the therapeutic use of this drug in psychic depression. It is known that iproniazid inhibits the action of monoamine oxidase, an enzyme which destroys serotonin, and it has been shown that iproniazid increases the levels of this amine in the brain (41).

There are certain inconsistencies in the data cited above to support the serotonin hypotheses, and no single theory has been found to explain all of the findings, even though full use is made of the concept of "free" and "bound" forms and of the common pharmacological principle of stimulant and depressant effects from the same drug under different circumstances. Moreover, certain weaknesses have appeared in each of the main supporting hypotheses, and these should be noted.

Although the ability of the hallucinogen lysergic acid diethylamide to block effects of serotonin on smooth muscle prompted the development of the hypotheses relating serotonin to mental function or disease, a number of lysergic acid derivatives have since been studied, and the correlation between mental effects and antiserotonin activity in the series as a whole is quite poor (46). One of these compounds is 2-bromo-lysergic acid diethylamide; this has 1.5 times the antiserotonin activity of lysergic acid diethylamide, and through this property, its presence in the brain, after systemic administration, can be demonstrated, but in doses more than 15 times as great it produces none of the mental effects of lysergic acid diethylamide (46). A recent report that, at least in one preparation, lysergic acid diethylamide in low concentration behaves like serotonin and does not antagonize it (47) seems to reconcile some of the empirical inconsistencies in the field, although it is quite at odds with the original hypotheses based on the antagonistic action of lysergic acid diethylamide.

Levels of norepinephrine as well as serotonin are markedly lowered in the brain following administration of reserpine (48). In fact, the brain concentrations of these two amines follow each other so closely in their response to reserpine as to suggest some mechanism common to both and perhaps obtaining as well for other active amines in the brain. In one study, 3,4-dihydroxyphenylalanine, a precursor of norepinephrine, was capable of counteracting the behavioral effects of reserpine, whereas the precursor of serotonin was ineffective (49). Moreover, the effects of iproniazid are not limited to brain serotonin; a comparable effect on norepinephrine has been reported (50), and it is possible that other amines or substances still to be discovered in the brain may be affected by what may be a nonspecific inhibitor of a relatively nonspecific enzyme. Of great interest in this connection are recent studies of Olds and Olds (51) indicating a positive behavioral response for iproniazid injected into the hypothalamus but not for serotonin or norepinephrine.

Chlorpromazine, which has the same therapeutic efficacy as reserpine in disturbed behavior, is apparently able to achieve this action without any known effect on serotonin. In addition, the provocative observation that iproniazid, which elevates serotonin levels in the brain, can cause a toxic psychosis loses some of its impact when one realizes that isoniazid, which does not inhibit monoamine oxidase and can hardly raise the brain serotonin concentration, produces a similar psychosis (45, 52).

It seems reasonable to conclude that the serotonin as well as the norepinephrine in the brain have some important functions there, and the evidence in general supports this thesis, even though it also suggests that their roles still remain to be defined.

If the picture of the role which serotonin plays in central nervous function is blurred, the direct evidence to support the early speculations that it is involved in mental illness is meager and contradictory. From all of the evidence cited above, one could find a basis for predicting that in schizophrenia the serotonin levels in the brain, if they are altered at all, should be quite low or quite high. Results confirming both predictions have been reported.

The urinary excretion of 5-hydroxyindoleacetic acid has been used as an indicator of the portion of ingested tryptophan which is metabolized through serotonin to form that end product. Although excretion of 5-hydroxyindoleacetic acid is normal in schizophrenic patients under ordinary circumstances (53), it may be altered by challenging the metabolic systems with large doses of tryptophan. Zeller and his associates have reported a failure on the part of schizophrenics, under these circumstances, to increase their output of 5-hydroxyindoleacetic acid, while nonpsychic controls double theirs (54). Banerjee and Agarwal, on the other hand, have reported exactly the opposite results; in their study it was the schizophrenics who doubled their output of the serotonin end product, while the output of the controls remained unchanged (55).

Kopin, of our laboratory, has had the opportunity to perform a similar study on schizophrenics and normal controls maintained on a good and reasonably controlled diet and given no drugs. In each group there was a slightly greater than twofold increase in output of 5-hydroxyindoleacetic acid following a tryptophan load, and there was no significant deviation from this pattern in any single case (56).

That the heuristic speculations of Woolley and Shaw, and of Gaddum, have not yet been established does not mean that they are invalid. The widespread experimental activity which they stimulated has broadened and deepened our knowledge of the metabolism and pharmacology of serotonin and of its effects on behavior and may lead the way to definitive evaluation of its possible role in normal and pathological states.

Genetics and Schizophrenic Disorders

Many of the current hypotheses concerning the schizophrenia complex are original and attractive even though, up to this time, evidence directly implicating any one of them in the disease itself is hardly compelling. There is, nevertheless, cogent evidence that is responsible to a large extent for the present reawakening of the long dormant biochemical thinking in this area and sufficiently convincing to promote its continued development. Genetic studies have recently assumed such a role, and it appears worth while briefly to review them in the present context.

In earlier studies on large populations, a remarkable correlation was reported between the incidence of schizophrenia and the degree of consanguinity in relatives of known schizophrenics (57). These findings were not conclusive, however, since the influence of socioenvironmental factors was not controlled. Better evidence is obtained from the examination of the co-twins and siblings of schizophrenics; a number of such studies have been completed and are summarized in Table 1 (57–59). The concordance rate for schizophrenia is extremely high for monozygotic twins in all the studies, while that for dizygotic twins is low and not significantly different from that in siblings, to which, of course, dizygotic twins are quite comparable genetically. Even these studies, however, are not completely free from possible sources of error, and this makes it difficult to arrive at a definitive conclusion regarding the role of genetic factors in this disease. One cannot assume that environmental similarities and mutual interactions in identical twins, who are always of the same sex and whose striking physical congruence is often accentuated by parental attitudes, play an insignificant role in the high concordance rate of schizophrenia in this group. This factor could be controlled by a study of twins separated at birth (of such twins no statistically valid series has yet been compiled) or by a comparison of the concordance rates in monozygotic twins and in dizygotic twins whose zygosity had been mistakenly evaluated by the twins themselves and by their parents and associates. Another possible means of better controlling the environmental variables would be to make a careful study of schizophrenia in adopted children, with comparison of the incidence in blood relatives and in foster relatives. Perhaps only a survey on a national scale would provide the requisite numbers of cases for any of these studies.

A less satisfactory resolution of this problem can be obtained by an appraisal of environmental similarities in normal fraternal and identical twins. Such a study, on over 100 specific aspects of the environment, has been made (60), and I have assembled the results into a rough index of environmental similarity (Table 2). Although a difference is apparent, in the crude measurement of environmental congruence, between identical and fraternal twins of like sex, it is not statistically significant and can account for only a small fraction of the large difference in concordance with respect to schizophrenia between these types of twins. On the other hand, there is a highly significant difference in environmental similarity between fraternal twins of like and unlike sex which is sufficient to account for the difference in concordance with respect to schizophrenic psychosis between them, for which, of course, there is no tenable genetic explanation.

Two recent reports have been used, but by no means conclusively, in support of the position that too much significance has been attached to environmental factors as determining causes in this disease group. Chapman (61), reporting a case of concordant early infantile autism in identical twins, points

out that this disorder has never been reported as concordant in fraternal twins, whereas it has been described in three sets of identical twins. Since fraternal twins occur nearly three times as frequently as identical twins, the evidence cited is suggested, in spite of the small numbers involved; furthermore, the disease may develop before the personal identifications and interactions peculiar to monozygotic twins have had much chance to operate. Another interesting finding in over 150 families with a single schizophrenic member is that no ordinal position in the family appears to carry specific vulnerability to schizophrenia (62)—a finding completely compatible with genetic theory but more difficult to reconcile with theories of environmental etiology if the assumption is correct that different positions within the family are subject to varying degrees of stress. Of course one may argue quite properly that schizophrenogenic stress exists and can be evaluated only in terms of the reaction between each individual and his own environment, so that any position on a social, economic, occupational, or birth-order scale may be associated with greatly different degrees of stress for different individuals.

Another possible source of error in the twin studies which have been reported is the personal bias of the investigators who made the judgment of zygosity and the diagnosis of schizophrenia in the co-twins. Until a more definitive study is carried out in which these judgments are made independently, a rough evaluation is possible, at least for the diagnosis of schizophrenia, if not for zygosity, on the basis of diagnoses arrived at in the various hospitals to which the co-twins may have been admitted before or irrespective of their involvement in the study—diagnoses which are not likely to have been contaminated by knowledge about their zygosity. Kallmann has been kind enough to review the material collected in his 1946–49 survey from that point of view. Of 174 monozygotic co-twins of schizophrenic index cases, 103, or 59 percent, had been diagnosed schizophrenic by Kallmann, while 87, or 50 percent, had received a psychiatric hospital diagnosis of schizophrenia prior to any examination made by him. On the other hand, he had made the diagnosis of schizophrenia in 47, or 9.1 percent, of 517 dizygotic co-twins as compared to a hospital diagnosis in 31, or 6 percent. Although the concordance rates based only on hospital diagnoses are lower in both types of twins, for obvious reasons, the striking difference between the two concordance rates remains. Slater (59) has published individual protocols of his cases from which I have made judgments of zygosity and schizophrenia. Of 21 pairs of twins who could be considered definitely uniovular, 15, or 75 percent, were concordant with respect to the simple criterion of admission to a mental hospital, whereas in only 12, or 10.3 percent, of 116 binovular or questionably binovular pairs was there a history of the co-twin's having been admitted to a mental hospital for any psychosis. On the basis of this analysis of the two most recent series, it seems that only a small component of the great difference in concordance rates reported for schizophrenia between uniovular and binovular twins can be attributed to the operation of personal bias in the diagnosis of the disease in the co-twin.

Even the most uncritical acceptance of all the genetic data, however, cannot lead to the conclusion that the schizophrenic illnesses are the result of genetic factors alone. In 14 to 30 percent of the cases in which schizophrenia occurs in one of a pair of monozygotic twins, the genetically identical partner is found to be free of the disorder (Table 1). Attention has already been called (Table 2) to the higher concordance with respect to schizophrenia and the greater environmental similarities in like-sexed fraternal twins or siblings than in those of unlike sex, and from the same source (57) a difference in concordance is reported between monozygotic twins separated some years before the study (77.6 percent) as opposed to those not separated (91.5 percent). Neither of these observations is compatible with a purely genetic etiology of the disease, and both suggest the operation of environmental factors. Rosenthal (63) and Jackson (64) have pointed out the striking preponderance of female over male pairs concordant for schizophrenia in all of the reported series, whether they be monozygotic or dizygotic twins, siblings, or parent-child pairs. If sampling errors resulting from the greater mobility of males are excluded and the observations are taken as a reflection of the true incidence of this phenomenon, several explanations for it on the basis of social interaction can be given, but none based on purely genetic grounds, unless sex linkage is invoked, for which there is no other evidence.

Clausen has critically reviewed the extensive literature supporting the importance of environmental factors in the etiology of schizophrenic disorders (65). The evidence there seems quite as suggestive as the genetic evidence but by no means more conclusive, since few studies in either field have been completely objective or adequately controlled.

It is both interesting and important to note that even if the conclusions of both the genetic and the environmental approaches to the etiology of schizophrenic psychoses are accepted uncritically, they are not mutually exclusive.

Both are compatible with the hypothesis that this group of diseases results from the operation of socioenvironmental factors on some hereditary predisposition, or from an interaction of the two, each being necessary but neither alone sufficient. An excellent example of such a relationship is seen in tuberculosis, where the importance of the environment microbial factor is undisputed and where, as Lurie (66) has shown, genetic susceptibility is likewise important; a population sufficiently heterogeneous with respect to susceptibility and exposure to tuberculosis yields results in contingency and twin studies (67) which, before the discovery of the tubercle bacillus, could casily have been used to prove a primary genetic cause—almost as convincingly as the results of similar studies have been used to prove such a cause in schizophrenia. Interestingly enough, studies of tuberculosis made from the socioenvironmental point of view would obviously provide data offering equally convincing proof that exogenous, social, and economic factors play a part. One hypothesis with respect to the schizophrenic psychoses which remains compatible with all the evidence from the genetic as well as the psychosocial disciplines is that these disorders, like tuberculosis, require the operation of environmental factors upon a genetically determined predisposition.

RÉSUMÉ

Although the evidence for genetic and therefore biological factors as important and necessary components in the etiology of many or all of the schizophrenias is quite compelling, the sign-posts pointing the way to their discovery are at present quite blurred and, to me at least, illegible.

Genetic factors may operate through some ubiquitous enzyme system to effect general changes in one or another metabolic pathway—changes detectable through studies of blood or urine—and it is to be hoped that the currently active search in these areas will continue.

It is at least equally possible, however, that these genetic factors may operate only through enzymes or metabolic processes peculiar to or confined within the brain, or even within extremely localized areas of the brain. We are in need of new hypotheses such as those of Elkes (68) and many already discussed. In this connection, gamma-amino-butyric acid appears to be just as interesting a substance about which to construct working hypotheses as are the catechols or the indoles. It has been isolated only from nervous tissue, and its metabolism in such tissue has been investigated in some detail (69), while its neurophysiological properties appear to be better defined than are those of the other two groups (70); in addition, its inhibitory properties may have special relevance to diseases where a failure in central inhibition seems to be involved.

Amphetamine possesses remarkable psychotomimetic properties which should not be overlooked. Its ability to produce a clinical syndrome often indistinguishable from schizophrenia (71) and the possible relation of amphetamine to the naturally occurring catechol amines make it at least as interesting as lysergic acid diethylamide.

In addition to techniques at present available in neurochemistry, neurophysiology, and behavioral pharmacology, the development of new methods designed to yield information on processes occurring within the psychotic brain will be needed before our explorations in this field have been exhausted.

But the biochemist must not lose sight of the possibility, which is certainly as great as any of the others, that the genetic factors in schizophrenia operate to

Table 1
Concordance Rates for Schizophrenia Found in Studies of Twins

Investigator	Number of pairs		Concordance rate* (%)	
	Dizygotic	Monozygotic	Dizygotic	Monozygotic
Luxenburger (1928)	48	17	2	59 (67)
Rosanoff et al. (1934)	101	41	10	61
Kallmann (1946)	517	174	10 (15)	69 (86)
Slater (1953)	115	41	11 (14)	68 (76)

* Figures in parentheses indicate rate after correction for the chance that a co-twin, normal at the time of observation, may develop the disease later.

determine inappropriate interconnections or interaction between chemically normal components of the brain; if that should prove to be the case, the physiological psychologist, the neurophysiologist, or the anatomist is likely to find meaningful information long before the biochemist does. It would take many biochemists a long time to find a noisy circuit in a radio receiver if they restricted themselves to chemical techniques.

These possibilities are mentioned only to indicate how large is the haystack in which we are searching for the needle; one cannot avoid a feeling of humility when one realizes how slight the chance is that any one of us has already found it, or will find it in a relatively short time.

That is no cause for discouragement, however. It is not necessary that one be convinced of the truth of a particular hypothesis to justify devoting one's energies to testing it. It is enough that one regard it as worth testing, and that the tools be adequate. Modern biochemistry, with its wealth of new knowledge of intermediary metabolism and its array of new techniques for the separation and identification of compounds and the tracing of their metabolic pathways, has provided the biologist interested in mental illness with an armamentarium which his predecessor of only a generation ago could hardly have envisioned. If he chooses from among the approaches which may lead to a definition of the biological factors in schizophrenia those

Table 2
Environmental Factors in Studies of Schizophrenia in Twins

Sex	Environmental similarity in normal twins* (%)	Number of pairs	Concordance with respect to schizophrenia† (%)	Number of pairs
Identical twins				
Same	61	70	86	174
Fraternal twins				
Same	53	69	18	296
Different	26	55	10	221
Siblings				
Same			16	
Different			12	

* Estimated from data of P. T. Wilson (1934).
† From data of F. J. Kallmann (1946).

which will in any case lead to a better understanding of the nervous system and of thought processes and behavior, the present surge of enthusiasm will not have been misdirected.

REFERENCES AND NOTES

1. S. Akerfeldt, *Science* 125, 117 (1957).
2. F. A. Gibbs, Ed., *Blood Tests in Mental Illness* (Brain Research Foundation, Chicago, 1957).
3. C. G. Holmberg and C. B. Laurell, *Scand. J. Clin. & Lab. Invest.* 3, 103 (1951).
4. B. E. Leach and R. G. Heath, *A.M.A. Arch. Neurol. Psychiat.* 76, 444 (1956).
5. B. E. Leach, M. Cohen, R. C. Heath, S. Martens, *ibid.* 76, 635 (1956).
6. W. Keup, *Monatsschr. Psychiat. Neurol.* 128, 56 (1954).
7. C. G. Holmberg and C. B. Laurell, *Acta Chem. Scand.* 2, 550 (1948).
8. H. Markowitz, C. J. Gubler, J. P. Mahoney, G. E. Cartwright, M. M. Wintrobe, *J. Clin. Invest.* 34, 1498 (1955).
9. L. G. Abood, F. A. Gibbs, E. Gibbs, *A.M.A. Arch. Neurol. Psychiat.* 17, 643 (1957).
10. R. K. McDonald, "Plasma ceruloplasmin and ascorbic acid levels in schizophrenia," paper presented at the annual meeting of the American Psychiatric Association, Chicago, Ill., 1957.
11. I. H. Scheinberg, A. G. Morell, R. S. Harris, A. Berger, *Science* 126, 925 (1957); M. K. Horwitt, B. J. Meyer, A. C. Meyer, C. C. Harvey, D. Haffron, *A.M.A. Arch. Neurol. Psychiat.* 78, 275 (1957); C. E. Frohman, M. Goodman, E. D. Luby, P. G. S. Beckett, R. Senf, *ibid.* 79, 730 (1958); M. H. Aprison and H. J. Grosz, *ibid.* 79, 575 (1958).
12. M. H. Aprison and A. L. Drew, *Science* 127, 758 (1958).
13. A. M. Ostfeld, L. G. Abood, D. A. Marcus, *A.M.A. Arch. Neurol. Psychiat.* 79, 317 (1958).
14. C. Angel, B. E. Leach, S. Martens, M. Cohen, R. G. Heath, *ibid.* 79, 500 (1957).
15. R. G. Heath, S. Martens, B. E. Leach, M. Cohen, C. A. Feigley, *Am. J. Psychiat.* 114, 917 (1958).
16. R. G. Heath, B. E. Leach, L. W. Byers, S. Martens, C. A. Feigley, *ibid.* 114, 683 (1958).
17. R. G. Heath, S. Martens, B. E. Leach, M. Cohen, C. Angel, *ibid.* 114, 14 (1957).
18. R. Fischer, *Proc. Intern. Physiol. Congr., 19th Congr.* (1953), pp. 350–351.
19. F. Georgi, H. P. Rieder, R. Weber, *Science* 120, 504 (1954).
20. C. B. Edisen, *Diseases of Nervous System* 17, 77 (1956).
21. S. Fedoroff, *Anat. Record* 121, 394 (1955).
22. ——— and A. Hoffer, *J. Nervous Mental Disease* 124, 396 (1956).
23. J. Wada, *Proc. Soc. Biol. Psychiatrists, 12th Ann. Conv.* (1957).
24. H. P. Rieder, *Psychiat. et Neurol.* 134, 378 (1957).
25. K. Smith and A. C. Moody, *Diseases of Nervous System* 17, 327 (1956).
26. A. K. Shapiro, *J. Nervous Mental Disease* 123, 65 (1956).
27. C. A. Winter and L. Flataker, *Proc. Soc. Biol. Psychiatrists, 12th Ann. Conv.* (1957).
28. ———, *A.M.A. Arch. Neurol. Psychiat.* 80, 441 (1958).
29. C. Kornetsky, personal communication; L. Ghent and A. M. Freedman, *Am. J. Psychiat.* 115, 465 (1958).
30. B. Minz and E. J. Walaszek, *Compt. rend.* 244, 1974 (1957).
31. R. K. McDonald, *J. Chronic Diseases* 8, 366 (1958); A. J. Barak, F. L. Humoller, J. D. Stevens, *A.M.A. Arch. Neurol. Psychiat.* 80, 237 (1958).
32. E. Robins, K. Smith, I. P. Lowe, in "Neuropharmacology," *Trans. Josiah Macy, Jr. Foundation, 4th Conf.* (1957).
33. S. S. Kety, in *ibid.* (1957).
34. H. I. Lief, *A.M.A. Arch. Neurol. Psychiat.* 78, 624 (1957).
35. A. H. Amin, T. B. B. Crawford, J. H. Gaddum. *J. Physiol.* (London) 126, 596 (1954).
36. D. W. Woolley and E. Shaw, *Science* 119, 587 (1954).
37. J. H. Gaddum, in *Ciba Foundation Symposium on Hypertension* (Little, Brown, Boston, 1954).

38. D. F. Bogdanski, H. Weissbach, S. Udenfriend, *J. Neurochem.* 1, 272 (1957); M. K. Passonen, P. D. MacLean, N. J. Giarman, *ibid.* 1, 326 (1957).

39. E. V. Evarts, *A.M.A. Arch. Neurol. Psychiat.* 75, 49 (1956); H. D. Fabing and J. R. Hawkins, *Science* 123, 886 (1956).

40. P. A. Shore, A. Pletscher, E. G. Tomich, A. Carlsson, R. Kuntzman, B. B. Brodie, *Ann. N.Y. Acad. Sci.* 66, 609 (1957).

41. S. Udenfriend, H. Weissbach, D. F. Bogdanski, *ibid.* 66, 602 (1957).

42. D. W. Woolley, *Science* 125, 752 (1957).

43. L. H. Rudy, E. Costa, F. Rinaldi, H. E. Himwich, *J. Nervous Mental Disease* 126, 284 (1958).

44. G. E. Crane, *ibid.* 124, 322 (1956).

45. H. Pleasure, *A.M.A. Arch. Neurol. Psychiat.* 72, 313 (1954).

46. E. Rothlin, *Ann. N.Y. Acad. Sci.* 66, 668 (1957).

47. J. H. Welsh and A. C. McCoy, *Science* 125, 348 (1957).

48. M. Holzbauer and M. Vogt, *J. Neurochem.* 1, 8 (1956); M. Vogt, in *Metabolism of the Nervous System,* D. Richter, Ed. (Pergamon, London, 1957), pp. 553–565.

49. A. Carlsson, M. Lindqvist, T. Magnusson, *Nature* 180, 1200 (1957).

50. S. Spector, D. Prockop, P. A. Shore, B. B. Brodie, *Science* 127, 704 (1958).

51. J. Olds and M. E. Olds, *ibid.* 127, 1175 (1958).

52. S. L. O. Jackson, *Brit. Med. J.* 2, 743 (1957).

53. G. A. Buscaino and L. Stefanachi, *A.M.A. Neurol Psychiat.* 80, 78 (1958); A. Feldstein, H. Hoagland, H. Freeman, *Science* 128, 358 (1958).

54. E. A. Zeller, J. Bernsohn, W. M. Inskip, J. W. Lauer, *Naturwissenschaften* 44, 427 (1957); J. W. Lauer, W. M. Inskip, J. Bernsohn, E. A. Zeller, *A.M.A. Arch. Neurol. Psychiat.* 80, 122 (1958).

55. S. Banerjee and P. S. Agarwal, *Proc. Soc. Exptl. Biol. Med.* 97, 657 (1958).

56. I. J. Kopin, *Science* 129, 835 (1959).

57. F. J. Kallmann, *Am. J. Psychiat.* 103, 309 (1946).

58. H. Luxenburger, *Z. ges. Neurol. Psychiat.* 116, 297 (1928); A. J. Rosanoff, L. M. Handy, I. R. Plesset, S. Brush, *Am. J. Psychiat.* 91, 247 (1934).

59. E. Slater, "Psychotic and Neurotic Illnesses in Twins," *Medical Research Council Special Report* No. 278 (H.M. Stationery Office, London, 1953).

60. P. T. Wilson, *Human Biology* 6, 324 (1934).

61. A. H. Chapman, *A.M.A. Arch. Neurol. Psychiat.* 78, 621 (1957).

62. H. J. Grosz and I. Miller, *Science* 128, 30 (1958).

63. D. Rosenthal, *J. Nervous Mental Disease,* in press.

64. D. D. Jackson, in "The Study of Schizophrenia," D. D. Jackson, Ed. (Basic Books, New York, in press).

65. J. A. Clausen, *Sociology Today,* Merton, Broom, and Cottrell, Eds. (Basic Books, New York, 1959).

66. M. B. Lurie, S. Abramson, A. Heppelston, *J. Exptl. Med.* 95, 119 (1952).

67. K. Planansky and G. Allen, *Am. J. Human Genet.* 5, 322 (1953).

68. J. Elkes, in "Neuropharmacology," *Trans. Josiah Macy, Jr. Foundation, 3rd Conf.* (1956).

69. E. Roberts and S. Frankel, *J. Biol. Chem.* 187, 55 (1950); E. Roberts, M. Rothstein, C. F. Baxter, *Proc. Soc. Exptl. Biol. Med.* 97, 796 (1958).

70. D. P. Purpura, M. Girardo, H. Grundfest, *Science* 125, 1200 (1957); K. Iwama and H. H. Jasper, *J. Physiol. (London)* 138, 365 (1957).

71. P. H. Connell, *Biochem. J.* 65, 7p (1957).

Of Flies and Men[1]

Theodosius Dobzhansky

One of the assertions which have gained acceptance by dint of frequent repetition is that science is competent to deal only with what recurs, returns, repeats itself. To study something scientifically, this something must be made representative of a class, group, or assemblage. A single *Drosophila* fly is of no interest whatsoever. A fly may merit some attention only if it is taken as a representative of its species. An individual person may, to be sure, merit attention. However, it is allegedly not in the province of science, but of insight, empathy, art, and literature to study and understand a person in his uniqueness.

I wish to challenge this view. Individuality, uniqueness, is not outside the competence of science. It may, in fact it must, be understood scientifically. In particular, the science of genetics investigates individuality and its causes. The singularity of the human self becomes comprehensible in the light of genetics. You may, of course, object that what science comprehends is not really a singularity but a plurality of singularities. However, an artist, no less than a biologist, becomes aware of the plurality because he has observed some singularities.

In the main, genetics is a study of differences among living beings. Genetics would be superfluous if all living beings were exactly alike. If all members of a species were exactly alike genetics could do very little. Since Mendel, the most powerful method of genetics is to observe differences among individuals in the progenies of parents which differed in some ways. Heredity and variation are the two sides of the same coin. Geneticists are always on the lookout for genetic diversity. Variety is said to be the spice of life. It is a staple necessity to geneticists. (This applies, of course, to Mendelian genetics proper. The great discoveries of the role of chromosomes in the development, and the relationships between DNA, RNA, and protein synthesis could conceivably have been made even if Mendel's laws remained unknown.)

That every person differs from every other person is so obvious that this is taken usually for granted. What continues controversial is to what extent the human differences are due to genetic and in what measure to environmental variations. Though in a new guise, the old nature-nurture problem is still with us. Now, the individuality of flies is rather less evident than human individuality. I do not claim to recognize every *Drosophila* by her face. The drosophiline individuality is nevertheless easier to analyze, and this analysis helps to throw some needed light on human individuality.

The theory of genetic individuality is simple enough. It stems directly from Mendel's second law, the law of independent assortment. An individual heter-

Reprinted from *American Psychologist*, 1967, vol. 22, pp. 41–48 with the permission of the American Psychological Association and the author.

[1] Invited address presented at American Psychological Association, New York, September 1966. Some of the experimental work referred to in the text supported under Contract No. AT-(30-1)-3096, United States Atomic Energy Commission.

ozygous for n genes has the potentiality of producing 2^n genetically different kinds of sex cells. Two parents, each heterozygous for the same n genes, can give rise to 3^n genotypes among the progeny, and parents heterozygous each for n different genes may produce 4^n genotypes. To be sure, not all of these genotypes are equally probable, because the linkage of genes in the same chromosome limits their independent assortment. Linkage disequilibrium delays but does not prevent eventual realization of the genetic variety. More important is the problem how large is n, that is, for how many genes an average individual is heterozygous, or how many genes are represented each by two or more variants in the populations of a species, such as man or a *Drosophila*.

The disagreement among geneticists on this point is rife. Those who espouse the classical theory of population structure believe that most genes are uniform, not only in all individuals of a species but even in different species not too remote in the biological system. The unfixed genes are a minority, perhaps of the order of some tens. Moreover, among the unfixed genes one variant, one allele, is normal and adaptively superior, while others are inferior and are maintained in populations by recurrent mutation. Though adherents of the classical theory are reluctant to admit this, the theory is a product of typological thinking. Lurking behind the facade of the variability, they like to envisage the Platonic archetype of the Normal Man, homozygous for all good with no bad genes.

The balance theory of population structure would assume numbers of variable genes of the order of hundreds, perhaps even thousands. An appreciable part of this variety is maintained in populations by several kinds of balancing natural selection. The kind most often discussed is the heterotic selection, operating be-

cause of hybrid vigor. There are, indeed, genetic variants which are adaptively favorable when heterozygous and unfavorable when homozygous. The gene which in homozygous condition causes sickle-cell anemia in man is a classical example; in heterozygous condition it confers a relative immunity to *falciparum* malaria. Perhaps even more important in evolution is diversifying natural selection. This can be explained most simply by pointing out that every living species faces not just one environment but a variety of environments. Human environments are certainly diverse, and moreover the diversity is growing. It is improbable that genes can be found to show optimal performance in all environments. More likely, different genes will be relatively more adaptive in different environments. Genetic variety is a method to cope with variety of environments.

Theoretical arguments cannot settle the questions for how many genes is an average individual heterozygous, and what proportion of the genes are represented by different alleles in different individuals of a species. Geneticists are busy working on these matters. I can cite here only the brilliant work of Lewontin and Hubby (1966), of the University of Chicago, as an example. Since the total number of genes is unknown, but is surely too large to have the whole set examined one by one, Lewontin and Hubby have decided to study what they believe is a random sample of genes. They chose a battery of enzymes that can be detected by electrophoresis in single individuals of the fly, *Drosophila pseudoobscura*. Some of these enzymes did and others did not show detectable genetic variations. The authors, after making a thorough examination of the possible biases and pitfalls, came to the conclusion that an individual fly was heterozygous for on the average between 10% and 15% of the genes in a sex cell can hardly be less than 10,000;

an average fly may, then, be heterozygous for a number of genes of the order of 1,000.

Do these results have any bearing on man? Although man is not an overgrown *Drosophila*, he must have as many or more genes than *Drosophila* does. If the degree of heterozygosity in man is anything like it is in *Drosophila*, brothers or sisters are quite unlikely to inherit from their parents the same genes. The likelihood that any two unrelated persons are genetically identical is practically nil. Only identical twins may be genetically identical, since they arise by asexual division of a sexually produced fertilized egg. Even there the possibility of mutation and of cytoplasmic difference must be reckoned with. Human nature is, then, not unitary but multiform; the number of human natures is almost as great as the number of humans. Every person is unique, unprecedented, and unrepeatable.

The demonstration of the genetic uniqueness of individuals only opens, rather than solves, the problem as far as behavioral and social sciences are concerned. There seems little point in belaboring the truism that behavior as such is not inherited. Only genes can be inherited, in the sense of being handed down from parents to offspring. Even so, I have mostly division products, true copies of the genes I have inherited from my parents, rather than these genes themselves. The skin color is not inherited either, because the skin pigment is not carried in the sex cells. However, I am yet to meet anybody who would contend that one's genes have nothing to do with one's skin color. Human, as well as animal, behavior is the outcome of a process of development in which the genes and the environment are components of a system of feedback relationships. The same statement can be made equally validly with respect to one's skin color, the shape of one's head, blood chemistry,

and somatic, metabolic, and mental diseases.

There are some authors who go so far as to question the existence of problems of genetics of behavior, distinct from genetics of anything else. They are right only inasmuch as there is not likely to exist a special brand of DNA concerned with behavior, different from that in other kinds of genes; moreover there are no genes "for" behavior, as there are no genes "for" the shape of one's nose. The problem is more subtle. It is the problem, or rather problems, of the genetic architecture of behavioral differences. We want to know how many genes are usually involved in such differences, the magnitude of their effects, the nature of their interactions, the parts played by mutation pressure, hybrid vigor, environmental heterogeneities, and by all forms of natural selection in the formation, in maintenance, and in normal and pathological variations of behavior. In this sense, the genetics and the evolution of behavior may well be different from, let us say, the genetics and the evolution of blood chemistry, or of metabolism, or of chromosomal polymorphism, or of concealing colorations, or mimetic resemblances. And in this sense, which is the only meaningful sense, the genetics of behavior, especially the experimental genetics of behavior, is not yet even a fledgling field, although it has recently begun to chirp rather lively.

In this article I can discuss only one example of a study of genetics of behavior, that made by my colleague B. Spassky and myself on phototaxis and geotaxis in *Drosophila pseudoobscura*. Hirsch and his students (Erlenmeyer-Kimling, Hirsch, & Weiss, 1962; Hirsch, 1962; Hirsch & Erlenmeyer-Kimling, 1962) have constructed a classification maze (Figure 1), and selected populations of *Drosophila melanogaster* which were clearly positively and others nega-

Figure 1 The classification maze for selection of *Drosophila* flies for geotactic behavior. (The starting tube is on the right. The terminal tubes are on the left, No. 1 being the uppermost, and No. 16 the lowermost.)

tively geotactic in their behavior. They showed furthermore that the genetic basis of this behavior was polygenic, the three large pairs of chromosomes all influencing the result. Hadler (1964a, 1964b) made a similar maze for selection for phototaxis (Figure 2), and succeeded in obtaining positively and negatively phototactic strains of *Drosophila melanogaster*. Dobzhansky and Spassky (1962), using Hirsch's maze, selected positively and negatively geotactic strains of *Drosophila pseudoobscura*. Their starting population was polymorphic for some inverted sections in the third chromosomes, and one of the variant chromosomes proved to favor negative geotaxis, while chromosomal heterozygosis favored positive geotaxis.

The results of newer experiments on selection for positive and negative phototaxis and geotaxis in *Drosophila pseudoobscura* are presented in Figures 3 and 4. The ordinates show the phototactic or the geotactic scores, i.e., the averages of the 16 terminal tubes of the mazes into which the flies distribute themselves. On the geotaxis maze the tube No. 1 is the uppermost and No. 16 the lowermost, on the phototaxis maze No. 1 is reached by 15 choices of dark passages and No. 16 by 15 choices of light passages. The selection is made by running through the maze 300 females or 300 males; the 25 most positive, or most negative, individuals of each sex are selected to be the parents of the next generation. The initial populations in our experiments were photo- and geotactically neutral on the average. Or, to be more precise, these initial populations had positive, neutral, and negative individuals in such proportions that the average scores were between 8 and 9 (an average of 8.5 is exact neutrality). After 15 generations of selection, the positively phototactic line had average scores 13.4 and 14.5 for females and males respectively, the negatively phototactic line 2.4 and 3.1, the positively geotactic line 12.1 and 12.5, and the negatively geotactic line 4.7 and 6.1. The frequency distributions overlap only slightly in the middle, i.e., only few flies of the selected strains end up in the terminal tubes Nos. 8 and 9.

Is it, then, the heredity which makes a *Drosophila* walk towards lights or darkness, climb up or descend? Even with flies, not only with men, the situation is more complex than that. From the effects of the selection in the first generation, the heritability of the photo- and geotactic responses can be calculated to lie between .15 and .20. This is somewhat oversimplifying the issue, but one can say that, as a first approximation, the genetic component of the behavior of the fly in our mazes is only 15% to 20%,

Figure 2 The classification maze for selection of *Drosophila* flies for phototactic behavior. (The starting tube is on the lower left. The terminal tube No. 1, shown on the upper left, is reached by 15 dark passages. The terminal tube No. 16, at the extreme right, is reached by 15 light passages.)

while random chance and environment is responsible for 80% to 85%. Nor is this all. Taking the data for the 15 generations of selection as a whole, we can compute the so-called realized heritability, that is to say the efficiency of the response to the selection. This turns out to be very small, only about 9% for the phototaxis, and only about 3% for the geotaxis. In other words, a prediction of what the selection could accomplish in 15 generations, based on the initial heritability figure, would be a gross overestimate. There are several factors responsible for this situation, among which I shall single out just one, which seems most interesting.

In our first experiments (Dobzhansky & Spassky, 1962) we made selection in three populations of *Drosophila pseudoobscura* during 18 generations for positive and for negative geotaxis. After the positive and the negative populations have diverged about as much as the populations on Figure 4, the populations were split each into two. In one member of each pair the selection was reversed, i.e., a population formerly selected for the positive was now selected for a negative geotaxis, and vice versa. In another subpopulation the selection was relaxed, i.e., the subpopulation was propagated without selecting either the positive or the negative individuals. The selective gains obtained through 18 generations of the original selection were almost erased in

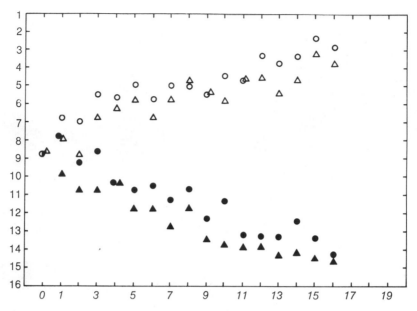

Figure 3 Selection for negative (light symbols) and positive (dark symbols) phototaxis. (Circles—females, triangles—males. Abscissa—generations of selection, ordinate—the phototactic score.)

6 generations of the reverse selection. The simple relaxation of the selection resulted in a loss of about half of the selection gains.

A partial, or even complete, loss upon abandonment of selection of what had been gained by previous selection is a phenomenon well known to breeders of agricultural plants and animals. Lerner (1954) has called this the genetic homeostasis. Very simply, the average height, weight, speed of maturation, and many other characteristics of a population which are determined by cooperation of numerous polygenes, are held by natural selection at levels near optimal for the population in the environments in which that population usually lives. When a breeder selects toward higher or toward lower levels of certain characteristics, he does so for his benefit, not necessarily for the benefit of the animal or the plant in its original environments. In other words, the artificial selection is often pitted against natural selection. As the artificial selection progresses it becomes more and more frustrated by natural selection. When the artificial selection is stopped, natural selection is given an opportunity to undo what the artificial one had gained; and reverse selection is highly effective because the artificial and the natural selections then work in the same direction, in alliance rather than in opposition.

Biologically, adaptively, this is an excellent strategy for evolution to follow. It combines high adaptedness to the existing environmental conditions with high adaptability to environmental changes. This strategy is, however, not at all what the classical theory of genetic population structure envisages. If the environment were uniform, constant, and favoring phototactically and geotactically neutral *Drosophilae*, then the simplest solution of the adaptive problem would seem to be to make all members of the species homozygous for the genes favoring photo- and geotactic neutrality. "Normal" or "typical" flies would then be neutral, and positive and negative ones would be abnormal or atypical. But this is not what is observed. The populations, though neutral on the average, contain also positive and negative genetic variants.

The availability in the populations of this genetic variance confers upon them evolutionary plasticity. A change in the environment that favors a positive or a negative photo- or geotaxis makes the population respond rapidly by adaptive genetic changes. Such responses might occur also in a genetically uniform and homozygous population, but they would be much slower. They would have to wait for the occurrence of mutations. These mutations would have to produce genetic variants which were unfavorable in the old but adaptive in the new environments. The rapidity of the genetic adjustment is, however, not the whole story.

A genetically polymorphic population not only responds adaptively to environmental challenges, but in so doing it does not, so to speak, burn the bridges for retreat. It is hedged against the contingency that the environmental change to which it is adapting may only be a temporary one. If it is indeed temporary, and the original environment returns, the population can readapt itself speedily, by returning to its former genetic composition.

And yet genetic homeostasis does not stand in the way of permanent, irreversible, progressive evolutionary changes. If a new environment or a new way of life endures, a new genetic system becomes stabilized. This genetic system will be buffered against the vagaries of the new environments, but no longer able to retrace its steps to the conditions of the bygone age. If these conditions returned, the species would probably become adapted to them in some new way. One of the most interesting lessons that evolu-

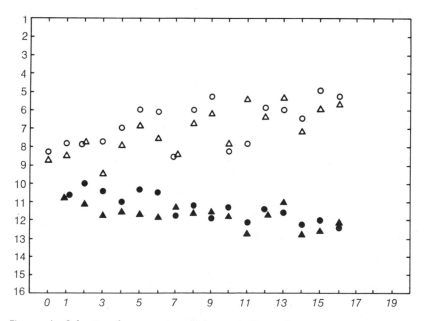

Figure 4 Selection for negative (light symbols) and positive (dark symbols) geotaxis. (Circles—females, triangles—males. Abscissa—generations of selection, ordinate—the geotactic score.)

tionary biology teaches us is that there may be many more than a single method to eke out a living from an environment. Major evolutionary changes are irreversible and unrepeatable.

This point is so central that it must be reiterated: Man is not just an overgrown *Drosophila*. We reject the belief that man is nothing but an animal. Yet he is, among other things, also an animal. Like *Drosophila*, he is a sexually reproducing, outbreeding species, and his populations are abundantly provided with genetic variability. The genetic diversity affects all kinds of traits—morphological, physiological, and behavioral. The discrete, clear-cut, and usually pathological genetic variations of behavior, such as the so-called Mongoloid idiocy or phenylketonuria, need not be considered in the present discussion. The genetic variations among healthy persons are no less interesting, though much harder to study. The same situation exists also in *Drosophila*: sharp, easily distinguishable, and poorly viable mutants of classical genetics, versus slight, quantitative, polygenic variations. The difficulty, in human as well as in *Drosophila* genetics, arises because in the phenotypic variance of the second kind of traits the genetic and the environmental influences are intermingled.

Neither in the most highly selected, nor in the unselected, photo- or geotactic lines of *Drosophila* is the behavior of an individual rigidly determined. We have seen that the heritability of these behavioral traits is rather low. Whether at a given point of the maze an individual climbs upwards or downwards, takes a light or a dark passage, is in part a matter of environment, or simply of chance. The evidence is nevertheless conclusive that the genotype does bias the choices. Some flies are inclined to walk more often upward and others downward. Are the behavioral traits in human populations also

conditioned by genetic variations? I shall be among the first to insist that the evidence is incomplete, and that more data must be collected. Yet the existing evidence, for a variety of traits ranging from IQ measurements to smoking habits, indicates that at least some genetic conditioning is involved, of course relatively more for some traits and less for others.

It is no secret that the study of the genetic conditioning of human behavior is hampered by the emotional reactions which this issue elicits in many people. Some wish to give an aura of scientific respectability to their race and class biases. Differences in material well-being and in social position are represented as just and necessary outcomes of the genetic differences. Others cling obstinately to the old tabula rasa theory. Man is a product of his environment and social conditions, and his genes are simply irrelevant. I submit that, irrespectively of your preconceptions, modern biology makes it necessary to state the problems of genetic conditioning of behavior in terms rather different from the traditional ones. This is because one of the most significant changes in the biological theory in the recent decades has been a shift from typological to populational models and concepts. This conceptual reformation has been discussed with admirable clarity and discernment, particularly by Simpson (1961) and by Mayr (1963), making it possible to state what is essential for us here very briefly.

To a typologist, what is real and important is the species or the race to which an organism belongs. Differences among individuals of the same species and race are, of course, too obvious to be denied. A typologist regards them, however, as merely a kind of troublesome noise in the biological system. He tries, as it were, to recognize the melody obfuscated by the noise; he seeks to identify, classify, and name the species and the races. He hopes that once he can determine to which species and race an individual belongs, that individual is thereby adequately described.

A populationist, on the contrary, regards the individuals and their diversity as the prime observable reality. The biological validity of species and races is not thereby refuted (although some extremists try to do just that, in my opinion ill advisedly). Species and races are, however, derivative from individuals, not the other way around. Species and races are Mendelian populations, reproductive communities of sexually reproducing organisms, forms of adaptive ordering of systems of individuals, evolved because they have made the evolutionary feedback processes between the organisms and their environments most efficient and successful.

Man in the street is a spontaneous typologist. To him, all things which have the same name are therefore alike. All men have the human nature, and an alleged wisdom has it that the human nature does not change. All Negroes are alike because of their negritude, and all Jews are alike because of their jewishness. Populationists affirm that there is no single human nature but as many human natures as there are individuals. Human nature does change. Race differences are compounded of the the same ingredients as differences among individuals which compose a race. In fact, races differ in relative frequencies of genes more often than they differ qualitatively, one race being homozygous for a certain gene and the other lacking it entirely. The extremists who deny that races exist are disappointed typologists who have discovered for themselves the gene gradients between race populations. They fail to understand that such gradients elucidate the nature of race as a biological phenomenon; the facts warrant the conclu-

sion that Platonic types of races do not exist, not that races do not exist.

The typological and populational operational approaches are characteristically different. A race of typology is described in terms of means or averages of height, weight, cephalic index, intelligence, etc. Populationists regard variances at least as important as means. Genetic variance characterizes not only the status but also the evolutionary possibilities of a population. The *Drosophila* populations with which Hirsch and his colleagues as well as ourselves began our experiments were photo- and geotactically neutral on the average. Yet the experiments have shown that the average neutrality did not mean that all individuals were neutral. Selection has attested the presence in the populations of genetic elements for positive and negative photo- and geotaxis. This does not quite mean that the original populations contained individuals as sharply positive and negative as are individuals of the selected strains. Natural and artificial selection do not act as simple sieves which isolate genotypes which were there before selection. Selection creates novelty, because it compounds genotypes the origin of which without selection would be altogether improbable.

All human beings have certain universally recognized rights because they are members of the species Homo sapiens. Members of other species do not have the same rights. Cows are sacred to Hindus, but even in India cows are not treated exactly like humans. An imaginative French writer, Vercors, has given a thought-provoking discussion of legal and other problems that might arise if a hybrid of man and some anthropoid species were produced. Anyway, membership in a group, be that a species or a race, does not define all the characteristics of individuals. The notion that it does is implicit in race pride, exclusiveness, and bias.

Racists busy themselves attempting to scrape up any kind of evidence that Race X has a lower mean IQ, or smaller mean brain volume, or greater emotionality than Race Y. How large is the genetic component in such differences is questionable. The partitioning of the genetic and environmental variances obtained through studies on monozygotic and dizygotic twins cannot be used as a measure of the genetic and environmental components of the group differences. The basic assumption of the twin method is that the environments of the cotwins are uniform. This is obviously not true when different social classes, castes, and races are compared. Even if we had much more complete data on twins than are actually available, this would still leave the question of the magnitude of the genetic component in the group differences wide open. The argument that about one-half of the interracial variance in IQ must be genetic because this appears to be so among cotwins is a misinterpretation when it is not an intentional obfuscation.

To say that we do not know to what extent group differences in psychological traits are genetic is not the same as saying that the genetic component does not exist. It is a challenge to find out. If individuals within populations vary in some character, be that blood grouping, or stature, or intelligence, it is quite unlikely that the population means will be exactly the same. What matters is how great is the intrapopulational variance compared to the interpopulational variance. This is different for different characters. Skin pigmentation is individually variable in probably all races, but the interracial variance is evidently larger. Although precise data are not available, it is at least probable that the relation is reversed for psychological traits. In simplest terms, the brightest individuals in every class, caste, and race are undoubtedly brighter than the average in any other class, caste, or race. And vice versa—the dullest individuals in any of these groups are duller than the average of any group. There are sound biological reasons why this should be so. Very briefly, in the evolution of mankind the natural selection has worked, nearly always and everywhere, to increase and to maintain the behavioral plasticity and diversity, which are essential in all human cultures, primitive as well as advanced.

True enough, an individual taken from a population with a higher mean of some trait, say a higher intelligence, has a higher statistical probability to possess this trait more developed than an individual from a population with a lower mean. When we select *Drosophilae* for stronger or weaker photo- or geotaxis, we generally breed the high and the low selection lines separately. Spassky and myself have, however, some experiments in progress, in which pairs of populations exchange migrants in every generation. The migrants are selected for high or for low photo- or geotaxis or for some other genetically conditioned trait. This may be considered to represent to some extent an experimental simulation of social mobility in human populations. The preliminary results of these experiments are, at least to us, fascinating. Genetically selective social mobility seems to be a powerful evolutionary agent.

A day may conceivably arise when mankind will embark on some all-out eugenical breeding program. This day is not yet in sight, because mankind has not reached a level of wisdom when it could decide with anything approaching unanimity what combination of genetic qualities should the ideal man have. It is rather easier to agree what qualities he should not have. As for positive ideals, we can only recommend that a diversity of tastes, preferences, abilities, and temperaments should be preserved and perhaps even increased. Anyway, when we consider the social implications of the human genetic diversity we are not usually preoccupied with eugenical breeding programs. The genetic diversity is, for example, most relevant to educational problems. The students are, however, selected for study, not for stud.

Insofar as the genetic component is concerned, the intelligence, or temperament, or special abilities of the parents have little predictive value for these qualities in an individual child. This does not mean that such genetic components do not exist, as some authors have over-hastily concluded. It means two things. First, the heritability is fairly low, as it is low in the photo- and geotactic behavior of our flies. In other words, the environmental variance is high, and in man the parent-offspring similarities in behavioral traits may well be due more to the cul-tural than to the biological inheritance. Second, one cannot too often be reminded of the fact that we do not inherit the genotypes of our parents but only one half of their genes. The genes do not produce their effects in development each independently of the others. The genes interact; the genetic "nature" of an individual is an emergent product of the particular pattern or constellation of the genes he carries. This is often the reason why a child is sometimes so strikingly dissimilar to his parents in some traits, even if the environment is kept constant.

How can I summarize the contents of this article, which is itself a summary of thinking concerning a variety of issues? Perhaps the best way is to say that genetics bears out John Dewey's emphasis of "the infinite diversity of active tendencies and combinations of tendencies of which an individual [human] is capable."

Personality Dysfunction

6

Values:
The Meanings
of Mental
Health and
Illness

There is a popular view of mental health and illness that looks at these matters quite simply: psychotherapy is merely making people well. Mental illness is simply the opposite of mental health, and normality is mental health, what we all aspire to. If only the appropriate techniques could be found, all people could be mentally healthy.

In this simple view, technique is the critical word. Some think we only need to find *the* technique, perhaps one combining the exorcism of yesterday's religious magic with the precision of modern surgery. Indeed, one ought to be able to treat mental illness as one treats a disfiguring wart: cut it away, and forget about it. These are the hopes of the people who take themselves or their children to a psychiatrist's office to become quickly, maybe painlessly, well.

What is this sickness which we seek to cure? Is it that the patient's behavior is odd, that it deviates noticeably from that of his fellow man? Then the therapy

ought to make him conform. But—and here is the troubling question—do we want to inculcate conformity? Do we really *value* conformity?

What if we have a patient who suffers some apparently psychophysiological dysfunction. Perhaps he is married to a truly hateful person and is sexually impotent with her. Of what shall the therapy then consist? Shall we recommend divorce? Or extramarital relations? Or simply urge him to do without sexual relations? *Value* is an important part of each recommendation: but which value is best?

Some people think we can avoid the issue of value altogether. They suggest we might create, for instance, a therapeutic environment in which each person can locate his own values and implement them. In such an environment, properly conceived and conducted, the therapist might have no need to make value judgments, but could allow the patient to search for and develop his own. This oversimplifies the matter. For one thing, it is doubtful whether any therapeutic interaction can occur in a value vacuum. Even if it can, is it then possible for a therapist to so restrain and control his values that they do not intrude into the relationship? Finally, even assuming that all this can be done, do we really want a person to simply discover and implement his own values, even if he were to discover antisocial values or values that we ordinarily associate with mental illness?

Value permeates the entire diagnostic and therapeutic endeavor. There are, certainly, some psychological disabilities in which there is complete value consensus. Fear of high or closed places, and unwanted auditory and visual hallucinations, are a few of the problems that would not cause disagreement. Excise the phobia, abolish the hallucination, as quickly as you can so long as you do not tamper with underlying value systems in the process! But phobias and hallucinations are not adequate models for other kinds of psychological dysfunction. The main problem in existential neurosis, for example, which is examined in Chapter 7, is one of values and valuing, and not much else. Value cannot be avoided for long by focusing on, say, the technical aspects of psychotherapy. And, as the following papers indicate, it is not easily resolved.

In the first selection, O. Hobart Mowrer makes clear an hypothesis that he has long held—that normal man is a moral man. Mowrer explicates this thesis further in his essay, " 'Sin,' the Lesser of Two Evils." He freely grants that the notion of sin is irritating to most scientists. But he is nevertheless captured by the two primary connotations of the word: the willful violation of a system of ethics, and the subsequent punishment that attends that violation. Sin implies personal responsibility, while

illness is something we fall prey to. Most theories of mental illness hold that the seeds of disorder are sown when the child is very young, that they invade and overcome the normal maturation process, and that the individual is essentially helpless in face of the onslaught. Mowrer holds that these theories not only lack adequate proof, but that they also erode the social fabric while retaining the "ill" in their presumed illness.

Thomas Szasz arrives at very much the same view, but from a quite different starting place. He finds few compelling analogies between physical illness and what is called mental illness. In Szasz' view the latter term is neither descriptive nor causal, and could be profitably abandoned. To him, the problems of mental illness are really problems of living, problems that may be exacerbated by the increasing complexity of society, but problems which are, in any event, the individual's responsibility.

The notion of mental illness and mental health is not held useless by everyone. David Ausubel, in the next essay, argues that it is possible to locate responsibility and morality within the individual and still find mental illness a useful term. The matter remains open, and the reader can decide for himself which uses of the terms "mental illness," "mental health," and "normality" are most compelling.

Even if our notions of ordered and disordered behavior did not require the inclusion of values, psychology would still need to deal with them, if only because there is a powerful popular demand to know which values are the best to live by. Psychologists are continually asked to expound on the value of what is required for mental health, for education and child rearing; they are asked to become secular priests and to replace with scientific authority what was previously the domain of tradition and religion. What shall they say? And how shall they go about it?

M. Brewster Smith says behavioral scientists need to become involved in the issues of values, that they can no longer divorce scientific and humane cultures, and that they may have a special contribution to make to the understanding of values. But *which* values qualify for the list of ideal values is not a matter that science can handle directly. No one can stipulate *in the name of science* which values are associated with positive mental health. One can only make clear his own values, make them public, and not pretend either that his pronouncements are value-free or that the values they imply have great scientific merit. There may come a time, Smith argues, when certain values may acquire preeminence because they satisfy empirical criteria.

The acquisition of values and the conditions under which they become salient to the individual is the substance of Carl Rogers' essay. The infant, Rogers suggests, knows his values: that pain and hunger are bad and that food is good. These values are part of his immediate experience. Something occurs in the process of growing up, however, that makes experience increasingly remote from values, and that may eventually make one wonder what his own values are, or even if he has any. The distance between self and value seems to grow as a result of social rejection. The search for, and discovery of, personal values can occur in therapy, as it can in any fully accepting relationship where the individual is able to experience his own worth and to savor again his personal explorations. From his therapeutic experience, Rogers finds that when an individual has been prized as a person he will not select antisocial values, but will instead choose values that further his own growth and that of those around him.

"Sin," the Lesser of Two Evils

O. Hobart Mowrer

Following the presentation of a paper on "Constructive Aspects of the Concept of Sin in Psychotherapy" at the 1959 APA convention in Cincinnati, I have repeatedly been asked by psychologists and psychiatrists: "But *why* must you use that awful word 'sin,' instead of some more neutral term such as 'wrongdoing,' 'irresponsibility,' or 'immorality'?" And even a religious layman has reproached me on the grounds that "Sin is such a

Reprinted from *American Psychologist*, 1960, vol. 15, pp. 301–304 with the permission of the American Psychology Association and the author.

strong word." Its *strength*, surely, is an asset, not a liability; for in the face of failure which has resulted from our erstwhile use of feebler concepts, we have very heavy work for it to do. Besides, sin (in contrast to its more neutral equivalents) is such a handy *little* word that it would be a pity to let it entirely disappear from usage. With Humpty-Dumpty, we ought to expect words to be "well-behaved" and to mean what *we* want them to!

A few years ago I was invited to teach in the summer session at one of our great Pacific Coast universities; and toward the end of the term, a student in my class on Personality Theory said to me one day: "Did you know that near the beginning of this course you created a kind of scandal on this campus?" Then he explained that I had once used the word "sin" without saying "so-called" or making a joke about it. This, the student said, was virtually unheard-of in a psychology professor and had occasioned considerable dismay and perplexity. I did not even recall the incident; but the more I have thought about the reaction it produced, the more frequently I have found myself using the term—with, I hope, something more than mere perversity.

Traditionally, sin has been thought of as whatever causes one to go to Hell; and since Hell, as a place of otherwordly retribution and torment, has conveniently dropped out of most religious as well as secular thought, the concept of sin might indeed seem antiquated and absurd. But, as I observed in the Cinicinnati paper, Hell is still very much with us in those states of mind and being which we call neurosis and psychosis; and I have come increasingly, at least in my own mind, to identify anything that carries us toward these forms of perdition as *sin*. Irresponsibility, wrongdoing, immorality, sin: what do the terms matter if we can thus understand more accurately the nature of psychopathology and gain greater practical control over its ramified forms and manifestations?

But now the fat is in the. fire! Have we not been taught on high authority that personality disorder is not one's own "fault," that the neurotic is *not* "responsible" for his suffering, that he has done nothing wrong, committed no "sin"? "Mental illness," according to a poster which was widely circulated a few years ago, "is no disgrace. It might happen to anyone." And behind all this, of course, was the Freudian hypothesis that neurosis stems from a "too severe superego," which is the product of a too strenuous socialization of the individual at the hands of harsh, unloving parents and an irrational society. The trouble lay, supposedly, not in anything wrong or "sinful" which the individual has himself *done*, but in things he merely *wants* to do but cannot, because of *repression*.

The neurotic was thus not sinful but *sick*, the helpless, innocent victim of "the sins of the fathers," and could be rescued only by a specialized, esoteric form of *treatment*. Anna Russell catches the spirit of this doctrine well when she sings in "Psychiatric Folksong,"

> At three I had a feeling of
>   Ambivalence toward my brothers,
> And so it follows naturally
>   I poisoned all my lovers.
> But now I'm happy; I have learned
>   The lesson this has taught;
> That everything I do that's wrong
>   Is someone else's fault.[1]

Freud saw all this not only as a great scientific discovery but also as a strategic gain for the profession which had thus far treated him so indifferently. It was, one may conjecture, a sort of gift, an offering or service which would place medicine in such debt to him that it could no longer ignore or reject him. In his *Autobiography* Freud (1935) puts it thus:

> My medical conscience felt pleased at my having arrived at this conclusion [that neurosis has a sexual basis]. I hoped that I had filled up a gap in medical science, which, in dealing with a function of such great biological importance, had failed to take into account any injuries beyond those caused by infection or by gross anatomical lesions. The medical aspect of the matter was, moreover, sup-

[1] Used with the permission of Miss Anna Russell.

ported by the fact that sexuality was not something purely mental. It had a somatic side as well. . . . (p. 45)

In his book on *The Problem of Lay Analysis*, Freud (1927) later took a somewhat different position (see also Chapter 9 of the third volume of Jones' biography of Freud, 1957); but by this time his Big Idea had been let loose in the world and was no longer entirely under his control.

Psychologists were, as we know, among the first of the outlying professional groups to "take up" psychoanalysis. By being analyzed, we not only learned—in an intimate, personal way—about this new and revolutionary science; we also (or so we imagined) were qualifying ourselves for the practice of analysis as a form of therapy. Now we are beginning to see how illusory this all was. We accepted psychoanalytic theory long before it had been adequately tested and thus embraced as "science" a set of presuppositions which we are now painfully having to repudiate. But, more than this, in accepting the premise that the neurotically disturbed person is basically *sick*, we surrendered our professional independence and authenticity. Now, to the extent that we have subscribed to the doctrine of mental *illness* (and tried to take part in its "treatment"), we have laid ourselves open to some really very embarrassing charges from our friends in psychiatry.

In 1954 the American Psychiatric Association, with the approval of the American Medical Association and the American Psychoanalytic Association, published a resolution on "relations between medicine and psychology," which it reissued (during the supposed "moratorium") in 1957. This document needs no extensive review in these pages; but a few sentences may be quoted to indicate what a powerful fulcrum the sickness conception of neurosis provides for the aggrandizement of medicine.

For centuries the Western world has placed on the medical profession responsibility for the diagnosis and treatment of illness. Medical practice acts have been designed to protect the public from unqualified practitioners and to define the special responsibilities assumed by those who practice the healing art. . . . Psychiatry is the medical specialty concerned with illness that has chiefly mental symptoms. . . . Psychotherapy is a form of medical treatment and does not form the basis for a separate profession. . . . When members of these [other] professions contribute to the diagnosis and treatment of illness, their professional contributions must be coordinated under medical responsibility. (pp. 1–2)

So long as we subscribe to the view that neurosis is a bona fide "illness," without moral implications or dimensions, our position will, of necessity, continue to be an awkward one. And it is here I suggest that, as between the concept of sin (however unsatisfactory it may in some ways be) and that of sickness, sin is indeed the lesser of two evils. We have tried the sickness horn of this dilemma and impaled ourselves upon it. Perhaps, despite our erstwhile protestations, we shall yet find sin more congenial.

We psychologists do not, I believe, object *in principle* to the type of authority which psychiatrists wish to exercise, or to our being subject to other medical controls, if they were truly functional. But authority and power ought to go with demonstrated competence, which medicine clearly has in the physical realm but, equally clearly, does not have in "psychiatry." Despite some pretentious affirmations to the contrary, the fact is that psychoanalysis, on which modern "dynamic" psychiatry is largely based, is in a state of virtual collapse and imminent demise. And the tranquilizers and other forms of so-called chemo-therapy are admittedly only ameliorative, not basically curative. So now, to the extent that we have accepted the "ill-ness" postulate and thus been lured under the penumbra of medicine, we are in the ungraceful maneuver of "getting out."[2]

But the question remains: Where do we *go*, what do we *do*, now? Some be-lieve that our best policy is to become frankly agnostic for the time being, to admit that we know next to nothing about either the cause or correction of psychopathology and therefore ought to concentrate on *research*. This is certainly a safe policy, and it may also be the wisest one. But since this matter of man's total adjustment and psychosocial sur-vival does not quickly yield up its inner-most secrets to conventional types of scientific inquiry, I believe it will do no harm for us at the same time to be thinking about some frankly ideological matters.

For several decades we psychologists looked upon the whole matter of sin and moral accountability as a great in-cubus and acclaimed our liberation from it as epoch-making. But at length we have discovered that to be "free" in this sense, i.e., to have the excuse of being "sick" rather than *sinful*, is to court the danger of also becoming *lost*. This danger is, I believe, betokened by the widespread interest in Existentialism which we are presently witnessing. In

becoming amoral, ethically neutral, and "free," we have cut the very roots of our being; lost our deepest sense of self-hood and identity; and, with neurotics them-selves, find ourselves asking: Who *am* I? What is my *destiny*? What does liv-ing (existence) *mean*?

In reaction to the state of near-limbo into which we have drifted, we have become suddenly aware, once again, of the problem of *values* and of their cen-trality in the human enterprise. This trend is clearly apparent in the programs at our recent professional meetings, in journal articles, and, to some extent al-ready, in our elementary textbooks. Something very basic is obviously hap-pening to psychologists and their "self-image."

In this process of moving away from our erstwhile medical "entanglements," it would be a very natural thing for us to form a closer and friendlier relation-ship than we have previously had with religion and theology. And something of this sort is unquestionably occurring. At the APA Annual Convention in 1956 there was, for the first time in our his-tory I believe, a symposium on religion and mental health; and each ensuing year has seen other clear indications of a developing rapprochement.

However, here too there is a difficulty—of a most surprising kind. At the very time that psychologists are becoming distrustful of the sickness approach to personality disturbance and are begin-ning to look with more benign interest and respect toward certain moral and religious precepts, religionists themselves are being caught up in and bedazzled by the same preposterous system of thought as that from which we psychologists are just recovering. It would be possible to document this development at length; but reference to such recent "theological" works as Richard V. McCann's *Delin-quency—Sickness or Sin?* (1957) and

---

[2] Thoughtful psychiatrists are also beginning to question the legitmacy of the disease concept in this area. In an article entitled "The Myth of Mental Illness" which appeared after this paper went to press, Thomas S. Szasz (1960) is par-ticularly outspoken on this score. He says: ". . . the notion of mental illness has outlived whatever usefulness it might have had and . . . now functions merely as a convenient myth. . . . mental illness is a myth, whose function it is to disguise and thus render more palatable the bitter pill of moral conflicts in human rela-tions" (p. 118). Szasz' entire article deserves careful attention.

Carl Michalson's *Faith for Personal Crises* (1958, see especially Chapter 3) will suffice.

We have already alluded to Anna Russell's "Psychiatric Folksong" and, in addition, should call attention to Katie Lee's 12-inch LP recording "Songs of Couch and Consultation." That entertainment and literary people are broadly rejecting psychoanalytic froth for the more solid substance of moral accountability is indicated by many current novels and plays. It is not without significance that Arthur Miller's *Death of a Salesman*, written in the philosophical vein of Hawthorne's great novel *The Scarlet Letter*, has, for example, been received so well.

How very strange and inverted our present situation therefore is! Traditionally clergymen have worried about the world's entertainments and entertainers and, for a time at least, about psychology and psychologists. Now, ironically, the entertainers and psychologists are *worrying about the clergymen*. Eventually, of course, clergymen will return to a sounder, less fantastic position; but in the meantime, we psychologists can perhaps play a socially useful and, also, scientifically productive role if we pursue, with all seriousness and candor,. our discovery of the essentially moral nature of human existence and of that "living death" which we call psychopathology. This, of course, is not the place to go deeply into the substantive aspects of the problem; but one illustration of the fruitfulness of such exploration may be cited.

In reconsidering the possibility that sin must, after all, be taken seriously, many psychologists seem perplexed as to what attitude one should take *toward the sinner*. "Nonjudgmental," "nonpunitive," "nondirective," "warm," "accepting," "ethically neutral": these words have been so very generally used to form

the supposedly proper therapeutic imago that reintroduction of the concept of sin throws us badly off balance. *Our* attitudes, as would-be therapists or helping persons, toward the neurotic (sinner) are apparently less important than his attitude *toward himself*; and, as we know, it is usually—in the most general sense—a rejecting one. Therefore, we have reasoned, the way to get the neurotic to accept and love himself is for us to love and accept *him*, an inference which flows equally from the Freudian assumption that the patient is not really guilty or sinful but only fancies himself so and from the view of Rogers that we are all inherently good and are corrupted by our experiences with the external, everyday world.

But what is here generally overlooked, it seems, is that recovery (constructive change, redemption) is most assuredly attained, not by helping a person reject and rise above his sins, but by helping him *accept them*. This is the paradox which we have not at all understood and which is the very crux of the problem. Just so long as a person lives under the shadow of real, unacknowledged, and unexpiated guilt, he *cannot* (if he has any character at all) "accept himself"; and all *our* efforts to reassure and accept him will avail nothing. He will continue to hate himself and to suffer the inevitable consequences of self-hatred. But the moment he (with or without "assistance") begins to accept his guilt and his sinfulness, the possibility of radical reformation opens up; and with this, the individual may legitimately, though not without pain and effort, pass from deep, pervasive self-rejection and self-torture to a new freedom of self-respect and peace.

Thus we arrive, not only at a new (really very old) conception of the nature of "neurosis" which may change our entire approach to this problem, but also at an understanding of one of the most fundamental fallacies of Freudian psychoanalysis and many kindred efforts at psychotherapy. Freud observed, quite accurately, that the neurotic tortures himself; and he conjectured that this type of suffering arose from the irrationality and overseverity of the superego. But at once there was an empirical as well as logical difficulty which Freud (unlike some of his followers) faithfully acknowledged. In the *New Introductory Lectures on Psychoanalysis* (1933), he said:

> The superego [paradoxically] seems to have made a one-sided selection [as between the loving and the punitive attitudes of the parents], and to have chosen only the harshness and severity of the parents, their preventive and punitive functions, while their loving care is not taken up and continued by it. If the parents have really ruled with a rod of iron, we easily understand the child developing a severe superego, but, contrary to our expectations, experience shows that the superego may reflect the same relentless harshness even when the upbringing has been gentle and kind. (p. 90)

And then Freud adds, candidly: "We ourselves do not feel that we have fully understood it." In this we can fully agree. For the only way to resolve the paradox of self-hatred and self-punishment is to assume, not that it represents merely an "introjection" of the attitudes of others, but that the self-hatred is realistically justified and will persist until the individual, by radically altered attitude *and action*, honestly and realistically comes to feel that he now deserves something better. As long as one remains, in old-fashioned religious phraseology, hard-of-heart and unrepentant, just so long will one's conscience hold him in the vise-like grip of "neurotic" rigidity and suffering. But if, at length, an individual confesses his past stupidities and errors and makes what poor attempts he can at restitution, then the superego (like the parents of an earlier day—and society in general) forgives and relaxes its stern hold; and the individual once again is free, "well" (Mowrer, 1959).

But here we too, like Freud, encounter a difficulty. There is some evidence that human beings do not change radically unless they first acknowledge their sins; but we also know how hard it is for one to make such an acknowledgment unless he has *already changed*. In other words, the full realization of deep worthlessness is a severe ego "insult"; and one must have some new source of strength, it seems, to endure it. This is a mystery (or is it only a mistaken observation?) which traditional theology has tried to resolve in various ways—without complete success. Can we psychologists do better?

The Myth of Mental Illness

Thomas S. Szasz

My aim in this essay is to raise the question "Is there such a thing as mental

Reprinted from *American Psychologist*, 1960, vol. 15, pp. 113–118 with the permission of the American Psychological Association and the author.

illness?" and to argue that there is not. Since the notion of mental illness is extremely widely used nowadays, inquiry into the ways in which this term is employed would seem to be especially indicated. Mental illness, of course, is not literally a "thing"—or physical object— and hence it can "exist" only in the same sort of way in which other theoretical concepts exist. Yet, familiar theories are in the habit of posing, sooner or later —at least to those who come to believe in them—as "objective truths" (or "facts"). During certain historical periods, explanatory conceptions such as deities, witches, and microorganisms appeared not only as theories but as self-evident *causes* of a vast number of events. I submit that today mental illness is widely regarded in a somewhat similar fashion, that is, as the cause of innumerable diverse happenings. As an antidote to the complacent use of the notion of mental illness—whether as a self-evident phenomenon, theory, or cause—let us ask this question: What is meant when it is asserted that someone is mentally ill?

In what follows I shall describe briefly the main uses to which the concept of mental illness has been put. I shall argue that this notion has outlived whatever usefulness it might have had and that it now functions merely as a convenient myth.

MENTAL ILLNESS AS A SIGN OF BRAIN DISEASE

The notion of mental illness derives its main support from such phenomena as syphilis of the brain or delirious conditions—intoxications, for instance—in which persons are known to manifest various peculiarities or disorders of thinking and behavior. Correctly speaking, however, these are diseases of the brain, not of the mind. According to one school of thought, *all* so-called mental illness is of this type. The assumption is made that some neurological defect, perhaps a very subtle one, will ultimately be found for all the disorders of thinking and behavior. Many contemporary psychiatrists, physicians, and other scientists hold this view. This position implies that people *cannot*

have troubles—expressed in what are *now called* "mental illnesses"—because of differences in personal needs, opinions, social aspirations, values, and so on. *All problems in living* are attributed to physicochemical processes which in due time will be discovered by medical research.

"Mental illnesses" are thus regarded as basically no different than all other diseases (that is, of the body). The only difference, in this view, between mental and bodily diseases is that the former, affecting the brain, manifest themselves by means of mental symptoms; whereas the latter, affecting other organ systems (for example, the skin, liver, etc.), manifest themselves by means of symptoms referable to those parts of the body. This view rests on and expresses what are in my opinion, two fundamental errors.

In the first place, what central nervous system symptoms would correspond to a skin eruption or a fracture? It would *not* be some emotion or complex bit of behavior. Rather it would be blindness or a paralysis of some part of the body. The crux of the matter is that a disease of the brain, analogous to a disease of the skin or bone, is a neurological defect, and not a problem in living. For example, a *defect* in a person's visual field may be satisfactorily explained by correlating it with certain definite lesions in the nervous system. On the other hand, a person's *belief*—whether this be a belief in Christianity, in Communism, or in the idea that his internal organs are "rotting" and that his body is, in fact, already "dead"— cannot be explained by a defect or disease of the nervous system. Explanations of this sort of occurrence—assuming that one is interested in the belief itself and does not regard it simply as a "symptom" or expression of something else that is *more interesting*—must be sought along different lines.

The second error in regarding complex psychosocial behavior, consisting of communications about ourselves and the world about us, as mere symptoms of neurological functioning is *epistemological*. In other words, it is an error pertaining not to any mistakes in observation or reasoning, as such, but rather to the way in which we organize and express our knowledge. In the present case, the error lies in making a symmetrical dualism between mental and physical (or bodily) symptoms, a dualism which is merely a habit of speech and to which no known observations can be found to correspond. Let us see if this is so. In medical practice, when we speak of physical disturbances, we mean either signs (for example, a fever) or symptoms (for example, pain). We speak of mental symptoms, on the other hand, when we refer to a patient's *communications about himself, others, and the world about him.* He might state that he is Napoleon or that he is being persecuted by the Communists. These would be considered mental symptoms *only* if the observer believed that the patient was *not* Napoleon or that he was *not* being persecuted by the Communists. This makes it apparent that the statement that "X is a mental symptom" involves rendering a judgment. The judgment entails, moreover, a covert comparison or matching of the patient's ideas, concepts, or beliefs with those of the observer and the society in which they live. The notion of mental symptom is therefore inextricably tied to the *social* (including *ethical*) *context* in which it is made in much the same way as the notion of bodily symptom is tied to an *anatomical* and *genetic context* (Szasz, 1957a, 1957b).

To sum up what has been said thus far: I have tried to show that for those who regard mental symptoms as signs of brain disease, the concept of mental illness is unnecessary and misleading. For what they mean is that people so labeled suffer from diseases of the brain; and, if

that is what they mean, it would seem better for the sake of clarity to say that and not something else.

MENTAL ILLNESS AS A NAME FOR PROBLEMS IN LIVING

The term "mental illness" is widely used to describe something which is very different than a disease of the brain. Many people today take it for granted that living is an arduous process. Its hardship for modern man, moreover, derives not so much from a struggle for biological survival as from the stresses and strains inherent in the social intercourse of complex human personalities. In this context, the notion of mental illness is used to identify or describe some feature of an individual's so-called personality. Mental illness—as a deformity of the personality, so to speak—is then regarded as the *cause* of the human disharmony. It is implicit in this view that social intercourse between people is regarded as something *inherently harmonious*, its disturbance being due solely to the presence of "mental illness" in many people. This is obviously fallacious reasoning, for it makes the abstraction "mental illness" into a *cause*, even though this abstraction was created in the first place to serve only as a shorthand expression for certain types of human behavior. It now becomes necessary to ask: "What kinds of behavior are regarded as indicative of mental illness, and by whom?"

The concept of illness, whether bodily or mental, implies *deviation from some clearly defined norm*. In the case of physical illness, the norm is the structural and functional integrity of the human body. Thus, although the desirability of physical health, as such, is an ethical value, what health *is* can be stated in anatomical and physiological terms. What is the norm deviation from which is regarded as mental illness? This question cannot be easily answered. But whatever this norm might be, we can be certain of only one thing: namely, that it is a norm that must be stated in terms of *psychosocial, ethical,* and *legal* concepts. For example, notions such as "excessive repression" or "acting out an unconscious impulse" illustrate the use of psychological concepts for judging (so-called) mental health and illness. The idea that chronic hostility, vengefulness, or divorce are indicative of mental illness would be illustrations of the use of ethical norms (that is, the desirability of love, kindness, and a stable marriage relationship). Finally, the widespread psychiatric opinion that only a mentally ill person would commit homicide illustrates the use of a legal concept as a norm of mental health. The norm from which deviation is measured whenever one speaks of a mental illness is a *psychosocial and ethical one.* Yet, the remedy is sought in terms of *medical* measures which—it is hoped and assumed—are free from wide differences of ethical value. The definition of the disorder and the terms in which its remedy are sought are therefore at serious odds with one another. The practical significance of this covert conflict between the alleged nature of the defect and the remedy can hardly be exaggerated.

Having identified the norms used to measure deviations in cases of mental illness, we will now turn to the question: "Who defines the norms and hence the deviation?" Two basic answers may be offered: (*a*) It may be the person himself (that is, the patient) who decides that he deviates from a norm. For example, an artist may believe that he suffers from a work inhibition; and he may implement this conclusion by seeking help *for* himself from a psychotherapist. (*b*) It may be someone other than the patient who decides that the latter is deviant (for example, relatives, physicians, legal authorities, society generally, etc.). In such

a case a psychiatrist may be hired by others to do something *to* the patient in order to correct the deviation.

These considerations underscore the importance of asking the question "Whose agent is the psychiatrist?" and of giving a candid answer to it (Szasz, 1956, 1958). The psychiatrist (psychologist or non-medical psychotherapist), it now develops, may be the agent of the patient, of the relatives, of the school, of the military services, of a business organization, of a court of law, and so forth. In speaking of the psychiatrist as the agent of these persons or organizations, it is not implied that his values concerning norms, or his ideas and aims concerning the proper nature of remedial action, need to coincide exactly with those of his employer. For example, a patient in individual psychotherapy may believe that his salvation lies in a new marriage; his psychotherapist need not share this hypothesis. As the patient's agent, however, he must abstain from bringing social or legal force to bear on the patient which would prevent him from putting his beliefs into action. If his *contract* is with the patient, the psychiatrist (psychotherapist) may disagree with him or stop his treatment; but he cannot engage others to obstruct the patient's aspirations. Similarly, if a psychiatrist is engaged by a court to determine the sanity of a criminal, he need not fully share the legal authorities' values and intentions in regard to the criminal and the means available for dealing with him. But the psychiatrist is expressly barred from stating, for example, that it is not the criminal who is "insane" but the men who wrote the law on the basis of which the very actions that are being judged are regarded as "criminal." Such an opinion could be voiced, of course, but not in a courtroom, and not by a psychiatrist who makes it his practice to assist the court in performing its daily work.

To recapitulate: In actual contemporary social usage, the finding of a mental illness is made by establishing a deviance in behavior from certain psychosocial, ethical, or legal norms. The judgment may be made, as in medicine, by the patient, the physician (psychiatrist), or others. Remedial action, finally, tends to be sought in a therapeutic—or covertly medical—framework, thus creating a situation in which *psychosocial, ethical,* and/or *legal deviations* are claimed to be correctible by (so-called) *medical action.* Since medical action is designed to correct only medical deviations, it seems logically absurd to expect that it will help solve problems whose very existence had been defined and established on non-medical grounds. I think that these considerations may be fruitfully applied to the present use of tranquilizers and, more generally, to what might be expected of drugs of whatever type in regard to the amelioration or solution of problems in human living.

THE ROLE OF ETHICS IN PSYCHIATRY

Anything that people *do*—in contrast to things that *happen* to them (Peters, 1958)—takes place in a context of value. In this broad sense, no human activity is devoid of ethical implications. When the values underlying certain activities are widely shared, those who participate in their pursuit may lose sight of them altogether. The discipline of medicine, both as a pure science (for example, research) and as a technology (for example, therapy), contains many ethical considerations and judgments. Unfortunately, these are often denied, minimized, or merely kept out of focus; for the ideal of the medical profession as well as of the people whom it serves seems to be having a system of medicine (allegedly) free of ethical value. This sentimental notion is expressed by such things as the doctor's willingness to treat and help patients irrespective of their religious or political beliefs, whether they are rich or poor, etc. While there may be some grounds for this belief—albeit it is a view that is not impressively true even in these regards—the fact remains that ethical considerations encompass a vast range of human affairs. By making the practice of medicine neutral in regard to some specific issues of value need not, and cannot, mean that it can be kept free from all such values. The practice of medicine is intimately tied to ethics; and the first thing that we must do, it seems to me, is to try to make this clear and explicit. I shall let this matter rest here, for it does not concern us specifically in this essay. Lest there be any vagueness, however, about how or where ethics and medicine meet, let me remind the reader of such issues as birth control, abortion, suicide, and euthanasia as only a few of the major areas of current ethicomedical controversy.

Psychiatry, I submit, is very much more intimately tied to problems of ethics than is medicine. I use the word "psychiatry" here to refer to that contemporary discipline which is concerned with *problems in living* (and not with diseases of the brain, which are problems for neurology). Problems in human relations can be analyzed, interpreted, and given meaning only within given social and ethical contexts. Accordingly, it *does* make a difference—arguments to the contrary notwithstanding — what the psychiatrist's socioethical orientations happen to be; for these will influence his ideas on what is wrong with the patient, what deserves comment or interpretation, in what possible directions change might be desirable, and so forth. Even in medicine proper, these factors play a role, as for instance, in the divergent orientations which physicians, depending on their religious affiliations, have toward such things as birth control and therapeutic abortion. Can anyone really believe that a psychotherapist's ideas concerning religious belief, slavery, or other similar issues play no role in his practical work? If they do make a difference, what are we to infer from it? Does it not seem reasonable that we ought to have different psychiatric therapies—each expressly recognized for the ethical positions which they embody—for, say, Catholics and Jews, religious persons and agnostics, democrats and communists, white supremacists and Negroes, and so on? Indeed, if we look at how psychiatry is actually practiced today (especially in the United States), we find that people do seek psychiatric help in accordance with their social status and ethical beliefs (Hollingshead & Redlich, 1958). This should really not surprise us more than being told that practicing Catholics rarely frequent birth control clinics.

The foregoing position which holds that contemporary psychotherapists deal with problems in living, rather than with mental illnesses and their cures, stands in opposition to a currently prevalent claim, according to which mental illness is just as "real" and "objective" as bodily illness. This is a confusing claim since it is never known exactly what is meant by such words as "real" and "objective." I suspect, however, that what is intended by the proponents of this view is to create the idea in the popular mind that mental illness is some sort of disease entity, like an infection or a malignancy. If this were true, one could *catch* or *get* a "mental illness," one might *have* or *harbor* it, one might *transmit* it to others, and finally one could get *rid* of it. In my opinion, there is not a shred of evidence to support this idea. To the contrary, all the evidence is the other way and supports the view that what people now call mental illnesses are for the most part *communications* expressing unacceptable ideas,

often framed, moreover, in an unusual idiom. The scope of this essay allows me to do no more than mention this alternative theoretical approach to this problem (Szasz, 1957c).

This is not the place to consider in detail the similarities and differences between bodily and mental illnesses. It shall suffice for us here to emphasize only one important difference between them: namely, that whereas bodily disease refers to public, physicochemical occurrences, the notion of mental illness is used to codify relatively more private, sociopsychological happenings of which the observer (diagnostician) forms a part. In other words, the psychiatrist does not stand *apart* from what he observes, but is, in Harry Stack Sullivan's apt words, a "participant observer." This means that he is *committed* to some picture of what he considers reality—and to what he thinks society considers reality—and he observes and judges the patient's behavior in the light of these considerations. This touches on our earlier observation that the notion of mental symptom itself implies a comparison between observer and observed, psychiatrist and patient. This is so obvious that I may be charged with belaboring trivialities. Let me therefore say once more that my aim in presenting this argument was expressly to criticize and counter a prevailing contemporary tendency to deny the moral aspects of psychiatry (and psychotherapy) and to substitute for them allegedly value-free medical considerations. Psychotherapy, for example, is being widely practiced as though it entailed nothing other than restoring the patient from a state of mental sickness to one of mental health. While it is generally accepted that mental illness has something to do with man's social (or interpersonal) relations, it is paradoxically maintained that problems of values (that is, of ethics) do not arise in this process.[1] Yet, in one sense, much of psychotherapy may revolve around nothing other than the elucidation and weighing of goals and values—many of which may be mutually contradictory— and the means whereby they might best be harmonized, realized, or relinquished.

The diversity of human values and the methods by means of which they may be realized is so vast, and many of them remain so unacknowledged, that they cannot fail but lead to conflicts in human relations. Indeed, to say that human relations at all levels—from mother to child, through husband and wife, to nation and nation—are fraught with stress, strain, and disharmony is, once again, making the obvious explicit. Yet, what may be obvious may be also poorly understood. This I think is the case here. For it seems to me that—at least in our scientific theories of behavior—we have failed to *accept* the simple fact that human relations are inherently fraught with difficulties and that to make them even relatively harmonious requires much patience and hard work. I submit that the idea of mental illness is now being put to work to obscure certain difficulties which at present may be inherent—not that they need be unmodifiable—in the social intercourse of persons. If this is true, the concept functions as a disguise; for instead of calling attention to conflicting human needs, aspirations, and values, the notion of mental illness provides an amoral and impersonal "thing" (an "illness") as an

explanation for *problems in living* (Szasz, 1959). We may recall in this connection that not so long ago it was devils and witches who were held responsible for men's problems in social living. The belief in mental illness, as something other than man's trouble in getting along with his fellow man, is the proper heir to the belief in demonology and witchcraft. Mental illness exists or is "real" in exactly the same sense in which witches existed or were "real."

CHOICE, RESPONSIBILITY, AND PSYCHIATRY

While I have argued that mental illnesses do not exist, I obviously did not imply that the social and psychological occurrences to which this label is currently being attached also do not exist. Like the personal and social troubles which people had in the Middle Ages, they are real enough. It is the labels we give them that concerns us and, having labelled them, what we do about them. While I cannot go into the ramified implications of this problem here, it is worth noting that a demonologic conception of problems in living gave rise to therapy along theological lines. Today, a belief in mental illness implies—nay, requires—therapy along medical or psychotherapeutic lines.

What is implied in the line of thought set forth here is something quite different. I do not intend to offer a new conception of "psychiatric illness" nor a new form of "therapy." My aim is more modest and yet also more ambitious. It is to suggest that the phenomena now called mental illnesses be looked at afresh and more simply, that they be removed from the category of illnesses, and that they be regarded as the expressions of man's struggle with the problem of how he should live. The last mentioned problem is obviously a vast one, its enormity reflecting not only man's inability to cope

---

[1] Freud went so far as to say that: "I consider ethics to be taken for granted. Actually I have never done a mean thing" (Jones, 1957, p. 247). This surely is a strange thing to say for someone who has studied man as a social being as closely as did Freud. I mention it here to show how the notion of "illness" (in the case of psychoanalysis, "psychopathology," or "mental illness") was used by Freud—and by most of his followers—as a means for classifying certain forms of human behavior as falling within the scope of medicine, and hence (by *fiat*) outside that of ethics!

with his environment, but even more his increasing self-reflectiveness.

By problems in living, then, I refer to that truly explosive chain reaction which began with man's fall from divine grace by partaking of the fruit of the tree of knowledge. Man's awareness of himself and of the world about him seems to be a steadily expanding one, bringing in its wake an ever larger *burden of understanding* (an expression borrowed from Susanne Langer, 1953). *This burden, then, is to be expected and must not be misinterpreted.* Our only *rational* means for lightening it is *more understanding*, and appropriate *action* based on such understanding. The main alternative lies in acting as though the burden were not what in fact we perceive it to be and taking refuge in an outmoded theological view of man. In the latter view, man does not fashion his life and much of his world about him, but merely lives out his fate in a world created by superior beings. This may logically lead to pleading nonresponsibility in the face of seemingly unfathomable problems and difficulties. Yet, if man fails to take increasing responsibility for his actions, individually as well as collectively, it seems unlikely that some higher power or being would assume this task and carry this burden for him. Moreover, this seems hardly the proper time in human history for obscuring the issue of man's responsibility for his actions by hiding it behind the skirt of an all-explaining conception of mental illness.

CONCLUSIONS

I have tried to show that the notion of mental illness has outlived whatever usefulness it might have had and that it now functions merely as a convenient myth. As such, it is a true heir to religious myths in general, and to the belief in witchcraft in particular; the role of all these belief-systems was to act as *social tranquilizers*, thus encouraging the hope that mastery of certain specific problems may be achieved by means of substitutive (symbolic-magical) operations. The notion of mental illness thus serves mainly to obscure the everyday fact that life for most people is a continuous struggle, not for biological survival, but for a "place in the sun," "peace of mind," or some other human value. For man aware of himself and of the world about him, once the needs for preserving the body (and perhaps the race) are more or less satisfied, the problem arises as to what he should do with himself. Sustained adherence to the myth of mental illness allows people to avoid facing this problem, believing that mental health, conceived as the absence of mental illness, automatically insures the making of right and safe choices in one's conduct of life. But the facts are all the other way. It is the making of good choices in life that others regard, retrospectively, as good mental health!

The myth of mental illness encourages us, moreover, to believe in its logical corollary: that social intercourse would be harmonious, satisfying, and the secure basis of a "good life" were it not for the disrupting influences of mental illness or "psychopathology." The potentiality for universal human happiness, in this form at least, seems to me but another example of the I-wish-it-were-true type of fantasy. I do believe that human happiness or well-being on a hitherto unimaginably large scale, and not just for a select few, is possible. This goal could be achieved, however, only at the cost of many men, and not just a few, being willing and able to tackle their personal, social, and ethical conflicts. This means having the courage and integrity to forego waging battles on false fronts, finding solutions for substitute problems—for instance, fighting the battle of stomach acid and chronic fatigue instead of facing up to a marital conflict.

Our adversaries are not demons, witches, fate, or mental illness. We have no enemy whom we can fight, exorcise, or dispel by "cure." What we do have are *problems in living*—whether these be biologic, economic, political, or sociopsychological. In this essay I was concerned only with problems belonging in the last mentioned category, and within this group mainly with those pertaining to moral values. The field to which modern psychiatry addresses itself is vast, and I made no effort to encompass it all. My argument was limited to the proposition that mental illness is a myth, whose function it is to disguise and thus render more palatable the bitter pill of moral conflicts in human relations.

Personality Disorder is Disease

David P. Ausubel

In two recent articles in the *American Psychologist*, Szasz (1960) and Mowrer (1960) have argued the case for discarding the concept of mental illness. The essence of Mowrer's position is that since medical science lacks "demonstrated competence . . . in psychiatry," psychology would be wise to "get out" from "under the penumbra of medicine," and to regard the behavior disorders as manifestations of sin rather than of disease (p. 302). Szasz' position, as we shall see shortly, is somewhat more complex than Mowrer's, but agrees with the latter in emphasizing the moral as opposed to the psychopathological basis of abnormal behavior.

For a long time now, clinical psychology has both repudiated the relevance of moral judgment and accountability for assessing behavioral acts and choices, and has chafed under medical (psychiatric) control and authority in diagnosing and treating the personality disorders. One can readily appreciate, therefore, Mowrer's

Reprinted from *American Psychologist*, 1961, vol. 16, pp. 69–74 with the permission of the American Psychological Association and the author.

eagerness to sever the historical and professional ties that bind clinical psychology to medicine, even if this means denying that psychological disturbances constitute a form of illness, and even if psychology's close working relationship with psychiatry must be replaced by a new rapprochement with sin and theology, as "the lesser of two evils" (pp. 302–303). One can also sympathize with Mowrer's and Szasz' dissatisfaction with prevailing amoral and nonjudgmental trends in clinical psychology and with their entirely commendable efforts to restore moral judgment and accountability to a respectable place among the criteria used in evaluating human behavior, both normal and abnormal.

Opposition to these two trends in the handling of the behavior disorders (i.e., to medical control and to nonjudgmental therapeutic attitudes), however, does not necessarily imply abandonment of the concept of mental illness. There is no inconsistency whatsoever in maintaining, on the one hand, that most purposeful human activity has a moral aspect the reality of which psychologists cannot afford to ignore (Ausubel, 1952, p. 462), that man is morally accountable for the majority of his misdeeds (Ausubel, 1952, p. 469), and that psychological rather than medical training and sophistication are basic to competence in the personality disorders (Ausubel, 1956, p. 101), and affirming, on the other hand, that the latter disorders are genuine manifestations of illness. In recent years psychology has been steadily moving away from the formerly fashionable stance of ethical neutrality in the behavioral sciences; and in spite of strident medical claims regarding superior professional qualifications and preclusive legal responsibility for treating psychiatric patients, and notwithstanding the nominally restrictive provisions of medical practice acts, clinical psychologists have been assuming an increasingly more important, independent, and responsible role in treating the mentally ill population of the United States.

It would be instructive at this point to examine the tactics of certain other medically allied professions in freeing themselves from medical control and in acquiring independent, legally recognized professional status. In no instance have they resorted to the devious stratagem of denying that they were treating diseases, in the hope of mollifying medical opposition and legitimizing their own professional activities. They took the position instead that simply because a given condition is defined as a disease, its treatment need not necessarily be turned over to doctors of medicine if other equally competent professional specialists were available. That this position is legally and politically tenable is demonstrated by the fact that an impressively large number of recognized diseases are legally treated today by both medical *and* nonmedical specialists (e.g., diseases of the mouth, face, jaws, teeth, eyes, and feet). And there are few convincing reasons for believing that psychiatrists wield that much more political power than physicians,

maxillofacial surgeons, ophthalmologists, and orthopedic surgeons, that they could be successful where these latter specialists have failed, in legally restricting practice in their particular area of competence to holders of the medical degree. Hence even if psychologists were not currently managing to hold their own vis-à-vis psychiatrists, it would be far less dangerous and much more forthright to press for the necessary ameliorative legislation than to seek cover behind an outmoded and thoroughly discredited conception of the behavior disorders.

THE SZASZ-MOWRER POSITION

Szasz' (1960) contention that the concept of mental illness "now functions merely as a convenient myth" (p. 118) is grounded on four unsubstantiated and logically untenable propositions, which can be fairly summarized as follows:

1. Only symptoms resulting from demonstrable physical lesions qualify as legitimate manifestations of disease. Brain pathology is a type of physical lesion, but its symptoms properly speaking, are neurological rather than psychological in nature. Under no circumstances, therefore, can mental symptoms be considered a form of illness.

2. A basic dichotomy exists between *mental* symptoms, on the one hand, which are subjective in nature, dependent on subjective judgment and personal involvement of the observer, and referable to cultural-ethical norms, and *physical* symptoms, on the other hand, which are allegedly objective in nature, ascertainable without personal involvement of the observer, and independent of cultural norms and ethical standards. Only symptoms possessing the latter set of characteristics are genuinely reflective of illness and amenable to medical treatment.

3. Mental symptoms are merely expres-

sions of problems of living and, hence, cannot be regarded as manifestations of a pathological condition. The concept of mental illness is misleading and demonological because it seeks to explain psychological disturbance in particular and human disharmony in general in terms of a metaphorical but nonexistent disease entity, instead of attributing them to inherent difficulties in coming to grips with elusive problems of choice and responsibility.

4. Personality disorders, therefore, can be most fruitfully conceptualized as products of moral conflict, confusion, and aberration. Mowrer (1960) extends this latter proposition to include the dictum that psychiatric symptoms are primarily reflective of unacknowledged sin, and that individuals manifesting these symptoms are responsible for and deserve their suffering, both because of their original transgressions and because they refuse to avow and expiate their guilt (pp. 301, 304).

Widespread adoption of the Szasz-Mowrer view of the personality disorders would, in my opinion, turn back the psychiatric clock twenty-five hundred years. The most significant and perhaps the only real advance registered by mankind in evolving a rational and humane method of handling behavioral aberrations has been in substituting a concept of disease for the demonological and retributional doctrines regarding their nature and etiology that flourished until comparatively recent times. Conceptualized as illness, the symptoms of personality disorders can be interpreted in the light of underlying stresses and resistances, both genic and environmental, and can be evaluated in relation to *specifiable* quantitative and qualitative norms of appropriately adaptive behavior, both cross-culturally and within a particular cultural context. It would behoove us, therefore, before we abandon the concept of mental

illness and return to the medieval doctrine of unexpiated sin or adopt Szasz' ambiguous criterion of difficulty in ethical choice and responsibility, to subject the foregoing propositions to careful and detailed study.

Mental Symptoms and Brain Pathology

Although I agree with Szasz in rejecting the doctrine that ultimately some neuroanatomic or neurophysiologic defect will be discovered in *all* cases of personality disorder, I disagree with his reasons for not accepting this proposition. Notwithstanding Szasz' straw man presentation of their position, the proponents of the extreme somatic view do not really assert that the *particular nature* of a patient's disordered beliefs can be correlated with "certain definite lesions in the nervous system" (Szasz, 1960, p. 113). They hold rather that normal cognitive and behavioral functioning depends on the anatomic and physiologic integrity of certain key areas of the brain, and that impairment of this substrate integrity, therefore, provides a physical basis for disturbed ideation and behavior, but does not explain, except in a very gross way, the particular kinds of symptoms involved. In fact, they are generally inclined to attribute the *specific* character of the patient's symptoms to the nature of his preillness personality structure, the substrate integrity of which is impaired by the lesion or metabolic defect in question.

Nevertheless, even though this type of reasoning plausibly accounts for the psychological symptoms found in general paresis, various toxic deleria, and other comparable conditions, it is an extremely improbable explanation of *all* instances of personality disorder. Unlike the tissues of any other organ, brain tissue possesses the unique property of making possible awareness of and adjustment to the world of sensory, social, and symbolic stimulation. Hence by virtue of this unique relationship of the nervous system to the environment, diseases of behavior and personality may reflect abnormalities in personal and social adjustment, quite apart from any structural or metabolic disturbance in the underlying neural substrate. I would conclude, therefore, that although brain pathology is probably not the most important cause of behavior disorder, it is undoubtedly responsible for the incidence of *some* psychological abnormalities *as well as* for various neurological signs and symptoms.

But even if we completely accepted Szsaz' view that brain pathology does not account for any symptoms of personality disorder, it would still be unnecessary to accept his assertion that to qualify as a genuine manifestation of disease a given symptom must be caused by a physical lesion. Adoption of such a criterion would be arbitrary and inconsistent both with medical and lay connotations of the term "disease," which in current usage is generally regarded as including any marked deviation, physical, mental, or behavioral, from normally desirable standards of structural and functional integrity.

Mental versus Physical Symptoms

Szsasz contends that since the analogy between physical and mental symptoms is patently fallacious, the postulated parallelism between physical and mental disease is logically untenable. This line of reasoning is based on the assumption that the two categories of symptoms can be sharply dichotomized with respect to such basic dimensions as objectivity-subjectivity, the relevance of cultural norms, and the need for personal involvement of the observer. In my opinion, the existence of such a dichotomy cannot be empirically demonstrated in convincing fashion.

Practically all symptoms of bodily disease involve some elements of subjective judgment—both on the part of the patient and of the physician. Pain is perhaps the most important and commonly used criterion of physical illness. Yet, any evaluation of its reported locus, intensity, character, and duration is dependent upon the patient's subjective appraisal of his own sensations and on the physician's assessment of the latter's pain threshold, intelligence, and personality structure. It is also a medical commonplace that the severity of pain in most instances of bodily illness may be mitigated by the administration of a placebo. Furthermore, in taking a meaningful history the physician must not only serve as a participant observer but also as a skilled interpreter of human behavior. It is the rare patient who does not react psychologically to the signs of physical illness; and hence physicians are constantly called upon to decide, for example, to what extent precordial pain and reported tightness in the chest are manifestations of coronary insufficiency, of fear of cardiac disease and impending death, or of combinations of both conditions. Even such allegedly objective signs as pulse rate, BMR, blood pressure, blood cholesterol have their subjective and relativistic aspects. Pulse rate and blood pressure are notoriously susceptible to emotional influences, and BMR and blood cholesterol fluctuate widely from one cultural environment to another (Dreyfuss & Czaczkes, 1959). And anyone who believes that ethical norms have no relevance for physical illness has obviously failed to consider the problems confronting Catholic patients and/or physicians when issues of contraception, abortion, and preferential saving of the mother's as against the fetus' life must be faced in the context of various obstetrical emergencies and medical contraindications to pregnancy.

It should now be clear, therefore, that symptoms not only do not need a physical basis to qualify as manifestations of illness, but also that the evaluation of *all* symptoms, physical as well as mental, is dependent in large measure on subjective judgment, emotional factors, cultural-ethical norms, and personal involvement on the part of the observer. These considerations alone render no longer tenable Szasz' contention (1960, p. 114) that there is an inherent contradiction between using cultural and ethical norms as criteria of mental disease, on the one hand, and of employing medical measures of treatment on the other. But even if the postulated dichotomy between mental and physical symptoms were valid, the use of physical measures in treating subjective and relativistic psychological symptoms would still be warranted. Once we accept the proposition that impairment of the neutral substrate of personality can result in behavior disorder, it is logically consistent to accept the corollary proposition that other kinds of manipulation of the same neutral substrate can conceivably have therapeutic effects, irrespective of whether the underlying cause of the mental symptoms is physical or psychological.

Mental Illness and Problems of Living

"The phenomena now called mental illness," argues Szasz (1960), can be regarded more forthrightly and simply as "expressions of man's struggle with the problem of how he should live" (p. 117). This statement undoubtedly oversimplifies the nature of personality disorders; but even if it were adequately inclusive it would not be inconsistent with the position that these disorders are a manifestation of illness. There is no valid reason why a particular symptom cannot both reflect a problem in living *and* constitute a manifestation of disease. The notion of mental illness, conceived in this way, would not "obscure the everyday fact that life for most people is a continuous struggle . . . for a 'place in the sun,' 'peace of mind,' or some other human value" (p. 118). It is quite true, as Szasz points out, that "human relations are in-

herently fraught with difficulties" (p. 117), and that most people manage to cope with such difficulties without becoming mentally ill. But conceding this fact hardly precludes the possibility that some individuals, either because of the magnitude of the stress involved, or because of genically or environmentally induced susceptibility to ordinary degrees of stress, respond to the problems of living with behavior that is either seriously distorted or sufficiently unadaptive to prevent normal interpersonal relations and vocational functioning. The latter outcome—gross deviation from a designated range of desirable behavioral variability —conforms to the generally understood meaning of mental illness.

The plausibility of subsuming abnormal behavioral reactions to stress under the general rubric of disease is further enhanced by the fact that these reactions include the same three principal categories of symptoms found in physical illness. Depression and catastrophic impairment of self-esteem, for example, are manifestations of personality disorder which are symptomologically comparable to edema in cardiac failure or to heart murmurs in valvular disease. They are indicative of underlying pathology but are neither adaptive nor adjustive. Symptoms such as hypomanic over-activity and compulsive striving toward unrealistically high achievement goals, on the other hand, are both adaptive and adjustive, and constitute a type of compensatory response to basic feelings of inadequacy, which is not unlike cardiac hypertrophy in hypertensive heart disease or elevated white blood cell count in acute infections. And finally, distortive psychological defenses that have some adjustive value but are generally maladaptive (e.g., phobias, delusions, autistic fantasies) are analogous to the pathological situation found in conditions like pneumonia, in which the excessive outpouring of serum and phagocytes in defensive response to pathogenic bacteria literally causes the patient to drown in his own fluids.

Within the context of this same general proposition, Szasz repudiates the concept of mental illness as demonological in nature, i.e., as the "true heir to religious myths in general and to the belief in witchcraft in particular" (p. 118) because it allegedly employs a reified abstraction ("a deformity of personality") to account in causal terms both for "human disharmony" and for symptoms of behavior disorder (p. 114). But again he appears to be demolishing a straw man. Modern students of personality disorder do not regard mental illness as a cause of human disharmony, but as a co-manifestation with it of inherent difficulties in personal adjustment and interpersonal relations; and in so far as I can accurately interpret the literature, psychopathologists do not conceive of mental illness as a cause of particular behavioral symptoms but as a generic term under which these symptoms can be subsumed.

Mental Illness and Moral Responsibility

Szasz' final reason for regarding mental illness as a myth is really a corollary of his previously considered more general proposition that mental symptoms are essentially reflective of problems of living and hence do not legitimately qualify as manifestations of disease. It focuses on difficulties of ethical choice and responsibility as the particular life problems most likely to be productive of personality disorder. Mowrer (1960) further extends this corollary by asserting that neurotic and psychotic individuals are responsible for their suffering (p. 301), and that unacknowledged and unexpiated sin, in turn, is the basic cause of this suffering (p. 304). As previously suggested, however, one can plausibly accept the proposition that psychiatrists and clinical psychologists have erred in trying to divorce behavioral evaluation from ethical consider-

ations, in conducting psychotherapy in an amoral setting, and in confusing the psychological explanation of unethical behavior with absolution from accountability for same, *without* necessarily endorsing the view that personality disorders are basically a reflection of sin, and that victims of these disorders are less ill than responsible for their symptoms (Ausubel, 1952, pp. 392–397, 465–471).

In the first place, it is possible in most instances (although admittedly difficult in some) to distinguish quite unambiguously between mental illness and ordinary cases of immorality. The vast majority of persons who are guilty of moral lapses knowingly violate their own ethical precepts for expediential reasons—despite being volitionally capable at the time, both of choosing the more moral alternative and of exercising the necessary inhibitory control (Ausubel, 1952, pp. 465–471). Such persons, also, usually do not exhibit any signs of behavior disorder. At crucial choice points in facing the problems of living they simply choose the opportunistic instead of the moral alternative. They are not mentally ill, but they are clearly accountable for their misconduct. Hence, since personality disorder and immorality are neither coextensive nor mutually exclusive conditions, the concept of mental illness need not necessarily obscure the issue of moral accountability.

Second, guilt may be a contributory factor in behavior disorder, but is by no means the only or principal cause thereof. Feelings of guilt may give rise to anxiety and depression; but in the absence of catastrophic impairment of self-esteem induced by *other* factors, these symptoms tend to be transitory and peripheral in nature (Ausubel, 1952, pp. 362–363). Repression of guilt is more a consequence than a cause of anxiety. Guilt is repressed in order to avoid the anxiety producing trauma to self-esteem that would otherwise result if it were acknowledged. Repression per se enters the causal picture in anxiety only secondarily—by obviating "the possibility of punishment, confession, expiation, and other guilt reduction mechanisms" (Ausubel, 1952, p. 456). Furthermore, in most types of personality disorder other than anxiety, depression, and various complications of anxiety such as phobias, obsessions, and compulsion, guilt feelings are either not particularly prominent (schizophrenic reactions), or are conspicuously absent (e.g., classical cases of inadequate or aggressive, antisocial psychopathy).

Third, it is just as unreasonable to hold an individual responsible for symptoms of behavior disorder as to deem him accountable for symptoms of physical illness. He is no more culpable for his inability to cope with sociopsychological stress than he would be for his inability to resist the spread of infectious organisms. In those instances where warranted guilt feelings *do* contribute to personality disorder, the patient is accountable for the misdeeds underlying his guilt, but is hardly responsible for the symptoms brought on by the guilt feelings or for unlawful acts committed during his illness. Acknowledgment of guilt may be therapeutically beneficial under these circumstances, but punishment for the original misconduct should obviously be deferred until after recovery.

Lastly, even if it were true that all personality disorder is a reflection of sin and that people are accountable for their behavioral symptoms, it would still be unnecessary to deny that these symptoms are manifestations of disease. Illness is no less real because the victim happens to be culpable for his illness. A glutton with hypertensive heart disease undoubtedly aggravates his condition by overeating, and is culpable in part for the often fatal symptoms of his disease, but what reasonable person would claim that for this reason he is not really ill?

CONCLUSIONS

Four propositions in support of the argument for discarding the concept of mental illness were carefully examined, and the following conclusions were reached:

First, although brain pathology is probably not the major cause of personality disorder, it does account for *some* psychological symptoms by impairing the neural substrate of personality. In any case, however, a symptom need not reflect a physical lesion in order to qualify as a genuine manifestation of disease.

Second, Szasz' postulated dichotomy between mental and physical symptoms is untenable because the assessment of *all* symptoms is dependent to some extent on subjective judgment, emotional factors, cultural-ethical norms, and personal involvement of the observer. Furthermore, the use of medical measures in treating behavior disorders—irrespective of whether the underlying causes are neural or psychological—is defensible on the grounds that if inadvertent impairment of the neural substrate of personality can have distortive effects on behavior, directed manipulation of the same substrate may have therapeutic effects.

Third, there is no inherent contradiction in regarding mental symptoms both as expressions of problems in living *and* as manifestations of illness. The latter situation results when individuals are for various reasons unable to cope with such problems, and react with seriously distorted or maladaptive behavior. The three principal categories of behavioral symptoms—manifestations of impaired functioning, adaptive compensation, and defensive overreaction—are also found in bodily disease. The concept of mental illness has never been advanced as a demonological cause of human disharmony, but only as a co-manifestation with it of certain inescapable difficulties and hazards in personal and social adjustment. The same concept is also generally accepted as a generic term for all behavioral symptoms rather than as a reified cause of these symptoms.

Fourth, the view that personality disorder is less a manifestation of illness than of sin, i.e., of culpable inadequacy in meeting problems of ethical choice and responsibility, and that victims of behavior disorder are therefore morally accountable for their symptoms, is neither logically nor empirically tenable. In most instances immoral behavior and mental illness are clearly distinguishable conditions. Guilt is only a secondary etiological factor in anxiety and depression, and in other personality disorders is either not prominent or conspicuously absent. The issue of culpability for symptoms is largely irrelevant in handling the behavior disorders, and in any case does not detract from the reality of the illness.

In general, it is both unnecessary and potentially dangerous to discard the concept of mental illness on the grounds that only in this way can clinical psychology escape from the professional domination of medicine. Dentists, podiatrists, optometrists, and osteopaths have managed to acquire an independent professional status without rejecting the concept of disease. It is equally unnecessary and dangerous to substitute the doctrine of sin for illness in order to counteract prevailing amoral and nonjudgmental trends in psychotherapy. The hypothesis of repressed guilt does not adequately explain most kinds and instances of personality disorder, and the concept of mental illness does not preclude judgments of moral accountability where warranted. Definition of behavior disorder in terms of sin or of difficulties associated with ethical choice and responsibility would substitute theological disputation and philosophical wrangling about values for specifiable quantitative and qualitative criteria of disease.

"Mental Health" Reconsidered: A Special Case of the Problem of Values in Psychology[1]

M. Brewster Smith

The signs are increasingly clear that "mental health" and its complement,

Reprinted from American Psychologist, 1961, vol. 16, pp. 299–306 with the permission of the American Psychological Association and the author.

[1] Adapted from a paper prepared for the Work Conference on Mental Health–Teacher Education Research Projects, Madison, Wisconsin, November 10–18, 1960. I am indebted to Barbara Biber, Robert Peck, Fred Wilhelms, John Withall, Nicholas Hobbs, Erich Lindemann, Ronald Lippitt, Ralph Ojemann, Hildegard Peplau, Carl Rogers, and the other participants in the conference for their reactions to the earlier version of the paper.

"mental illness," are terms that embarrass psychologists. Many of us do not like them (cf. APA, 1959). Unable to define or to conceptualize them to our satisfaction, we use the terms in spite of ourselves, since they label the goals, however nebulous, of many of our service activities and the auspices of much of our research support. Even when we try to avoid them, we are swept along in the social movement of which they are shibboleths, and our scruples make little difference. Little wonder, then, that we and our colleagues in the other "mental health professions" seek to clear our consciences by continuing to engage in sporadic attempts to give them more precise and explicit meaning.

Having contributed from time to time to this discussion, I feel entitled to some skepticism about where it has got us. True, we have made some gains in disposing of several unprofitable ways of thinking about mental health that used to be prevalent. We have come to see that statistical notions of "normality" are no real help in giving psychological meaning to mental health and illness: they beg the question or fail to come to grips with it. We have become suspicious of the once regnant concept of adjustment, as it has fallen into disrepute at the hands of social critics and moralists (e.g., Riesman, 1950) who see it as a pseudo-scientific rationalization for conformist values, and of psychological theorists (e.g., White, 1959) who are challenging the sufficiency of the equilibrium model in which it is rooted. And from many quarters we encounter the call for a more positive view of mental health than is involved in the mere absence of manifest mental disorder. Since the appearance of Jahoda's useful book (1958) that reviewed the considerable array of proposals toward such a conception of optimal human functioning, the flow of suggestions has not abated. The discussion goes on in articles, conferences, and symposia, with little evidence of consensus in the offing.

The various lists of criteria that have been proposed for positive mental health reshuffle overlapping conceptions of desirable functioning without attaining agreement—or giving much promise that agreement can be reached. The inventories repeat themselves, and indeed it is inevitable that they should, since each successor list is proposed by a wise psychologist who scrutinizes previous pro-

posals and introduces variations and emphases to fit his own values and preferences. Some give greater weight to the cognitive values of accurate perception and self-knowledge (e.g., Jahoda, 1955); some to moral values, to meaningful commitment, to social responsibility (e.g., Allport, 1960; Shoben, 1957); some to working effectiveness (e.g., Ginsberg, 1955); some to the blander social virtues (e.g., aspects of Foote & Cottrell, 1955); some to zest, exuberance, and creativity (e.g., Maslow, 1954). The terms recur, but in different combinations and with connotations that slant in divergent directions. By way of illustration, Table 1 gives the six headings under which

Table 1
Two Illustrative Conceptions of Positive Mental Health in Terms of Multiple Criteria

Jahoda (1958)	Allport (1960)
attitudes toward the self	self-objectification
growth and self-actualization	ego-extension
integration	unifying philosophy of life
autonomy	
perception of reality	realistic coping skills, abilities, and perceptions
	warm and deep relation of self to others
environmental mastery	compassionate regard for all living creatures

Note: Rubrics are rearranged to bring out parallels.

Jahoda (1958) organized the proposals for mental health criteria that she encountered in her review of the literature, and Allport's most recent proposal (1960), rearranged to bring out correspondences and discrepancies in the two lists. While it is an advance that psychologists are now looking for multiple criteria of good functioning rather than seeking the single touchstone of a unitary definition of mental health, we may well ask: How are psychologists to decide what items belong in such a list? By what warrant may we assign priorities to alternative criteria? Surely we need something closer to *terra firma* on which to build our research, from which to guide our practice.

There is little to be gained, I think, from adding to these competing lists. Conceptual clarification, on the other hand, may be more profitable, and my attempt in the present essay lies in that direction. Starting from the now prevalent recognition that mental health is an evaluative term, that personal and social values as standards of the preferable are somehow crucially involved in any discourse about mental health, I try first to show that this intrusion of values into psychology, lamented by some, applauded by others, is entirely legitimate. But I question, secondly, whether there is any profit in the argument about which evaluative criteria for appraising human personality and behavior are to be included in a concept of mental health. Rather, I suggest that, at least in the present stage of personality theory, "mental health" should not be regarded as a theoretical concept at all, but as a rubric or chapter heading under which fall a variety of evaluative concerns. I try to show that such a view of the term may help to clear the ground for both practical and theoretical purposes.

In an earlier effort (1959) at clarification in this area, I observed that at the crux of the difficulty of assimilating "mental health" to psychology is the fact that "science has not yet learned how to deal surefootedly with values" (p. 673). Any progress toward clarity in psychological thinking about mental health, I am increasingly convinced, depends on our becoming clearer, as psychologists,

about how we are to think about values. Whatever advances we make on the problem of values in this setting should also stand us in good stead in other contexts where issues of value confront psychology. The value problem is worth a close and sustained look.

WHY THE SEARCH FOR A VALUE-LADEN CONCEPTION OF POSITIVE MENTAL HEALTH?

While evaluative criteria and judgments are involved in the notion of mental disorder, our consensus about what is *undesirable* is close enough for practical purposes that the role of values tends to remain implicit. It is when we want to talk about positive criteria of psychological functioning that we encounter the value problem head on. A good starting point for the present discussion, then, is to ask why we ever got ourselves into this difficult, intellectually treacherous business of positive mental health. Are not the problems of mental disorder enough? Why should the mental health movement be impelled, as it has been since the days of Clifford Beers (cf. Joint Commission on Mental Illness and Health, 1961), to extend itself to concern with the "mental hygiene" of promoting positive mental health—in the absence of firm knowledge or clear guidelines?

The answer to such a question cannot be simple. But I think a generally critical onlooker from England, R. S. Peters (1960), has hit the essential point when he addressed the BBC audience thus:

> We have a highly specialized society and we are often warned that we are developing not merely two nations but a league of nations without a common culture and shared ideals. This should not surprise us; for where are such unifying ideals to be fostered? The study of literature, history, and the classics has had to be cut down to make room for the

vast expansion in scientific education without which our society cannot survive, and the Church is rapidly losing the authority it once had as a source of unifying ideals. We tend to treat the doctor who looks after our bodies and the psychiatrist who advises us about our minds with more respect than we treat the priest who advises us about our souls—if we still think we have one. For they are scientists; and it is scientists who are now coming to be thought of as the repositories of wisdom about the mysteries of life.

This general trend explains why the educationist sometimes inclines his ear towards a new expert, the psychologist, when he is at a loss to find new unifying educational ideals to replace the old religious ones. There is thus much talk in educational circles of "the mental health of the child," "wholeness," "integration," "adjustment," and all that sort of thing. We no longer talk of turning out Christian gentlemen; we talk of letting people develop mental health or mature personalities. Indeed in America Freud's priestly role is much more explicitly acknowledged. . . . Nevertheless the general trend is [also] with us, as is shown in the frequent references to psychological notions such as "mental health" in discussion about educational ideals. (p. 46)

Discount the bias of perspective arising from Peters' assured stance in the tradition of British class education, and hold in abeyance reaction to his critical undertones: his point remains that a good many thoughtful people have turned, appropriately or otherwise, to notions of mental health in order to fill a void left by the attrition of traditionally or religiously sanctioned values. There is consumer demand for psychologists to enter the discussion of goals and aspirations for human behavior; but we had better be clear about our warrant for doing so.

The demand for a psychologically informed phrasing of objectives—for conceptions of positive mental health—comes most compellingly from those concerned with the rearing and education of children. The psychologist or psychiatrist who mainly deals with hospitalized psychotics has enough to do in trying to treat severe mental disorder and get his patients to function at some minimally adequate level; since consensus on these objectives is immediately given, the value problem hardly rises to the surface. But responsibility for the raising of children calls for positive criteria against which the success of one's efforts on their behalf can be measured. Perhaps a counselor may appropriately leave it to his adult client to set the goals for his therapy; the case can hardly be extended to the child as ward of teacher and parent—who in turn look to the psychologist for guidance.

Of course there are intellectual positions from which the responsibility appears to be minimized. If you take a Rousseau-like view that regards optimal development as the unfolding of a benign inner potential, you can at least pretend to leave goal setting entirely to the child's own nature. This doctrine of benign potentiality, which is still very much alive in educational and psychological theory (witness Maslow, 1954), strikes me as involving psychological half-truths and philosophical error. It is we ourselves, in terms of our tacit values, who single out, as optimal, one of an infinite set of possible environments for the developing child, and distinguish the way he develops in such an auspicious setting as the actualization of a naturally given potential. We ignore the infinite variety of other developmental trends that he simultaneously has the potential to actualize, many of which we would not think highly of—and ignore the silent and therefore not fully responsible intrusion of our own values involved in distinguishing one class of possible trends as self-actualizing.

Another way of minimizing responsibility for educational goal setting in terms of mental health is to accept as ultimate the values of the culture, to define the function of education as cultural transmission and, in effect, leave matters of value-choice to parents and school board. The trouble is that this option is no longer really available, even if we prefer it. The state of affairs evoked by Peters is with us: there is no longer such a solid traditional consensus for us to fall back on. Parents and school boards too are confused and involved in the fray. Under these circumstances education can hardly avoid a complex role that combines and balances cultural transmission, on the one hand, and social criticism and reconstruction on the other. This characteristic American philosophy of education has thus become virtually a policy of necessity. It calls for clear-headedness about goals, and has tended to draw on psychology for their formulation.

Insofar as we take the requirements of education seriously, then, we cannot help trying to grapple with conceptions of optimal human functioning. We also need them in planning and assessing programs of counseling and of environmental change. In the face of a waning consensus on traditional values, we join our lay clientele in hoping that psychology can help in this endeavor. But hope does not guarantee success. The strength of our needs may head us the more rigidly down blind alleys, unless we have our wits about us.

THE VALUE PROBLEM

The skeptical reader imbued with the distinction between scientific objectivity, on the one hand, and the humanistic cultivation of values on the other will have balked at an earlier point, and stayed with the question: By what warrant do psychologists assume the right to posit any set of human values, as we do when we propose criteria of positive mental health? The psychologist has no more right to do so, he will say, than anyone else. Let him stick to his last, and recognize the limits of his competence. My serious rejoinder, which requires somewhat of a detour to develop, reverses this conventional view: the psychologist has *as much* right to posit values as anyone else, in some important respects more. It is time to dispel the shopworn bromide that the humanist (or moralist or philosopher) has a corner on pronouncements about values, while the psychologist (or sociologist or scientist generally) must restrict himself to facts. Things are just not that simple.

For most of us, the two sources to which everyone once looked for what were then regarded as "absolute" values— Tradition and Theology—speak only equivocally if at all. We are still suffering from the crisis of personal and social readjustment occasioned by this loss. As we regain our bearings, our nostalgia for the old illusion of Absoluteness, of givenness in the eternal scheme of things, begins to fade. But in spite of the pessimism of those who hunger after Absoluteness, we still have values, in the sense of personal standards of desirability and obligation. We see them, now, as committing choices that people make (often unwittingly) in the interplay of cultural tradition and individual experience. We see them as "relative," yes, but relative not only to culture (an exclusive focus on *cultural* relativism was the mistake of the last generation of anthropologists). They are relative also to human nature—in the diverse varieties of this nature that have emerged in human history with a degree of continuity and cumulativeness—and relative to the opportunities and limitations of human situations. Thus the warrior virtues held validity for the traditional Sioux; for the reservation Sioux they no longer make any sense (MacGregor, 1946). And one can fairly doubt whether the petty competitive values of the Alorese studied by Cora DuBois (1944) ever made much sense: she showed them to be part and parcel of a wretched and demeaning way of life that I doubt whether any Alorese would choose were some magic to give him a wider range of opportunity.

If values are social products, they rest, ultimately, on a personal commitment. Everybody, scientist or humanist or man in the street, has the right to posit values. And, since people in society are interdependent, everyone has a right to try to persuade others to his ways of valuing: *de gustibus non disputandum est* may apply to tastes and preferences, but it has never prevented controversy about values, as the course of human history well reveals. We *all* have the right to dispute values, and most of us do it. The humanist and the humane scientist nevertheless have potentially different specialized roles in the argument.

Their roles arise from the peculiar nature of argument about values that follows from the basis of values in an optional personal commitment. If you want to persuade someone to value something as you do, you can follow one of at least two strategies (assuming that physical or social coercion is ruled out, which historically has unfortunately not been the case): You can, first, try to open his eyes to new ways of seeing things—increase the range of possibilities of which he is aware, create the conditions for differentiations and restructurings in his experience from which it is possible (not necessary) that, seeing things like yourself, he may come to value them likewise. Or, second, you can give him evidence that the position he takes on a particular value has consequences for other values to which he is also com-

mitted. For the fact that values rest on a personal option does not make them arbitrary in the sense of being detached from cause or consequence. If you show a person that his chosen value of racial purity conflicts with the values of the American Creed that he also embraces, he *may* reconsider it (Myrdal, 1944). Or if you show him that his prejudiced value rests causally on evasive covert tactics of defense against inner weakness, you again have a chance to win out (Adorno, Frenkel-Brunswik, Levinson, & Sanford, 1950). The *ad hominem* argument, in ill favor as it is, is fair play in this peculiar and important realm, so long as it is not taken as conclusive. Since values rest on personal option, *no* argument is conclusive, though many can be persuasive, and appropriately so.

I am thus suggesting that the humanist and the moral philosopher are especially equipped to employ the first of these strategies: drawing on the fund of human history and culture, with its stock of transmitted discriminations, they can sensitize us to differentiations and potentialities of human experience which, unaided, we could never attain individually. Our value choices are enriched and modified by this exposure. The second strategy, that of displaying the causal network in which value choice is embedded, is one for which the humane or behavioral scientist is uniquely qualified.

The old myth had it that man lost his precultural innocence when, biting the fruit of the Tree of Knowledge, he became aware of Good and Evil. In becoming modern, Man has taken a second portentous bite of the same fruit. There are alternative versions of Good and Evil, he discovers to his discomfiture, and it is up to him to chose the commitments he is to live by. From this emerging view that can no longer turn to authoritative interpretations of tradition or divine revelation to resolve questions of value, it makes no sense at all for us to encyst ourselves behind a pass-the-buck notion that we can leave value judgments to some other discipline that specializes in them. There is no discipline that has this mythical competence: the humanist and the theologian speak with no greater authority than we. We are all in it together.

THE LIST PROBLEM

I think I have shown the legitimacy, the clear warrant, for psychologists to concern themselves with values, as we do when we involve ourselves with mental health. But my argument gives no help at all on the other problem: what value dimensions are to get on our lists of mental health criteria, and why? If anything, it makes things more difficult. For if values are matters of a committing personal option, how are psychologists—let alone people at large—to come to agree on any particular list any more closely than the limited extent to which they already do? Even with a richer exposure to the humanistic tradition than is customary for psychologists, even with a far more adequate fund of causal knowledge than is presently available, psychological "experts" are not going to agree on the proper goals for human nature, and these are what we are talking about.

The actual situation is well typified by the experience of the Cornell Conference (National Assembly on Mental Health Education, 1960). To quote the conference report:

> Everyone at Cornell seemed to agree that the good life for all was to be desired. They split, however, on what that good life was—as they had split on the definition of mental health, and they split on who, if anyone, should have the right to try to "impose" it on others. (p. 20)

The definition of mental health, of course, *involves* a conception of the good life, which nobody *can* impose on anyone else (barring "brainwashing" and physical coercion), though, at least among colleagues and equals, it is fair enough for each of us to try to persuade the rest.

But the time has come to cut the Gordian knot, to restructure the problem along more profitable lines. The place to cut, I think, is the notion that the lists we have been considering itemize criteria of some entity called "positive mental health," and are equivalent to a definition of it. Even though we may have forsaken the view of mental health as a unitary phenomenon, and may have no intention of adding up a single score across our multiple criteria, we remain beguiled by the assumption that an articulate theoretical concept or construct of mental health lurks somewhere ready to be discovered. It is the pursuit of this will-of-the-wisp that has made the procession of lists of mental health criteria so fruitless.

As we actually study effective functioning—or commit ourselves to social or educational programs that seek in various ways to promote it—our focus then becomes, not "mental health" variously indexed, but any or all of a number of much more specific evaluative dimensions of human functioning: any that we are ready to commit ourselves to take seriously as relevant and valued potential psychological outcomes of the programs that we are working with, any that we can begin to pin down in operational terms, as many of them as seem important to us and as we can feasibly cope with. Here I find myself in essential agreement with the position recently taken by Levine and Kantor (1960).

From the standpoint of research, the problem of attaining consensus on criteria is thus scaled down to the workaday dimensions we are used to: the practical difficulty of trying to convince at least some of our colleagues to study some of the same things we are studying by similar methods, so that our results can dovetail or add up. There is no reason at all why study of the causes, consequences, and interrelations of standing on various mental health dimensions has to await consensus on a common list that may never be attained—and by my personal value commitments would not even be desirable!

In the long run, it is possible that our understanding of interrelated system properties of personality may advance to a point that warrants a more theoretical conception of mental health—one related, say, to empirically based estimates of such properties as self-maintenance, growth, and resilience (cf. Smith, 1959). We are certainly still far from being able to envision such a conception except in the most schematic terms. But if it is to be attained at all, the road to it should lie through nonevaluative research on personality development and functioning, on the one hand, and, on the other, through the strategy I have just been advocating: modestly exploring the empirical correlates of valued attributes of personality.

But what of the public demands for mental health "expertise" with which we started? What implications does our analysis have for the role of the psychologist in school, clinic, or consulting room? The very fact that no simple rule book of prescribed conduct seems to follow from it gives me greater confidence in the appropriateness of the approach we have taken.

Knowing that he lacks a scientifically sanctioned single set of mental health criteria, the psychologist in his consulting or service or educational relationships will hesitate to prescribe the nature of the good life to others in the name of psychology. Since values rest on a personal option, he will find it easiest to

keep a clear scientific and professional conscience when he can use his knowledge and skill to help others identify, clarify, and realize their value commitments—provided that he can reconcile them with the values that he himself is committed to. Yet his own psychologically informed personal commitments about the nature of good human functioning cannot exist in a vacuum. They may lead him to avoid or to terminate service relationships that appear to violate them, to seek relationships that promote them. When his role as teacher or therapist vests him with more direct and personal responsibilities for goal setting, he will not hesitate to act in terms of his convictions about what is desirable in the relationship and of the best knowledge and wisdom he can muster. But he will seek to move such relationships in the direction of increasing the responsibility of the other party for choosing his own goals. To his colleagues in and out of psychology and to various publics, he may often appear as an advocate of particular values. But his advocacy will consist in displaying the nature of his personal commitment and of using his psychological knowledge and insight to explore the linkage between holding or attaining a value and its conditions and consequences. In a word, explicitness about values goes with responsible scientific and professional behavior, and when we are explicit about such values as truthfulness, competence, care, responsibility, creativity, we add nothing consequential by labeling them as dimensions or criteria of positive mental health.

MENTAL HEALTH AS A RUBRIC

If "mental health" is to lose its presumptive conceptual standing, what does its status become? I see it rather as a rubric, a chapter title, a label for the common concern of various disciplines involved in evaluating human functioning from the perspective of the psychology of personality. Its usefulness in this respect does not depend on its dubious status as a theoretical concept. As chapter title, "mental health" is analogous to "mechanics" in classical physics: a rubric under which we treat a number of theoretical constructs (e.g., mass, force, velocity) and the laws relating them. You do not argue very violently about where chapter boundaries should be drawn.

There remain many meaningful problems concerning the contents and organization of such a chapter, even about its name. Personally, I agree with Levine and Kantor (1960) and with Szasz (1960) that the term "mental health" is unfortunate for our present purposes, biasing the issues as it does toward a model of physical health and illness that seems quite inappropriate to the analysis of effective and disordered conduct. But with the focus shifted to specific evaluative dimensions, I do not find myself caring very much about this argument, any more than I worry about the chapter titles in a book of applied science. This is an editorial problem, not a substantive one.

As for the contents of the mental health chapter, a variety of pragmatic considerations come to mind to assist in culling, augmenting, and refining the items in the available lists. Candidates for treatment as dimensions of mental health or of goodness of psychological functioning might be expected to meet most of the following criteria, none of which seems to require elaborate justification:

1. They should be serious contenders in the arena of human values (though an impossible consensus is of course not required). The posited value should be explicit.
2. They should be capable of measurement or of inference from identifiable aspects of behavior.
3. They should articulate with personality theory (a weak requirement, since the proviso must be added immediately that personality theories will probably need to be extended and modified to make contact with value dimensions chosen on other grounds).
4. They should be relevant to the social context for which the chapter is being written. In the context of education, for instance, this is to ask: What kinds of psychological assets would we like to see the schools develop in our children? Quite different considerations would come to the fore in the context of a correctional agency.

Considerations such as these make it unlikely that the entire range of moral, esthetic, and cognitive values will vie for inclusion in the mental health chapter. But no harm is done if a venturesome soul decides to study the natural history of some utterly "unpsychological" value under mental health auspices.

A more fundamental choice concerns short vs. long versions of the chapter: in other words, minimal vs. extended conceptions of mental health. I can illustrate this choice best if I introduce at the same time a possible principle for organizing the chapter. Jahoda (1958) observed that "one has the option of defining mental health in at least two ways: as a relatively constant and enduring function of the personality . . . ; or as a momentary function of personality and situation" (pp. 7–8). Klein (1960) makes a similar point in his distinction between soundness or general stability, and well-being. We want, that is, to distinguish, on the one hand, the person's present state and behavior as an interactive resultant of his personality and features of the momentary situation that he confronts, and, on the other, the corresponding dispositions of his present personality, with situational effects discounted. Add a time dimension—here in terms of an assessment of mental health in childhood with prognosis to adulthood, since a primary ingredient of our interest in the mental health of children is the foundation it is assumed to provide for adult functioning—and minimal vs. extended views of mental health may be illustrated as in Table 2.

To me, this way of mapping the contents of the chapter seems clarifying. As I look at the top row, the narrow conception of the scope of mental health seems thoroughly viable. I am led to think that Jahoda (1958) may have dismissed this version too quickly, that the psychiatrist Walter Barton in his postscript to her volume was certainly right about its relevance and adequacy for the context of institutional psychiatry. But as I compare the top and bottom lines, I agree with her that the narrow version of the chapter is not in itself adequate to the evaluative concerns of education—to pick one relevant context with which psychologists are involved. And it is of course the bottom line, the extended version, that potentially expands greatly as various dimensions of good functioning are specified. Comparison of the two lines reminds me to agree with Clausen (1956) that we know very little about their relationship to one another: no longer regarding mental health as a theoretical concept, we have no particular reason to expect resistance to mental disorder to correlate with various aspects of positive functioning, but the problem calls for research. And finally, the presence of the right-hand column calls to mind how little we know about the continuities of behavior seen in evaluative terms.

So long as we grope futilely toward a *concept* of "mental health," minimal or maximal, the advantages of specificity and researchability appear to be on the side of the minimal conception. Viewing these versions as different locations of chapter boundary lines, however, we can be as specific as we want about our positively valued criteria. It may well turn out to be the case, then, that the extended version includes the valued dimensions of behavior and personality that are most responsive to our interventions. "Mental health promotion" in this sense may not be as impractical as some of us have come to assume.

CONCLUSION

Where has this analysis of "mental health" as a problem of values led us? It may free us, I hope, from some of the embarrassment that has motivated psychologists' attempts to treat it as a theoretical concept—attempts that have not been additive and have not made

Table 2
Illustration of Narrow and Broad Conceptions of Mental Health

Scope	Mental Health of Child		
	Present Behavior	Present Disposition	Adult Prognosis
Minimal conception	Freedom from incapacitating symptoms	Good resistance to stress	Absence of mental disorder in adulthood
Extended conception	Momentary well-being (in specified respects)	Capacities for competent, happy, zestful, etc. child life	Capacities for competent, happy, zestful, etc. adult life.

the term theoretically respectable. If we understand "mental health" not as an unsatisfactory and vague theoretical concept but as a reasonably adequate rubric or label for an evaluative psychological perspective on personality—even though the term is not of our own choosing— we can get about our business without wasting our efforts on the search for consensus on a unique set of mental health criteria when consensus is not to be had.

Under this rubric, our business, be it research or service, is properly concerned with specific valued dimensions or attributes of behavior and personality. In our focus on these dimensions we are not at all handicapped by the lack of a satisfactory conceptual definition of mental health.

Nor need we be embarrassed by the intrusion of values in our focus on various specified aspects of desirable or undesirable psychological functioning. What is to be avoided is the *surreptitious* advocacy of values disguised under presumptive scientific auspices. The lists of psychological desiderata that psychologists have continued to propose, each reflecting the value commitments of its proponent, have this drawback insofar as they are offered as "criteria of positive mental health." But there is nothing surreptitious, nothing illegitimate, in using evaluative dimensions such as those that appear on these lists to appraise behavior and personality, so long as the value position one takes is explicit. And there is much to be gained from psychological study of the empirical antecedents, consequences, and interrelations of realizing different values in the sphere of personality.

In the study of optimal human functioning, I have argued, behavioral and social scientists can put their special qualifications to work toward the clarification of values among which people must choose and of the causal relations that are relevant to value choice. From it we should not only increase our knowledge about ways and means of attaining the values we agree on; we should also bring to light factual relationships that have a bearing on our choice of what values to pursue, individually and socially. To the extent that the behavioral sciences develop in this direction, they contribute to providing a badly needed bridge between what C. P. Snow (1959) has called "the two cultures" of the scientists and the humanistic intellectuals.

Toward a Modern Approach to Values: The Valuing Process in the Mature Person

Carl R. Rogers

There is a great deal of concern today with the problem of values. Youth, in almost every country, is deeply uncertain of its value orientation; the values associated with various religions have lost much of their influence; sophisticated individuals in every culture seem unsure and troubled as to the goals they hold in esteem. The reasons are not far to seek. The world culture, in all its

Reprinted from the *Journal of Abnormal and Social Psychology*, 1964, vol. 68, pp. 160–167 with the permission of the American Psychological Association and the author.

aspects, seems increasingly scientific and relativistic, and the rigid, absolute views on values which come to us from the past appear anachronistic. Even more important, perhaps, is the fact that the modern individual is assailed from every angle by divergent and contradictory value claims. It is no longer possible, as it was in the not too distant historical past, to settle comfortably into the value system of one's forebears or one's community and live out one's life without ever examining the nature and the assumptions of that system.

In this situation it is not surprising that value orientations from the past appear to be in a state of disintegration or collapse. Men question whether there are, or can be, any universal values. It is often felt that we may have lost, in our modern world, all possibility of any general or cross-cultural basis for values. One natural result of this uncertainty and confusion is that there is an increasing concern about, interest in, and a searching for, a sound or meaningful value approach which can hold its own in today's world.

I share this general concern. As with other issues the general problem faced by the culture is painfully and specifically evident in the cultural microcosm which is called the therapeutic relationship, which is my sphere of experience.

As a consequence of this experience I should like to attempt a modest theoretical approach to this whole problem. I have observed changes in the approach to values as the individual grows from infancy to adulthood. I observe further changes when, if he is fortunate, he continues to grow toward true psychological maturity. Many of these observations grow out of my experience as therapist, where I have had the mind stretching opportunity of seeing the ways in which individuals move toward a richer life. From these observations I believe I see some directional threads emerging which

might offer a new concept of the valuing process, more tenable in the modern world. I have made a beginning by presenting some of these ideas partially in previous writings (Rogers, 1951, 1959); I would like now to voice them more clearly and more fully.

Some Definitions

Charles Morris (1956, pp. 9–12) has made some useful distinctions in regard to values. There are "operative values," which are the behaviors of organisms in which they show preference for one object or objective rather than another. The lowly earthworm, selecting the smooth arm of a Y maze rather than the arm which is paved with sandpaper, is giving an indication of an operative value.

There are also "conceived values," the preference of an individual for a symbolized object. "Honesty is the best policy" is such a conceived value.

There is also the term "objective value," to refer to what is objectively preferable, whether or not it is sensed or conceived of as desirable. I will be concerned primarily with operative or conceptualized values.

Infant's Way of Valuing

Let me first speak about the infant. The living human being has, at the outset, a clear approach to values. We can infer from studying his behavior that he prefers those experiences which maintain, enhance, or actualize his organism, and rejects those which do not serve this end. Watch him for a bit:

Hunger is negatively valued. His expression of this often comes through loud and clear.

Food is positively valued. But when he is satisfied, food is negatively valued, and the same milk he responded to so eagerly is now spit out, or the breast which seemed so satisfying is now rejected as he turns his head away from the nipple with an amusing facial expression of disgust and revulsion.

He values security, and the holding and caressing which seem to communicate security.

He values new experience for its own sake, and we observe this in his obvious pleasure in discovering his toes, in his searching movements, in his endless curiosity.

He shows a clear negative valuing of pain, bitter tastes, sudden loud sounds.

All of this is commonplace, but let us look at these facts in terms of what they tell us about the infant's approach to values. It is first of all a flexible, changing, valuing *process*, not a fixed system. He likes food and dislikes the same food. He values security and rest, and rejects it for new experience. What is going on seems best described as an organismic valuing process, in which each element, each moment of what he is experiencing is somehow weighed, and selected or rejected, depending on whether, at that moment, it tends to actualize the organism or not. This complicated weighing of experience is clearly an organismic, not a conscious or symbolic function. These are operative, not conceived values. But this process can nonetheless deal with complex value problems. I would remind you of the experiment in which young infants had spread in front of them a score or more of dishes of natural (that is, unflavored) foods. Over a period of time they clearly tended to value the foods which enhanced their own survival, growth, and development. If for a time a child gorged himself on starches, this would soon be balanced by a protein "binge." If at times he chose a diet deficient in some vitamin, he would later seek out foods rich in this very vitamin. The physiological wisdom of his body guided his behavioral movements, resulting in what

we might think of as objectively sound value choices.

Another aspect of the infant's approach to values is that the source or locus of the evaluating process is clearly within himself. Unlike many of us, he *knows* what he likes and dislikes, and the origin of these value choices lies strictly within himself. He is the center of the valuing process, the evidence for his choices being supplied by his own senses. He is not at this point influenced by what his parents think he should prefer, or by what the church says, or by the opinion of the latest "expert" in the field, or by the persuasive talents of an advertising firm. It is from within his own experiencing that his organism is saying in nonverbal terms, "This is good for me." "That is bad for me." "I like this." "I strongly dislike that." He would laugh at our concern over values, if he could understand it.

Change in the Valuing Process

What happens to this efficient, soundly based valuing process? By what sequence of events do we exchange it for the more rigid, uncertain, inefficient approach to values which characterizes most of us as adults? Let me try to state briefly one of the major ways in which I think this happens.

The infant needs love, wants it, tends to behave in ways which will bring a repetition of this wanted experience. But this brings complications. He pulls baby sister's hair, and finds it satisfying to hear her wails and protests. He then hears that he is "a naughty, bad boy," and this may be reinforced by a slap on the hand. He is cut off from affection. As this experience is repeated, and many, many others like it, he gradually learns that what "feels good" is often "bad" in the eyes of significant others. Then the next step occurs, in which he comes to take the same attitude toward himself which these others have taken. Now, as he pulls his sister's hair, he solemnly intones, "Bad, bad boy." He is introjecting the value judgment of another, taking it in as his own. To that degree he loses touch with his own organismic valuing process. He has deserted the wisdom of his organism, giving up the locus of evaluation, and is trying to behave in terms of values set by another, in order to hold love.

Or take another example at an older level. A boy senses, though perhaps not consciously, that he is more loved and prized by his parents when he thinks of being a doctor than when he thinks of being an artist. Gradually he introjects the values attached to being a doctor. He comes to want, above all, to be a doctor. Then in college he is baffled by the fact that he repeatedly fails in chemistry, which is absolutely necessary to becoming a physician, in spite of the fact that the guidance counselor assures him he has the ability to pass the course. Only in counseling interviews does he begin to realize how completely he has lost touch with his organismic reactions, how out of touch he is with his own valuing process.

Perhaps these illustrations will indicate that in an attempt to gain or hold love, approval, esteem, the individual relinquishes the locus of evaluation which was his in infancy, and places it in others. He learns to have a basic *dis*trust for his own experiencing as a guide to his behavior. He learns from others a large number of conceived values, and adopts them as his own, even though they may be widely discrepant from what he is experiencing.

Some Introjected Patterns

It is in this fashion, I believe, that most of us accumulate the introjected value patterns by which we live. In the fantastically complex culture of today, the patterns we introject as desirable or undesirable come from a variety of sources and are often highly contradictory. Let me list a few of the introjections which are commonly held.

Sexual desires and behaviors are mostly bad. The sources of this construct are many—parents, church, teachers.

Disobedience is bad. Here parents and teachers combine with the military to emphasize this concept. To obey is good. To obey without question is even better.

Making money is the highest good. The sources of this conceived value are too numerous to mention.

Learning an accumulation of scholarly facts is highly desirable. Education is the source.

Communism is utterly bad. Here the government is a major source.

To love thy neighbor is the highest good. This concept comes from the church, perhaps from the parents.

Cooperation and teamwork are preferable to acting alone. Here companions are an important source.

Cheating is clever and desirable. The peer group again is the origin.

Coca-Colas, chewing gum, electric refrigerators, and automobiles are all utterly desirable. From Jamaica to Japan, from Copenhagen to Kowloon, the "Coca-Cola culture" has come to be regarded as the acme of desirability.

This is a small and diversified sample of the myriads of conceived values which individuals often introject, and hold as their own, without ever having considered their inner organismic reactions to these patterns and objects.

Common Characteristics of Adult Valuing

I believe it will be clear from the foregoing that the usual adult—I feel I am speaking for most of us—has an approach to values which has these characteristics:

The majority of his values are introjected from other individuals or groups significant to him, but are regarded by him as his own.

The source or locus of evaluation on most matters lies outside of himself.

The criterion by which his values are set is the degree to which they will cause him to be loved, accepted, or esteemed.

These conceived preferences are either not related at all, or not clearly related, to his own process of experiencing.

Often there is a wide and unrecognized discrepancy between the evidence supplied by his own experience, and these conceived values.

Because these conceptions are not open to testing in experience, he must hold them in a rigid and unchanging fashion. The alternative would be a collapse of his values. Hence his values are "right."

Because they are untestable, there is no ready way of solving contradictions. If he has taken in from the community the conception that money is the *summum bonum* and from the church the conception that love of one's neighbor is the highest value, he has no way of discovering which has more value for *him*. Hence a common aspect of modern life is living with absolutely contradictory values. We calmly discuss the possibility of dropping a hydrogen bomb on Russia, but find tears in our eyes when we see headlines about the suffering of one small child.

Because he has relinquished the locus of evaluation to others, and has lost touch with his own valuing process, he feels profoundly insecure and easily threatened in his values. If some of these conceptions were destroyed, what would take their place? This threatening possibility makes him hold his value conceptions more rigidly or more confusedly, or both.

Fundamental Discrepancy

I believe that this picture of the individual, with values mostly introjected, held as fixed concepts, rarely examined or tested, is the picture of most of us. By taking over the conceptions of others as our own, we lose contact with the potential wisdom of our own functioning, and lose confidence in ourselves. Since these value constructs are often sharply at variance with what is going on in our own experiencing, we have in a very basic way divorced ourselves from ourselves, and this accounts for much of modern strain and insecurity. This fundamental discrepancy between the individual's concept and what he is actually experiencing, between the intellectual structure of his values and the valuing process going on unrecognized within— this is a part of the fundamental estrangement of modern man from himself.

Restoring Contact with Experience

Some individuals are fortunate in going beyond the picture I have just given, developing further in the direction of psychological maturity. We see this happen in psychotherapy where we endeavor to provide a climate favorable to the growth of the person. We also see it happen in life, whenever life provides a therapeutic climate for the individual. Let me concentrate on this further maturing of a value approach as I have seen it in therapy.

As the client senses and realizes that he is prized as a person[1] he can slowly begin to value the different aspects of

[1] The therapeutic relationship is not devoid of values. When it is most effective it is, I believe, marked by one primary value, namely, that this person (the client) has *worth*.

himself. Most importantly, he can begin, with much difficulty at first, to sense and to feel what is going on within him, what he is feeling, what he is experiencing, how he is reacting. He uses his experiencing as a direct referent to which he can turn in forming accurate conceptualizations and as a guide to his behavior. Gendlin (1961, 1962) has elaborated the way in which this occurs. As his experiencing becomes more and more open to him, as he is able to live more freely in the process of his feelings, then significant changes begin to occur in his approach to values. It begins to assume many of the characteristics it had in infancy.

Introjected Values in Relation to Experiencing

Perhaps I can indicate this by reviewing a few of the brief examples of introjected values which I have given, and suggesting what happens to them as the individual comes closer to what is going on within him.

The individual in therapy looks back and realizes, "But I *enjoyed* pulling my sister's hair—and that doesn't make me a bad person."

The student failing chemistry realizes, as he gets close to his own experiencing, "I don't like chemistry; I don't value being a doctor, even though my parents do; and I am not a failure for having these feelings."

The adult recognizes that sexual desires and behavior may be richly satisfying and permanently enriching in their consequences, or shallow and temporary and less than satisfying. He goes by his own experiencing, which does not always coincide with social norms.

He recognizes freely that this communist book or person expresses attitudes and goals which he shares as well as ideas and values which he does not share.

He realizes that at times he experiences cooperation as meaningful and valuable to him, and that at other times he wishes to be alone and act alone.

Valuing in the Mature Person

The valuing process which seems to develop in this more mature person is in some ways very much like that in the infant, and in some ways quite different. It is fluid, flexible, based on this particular moment, and the degree to which this moment is experienced as enhancing and actualizing. Values are not held rigidly, but are continually changing. The painting which last year seemed meaningful now appears uninteresting, the way of working with individuals which was formerly experienced as good now seems inadequate, the belief which then seemed true is now experienced as only partly true, or perhaps false.

Another characteristic of the way this person values experience is that it is highly differentiated, or as the semanticists would say, extensional. The examples in the preceding section indicate that what were previously rather solid monolithic introjected values now become differentiated; tied to a particular time and experience.

Another characteristic of the mature individual's approach is that the locus of evaluation is again established firmly within the person. It is his own experience which provides the value information or feedback. This does not mean that he is not open to all the evidence he can obtain from other sources. But it means that this is taken for what it is—outside evidence—and is not as significant as his own reactions. Thus he may be told by a friend that a new book is very disappointing. He reads two unfavorable reviews of the book. Thus his tentative hypothesis is that he will not value the book. Yet if he reads the book his valuing will be based upon the reactions it stirs in *him*, not on what he has been told by others.

There is also involved in this valuing process a letting oneself down into the immediacy of what one is experiencing, endeavoring to sense and to clarify all its complex meanings. I think of a client who, toward the close of therapy, when puzzled about an issue, would put his head in his hands and say, "Now what *is* it that I'm feeling? I want to get next to it. I want to learn what it is." Then he would wait, quietly and patiently, trying to listen to himself, until he could discern the exact flavor of the feelings he was experiencing. He, like others, was trying to get close to himself.

In getting close to what is going on within himself, the process is much more complex than it is in the infant. In the mature person it has much more scope and sweep. For there is involved in the present moment of experiencing the memory traces of all the relevant learnings from the past. This moment has not only its immediate sensory impact, but it has meaning growing out of similar experiences in the past (Gendlin, 1962). It has both the new and the old in it. So when I experience a painting or a person, my experiencing contains within it the learnings I have accumulated from past meetings with paintings or persons, as well as the new impact of this particular encounter. Likewise the moment of experiencing contains, for the mature adult, hypotheses about consequences. "It is not pleasant to express forthrightly my negative feelings to this person, but past experience indicates that in a continuing relationship it will be helpful in the long run." Past and future are both in this moment and enter into the valuing.

I find that in the person I am speaking of (and here again we see a similarity to the infant), the criterion of the valuing process is the degree to which the object of the experience actualizes the individual himself. Does it make him a richer, more complete, more fully developed person? This may sound as though it were a selfish or unsocial criterion, but it does not prove to be so, since deep and helpful relationships with others are experienced as actualizing.

Like the infant, too, the psychologically mature adult trusts and uses the wisdom of his organism, with the difference that he is able to do so knowingly. He realizes that if he can trust all of himself, his feelings and his intuitions may be wiser than his mind, that as a total person he can be more sensitive and accurate than his thoughts alone. Hence he is not afraid to say, "I feel that this experience [or this thing, or this direction] is good. Later I will probably know *why* I feel it is good." He trusts the totality of himself, having moved toward becoming what Lancelot Whyte (1950) regards as "the unitary man."

It should be evident from what I have been saying that this valuing process in the mature individual is not an easy or simple thing. The process is complex, the choices often very perplexing and difficult, and there is no guarantee that the choice which is made will in fact prove to be self-actualizing. But because whatever evidence exists is available to the individual, and because he is open to his experiencing, errors are correctable. If this chosen course of action is not self-enhancing this will be sensed and he can make an adjustment or revision. He thrives on a maximum feedback interchange, and thus, like the gyroscopic compass on a ship, can continually correct his course toward his true goal of self-fulfillment.

Some Propositions Regarding the Valuing Process

Let me sharpen the meaning of what I have been saying by stating two propositions which contain the essential elements of this viewpoint. While it may not be possible to devise empirical tests of each proposition in its entirety, yet each is to some degree capable of being tested through the methods of psychological science. I would also state that though the following propositions are stated firmly in order to give them clarity, I am actually advancing them as decidedly tentative hypotheses.

Hypothesis I. There is an organismic base for an organized valuing process within the human individual.

It is hypothesized that this base is something the human being shares with the rest of the animate world. It is part of the functioning life process of any healthy organism. It is the capacity for receiving feedback information which enables the organism continually to adjust its behavior and reactions so as to achieve the maximum possible self-enhancement.

Hypothesis II. This valuing process in the human being is effective in achieving self-enhancement to the degree that the individual is open to the experiencing which is going on within himself.

I have tried to give two examples of individuals who are close to their own experiencing: the tiny infant who has not yet learned to deny in his awareness the processes going on within; and the psychologically mature person who has relearned the advantages of this open state.

There is a corollary to this second proposition which might be put in the following terms. One way of assisting the individual to move toward openness to experience is through a relationship in which he is prized as a separate person, in which the experiencing going on within him is empathically understood and valued, and in which he is given the freedom to experience his own feelings and those of others without being threatened in doing so.

This corollary obviously grows out of therapeutic experience. It is a brief statement of the essential qualities in the therapeutic relationship. There are already some empirical studies, of which the one by Barrett-Lennard (1962) is a good example, which give support to such a statement.

Propositions Regarding the Outcomes of the Valuing Process

I come now to the nub of any theory of values or valuing. What are its consequences? I should like to move into this new ground by stating bluntly two propositions as to the qualities of behavior which emerge from this valuing process. I shall then give some of the evidence from my experience as a therapist in support of these propositions.

Hypothesis III. In persons who are moving toward greater openness to their experiencing, there is an organismic commonality of value directions.

Hypothesis IV. These common value directions are of such kinds as to enhance the development of the individual himself, of others in his community, and to make for the survival and evolution of his species.

It has been a striking fact of my experience that in therapy, where individuals are valued, where there is greater freedom to feel and to be, certain value directions seem to emerge. These are not chaotic directions but instead exhibit a surprising commonality. This commonality is not dependent on the personality of the therapist, for I have seen these trends emerge in the clients of therapists sharply different in personality. This commonality does not seem to be due to the influences of any one culture, for I have found evidence of these directions in cultures as divergent as those of the United States, Holland, France, and Japan. I like to think that this commonality of value directions is due to the fact that we all belong to the same species—that just as a human infant tends, individually, to select a diet similar to that selected by other human infants, so a client in therapy tends, individually, to choose value directions similar to those chosen by other clients. As a species there may be certain elements of experience which tend to make for inner development and which would be chosen by all individuals if they were genuinely free to choose.

Let me indicate a few of these value directions as I see them in my clients as they move in the direction of personal growth and maturity.

They tend to move away from façades. Pretense, defensiveness, putting up a front, tend to be negatively valued.

They tend to move away from "oughts." The compelling feeling of "I ought to do or be thus and so" is negatively valued. The client moves away from being what he "ought to be," no matter who has set that imperative.

They tend to move away from meeting the expectations of others. Pleasing others, as a goal in itself, is negatively valued.

Being real is positively valued. The client tends to move toward being himself, being his real feelings, being what he is. This seems to be a very deep preference.

Self-direction is positively valued. The client discovers an increasing pride and confidence in making his own choices, guiding his own life.

One's self, one's own feelings come to be positively valued. From a point where he looks upon himself with contempt and despair, the client comes to value himself and his reactions as being of worth.

Being a process is positively valued. From desiring some fixed goal, clients come to prefer the excitement of being a process of potentialities being born.

Sensitivity to others and acceptance of others is positively valued. The client comes to appreciate others for what they are, just as he has come to appreciate himself for what he is.

Deep relationships are positively valued. To achieve a close, intimate, real, fully communicative relationship with another person seems to meet a deep need in every individual, and is very highly valued.

Perhaps more than all else, the client comes to value an openness to all of his inner and outer experience. To be open to and sensitive to his own *inner* reactions and feelings, the reactions and feelings of others, and the realities of the objective world—this is a direction which he clearly prefers. This openness becomes the client's most valued resource.

These then are some of the preferred directions which I have observed in individuals moving toward personal maturity. Though I am sure that the list I have given is inadequate and perhaps to some degree inaccurate it holds for me exciting possibilities. Let me try to explain why.

I find it significant that when individuals are prized as persons, the values they select do not run the full gamut of possibilities. I do not find, in such a climate of freedom, that one person comes to value fraud and murder and thievery, while another values a life of self-sacrifice, and another values only money. Instead there seems to be a deep and underlying thread of commonality. I believe that when the human being is inwardly free to choose whatever he deeply values, he tends to value those objects, experiences, and goals which make for his own survival, growth, and

PERSONALITY DYSFUNCTION

development, and for the survival and development of others. I hypothesize that it is *characteristic* of the human organism to prefer such actualizing and socialized goals when he is exposed to a growth promoting climate.

A corollary of what I have been saying is that in *any* culture, given a climate of respect and freedom in which he is valued as a person, the mature individual would tend to choose and prefer these same value directions. This is a significant hypothesis which could be tested. It means that though the individual of whom I am speaking would not have a consistent or even a stable system of conceived values, the valuing process within him would lead to emerging value directions which would be constant across cultures and across time.

Another implication I see is that individuals who exhibit the fluid valuing process I have tried to describe, whose value directions are generally those I have listed, would be highly effective in the ongoing process of human evolution. If the human species is to survive at all on this globe, the human being must become more readily adaptive to new problems and situations, must be able to select that which is valuable for development and survival out of new and complex situations, must be accurate in his appreciation of reality if he is to make such selections. The psychologically mature person as I have described him has, I believe, the qualities which would cause him to value those experiences which would make for the survival and enhancement of the human race. He would be a worthy participant and guide in the process of human evolution.

Finally, it appears that we have returned to the issue of universality of values, but by a different route. Instead of universal values "out there," or a universal value system imposed by some group—philosophers, rulers, priests, or psychologists—we have the possibility of universal human value directions *emerging* from the experiencing of the human organism. Evidence from therapy indicates that both personal and social values emerge as natural, and experienced, when the individual is close to his own organismic valuing process. The suggestion is that though modern man no longer trusts religion or science or philosophy nor any system of beliefs to *give* him values, he may find an organismic valuing base within himself which, if he can learn again to be in touch with it, will prove to be an organized, adaptive, and social approach to the perplexing value issues which face all of us.

7

Psychopathology

The four papers presented in this chapter are a small sample of the research on these two questions: How, if at all, shall we categorize the mental illnesses? And what are their stable properties?

Both questions have drawn interest and controversy for nearly a century. The matter of categorization is enormously complex, and the complicated scientific issues are often further obscured by value judgments and personal judgments. Yet the problems are exciting. Consider the psychogenic ailment that involves either paralysis of a limb or the distinct anesthetization of an area of the body. It was this kind of disorder that interested Charcot, Bernheim, and later Freud, who concluded that this apparently physiological disorder is really psychological in origin. In that day it was widespread and homogeneous disorder that easily lent itself to symptomatic diagnosis. It was called hysteria then, as it had been for centuries earlier. That ailment has almost disappeared today, and although the diagnostic term "hysteria" is still used, it has little of the overt behavioral meaning it once had.

The forms that psychopathologies take seem to change with each era, if not from one decade to the next. The existential neurosis, which Salvatore Maddi examines in the first paper in this chapter, does not seem to have existed a century ago. Or if it did, it appeared in a quite different guise from the one it wears today. One has reason to believe that it is now widespread: certainly both social theorists and practicing therapists often remark its presence and speculate on procedures for its cure. It is a curious neurosis from many points of view. Overtly, the patient seems very much intact: successful, competent, often charming. It is his inner world that seems amiss, and this contrast provides a painful rebuttal to the notion that all disorder is essentially behavioral.

The two papers by Arnold Buss and

Peter Lang contain the results of an exhaustive survey of the experimental literature on schizophrenia. Various theories of schizophrenia are assessed against the available data. The authors conclude that schizophrenia involves some kind of sensorimotor deficit, a view challenged in the next paper.

One often gets the impression that the mentally ill who are chronically hospitalized are quite withdrawn from social realities. Indeed, the stereotyped view of the "burnt out" schizophrenic includes the notions of withdrawn passivity, of affectlessness, of being little more than vegetable. The paper by Benjamin and Dorothea Braginsky may serve to counter that view. Schizophrenics, in their own way, and in accord with their own psychological needs, are shown to be quite sensitive and responsive to the conditions of their environment. In formal psychiatric interviews they are quite capable of giving relatively positive impressions when these suit their desires and further their goals, and distinctly negative ones when their goals are threatened. This paper will show the reader that notions of deficit and illness are not universally believed, even in regard to the chronically mentally ill.

The Existential Neurosis

Salvatore R. Maddi

Social critics, philosophers, sociologists, and psychotherapists are raising the cry that alienation and the problems of existence form the sickness of our times. Even though a significant proportion of the statements has been vague and polemical, more and more people are haging on every word. I do not think this is merely the new fad. There is too much insistence and desperation in people's attempts to understand the commentaries that have been made in some terms that will make a difference in their lives. It is too hard to overlook the evidence that people seeking psychotherapy do so in ever increasing numbers because they are deeply dissatisfied with the nature and bases of their living. It is too obvious that even those who do not seek psychotherapy often feel alone and empty.

Reprinted from the *Journal of Abnormal Psychology*, vol. 72, pp. 311–325 with the permission of the American Psychological Association and the author.

Under the circumstances, the best thing serious students of the human condition can do is try for clarity and precision in thinking about alienation and the problems of existence. My task in this paper falls within this category of endeavor. What I will do is offer a model for the understanding of psychopathology and then use the model in ordering the various themes common in existential writings. Sometimes I will agree with writers in this field, and sometimes I will be reinterpreting their views. My basic aim in all this is to attempt to bring order and structure to an amorphous and complex literature in a way that clarifies the parts of it bearing on psychopathology and on mental health.

A MODEL FOR NEUROSIS

At the outset we need a model for neurosis that can serve as a heuristic device, a thread of Ariadne, lest we lose our way in the labyrinth of words that has been created. The model I suggest we adopt represents fairly standard thinking in the area, happily enough. It starts with the notion of a neurosis as a set of symptoms that can be distinguished not only from mental health but also from other psychopathological states. So the hysterical neurosis, for example, can be described as a set of cognitive and motor symptoms that are absent not only in the healthy state, but also in other classes of illness, like psychosis, and other neuroses, like obsessive-compulsiveness. When we discuss the existential neurosis, then, we will be searching for a set of relevant symptoms that are clearly different both from whatever we consider to be mental health and from other forms of psychopathology.

Further, the model distinguishes between the neurosis itself and the premorbid personality out of which the neurosis may come through a process of breakdown. For example, if you are working within a psychoanalytic framework, you would say that the obsessive-compulsive neurosis represents the breakdown of the anal character type. While the anal character type bears some strong resemblances to the obsessive-compulsive neurosis (e.g., the reliance upon defense mechanisms of intellectualization, isolation, and undoing), the latter includes symptoms (e.g., obsessions and compulsions) that are considered pathological and that appear in only minimal form in the former. The premorbid personality is within the category of normality, though like the neurosis it can be distinguished from other types of premorbid personality. As there is an anal character type, so also are there phallic and oral character types. The differences between the premorbid personalities define predispositions to different kinds of neuroses. The significance of all this for discussion of the existential neurosis is that we will want to define a premorbid personality for which the neu-

rosis itself is a believable breakdown product.

Premorbid personalities define predispositions to particular neurotic manifestations because they incorporate vulnerabilities to particular kinds of stress. The next aspect of the model, stress, is best considered to be something objectively describable, whether originating inside or outside the person, that represents a comprehensive enough threat to the personality to disrupt the premorbid balance or adjustment. Obviously, stress has to be defined with the characteristics of premorbid personality in mind. Loss of a strong loved one may be especially stressful to the person with an oral character, because in that character satisfaction of dependency is especially important for adequate functioning. Stress can be a sudden occurrence, or an accumulation of undermining events, as long as what is called stress is reasonably specifiable.

The model states that neurosis is some joint function of premorbidity and stress. Without attempting to state the exact nature of the function, some facets of the relationship are apparent. If there is zero stress, there should be no neurosis. Further, the amount of stress necessary to precipitate a neurosis should depend upon the intensity of the vulnerability constituted by the premorbid characteristics. But it should be kept in mind that the stress must match the nature of the vulnerability if undermining of the premorbid adjustment is to be possible. In considering the existential neurosis, I will try to identify the kinds of stress that are relevant, though it will be very difficult to make any qualitative statements about how much stress is too much.

Any model which involves the notion of premorbidity, or that which predisposes to illness, also involves the notion of what the ideal personality would be. What I am saying is not very mysterious or new. In psychoanalytic thinking, the ideal is genital personality, whereas in Rogerian thinking, the ideal is the fully functioning person. The ideal personality is usually a null class, which nonetheless has the very important theoretical function of permitting specification of what it is about the premorbid personality that predisposes to illness. In discussing the existential neurosis, we should expect to understand at least those aspects of the ideal personality that insure against the likelihood of that disorder. It may, in addition, be possible to gain an even more comprehensive sense than that of what is ideal.

The rest of the model refers to development. There is first ideal development, or that series of early life experiences that culminate in the ideal personality. Second, there is what might be called deviant development—a series of life experiences leading to premorbidity. It should be possible to specify the particular developmental deviancy that accounts for particular premorbid personalities. It will be important in this article to consider the developmental vicissitudes producing the premorbid state out of which the existential neurosis may come, and, in this consideration, a sense of what would be developmentally more ideal will necessarily be gained.

Without a doubt there are vexing questions that can be raised concerning this model. But rather than raise them here, let me encourage you to consider the general outlines of the model as no more than an interesting and plausible heuristic device. In that spirit, let us plunge in.

THE SYMPTOMS CALLED EXISTENTIAL NEUROSIS

Like all neuroses, we should expect the existential neurosis to have cognitive, affective, and actional components. Once we have accepted the heuristic notion that there are existential manifestations some of which are neurotic and some of which are not, we have already begun to find the road to clarity. The cognitive component of the existential neurosis is meaninglessness, or chronic inability to believe in the truth, importance, usefulness, or interest value of any of the things one is engaged in or can imagine doing. The most characteristic features of affective tone are blandness and boredom, punctuated by periods of depression which become less frequent as the disorder is prolonged. As to the realm of action, activity level may be low to moderate, but more important than amount of activity is the introspective and objectively observable fact that activities are not chosen. There is little selectivity, it being immaterial to the person what if any activities he pursues. If there is any selectivity shown, it is in the direction of ensuring minimal expenditures of effort and decision making.

It is important to recognize that the syndrome described above refers to a chronic state of the organism. I do not refer to stabs of doubt, in the cognitive domain, or occasional indifference and passivity, in the affective and actional domains. Rather, I refer to the settled state of meaninglessness, apathy, and aimlessness, such that contradictory states of commitment, enthusiasm, and activeness are the exception rather than the rule. The temporary state of doubt, though an existential manifestation, is not here defined as part of the existential neurosis. Indeed, doubt is a by-product of vigorous mental health, I shall argue later, no matter how painful it may be.

If my model is to be served, the existential neurosis must be distinguished from other forms of illness. I take it that the obviousness of its difference from such psychotic states as schizophrenia and senile psychosis, such character disorders as homosexuality and psychopathy, and such neuroses as obsessive-compulsiveness and hysteria, is clear without further attention. Of the traditional states of psychopathology, the existential neurosis probably most nearly resembles neuraesthenia and depression. It is from these two disorders that distinctions are important. The major difference between neuraesthenia and the existential neurosis is that the dreadful lack of energy and somatic decreptitude of the former is not present in the latter. There is certainly listlessness in existential neurosis, but it is not experienced as a primarily somatic disability. In addition, the cognitive state of meaninglessness is virtually absent in neuraesthenia.

The distinction between depression and the existential neurosis is harder to make, specifically because the latter state sometimes includes sadness, and usually includes low activity level. But in existential neurosis, depressive affect is the exception rather than the rule, with apathy—an actual absence of strong emotion—being the usual state. Apathy is not typical of depression, though it may occur occasionally in that disorder. In traditional terms, what I am calling the existential neurosis might actually be called depression, but this would involve an unwarranted stretching of the latter concept, taking some such form as inferring depressive affect hidden by defenses such that apathy was the visible resultant. But once we have decided that traditional terminology is not necessarily exhaustive in describing psychopathology, the syndrome I have called the existential neurosis is very likely to emerge as discriminably different from depression.

The way I have defined it, the existential neurosis is characterized by the belief that one's life is meaningless, by the affective tone of apathy and boredom, and by the absence of selectivity in actions. This symptom cluster is, to judge from the writing of many psychotherapists, sociologists, and social critics (e.g., Fromm, 1955; Josephson & Josephson, 1962; May, Angel, & Ellenberger, 1958; Sykes, 1964), rampant in contemporary life. It may seem as if what I am talking about as existential neurosis is much closer to alienation from self, than it is to alienation from society. But on reflection, it should be clear that the existential neurotic would be separated from deep interaction with others as well as from his own personal vitality. Therefore, I find the existential neurotic to be alienated both from self and from society. Indeed, the notions of self-alienation and societal alienation represent little more to me than biases reflecting whether the theorist considers the individual or the group to be the most important unit of analysis.

Nonetheless, it is true that traits sometimes considered under the rubric of alienation are not covered by my definition of the existential neurosis. Such things as anguish, rebelliousness, acute dissatisfaction, and civil disobedience are sometimes considered evidence of alienation. Alienation in such cases is usually taken to be from society and not at all from self. First, I should affirm that such traits are not to be considered part of the existential neurosis. The symptoms of the neurosis all point to a rather comprehensive psychological death, where there is no longer even anguish or anger to remind the person that he is a person, and a very dissatisfied one at that. But what can be said in understanding these traits that I have excluded? Sometimes, what is meant is doubt of the kind that I will later argue is quite healthy. Even when this is not the case, I have difficulty understanding why the traits are considered evidence of alienation in the first place. After all, a person acutely dissatisfied with society, and actively trying to change it through his own actions, is hardly alienated in any important sense. He is accepting the importance of society by the stance that it is worth changing, and feeling perhaps even more powerfully than most of us that he can produce a change. There is little here of the meaninglessness and powerlessness that are supposed to characterize alienation. The person with these traits may well have some psychological malady, but unless his social protest masks an underlying tendency toward meaninglessness, apathy, and aimlessness, the malady bears little relationship to either existential neurosis or what has been called alienation.

The character of Meursault in Camus' (1946) *The Stranger* is a perfect example of the existential neurotic. He frequently says, and even more frequently implies, that he believes life to be meaningless and his activities to be arbitrary. He is virtually always bored and apathetic. He never imagines or daydreams. He has no goals. He makes only the most minimal decisions, doing little more than is necessary to keep a simple job as a clerk. He walks in his mother's funeral cortege and makes love to a woman with the same apathy and indifference. He frequently says, "It's all the same to me." His perceptions are banal and colorless. The most difference anything makes is to be mildly irritating. He has this reaction, for example, to the heat of the sun, but then does nothing about it. Although it might seem remarkable that a novel about such a person could have any literary power at all, it is precisely because of the omnipresence of the symptom cluster we have been calling existential neurosis that the reader is intrigued and shocked. When Meursault finally murders a man without any emotional provocation or reaction, without any premeditation or reason, without any greater decision than is involved in resolving to take a walk, the reader is not even surprised. Anything is possible for Meursault, specifically because nothing is anything of importance.

His is a vegetative existence that amounts to psychological death. Some writers have called this a state of nonbeing (e.g., May et al., 1958; Sartre, 1956).

THE PREMORBID PERSONALITY

Turning to the premorbid personality out of which the existential neurosis can come through a process of breakdown precipitated by appropriate stress, I find that the concept of central importance is that of *identity*. I define identity in phenomenological terms, as that which you consider yourself to be. Although a person's identity is not necessarily expressed in verbal terms at any given time, it can be so stated if the person reflects upon the question of what he thinks he is. In focusing upon identity, therefore, I am not implying something that is barred from awareness.

Theorists having recourse to this kind of concept of identity or self have frequently considered of importance the discrepancy between one's sense of identity and one's natural potentialities as a human being. In following that lead, I would say that the premorbid personality corresponding to the existential neurosis is one in which the identity includes only some of the things that express the true nature of man. I will not discuss the true nature of man until the section of this paper on the ideal personality. It will suffice for initial purposes to say that the premorbid identity can be considered overly *concrete* and *fragmentary*. These are certainly ideas that are, in one form or another, common enough in the existential literature (e.g., Fromm, 1955; Kierkegaard, 1954; May et al., 1958). But to say this and nothing more is to fall short of the precision really necessary for adequate understanding of the etiology of existential neurosis. We must ask in what ways is the premorbid identity overly concrete and fragmentary?

The best way to summarize the problem is that the premorbid identity stresses qualities of man that are, among those he has, the ones least unique to him both as opposed to other species and to other men. In other words, the identity is insufficiently humanistic. For our society at this point in time, it is easy to say what an insufficiently humanistic identity looks like. Such an identity leads the person to consider himself to be nothing more than *a player of social roles and an embodiment of biological needs.* I must stress that the difficulty is not so much that man is not these two things, but that what he is in addition to them finds little representation in identity. Considering yourself to be an embodiment of biological needs certainly does not set you apart from other species. Neither does the view of yourself as a player of social roles, for most subhuman species have social differentiation of at least a rudimentary sort. And there is little in either of the two components of identity that permits much sense of difference between individual men, except in the trivial sense that the particular social roles played this moment may be different for me than for you, and the biological needs that I have right now may happen to be different than those you have. But tomorrow, or an hour from now, the situation may change, and we may not even have that small basis for distinguishing ourselves from one another. The overarching fact of life for a person with the premorbid personality I have described is that all men play a small number of social roles and all men embody a few biological needs, and that is that.

Consider what it means to view yourself as a player of social roles. First, you accept the idea that the social system—a set of interrelated institutions operating according to a different group of laws than those that govern individual existence—is a terribly real and important force in living. Second, you believe that the way you presently perceive the social system and have been taught it to be is its real and unchangeable nature. Finally, you consider it not only inevitable, but proper, that you conform to the pressures of the social system. A major aim in life becomes playing the roles that are necessarily yours as well as you can.

Also imagine what it means to consider yourself an embodiment of biological needs. First, you believe that such needs as that for food, water, and sex are terribly important and real forces in living. Second, you are convinced that an important gauge of the adequacy of the life is the degree to which these needs are satisfied. Finally, you believe that any alternative to direct expression of these needs, if an alternative were possible, would be unwise because it would constitute a violation of the true nature of man. All this means that a major aim in life becomes biological survival and satisfaction.

A person who has only these two themes represented in his identity would feel powerless in the face of social pressures from without, and powerless in the face of biological pressures from within. Both social and biological pressures would be considered independent variables, that is, variables that influence the behavior of the person without themselves being influenced by him. Naturally he tries to play his social roles well and to insure physical satisfaction and survival. Indeed, he *is* his social roles and biological needs. In other words, his identity is overly concrete. The goals of serving social roles and biological needs often lead in different, if not incompatible, directions. Generally speaking, the person will try to serve social and biological pressures at different times, or in different places, keeping possible incompatibilities from the eyes of others and from direct confrontation in his own awareness. In other words, this kind of identity is overly fragmentary.

For vividness, consider further the cognitive and affective state of the person with the premorbid personality under discussion. In the cognitive realm, the person would be rather consistently pragmatic and materialistic in his outlook on life. The pragmatism would come primarily from accepting the necessity of playing certain social roles. How often one hears that the world is the way it is, so one might as well be practical about it! The materialism would come primarily from the view that man is an embodiment of biological needs. The pursuit of material things is given the status of a natural process. How often one hears that narrow self-interest is the only real motivating force outside of society! Superimposed upon the fairly consistent pragmatism and materialism would be more transitory states of fatalism, cynicism, and pessimism. These transitory cognitive states would presumably mirror the moment-to-moment economy of social system and biological rewards and punishments. There is a final implication contained in the premorbid personality that is extremely important. If you consider yourself bound by certain rules of social interaction, on the one hand, and in need of certain material goods for satisfaction and survival, on the other hand, relationships between yourself and other people will be made on contractual grounds, rather than on the grounds of tradition or intimacy. The person with a premorbid personality will tend to look upon relationships as serving some specific social or biological end. His view of relationship will be rather coldblooded.

Turning to the affective realm, the person with a premorbid identity would tend to worry about such things as whether he is considered by others to be conscientious, whether he is seen to be a nice person, whether he is admired, whether people can guess the animal lusts within him, whether he can satisfy his needs without interfering too much with social role playing. His predominant affective states would be fear and anxiety, and these would be only aggravated by the frequent incompatibility between serving other-directed social aims and self-interested biological aims. The other affective states typical of the premorbid state stem from the continual emphasis upon contractual relationships. Since relationships are defined in terms of limited, specific goals, and in terms of the economic considerations of who is getting what out of interaction, social life will be rather structured and superficial. Contractual relationships are devoid of intimacy, commitment, and spontaneity because of the preemptiveness of role playing and need expression. Thus, important affective states associated with premorbidity would be loneliness and disappointment. On the one hand, the person feels anxious and afraid a good deal of the time, while on the other hand, he feels alone and as if something were missing from his life.

You will have recognized in the discussion of the premorbid personality many of the features common in writings on alienation. There is much in what I have said that is reminiscent of Fromm's (1955) marketing personality and Sartre's (1956) idea of bad faith, to name only two sources. I want to encourage you to think of the premorbid personality not as a sickness in itself, but rather as a predisposition to sickness of an existential sort. What I have described as premorbidity is simply too common and livable to be considered frank neurosis, though it is a state with its own characteristic sufferings and limitations. The premorbid person is still too much enmeshed in the problems of his living, still too much concerned with having a successful life, to be considered existentially neurotic, given the implications of detachment from life included in that idea.

PRECIPITATING STRESS

For the person with a premorbid identity, life may go on in a rather empty, though superficially adequate, way for a long time. He may even be reasonably successful in objective terms, keeping his vague dissatisfactions and anxieties to himself. But he may also be precipitated into an existential neurosis if he encounters stress of the right content and sufficient intensity to be undermining.

The stresses that will be effective are those that have content that strikes at the vulnerabilities inherent in defining yourself as nothing more than a player of social roles and an embodiment of biological needs. The stronger this self-definition the weaker can the stress be and still produce breakdown. In speaking of precipitating stress, I do not mean the things that merely make the person worry. The threat of social censure or biological deprivation are potent sources of concern for the premorbid personality we are discussing, but these things do not ordinarily cause the kind of comprehensive breakdown involved in the existential neurosis. *The stresses that can produce the neurosis are ones that disconfirm the premorbid identity by forcing recognition of its overly concrete, fragmentary, and nonhumanistic nature.*

Three stresses come readily to mind, though there are bound to be others as well. Perhaps the most effective of them is the concrete threat of imminent death. It is my impression that this threat must be to your own life in order to be very effective. Even the threatened death of someone reasonably close to you may not have the force I am about to describe. Perhaps those of you who have faced

the threat of death to yourself and to others will know what I mean. If the threat of death actually does lead to death, people with the premorbid identity tend to die *The Death of Ivan Ilych*, in the great novella by Tolstoi (1960). Ilych knows he is dying of a horrible disorder, and this colors all his perceptions and judgments. Most of the visitors to his bedside are business associates who, he comes to realize, are only performing what they experience as a distasteful obligation of their social role. Then he realizes that the same thing is true of his own family! None of these people is deeply touched by his drift toward death, for theirs is a contractual rather than intimate relationship to him. And even more horrible, he realizes the appropriateness of their behavior because he too has thought of and experienced them only in contractual, superficial terms. The triviality and superficiality of their materialism and social conformity—and his own —are thrown into sharp relief by the threat of death. He becomes acutely aware of his wasted life and can tell himself nothing that will permit a peaceful death. He realizes that he has always felt deprived of intimacy, love, spontaneity, and enthusiasm. By renouncing himself and the people around him, he is finally able to feel truly human and alive just at the point where he dies physically. This story is didactically and literarily powerful because this is a tragic way to die. What bankruptcy when it is death that frees us from the impoverishing shackles of social conformity and biological needs!

If the person with a premorbid identity who is faced with the threat of imminent death should actually recover rather than die he is likely to experience an existential neurosis. Before he dies, Ilych is certainly a good example of this. If the threat of death disconfirms your previous identity, then you have no identity to work with, and in an adult this is virtually the same as psychological death. The adequacy of recovery from the existential neurosis will be determined by whether the person can use, or be helped to use, the knowledge gained through facing death to build a more comprehensive, abstract, humanistic identity.

The second stress that can precipitate existential neurosis is gross disruption of the social order, through such things as war, conquest, and economic depression, leading to distintegration of social roles and even of the institutionalized mechanisms for satisfying biological needs. Such catastrophe has two effects on people with the premorbid identity. First, it makes it difficult to continue to obtain the usual rewards for playing social roles and expressing biological needs. Second, and more important, disruption of the social order demonstrates the relativity of society to someone who has been treating it as absolute reality. The premorbid person is left without much basis for living and an existential neurosis may well ensue. Thinking along very similar channels, Durkheim (1951) saw social upheaval, or anomie, as a factor increasing suicide rates.

The final stress is difficult to describe because it is less dramatic than threat of death and social upheaval. Not only is this stress less dramatic, but it is usually an accumulation of events rather than something that need happen only once. And yet, this final stress is probably the most usual precipitating factor in the existential neurosis. The stress I mean is the repeated confrontation with the limitation on deep and comprehensive experiencing produced by the premorbid identity. These confrontations usually come about through other people's insistence on pointing out the person's existential failures. The aggressive action of other people is more or less necessary because

the person with the premorbid identity usually avoids self-confrontation. But let there be a close relative who is suffering because of the person's premorbidity, and confrontations will be forced.

A good example of this kind of stress and its effects is to be found in Arthur Miller's (1964) *After the Fall*. During the first two-thirds of the play, Quentin discovers that his is what I would call a premorbid identity. The discovery is a terribly painful stress. It begins when his first wife, working up the courage for a separation and divorce, tries, after a long period of docility, to force him to recognize the limitations in their relationship and her deep dissatisfaction with him. In listening to his own attempts to answer her charges, and in considering her attacks he begins to recognize that his has been little more than a contractual commitment to her. He has been merely conforming to social roles in being husband and father. Under her scrutiny, he begins to recognize her superficial sexuality—a biological need—as well. He feels at fault for his limitations, but can do little about them, instead asking pathetically for understanding. His wife is also important in forcing recognition that his offer to defend his old law professor in court is not out of deep affection, or intimacy, or even loyalty, but rather out of an attempt to convince people that he feels these ways toward this man. Frightened and distraught by what he is learning about himself, Quentin finally begins to envy his wife for her ability to experience deeply and know what she wants.

After the breakup of his first marriage, Quentin moves impulsively into a second. His second wife, Maggie, idealizes him, and he feels reassured about himself, though he has not really changed much. It is only after they have been married for some time that Quentin begins to appreciate Maggie's extraordinary neediness and lack of differentiation as a person. Her adulation of him can no longer serve to reassure him, and to make matters worse, he has new evidence of his superficiality in his inability to reach her in any significant way. He must stand by and let her commit suicide, having decided that the most he can do is to save his own life! Whatever depth of personality could have saved her in a husband, he simply did not have.

After Maggie's death, Quentin spends 2 years or so in a state of meaninglessness, apathy, and aimlessness. He does not work, he does not relate to people, he merely drifts. This period is clearly one of existential neurosis, and can be seen as precipitated by a person's being forced repeatedly to confront the limitations on living produced by social conformity and expression of biological need.

THE IDEAL PERSONALITY

From the discussion of the premorbid personality, it will come as no surprise that the ideal identity from my point of view is abstract, unified, and humanistic. I would remind you of Emerson's (Atkinson, 1940) elegant plea for such an identity at the beginning of *The American Scholar*:

> It is one of those fables which out of an unknown antiquity convey an unlooked-for wisdom, that the gods, in the beginning, divided Man into men, that he might be more helpful to himself; just as the hand was divided into fingers, the better to answer its end.
> The old fable covers a doctrine ever new and sublime; that there is One Man —present to all particular men only partially, or through one faculty; and that you must take the whole society to find the whole man. Man is not a farmer, or a professor, or an engineer, but he is all. Man is priest, and scholar, and statesman, and producer, and soldier. In the *divided* or social state these functions are parcelled out to individuals, each of whom aims to do his stint of the joint work, whilst each other performs his. The fable implies that the individual, to possess himself, must sometimes return from his own labor to embrace all the other laborers. But, unfortunately, this original unit, this fountain of power, has been so distributed to multitudes, has been so minutely subdivided and peddled out, that it is spilled into drops, and cannot be gathered. The state of society is one in which the members have suffered amputation from the trunk, and strut about so many walking monsters—a good finger, a neck, a stomach, an elbow, but never a man.
> Man is thus metamorphosed into a thing, into many things. The planter, who is Man sent out into the field to gather food, is seldom cheered by any idea of the true dignity of his ministry. He sees his bushel and his cart, and nothing beyond, and sinks into the farmer, instead of Man on the farm. The tradesman scarcely ever gives an ideal worth to his work, but is ridden by the routine of his craft, and the soul is subject to dollars. The priest becomes a form; the attorney a statute-book; the mechanic a machine; the sailor a rope of the ship.
> In this distribution of functions the scholar is the delegated intellect. In the right state he is *Man Thinking*. In the degenerate state, when the victim of society, he tends to become a mere thinker, or still worse, the parrot of other men's thinking. [pp. 45–46]

This quote criticizes concretizations (e.g., when a man is a farmer, instead of man on the farm) and fragmentation (e.g., one can find a good finger, neck, etc., but never a man), and implies that the antidote to this ill is humanistic in nature (e.g., note the capitalization of man). Rousing and emotionally convincing though Emerson is, he does not give us a theory of man that makes this ideal identity rationally understandable. I shall try to present the rough outlines of such a theory, which is based on Emerson's intuitive lead and the writings of many other people concerned with the problems of existence.

First, let us assume that there are three sides to man's nature—social, biological, and psychological. The social side refers to interpersonal relationships, the biological side to physical survival and satisfaction, and the psychological side to mental processes, primarily symbolization, imagination, and judgment. Assume further that all three sides are of equal importance for successful living, and that curtailment of expression of any of them sets up some kind of premorbidity.

When you express your psychological side fully and vigorously, you generate symbols that represent concrete experiences in the general form that makes clear their similarities to and differences from other experiences. You also have an active and uninhibited imagination, which you use as a guide rather than substitute for action. In other words, you let your imagination reveal what you want your life to be, and then attempt to act on that knowledge. The psychological faculty of judgment functions as a check upon the validity of your imagination. When you act upon imagination, you can evaluate the nature of your ensuing experience in order to determine whether it is really what you seem to want. Does the action lead to satisfaction, or is it frightening or boring? Hence the knowledge gained through exercising judgment is also used as a guide to living.

Of the psychological, biological, and social sides of man, it is the psychological side that is most human. All subhuman species have biological requirements for survival and satisfaction, and these requirements are generally acted upon in a straightforward and simple manner. Most subhuman species have patterned social relationships. Indeed, sometimes subhuman society is quite complex and extensive. But even then it tends to be rigidly organized and characterized by social roleship. Only in man is it reasonable to consider the psychological side of life to be

of much importance. Indeed, when social and biological behavior is unusually subtle and complex in man it is because of his most human, or psychological, side.

Let me make my position more vivid by contrasting the lives of people with premorbid and ideal identities. Whereas both premorbid and ideal identities involve expression of the social and biological sides of man, only the ideal identity shows much representation of the psychological side. Because the premorbid person does not have available to him the generalizing, unifying, humanizing effect of psychological expression, encompassing as it does symbolization, imagination, and judgment, he achieves only the most obvious, common, superficial forms of social and biological expression. He accepts social roles as given, tries to play them as well as he can, and sees himself quite literally as the roles he plays. He accepts biological needs as given and acts on them in a way that is isolated and unreflective, however straightforward it may be. The best example of such biological expression is with regard to the sexual need. The premorbid person considers sexuality to be no more than an animalistic urge, and satisfies it as simply as possible, with little consideration of relationship, affection, or even comprehensiveness of attraction. Little wonder that though he seems very social, he frequently feels insecure, lonely, and without intimacy, and that though he seems very active in expressing biological needs, he frequently feels incompletely satisfied. The loneliness and incomplete satisfaction are signs that he is deprived of psychological expression.

As the premorbid person does not rely upon the processes of symbolization, imagination, and judgment, favoring instead the view that life is determined by social and biological considerations, he not only feels powerless to influence his actions, but also does indeed lead an existence that is rather stereotyped and unchanging. As no human being is completely without psychological expression, the premorbid person often has a glimmer of awareness that his life is not what it might be. This accumulated sense of missed opportunity is what May *et al.* (1958, pp. 37–91) have called ontological guilt.

With vigorous psychological expression, would come social and biological living that is more unified, subtle, deep, and rewarding than that I have described above. The person with the ideal identity would not feel powerless in the face of social and biological pressures, because he puts heavy reliance in living on his own processes of symbolization, imagination, and judgment. He would perceive many alternatives to simple role playing and isolated biological satisfaction. Because he sees himself to be the "fountain of power," to use Emerson's excellent phrase, his social and biological living transcend the concrete instance and involve anything that he can imagine and anything that is evaluated by him as worthwhile.

So, if contractual relationships leave him unsatisfied, he can choose to relate otherwise, such as on the basis of shared personal experience. He can even make a start on this by talking with others about his dissatisfaction with merely playing social roles. Once he does this, he will undoubtedly find some people who will be encouraged to share their own feelings of loneliness with him, and the road to more subtle, myriadly rewarding social relations has already been found. If simple, unreflective expression of biological urges leaves him unsatisfied, he can choose to explore other forms of expression. For example, instead of merely seeking food, he can make hunger the basis for more comprehensive satisfaction by cooking especially tasty dishes, or by eating in the company of people with whom he feels intimate. And the same with sex. He can make sexual expression a subtle,

complex, changing thing, indulged in with people toward whom he feels intimate and affectionate on other than simply sexual grounds. There will be many more parts to the life of the person with an ideal identity, and the parts will achieve much closer integration than is true for the premorbid person.

One important consequence of reliance upon his imagination and judgment as guides to living is that the ideal person is not a conformist. Some critics of my position would argue that it amounts to advocating the unleashing of monsters on the world. What is to stop a person from murdering, or robbing, if he feels so free to put his imagination into operation? Psychologists like Rogers (1961) would answer this criticism by contending that there is nothing basic to the organism that would lead in the direction of such monstrosities. As the individual is oriented toward survival, so too does his natural functioning support the survival of his species. One can easily develop an evolutionary argument for this position. Rogers would believe that only an imagination already perverted by psychopathogenic social pressures would lead the person in the direction of terrible aggressions toward his fellow men. I have considerable sympathy for this position, but would like to add to it the notion that judgment is a maturing supplement to imagination. Your imagination might even include the bases for catastrophic action, perhaps at a time when someone has hurt you badly, and still you might not act on the imagination if judgment provided some balance. I sincerely feel that although the ideal person might well make mistakes in life, he will not be a monster simply because he does not conform to the most obvious societal pressures.

It should be remembered that Emerson's (Atkinson, 1940, p. 148) conclusion that "whosoever would be a man must be a non-conformist" is echoed by many of the world's finest thinkers. If a critic responds by claiming that this kind of thinking permits such abominations as Hitler, I would suggest that he was a badly twisted man who showed less imagination than repetitive, compulsive preoccupations, and less judgment than megalomanic overconfidence. It is only by losing the usual standards of what is meant by imagination and judgment that Hitler and the ideal identity can be discussed in the same breath! But a secondary argument could be made that the position I am taking makes it at least possible for some twisted person like Hitler to gain dangerous power because those around him believe enough in imagination and judgment as guides to living that they may not see that he is only a pseudo-example of this in time to do anything about it. This is a terribly weak argument. Indeed, it is much more likely that people who define themselves as social role players and embodiments of biological needs will not recognize or be able to stop a man like Hitler. It is to the point that Hannah Arendt (1964) subtitled her treatise on the enacting of the final solution to the "Jewish problem" *a report on the banality of evil*. To judge from reports, the rank-and-file Germans were simply following rules when they gassed people!

Another consequence of relying upon imagination and judgment as guides to action is that the life of the ideal person will be a frequently changing, unfolding thing. New possibilities will be constantly developing, though it is unlikely that the process of change will be without pattern or continuity. The reliance upon judgment insures that there will be values and principles represented in the personality, and these would be slow to change. But more concrete experiential possibilities would change, presumably in an orderly fashion, due to the abstract view of experience and the play of imagination. The person with an ideal identity would not, then, be beset by boredom or by ontological guilt. Indeed, he would feel emotions deeply and spontaneously, be they pleasant or unpleasant. He would be enthusiastic and committed.

But his life would not be quite that rosy. When you are in a rather continual process of change, you cannot predict what existential outcomes will be. Interestingly enough, we find that doubt (Frankl, 1955) or existential anxiety (May et al., 1958, pp. 37–91) is a necessary concomitant of the ideal identity. When you stop to think about it, it is quite understandable that someone who is his own standard of meaning would be unsure and anxious at times when he was changing.

Looked at in this way, doubt (existential anxiety) is actually a sign of strength, rather than illness. This is precisely what was meant by Camus (1955) when he said, "I cherish my nights of despair," and Tillich (1952) when he designated doubt to be the "god above God." Powerful expression to doubt as an aspect of humanism, and therefore strength, is given by Frankl (1955) when he says:

> Challenging the meaning of life can . . . never be taken as a manifestation of morbidity or abnormality; it is rather the truest expression of the state of being human, the mark of the most human nature in man. For we can easily imagine highly developed animals or insects—say ants or bees—which in many aspects of their social organization are actually superior to man. But we can never imagine any such creature raising the question of the meaning of its own existence, and thus challenging this existence. It is reserved for man alone to find his very existence questionable, to experience the whole dubiousness of being. More than such faculties as power of speech, conceptual thinking, or walking erect, this factor of doubting the significance of his own existence is what sets man apart from animal. [p. 30]

On logical grounds alone, nothing so basic to man's nature as doubt could ever be defined as psychopathological, for to do so would be to call everyone sick by virtue of his true nature. This logical argument is made more psychologically compelling by recognizing that when one is one's own standard of meaning, that will entail accepting and even valuing doubt because it is the necessary concomitant of the uncertainty produced by personal change. To avoid doubt is to avoid change and to give over the power in living to social and biological considerations. This is too big a price to pay for comfort alone. In avoiding the tragedies you also lose the potentiality of triumphs.

PRECIPITATING STRESS AND THE IDEAL PERSONALITY

If the ideal identity is truly an improvement over the premorbid identity, then the stresses that precipitate breakdown in the latter should be ineffective in the former. You will recall that the three stresses mentioned earlier are the threat of imminent death, social upheaval, and the accumulated sense of failure in living deeply and commitedly.

The ideal person would be so actively and enthusiastically enmeshed in living socially, biologically, and psychologically that the therapeutic effect of threat of imminent death would be markedly diminished. You simply do not need the threat of death to remind you to take life seriously and live in the immediate moment, if you are already doing these things. To the ideal person, such a threat could be frightening to some degree, but it would not be helpful. A definite implication of my saying this is the belief that the emphasis on death as what makes life important, which appears in one form or another in so much existential writing, is only of relative importance. Only when you think in terms of premorbidity as the true nature of man and the world, do you celebrate the purifying effects of threat of imminent death.

If the ideal person actually does come to the point of death, he will die a much more graceful death than that of Ivan Ilych. Death for the ideal person will be no more than a very unfortunate interruption of an intense and gratifying life process. I contend that someone who is living well will more easily face death than someone who senses that he has not even lived at all. In any event, it seems clear that the threat of imminent death will hardly precipitate an existential neurosis in a person with the ideal identity.

As to social upheaval, it is interesting to note in detail Durkheim's (1951) point of view on anomic suicide:

> It is not true . . . that human activity can be released from all restraint. Nothing in the world can enjoy such a privilege. All existence being a part of the universe is relative to the remainder; its nature and method of manifestation accordingly depend not only on itself but on other beings, who consequently restrain and regulate it. Here there are only differences of degree and form between the mineral realm and the thinking person. Man's characteristic privilege is that the bond he accepts is not physical but moral; that is, social. He is governed not by a material environment brutally imposed on him, but by a conscience superior to his own, the superiority of what he feels. Because the greater, better part of his existence transcends the body, he escapes the body's yoke, but is subject to that of society.
>
> But when society is disturbed by some painful crisis . . . it is momentarily incapable of exercising this influence; thence come the sudden rises in the curve of suicides which we have pointed out. [p. 252]

Durkheim clearly believes that man's animalistic, self-interested urges must be held in check by social regulation of life. Naturally, then, social upheaval would lead to a rise in suicide and, incidentally, in existential neurosis. But it is also likely that times of social upheaval involve intense creativity. While some people are committing suicide, others are using to good advantage the freedom achieved by the breakdown of monolithic social institutions. We should remember that the Italian Renaissance was a time of extraordinary social upheaval, and while suicide must have been high, so too was creativity. That the increase in creativity might have been due to the existence of ideal persons, for whom freedom from social pressures was helpful, is suggested by the following quote from the *Oration on the Dignity of Man*, written by Pico della Mirandola (1956), a most Renaissance man:

> Neither heavenly nor earthly, neither mortal nor immortal have we created thee, so that thou mightest be free according to thy own will and honor, to thy own creator and builder. To thee alone we gave growth and development depending on thy own free will. Thou bearest in thee the germs of a universal life. [p. 17]

Rather than constituting a stress, social upheaval may well be a boon for the person with the real identity.

Finally, there is the matter of an accumulated sense that your life is a failure in terms of depth and committedness of experience. Actually, I am speechless here. It is simply incomprehensible that a person with an ideal identity would ever experience the painful course of self-revelation leading to existential neurosis seen in Arthur Miller's Quentin. The person with an ideal identity will certainly make mistakes, and suffer for them, but will not go for as long as Quentin with no cognizance for his superficiality and attendant frustration, and, hence, will not be in the position of condemning his life.

IDEAL AND DEVIANT DEVELOPMENT

It is natural at this point to raise the question of how ideal and premorbid identities develop. But before launching into considerations of early experience and their effects on later personality, one obviously relevant and thorny problem should be raised. It is the problem of free will.

Some of you may have long since decided that I have left the scientific fold with all this emphasis upon the person himself as the "fountain of power." Does this not mean, you will ask, that according to me man's actions are not determined by anything but his own will? And is this not a view antithetical to science? Let me try to explain why I think what I am saying is quite scientific. *I am explicating the way in which a particular set of beliefs about oneself and the nature of the world can lead to actions that are more varied, active, and changeable than is true when that set of beliefs is absent.* In the psychologist's terms, I am focusing upon proactive and reactive behavior, and attempting to explain the differences between them on the basis of differences in sense of identity. The functioning of the ideal person is well summarized by the concept of proactive behavior, with its emphasis on the person as an influence on his environment. In contrast, reactive behavior, which is influenced by the environment, is very descriptive of the premorbid person. But just because proactive behavior is more varied, flexible, and original is no reason to presume it is not caused in a scientifically specifiable way. In my view, proactive behavior is caused by the characteristics of the ideal personality, namely, the humanistic belief in oneself as the fountain of power, and the associated preparedness to exercise fully the psychological as well as social and biological sides of man. Further, the ideal personality is not a mysterious implant of God, like the concept of soul. The ideal personality, like the premorbid personality, is formed out of early life experiences. I propose to sketch these experiences in the paragraphs that follow. Clearly, my position assumes that all action is determined in a specifiable scientific way. My approach amounts to availing oneself of the value in recognizing that some behavior is active while some is passive without assuming anything about a soul, or divine inspiration, or mysterious freedom.

In developing an ideal identity it certainly helps to start out with a minimum of average intelligence, but once having this, the rest depends upon the parent-child relationship, and the supplementation of this in later relationships that are significant. Even relationship of child to teacher needs to be considered. One route to ideal development is for the person to experience in his relationships with significant people in his life what Rogers (1959) has called unconditional positive regard. This means that the person is appreciated as a human being and knows it. With such appreciation, the person comes to value his own humanness, and is able to act without fear and inhibition from all three sides of himself. But unconditional positive regard is not enough. There must be something better suited to point the young person in particular directions rather than others. The people around him must value symbolization, imagination, and judgment and encourage and support the child when he shows evidence of these psychological processes. But in this, the emphasis must be upon the child's own psychological processes, rather than on his parroting those of others. In addition, the child's range of experience must be broad, so that the generalizing function of symbolization, and the ordering function of judgment will have raw material with

which to work. A broad range of experience may also have the secondary value of firing the imagination. Finally, it is crucial that the significant people in the child's life recognize the importance of social and biological functioning as well, so that they can encourage him in such expression. Their encouragement, however, should not be in the service of accepting social roles and animalistic urges, so much as in the conviction that social and biological living is what you make it, and, in the final analysis, these two sides of man are not so separate from each other and from the life of the mind.

From this brief statement, it is easy to see what would be deviant development leading to premorbidity. All you need to develop a premorbid identity is to grow up around people in significant relationship to you who value only some aspects of you, who believe in social roles and biological needs as the only defining pressures of life, and who are either afraid of active symbolization, imagination, and judgment, or see no particular relevance of these processes to living. Have these significant people act on their views in interaction with the child, and he will develop a premorbid identity.

While my brief remarks may seem somewhat flippant, I urge you to recognize that the two kinds of identity are almost that simply caused.

CONCLUDING REMARKS

If I have succeeded in my purpose, you should have a clearer, potentially research-oriented sense of existential disorder, its precursors, and its opposite, than you did before. In addition, you should have found documented here aspects of your own life and those of the people you know well.

If I have drawn the outlines of premorbid identity at all well, you will have recognized its great frequency in our contemporary Western world. While one can point to a set of early experiences in explaining the development of premorbidity, this does not help very much in understanding why this type of personality should be so prevalent these days. Inevitably, the question is raised of why so many parents and significant people in the life of modern-day youngsters instill in them the seeds of premorbidity. This question requires an answer concerning the general cultural milieu in which both adult and child exist. It is as products of their culture that adults influence the young.

Much has been written about the cultural causes of conformity, materialism, and shallow living, and I do not intend to review that literature here. But I would like to point to three broad views, of special interest to psychologists, that have gone far toward creating a cultural climate congenial to premorbidity. The men usually associated with these views are Darwin, Weber, and Freud.

Darwin argued a kinship between all animals, and this view has been sloppily interpreted by many to mean that man is very little different from lower animals. Any characteristics of man that do not seem amply represented in lower animals must be epiphenomenal, or reducible to simpler, animalistic things. Inevitably, such a view undercuts the importance of psychological processes and humanistic doctrines. And that is just what happened. I would like to point out, however, that there is nothing in the concept of a phylogenetic scale that justifies overlooking the importance of characteristics that seem to emerge at one level, having appeared in what may be only minimal proto-typical form at lower levels. Add this to the reasonable view that man is really quite far on the scale from his next lower kin, and you have a form of Darwinism that is not so incompatible with my view of the ideal identity, and that

would not be a cultural seed for the existential neurosis. To those psychologists who have rashly made what Murray (1954, p. 435) calls "the audacious assumption of species equivalence" between man and white rat I would say that a meaningful comparative psychology is as much interested in the differences as the similarities between species.

The sociologist Weber was certainly among the first to formally specify that modern, industrial society is necessarily bureaucratic in nature. This view has been considered to mean that the social roles a person is delegated are the most important things about him. Indeed, many a modern sociologist will define personality as the sum total of the social roles played by a person. Anyone who accepts such a view of himself without looking more deeply into the matter will very likely either be on the road to premorbidity himself, or be the kind of parent that breeds premorbidity in his children. In trying to show that there is an alternative to this view, let me agree that all behavior can be analyzed as social role playing, but point out that this does not necessarily mean that the social system is unchangeable and an irresistible shaper of individual living. The first step in convincing yourself of this is recognizing that there are different types of social roles. Social roles differ in their rigidity, preemptiveness, status, initiative requirements, and even in the degree to which they involve the person in changing existing social roles. The import of all this is that some social roles encourage the expression of symbolization, imagination, and judgment. Clear examples are roles of leadership, power, and aestheticism. The second step in convincing yourself that the social system is not necessarily the prime mover of individual life is to ask yourself the question of how any person comes to play certain types of roles as opposed to others. In any society that does not restrict competition for roles, the roles that a person actually does come to play will be determined in part by his view of the good life and his sense of personal identity. The person with the ideal identity will gravitate toward roles involving symbolization, imagination, and judgment, while the person with the premorbid identity will avoid these roles. Indeed, the sense of powerlessness and despair pointed to by Marx in people playing social roles that are inhuman may be a psychological problem as much as a sociological one.

Finally, we come to Freud. It may not have escaped your recognition that Freud, in classical libido theory, gives expression to the belief that life represents a compromise between the necessity of playing social roles and of expressing biological needs. He makes what I have called pre-morbidity the ideal! Further, for Freud the psychological processes are defensive in nature, reflecting at most no more than a pale shadow of the truth. It is not hard to believe that our current-day outlook that thought processes are not to be trusted and that man's self-interested sexual nature needs to be checked by society was given great impetus by Freud's theory. Interestingly enough, his theory may well have served as a necessary corrective in his day, when thought had become arid through neglect of the biological side of man and too heavy in emphasis upon judgment to the detriment of imagination. But because his theory was a corrective rather than something more comprehensively adequate, its acceptance into the general culture has contributed to setting the stage for a new emphasis in psychopathology, namely, the existential neurosis.

Psychological Deficit in Schizophrenia: Affect, Reinforcement, and Concept Attainment

Arnold H. Buss and Peter J. Lang

The term *psychological deficit* was coined by Hunt and Cofer (1944) who wanted a neutral phrase to describe the decrement shown by psychiatric patients in comparison to normals on various laboratory and intellectual tasks. They reviewed the substantial body of research accumulated prior to World War II.

Since that time there has been a prolific output of research on deficit, too much to encompass within a single re-view. Therefore we shall consider only laboratory studies of psychological deficit in schizophrenia, omitting reports of tests and clinical observations.

Organizing the voluminous literature proved to be a difficult task. One possibility was to group studies on the basis of the major theoretical approaches to deficit, since theories of deficit are essentially theories of schizophrenia: but this would have led to excessive repetition. Therefore the literature has been organized around seven areas defined in part by theory but more broadly in terms of issues and methods of investigation: (*a*)

Reprinted from the *Journal of Abnormal Psychology*, 1965, vol. 70, pp. 2–24 with the permission of the American Psychological Association and the authors.

affect and reinforcement, (*b*) concept attainment, (*c*) attention, (*d*) set, (*e*) associative interference, (*f*) drive, and (*g*) somatic arousal.

The dominant orientation in the affect and reinforcement area might be called a social-motivational view, which has two main variants. One suggests that schizophrenics are over-sensitive to punishing and/or affective stimuli, which cause them to withdraw and which produce performance deficit. The other assumes that schizophrenics are already so withdrawn from interpersonal situations that the usual incentives, rewards, and punishments employed in experimental situations do not motivate them, and their performance suffers.

In the concept attainment area, research relevant to four explanatory concepts is reviewed. The first approach holds that both schizophrenics and brain-damaged patients suffer from a loss of the "abstract attitude." A second view argues that deficit is attributable to a communication disturbance, and a third emphasizes regression: later, more mature modes of functioning are ostensibly given up for earlier, more concrete, and less efficient modes. Finally, more recent research suggests that differences in the concepts of normals and schizophrenics occur because the latter are distractible and respond to irrelevant cues.

Research on attention, set, and association further emphasizes the importance of interference effects in deficit. The schizophrenic is regarded as being excessively distracted by both incidental, external stimuli and intrusive associations, as failing to maintain a proper set or orientation, and as failing to alter the set when such a change is appropriate.

Two drive theories are evaluated. The better known theory assumes that the schizophrenic is extremely anxious, this anxiety being a high drive state that worsens performance, especially on complex tasks. The lesser known theory suggests that in schizophrenia there is a protective (cortical) inhibition that slows down learning and increases reminiscence. Interpretations of deficit in terms of the neurophysiological concept of arousal are also considered, and the relevant research on the somatic responses of schizophrenics is evaluated.

The exposition is divided into two papers. In this first paper we review the affect-reinforcement and concept-regression areas. A subsequent paper considers research on interference effects (attention, set, and associative interference) and activation (drive and arousal) as well as general problems of method in deficit research.

AFFECT AND REINFORCEMENT

Social Censure

Rodnick and Garmezy (1957) have been the most forceful advocates of the censure hypothesis:

> We have indicated that clinical psychiatric reports stress the sensitivity of the schizophrenic patient to the threat of criticism or rebuff inherent in almost any social situation. If such criticism does accentuate the patient's difficulty in differentiating cues in his environment, then it would follow that the experimental introduction of censure should produce greater discrimination decrements in schizophrenic patients than in normal individuals. [p. 118]

Rodnick and Garmezy have attempted to confirm the censure hypothesis in a series of experiments conducted by themselves or by their students. Garmezy (1952) showed that after censure (the word WRONG flashed after a response) schizophrenics had flatter generalization gradients and more errors than after praise (the word RIGHT flashed after a response); the performance of normals improved with censure. Webb (1955) found that failure led to poorer performance on a conceptual task, whereas a control group *improved* in their performance. All subjects were schizophrenics, and it is not known whether failure would have led to poorer performance in normals.

Bleke (1955) compared normals, good premorbid, and poor premorbid schizophrenics on a memory task. The subjects were either rewarded (RIGHT) or punished (WRONG) during learning. The poor premorbid schizophrenics manifested significantly better reminiscence and relearning than did good premorbids or normals. This was interpreted in terms of the effect of censure: criticism interfered with the learning of the poor premorbids, but on later testing for recall in the absence of censure they improved.

Smock and Vancini (1962) followed up Bleke's study, using a similar task but without differentiating between good and poor premorbid schizophrenics. After a practice session, half the subjects were rewarded (told they had done well), and half were censured (told they had done poorly). The practice was followed by learning without reinforcement, and then recall. There were no differences between normals and schizophrenics or between praised and censured subjects in original learning, but the censured schizophrenics had significantly *less* reminiscence than both the praised schizophrenics and the normal subjects. These findings are opposed to Bleke's, but there are differences between the studies that might be important: the makeup of the schizophrenic sample (good and poor premorbid versus a mixed group), the task, and the way praise and censure were delivered (after each response versus after practice trials). The discrepancy in findings and the possible reasons for it suggest that the effects of praise and censure may be too complex to be handled within the Rodnick-Garmezy framework.

Alvarez (1957) had normals, good pre-morbids, and poor premorbids make judgments about pictures. The judgments were either censured (WRONG) or praised (RIGHT), and later preference for the pictures was assessed. Poor premorbid schizophrenics were more susceptible to the effects of censure than good premorbids or normals, that is, the poor premorbids showed the greatest decline in preference for the pictures associated with WRONG. Thus the poor premorbids were more sensitive to WRONG, as judged by their preference scores; note that this does not mean that WRONG disrupted their performance, for this was not assessed. Similar results have been reported by Neiditch (1963), who found that functional psychotics lowered their preference for tasks which followed a failure situation significantly more than normals. He interpreted these data in terms of an inappropriate set.

Finally, Zahn (1959) tested the perceived size of pictures denoting scolding and feeding of a child by a mother. The size estimates were rewarded (RIGHT) for some subjects and punished (WRONG) for others. Good premorbid schizophrenics tended to *overestimate* the size of the punished pictures, whereas normals and poor premorbids did not.

> The results are interpreted in terms of a high degree of anxiety or affective responsivity in the Goods and the predominance of avoidance and withdrawal mechanisms in the Poors. [Zahn, 1959, pp. 46–47]

Most of these experiments were conducted under the aegis of Rodnick and Garmezy (1957). Taken at face value, they offer some support for the social censure hypothesis: failure or being told WRONG seems to produce schizophrenic deficit, an effect more striking in poor premorbid than in good premorbid schizophrenics. However, the evidence is weak, and individual experiments are open to a variety of interpretations. We shall return to these issues in the larger context of reward and punishment.

"Affective Stimuli"

Censure stimuli. The social censure hypothesis has a corollary pertaining to stimuli: schizophrenics are oversensitive to, and therefore disrupted by, stimuli connoting parental punishment or negative parent figures. This corollary has been tested mainly by students of Rodnick and Garmezy.

Dunn (1954) presented pictures of scolding, whipping, feeding, and neutral objects to schizophrenics and normals. For each scene there was a standard picture and five variations; the task was to judge whether the standard and the variations (presented in pairs) were the same or different. The schizophrenics judged more of the scolding variations as being the same as the standard than did the normals, but the other scenes yielded no differences. Dunn also discovered that a history of maternal conflict led to more judgments of "same" on the scolding scene. Two issues make it difficult to interpret these findings. First, the scolding scene is less clearly represented and might depict a number of different interactions, whereas the raised whip and the food in hand leave no doubt about the relationships presented. Thus ambiguity might account for the results, assuming that schizophrenics have more difficulty with complex stimuli which elicit many alternate responses. Second, if it were established that scolding (but not whipping or feeding) is the major trauma in the parent-child interactions of schizophrenics, the social censure hypothesis might be supported by these data. However, there is at present no basis for assuming that scolding is a more prominent problem for schizophrenics than whipping or feeding difficulties.

Dunn's results are only partially corroborated by those of Turbiner (1961), whose procedure was almost identical. In addition to neutral pictures, Turbiner had pictures of scolding and of affection. The schizophrenics' judgments were the same as the normals' for neutral stimuli but poorer than normals' for *both* positive and negative affective pictures.

Garmezy and Rodnick (1959) suggested that good and poor premorbid schizophrenics are not equally sensitive to censure from both parents. Specifically, they proposed that good premorbid schizophrenics are disrupted by paternal censure and poor premorbids by maternal censure. Two of their students, Dunham (1959) and Kreinik (1959), attempted to verify this hypothesis.

Dunham repeated Dunn's experiment, with minor modifications. Compared to normal subjects, good premorbid schizophrenics showed deficit only on slides depicting father censure and poor premorbids showed deficit on both mother censure and neutral slides. These are positive findings, but the poor premorbids' deficit with neutral slides is difficult to reconcile with the hypothesis.

Kreinik's experiment is open to two interpretations. She employed a conceptual task in which all subjects were presented with stimuli connoting positive fathers, negative fathers, positive mothers, negative mothers, and neutrality (nonhuman). There were two sessions, and only two groups failed to show improvement in the second session. These were the good premorbids with positive father stimuli and the poor premorbids with positive mother stimuli. Kreinik attributed these results to sequence effects. The Goods presented with negative father stimuli in the first session failed to improve with positive father stimuli in the second session. The results were the same for Poors with mother stimuli. Kreinik assumed that the deleterious effects of the negative parental stimuli carried over to the session with the positive stimuli. The problem with this interpretation is that the sessions were 1 day apart, and it appears doubtful that any effects would be sustained for 24 hours. The alternate explanation is more parsimonious: Goods and Poors are negatively affected by positive father and mother figures, respectively.

Two other studies are relevant. Baxter and Becker (1962) used TAT cards depicting mother-son and father-son relationships, scoring the stories for anxiety. Poor premorbids scored higher in anxiety than good premorbids on the mother-son picture, and the reverse was true for the father-son picture. However, two issues make it difficult to interpret these results unequivocally. First, the Goods scored approximately the same in anxiety on the mother-son and father-son pictures. Second, there was no control group of normal subjects, which means we do not know how much anxiety ordinarily appears in stories about these pictures.

Lebow and Epstein (1963) used TAT-like stimuli depicting mother, father, and peer interactions in nurturant, rejecting, and ambiguous situations. The subjects were good premorbid schizophrenics and medical patients. In the present context the only relevant measure was a rating of the stories, called goodness of response. Concerning this measure,

> there was a strong tendency for the schizophrenics to tell their poorest stories to the nurturant cues and their best stories to the ambiguous cues. Thus, if anything, the schizophrenics find nurturant as well as rejecting cues disruptive, and the former more so. Rather than a specific censure-cue deficit, the schizophrenic exhibits a general deficit for cues associated with emotional involvement, whether of a positive or a negative nature. [p. 32]

Size estimation has also been used as an index of the distorting effects of affective stimuli. Harris (1957) presented pictures of the mother-son interaction. Normals made few mistakes in size estimation, and good premorbids underestimated the size of the pictures. In a similar study Zahn (1959) tested perceived size of scolding and feeding pictures. In addition the pictures were associated with RIGHT for some subjects and with WRONG for others. Good premorbids, in relation to the rewarded and the feeding pictures, overestimated the size of scolding pictures and pictures associated with WRONG. There were no similar relationships for normals or poor premorbids. In attempting to explain the discrepancy (Harris' good premorbids *under*estimated, Zahn's good premorbids *over*estimated), Zahn pointed out that his schizophrenics had been hospitalized longer than Harris', although it is not clear how this accounts for the discrepancy.

Moriarty and Kates (1962) matched normals, good premorbid, and poor premorbid schizophrenics for concept attainment with neutral stimuli and tested them with stimuli connoting parental approval and disapproval. For *both* approval and disapproval stimuli the normals performed significantly better than the good premorbids, who performed significantly better than the poor premorbids. Evidently, "social" stimuli disrupted the performance of the schizophrenics. Concerning specific effects of parental disapproval,

> all groups show deficit behavior on social materials suggesting censure, with the psychiatric and the normal groups showing about the same relative decrements on the disapproval cards. [p. 362]

Taken together, these studies do not support the hypothesis that the performance of schizophrenics is disrupted by stimuli connoting censure, especially parental censure. Positive findings have been reported, but they have been open to alternate interpretations because of methodological problems (e.g., Dunn, 1954; Kreinik, 1959) or unclear results (e.g., Dunham, 1959; Baxter & Becker, 1962). Early positive results have been either contradicted by later results (e.g., Harris, 1957; Zahn, 1959) or only weakly corroborated by later results (e.g., Dunn, 1954; Turbiner, 1961). There have also been negative findings: schizophrenics are adversely affected not only by censure stimuli but also by stimuli connoting affection, nurturance, and approval.

Affective stimuli in general. If the social censure hypothesis is correct, deficit should be produced *only* by stimuli associated with censure or parental punishment. An alternate hypothesis is that schizophrenics are oversensitive to *all* affective stimuli, not merely those connoting censure. A number of studies have attempted to test this hypothesis.

Culver (1961) had subjects estimate the size of pictures of a mother and a neutral object. *Both* good and poor premorbids underestimated the size of the mother, whereas normals did not. All three groups were similar in size estimation of the square. Raush (1956) tested for perceived size of a neutral object (overcoat button) and symbolic objects (ice cream cone and cigar). Using the estimated size of the neutral object as a base, he found that schizophrenics overestimated the size of the symbolic objects in comparison to the normals. Ehrenworth (1960) had subjects estimate the relative size of drawings of geometric figures and themes of heterosexuality, autonomy, competition, affiliation, and authority (all affective themes). Schizophrenics' size estimates of the affective stimuli were significantly poorer than both their estimates of the neutral stimuli and normals' estimates of the affective stimuli.

Pishkin, Smith, and Leibowitz (1962) used figures dressed as psychiatric aides or patients, and the subjects judged the relative size of the figures versus a silhouette. For the aide figure the errors of schizophrenics and normals were similar; for the patient figure the schizophrenics made significantly more errors. Assuming the patient figure was more symbolic, Pishkin *et al.* concluded that

> it is the symbolic or emotional value of the stimulus which accounts for schizophrenic deficit on perceptual tasks. [p. 329]

De Wolfe (1962) showed that good premorbids are more emotionally responsive to affective words than both poor premorbids and normals in a verbal conditioning task. Feldstein (1962) tested speech disturbance to affective and neutral materials and found no differences between schizophrenics and normals.

Four studies reported significant results using the human-nonhuman dichotomy. Davis and Harrington (1957) matched subjects on the basis of their ability to utilize information about nonhuman stimuli in a conceptual-discrimination problem. Schizophrenics were severely disrupted by human stimuli in a comparable problem, whereas normals were not. Marx (1962) divided his schizophrenic subjects into "early" and "late" patients (similar to acute versus chronic). In a conceptual task, human stimuli disrupted the early schizophrenics more than the late schizophrenics. Whiteman (1954) had subjects learn formal concepts (based on physical properties or size relationships) and social concepts (based on interactions among people, such as cooperation or encouragement). Although the schizophrenics were poorer than normals on the formal, nonhuman concepts, their performance significantly worsened on the social, human concepts. Brodsky (1961) compared schizophrenics and nonpsychotic hospital patients on a conceptual task involving people and nonhuman stimuli. The schizophrenics' conceptual performance was less adequate than normals' only with human stimuli.

Feffer (1961) tested the perception of affective and neutral words. He divided his schizophrenic subjects into "pathologically-concrete" and "adequately-conceptualizing" groups on the basis of tests of conceptual thinking. On the perceptual task the adequately-conceptualizing schizophrenics were especially vigilant in the presence of affective stimuli; the pathologically-concrete schizophrenics tended to avoid affective stimuli; and the normals showed no particular reaction to affective stimuli.

Silverman (1963) reported similar findings when words were presented tachistoscopically. Schizophrenics were especially sensitive to unpleasant words, identifying them more correctly than did normals. There were two kinds of schizophrenics, paranoid and nonparanoid. The paranoids placed between nonparanoids and normals in their differential sensitivity to unpleasant words. These results raise the possibility that Feffer's pathologically-concrete and adequately-conceptualizing schizophrenics may have been nonparanoid and paranoid, respectively.

One study failed to find a difference in perception between schizophrenics and normals. Nelson and Caldwell (1962) measured depth perception, using as stimuli drawings of a man, a woman, a dog, and a circle. There were no significant differences in perception for different stimuli or between normals and schizophrenics.

Arey (1960) tested subjects for recognition of sexual and neutral pictures. He found that schizophrenics were more affected by the sexual pictures, i.e., their recognition performance on sexual pictures compared to nonsexual pictures was significantly poorer than normals.

These various studies indicate that schizophrenic deficit occurs in response to many different kinds of stimuli, not merely those connoting censure. Thus the censure hypothesis is not sufficiently encompassing to account for the data. The results can be better explained by the alternate hypothesis that schizophrenics are oversensitive to all affective stimuli.

This latter hypothesis suggests that schizophrenics are disturbed by certain kinds of stimuli and that such disturbance leads to a deterioration in performance. The central problem is to define the term *affective*, whose meaning appears to change from one experiment to the next. It can have taboo aspects, as in the sexual stimuli used by Arey (1960); it may refer to human, as opposed to nonhuman stimuli; it may be symbolic, as opposed to nonsymbolic stimuli (Raush, 1956); or it may be defined empirically, by means of Luria free association indices (Feffer, 1961). In the face of such diverse operational definitions, it is difficult to maintain a clear referent for "affective stimuli."

Another way of approaching this issue is to regard affective stimuli as being better able to elicit associations from subjects. It is reasonable to assume that human, symbolic, sexual, and aggressive stimuli are more capable of setting off a train of personal and idiosyncratic associations than are more neutral and impersonal stimuli. One way of accounting for the deleterious effect of affective stimuli is to assume that they trigger more associations than do neutral stimuli. This assumption has been verified by Deering (1963), who had subjects associate to affective (pleasant and unpleasant) and neutral words matched for familiarity. Schizophrenics gave significantly more associations to affective words than did normals, but the groups did not differ in the number of associations to neutral words. Presumably, the greater the number of associations to any stimuli, the more the responder will be distracted and the more his performance will suffer.

Insufficient Motivation

Clinical descriptions of schizophrenics usually include apathy and isolation, or at least a tendency to withdraw from interpersonal contacts. The social censure hypothesis attempts to explain the withdrawal (as well as psychological deficit) in terms of the schizophrenic's inordinate sensitivity to rejection. The insufficient motivation hypothesis accepts the disinterest in social contacts as a given and uses it to account for deficit. The schizophrenic is ostensibly unmotivated to perform well on experimental tasks, whereas the normal subject tries to please the experimenter and perseveres at meaningless tasks in the face of boredom and fatigue (Orne, 1962). The schizophrenic, it is suggested, tends to be uncooperative, disinterested, and relatively unmotivated by laboratory criteria of success or by pleasing the experimenter. Supporting this view, Slechta, Gwynn, and Peoples (1963) showed that when such casual social reinforcers as nods of the interviewer's head or "mmm-hm" follow particular verbal behaviors, normal subjects yield a significantly greater percentage of criterion responses than do schizophrenics.

The deficit, then, is not in the schizophrenic's ability but in his motivation. It follows that if the schizophrenic could be urged to cooperate or if he were given appropriate incentives, rewards, or punishments, his performance would equal that of normals.

Cooperation and urging. Wittman (1937) estimated the cooperativeness of schizophrenics, paretics, and nonpsychiatric patients from the response of attendants and physicians to rating scales and checklists. The schizophrenics' cooperativeness scores were generally lower than those of the other two groups, and the schizophrenics were the only group to have high negative correlations between cooperativeness ratings and a memory-reasoning test. Similar findings have been reported by Shakow (1962) for a variety of tasks, and Spohn and Wolk (1963) and Wing and Freudenberg (1961) showed that sustained social stimulation can lead to improved performance and improved ward behavior.

Several experiments were based on the following line of reasoning: (*a*) schizophrenics perform worse than normals, (*b*) schizophrenics are less cooperative or less motivated than normals, (*c*) therefore schizophrenics should improve more than normals when both are urged.

Stotsky (1957) studied the effect of a "motivational incentive" on the psychomotor performance of remitted, regressed schizophrenics and normal subjects. The incentive took the form of encouragement, from their psychotherapist for the patients and from the experimenter for the normal subjects, during an interim between tasks. Both patients and normals were responsive to the motivational condition: the regressed schizophrenics showed significantly greater improvement than normals in simple reaction time (RT), but the normals showed significantly greater improvement than the patients on the disjunctive RT task. D'Alessio and Spence (1963) reported no difference in degree of improvement on a simple motor task between normal and chronic schizophrenic patients. Benton, Jentsch, and Wahler (1960) found that both normal and schizophrenic subjects improved RT performance equally when administered positive "motivating" instructions, and the improvement of the schizophrenic subjects was not significantly different from that of a group of similarly-treated brain-damaged patients (whose data were available from Blackburn, 1958). Olson (1958) reported that schizophrenics improved their performance on a digit-symbol task following either depreciation or praise of a previous performance, whereas normals improved only after praise. However, Goodstein, Guertin, and Blackburn (1961) found no difference in the RT improvement of schizophrenics and normals, both groups improving most following failure instructions. Shankweiler (1959) reported that like schizophrenics, brain-damaged subjects also improve on a psychomotor task subsequent to failure instructions.

Johannsen (1962) had nonparanoid and paranoid schizophrenics and normals cancel the letter f in prose material. At the end of each 2-minute trial subjects were told their performance was good or poor, or they were told nothing. The criticized subjects showed the greatest improvement, the praised subjects were next, and the control subjects were last; these results held for both schizophrenic and normal subjects. The order of improvement for diagnostic groups was: normals, paranoids, and nonparanoids.

Schooler and Spohn (1960) studied schizophrenics and normals in an Asch situation and found both groups equally responsive to social pressure. Felice (1961) examined the effects of interpersonal (experimenter present) and impersonal (experimenter absent) administration on the performance of normals and schizophrenics on a variety of laboratory tasks. Task, diagnosis, and method of administration interacted to produce highly variable results. On some tests schizophrenic performance was depressed by the presence of the experimenter, on other tasks it made no difference, and on some the normals did poorest during the interpersonal administration. However, in these experiments the experimenter's status as a social or affective stimulus may not be the relevant variable. He may simply be an additional distracting element or a source of reduced cues which aid the subject in his task.

In summary, the data on both positively and negatively oriented urging do not support a motivational interpretation of deficit. Normals, schizophrenics, and brain-damaged patients all tend to respond with equal improvement on these conditions. At least one researcher has reported urging instructions to be completely ineffective in modifying schizophrenic psychomotor behavior (Ladd, 1960). In any event, the schizophrenic's deficit has never been completely overcome by these methods. Only Stotsky's (1957) "remitted" group could not be differentiated from normals, and this occurred on some tasks before additional motivations were introduced.

Nonverbal reward and punishment. While the schizophrenic may be insensitive to the rewards of social interaction (pleasing the experimenter, etc.), he might still be affected by more tangible or biologically pertinent reinforcers. Thus an attempt may be made to eliminate his performance deficit by using such nonverbal rewards (cigarettes, money, pleasant stimuli) or punishments (electric shock and "white noise").

Peters (1953) and Peters and Jenkins (1954) studied the motor learning and problem-solving behavior of schizophrenics receiving subshock insulin, providing a "sweet nutrient" as a reward for correct responses. On the basis of his first study, Peters concluded that although the reward did increase operant rate, it did little to eliminate errors. In the second study, using the same incentive condition, an attempt was made to use rewarded problem-solving as an adjunct to therapy. It was anticipated that rewarded achievement on simple motor tasks would provide a base for success in more complex social tasks, and hence would transfer to routine, day to day behavior. It was found that the experimental group had significantly fewer "negative ward incidents" than the control group, but the ratings of ward personnel did not distinguish between the groups. The weak effect found in these studies is consistent with Michaux's (1955) study of apperception as a function of hunger. He reported that unlike normals, schizophrenics show no increase in food completions on a verbal task under hunger conditions.

Schizophrenics, brain-damaged patients, and medical controls were promised money for better performance in a study by Burday (1962). The task involved conceptual sorting, and the money incentive yielded no significant differences among the three groups. However, Rodnick and Garmezy (1957) reported informally that candy, cigarettes, and an attractive scoreboard raise the performance level of schizophrenic subjects. At the beginning of their experiments the performance of good premorbid patients has frequently been no different from that of normal subjects.

Lindsley and Skinner (1954) found results similar to those for dogs, rats, and pigeons, in schizophrenic patients conditioned to pull levers for candy, cigarettes, or projected colored slides. They concluded that psychotic behavior is controlled "to some extent" by the reinforcing properties of the immediate physical environment. Isaacs, Thomas, and Goldiamond (1960) reinstated verbal behavior in two catatonic patients, using operant conditioning methods, and Tilton (1956) reported an improved "general level of functioning" in schizophrenics treated by instrumental learning. However, in Lindsley's study (1960) schizophrenics sometimes abruptly ceased their operant responding without the introduction of any extinction procedure. Furthermore, King, David, and Lovinger (1957) failed to confirm the hypotheses that severity of neuropsychiatric illness is inversely related to rewarded operant rate and that clinical improvement is positively related to this variable. Contrary to Lindsley and Skinner, they concluded that "operant motor behavior seems best classified as a peripheral variable in terms of psychopathology [1957, p. 325]."

As with urging instructions, tangible positive rewards appear somewhat to ameliorate the poor performance of schizophrenics, and less severely disturbed patients may approach the performance of normals on some tasks. However, there is no clear evidence that for schizophrenics, positive tangible rewards are superior to verbal encouragement. Killberg (1962) found that improvement in a verbal learning task was greater for verbally reinforced normal subjects than for similarly treated schizophrenics and that schizophrenics and normals did not differ in improvement when cigarettes were used as a reinforcer. However, the difference between the schizophrenic subjects under the two conditions of reinforcement was not significant.

Whereas monetary reward improved the performance of normals on a serial anticipation task, Topping and O'Connor (1960) found that nonparanoids did not improve and paranoid schizophrenics worsened under the same conditions. Clearly, positive rewards do not exert any consistent control over schizophrenic behavior and probably vary considerably in their consequences with changes in population and experimental setting.

Physical punishment has proved to be the most consistent and effective reinforcer of behavior in schizophrenic subjects. Pascal and Swenson (1952) found no difference between a group of schizophrenic and normal subjects on initial trials of a complex, discrimination RT task, but on subsequent trials the normals improved and the schizophrenics did not. At this point a strong, aversive stimulus was introduced in the form of high intensity noise delivered through earphones, and subjects were told that the noise would be turned off only after a correct response. Under these conditions both groups improved, the schizophrenics showing a greater reduction in latency scores than the normal subjects. Analysis of the final trials revealed no significant difference between the schizophrenic and normal groups.

Cohen (1956) evaluated the performance of chronic schizophrenic and normal subjects on an apparatus which presented patterned visual stimuli. Subjects responded by moving a handle either left or right, depending on the pattern. After a number of trials under the usual conditions of administration, half of the normal group and half of the schizophrenics received a shock at stimulus onset, which was terminated by a correct response. The schizophrenics consistently required more trials to learn and made more errors than did the normals. However, although the unshocked schizophrenics showed a decrement in performance on later trials, the shocked schizophrenics maintained their previous level of performance. This difference between control and experimental groups was not present in the results of the normals.

A study of RT in schizophrenia by Rosenbaum, Mackavey, and Grisell (1957a) suggests that schizophrenics are able to improve their performance under shock conditions. Male and female schizophrenics and hospital employees were first tested in a simple RT situation under standard conditions. Half of each group was then tested under shock conditions, while the remainder continued responding in the previous manner. The task was a simple finger lift from a key in response to an auditory stimulus. In the shock condition subjects were stimulated electrically in the finger to be withdrawn, simultaneously with the sounding of the buzzer. The hospital employees were significantly faster than the psychotics under all conditions of the ex-

periment, but the schizophrenics showed significantly greater improvement than the normals from nonshock to shock conditions. In fact, the electric shock raised the scores of the schizophrenic men to the level of the normals. These results cannot be attributed to an increased "need" to respond quickly because the shock, which was administered to the responding finger, actually replaced sound as the discriminative stimulus. The improvement can as easily be assigned to an increased stimulus dynamism.

In a subsequent study Rosenbaum, Grisell, and Mackavey (1957b) tested the RTs of female schizophrenics and college students. There were several conditions, involving particular combinations of "ready" interval (regular or irregular) and shock. The conditions were called "social motivation," "anxiety motivation," and "biological motivation," respectively. The authors report that:

> The normals were superior to the schizophrenics on all measures, but could be significantly differentiated from the younger, privileged group only on anxiety reaction time [during the anxiety reaction time trials, the shock was presented in an unpredictable manner]. [p. 206]

Two other studies are particularly worthy of mention in that a concept formation rather than a psychomotor test provided the experimental task. Cavanaugh (1958) compared the performance of chronic schizophrenics and nonpsychiatric patients and found that under the usual conditions of administration, schizophrenics were inferior. However, when an aversive stimulus was introduced (high intensity noise presented with the concept materials and terminated by a correct response), schizophrenic experimental subjects performed significantly better (in terms of the number of correct concepts and latency scores) than a control (no noise) group. Furthermore, there was no difference in performance between this schizophrenic noise group and a group of similarly tested nonpsychiatric patients. Brown (1961) substantially confirmed Cavanaugh's findings in a study in which incorrect responses were followed by aversive noise.

In brief, in all studies employing physical punishment as an incentive there has been a definite reduction, and in a few instances the temporary elimination, of psychological deficit. These results are consistent with this variant of motivation theory: deficit is a consequence of lowered social motivation, and thus may be reduced when biologically intense reinforcers are used. However, they can also be explained by interference theory: the important fact in the introduction of intense stimuli may be the change in attention and set, with a sharper differentiation between relevant and irrelevant inputs being created.

Verbal reward and punishment. Many studies of schizophrenia have been designed to evaluate the effects of specific verbal cues or reinforcers on the course of psychological tasks. This research has been less concerned with overcoming deficit than with the differential effects of verbal reward and punishment. It will be recalled that Rodnick and Garmezy (1957) hold that social censure or disapproval disrupts the performance of schizophrenics. However, studies of physical punishment and studies which found improvement after negatively oriented urging suggest that the schizophrenic's performance is specifically facilitated by censure.

In a series of experiments Buss and colleagues (Buss & Buss, 1956; Buss, Braden, Orgel, & Buss, 1956; Buss, Wiener, & Buss, 1954) found that the word WRONG, following an incorrect response, yields more effective learning than RIGHT for correct answers. The sub-

jects were mixed groups of psychiatric patients, the majority being schizophrenic. Leventhal (1959) confirmed these findings in a study of diagnosed schizophrenics; "Not so good" was more effective in facilitating verbal conditioning than "Good." Atkinson and Robinson (1961) and Koppenhaver (1961) compared verbal reward and punishment in a paired-associates learning task and found that punishment improved schizophrenic learning, relative to that obtained with reward.

Losen (1961) matched good premorbid schizophrenics with normals on the basis of arithmetic ability and tested them on arithmetic and short-term memory tasks. There were four experimental groups. One group was shown their scores without comment following each response; the other three groups were administered 100%, 50%, and 0% censure schedules. The censure was verbal: "No, that was wrong." None of the experimental conditions significantly altered the performance of normal subjects. For schizophrenics, the 0% censure group and the group that was simply shown their scores did not change, but both the 100% and 50% censure groups showed significant improvement. In all of the above studies mild verbal censure of the type used by Garmezy and Rodnick and their students *facilitated* the performance of schizophrenics.

A number of experiments suggest that the ameliorative effects of censure cannot be attributed to the personal or social character of these reinforcers. Lang (1959) found that chronic schizophrenics significantly improved RT scores when a neutral tone followed responses slower than a previously established standard. A subsequent study (Cavanaugh, Cohen, & Lang, 1960) showed that verbal reward was ineffective in improving RT but that verbal censure and the same information about errors used in the previous experiment led to nearly equal improvement. Atkinson and Robinson (1961) found no difference between the facilitating effect of verbal censure and the results obtained when incorrect responses were followed by the sound of an adding machine in operation. On the other hand, Maginley (1956) employed a visual rather than an auditory cue as a nonsocial reinforcer and found that schizophrenics performed less well than normals on the later trials of a concept formation task. However, he attributed this effect to the "diminished interest and attention" occasioned by the light. Johannsen (1961) studied the performance of normals and two schizophrenic groups on a double alternation task. The reinforcers were either verbal right and wrong or differentially colored light. Paranoid schizophrenics were no different under conditions of social and nonsocial reinforcement but the performance of nonparanoid schizophrenics was significantly poorer when social reinforcers were employed.

The thesis that punishment invariably disrupts performance is clearly not tenable. Both a negative evaluation and specific verbal or physical punishment for errors can lead to significant improvement in performance rather than further deficit. The fact that this improvement occurs in both the presence and absence of socially or personally punitive conditions suggests that the significant factor is information about inadequate responses rather than the interpersonal context.

Knowledge of results is important to any task in which improvement is expected with practice, and in general the normal subject recognizes the correctness or wrongness of a response as soon as it occurs, and no assistance is required. However, schizophrenics seem to be less able to instruct themselves and less able

to maintain or usefully alter a response set (Shakow, 1962). Furthermore, studies of incidental learning (Greenberg, 1954; Winer, 1954) reveal that relative to normals, schizophrenics fail to observe objects or relationships towards which their attention has not been specifically directed. Thus, informational cues introduced by the experimenter have greater importance for the psychotic subject in certain tasks.

In the experiments of Lang (1959), Cavanaugh et al. (1960), and Losen (1961) normal subjects performed asymptote under the usual conditions of administration; additional cues did not lead to improvement. Starting at a lower performance level, schizophrenics were able to profit from information about errors and thereby improve their performance. On a task with more ceiling, however, normal subjects can accomplish the same result, Buss and Buss (1956) demonstrated that in concept formation, normals yield a reward-punishment hierarchy no different from that originally found with patients, i.e., punishing errors is more effective in improving performance than rewarding correct responses.

Studies of normal subjects indicate there is considerable difference in the effectiveness of reward and punishment, depending on the experimental task (Meyer & Offenbach, 1962). If the task is a simple one (few alternate responses) and the correct response is already in the respondent's behavioral repertoire, reward is likely to be effective in maintaining the wanted behavior. However, if the task is complex (many alternate responses) and if the correct response is not currently in the subject's repertoire or readily elicited, punishment will provide the better guide. In essence, verbal approval confirms the aptness of a response already made; punishment signals a need for change. In nearly all the experiments under consideration the question raised was to what extent could subjects improve or change, and information about errors generally proved to be the most valuable experimental manipulandum for *both* normal and schizophrenic subjects.

Nevertheless, diagnosis and the specific experimental task interact, and results at variance with this trend are not surprising. Both Atkinson and Robinson (1961) and Leventhal (1959) report that schizophrenics learn fastest when punished for errors, while nonpsychotics show most rapid learning with reward. The former authors attribute these findings to the fact that punishment tends to break up the perseverative behavior unique to schizophrenic subjects, an interpretation consistent with the set hypothesis proposed earlier.

Garmezy's study of generalization (1952) can also be interpreted as suggesting that punishing errors is a more effective method for schizophrenic than normal subjects. The subjects were instructed either to pull a lever if a tone was the same as a training stimulus or to push the lever if it was different. Extreme incorrect pull responses were punished, and correct pull responses were rewarded: in effect, the subject was both rewarded and punished for the same behavior. Under these circumstances the incidence of pull responses among schizophrenic subjects dropped to all tones. They simply learned to avoid the word WRONG, rather than to make the discrimination accomplished by the normal subjects. Maginley (1956) reported similar data in a concept formation task. Reward was superior to a combination of punishment for errors and reward for correct responses, and this held for *both* normal and schizophrenic subjects. It is not clear whether the performance difference may be attributed to censure or the different information provided by the two kinds of cues.

Waters (1962) attempted to separate the effects of censure and information about errors in a two-choice learning task. As might be expected, chronic schizophrenics performed best when provided with maximal cues. Paradoxically, the acute patients had fewer errors under the minimal cue condition. Both groups showed poorer performance when social censure was introduced.

Fischer (1963) used both specific criticism for responses and general criticism for performance, as well as specific praise, general praise, and a control. The task was to repeat a series of lights, and the performance measure was response speed. All subjects improved from the first series to the second, and in order of improvement the conditions were criticism (general and specific), praise (general and specific), and the control. An additional finding was that the subjects performed better in the experimenter's absence (comments delivered via earphones) than in his presence.

In neither Waters' nor Fischer's experiment were there normal subjects, but there were normals in a related study by Brooker (1962), who compared task-relevant criticism (WRONG) and praise (RIGHT) with task-irrelevant criticism and praise. The relevant task was the Wisconsin Card Sorting Test, and the irrelevant task was judging a weight every five trials of the card sorting. Normals and schizophrenics both learned better with task-relevant criticism than with task-relevant praise. In the task-irrelevant condition, criticism led to poorer learning than reward for schizophrenics, but there were no differences for normals. These results can be interpreted as supporting both the social censure and interference theories. In light of the complexities that have cropped up in previous research, the separation of censure from information about errors should be part of any experiment on verbal punishment and deficit.

Summary

The research on affect and reinforcement will be summarized under four headings: affective stimuli, information, punishment, and diagnosis.

Affective stimuli. Certain "affective" stimuli disturb schizophrenics enough to produce psychological deficit, but the stimuli are so varied that this term has no precise referent. Concerning affective stimuli, the social censure hypothesis appears to be incorrect. Schizophrenic deficit occurs not only with stimuli connoting censure but also with human, symbolic, and taboo stimuli. A promising hypothesis is that affective stimuli elicit more associations from schizophrenics and that these associations interfere with performance.

Information. It is clear that schizophrenic subjects improve when they are given information about their responses, and they can profit from cues that may be superfluous to normals. Lang (1959) and Losen (1961) have pointed out that schizophrenics, unlike normals, fail to make statements during tasks which suggest self-guidance (e.g., "I got that one wrong"; "I'll have to watch it next time."). It seems likely that external reinforcing cues serve a directive purpose in schizophrenics that normal subjects accomplish for themselves.

The task usually determines whether positive or negative information is more valuable in improving performance. Most tasks have been complex (initiate many alternate responses), and change (improvement), rather than the maintenance of an initially offered response, has been the desired result. If the task also has sufficient ceiling, both normals and schizophrenics profit more from information about errors than they do from knowledge of successes.

Punishment. In some tasks psychotics make more use of punishment than reward, relative to normal subjects, but there is little evidence to suggest this is due to schizophrenics' personal reaction to social censure. Punishment seems to assist the schizophrenic by breaking up perseverative tendencies, whereas reward maintains a previously correct response that is wrong on subsequent trials. This could happen in paired-associate learning, in which a correct response to one stimulus word is wrong for every other stimulus. The process is probably dependent on instructions the subject gives to himself, and it is here that schizophrenics appear to be deficient.

Physical punishment facilitates the performance of schizophrenics, and in fact it is the only contingency that has led to a complete elimination of deficit on some tasks (concept formation). However, it is conceivable that "noise" and shock serve a focusing or arousal function, rather than the traditional role of incentive or reinforcer.

Diagnosis. Response to motivating instructions, social stimuli, and information about performance all seem to vary with diagnosis. These variables are sensitive to personality differences in normal subjects, and perhaps at least an equal effect should be anticipated in schizophrenics. Because of the variety of populations and experimental situations employed, generalizations about the consequences of motivational factors are difficult. However, paranoid-nonparanoid, good premorbid versus poor premorbid, and the acute-chronic typologies have all proved to be experimentally distinct and cannot be ignored in research with schizophrenics.

CONCEPT ATTAINMENT

Schizophrenics show deficit in conceptual tasks, just as they do in tasks involving simple learning, perception, and psychomotor behavior. In fact, studies on concept learning predominate in the older literature on deficit. There are four main hypotheses in this area: loss of abstractness, loss of communication, regression, and interference.

Loss of Abstractness

Goldstein (1946), analogizing from his research with brain-damaged patients, suggested that the fundamental thinking disorder in schizophrenia is the inability to form abstract concepts. He postulates a disturbance of the "abstract attitude," which has the following characteristics:

1. To assume a mental set voluntarily.
2. To shift voluntarily from one aspect of the situation to another.
3. To keep in mind simultaneously various aspects.
4. To grasp the essentials of a given whole; to break up a given whole into parts and to isolate them voluntarily.
5. To generalize; to abstract common properties; to plan ahead ideationally; to assume an attitude toward the "mere possible," and to think or perform symbolically.
6. To detach our ego from the outer world. [p. 19]

The ability to assume the abstract attitude develops gradually being preceded by the "concrete attitude," which is merely a response to immediate sense impression. Goldstein's (1959) major hypothesis is that both organic brain-damaged patients and schizophrenics have lost the abstract attitude and can function in thought and language only at the concrete level. He was careful not to conclude that schizophrenia is the same as organic brain damage, but it is clear from his writings that he attributed

schizophrenic deficit in conceptual tasks to a loss of function similar to that seen in neurological conditions.

Goldstein cited as evidence for this theory the relatively poor performance of schizophrenics on the Goldstein-Scheerer test (Bolles & Goldstein, 1938; Goldstein & Scheerer, 1941). Similar results were obtained with the Vigotsky blocks, a test of concept formation (Hanfmann & Kasanin, 1937, 1942; Kasanin, 1946). However, Fisher (1950) found that schizophrenics and hysterics were not significantly different in their performance with the Vigotsky blocks. It is difficult to interpret this body of data. The Goldstein-Scheerer test is nonquantitative and requires a rating of concreteness by the experimenter. The Vigotsky test uses a combination time-help score that confounds slowness with poor performance. Furthermore, in many of the studies adequate control groups were absent. Thus these early studies are inconclusive.

Later investigators, using quantitative techniques and adequate control groups, have demonstrated that schizophrenics are *not* abnormally concrete (Chapman & Taylor, 1957; Fey, 1951; Lothrop, 1960; McGaughran, 1954; McGaughran & Moran, 1956, 1957; Rashkis, 1947; White, 1949, and Williams, 1962). They showed that schizophrenics are capable of responding with abstract concepts, but the concepts are often unusual and idiosyncratic. The problem with schizophrenics is therefore not a loss of the abstract attitude but a tendency to verbalize concepts that are deviant and difficult for normals to understand. One way of interpreting these results is to assume an inability to communicate with others.

Loss of Communication

This theory holds that the problem in schizophrenia is not a loss but a basic lack of communication. The schizophrenic's concepts are bizarre and unacceptable to others because he is withdrawn and asocial. The first one to advance this view was Sullivan (1946), who emphasized language problems. Cameron (1946) elaborated it in terms of fantasy:

> Social communication is gradually crowded out by fantasy; and fantasy itself, because of its nonparticipation in and relation to action, becomes in turn less and less influenced by social patterns. The result is a progressive loss of organized thinking. . . . [pp. 51–52]

As McGaughran (1954; McGaughran & Moran, 1956) has indicated loss of communication and loss of abstractness represent two dimensions of concepts: public-private and open-closed. The public-private dimension is the one emphasized by Sullivan and later Cameron (1946). Schizophrenics ostensibly give an idiosyncratic, private basis for the way they sort objects, whereas normals give a common, public basis. The open-closed dimension is the one emphasized by Goldstein and Kasanin. Schizophrenics give a more closed, narrow, stimulus-bound basis for sorting objects, whereas normals give an open, more inclusive, stimulus-free basis for sorting.

McGaughran and Moran (1956) used a quantified object-sorting task to test these two theories. Sorting performance was scored for both the open-closed and public-private dimensions. Schizophrenics gave slightly fewer public bases for sorting and slightly more open bases than matched normals, but neither difference met the usual level of statistical significance. Furthermore, intelligence was found to be related to the public-private dimension: the more intelligent schizophrenics gave more public bases for sorting than did the less intelligent schizophrenics.

Some of these results were corroborated by Payne and Hewlitt (1960), who included in their battery tests of concreteness. While schizophrenics did perform relatively poorly on three measures of concreteness, performance on these measures was determined mainly by intelligence. These authors also noted that many of the unusual responses of schizophrenics tend to be scored as concrete.

Not all investigators have demonstrated conceptual deficit in schizophrenics. Nathan (1962) compared acute and chronic schizophrenics and normals on eight conceptual tasks, which varied on three dichotomous dimensions: formal versus social, verbal versus nonverbal, and abstract versus subsuming. There were no significant differences between schizophrenics in these tasks.

Evidence that schizophrenics are abnormally concrete is again weak. Their concepts do tend to be eccentric and thus difficult for normals to understand. However, this is a property of the concepts, not a defect in the manner in which they are communicated. Furthermore, both dimensions appear to be related to general intelligence, suggesting that evidence for the concreteness or privacy of concepts is confounded with a more general intellectual disability.

Regression to Childish Thinking

Goldman (1962) elaborated Werner's (1948) developmental approach, combining the loss of abstractness and the loss of communication views into a single theory. He distinguished three dimensions believed to be important in the development of thinking in children. First, the child's concepts and ideas are initially personal and idiosyncratic, but they gradually become more public and common. Second, early concepts are labile and shifting, whereas later ones are more stable. Third, early concepts are more concrete and tied to the stimulus context, but later concepts are more abstract and free of the stimuli or events with which they were originally associated.

In support of his position Goldman cited qualitative findings with children and clinical reports on schizophrenics' concreteness (Arieti, 1955; Cameron, 1938; and Kasanin, 1946). Unfortunately these findings lack quantification or adequate controls. As additional evidence Goldman noted that schizophrenics tend to define words more concretely than normals (Choderkoff & Mussen, 1952; Feifel, 1949; Flavell, 1956; Harrington & Ehrmann, 1954). However, as we noted above, bizarre and eccentric responses tend to be scored as concrete, which renders such evidence inconclusive. Furthermore, a number of experiments have demonstrated that schizophrenics give abstract concepts.

Going beyond these considerations, there is the more general issue of the regression hypothesis: does the thinking of schizophrenics resemble that of children? Feifel (1949) showed that children and schizophrenics defined words in a similar pattern that deviated from normal adult definitions. Ellsworth (1951) found that children and schizophrenics were similar in the way they used different parts of speech. Burstein (1959, 1961) demonstrated that children and schizophrenics both tended to equate antonyms with synonyms to a greater extent than normals. On the other hand, Cameron (1938) found that children were very different from schizophrenics in the way they completed incomplete sentences involving causality.

Chapman, Burstein, Day, and Verdone (1961) pointed out a possible artifact in these studies:

> the tasks were such that both children and schizophrenics were characterized by deviant performance relative to normal adults. However, as a result of restrictions either on the response alternatives available or on the investigator's cate-

gorization of the responses, each task provided relatively few avenues along which deviations could occur. The tasks tended to measure undifferentiated deviation rather than different kinds of specific deviation. Therefore the likelihood that schizophrenics and children would appear similar was very great. [p. 541]

Chapman *et al.* administered two ferent thinking tasks to children, schizophrenics, and brain-damaged patients. On one task the younger children resembled schizophrenics but not brain-damaged patients. On the other task the younger children resembled brain-damaged patients but not schizophrenics. They concluded:

> There is no blanket similarity between the error patterns of children and of either schizophrenics or brain-damaged patients, and the use of the term "regression" to imply such a blanket similarity is not justified. [p. 545]

To the extent that these comments are true, we may question the conclusion that the thinking of schizophrenics and children is similar. In brief, the evidence for regression of thought processes is equivocal, and there are opposing findings; we regard the regression hypothesis as not proved.

Interference Theory

In searching for an approach to conceptual deficit, one possibility is interference theory. There are two variants, one emphasizing overinclusion or excessive generalization and the other a deficit in attention.

Overinclusion. Overinclusion is the tendency to include irrelevant and extraneous aspects in responding to stimuli. In Cameron's (1938) early work he demonstrated that schizophrenics have difficulty in maintaining boundaries, their concepts spilling over into nontask stimuli such as objects in the room and even the experimenter. Cameron labeled this *interpenetration:* the intrusion of personal and idiosyncratic themes into the schizophrenic's speech and concepts.

Cameron and Magaret (1951) have pointed out that *exclusion* is necessary for success on a given task. At first the subject attends to too many aspects of the stimulus situation, and much of his response is superfluous. Gradually he focuses on the crucial aspects of the stimulus situation, ignoring irrelevant aspects; similarly, he drops out motor responses he does not need. Presumably the schizophrenic cannot exclude nonessential stimulus elements, and his overinclusiveness impairs performance on conceptual tasks.

That schizophrenics are overinclusive has been established by a number of experiments since Cameron's original observations. Zaslow (1950) showed that schizophrenics included more stimuli in the concepts of circularity and triangularity than did normals, although Kugelmass and Fondeur (1955) did not replicate these results with early schizophrenics.

Epstein (1953) and Moran (1953) presented subjects with a stimulus word and a number of response words. The task was to underline response words that were an essential part of the concept denoted by the stimulus. In both studies schizophrenics underlined significantly more response words, especially more distantly related words, than did normals. In addition Moran found that the schizophrenics' associations to the stimulus words were more distant and their synonyms were less precise than those of normals.

Lovibond (1954) quantified object-sorting performance and found that schizophrenics were more overinclusive than normals. Chapman (1956) and Chapman and Taylor (1957) presented pictures of different objects and had subjects sort them under specific headings or concepts such as clothing, furniture, and fruit. In comparison to normals, schizophrenics were more influenced by irrelevant and distracting elements, their conceptual performance being severely impaired by extraneous stimuli.

Payne and his collaborators (Payne & Hewlitt, 1960; Payne, Matussek & George, 1959) used as conceptual tasks a set of proverbs, two sorting tests, and Epstein's word-grouping test. The results were in the expected direction and for the most part significant: schizophrenics were overinclusive in comparison to normals. A number of the schizophrenics were no more overinclusive than the normals, but they were somewhat slow in their motor responses. Payne and Hewlitt speculated that paranoid and catatonic schizophrenics behave differently in these tasks. Paranoids, they suggested, tend to overgeneralize, their overinclusiveness showing up both in ideas of reference and in laboratory conceptual tasks; but they are neither slower nor less abstract than normals. Catatonics do not overgeneralize and are not overinclusive, but they tend to be slower and less abstract than normals.

Attention. Chapman (1961), who reported strong evidence for the overinclusion hypothesis, was not completely satisfied with it. He argued that schizophrenic concreteness is really *underinclusion* (overexclusion), which means that schizophrenics are both overinclusive and underinclusive:

> what may in part underlie the frequently observed inappropriate enlarging or restricting of the application of common concepts is in fact a preference for concepts of a particular breadth [p. 514].

He used two kinds of tasks, one tending to elicit errors of overinclusion and one tending to elicit errors of overexclusion. Schizophrenics were found to make both kinds of errors, although there was a predominance of overinclusion errors. When the task called for broad concepts, there were more overexclusion errors and fewer overinclusion errors. The same tendency was observed in normals, although greatly diminished. Thus the schizophrenics' predilection for concepts of a particular breadth may be merely an exaggeration of a similar finding in normals.

This suggestion is supported by a study by Seth and Beloff (1959) on schizophrenics and tubercular controls. The schizophrenics, who were inferior on verbal tasks, manifested a language decrement and a tendency not to use abstract concepts spontaneously. The errors made by the schizophrenics were exaggerations of the error tendencies of the controls, and the authors suggested that the underlying reason for this was a lowering or alternation of the attention process.

These results lead to the second variant of the interference hypothesis:

> Both disorders of perception and thinking in schizophrenic patients are secondary to a disorder of the span of attention, which can be too broad or too narrow, or may alternate between the two. Constancy of perception . . . depends on the ability to perceive a thing in its context, or to take into account all the "cues" existing in the whole perceptual field. Thus it is related to "broadness of attention." "Overinclusiveness" or wide span of schizophrenic concepts is related also to "overbroadness" of their attention, which makes them incapable of excluding irrelevant stimuli. On the other hand, the ability to perceive embedded figures is related to "narrowness" of attention which causes the distracting, embedded figure to be excluded. [Weckowicz & Blewitt, 1959, p. 914]

Note that this hypothesis, introduced before Chapman's results appeared, explains his results. Excessively broad attention should lead to overinclusive concepts; excessively narrow attention should lead to overexclusive concepts; alternating between too-broad and too-short attention

should lead to both overinclusive errors and overexclusive errors, such as were found in schizophrenics by Chapman (1961).

Weckowicz and Blewitt were able to test one implication of their hypothesis. In maintaining constancy of perception it is necessary to accept certain cues and reject others. There must be some kind of "filter" mechanism that avoids the errors of both overinclusiveness and overexclusiveness in conceptual performance as well as in size perception. They obtained high correlations (in the fifties) between abstraction scores on a sorting test and size constancy, thus substantiating the hypothesis. More evidence of this kind is needed, but at present his second variant of the interference hypothesis appears to be a promising explanation of schizophrenic deficit in the conceptual area.

Summary

This section has considered four interpretations of schizophrenic deficit in concept attainment. The loss of abstractness theory appears to be incorrect: schizophrenics' concepts are not especially concrete although they tend to be eccentric and deviant. Schizophrenics' concepts are not necessarily childlike, and the evidence for such regression may be attributed to both the limited responses available on the tasks used and to the scoring of idiosyncratic responses as concrete.

Concerning lack of communication, there is no doubt that schizophrenics have difficulty in making their concepts comprehensible to others. However, this appears to be due to the bizarre nature of the concepts rather than an inability to communicate them. Thus the disorder appears to involve thought processes rather than communication skills.

Interference theory appears to be the most promising approach. The overinclusion hypothesis has been sustained by a number of studies: schizophrenics' concepts are excessively broad, and they suffer from the intrusion of extraneous and irrelevant elements. Whether this is true of all schizophrenics or mainly of paranoids is an interesting question. One possibility is that paranoids are more inclusive and less deteriorated than nonparanoids (catatonics and hebephrenics).

DISCUSSION

This section will focus on five theories that attempt to explain schizophrenic deficit in the two research areas covered in this paper. Three theories emphasize interpersonal and social aspects: social censure, sensitivity to affective stimuli, and insufficient motivation. The other two, while not ignoring interpersonal aspects completely, emphasize more impersonal aspects of psychological functioning: regression and interference.

Social Censure

This theory exists in two basic forms, one general and the other a specific corollary. The general theory holds that schizophrenics are abnormally sensitive to, and disrupted by, social censure and stimuli connoting censure. In its support is the fact that in some experiments deficit has been found to increase when censure stimuli are introduced. However, other research has found no difference in the censure response of schizophrenics and normals, or effects for one type of schizophrenic and not for another. Furthermore, data interpreted in support of censure theory are often more parsimoniously explained in other terms (differential information or the saliency of cues). The strongest negative evidence is that on a great variety of tasks social censure *reduces* deficit in schizophrenia rather than increases it, i.e., facilitates performance relative to praise or no reinforcement.

The specific censure theory argues that schizophrenics with good and poor premorbid histories are differentially responsive to parental chastisement: the former are disturbed by paternal and the latter by maternal censure. While there are data consistent with this view, replication has infrequently supported original studies, and methodological problems abound. Both schizophrenic groups have shown disturbance with parental stimuli, regardless of whether the stimuli were positive or negative; both types of schizophrenics have, in specific experiments, been similar to normals in their response to censure.

Furthermore, while distinctions are made within the schizophrenic group, control subjects are treated as a homogeneous population. We cannot help but speculate that the subdivision of a hospital attendant or neurotic group—following similar criteria of general social or sexual adequacy—might yield similar differences in response to parental stimuli. In other words, we do not know that the findings are in any way unique to schizophrenia. In fact, while good and poor premorbid patients are treated as subtypes of schizophrenia, group assignment is actually determined by a scale defining a continuous dimension of social maturity (Phillips, 1953). The scales' author has already provided strong evidence:

> that the relationship of achieved level of maturity (defined in terms of premorbid social competence) to certain dimensions of psychopathology is not unique to schizophrenia, but instead cuts across all forms of functional mental disorder. [Zigler & Phillips, 1962, p. 216]

As a general theory of deficit the social censure approach is not sufficiently comprehensive and involves a major inconsistency: stimulus conditions other than censure have been found to yield deficit in schizophrenia, and censure may reduce rather than increase deficit. The specific theory involves a questionable typology. It also needs the support of less equivocal experiments. Dividing schizophrenics into good and poor premorbid groups does not account for the variable effects of censure, a full explanation of which must include *task variables*.

This evaluation does not necessarily negate the clinical theory from which the social censure hypothesis originated. Parental censure may still be an important variable in the histories of schizophrenics and may shape some symptoms. However, social censure does not provide a general explanation for schizophrenic deficit in the laboratory.

Sensitivity to Affective Stimuli

This theory resembles social censure theory, but it is broader in that it assumes that schizophrenics are specially sensitive to, and disrupted by, *all* affective stimuli. This assumption has been verified in many experiments which have demonstrated poorer performance by schizophrenics with affective stimuli than with neutral stimuli. The difficulty with this evidence is that so many stimuli have been labeled *affective* that the term no longer has precise referents. The underlying assumption in this theory is that past events in schizophrenics' lives have rendered them abnormally sensitive to stimuli that connote traumatic situations or anxiety-laden interpersonal relationships. While some of the affective stimuli that lead to deficit pertain to special areas of maladjustment such as sexuality, censure, or competition, others have only a vague connection with personal adjustment or emotion, e.g., human-nonhuman, symbolic-nonsymbolic, and patient-attendant stimulus dimensions have all been shown to influence the performance of schizophrenics. Furthermore, as we have seen with censure stimuli, the effect

of specific affective contents varies considerably from experiment to experiment, and perhaps from subject to subject.

The dilemma is as follows. If the term affective is loosely defined, the theory can account for all the data, but it lacks precision. If the term affective is restricted to a narrow, precise meaning, then the reliability of the phenomenon must be questioned; furthermore, nonaffective stimuli have been found to produce deficit. Shakow (1962) has suggested that the associations of schizophrenics constitute a kind of apperceptive mass,

> full of elements—both affective and nonaffective—of past experience. For the schizophrenic, many of these elements are floating around on top of the barrel, ready to be attached to almost any new situation. [p. 9]

This conception accommodates the data and provides the basis for an interference explanation. Evidence for this view will be assessed in the next paper. However, the psychodynamic concept of affective stimuli is clearly not a sufficient theory of schizophrenic deficit.

Insufficient Motivation

Another group of theorists argue that schizophrenic deficit is attributable not to an oversensitivity to social stimuli but to a reduced sensitivity to such inputs. Schizophrenics are held to be unmotivated, uninterested in pleasing the experimenter, or uninterested in meeting task requirements; Hunt and Cofer (1944) suggested that responses to social stimuli have been extinguished in schizophrenic patients. In general, the evidence is against this formulation. Testable schizophrenics are as responsive to persuasion as normals or brain-damaged patients whether the social pressure is based on encouragement or on critical admonishment. Many studies stimulated by this theory have confounded the effects of praise and criticism or reward and punishment with the effects of giving subjects different information about their task performance. Evaluating their separate effects is difficult. Nevertheless, schizophrenics and normals generally show a similar pattern of responding: on most tasks information about errors leads to better performance than the signaling of correct responses. However, the importance of this additional information seems to be greater for schizophrenics than for normal subjects. Schizophrenics show relatively greater improvement with clear supplementary cues than do normals, and there is some evidence that information about errors is particularly useful to schizophrenics. The effect of these cues does not appear to be social motivational but rather to help maintain attention and guide responding. It has been suggested that the schizophrenic fails to instruct himself as normals do, and the additional information provided after each response fulfills this guidance function.

Physical punishment tends to facilitate the performance of schizophrenics, and it has occasionally eliminated schizophrenic deficit. This fact has been used to support the lowered motivation hypothesis: if schizophrenics are able to approach normal functioning when reinforced with pain termination but not when social reinforcers are administered, a deficit in social motivation is implied. An alternate view is that physical punishment may be a better source of information about errors, breaking up incorrect sets, and guiding responding. The importance of cue emphasis as opposed to motivational instigation has been demonstrated in studies of normal subjects, in which improvement was occasioned by delivering electric shock for correct responses. Furthermore, when intense stimuli are coincident with important discriminative stimuli, the

latter are lent emphasis and more clearly separated from the irrelevant cues in the situation. Evidence for these alternate motivation and interference interpretations of studies employing aversive stimuli will be evaluated in the subsequent paper.

Regression

The loss of abstractness theory received support mainly from early studies, but later work revealed that the excessive concreteness of schizophrenics may be attributed to methods of scoring responses rather than to a loss of the abstract attitude. Schizophrenics are capable of attaining abstract concepts, although their concepts may be bizarre, eccentric, and deviant from those given by normals.

The loss of abstractness theory is but one variant of regression theory, which includes not only Goldstein's formulation but those of Freud, Arieti (1955), and Werner (1948). Regression theory makes two fundamental assumptions: (a) there is a fixed sequence of developmental stages that ends in maturity or adult normality, and (b) psychopathology represents a retracing of these developmental steps. Concerning deficit, the theory should demonstrate: (a) a fixed sequence or hierarchy of psychomotor learning and thinking behavior in childhood, and (b) a retracing of the sequence in psychopathology. The only one to attempt such a specific formulation with respect to schizophrenic deficit has been Goldman (1962), using Werner's developmental approach. Whether or not one accepts Goldman's developmental sequence of learning and thinking, there is considerable doubt that the learning and thinking of schizophrenics resembles those of children of any given age. There are occasional similarities between schizophrenics' concepts and those of children: tendencies toward more primitive concepts and deviance from adult concepts. However, there are also marked differences between children's and schizophrenics' concepts: those of schizophrenics are usually more abstract, bizarre, and eccentric than those of children.

Furthermore, it is not sufficient to demonstrate vague similarities between schizophrenics and children. It must be shown that as an individual becomes schizophrenic, he retraces the developmental sequence (if there is one) of learning and thinking; as he recovers, he again moves forward toward demonstrably more mature modes of learning and thinking. These corollaries of regression theory have yet to be established empirically, and therefore we conclude that the regression theory of schizophrenic deficit is unproved.

Interference

This theory assumes that when a schizophrenic is faced with a task, he cannot attend properly or in a sustained fashion, maintain a set, or change the set quickly when necessary. His ongoing response tendencies suffer interference from irrelevant, external cues and from "internal" stimuli which consist of deviant thoughts and associations. These irrelevant, distracting, mediated stimuli prevent him from maintaining a clear focus on the task at hand, and the result is psychological deficit.

If the schizophrenic has difficulty in shifting to a new set, he should benefit from stimuli that break the old set. This is precisely what has been established. Schizophrenics benefit from punishment, which eliminates previously correct response tendencies that are no longer appropriate. Physical punishment, in some instances, has been found to eliminate schizophrenic deficit entirely.

If the presence of distracting, internal stimuli prevents the schizophrenic from giving self-instructions (as normals do),

he should benefit from external cues. It has been established that schizophrenics are helped more than normals by external reinforcing cues which help direct responses, although normals are also helped. Thus interference theory has an explanation for the effects of punishment and of the rewarding and punishing stimuli that follow responses.

Interference theory can account for schizophrenic deficit with affective stimuli. The theory assumes that the schizophrenics' associations distract him, thereby producing disturbance of performance. The more associations, the greater the deficit. Since affective stimuli elicit more associations than neutral stimuli (Deering, 1963), it follows that they should produce more schizophrenic deficit.

Conceptual deficit is explained by assuming excessive variability in attention. The schizophrenic is either overinclusive because he allows irrelevant stimuli to intrude or overexclusive because he attempts to defend against the distracting, internal stimuli. It follows that some schizophrenics should be overinclusive, some overexclusive, and some alternating between the two; all three possibilities have been found to exist in schizophrenics when they are confronted with conceptual tasks.

Interference theory may be viewed as a devil's advocate in that in each research area it offers an alternative to the theories of social censure, sensitivity to affective stimuli, insufficient motivation, and regression. Obviously, the theory is sufficiently comprehensive, but a theory must do more than merely offer alternatives. Also needed is evidence that tests specific hypotheses, in this instance about the particular interfering effects of environmental, associational, and also somatic stimuli. Such evidence is reviewed in the subsequent paper.

Psychological Deficit in Schizophrenia: Inference and Activation[1]

Peter J. Lang and Arnold H. Buss

During the last 20 years a voluminous research literature has appeared on the subject of psychological deficit in schizophrenia, and the relative incapacity of this patient group has been demonstrated with a host of different laboratory tasks. In a previous paper (Buss & Lang, 1965), the authors reviewed deficit experiments concerned with concept formation, the possible disrupting character of social censure and affective stimuli, and the enhancing effect on performance of various reinforcers and motivational devices.

These findings revealed that testable schizophrenics are about as responsive to social pressure (reward or punishment) as other patients and normal controls. The hypothesis that in schizophrenia social censure invariably leads to deficit is not tenable. Regression theory interpretations of psychotic behavior receive little specific empirical corroboration.

A large body of literature indicates that affective stimuli in general disrupt the functioning of schizophrenics, but this may be due to a broader inability to inhibit any interfering stimulus. Similarly,

Reprinted from the *Journal of Abnormal Psychology*, 1965, vol. 70, pp. 77–106 with the permission of the American Psychological Association and the authors.

[1] The following abbreviations will be used: reaction time (RT), preparatory interval (PI), critical flicker frequency (CFF), galvanic skin response (GSR), electroencephalograph (EEG), electromyograph (EMG), autonomic nervous system (ANS), and stimulus generalization (SG).

while schizophrenics do not appear to have lost the capacity to form concepts, the concepts achieved are deviant—overinclusive or overexclusive—a flaw often traceable to the intrusion of task-irrelevant events. On the positive side, deficit can be significantly reduced by extra instructions, feedback about responses, and intense, physical reinforcers.

Guided by these considerations, the present paper is oriented around two broad conceptions: interference and activation. The first of these directly concerns schizophrenics' ability to attend to specific stimuli and to inhibit inappropriate responses. The relevant literature on attention, set, and association is explored. In general, schizophrenics show interference effects in all three of these areas. They are distracted by external stimuli. Responses are more likely to be determined by incidental physical properties of the perceptual field than by meaningful relationships. There is difficulty in initiating and maintaining a set over time and in changing a set that is no longer suitable to the experimental task. Finally, schizophrenics' associations are uncommon, intrusive, and interfere with performance.

While the first paper suggested that social motivational constructs have limited value, the fact of greatly reduced responsivity in schizophrenia argues for a thorough exploration of formal theories of motivation or activation. Experimental studies relevant to two classical drive theories are reviewed. One holds that the associational disturbance of schizophrenics is a consequence of high-anxiety drive; the other stresses reactive inhibition, which slows down learning and increases reminiscence. The drive approach is complemented by the neurophysiological concept of arousal. From this perspective, schizophrenics have been viewed both as underaroused and as so hyperactivated that effective responding is impossible. Evidence for these conceptions is evaluated in a review of research on the somatic response system in schizophrenia.

Thus, the present paper considers five specific topics: attention, set, associative interference, drive, and somatic arousal. A final discussion of deficit theory and a consideration of methodological problems follows the research review.

ATTENTION

The improvement of schizophrenics under aversive stimulus conditions has generally been explained in terms of an increase in motivation or "need" to respond. However, Lang (1959) suggested that the improvement is attributable to a stimulus-intensity dynamism and undertook a test of this hypothesis. Schizophrenics and normals performed a visual disjunctive reaction-time (RT) task under five conditions: escape, excitation, avoidance, information, and control. Following a pretest series the escape subjects were administered an aversive white noise stimulus, simultaneous with the onset of the visual cue and terminated by a correct response. Excitation subjects received the same ancillary stimulus, but the noise was terminated at random intervals unrelated to the subject's response. Escape and excitation both yielded significantly greater improvement in RT than did the control condition. Avoidance training subjects were administered aversive noise following responses slower than their pretest median. Information subjects received a nonaversive signal under the

same conditions. The information group significantly lowered their RT; the avoidance procedure did not lead to significantly greater improvement than that obtained for control subjects. While the positive effects of the escape and excitation conditions did not persist into a posttest series, the positive effects of information did. These data strongly suggest that aversive stimuli improve the performance of schizophrenics via a stimulus-intensity dynamism or better definition of the task-relevant stimuli rather than via an alteration of the subject's need to respond.

Tizard and Venables (1957) found that schizophrenics improved visual RT on trials accompanied by white noise. They also found regular decreases in auditory RTs to pure tones or white noise with increases in the physical intensity of the stimulus (Venables & Tizard, 1958). King (1962b) and Grisell and Rosenbaum (1963) confirmed this result and showed that the intensity-latency gradient is steeper for chronic schizophrenics than for normal subjects. However, King reported that in both chronic schizophrenics and normals the degree of RT reduction attendant on intensity increase covaried with the subject's base latency at more moderate stimulus intensities. Furthermore, both populations showed a similar reduction in intraindividual variability with stimulus-intensity increase. King (1962b) concluded that schizophrenics and normals

> are equally sensitive to change in the variable, in a relative sense, although patient response is initially slower and thereby subject to greater reduction in absolute value. [p. 304]

The effects of intensity on visual RT are not clear.[2] An initial experiment

[2] Venables and O'Connor (1959) reported that unlike normal subjects, schizophrenics yield relatively faster RTs to light than to an auditory stimulus. Analysis of the data revealed this to

yielded variable results for different light intensities but no regular order (Venables & Tizard, 1956a). A second investigation (Venables & Tizard, 1956b) reported paradoxical effects, but these did not hold up on retest. The variable results may be due to the short intertrial period (8 seconds) used in these experiments, and possible differences between normal and schizophrenic subjects in recovery time to visual stimuli should be explored. Cohen (1949a, 1949b) reported anomalies in the eye grounds of schizophrenic patients and suggested that their visual pathways may be affected by some pathological process. In any event, withdrawn schizophrenics did yield significantly faster auditory RTs in a bright room than under conditions of dim illumination (Tizard & Venables, 1957). These authors proposed that schizophrenics suffer from a defect in the arousal system, and that

> an increase in sensory input might be expected to have nonspecific facilatory effects on cortical and sub-cortical activities. [p. 303]

Karras (1962) attempted to test the alternate reinforcement and arousal interpretations of the deficit reduction attendant on aversive stimulation. Chronic male schizophrenics responded in a visual RT task under one of five experimental conditions. The first two groups escaped from either a low- or an intense-noise stimulus; two other groups performed while either a low- or an intense-noise was continuously administered. All four groups were compared with a no-noise control. Both escape groups had faster RTs than the two stimulation conditions,

and Karras held that these findings favored a reinforcement interpretation. However, another conclusion is suggested by comparison with other data. In the previously considered experiments (Lang, 1959; Tizard & Venables, 1957) the sound was not on continuously. Tizard and Venables administered the sound only during a few trials in a long series. In the Lang experiment it was initiated at the same time as the visual stimulus and thus may have functioned both as a stimulus dynamism (arousal) and as a signal to emphasize the appropriate instant for a response (a focusing function). In the Karras (1962) experiment the continuous white noise might have aroused the subject, but it was also an irrelevant stimulus, unrelated to the task at hand. As such, it would be expected to initiate competing responses. Consistent with this interpretation is the fact that Karras's low-stimulation group yielded slower RTs than the high-stimulation group. Both the high and low stimuli were distracting, but it appears that the high-intensity sound also served a positive arousal function. Furthermore, the low-intensity stimulus was not reported as unpleasant when presented suddenly. Nevertheless, when presented coincident with the discriminative stimulus (escape), the low-intensity stimulus yielded faster RTs than the two general stimulation conditions and consistently faster RTs than the control group, although this latter difference was not significant. These effects cannot be attributed to escape from an aversive stimulus and must therefore be attributed to the increased focusing of a more marked onset change.[3]

Wienckowski (1959) also re-examined the effects of collateral stimuli on the RT task, using a modification of Lang's apparatus (1959). In addition to a con-

---

be an artifact of relative speed. Slow normals also showed the light stimulus superiority, whereas fast schizophrenics had relatively better auditory RTs. However, cross modality investigations involve many procedural problems, and further study is needed before the importance of these results can be assessed.

[3] An alternate interpretation of the Lang and Karras studies is offered by Silverman (1963).

trol situation, the performances of acute and chronic schizophrenics and normals were evaluated under three experimental conditions: (*a*) a light and a brief buzzer initiated the preparatory interval (PI); the light alone was maintained throughout the PI and terminated with the onset of the discriminative stimulus; (*b*) both buzzer and center light continued throughout the foreperiod and were terminated with discriminative stimulus onset; (*c*) the buzzer and center light were not terminated until the subject completed his response. Under Condition *b*, both the chronic and acute schizophrenics showed a greater reduction in RT than either schizophrenic controls or normals performing under the same experimental condition. Neither Condition *a* nor *c* resulted in improved scores for any group, although the latter condition resulted in a nonsignificant lengthening of the mean RT of the chronic patients. Thus schizophrenics showed positive effects from collateral stimuli only when there was a significant net change in total stimulation at the onset of the discriminative stimulus (Condition *b*). Stimuli introduced at other times were ineffective or, in the case of the chronic group, showed a tendency to disrupt performance when they continued throughout the trial period (Condition *c*).

On the basis of their clinical observations, McGhie and Chapman (1961) attributed schizophrenic deficit to a disturbance of "selective attention," the disturbance being greatest when the patient must inhibit information in one sensory channel and attend to another. They noted that schizophrenics are particularly distracted by irrelevant auditory stimuli but that any unrelated sensory input disturbs a smooth sequence of motor responses. Substantial support for this view was obtained in an experimental study (Chapman & McGhie,

1962). When a sporadic, high-pitched noise was introduced, schizophrenics displayed a greater increase in errors on a visual tracking task than either normals or nonschizophrenic psychiatric patients. Similar differences were found when subjects were instructed to spin a wheel at a constant rate while listening to varying rates from a taped metronome. Shakow (1950) also reported interfering effects of distracting stimuli. Chapman and Mc-Ghie (1962) found the same effects for visual distractors; when subjects were instructed to attend only to auditory information while being simultaneously presented with competing visual cues, schizophrenics showed great disturbance of performance relative to normals or other psychiatric patients. Sutton, Hakerem, Zubin, and Portnoy (1961) studied a serial RT task and found that schizophrenics showed greater lengthening of RT to a second stimulus in a different modality than did normal subjects.

The inability of schizophrenics to exclude distracting stimuli has also been observed in cognitive tasks. Chapman (1956) had schizophrenic and normal subjects sort cards according to concepts. In addition to a "correct" figure the cards shared communalities that were not appropriate to the correct response. The schizophrenics used the incorrect distractor communalities as a basis for the sorting more than did normals. Weckowicz (1960) found that schizophrenics and brain-damaged patients performed worse than other nonschizophrenic psychiatric patients on a Hidden Figure Test, which required subjects to select relevant and disregard irrelevant information. Recently, Draguns (1963) studied a task in which subjects interpreted pictures that became progressively clearer with successive presentations. In addition to making more recognition errors, chronic schizophrenics were less able than normals to inhibit responses to the earlier, ambiguous pictures.

In addition to their inability to exclude or inhibit unwanted sensory inputs, schizophrenics have difficulty in integrating related stimuli. When this is done by the experimenter's presenting stimuli simultaneously as in the Lang and Wienckowski studies, a marked facilatory effect is observed. However, when stimuli are only slightly out of phase, the schizophrenic is unable to compensate and relative deterioration results. Chapman and McGhie (1962) found schizophrenics' performance to be markedly disturbed when they were required to repeat information presented on alternate visual and auditory channels. Schizophrenics also had greater discrepancies than other psychiatric patients between their scores on a dual task (they were instructed to indicate which figures appeared in a series twice *and* locate their position) and performance when instructed to do only one of these tasks.

Distractibility and disrupted information processing may underly schizophrenic deficit in a variety of perceptual tasks. Cohen, Senf, and Huston (1956) and Johannsen, Friedman, and Liccione (1963b) studied pattern recognition in schizophrenics, using the Street Visual Gestalt Test. They found inferior closure in chronic patients relative to both acute schizophrenics and normal controls. Eysenck, Granger, and Brengelmann (1957) reported a lower than normal (although not significant) mean Street Test score for a small group of psychotics; a significant closure deficit was found on a Kohs blocks task when these patients were compared to either normals or neurotics. Snyder, Rosenthal, and Taylor (1961) reported a closure deficit in schizophrenics, based on drawings of incomplete figures. However, Snyder (1961) found a greater than normal tendency to closure in a group of acute, paranoid patients, which

he attributed to emotionality associated with disease onset. Johannsen *et al.* (1963b) reported a significant interaction between the paranoid-nonparanoid dimension and chronicity. Their paranoid subjects maintained normal closure test scores except for the most extreme chronic group, but nonparanoid schizophrenics showed progressive deterioration with chronicity.

Although evidence is limited, a few studies suggest differences between schizophrenics and normal controls in critical flicker frequency (CFF). Dillon (1959) reported higher CFF thresholds in functional psychotics than in a control group, but the patients were a specially selected treatment sample. McDonough (1960) also found higher than normal mean CFFs in reactive schizophrenics but no differences between process schizophrenics and normals. Recently, Johannsen *et al.* (1963b) reported that acutes showed a high CFF, but with increasing chronicity there was a progressive reduction in thresholds to a point well below that of normal subjects. The conflicting findings may be due to the competing effects of high distractibility and high activation level in schizophrenia. These two factors tend to influence CFF thresholds in opposite ways. The most extensive study (Johannsen *et al.*, 1963b) is consistent with the hypothesis of decreased vigilance in chronic patients.

A number of researchers report deficit in size or distance constancy in chronic schizophrenics (Cooper, 1960; Crooks, 1957; Lovinger, 1956; Reynolds, 1954; Weckowicz, 1957, 1958, 1960; Weckowicz & Blewitt, 1959; Weckowicz & Hall, 1960; Weckowicz, Sommer, & Hall, 1958). Nevertheless, Reisman (1961) failed to find differences in size constancy between normals and two schizophrenic groups. Raush (1952, 1956) found that "fairly young, fairly well oriented" paranoid schizophrenics showed higher constancy scores than normal subjects. Sanders and Pacht (1952) also reported what amounts to "overconstancy" (distant objects seen as larger than they actually were) in a group of psychotic outpatients. However, Kidd (1964) found subnormal monocular depth perception in schizophrenics within 48 hours after they were admitted to a state hospital. Unfortunately, it is not clear whether these were first admissions, nor is there information on the subtype or chronicity of these patients. Perhaps the most comprehensive data on these variables is provided by Johannsen et al. (1963b) who studied depth perception in a large group of schizophrenics classified according to duration of illness. They found a low mean error score for acute patients; chronic patients generally made significantly more errors than either acute psychotics or normal controls, although the most extreme chronic group evidenced some restitution of ability.

Thus, the closure, size constancy, and distance constancy studies reviewed here found deficit in schizophrenics more often than not. However, experiments with acute schizophrenics, and particularly with early paranoid patients, suggest the presence of compensatory efforts in these subjects, which result in normal or occasionally above-average functioning. Chronic patients show the greatest deterioration, but even this result is not wholly reliable.

Perhaps much of this variability between experiments reflects the schizophrenic's response to characteristics of the specific task or task setting that do not affect normal subjects. The perceptual judgments of schizophrenics appear to be readily manipulated by minor alterations of experimental stimuli. Weckowicz (1964) found inferior shape constancy in schizophrenics when the stimulus objects were inclined at 60 degrees, but not when the angle of inclination was only 30 degrees. The findings of

Raush (1956) and Pishkin, Smith, and Leibowitz (1962) among others, show significant constancy differences attributable to the symbolic value of stimulus objects. It has already been suggested (Buss & Lang, 1965) that these results are due to the greater number of associations occasioned in schizophrenics by these stimuli and their intrusion into the task at hand. Salzinger (1957) reported no initial differences between schizophrenics and normals in ability to discriminate weights. However, when required to make estimates following the lifting of a heavy anchor stimulus, the patient group showed a significantly greater shift in judgment than controls. Lovinger (1956) found deterioration in the size constancy of schizophrenics only under minimal cue conditions. Leibowitz and Pishkin (1961) reported no size constancy deficit in schizophrenics under maximum cue conditions, but a follow-up investigation (Pishkin et al., 1962) revealed a significant difference in size estimation errors between normals and chronic schizophrenics. In this latter experiment the subjects had to illuminate the stimulus objects themselves by closing a switch; in addition to making more errors, schizophrenics tended to illuminate the field significantly more often than controls. Pishkin and his associates attributed these differences to the schizophrenics' greater difficulty in selecting and attending to relevant cues. Further evidence for an attention deficit is provided by tachistoscopic studies, e.g., McGinnies and Adornetto (1952) found that schizophrenics have higher recognition thresholds than normal for *both* emotionally toned and neutral verbal material.

Schizophrenics appear to live in a subjective world determined by the physical size and intensity of stimuli, poorly integrated with the information about relationships between objects, which modulates the perception of normal subjects.

Perhaps because attention is so wavering, the static, formal characteristics of the physical field determine behavior, and schizophrenics fail to show normals' flexible, meaningful perceptual experience. Thus, deficit is greatest when the schizophrenic must pay attention to more than one stimulus input, switch his attention from one stimulus to another, or ignore irrelevant stimuli in favor of physically weak, task-relevant inputs. Deficit is least when the irrelevant stimuli are few, the task stimulus is intense and unequivocal, or any collateral inputs are temporally in phase. Under these latter conditions chronic schizophrenics may approach the functioning level of normal subjects.

SET

Analogous to the difficulty with concurrent stimuli described above is the schizophrenic's frequent failure to inhibit inappropriate responses initiated by sequences in time. This was already suggested by the Chapman and McGhie (1962) experiment in which patients failed to spin a wheel at a constant speed while listening to varied tempi from a metronome. A number of studies indicate a time estimation deficit in schizophrenia. Rabin (1957) found schizophrenics to be significantly poorer than nonpsychotics in estimating the length of a psychological interview. Lhamon and Goldstone (1956), H. E. King (1962a), and Pearl and Berg (1963) all reported that schizophrenics systematically overestimate short time intervals (.5 to 30 seconds). King's interval-matching study indicated that normal subjects consistently underestimate the same intervals, and he suggested that the deficit of schizophrenics may be attributed to their characteristic psychomotor retardation. Pearl and Berg (1963) had schizophrenics and normals estimate the presentation time of neutral and affect

arousing pictures and found that psychotics displayed greater overestimation to the affective materials.

The schizophrenic's performance is markedly disturbed whenever he must initiate a response at a fixed point in time. Shakow (1962) has noted that schizophrenics show less deficit on tasks such as tapping, in which time of onset and termination is not important to adequate performance, than on tasks like RT, which require preparation for a response at the discretion of the experimenter. Furthermore Rosenthal, Lawlor, Zahn, and Shakow (1960), and H. E. King (1954, 1961) have demonstrated a high positive relationship between RT and mental health ratings.

The latencies of schizophrenics are readily manipulated by slight variations in the foreperiod or preparatory interval (PI). The RT of chronic patients increases disproportionately with the lengthening of a regular PI (Huston, Shakow, & Riggs, 1937; Rodnick & Shakow, 1940). Zahn, Shakow, and Rosenthal (1961) demonstrated that this effect is attributable not to the slower pace of the task but to foreperiod length; it is also partially a function of the preceding sequence of foreperiods. When a single long PI occurs in a series of shorter ones, the RT latency is relatively shorter than if the preceding foreperiods were of equal length (Rodnick & Shakow, 1940; Tizard & Venables, 1956). Similarly,

> when a single long PI trial was followed by a single short PI trial, RT on the latter trial was disproportionately lengthened in schizophrenic as compared with normal subjects. [Zahn, Rosenthal, & Shakow, 1961, p. 167]

Zahn et al. (1961, 1963) demonstrated that if the length of the PI is systematically varied during the task, the RT of schizophrenics changes in characteristic ways. When successive PIs were administered in order of increasing length, RT was an increasing function of foreperiod length for both schizophrenics and normals, but the slope of the curve was significantly greater for the former population. The RTs of the schizophrenics tended to be the same for all PIs and relatively slow when a descending order of administration was employed, whereas the curve for normal subjects was virtually identical to that when length was increased.

In summary, the RT of schizophrenics is controlled to a great extent by the context of PIs and more particularly by the immediately preceding foreperiod. As with concurrent stimuli, temporal sequence may be manipulated to produce increases or decreases in deficit.

Blaufarb (1962) demonstrated a facilatory effect of context on a verbal task. Schizophrenics and normals were administered proverb tasks in two sessions. In one session they were asked to give the meaning of a single proverb, and in the other session they were asked to give the meaning of a set of proverbs, all of which had the same meaning. The chronic schizophrenics were significantly poorer than normals under the single proverb condition. Schizophrenics showed significantly greater improvement with proverb sets and under this condition could not be distinguished from the normal group.

However, tasks may be selected so as to produce inappropriate sets, thereby increasing deficit. Mandl (1954) found that paranoid schizophrenics showed greater rigidity than normals on a perceptual task. Shakow (1950) noted that distractors disrupted the performance of both normals and schizophrenics, but the deleterious effects carried over to subsequent nonstress trials only for the psychotic patients. In W. O. Smith's (1959) study of the pursuit rotor task, process schizophrenics showed less improvement

with modification of the experimental conditions than did reactive patients. Similarly, Crumpton (1963) showed that schizophrenics persisted in a previously rewarded but now incorrect response for significantly more trials than a normal control sample. Furthermore, this tendency to persist with a maladaptive response appeared to be related to the severity of the schizophrenic process.

ASSOCIATIVE INTERFERENCE

It was Bleuler (1950) who first pointed to association as the crucial issue in schizophrenia. He believed that many schizophrenic symptoms (hallucinations, delusions, etc.) were only elaborations of, and secondary to, the primary disturbance in association. This disturbance in association may be seen in bizarre ideas, loose associations, fragmented thinking, and the blocking of the usual and common chains of associations and ideas.

What is the role of associative disturbance in schizophrenic deficit? Specifically, how would difficulty in association disturb attention or set and therefore worsen performance on psychomotor, perceptual, and learning tasks? The answer may be framed in the context of the psychological demands of such tasks. The subject is required to maintain a state of vigilance, a readiness to respond to oncoming stimuli. He must also react to stimuli and instructions in a normative manner, that is, on the basis of the common meanings of stimuli and instructions. To the extent that stimuli have individual, idiosyncratic meanings (associations) for the subject, he will be handicapped in responding to them. For example, stimuli seen as relatively neutral by normals, may be provocative for schizophrenics, who perceive simple stimuli in idiosyncratic ways (Feldman & Drasgow, 1951).

In maintaining a state of vigilance as preparation for oncoming stimuli, the subject needs to be free from distractions. He must inhibit responses not only to inappropriate external stimuli but also to extraneous thoughts and associations that may divert his attention. The research on psychomotor performance discussed earlier shows that the schizophrenic is unable to accomplish the first of these tasks. Clinical reports suggest that he also cannot prevent the intrusion of bizarre ideas and associations that pull his attention from the task at hand. The idiosyncratic associations of schizophrenics distract them, thus degrading their performance. This formulation leads to two testable hypotheses.

The Associations of Schizophrenics Are Uncommon

Several studies have sustained this assertion. Moran (1953) tried a word association task with schizophrenics and normals, the stimulus words having previously been defined by the subjects. The schizophrenics' associations were significantly less related to the stimulus words than the associations of the normals. These findings were corroborated by Johnson, Weiss, and Zelhart (1964) who found that schizophrenics produced more idiosyncratic word associations than normals.

Sommer, Dewar, and Osmond (1960) compared the associations of schizophrenics and normals to the words on the Kent-Rosanoff list. Schizophrenics gave significantly more uncommon associations, and they were extremely variable in terms of both stability of responses over time and comparisons between subjects. Sommer, Witney, and Osmond (1962) followed up this experiment by trying to condition common associations. While alcoholics conditioned rapidly, schizophrenics showed very little conditioning.

Wynne (1963) found that the free associations of acute schizophrenics differed little from those of normals. However, when instructed to give the associations "most people do," normals gave more common associations but schizophrenics did not. Maltzman, Seymore, and Licht (1962) attempted to condition normal subjects to give common or uncommon associations. They learned to give more common associations but did not learn to give more uncommon associations. Maltzman, Cohen, and Belloni (1963) found that schizophrenic children give more uncommon associations than normal children.

On the basis of these various studies, we may conclude that schizophrenics tend to give uncommon associations but cannot learn common associations, whereas normals tend to give common associations but cannot learn uncommon associations.

Intrusive Associations Worsen the Performance of Schizophrenics More Than of Normals

Chapman (1958) used a verbal concept formation task, with a stimulus word and three response words. One response was the correct concept, one an (irrelevant-to-the-task) association, and one neither. The associations were of high and low strength. Schizophrenics showed significantly more associative intrusions than normals.

Donahoe, Curtin, and Lipton (1961) questioned whether associative intrusions in schizophrenics occurred only with meaningful stimuli (words) or with all stimuli (words and nonsense syllables). They tested the effect of experimentally built-in intrusive associations on the learning nonsense syllables and found an equal decrement in normals and schizophrenics. Downing, Ebert, and Shubrooks (1963) studied the number of errors schizophrenics produced on a concept test by different types of distractor words. Associatively linked words produced more errors than either contiguity or rhyme-clang distractors. Thus it is the restrictive hypothesis that appears to be correct: schizophrenics suffer especially from the intrusion of meaningful irrelevant associations and not all types of irrelevant associations.

A number of studies have produced more direct evidence on the intrusion of associations in schizophrenia. Lang and Luoto (1962) had subjects learn two lists of paired associates (words). On the second list, half the response terms were associates of the response terms used in the first list. The response terms of the other half were also associates, but they were not assigned to the correct stimulus term, thereby creating an interference list. The results showed that the schizophrenics' mediational processes were not significantly different from the normals. However, schizophrenics showed significantly poorer performance than normals on the early trials of the interference list. Furthermore, while normals seldom again offered the response terms of pairs already learned, these words tended to persist as responses for schizophrenics, interfering with subsequent learning.

Spence and Lair (1964) failed to find differences between the paired-associate learning of normals and schizophrenics, consistent with Mednick's theory (1958). However, an analysis of errors did differentiate the two groups. Acute schizophrenics tended to give more overt, inappropriate responses, stemming from both intralist and extralist sources. Normals produced more errors of omission. Thus, schizophrenics seem unable to inhibit the overt expression of intruding associations.

Further evidence of intrusiveness comes from an experiment by Lauro (1962), who used words that varied in

clustering tendency. There were no differences in recall between normals and schizophrenics in the easy clustering list, but in the difficult clustering list the schizophrenics "imported" more irrelevant words than did normals.

There should be more associative interference when words have several meanings than when they have only one meaning. Faibish (1961) had normals and schizophrenics define and free associate to words with either one meaning or multiple meanings. Both normals and schizophrenics showed poorer word association and vocabulary performance with the multiple-meaning words, but the schizophrenics' decrement was greater than the normals. The schizophrenics were disrupted by the multiple meanings, and Faibish concluded that "the majority of the results can be understood in terms of interference effects [p. 423]."

Finally, Lester (1960) studied restricted association in normals, hebephrenic and paranoid schizophrenics, and epileptics. The patient groups showed more intereference than the normals in the selection of associates, the interference occurring because of the intrusion of extraneous associations. The interference was greatest for epileptics, followed by hebephrenics, paranoids, and normals, in decreasing order.

In brief, the hypothesis of associative interference has been verified. Schizophrenics have more unique, nonshared associations, and these associations, like external distractors, serve to deteriorate performance because of their intrusive nature. Shakow's (1962) summation of his RT studies aptly describes both inner (associational) and outer distractors:

Here we see particularly the various difficulties created by *context*, the degree to which the schizophrenic is affected by irrelevant aspects of the stimulus surroundings—inner and outer—which prevent his focusing on the "to-be-responded-to" stimulus. It is as if, in the scanning process which takes place before the response to a stimulus is made, the schizophrenic is unable to select out the material relevant for optimal response. He apparently cannot free himself from the irrelevant among the numerous possibilities available for choice. In other words, that function which is of equal importance as the response *to* stimuli, namely, the protection *against* the response to stimuli, is abeyant. [p. 25]

DRIVE

Two drive theories of schizophrenic deficit have been proposed, each associated with different behaviors. Positive drive theory, which identifies anxiety as the crucial variable, is intended to explain aspects of the schizophrenic's associational disturbance. Negative drive theory focuses on inhibition during conditioning and the phenomenon of reminiscence.

Anxiety and Associational Deficit

The hypothesis of continuity between neurosis and psychosis has long been popular with theorists and practicing clinicians. From this perspective, the symptoms of schizophrenia result from a failure of neurotic defenses. The individual is finally overwhelmed by social or personal anxiety, and he retreats to the pseudoworld of psychosis. Fenichel (1945) and Arieti (1955) provide classical examples of this approach to clinical phenomena.

Mednick (1958) has recently attempted an analogous, though more rigorous, explanation of the schizophrenic's associational disturbance. Anxiety is again taken to be the central construct, but it is equated with the Hull-Spence concept of drive.

The term *drive* is frequently used to denote physiological activation; it is not considered here in that context (see the following section on arousal). In the Hull-Spence framework, drive is generally defined by deprivation time or stimulus intensity and measured by performance. As an intervening variable it bears a mathematical relationship to response strength, learning, and generalization; Mednick's hypotheses are deduced within this theoretical system. Experimental evidence is sought at a number of crucial points, and the following review is concerned mainly with this empirical support.

Mednick (1958) assumes anxiety to be intense in the schizophrenic. High drive (intense anxiety) leads to excessive stimulus generalization and associative generalization. A phobic defense may be successful in maintaining a precarious balance, as seen in schizoid, withdrawing personalities, but the balance may be upset by a precipitating event, which elevates the anxiety level. This increase in drive leads to still more generalization, and now many more stimuli are fear-invoking. Furthermore, the higher drive level increases the intensity of previously present fear responses.

As the spiral of anxiety and generalization mounts, his drive level may increase to an almost insupportable degree. As this is taking place, his ability to discriminate is almost totally eclipsed by his generalization tendencies. Any unit of a thought sequence might call up [still another] remote associate. . . . Clang associates based on stimulus-response generalization may be frequent. . . . His speech may resemble a "word salad." He will be an acute schizophrenic with a full-blown thinking disorder. [p. 322]

Mednick recognized that, in contrast to acute schizophrenics, chronic schizophrenics tend not to give overt evidence of intense anxiety. Therefore he proposed the following transition from acute to chronic schizophrenia. The excessive generalization of the high drive (anxiety) state may lead to a "highly generalized, remote, irrelevant, tangential associate." A remote association diverts the individual's attention from anxiety-provoking stimuli, and the resulting drive (anxiety) reduction is reinforcing. Continued repetition of the strongly reinforced tendency to escape anxiety via remote associations leads to deviant, disorganized thinking. Thinking irrelevant thoughts proves to be so effective in reducing anxiety that the schizophrenic may appear emotionally phlegmatic. Now the well-learned tendency toward remote and tangential associations is maintained even in the absence of a high anxiety level. In deriving his theory Mednick made four assumptions.

Schizophrenics acquire classically conditioned responses faster than normals. Two studies support this assumption. Pfaffman and Schlosberg (1936) demonstrated more frequent conditioned patellar tendon reflexes in schizophrenics than in normals. Spence and Taylor (1953) reported similar results for eyelid conditioning.

On the other hand, six studies have shown that normals condition at least as well as, or better than, schizophrenics. Shipley (1934) and Pishkin and Hershiser (1963) found better conditioning for normals with the GSR, and Howe (1958), also using GSR conditioning, failed to obtain significant differences between normals and schizophrenics. Franks (1954), Peters and Murphree (1954), and O'Connor and Rawnsley (1959) also found that schizophrenics fail to learn faster or better than normals on a variety of conditioning tasks. Thus the weight of evidence is against the hypothesis, which receives little support from the studies just cited.

In more complex situations schizophrenics learn slower. This assumption is linked to the first one in an attempt to apply drive theory to two types of learning situations. In simple situations (e.g., classical conditioning) high drive leads to faster learning; in complex situations high drive enhances irrelevant and incorrect responses, causing a decrement in learning. Schizophrenics, having greater anxiety and therefore higher drive, should learn faster in simple situations and slower in complex situations. The second part of this statement is true: schizophrenics do learn slower in complex situations. However, the first part is probably untrue. Except for classical conditioning, where the evidence is admittedly equivocal, schizophrenics learn *slower* than normals in simple situations. (See the sections on Insufficient Motivation, Attention, Set, and Associative Interference.)

Actually the facts already reviewed are a good deal more complex than the hypothesis allows. While chronic schizophrenics rarely show superior learning to normals, they may approach normal functioning when the response alternatives are reduced and distractions are few. If such conditions define task simplicity, these facts may bring the drive theorist some solace. Furthermore, in a few experiments acute paranoid patients have actually emerged superior to their normal controls. Unfortunately, one must pick and choose among the data to find support for what pretends to be a comprehensive theory. Since schizophrenics in general learn both simple and complex tasks more slowly than normals, the evidence is not consistent with drive theory.

Schizophrenics overgeneralize in comparison to normals. Mednick cited four experiments that ostensibly found elevated generalization gradients in schizophrenics. The first is a study by Bender and Schilder (1930), who present data that are difficult to interpret in terms of generalization gradients and who did not employ normal controls. The second is Garmezy's study (1952), which is open to several interpretations, as we showed in the previous paper (Buss & Lang, 1965). The third is Mednick's (1955) doctoral dissertation, in which he wrote:

> With respect to the hypothesis that schizophrenics would display a more elevated GSR (gradient of stimulus generalization) than normals, the results are not conclusive. While the C (normal) and S (schizophrenic) groups differ, the differences occur both in the predicted direction and counter to it. [p. 540]

The fourth study is that of Dunn (1954) who found an elevated generalization gradient in schizophrenics in one experimental condition and no differences between the gradients of schizophrenics and normals in three other conditions. The most neutral comment to be made about these four studies is that they do not offer support for this third hypothesis.

There is considerable evidence that schizophrenics tend to be overinclusive, including in their vocabulary definitions and conceptual sortings more stimuli than do normals (Buss & Lang, 1965).

> Phenomena of this sort tempt one to describe schizophrenics as showing a heightened and broadened gradient of secondary stimulus generalization. However, the experimental evidence seems to contradict this interpretation. At least three different investigators have compared schizophrenics and normals on tasks which are usually thought of as measuring propensities toward heightened semantic generalizations. All of these studies have uniformly obtained negative results, that is, they find no difference between schizophrenics and normals on semantic generalization. [Chapman, 1962]

Chapman went on to report an experiment demonstrating that schizophrenics were *less* inclusive than normals. Thus the assumption that schizophrenics overgeneralize is not supported by the evidence.

High anxiety leads to overgeneralization and to faster conditioning. This assumption receives some support from the literature, which is too remote from schizophrenic deficit to review here. It should be noted that research with the Taylor Manifest Anxiety scale (the major instrument in these studies) has tended to produce controversial and, at times, unreliable results. Mednick himself (1957) found that middle-anxious subjects had flatter stimulus generalization (SG) gradients than did high- and low-anxious psychiatric patients. Thus there has been both positive and negative evidence on the relationship between anxiety and overgeneralization.

The results concerning anxiety and classical conditioning have been more clearly positive: high-anxious subjects do condition faster than low-anxious subjects. However, the potency of anxiety as a determiner of conditioning is slight, a fact that is admitted by drive theorists:

> While previous studies have demonstrated a relationship between conditioning and manifest anxiety, variously defined, correlation coefficients that have been reported between those two variables indicate that a relatively small amount of the variability among Ss can be accounted for in terms of anxiety. [Taylor & Spence, 1954, p. 502]

Thus the evidence of this fourth assumption tends to be equivocal.

Examination of Mednick's four assumptions indicates that supporting evidence is either equivocal or lacking. Since these assumptions are the base of his drive theory, the theory itself is weakened to the extent that the assumptions lack verification.

The theory places all its eggs in one basket in that it accounts for schizophrenia solely in terms of anxiety. The difficulty is that, with anxiety so prevalent, it is necessary to explain why schizophrenia is still relatively rare in the population. Mednick (1958) was aware of this issue of "over-explanation:"

> Why doesn't everybody proceed to schizophrenia after an extremely anxiety provoking event? The answer lies in three factors: the individual's original drive level, his rate of recovery from anxiety states, and the number of stimuli that elicit anxiety responses from the individual . . . high drive, slow recovery rate, and the number of fear arousing stimuli are highly correlated factors. [p. 323]

Only those with all three factors tend to become schizophrenic, but Mednick himself admitted that the three factors are all highly correlated. Thus an extremely anxious individual, being high on all three factors, should become schizophrenic. Clearly, Mednick has not answered his own question. We may guess that he cannot answer it because he identifies anxiety as the sole cause of the thinking disorder in schizophrenia. This explanation will not be acceptable to the majority of psychologists. It is evident that many individuals with extremely high levels of anxiety never become schizophrenic, whereas Mednick's drive theory clearly implies that they should.

Reactive Inhibition and Reminiscence

Pavlov (1941) suggested that in schizophrenia inhibition predominates over excitation, the theory being labeled "protective inhibition." Several English investigators have developed this idea in terms of a negative drive, reactive inhibition (Claridge, 1960; Eysenck, 1961; Rachman, 1963; Venables & Tizard, 1956c). Thus schizophrenics are believed to develop reactive inhibition faster than normals and to dissipate it slower. If this is true, schizophrenics should learn more slowly than normals, and, more important, show greater reminiscence. The

prediction is straightforward: after a rest period schizophrenics should have a greater increment in performance (reminiscence) than do normals.

This prediction has been unequivocally confirmed in only one study. Huston and Shakow (1948, 1949) tested schizophrenics and normals on a pursuit rotor task at 3-month intervals. Normals performed significantly better than schizophrenics, but whereas normals showed no reminiscence after a 3-month interval, schizophrenics manifested a clear improvement in performance.

Venables and Tizard (1956c) used a repetitive choice task and a 1-minute rest period. Schizophrenics showed slightly more reminiscence than psychotic depressives; there were no normal subjects. Bleke (1955) used a memory task under conditions of reward or punishment. With verbal punishment, poor premorbid schizophrenics showed more reminiscence than either good premorbid schizophrenics or normals. With verbal reward, there were only chance differences in reminiscence. Smock and Vancini (1962) obtained *less* reminiscence in schizophrenics after censure; after reward there were no differences in reminiscence between schizophrenics and normals. Higgins and Mednick (1963) had early and advanced schizophrenics copy the alphabet upside down and backward. They found more reminiscence in early than in advanced schizophrenics. The discrepancies among these last three studies may be due to the way punishment was administered, the difference in tasks, or sampling differences in the subjects.

Taken as a whole, these studies offer little support for the hypothesis that schizophrenics build up reactive inhibition faster than normals and therefore show greater reminiscence. Six experiments have yielded clearly negative results. Campbell (1957) used paper-and-pencil mazes, Rosenbaum, Cohen, Luby, Gottlieb, and Yelen (1959) employed the pursuit rotor, and Venables (1959) used a repetitive choice task; none of these workers found any difference in reminiscence between normals and schizophrenics. O'Connor (1957), Claridge (1960), and Rachman (1963), with varying tasks and rest periods, all found greater reminiscence in normals than in schizophrenics.[4]

In summary, there appear to be no consistent remiscence differences between schizophrenics and normals. Some of the discrepancies among results are undoubtedly due to variations in task, in rest period, and in composition of the subject samples. Regardless of methodological considerations, it seems safe to conclude that the negative drive hypothesis has not been corroborated.

SOMATIC AROUSAL

Autonomic, cortical, and neuromuscular response systems are of considerable relevance to both activation and interference interpretations of schizophrenic deficit. The basic concept of an arousal system in the lower brain was initially dependent on electroencephalogram (EEG) findings rather than on overt behavioral data. Malmo (1958) has stressed the importance of peripheral physiological responses (GSR, EMG, cardiac rate, and blood pressure) as concomitant estimates of drive or the aroused state. Furthermore, the work of Lacey and Lacey

[4] Rachman studied length of the intervening time period and amount of reminiscence. He found that schizophrenics show greater reminiscence after 24 hours than they do after 10 minutes. Furthermore, a comparison with data published elsewhere (Rachman, 1962) suggests that the degree of reminiscence, when measured at the first trial following a 10 minute rest period, is less for schizophrenics than for normal subjects. The relationship between time interval and reminiscence is complex and in general outside the scope of the present review. The reader is referred to the Rachman papers for a discussion of these issues and the related topic of disinhibition.

(1958a), Gellhorn (1957), and Barratt (1962) indicates that feedback from autonomic nervous system (ANS) activity and muscle tension may have important effects on cortical functioning and thus determine temperament, alertness, and adequacy of psychomotor control. It has been suggested that schizophrenic deficit is attributable to *diminished* feedback from peripheral sensors or effector systems, with a resultant disturbance of control and orientation. Others propose that *excessive* feedback of ANS activity interferes with organized behavior in a manner analogous to that of irrelevant associations or intrusive external stimuli.

Research on these covert responses in schizophrenics may be divided into two broad areas: *habitual levels of activity* and *reactivity*. The first term refers to the base amount of ANS or neuromuscular responding characteristic of an individual at rest, when external stimuli are abeyant. The second term refers to the form or amplitude of responses to specific stimuli introduced by the experimenter.

Habitual Level of Activity

At the time Hunt and Cofer (1944) reviewed literature on psychological deficit, no consistent differences between normal and schizophrenic subjects in resting ANS response level had been found (Freeman & Pathman, 1943). A later review (Hoskins, 1946) noted that schizophrenics were less variable than normals in blood pressure and the oral-rectal temperature differential.

Early investigators sought unsuccessfully for evidence of ANS hypoactivity to parallel the clinically observed withdrawal and flattened affect. In addition to this theoretical bias they were hampered by a tendency to consider single measures of specific physiological functions—heart rate or skin resistance—both as adequate estimates of overall ANS functioning and as indicants of general emotionality or

arousal. However, the experimental literature (Lacey & Lacey, 1958b) suggests that
the relationships between somatic responses are complex and that more than
one system must be considered in such
evaluations. In the subsequent few paragraphs studies of basal skin resistance,
cardiovascular and respiration responses,
and muscle activity in schizophrenia are
reviewed.

Basal skin resistance. Hock, Kubis, and
Rouke (1944) noted that withdrawn psychotics show increasing skin resistance
over time periods in which normals are
relatively stable. Experiments by Jurko,
Jost, and Hill (1952) and Howe (1958)
found higher resting resistance levels for
schizophrenic patients than for normal
controls. Malmo and Shagass (1949),
DeVault (1957), Ray (1963) in a study
of female patients, and Pishkin and
Hershiser (1963) reported no difference in
resistance between normals and schizophrenics. Only two studies found low
basal skin resistance in schizophrenics.
Zahn, Rosenthal, and Lawlor (1963) report both lower than normal skin resistance and greater spontaneous activity in
schizophrenics. Williams (1953) also
found lower than normal resting levels
for what he described as an "early chronic
schizophrenic" group. However, this difference barely reached significance and
was not maintained during the experimental conditions. Previous studies by Syz
(1926) and Syz and Kinder (1928) attempted to distinguish between patient
subtypes. They found high basal resistance for catatonics, the paranoids' mean
fell between those obtained from two
normal control samples, and there was
more spontaneous activity in paranoids
than catatonic patients.

Cardiovascular system and respiration.
Gunderson (1953), Williams (1953),
and Jurko *et al.* (1952) reported faster
resting heart rates for schizophrenics than
normal controls. DeVault (1957) ob-

tained similar results for chronic, reactive
patients but not for process schizophrenics. However, Reynolds (1962) found
process schizophrenics had a significantly
higher basal pulse than reactive patients,
and normal controls yielded the lowest
rates.

Altschule and Sulzbach (1949) reported vasoconstriction, particularly of
the hand, to be a habitual condition in
many schizophrenics. Data collected by
Henschel, Brozek, and Keys (1951) also
suggested that the skin vessels of schizophrenics have a high resting tonus level.
Consistent with these views, Malmo and
Shagass (1952) found habitual high
diastolic pressure in chronic schizophrenics, combined with lowered pulse pressure.
Both diastolic and systolic pressures
tended to be higher in process schizophrenics than normal subjects in the
Reynolds (1962) experiment, but a significant difference was obtained for only
one of four resting samples.

Gunderson (1953), Jurko *et al.* (1952),
and Williams (1953) reported that schizophrenics had faster respiration rates than
normals. Reynolds' data show a nonsignificant tendency for process schizophrenics
to have faster rates.

Muscle activity. Malmo and his associates (Malmo, & Shagass, 1949; Malmo,
1950; Malmo, Shagass, & Smith, 1951)
reported a high resting electromyograph
(EMG) in schizophrenics, with the highest levels among chronic patients. Martin
(1956), Whatmore and Ellis (1958), and
Petursson (1962) also found evidence of
higher than normal muscle tension in
schizophrenics. Reynolds (1962) reported
a significantly higher resting EMG response in process schizophrenics than
normal subjects; reactive patients fell between these two groups. Jurko *et al.*
(1952) found considerable adventitious
muscle activity in schizophrenics relative
to normals. Malmo and Shagass (1949),
Edwards and Harris (1953) and later

Gindis (1960) reported disturbance of finger movement in a variety of schizophrenics.

EMG investigations parallel psychomotor studies (King, 1962b) in that schizophrenics show high intraindividual variability. Malmo *et al.* (1951) found that increases in painful stimuli yielded increased action potentials in the neck muscle of schizophrenic patients, but unlike normals, these subjects failed to show such changes in potentials taken from from arm electrodes. Reynolds (1962) also reported high variability in response to stressors and within and between subjects during rest.

The psychophysiological studies described above generally included only one testing session, and little information is available on trends in variability. Recently Carrigan (1963) reported that daily polygraph tests yielded few differences in intraindividual variability between a group of nonparanoid schizophrenics and normal controls. Acker (1963) compared a small group of schizophrenics on tranquilizers and normal subjects. The two groups yielded different trends for different physiological systems. Schizophrenics showed heart rate adaptation over sessions, but unlike the normal controls, blood pressure measures did not show this effect. Both psychophysiological variability and adaptation effects in schizophrenia deserve further study.

In summary, the habitual level of somatic activity in schizophrenics appears to have the following characteristics. Skin resistance levels are generally similar to those of normals, although two samples were clearly higher and at least one was lower than those of control subjects. During experiments the cardiovascular systems of schizophrenics tend to be at a higher activation level than those of normal controls. However, the relationship between cardiac functioning and such dimensions as process-reactive or chronic-acute is not yet clear. All reports indicate higher than normal muscle tension in schizophrenics, the highest levels being associated with chronicity and the process label.

The conclusion that schizophrenics are underaroused or at a normal level of arousal during experiments (i.e., Ray, 1963) is not consistent with a major part of the data. Only the skin resistance findings lend support to this position, while the cardiovascular and neuromuscular systems point to a heightened level of activation. The reason for this division has been variously interpreted. Jurko *et al.* (1952) point out the close relationship between sweat gland activity, attention, and ideation—functions particularly disturbed in schizophrenics. They suggest that energy discharge via muscular tension represents a phylogenetically more primitive way of maintaining energy balance than through the electrodermal response.

The skin resistance findings seem inconsistent with Wenger's (Wenger, 1956; Wenger, Jones, & Jones, 1959) conclusion that the autonomic activity of schizophrenics is dominated by the sympathetic system. However, Solomon, Darrow, and Blaurock (1939) remind us that sweat gland activity, though sympathetically activated, is a cholinergic mechanism. They suggest that the neurohormonal inhibition of cholinergic response systems may be related to psychotic withdrawal. More recently, Rubin (1962) has suggested that an adrenergic-cholinergic unbalance is an important aspect of functional psychosis. Perhaps sweat gland activity is a sensitive measure of small increases in arousal level, but the action of adrenin inhibits this system under high levels of sympathetic activation.

The cardiovascular results and particularly the muscle tension findings suggest that the level of "biological noise" is quite high in schizophrenics. A number of authors have proposed that this directly accounts for schizophrenic symptoms. Angyal (1935, 1936) suggested that disturbance of muscle tension may be the perceptual basis of somatic delusions in schizophrenia, and Gould (1950) proposed that auditory hallucinations could be traced to a motor disturbance of the speech mechanism. Furthermore, diffuse neuromuscular activity may contribute to deficit in psychomotor or perceptual tasks by interfering directly with coordinated behavior (Freeman, 1948; Luria, 1932). Wishner (1955, 1962) has maintained that an increase in degree of psychopathology is signaled by a decrease in efficiency, with efficiency defined as the ratio of focused to diffuse activity. Normals orient their activity to the task requirements, and there is a minimum of diffuse random activity in either the musculature or the ANS. In psychopathology less of the total activity is directed to the task at hand, and more of the total behavior output is diffuse and random. Schizophrenia represents the extreme of inefficiency.

Reynolds (1962) found that in process schizophrenics stress sometimes produces a decrease rather than the normal's increase in muscle tension level. He interpreted studies which show chronic schizophrenics improve under conditions of aversive stimulation (Cohen et al., 1956; Lang, 1959) in a manner that parallels Wishner's theory. Reynolds suggested that aversive stimuli reduce the general tension level in chronic schizophrenics, producing a temporarily favorable ratio of directed to diffuse muscular activity and an associated amelioration of psychomotor performance.

Reactivity and pathology. Many studies of reactivity to stimulations reveal a diminished ANS response in chronic schizophrenia. Stressors that have yielded hyporeactivity include the inhalation of heated air (Freeman & Rodnick, 1940) and cold baths (Buck, Carscallen, & Hobbs, 1950). Schizophrenics show reduced rotational and caloric nystagmus (Angyal & Blackman, 1940, 1941; Angyal & Sherman, 1942; Colbert, Koegler, & Markham, 1959; Freeman & Rodnick, 1942; Leach, 1960) and pupillary hypofunction in response to pain, light, or exercise (May, 1948). Astrup (1962) found inadequate vascular responses to cold in all types of schizophrenia, and Hall and Stride (1954) reported higher thresholds to thermal pain. Reduced GSR responses have been noted to Hock, Kubis, and Ronke (1944), Jurko et al. (1952) and Solomon et al. (1939).

Except for the GSR, hyporeactivity in chronic patients may be partly a function of their higher basal levels. The "law of initial values" (Lacey, 1956; Wilder, 1950) predicts reduced responses when psychological systems approach homeostatic limits. Williams' (1953) and Reynolds' (1962) data are consistent with this hypothesis. The latter author found that normals had the lowest basal levels and showed a typical increase in functioning under stress. Reactive schizophrenics displayed a reduced response but a higher base level; process patients yielded the highest initial values and showed the least change. Separating reactivity from base level will prove to be even more difficult if, as Shakow (1963) suggests, the rate of adaptation to stimuli is significantly slower in schizophrenics than normals.

Reactivity is often less in chronic than acute schizophrenics, and lower in process than reactive patients. Malmo and Shagass (1949) reported that early schizophrenics are hyperreactive and resemble anxiety neurotics in the EMG response to pain. Chronic patients showed a reduced muscular response to the same stimulus, although this was not true for heart rate (Malmo et al., 1951). King (1958) found reactive schizophrenics hospitalized less than 8 weeks to be hyperreactive to mecholyl. Process schizophrenics proved to be hyporeactive. DeVault (1957) reported negative heart rate changes to his experimental stimuli in process patients, while reactive schizophrenics tended to show the same positive increases as normal controls.

Venables and Wing (1962) studied the relationship between arousal and ratings on a withdrawal scale (Venables & O'Connor, 1959) by schizophrenic patients' charge nurse. Arousal was measured by the two-flash threshold and the skin potential response. With the exception of those deluded patients who showed no incoherence of speech (essentially intact paranoid schizophrenics), increased physiological arousal was associated with increased ratings of social withdrawal.

The above findings are provocative but difficult to relate to other research. Most workers have measured resistance to an exosomatic current, a procedure not directly comparable with the recording of endosomatic potentials. Furthermore, the visual threshold measure has been infrequently used with psychiatric patients. In one study King (1962c) found no difference between schizophrenics and normals on the two-flash threshold, but his sample was small and distinctions within schizophrenics were not made. More recently Venables (1963b) repeated his results for withdrawal and found the two-flash threshold to be significantly related to the extent irrelevant information disturbed the card sorting behavior of nonparanoid schizophrenics. He also reported (Venables, 1963a) that, while normals are unaffected, the thresholds of schizophrenic patients are significantly altered by coincident noise. Further study of these phenomena is needed.

Funkenstein (1951) reported that amelioration of schizophrenic pathology is associated with a reduction in basal systolic blood pressure. Gellhorn (1953) and Gunderson (1953) also found that improvement in schizophrenia is correlated with a reduction in the ANS basal level of functioning. Weckowicz (1958) reported that reduced blood pressure response to the mecholyl test is associated with deteriorated size constancy. He suggested that the hyporeactivity in these patients is attributable to higher basal levels of sympathetic activity. An increase in GSR with clinical improvement has been noted by Solomon et al. (1939) and Hock et al. (1944). Finally, Reynolds (1962) found that polygraph profiles of schizophrenics receiving tranquilizing medication were more like those of normals than those of patients off medication at the time of his experiment.[5]

Reactivity and the properties of the stimulus. Paintal (1951) reported that psychotics gave a reduced GSR response to threat of pain. Ray (1963) failed to confirm this finding in a study of female schizophrenics, but he obtained significant set differences. With instructions simply to listen to a list of "loaded" and "neutral" words, no difference in GSR between schizophrenics and normals was noted; with instructions to respond with an association, however, the normal GSR increased considerably more than that of the schizophrenics. This was true regardless of whether the schizophrenics proved to be "adequate" or "inadequate" verbal responders. Furthermore, while the GSRs of normals were greatest to the loaded

[5] Tourney et al. (1962) reported that chronic schizophrenics show a disturbance in the mechanism concerned with the transformation of chemical to kinetic energy which seems to parallel the findings cited in this section. The specific activity of chemicals involved in carbohydrate breakdown is greater under basal conditions in chronic schizophrenic patients than normal subjects. However, the mobilization of these products in response to stimulation was significantly less in those patients than in normal controls.

words under both conditions, the schizophrenics yielded differential responses only when actually responding.

Venables (1960) found that the GSR of schizophrenic subjects varies with the stimulus context in a manner similar to RT. Schizophrenic and normal subjects were presented discrete visual and auditory stimuli, with or without a continuous, collateral stimulus of the opposite modality. The experimental conditions did not significantly affect the GSR of normal subjects. A low illumination and quiet condition was compared with a bright illumination and noisy condition; in "active schizophrenics" the former yielded more GSRs which were of greater intensity and shorter latency. In withdrawn schizophrenics the bright, noisy condition produced the same number of GSRs as the quiet condition, but latency was shorter. Thus, as with RT, additional stimuli appear to modify the speed of response, with the most intense stimuli affecting withdrawn schizophrenics the most.

Venables recalled that any sensory input may serve both a cue and a nonspecific arousal function (Hebb, 1955) and that this latter dimension may describe an inverted U function (Malmo, 1958). He suggested that with moderate stimulation active schizophrenics function at an optimal level. With increased intensity there is a paradoxical depression of response. On the other hand, moderate stimuli are less effective for withdrawn patients, and increases in stimulus intensity improve performance in a linear fashion. Unfortunately, no information was provided about basal potentials under both conditions of stimulation, rendering the result and the interpretation inconclusive.

Leach (1960) studied ocular nystagmus in response to rotation at various acceleration speeds. He reported that

with increasing intensity of the stimulus schizophrenic deficit decreased. This tendency is demonstrated most clearly in latency of nystagmus to onset rotation. Schizophrenic deficit was less than one-fourth for moderate and strong intensities than for a mild intensity. [p. 308]

The response of normals remained relatively constant in relation to changes in stimulus intensity. These findings parallel those of Venables and Tizard (1958), Lang (1959), and King (1962b), who reported a decrease in relative psychomotor deficit with increases in the physical intensity of the stimulus. The fact that the semicircular canals regulate muscle tonus in the body lends added meaning to this parallel. Furthermore, Angyal and Blackman (1940) showed an association within schizophrenia between nystagmic deficit and disturbance in muscular tonus.

Reduced caloric and rotational nystagmus has also been reported in childhood schizophrenia. Colbert, Koegler, and Markham (1959) found that all the subjects in the sample for whom nystagmus was absent carried the schizophrenic diagnosis. When nystagmus was present, the shorter its duration, the greater the probability of schizophrenia. It is interesting to note that, as with psychomotor behavior (King, 1954, 1961), intraindividual variability was as pathognomic for schizophrenia as the reduced response. These authors ruled out the possibility that a lesion in the major vestibular pathways could be the causal agent because none of the usual collateral symptoms were observed. They speculated that vestibular activity may be inhibited at the level of the caudal midbrain, in a manner neurologically analogous to the inhibition of auditory attention demonstrated by Hernandez-Péon and Associates (1956).

Another approach suggests that both vestibular and psychomotor deficit are attributable to a disturbance of proprioception. Rosenbaum et al. (1959) using shock and no shock conditions studied simple RT of chronic schizophrenics and normal subjects who were administered either LSD-25, amobarbital sodium, or phencyclidine hydrochloride (sernyl). Under nonshock conditions, the sernyl normals and schizophrenics had significantly slower latencies than the other two drug groups. With shock, both the schizophrenics and the sernyl subjects reduced their scores to the level of the other subjects. Similar parallels between schizophrenic and sernyl normals were noted in rotary pursuit learning and weight discrimination. Unlike LSD-25, sernyl seems to produce primary, rather than secondary, schizophrenic symptoms. Furthermore, when it is administered to schizophrenic patients, pathology is markedly exacerbated, and this condition may last for several weeks (Luby, Gottlieb, Cohen, Rosenbaum, & Domino, 1962).

In normal subjects sernyl depresses "central integrating mechanisms involving various sensory modalities such as touch, pain, and proprioception [Luby et al., 1962, p. 64]"; subjects report alterations of body image and feelings of estrangement and unreality, and they display progressive disorganization of thought, inability to maintain set, and impairment of abstract thinking. The drug effects show a further parallel to schizophrenia in that increased levels of respiratory and cardiovascular activity have been reported (Meyer, Greifenstein, & Devault, 1959). Cohen, Rosenbaum, Luby, & Gottlieb (1962) studied the effects of schizophrenia, sernyl, LSD, and amytal on proverb interpretation and a serial seven task. Under nondrug conditions, the normal groups were superior to the schizophrenic patients. LSD and amytal produced insignificant decrements in the performance of the normals. However, sernyl subjects approximated the level of the patients. Cohen et al. (1962) proposed that both sernyl normals and

schizophrenics suffer from a basic proprioceptive deficit, this failure of feedback accounting for both psychomotor and cognitive disturbance.

> The S is impaired in his ability to provide himself with those response-produced cues which normally function to enhance stimulus discrimination and relevant response selection. [p. 84]

This formulation meaningfully parallels the hypothesized breakdown in self-instruction previously raised to account for the findings of verbal reinforcement studies (Buss & Lang, 1965).

The fact that schizophrenics display increased deficit when many competing stimuli are present has already been amply documented. Recently a number of researchers have reported a decrease in behavior disturbance under conditions of decreased stimulation. Cohen, Rosenbaum, Dobe, and Gottlieb (1959), Harris (1959), and Smith, Thakurdas, and Lawes (1961) all found that schizophrenics who have experienced sensory deprivation show less discomfort and some improvement under these conditions. Reitman and Cleveland (1964) reported that schizophrenics showed an increase in tactile sensitivity and gave more accurate estimates of body size, following sensory deprivation. These positive effects were not observed in similarly treated normal subjects.

Cohen, Luby, Rosenbaum, and Gottlieb (1960) and Lawes (1963) studied the effects of sensory deprivation on normal subjects who had been administered sernyl. Like schizophrenics, sernyl normals evidenced less disorder of thought, attention, and perception under deprivation conditions than under normal conditions of stimulation. Lawes suggested that the schizophrenic is overwhelmed by normal levels of external stimulation and incapable of managing sensory inputs.

Callaway and Dembo (1958) described a narrowing of attention which they related to a kind of crowding out of meaningful stimuli by the high level of central sympathetic activity. These authors also reported disturbance of size constancy, reduced EMG, GSR reactivity, and learning deficit produced by drugs that initiate widespread sympathetic activity (nerve gas, amylnitrite, and amphetamine).

There are few studies of cortical responsitivity in schizophrenia that can be meaningfully related to psychological deficit. EEG abnormalities have frequently been reported (Ellingson, 1954), but differences have too often been judged rather than measured. Gromoll (1961) tested the hypothesis that reactive schizophrenics would be more responsive and show higher levels of cortical arousal than process patients or controls. No significant difference between groups were obtained on such measures as alpha blocking. However, the author reported that process subjects, rather than reactive schizophrenics, tended to maintain the highest activation levels.

Shagass and Schwartz (1961) have developed techniques for studying evoked responses in the somatosensory cortex of man. Subjects receive electric shock to the wrist, and potentials are recorded from EEG surface electrodes. By repeating the stimulation and averaging across trials, the form of evoked potentials may be determined. In a number of experiments a trial has consisted of two shocks separated by an interval varying in milliseconds. Normal subjects, neurotic depressives, and anxiety patients showed a response to the second shock at around 20 milliseconds that equalled the initial evoked potential. Psychotic depressives and schizophrenics showed a much reduced response in this early recovery phase (Shagass & Schwartz, 1961, 1962). Data consistent with these findings were reported by Purpura, Pool, Ransohoff,

Freeman, and Houspian (1957), who found that the direct stimulation of the exposed human cortex yielded much later recovery in two schizophrenic patients than in the nondiseased cortex of a patient with a tumor.

Shagass and Schwartz (1963) also studied the effects of shock intensity on evoked cortical potentials in different psychiatric patients. They reported that the intensity response gradients of a mixed group of patients (including schizophrenics and psychotic depressives) were steeper than those of normal subjects or dysthymic patients. These data parallel the intensity gradients obtained for RT and suggest that studies relating cortical potentials and psychomotor behavior may be of considerable value in studying schizophrenia.

Summary

The picture of schizophrenic deficit that emerges from these findings is remarkably consistent across a number of very different response systems. Latency and/or amplitude of psychomotor, vestibular, cardiovascular, sweat gland, and cortical EEG responses are reduced, relative to normal subjects. In at least three of the above systems and in verbal association, excessive intraindividual variability of response has also proved to be pathognomic of schizophrenic disorder. In addition, the levels of cardiovascular activity and muscular tension are unusually high among these patients. All these behaviors—reduced responsivity, deterioration of associational or psychomotor control, and high somatic tension—are positively related to increased withdrawal or clinically judged exacerbation of the illness. They are more marked for chronic and process schizophrenics than for acute and reactive patients. These relationships do not appear to hold for relatively intact paranoids, and perhaps not for early schizophrenics (recent, first admissions).

The experimental manipulation of stimulus intensity has yielded consistent data in studies of RT, ocular nystagmus, and cortical potentials. Deficit in chronic schizophrenia is greatest for low-intensity inputs and least when stimulus amplitude is high. Related to these findings are results of distractibility experiments, which reveal both the schizophrenic's susceptibility to irrelevant cues and his improved performance when background noise is reduced.

A host of studies indicate set disturbances in schizophrenia. On the one hand, schizophrenics are unable to maintain response readiness, and response latency increases if stimuli are presented in more than one modality. On the other hand, these patients seem unduly influenced by a previous set, and responses persist long after they are demonstrably ineffective.

In general, the hypothesis that schizophrenic deficit is attributable to the interference of competing stimuli, internal or external, receives considerable support. The theory that schizophrenics are underaroused may be maintained only if studies of activity level are ignored. This latter research argues that even long-term chronic patients may be physiologically hyperaroused relative to normal subjects, although the frequency and amplitude of overt behavior is greatly reduced.

DISCUSSION

Theory

In the previous review (Buss & Lang, 1965) three general theories of schizophrenic deficit were considered. The first of these can be roughly described as social or interpersonal in emphasis: deficit is variously attributed to social censure, oversensitivity to affective stimuli, or lowered social motivation. The second approach holds that schizophrenic deficit is a consequence of regression. A third view argues that associative interference underlies many instances of the schizophrenic's behavior disturbance.

Regression theory received little support from data summarized in the first paper, and the current review adds nothing that alters conclusions drawn there. In this discussion, three motivational constructs (social motivation, drive, and arousal) and a more broadly conceived interference theory will be considered as explanations of schizophrenic deficit.

Social motivation. The hypothesis that schizophrenics suffer from lowered social motivation was examined in the previous review. It was seen that schizophrenics and normals respond similarly to general encouragement or chastisement on laboratory tasks. Furthermore, when specific responses are reinforced, differences between groups may be attributed to the greater value of information about performance for the schizophrenic subject. A guidance function is served for patients, which normals apparently provide for themselves. For example, punishment breaks up the perseverative behavior of psychotics, resulting in a closer approximation of normal performance.

The fact that schizophrenics improve more than normals when aversive, physical reinforcers are used has been interpreted to mean that schizophrenics' response to social reward is reduced. However, the research reviewed in the present paper suggests that the intense stimuli employed in these experiments serve to emphasize relevant cues and focus attention, rather than function as special motivators for an indifferent patient.

Some theorists argue that the schizophrenic's problem is not *undersensitivity* to social motivators; it is held that their *oversensitivity* to the affective meaning of stimuli disrupts performance. While affective stimuli may increase deficit, this property is not restricted to one type, such as social censure. In fact, the considerable variety of stimuli (symbolic, human versus nonhuman, etc.) capable of producing these effects calls into question the value of a category so loosely defined. In the previous paper, the authors suggested that the deficit produced by so-called affective or emotionally arousing stimuli is due to an inability to inhibit irrelevant associations. Most of these stimuli instigate more associations than do the neutral comparison stimuli. Evidence presented here indicates that the capacity to suppress *any* intruding cognition is greatly reduced in schizophrenia.

In summary, the hypothesis that schizophrenics are indifferent to social stimuli or particularly sensitive to the affective meaning of stimuli, have very limited value. Experiments relevant to both views are more parsimoniously interpreted in the context of interference theory, which will be reconsidered after a discussion of drive and arousal.

Drive. Negative drive theory applies Pavlov's notion of protective inhibition in schizophrenia to the learning process. Specifically, schizophrenics are held to develop reactive inhibition faster than normals and should therefore show greater reminiscence. Concerning reactive inhibition, there is no consistent evidence that schizophrenics classically condition slower than normals. Concerning reminiscence, the results are similar: no established difference between schizophrenics and normals. It seems safe to conclude that negative drive theory is incorrect.

Mednick, labeling the potential schizophrenic as high-anxious, used the Spence-Taylor approach in making predictions: faster conditioning in simple situations, slower conditioning in complex situations, and flattened generalization gradi-

ents. As we showed earlier, these predictions have received only weak support, and there is strong opposing evidence. Thus Mednick's theory has, in general, not been sustained by research findings.

What appears to be wrong with the theory is its specification of anxiety as the crucial drive that leads to schizophrenia. While it is true that many schizophrenics appear anxious, this could as readily be a reaction to incapacity as a cause of it. The theory is embarrassed not only because the predictions from anxiety theory are not supported but also because more chronic and severe schizophrenics show less clinical anxiety. The fact that chronic, withdrawn patients frequently have high-somatic activity levels appears partially to save the theory. However, Mednick has already explained that the chronic schizophrenic's associational defense successfully eliminates anxiety!

These weaknesses of Mednick's theory do not necessarily apply to all drive theories. In fact, drive theory can be shown to be consistent with much research evidence if it is assumed that: (*a*) it is a generalized drive state rather than a specific one such as anxiety, and (*b*) generalized drive can be measured by, or is the same as, physiological arousal. Two sets of facts seem to fit a generalized drive theory. First, schizophrenics tend to be over-aroused, the physiological hyperactivity varying directly with chronicity and/or severity. Second, schizophrenic deficit also varies directly with chronicity and/or severity. These facts can be combined in a causal sequence: schizophrenic deficit is due to the disruptive effects of an excessively high arousal or generalized drive state. Stated this way drive theory can be seen to be one variant of interference theory.

Arousal. Complementary to drive theory is what may be called arousal theory. This view was originally based on the neurological speculations of Hebb (1955) and Lindsley (1951), the EEG work of the latter, and studies of the ANS and muscle tension system by Freeman (1948), Duffy (1962) and Malmo (1958). This conception orders behavior on a continuum from deep sleep to intense excitement. These behavioral states are held to be a function of the degree of diffuse activity in the lower brain, particularly in the reticular formation. From this site collateral impulses ascend to the cortex and descend to the ANS. Alertness, attention, and reactivity are thus determined by the organism's level of "arousal." As with the social motivational point of view, schizophrenics have been held to be both overaroused and underaroused.

The hypothesis that schizophrenics suffer from an underactive arousal mechanism would seem to receive support from studies demonstrating psychomotor and physiological hyporeactivity in chronic patients. However, Malmo (1958) argues cogently that activation is measured more directly in studies of basal physiological level than in research on responsivity. Thus, studies showing high resting somatic activity in schizophrenia would indicate that schizophrenics are generally hyperaroused rather than the opposite. Furthermore, their reduced responsivity is not inconsistent with this view. Malmo (1958), Lacey (1956), and Wilder (1950) have all presented evidence that responsivity progressively decreases when plotted on an abscissa of increasing activation (defined by base activity level). A similar function is obtained in normal subjects when "adequacy of performance" in a complex psychological task replaces responsivity on the ordinate. These facts not only argue that testable chronic schizophrenics are habitually in a hyperaroused state, but in this context the performance deterioration of schizophrenics appears to be analogous to the psychological stress response of a normal sub-

ject. However, the symmetry of this analogy is only apparent. Whereas it is complex functioning of normal subjects that mainly suffers under stress (while perhaps more primitive and less adequate but well organized responses emerge), the schizophrenic patient shows deterioration of the simplest and most fundamental behaviors. For example, the schizophrenic performs poorly on a RT task, not because he is anxious, an overready impulsive responder, but because the stimulus seems to arrive unexpectedly. He is not prepared or set, and the response is slow and reduced in amplitude. The psychomotor performance of chronic schizophrenics is more similar to that of aged normals or young adults with general cerebral damage than to that of psychologically stressed normals or anxiety neurotics.

In summary, the underarousal theory of schizophrenia, in terms of the nonspecific projection system, is directly contradicted by most of the psychophysiological research reviewed here, and it may be considered incorrect. The hypothesis that schizophrenics are overaroused receives some support. However, the exact mechanism by which overarousal can produce hyporesponsivity, high-response variability, inattention, disturbances of set and association, and the other symptoms of chronic schizophrenia is yet to be explained.

Interference theory. Interference theory has focused mainly on association and attention-set. The associations of schizophrenics are idiosyncratic and deviant, and they deteriorate performance because they serve as distractors. Schizophrenics have difficulty in focusing on relevant stimuli and excluding irrelevant stimuli, in maintaining a set over time, in shifting a set when it is necessary, in instructing themselves and in pacing themselves, and generally in performing efficiently, in Wishner's sense (1955). These difficulties are pervasive, occurring over a wide range of perceptual, motor, and cognitive tasks. In brief, interference theory, as a broad explanation of schizophrenic deficit, has clearly been supported by research findings and appears to be the only theory comprehensive enough to account for what is known.

The generality of interfering effects suggests a fundamental sensori-motor defect. However, the reactions of patients vary somewhat according to subtype. The defect is seen most clearly in the behavior of chronic, withdrawn patients; acute schizophrenics and particularly early paranoids seem to be compensating for their disability. In many tasks they are overprecise or overresponsive. The fact that in some experiments, among paranoid schizophrenics only the most chronic cases show deficit, suggests that their bizarre attempts at organizing the world may have functional value. Support is gained for Bleuler's contention that many of these behaviors are secondary symptoms—responses to the fundamental disturbance, rather than intrinsic expressions of it.

The locus of the sensori-motor defect is a matter for speculation. It seems clear that the defect is not at the level of the peripheral sensors[6] or effectors, although feedback from the musculature and the ANS may contribute to the disturbance. Lacey and Lacey (1958a) suggest that attention, set, and psychomotor control are directly influenced by autonomic feedback. They propose the carotid sinus as one such steering mechanism: blood pressure changes stimulate the carotid, which has "a profound tonic and inhibitory effect" on cortical electrical activity, and thus alters the organism's orientation to the environment.

Furthermore, these researchers have demonstrated a relationship between cardiac variability and failure to inhibit psychomotor responses. Recently, they have also shown that heart rate changes correlate with RT fore-period effects. This raises the interesting possibility that the motor and perceptual symptoms of schizophrenia are related to defects in this carotid cortical mechanism.

The disturbance that appears in all studies of deficit concerns the initiation of responses to selected stimuli and the inhibition of inappropriate responses. All intelligent behavior represents a compromise between the demands of the immediate environment and a previously established set of the organism, but the schizophrenic makes a uniquely poor bargain. External stimuli, associational and biological "noise," routinely suppressed by normal subjects, intrude, and responses to the appropriate stimuli are not made.

These facts suggest that researchers in schizophrenia should concentrate on the processes by which stimuli adapt out or habituate and response competition is resolved. The ascending reticular activating system is the neurological site of greatest relevance. In addition to general arousal, this system appears to have a specific alerting or focusing function. Hernandes-Péon and his associates (1956) demonstrated that cortical potentials in the cochlear nucleus of the cat, normally elicited by a tone, were suppressed when a competing odor of fish or a jar of mice was simultaneously presented. These authors write:

> Attention involves the selective awareness of certain sensory messages with the simultaneous suppression of others. . . . During the attentive state, it seems as though the brain integrates for consciousness only a limited amount of sensory information, specifically, those impulses concerned with the object of attention. [p. 332]

[6] Schizophrenics are no different from normals in pure tone threshold and speech reception but are disrupted more quickly and easily by auditory feedback and noise (Ludwig, Wood, & Downs, 1962).

The data on schizophrenic deficit are consistent with the hypothesis that such sensory inhibition centers are defective. These centers and the related behavior should be given extensive study in schizophrenic patients.

Methodological Considerations

It is appropriate that a research review should conclude on a methodological note. The issues raised are many, and their listing amounts to a set of guidelines and admonishments to future investigators.

1. A number of studies have shown that schizophrenics as a group are more variable than normals, and no one regards the nonpsychiatric population as being especially homogeneous. Furthermore, schizophrenics are known to vary in the extent of deficit in relation to several variables which are usually dichotomized: mild-severe, acute-chronic, reactive-process, good premorbid-poor premorbid, and paranoid-nonparanoid. It seems likely that these variables overlap, but empirical data are limited. We need studies relating these dimensions of schizophrenia to each other, as well as more precise data on their relation to deficit.

The paranoid-nonparanoid dichotomy is of special interest. For over a century there has been doubt about including paranoids under the heading of schizophrenia or keeping them separate as "paranoid conditions." Paranoids have been found to show less deficit (e.g., Payne & Hewlitt, 1960), and clinically they have been observed to show less thought disorder and less deterioration over time than have schizophrenics of other subgroups. However, these statements are not true of all paranoids; some patients with delusions do manifest considerable deficit and deterioration of thought processes. Perhaps the presence of delusions is less important than the relative absence of deficit. Stated another way, perhaps the important dimension is intactness of sensori-motor and intellectual processes, and the paranoid-nonparanoid distinction partially reflects or is partially correlated with this dimension.

Recently Johannsen and his associates (1963) examined correlations between different measures used to describe schizophrenics. High correlations were found between placement on process-reactive, acute-chronic, and good-poor premorbid scales. Only the paranoid-nonparanoid dimension appeared to be an independent dimension. Furthermore, this latter dichotomy was the only one that yielded a significant difference on a double alternation learning task. Whether delusional behavior is an epiphenomenon in low-deficit schizophrenics or a positive effort to reduce deficit as was suggested earlier, future investigators must consider paranoid symptoms in selecting experimental samples.

A less known source of variability among schizophrenics may be found in sex differences. The subjects in most research have been men, with a minority of experiments including both sexes or using women only. It is possible that results found with men cannot be generalized to women, and sex differences might account for some of the discrepancies in results that occur among studies otherwise comparable.

The importance of this issue is pointed up by Schooler's (1963) study of affiliation. He found that the relationships that held for men did not hold for women, and vice versa, which led him to conclude:

> A major implication of the study is that theories based on experimental findings with one sex cannot be generalized to explain the behavior of chronic schizophrenics of the other sex. [p. 445]

2. In many instances the range of tasks used to study deficit is not sufficient to sustain the broad conclusions of the investigators. For example, on the basis of demonstrated deficiency on conceptual tasks, some researchers have concluded that the basic problem of schizophrenic deficit is an inability to handle concepts. Taken at face value, this conclusion is an overgeneralization because of the absence of evidence that schizophrenics show no deficit on nonconceptual tasks. In the light of the evidence with non-conceptual tasks, the conclusion is patently false. Generalizations about schizophrenic deficit require a sampling of tasks that tap a variety of psychological functions.

It would be of considerable help if we knew more about what various tasks are measuring and their relations to each other. The appropriate tool is factor analysis, which has been employed mainly by English researchers such as Payne and his collaborators (Payne, Mattussek, & George, 1959; Payne & Hewlitt, 1960).

3. When the investigator is interested in particular characteristics of his stimuli, a special problem may arise. He may assume, for example, that some of his stimuli are "affect-laden" without having any evidence for this assertion. A priori statements that stimuli differ along a dimension such as "emotionally arousing" cannot be accepted. It behooves the investigator to present evidence on this point, and the evidence must be independent of the effects obtained with his dependent variable. A similar problem appeared in studies of positive and negative incentives. These experiments were generally interpreted in a social-motivational context, while the more important differences in the degree of information conveyed by these stimuli were largely ignored.

4. General methodological problems in psychophysiological research have been adequately described elsewhere (Lacey, 1956; Lacey & Lacey, 1958b). However, these difficulties are accentuated when schizophrenics are the experimental subjects. For example, the low-positive correlations between physiological measures noted in studies of normal subjects may be lower or even negative in schizophrenics. Single measures of arousal or drive are necessarily misleading. Thus, hypoactivity in schizophrenia is frequently found for skin resistance, while muscle tension is generally reported to be high. Such results are provocative, and further study of relationships between sweat gland, cardiovascular, and muscle tension systems may prove valuable.

The pervasive use of drugs in the treatment of psychosis creates problems for both the behavioral and psychophysiological investigator. For example, Reynolds (1962) found a significant interaction between diagnostic subtype (process-reactive) and tranquilizer-non-tranquilizer conditions in a study of somatic responses in schizophrenia. No research should be undertaken unless the drug variable is properly controlled.

Researchers have begun to emphasize individual variability in behavioral studies of schizophrenia. Investigations of somatic inter- and intrasession variability are also needed. Furthermore, there may be profit in studying somatic responses recorded concurrently with tasks that elicit deficit. Lacey and Lacey (1958a) have reported important relationships between autonomic activity and psychomotor functioning in normals, and studies cited here encourage this experimental strategy.

Better estimates are needed of resting somatic activity levels. Despite the elaborate care of some investigators, what purport to be differences in basal levels between psychotics and normals may actually be differences in reaction to the laboratory situation. Long-term studies are needed in which information is telemetered from patients while they proceed with the usual hospital routine.

5. While only psychological deficit in schizophrenia has been considered in this review, it is important to reaffirm that these patients share many of the characteristics of deficit with other psychiatric disorders and cases of cerebral damage. The psychomotor retardation, inattention, increased response variability, muscle tension and ANS hyperactivity, and even to some extent the associative disturbance, may be found in many aged, paretic, severe epileptic, or arterial sclerotic patients. Deficit behavior can be produced in normal subjects through the administration of drugs or surgical intervention, and there is some evidence that it may be manipulated by brain stimulation (Heath, 1954).

There is ample evidence that severity of psychopathology and psychological deficit are positively related. Some theorists hold that this is the only meaningful relationship between deficit and diagnosis, and they argue that specific consideration of schizophrenia is superfluous. They emphasize the unity of deficit in psychiatric illness and suggest a common neurological defect underlies all its manifestations.

Certainly, further demonstrations that schizophrenics differ from normals are not needed. If the schizophrenic label has experimental validity, the deficit specific to this diagnosis must be more clearly defined. Are variables such as maternal censure or pictures of hospital aids uniquely important to the behavior of schizophrenics, or might they similarly influence the responses of other patient groups? An answer to this question can only come from studies employing control subjects other than normals, i.e., anxiety neurotics, aged, epileptic, brain-damaged or other chronically ill patients. While some experiments have compared schizophrenics to these groups, the evidence is fragmentary and the interpretations usually emphasize the safer, more reliable distinction between normality and psychosis.

The theoretical point of studies in this area often needs sharpening. Deficit is simply performance decrement. In trying to explain it we must distinguish between what is basic to the disorder and what is epiphenomenal. For example: Is the schizophrenic's anxiety the instigator of deficit, or is it an individual reaction to an insidious and pervasive sensorimotor defect? Issues of this type will tax the ingenuity of the behavioral researcher.

In summary, the problem of psychological deficit remains as broad and as challenging now as in 1944. However, the last 20 years have done much to clarify fundamental symptoms and define conditions which increase or decrease deficit. Many theories have failed to receive empirical support and may now be discarded. Fruitful lines of investigation have also been revealed, and the researcher today, guided by this work, is better equipped to discover the basic nature of schizophrenia.

Schizophrenic Patients in the Psychiatric Interview: An Experimental Study of Their Effectiveness at Manipulation

Benjamin M. Braginsky and Dorothea D. Braginsky [1]

The present investigation is concerned with the manipulative behavior of hospitalized schizophrenics in evaluative interview situations. More specifically, the study attempts to answer the question: Can schizophrenic patients effectively control the impressions (impression management, Goffman, 1959) they make on the professional hospital staff?

Typically, the mental patient has been viewed as an extremely ineffectual and helpless individual (e.g., Arieti, 1959; Becker, 1964; Bellak, 1958; Joint Commission on Mental Illness and Health, 1961; Redlich & Freedman, 1966; Schooler & Parkel, 1966; Searles, 1965). For example, Redlich and Freedman (1966) described the mental patient and his pathological status in the following manner: "There is a concomitant loss of focus and coherence and a profound shift in the meaning and value of social relationships and goal directed behavior. This is evident in the inability realistically to implement future goals and present satisfactions; they are achieved magically or through fantasy and delusion. . . [p. 463]." Schooler and Parkel (1966) similarly underline the mental patients' in-

effectual status in this description: "the chronic schizophrenic is not Seneca's 'reasoning animal,' or Spinoza's 'social animal,' or even a reasonably efficient version of Cassirer's 'symbol using animal.' . . . Since he violates so many functional definitions of man, there is heuristic value in studying him with an approach like that which would be used to study an alien creature [p. 67]."

Thus, the most commonly held assumptions concerning the nature of the schizophrenic patient stress their ineffectuality and impotency. In this context one would expect schizophrenics to perform less than adequately in interpersonal situations, to be unable to initiate manipulative tactics, and, certainly, to be incapable of successful manipulation of other people.[2]

In contrast to the above view of the schizophrenic, a less popular orientation has been expressed by Artiss (1959), Braginsky, Grosse, and Ring (1966), Goffman (1961), Levinson and Gallagher (1964), Rakusin and Fierman (1963), Szasz (1961, 1965), and Towbin (1966). Here schizophrenics are portrayed in terms usually reserved for neu-

Reprinted from the *Journal of Consulting Psychology*, 1967, vol. 31, pp. 543–547 with the permission of the American Psychological Association and the authors.

[1] The authors would like to express their appreciation to Doris Seiler and Dennis Ridley for assisting with the data collection.

[2] This statement is explicitly derived from formal theories of schizophrenia and not from clinical observations. It is obvious to some observers, however, that schizophrenics do attempt to manipulate others. The discrepancy between these observations and traditional theoretical assumptions about the nature of schizophrenics is rarely, if ever, reconciled.

rotics and normal persons. Simply, the above authors subscribe to the beliefs that: (*a*) the typical schizophrenic patient, as compared to normals, is not deficient, defective, or dissimilar in intrapsychic functioning; (*b*) the typical schizophrenic patient is not a victim of his illness; that is, it is assumed that he is not helpless and unable to control his behavior or significantly determine life outcomes; (*c*) the differences that some schizophrenic patients manifest (as compared to normals) are assumed to be more accurately understood in terms of differences in belief systems, goals, hierarchy of needs, and interpersonal strategies, rather than in terms of illness, helplessness, and deficient intrapsychic functioning. This orientation leads to the expectation that schizophrenic patients do try to achieve particular goals and, in the process, effectively manipulate other people.

There is some evidence in support of this viewpoint (e.g., Artiss, 1959; Braginsky, Holzberg, Finison, & Ring, 1967; Levinson & Gallagher, 1964). Furthermore, a recent study (Braginsky *et al.*, 1966) demonstrated that schizophrenic patients responded, on a paper-and-pencil "mental status" test, in a manner that would protect their self-interests. Those who wanted to remain in the hospital (chronic patients) presented themselves as "sick," whereas those who desired to be discharged (first admissions) presented themselves as "healthy." That is, they effectively controlled the impressions they wished to make on others. Their manipulative performance, however, was mediated by an impersonal test.

Therefore, the following question is asked: Can schizophrenics engage in similar manipulative behaviors in a "face-to-face" interview with a psychologist? That is, will chronic schizophrenics who desire to remain in the hospital and live on open wards present themselves in an interview situation when they perceive that their open ward status is being questioned as (*a*) "healthy" and, therefore, eligible for open ward living, and in another interview situation when their residential status is being questioned as (*b*) "sick" and, therefore, ineligible for discharge? If so, are their performances convincing to a professional audience (i.e., psychiatrists)?

METHOD

A sample of 30 long-term (more than 2 continuous years of hospitalization) male schizophrenics living on open wards was randomly selected from ward rosters. Two days prior to the experiment the patients were told that they were scheduled for an interview with a staff psychologist. Although each patient was to be interviewed individually, all 30 were brought simultaneously to a waiting room. Each patient interviewed was not allowed to return to this room, to insure that patients who had participated would not communicate with those who had not.

Each patient was escorted to the interview room by an assistant, who casually informed the patient in a tone of confidentiality about the purpose of the interview (preinterview induction). Patients were randomly assigned by the assistant to one of three induction conditions (10 to each condition). The interviewer was unaware of the induction to which the patients were assigned, thereby eliminating interviewer bias.

Induction Conditions

Discharge induction. Patients were told: "I think the person you are going to see is interested in examining patients to see whether they might be ready for discharge."

Open ward induction.[3] Patients were told: "I think that the person you are going to see is interested in examining patients to see whether they should be on open or closed wards."

Mental status induction.[4] Patients were told: "I think the person you are going to see is interested in how you are feeling and getting along in the hospital."

After greeting each patient the interviewer asked: "How are you feeling?" Patients who responded only with physical descriptions were also asked: "How do you feel mentally?" whereas those who only gave descriptions of their mental state were asked: "How are you feeling physically?" The patients' responses were tape-recorded. The interview was terminated after 2 minutes,[5] whereupon the purpose of the experiment was disclosed.

Three staff psychiatrists from the same hospital separately rated each of the 30 tape-recorded interviews during two 40-minute sessions. The psychiatrists had no knowledge of the experiment, and they were unfamiliar with the patients; they were told by the experimenter that

these were mental patients residing in the hospital and that as a group they represented a wide range of diagnostic categories.

The psychiatrists rated the patients on the following dimensions: (a) the patient's degree of psychopathology, using a five-point scale ranging from "not at all ill" to "extremely ill"; (b) the amount of hospital control a patient needed, ranging on an eight-point scale from complete freedom ("discharge") to maximum control ("closed ward, continual observation"); and (c) the structural or qualitative aspects of the patient's speech, such as pressure of speech, affect, volume, etc. The score for each patient's speech characteristic was based on the sum of the psychiatrist's rating of 14 Lorr scale items (Lorr, 1953). Each item was rated on an eight-point scale ranging from not at all atypical to extremely atypical verbal behavior.

Predictions

If long-term patients are both motivated to live on open wards and to remain in the hospital and if, in addition, they effectively engage in impression management in order to realize these desires, then the following would be expected:

1. Psychiatrists will rate patients in the discharge and the mental status conditions as being similar with respect to psychopathology and need for hospital control. Mental status interviews are generally used by the hospital to evaluate patients for discharge; therefore, the mental status and discharge conditions offer the same potential consequences for patients. Thus, patients in both conditions will give the impression of being "sick" and in need of hospital control in order to decrease the probability of discharge. The purpose of including the discharge induction was to present the

---

[3] It may be suggested that the open ward induction was meaningless, since no patient enjoying open ward status would believe that he could be put on a closed ward on the basis of an interview. At the time this experiment was being conducted, however, this hospital was in the process of reorganization, and open and closed ward status was a salient and relevant issue.

[4] Mental status evaluation interviews are typically conducted yearly. Thus, patients who have been in the hospital for more than a year expect to be interviewed for the purposes of determining their residency status.

[5] Although, admittedly, psychiatrists would never base decisions concerning mental status and discharge on a 2-minute interview, it was adequate for the purposes of this study (namely, to determine if mental patients effectively engage in impression management). The 2-minute response to the single question provided sufficient information for psychiatrists to form reliable impressions of the patients. Interestingly, the typical mental status interview conducted by these psychiatrists is rarely longer than 30 minutes.

consequences of the interview as explicitly as in the open ward induction.

2. Psychiatrists will rate the patients in the open ward condition significantly less mentally ill and less in need of hospital control than patients in the discharge and mental status conditions. That is, patients in the open ward condition will give the impression of being "healthy" in order to maximize their chances of remaining on an open ward.

Subjects

The mean age of the patients was 47.4 years ($SD = 8.36$). The mean educational level of the group was 8.05 years of schooling ($SD = 3.44$). The median length of hospitalization was 10 years. In terms of diagnostic categories, 43% of the sample was diagnosed as chronic undifferentiated schizophrenic, 37% as paranoid schizophrenic, 10% as catatonic, and the remaining 10% as simple schizophrenic. There were no differences between the three experimental groups on any of the above variables.

RESULTS AND DISCUSSION

The reliability coefficients of the three psychiatrists' combined ratings of the patient interviews were as follows: (a) ratings of psychopathology—$r = .89$, $p < .01$; (b) need for hospital control—$r = .74$, $p < .01$; (c) normality of speech characteristics—$r = .65$, $p < .01$. Thus, it was concluded that there was significant agreement between the three psychiatrists.

The means of the psychopathology ratings by experimental conditions are presented in Table 1. The ratings ranged 1–5. The analysis of variance of the data yielded a significant condition effect ($F = 9.38$, $p < .01$). The difference between the open ward and discharge conditions was statistically significant ($p < .01$; Tukey multiple-range test). In addi-

tion, the difference between the open ward and the mental status condition was significant ($p < .01$). As predicted, there was no significant difference between the discharge and mental status conditions.

The means of the ratings of need for hospital control are presented in Table 1. These ratings ranged 1–8. The analysis of these data indicated a significant differ-

Table 1
Mean Psychopathology and Need-for-Hospital Control Ratings by Experimental Condition

Rating	Open ward		Mental status		Discharge	
	M	SD	M	SD	M	SD
Psycho-path-ology	2.63	.58	3.66	.65	3.70	.67
Need for hospital control	2.83	1.15	4.10	1.31	4.20	1.42

ence between the means ($F = 3.85$, $p < .05$). Again, significant differences (beyond the .05 level) were obtained between the open ward and the discharge conditions, as well as between the open ward and mental status conditions. No difference was found between the discharge and mental status conditions.

On the basis of these analyses it is clear that patients in the open ward condition appear significantly less mentally ill and in less need of hospital control than patients in either the discharge or mental status conditions. Obviously the patients in these conditions convey different impressions in the interview situation. In order to ascertain the manner by which the patients conveyed these different impressions, the following three manipulative tactics were examined: (a) number of positive statements patients made about themselves, (b) number of negative statements made about themselves (these include both physical and mental referents), and (c) normality of speech characteristics (i.e., how "sick" they sounded, independent of the content of speech). The first two indexes were obtained by counting the number of positive or negative self-referent statements a patient made during the interview. These counts were done by three judges independently, and the reliability coefficient was .95. The third index was based on the psychiatrists' ratings on 14 Lorr scale items of the speech characteristics of patients. A score was obtained for each patient by summing the ratings for the 14 scales.

Ratings of psychopathology and need for hospital control were, in part, determined by the frequency of positive and negative self-referent statements. The greater the frequency of positive statements made by a patient, the less ill he was perceived ($r = -.58, p < .01$) and the less in need of hospital control ($r = -.41, p < .05$). Conversely, the greater the frequency of negative statements, the more ill a patient was perceived ($r = .53, p < .01$) and the more in need of hospital control ($r = .37, p < .05$). It is noteworthy that patients were consistent in their performances; that is, those who tended to say positive things about themselves tended not to say negative things ($r = -.55, p < .01$).

When self-referent statements were compared by condition, it was found that patients in the open ward condition presented themselves in a significantly more positive fashion than patients in the discharge and mental status conditions. Only 2 patients in the open ward condition reported having physical or mental problems, whereas 13 patients in the mental status and discharge conditions presented such complaints ($\chi^2 = 5.40, p < .05$).

The frequency of positive and negative self-referent statements, however, cannot account for important qualitative components of the impressions the patients attempted to convey. For example, a patient may give only one complaint, but it may be serious (e.g., he reports hallucinations), whereas another patient may state five complaints, all of which are relatively benign. In order to examine the severity of symptoms or complaints reported by patients, the number of "psychotic" complaints, namely, reports of hallucinations or bizarre delusions, was tallied. None of the patients in the open ward condition made reference to having had hallucinations or delusions, while nine patients in the discharge and mental status conditions spontaneously made such reference ($\chi^2 = 4.46, p < .05$).

In comparing the structural or qualitative aspects of patient speech no significant differences were obtained between experimental conditions. Patients "sounded" about the same in all three conditions. The majority of patients (80%) were rated as having relatively normal speech characteristics. Although there were no differences by condition, there was a significant inverse relationship ($r = -.35, p < .05$) between quality of speech and the number of positive statements made. That is, patients were consistent to the extent that those who sounded ill tended not to make positive self-referent statements.

In summary then, the hypotheses were confirmed. It is clear that patients responded to the inductions in a manner which maximized the chances of fulfilling their needs and goals. When their self-interests were at stake patients could present themselves in a face-to-face interaction as either "sick" or "healthly," whichever was more appropriate to the situation. In the context of this experiment "sick" impressions were conveyed when the patients were faced with the possibility of discharge. On the other hand, impressions of "health" were conveyed when the patients' open ward status was questioned. Moreover, the impressions they conveyed were convincing to an audience of experienced psychiatrists.

One may argue, however, that the differences between the groups were a function of differential anxiety generated by the inductions rather than a function of the patients' needs, goals, and manipulative strategies. More specifically, the discharge and the mental status conditions would generate more anxiety and, therefore, more pathological behavior than the open ward condition. As a result, the psychiatrists rated the patients in the discharge and mental status conditions as "sicker" than patients in the open ward condition. According to this argument, then, the patients who were rated as sick were, in fact, more disturbed, and those rated healthy were, in fact, less disturbed.

No differences, however, were found between conditions in terms of the amount of disturbed behavior during the interview. As was previously mentioned, the psychiatrists did not perceive any differences by condition in atypicality of verbal behavior. On the contrary, the patients were judged as sounding relatively normal. Thus, the psychiatrists' judgments of psychopathology were based primarily on the symptoms patients reported rather than on symptoms manifested. Patients did not behave in a disturbed manner; rather, they told the interviewer how disturbed they were.

The traditional set of assumptions concerning schizophrenics, which stresses their irrationality and interpersonal ineffectuality, would not only preclude the predictions made in this study, but would fail to explain parsimoniously the present observations. It is quite plausible and simple to view these findings in terms of the assumptions held about people in general; that is, schizophrenics, like normal persons, are goal-oriented and are able to control the outcomes of their social encounters in a manner which satisfies their goals.

8

The Nature of Psychotherapy

How do we proceed to change a man?

Freud and his disciples seemed to have the answer. Neurotic behavior, they hypothesized, was guided by unseen, repressed forces. Altering the direction of those forces first required insight. Thus, understand the repressed force, gain insight into it, and you can then change the behaviors and feelings it guides.

But what is it that is repressed? All people respond to stress and conflict. Is there a single force (or small group of forces) that makes him suffer most in conflict? Freud thought there was. He pointed to the vicissitudes of instinct, to the fused and misdirected sexual and aggressive energies resulting from conflict. Others, however, were not so certain that these were the only major casualties of sustained human conflict. Adler asked, what of the sense of competence in rivalry? Sullivan asked, what of the capacity to perceive reality accurately? And Rogers asked about the sense of being unconditionally acceptable to others and the self.

Psychotherapists are practical men, and these differences in viewpoint arose because Freudian psychoanalysis was not an overwhelmingly successful treatment. The data on outcome in psychoanalysis were a long time coming and were difficult to assemble, and though there might be some disagreement regarding the precise meaning of the statistics, it was perfectly clear to all that psychoanalysis was a lengthy, expensive treatment with less success than it should have had.

The failures of psychoanalysis served in part to goad other theorists into an examination of the requirements of human happiness and maturity. The search for a theory of psychotherapy involves nothing less than this. The current status of that examination is summarized in the first selection offered here. It is an analysis of the insight therapies that require some kind of self-understanding in order for the individual to change. The road traveled to achieve such understanding varies from one insight theorist to another, and the nature of the desired understanding varies too. But the agreements between theories far outweigh their differences, and these points in common consist essentially of a search for motives: through the understanding of motives, and perhaps their alteration, comes the release from neurosis.

For quite a while it seemed that the varieties of Insight therapy were ideal for the healing of neuroses, and if these were not sufficient to the task, nothing else was. This was not the case, however, for during much of the period when psychoanalytic therapies were being developed, a small group of people were working on the Behavior or Action therapies. As the success of their efforts grew, they received increasing attention from psychologists, especially during the past decade.

These therapies differ markedly from the Insight therapies in at least two respects. First, they appear to take their inspiration, if not their actual theoretical substance, from the experimental psychologies, and particularly from classical conditioning and extinction. Second, they attempt to change behavior directly, by-passing entirely the search for motive that was so critical to the Insight therapies.

In three of the papers in this section, the reader will not only study the Action therapies, but may also deserve something of the single-mindedness and dogmatism that has characterized the appearance of all "new" psychotherapies. In the second paper, Louis Breger and James McGaugh take this dogmatism to task and analyze the scientific bases for the Action therapies. In the next paper, Stanley Rachman and Hans J. Eysenck, both important contributors to the development of the Action therapies, respond to the Breger and McGaugh critique. Their

response is rather acrimonious, and nothing palliative is offered in the subsequent counter-response by Breger and McGaugh to narrow the gap between these theorists. Thus, two groups of scientists, equally committed to a scientific form of psychotherapy developed from the laboratories of experimental psychology, find little ground to stand together on. Even so, the gap between them is certainly smaller than the one which separates all of them from the psychoanalytic and other insight therapists.

It may well be that a period of encapsulated incubation is necessary for the growth of an idea and that the ideas of psychotherapy require the "protection" of dogmatism because they touch so very near to the aspirations and values of men. But bad ideas are certainly better discarded than protected, and rapprochement between warring theoretical factions may be best of all, especially if it discards the worst and saves the best of two competing ideas. Bernard Weitzman's paper tries to do just this and, in so doing, may anticipate some of the future developments in this field. He seeks a "convincing and elegant penetration of the proper relationship between the data of behavior therapy and analytic therapy," and he presents compelling arguments that such a relationship does exist. Man's behavior can be altered only by a limited number of means, many of which share some things in common, and Weitzman indicates the precise nature of the points in common in the psychotherapies.

Hopefully, these papers and debates reflect a steady movement forward, fed by the interaction between data and theory in psychotherapy. This movement and these debates contribute to the excitement that characterizes research in this area.

The Secrets of the Heart: Insight Therapy

Perry London

Magazines, movies, plays, television programs, novels, short stories, and learned texts have all told much about Insight psychotherapy, often very accurately. Artists, poets, composers, and movie scenarists have all borrowed from it for their work, and if their renderings are less than clear expositions of it, still they are illustrations of its pervasiveness in this culture. It is unnecessary, to say the least, to introduce sophisticated readers to this discipline, for they have been introduced almost endlessly to one or another aspect of it in education, in entertainments, in cultural pursuits, in social relationships, and perhaps in their personal lives. This is even more true in metropolitan than in rural areas, for large cities have the resources to sustain formal societies of psychotherapists, and in such settings the educated public is likely to learn a good deal about the different trademarks of different psychotherapeutic denominations. The less initiated, on the other hand, are more likely simply to equate psychotherapy with psychoanalysis, a confusion which is given unwitting support by the many Insight therapists who simultaneously affirm and deny that they are psychoanalysts, usually by calling themselves "psychoanalytically oriented."

Far from belittling this equivalence, however, I shall argue that the apparently ignorant gathering of many psychotherapeutic sheep into a single fold is more justified than not, and that the many different Insight schools of therapy, instead of differing vitally from each other, as they

allege, in practice are united by more significant commonalities than they are separated by discords. The areas of disagreement are worth some attention because, among other reasons, they have been sources of intense personal argument among psychotherapists and have given rise historically to a large number of schools, some of which feel so strongly about their differences that they avoid contact or interaction with members of rival camps.[1] These differences have also consumed considerable space in the psychotherapeutic literature. But they are here regarded chiefly as curiosa, and one purpose in citing them will be to discount them.

The progenitor of all modern types of Insight therapy, if not of all psychotherapy, is Sigmund Freud's psychoanalysis, and as prototype, it has continued to this day to serve both as bible and whipping boy to all the subsequent developments in this field. It will do as much for this characterization of Insight psychotherapies, for the most vital attributes of psychoanalysis apply equally well to its progeny, justifying the allegation that they are all "psychoanalytically oriented" whether they say so or not.

Insight therapists vary considerably both in the degree of and the reasons for their divorcement from Freudian psychoanalysis. Disciples of the American psychiatrist Harry Stack Sullivan, for example, himself only a vicarious disciple of Freud, are likely to say that they differ

Reprinted from *The Mode and Morals of Psychotherapy*, copyright 1964, pp. 43–69 with the permission of Holt, Rinehart and Winston, Inc. and the author.

[1] They sometimes try to protect patients from them too, as when a Freudian therapist told a patient to make his wife stop seeing a Jungian because "we can't have two kinds of therapy going on in the same family."

radically from Freudians because of their different theory of personality, which asserts a cultural rather than biological origin of neurosis. But they also claim to differ on the technical grounds that the patients of Freudians have to lie down where they cannot see the therapist during their appointments while their own patients are permitted both to sit upright and to face their doctor.

Perhaps the Insight school which claims the greatest difference from psychoanalysis and for the most reasons is that founded by the psychologist Carl Rogers. It is variously known as Rogerian, nondirective, or client-centered therapy, and not only does it fail to specify any origins in psychoanalysis, but it also identifies the most critical aspect of its operations as critically different from psychoanalysis. Like the Sullivan school, it is an American product.

Existential analysis, on the other hand, originates in Europe and has become widely known in the United States only within the past few years. This movement, as its name implies, tries to blend the insights of psychoanalysis with the insights of existential philosophy to elicit insights from troubled people. Without totally disavowing psychoanalysis, it claims to be and do more than analysis.

THE TECHNICAL EQUIVALENCE
OF INSIGHT THERAPIES

To begin with their operations, there are two gross commonalities among all the Insight therapies, one positive and one negative, which dwarf both their many differences and all their other likenesses:

1. The simple allowable instrument of the therapy is talk, and the therapeutic sessions are deliberately conducted in such a way that, from start to finish, the patient, client, analysand, or counselee does most of the talking and most of the deciding of what will be talked about.

2. The therapist operates with a conservative bias against communicating to the patient important or detailed information about his own life, that is to say, the therapist tends to hide his personal life from the patient.

There are considerable differences in the rationale of these procedures among different schools, just as there are differences between them in the actual conduct of many details of therapy. But the foregoing characteristics are still sufficiently vital to determine the general appearance of all Insight therapy sessions, and even a superficial description of them does not require very many qualifications to incorporate the differences from one school to another.

The actual conduct of an Insight therapy session might proceed as follows:

The patient and doctor greet each other and take positions in the doctor's office. If the patient lies down on a couch (classical psychoanalysis), the doctor generally sits behind his head towards the side, in order to see him without being seen. If the patient sits (client-centered, Sullivanian, and so on), the doctor usually sits facing him. In either case, the positions tend to be fixed and constant for all sessions; neither party will ordinarily get up or move around the room during the session, nor will there ordinarily be any physical contact between them. Talk is the legal tender of expression and communication here, talk and not motion; there are therapists who say one must never take notes, but listen in rapt attention, motionless. For some even, talk means only speech and no other kind of words, as with therapists who discourage or forbid patients to make agendas or other notes about themselves or read them during the session; notes are words, but not talk.

As physical positions are established, and patient and doctor get "set," there may be some brief exchange of a conventional social kind, though many therapists frown on this. In any case, it is always desultory and impersonal, about the weather, the traffic, and so forth, a part of the preparatory activity. It is usually introduced by the patient, not the therapist, who probably makes no more response to it than necessary, partly because of its baldly social character, with its implications for his role in the relationship, but more because it is plainly not the *res gestae* of the therapy session. Some talk is worth more than other talk. Thus, if the patient begins the therapy session with irrelevant pleasantries rather than diving headlong into serious things, the casual conversation is as likely to die off into silence as to blossom into more momentous talk.

And the silence is likely to be maintained until and unless the patient begins talking, for it is the rule that, in the ordinary course of Insight therapy, all possible options on decisions belong to the patient. Once the decision to undergo therapy is made, along with arrangements for the business of its conduct, such as hours and fees, there is nothing left to opt except the decision to talk and the content of the talk. The explicit responsibility for both of these is never assumed by the therapist,[2] though he may appear to prod the patient into talking by comments or reflections upon his silence.

Even after the patient has begun to talk, the therapist is unlikely to make very explicit evaluations of his remarks, such as indicating that one thing is important and another not. Nor is he likely to assume even such passive responsibility for the interchange as directly answering most direct questions. Should the client hesitate, for example, to choose between

two things to talk about, the therapist would not choose either one—and if the client named the things and asked him outright which to speak of first, the therapist would almost certainly not say. On the contrary, Insight therapists devote a good deal of their energy, particularly in the early part of treatment, to subtly turning the patient's attention in upon himself and to accustoming him to become completely self-responsible for the entire flow of his consciousness. And this is done by practice rather than precept, for the therapist accomplishes this end by taking on himself essentially the reverse of that role he wishes the patient to adopt, leaving the patient with only the alternatives of carrying the ball himself or having no interaction. The therapist does not discourse or lecture; he merely responds suggestively.

If the foregoing description applies more literally to classical psychoanalysis than to other forms of Insight therapy, it is only because analysis is practiced more consistently and lasts longer than other Insight therapies. The procedural bias of them all lies in this direction, and it has long since been shown that the operations of trained therapists of different Insight schools are relatively hard to tell apart.

Fiedler's study is now more than fifteen years old, and its result apparently still stands, but the practical similarity in therapeutic work of different schools still comes as a surprise to many Insight therapists, the more so as they have been schooled in the comparison of differences. It might be useful therefore, at this point, assuming some general knowledge on the reader's part of individual Insight schools, to explore the semantics of technique they employ and see how critical their differences really are.

PSYCHOANALYSIS AND CLIENT-CENTERED THERAPY

The extremes of technical difference among the Insight school are represented

---

[2] Freudian psychoanalysts are kind enough to try to remove this responsibility from the patient as well by their "cardinal rule of analysis," which is to say whatever comes to mind. Analytic hypnotherapists may go even further by suggesting not only that the patient assume no responsibility for what he says, but also that he does not have to listen to it or remember it afterwards.

by the systems of Freud and Rogers respectively. Their differences in technique are mainly concerned with the therapist's instrument of response, his remarks, and the kind of material to which they should be addressed. Rogerians place primary reliance on the technique called "reflection," while Freudians give similar weight to one called "interpretation." Reflection is a therapist's remarks which tries to communicate that the patient has been thoroughly understood, while interpretation is one which, in addition to understanding, implies some elaboration, explanation, or assessment of meaning by the therapist. When a therapist reflects a remark, he might repeat the patient's very words or synonyms for them, whereas in interpreting a remark he would be freer to say things whose meaning was less obvious from the patient's words.

The distinction between reflection and interpretation is more apparent than real, however, when they are both considered in the context to which Rogerians and Freudians respectively recommend that psychotherapists apply themselves. Rogerians limit the therapeutic attack to the exposure of feelings in whatever connection they are presented to the therapist, while Freudians, though similarly interested in dealing with feelings, are concerned with identifying their sources as well. This difference may seem great, but its significance depends entirely on the extent to which reflections and interpretations can be distinguished from each other and can be seen to have different consequences. Neither is easy to do.

Since feelings are the pivotal contents of client-centered therapy, reflection is meaningfully directed towards feelings alone. The impact of the therapist's reflection of feelings is likely always to be greatest when the relevant feelings are implied rather than spoken, for it is in such situations that the reflective response can be most clearly seen to contain more empathy than mimicry. But to the ex-tent that it addresses the implicit rather than the explicit, the reflection is itself interpretive, for it both assesses and elaborates upon the actual content which has been presented.

Even when the feeling is explicit though, reflection may still be seen as nothing more than a relatively restricted response on precisely the same continuum where interpretation lies—both are counter-remarks or responses of the therapist to something the patient has elected to say. The difference between them would then be quantitative only, and since reflection is quantitatively more restricted than interpretation, its consequences might differ simply by being less effective in communicating the very messages of "acceptance," "empathy," and so on, for the facilitation of which it is specifically prescribed. In effect then, the risk of failing to communicate empathy may be no greater for an interpretation that says too much than for a reflection that says too little. In either case, moreover, the therapeutic effectiveness of the remark will depend upon the interpretation lent it by the patient, not the intention of the therapist. The peculiar emphasis that the Rogerians lay on reflection may thus have no operational significance.

But what of the importance of interpretation, the equivalent cornerstone of psychoanalytic responses? It involves a somewhat greater latitude of content on the part of therapists, but does it have any greater significance than reflection? Perhaps not, especially if interpretation eventuates as a communication from the Freudian therapist of meanings equivalent to those the Rogerian conveys by reflection. The difference between them would then be a function only of the difference between the theories on which they were based. My contention is that these distinctions of devices serve to satisfy some theoretical preferences of the therapists who use them, but without much difference in effects on patients.

The Freudian scheme of things is more complicated than the Rogerian, which suggests that it requires a more complicated approach for its implementation. Since the source of feelings may involve the examination of an individual's history, and since some people find history a less than obvious subject for discussion, the Freudian therapist permits himself greater latitude for comment than does the Rogerian. It takes more to direct the patient's attention where he wants it to go. The Rogerian, on the other hand, theoretically does not want to make the patient's attention go anywhere, which is one reason his therapy is called nondirective. Consequently, he neither requires nor permits himself the same latitude of deliberate interpretation. Of course, he does want the client's attention to be focused on his own feelings, but he regards his part in getting it there as a mirroring function only.

The difference in usage is then a matter of exposing feelings in the proper context. The Freudian requires more interpretive latitude in order to get them to appear in the context of history, while the Rogerian can afford merely to reflect because he will in any case interpret the exposed feelings with no reference to time. These different techniques are, then, both equally closely related to the different theories of the Freudians and Rogerians respectively. And therefore, to the extent that the theories have similar objectives in therapy, the techniques will mean the same thing. Both Freudians and Rogerians would argue that the differences in therapy theories are of cardinal importance, but there are some grounds for questioning this.

In the first place, the Freudian emphasis on history in the development of neurosis is not challenged by the Rogerian scheme; on the contrary, the latter simply does not consider it important to deal with history in the course of therapy, attending instead to phenomenology.

Any contradictions between them must then be sought in the present tense, where the sum of the difference seems to be that the Freudians claim to know a great deal about the structure and content of neurosis and the Rogerians claim that they do not. On the basis of what they believe to be their knowledge of neurotic development, the Freudians deduce a rather plausible scheme of treatment to unravel the neurosis. The Rogerians challenge the psychoanalytic genetics of personality as involving both unknowns and unknowables, but rather than contradicting it as wrong, they seem to believe simply that analytic therapy involves procedures which are unnecessary. The Rogerians then describe a treatment strategy of their own, which limits the therapist to doing only that minimum which is indispensably necessary for treatment to succeed. Their scheme thus ends up as a distillation of the Freudian, which does no real violence either to the theory of psychoanalysis or to the essence of its technique.

The single difference on which the whole technical controversy hinges may be seen as a dispute over the extent to which it is cricket for the therapist to cue the patient, and the difference here is not all that great. Freudians, for example, regard dreams as rich sources of therapeutically useful information and are therefore eager to hear their patients' dreams. But they do not prod the patient to produce them; they are much less likely to ask for dreams in the first place than they are simply to respond in a reinforcing way if a patient spontaneously brings up the subject. Similarly, they believe that the therapy sessions, to be completely effective, must involve a microcosmic repetition by the patient of important emotional experiences of earlier life, with the therapist placed in the same light as were the loved and hated figures of childhood. But the therapist hardly lectures to the patient about this expected transference of feeling, nor does he ask the patient to watch for it and let him know when some such mental spots appear. Essentially, the therapist simply waits for signs of its occurrence, and when they appear, he responds to them in such a manner as to support their exposure without demanding it. The Rogerian may accuse him of wasting time on irrelevancies by fiddling with dreams or history, but of little else, for he himself uses precisely the same general technique: he responds selectively to those unsolicited remarks of the patient that are most critically important for his treatment. The Rogerian tries to limit himself to selecting feeling tones and responding only to them, while the Freudian permits himself to respond to other things as well and to look for connections between things; but both regard the feelings as centrally important, however complicated they may be to untangle.

From the preceding discussion, it is clear that Insight psychotherapists of all kinds will go to some lengths to avoid giving information about their own personal lives to their patients. From the purely tactical side, this practice seems to be corollary to the rule that patient-opted talk be the focus of therapy. In other words, if the patient must do all the talking, then the therapist had better not, and if the patient is to be encouraged to talk about his most private feelings, then it might be ill advised for the therapist to talk about himself in any terms.

But it is not simply relevance that dictates this procedure, and it is anything but corollary—for by and large, the therapist masks himself from the patient outside the therapy session as well as within it, avoiding even casual social relationships. If that is plainly impossible to begin with, he will probably not accept the patient for treatment, and if social contacts later occur unavoidably, he will limit them and probably discuss them at length as part of the therapy. At all events, it is considered extremely improper by all Insight schools for therapists deliberately to undertake or even permit social relationships with their patients or clients.[3] However personal this relationship may be in some sense, it is not in any social sense—for to make it so would be to make it an extension of that ordinary existence in which people are mostly preoccupied by their engagements with other people and with objects, and the recipient of Insight therapy must be permitted to engage with nothing but himself. His interest in the therapist as a person must be transmuted into transference projections for the Freudian and deflected away from himself and onto others who, by virtue of their physical absence, are no more than extensions of the patient's thoughts. And for the Rogerian, this interest must be reflected back onto the patient from a therapist who, operating at his best, is suffused with *empathy*, that is, who feels the patient's feelings proper, not mere sympathetic kinship with them, and who, to the extent that he succeeds, is himself the patient's self in kindly form, so that the patient may learn to see himself in the image of this beautifying mirror.

To summarize the techniques of Insight Therapy: The patient initiates all critical talking and assumes responsibility for it, while the therapist reinforces that talk which is of the most personal and feeling kind, always maintaining himself as an object but never subject of what has its meaning ultimately as an elaborate monologue. He guides the patient, as it were, by following his lead, always

[3] This analysis pays no attention to those mundane reasons which have nothing to do with either technique or theory of therapy, but may still be important, such as the fact that therapist and patient may both be embarrassed by a tea party relationship after the intense interactions of their sessions, or that therapists in particular would just as soon not be bothered with the same people after hours, or that neurotics may be unpleasant company.

without letting his own identity be fully known, and without forewarning the patient where the path will lead, however many times the therapist has earlier guided others over similar paths through similar forests.

But where does the path lead? Curiously enough, for the Insight therapist this is a very secondary question to that which asks from where it originates, for the former is inexorably tied to the latter, and it is towards the clarification of that tie in the patient's mind that the therapist directs his functioning. This takes us to the examination of the theory that underlies the Insight techniques.

THE MOTIVES OF BEHAVIOR

If "insight" is the critical term that incorporates the technical objectives of the psychotherapy system we are discussing, then "motive" is the parallel term to caption the theory of personality it employs. For the cardinal assumption which unites all dissidents among the Insight schools is that the significant problems or behaviors which are the target of psychotherapy are the products of some equally significant motives, and that the solution to those problems and changes of behavior must result primarily from changes in the motives producing them. This same proposition can be put in several different ways, and it may be well to state them, for there is no overstating its importance to the understanding of Insight therapy:

In common parlance, it says that there are compelling reasons for everything one does, that these reasons are the sources or causes of one's acts, and that the only effective way of changing the acts in question is by changing the reasons which compel them.

Yet again, this theory says that people behave in whatever ways they do because they are driven to behave so, and they cannot be persuaded or induced to be-

have otherwise unless they are otherwise driven or their energies reduced.

What motivates a man, what drives him, what his needs are, or his tensions, what gratifies him, what his reasons are, or goals, or objectives—all these terms mean essentially the same thing, and all may be employed equally aptly in the basic formula of motivation theory, that motives determine and dictate acts. In the order of behavioral events, motives seem to occur prior to the acts they motivate. Their priority in sequence is taken as a basis by the Insight therapist, from which, adding on some secondary postulates, he builds an intellectual structure in which motives are prior in significance as well. At the extreme of this position, acts are left dangling as helplessly from their motives as puppets from their strings.

There is a biological basis to this argument which is so familiar to the experience of everyone that it seems like the most elementary common sense: We eat because we are hungry, sleep because we are tired, evacuate because our bowels are full, and so forth. In each case, these acts, which we may plainly observe in another person, are driven or compelled or motivated by things within him which we cannot see, but none can doubt that such acts are a consequence of their motives. And if this is the case in biology, it hardly strains credibility to extend it to psychology, proposing that more refined and less vital drives develop from fundamental ones, so that general hunger may eventually result in a specific craving for meat or bread or ice cream or even for money with which they can be procured. By such reasoning, one may finally reach the point of arguing that all behaviors may be explained by some motives which underlie them, and that all acts seek ultimately to satisfy unseen drives.

If this idea is applied to the symptoms that cause people to undergo psychotherapy, then all such symptoms can be properly understood as attempts to satisfy some need, as expressions of some drive, revelations of some longing or some fear. Far from being pointless, accidental, automated things irrelevant to the essence of one's life, as measles, broken legs, and staph infections are irrelevant, these symptoms are replete with meaning, derivatives of unseen needs, immeasurably significant of causes whose content may be vague, but that lurk beneath the symptom as surely as the symptom can itself be seen.

This view of symptoms bespeaks some hope or confidence that the world is a rational place in which results do not take place without causes, nor consequences without antecedents, and this suggests a strategy for treatment. Not only should the symptom be relieved, but tracing back its course to find its origin may make it possible to quell the flood of misery at its source—while failing to do so, and attacking the symptom alone, runs the risk of damming up one outlet only to leave the torrent free to break through at another point, in another symptom.

The implication for treatment is more ambiguous and has been less important, however, to Insight therapy than the model of disorder implied by this doctrine, for the suggestion that there is no such thing as a meaningless symptom, and that all symptoms have reference to ideas or feelings or impulses which go to the core of a man's being, intimates as well that all of his experiences are somehow important and worthy of his attention. And if he does not engage in any truly incidental behavior, then he must operate entirely on some pay-off principle that directs every motion, however minute, to the satisfaction of some need. But if that is the case, then the definition of a symptom is now clearly reduced to "that behavior which tries to gratify some need and fails to do so." Then the prob-

lem of understanding the nature of the disorder is one of tracing, in detective story fashion, the need whose satisfaction is the symptom's futile aim, and insofar as treatment involves the removal of symptoms, it becomes a matter of trying to do away with the need, which is generally unlikely, or more realistically, of finding and using means other than the symptom by which it can be satisfied. At all events, the belief that acts are essentially the consequences of their underlying motives forces one's attention to a consideration of the "meaning" of any act, for meaning means the pattern of events and circumstances which antecede, surround, and "cause" events. The motive of an act thus is its meaning, and this consideration ultimately demands, as we shall see, that as therapeutic discourse involves motives of increasing significance, the therapeutic situation itself evolves into an exploration of the meaning of one's life. This is least deliberately true, historically, of Freudian psychoanalysis, which is even today "classically" articulated as a system aimed at facilitating personal adjustment, in other words, at reducing psychological distress so that people may conduct their affairs without undue susceptibility to feelings of anxiety and guilt. The search for meaning is fostered more strongly, albeit passively, in the Rogerian system, which is built entirely on a concern with a capitalized, concretized entity called the Self, whose very definition must incorporate the meaning systems people use to judge themselves. But the search culminates actively, explicitly, and deliberately in the writing of the existential analysts, who identify psychological distress as a loss of meaning and treatment as the effort to discover or construct a meaning in life, regardless of the fate of the symptoms themselves. This is the situation which describes the patient who, when therapy is done, says that his tics and headaches are still there, but that his attitude has changed for the better, so that they no longer bother him. However ironical, this is a logical development in a system which posits, as its first principle, that the most apparent behavior is peripheral and less important than some unseen thing that lies behind it. It says in effect that the "real problem" is never what it seems to be.

The assumption of the prepotent effects of motivations lends an aura of indirection to the operations of Insight therapists. Symptoms must be flanked rather than attacked outright, not because they cannot be assaulted directly, nor even because symptomatic changes, when induced, might be unstable in and of themselves, but for another reason: The vital task is, to begin with, the discovery of the complex of motives from which the symptoms spring. And this is no simple matter, for not only are motives less than evident to others, but they are also often hidden from the sufferer himself. The significance of consciousness, or rather unconsciousness, is second in importance in the theories of Insight systems only to that of motivation. The main reason why people continue to manifest their symptoms over long periods of time despite their efforts to change is that their motives are hidden from themselves. The task of therapy is to expose those motives, not so much to the therapist as to the patient himself. The techniques of therapy are then systems for facilitating this exposure, for producing consciousness. And the occurrence in one's awareness of things of which he was previously unaware defines insight.

Insight is thus synonymous with consciousness, and the expansion of consciousness is indeed the productive goal of all Insight therapies. What then is the significance of the widely touted phenomena called unconscious processes? With the exception of classical psycho-analysis, this is a moot point. The Freudian system has assumed that motives were effective in producing neurotic symptoms somewhat in proportion to how thoroughly out of awareness they were, and a large scholarly industry has developed within psychotherapeutic writing and research on personality, as well as in practice itself, for analyzing, exploring, elaborating, elucidating, and otherwise inquiring into Unconsciousness and the mental mechanisms which sustain it. But the secondary position of such processes in Insight systems is clear enough if we keep in mind that unconscious contents are never dealt with directly; they are always inferred, never measured, and thus far, are not clearly measurable.[4] Most important, they are inferred primarily from that material which occurs in consciousness, whether free associations, dreams, or straightforward reports of experience. The very assumption of the existence of unconscious processes can be seen as a means of facilitating the expansion of consciousness, for it suggests that there is an endless supply of content within the mind of the patient which can be coaxed into awareness.

The minimum assumptions of Insight therapists about personality are that symptoms, like all behaviors, are significantly motivated and that their operations are sustained and their removal impeded by a relative dearth of consciousness. The activities of all Insight therapists must therefore involve some kind of insight-producing sequence of (1) exposure, whether by requiring free

[4] There may be important exceptions to this with respect to some physiological and psychological changes that unconsciously accompany some psychological states and may be controlled by them (see Blum and Razran), and (Eriksen). The argument does apply to unconscious "content" that is inferred from verbal reports, however, and is therefore applicable to virtually everything that happens in Insight therapy.

association or passively letting people say what they wish; (2) therapist operation on the exposed material, whether by analytic interpretation or empathic reflection; and (3) consciousness or insight within the patient, whether intellectual, a greater understanding of himself, or emotional, a feeling of awareness of himself.

But what is insight supposed to do in turn? How is it supposed to change anything? We find in Insight therapy a body of techniques of practice and assumptions about personality that are reasonably consistent with each other, and we are returned once more to the question of where the system is supposed to go.

THE USES OF CONSCIOUSNESS

To be fair and accurate, I believe that this question must be properly answered at two different levels, a *scientific* one, whose value now appears chiefly historical, and a *moralistic* one, which may finally propose more questions than it answers. The scientific answer is that insight is supposed to produce relief from the symptoms which have been troubling the person and to provide him with a greater degree of control over himself than he has previously felt. The moralistic answer is that insight is not supposed to do anything, that it is a quantum desirable in maximum amounts and sufficient unto itself, and that its achievement in proper measure represents the point in therapy at which the doctor has fulfilled his responsibility and may discharge his patient as cured. Cured of what? Of ignorance of self.

SCIENCE AND INSIGHT THERAPY

Insight therapy began as a thoroughly scientific enterprise in the work of Breuer and Freud, both at that time practicing physicians deeply concerned with finding means for treating neurotic symptoms. The discovery of the techniques from which psychoanalysis evolved, and the later elaborations of those techniques into a formal system of treatment, was directed primarily at an attack on a limited set of symptoms. Even the intricate personality theory that Freud's genius constructed out of a medley of clinical observations, personal experiences, and literary acumen was intended primarily as a means for deducing how neurotic symptoms arose and for predicting the course that psychoanalytic therapy might take towards their relief. In other words, the system started with the technical problem of the existence of neurotic symptoms and worked itself both backwards to a theory explaining their origins and forwards towards a means of hastening their end; but theory of any kind was, for a long time, entirely adjunct and subsidiary to a concern with curing symptoms, and success or failure of the therapy could be judged entirely in those simple but eminently scientific terms.

Insight came to be regarded as a curative agent because early Freudians viewed the development of symptoms as an immediate consequence of an unconsciousness-producing mental mechanism—repression. Repression prevented its victim from recognizing his motivations, which, continuing to operate sub rosa, eventually expressed themselves in the unhappy form of neuroses. Lifting the repression, permitting consciousness, or eliciting insight, might therefore be expected to relieve the pressure of the motive, so that it would not force its expression any longer in the form of symptoms. Once insight occurred, the symptom might go away by itself, as it were, without further attempts at decision. If not that, the occurrence of insight still meant that the patient would recognize his motives clearly, and this done, he would be able to find ways of fulfilling or handling them which would make the symptoms superfluous, thus atrophying them.[5]

As stated, the foregoing scientific rationale for Insight therapy remains a basic tenet to this day of all those schools of therapy that orient themselves towards psychoanalysis, whether "neo-Freudian" or "classical," for it is just this rationale that justifies the therapy of searching for underlying motives. But there are probably few adherents of this system who nowadays would state its doctrine in such an elementary form, for in that form it is, by and large, invalid. For most of the problems of most people, it seems generally to be the case that the achievement of insight, however detailed and precise, into their motivations, however unconscious, does not by itself solve their problems, reduce their symptoms, or change their lives in any but a gross intellectual or economic sense—they have an enormous body of information for talking about themselves at cocktail parties, and they are out so much and so much in analytic fees.

It is possible, of course, that whenever insight does not produce relief, it is false insight, with the true motives still remaining hidden, or that the insights achieved are valid but incomplete, with their motivations actually more complicated than was thought. Puristic adherents of insight make precisely such claims, and analysts who keep patients in treatment for ten or fifteen or twenty years are implicitly making them.[6] The

concept of "interminable analysis," a problem of some currency among psychoanalysts even during Freud's life, can be sustained by this argument. But if this idea is not false just because it is logically circular, it is still terribly wasteful; in scientific matters, merely reasonable arguments, which this one is, rarely succeed as explanations in competition with parsimonious ones, and a parsimonious argument here would be that insight is just not very effective by itself in solving most therapeutic problems.

Most modern Insight therapists have had too much experience with this situation to insist any longer that the achievement of insight spontaneously melts away all other problems, but they are still prone to approach therapeutic problems by asking about the underlying complexes of motives which produce them and by assuming, in the first instance, that these problems can be treated by insight methods. They are likely to rationalize the use of insight more in terms of somewhat indirect effects mentioned earlier. "True, achieving insight will not necessarily solve all problems or remove all symptoms," they say, "but what it will do is put the patient in a position where he can now control his behavior if he is sufficiently motivated to do so." To some extent, this position suffers from the same circularity as the previous one, for the only obvious index of whether the patient is sufficiently motivated is whether or not the relief of symptoms occurs. If it does not, then it becomes possible to say that the patient's claim was untrue that he wanted an end put to his symptoms, and the plea was

---

[5] The language of classical psychoanalysis is enormously more complicated than my statement suggests, but I do not think its ideas really are. Very many terms are used to describe the prevention of consciousness, such as "defenses," "denial," and "projection," but these are all variants of repression. Similarly, many terms describe the facilitation of consciousness—"abreaction," "working through," "screening," and so on but these all concern variations in the situations, processes, and experiences that culminate in insight.
[6] The figures used here are not literary but literal ones: a colleague recently brought to my attention that the analytic consultant to a dis-

tinguished mental hospital urged the psychotherapists there not to give up "too easily" on their cases. To illustrate, he told how he was now in the sixteenth year of treating a homosexual, though intensive treatment had been going on only for ten. He was pleased to report that the man was finally making such progress that "in another four years he should be able to make a heterosexual adjustment."

itself the result of hidden motives which require exploration. We are then back where we started, but this kind of risk is inherent in any argument that puts much emphasis or credence on the efficacy of unseen and essentially invisible and unmeasurable factors—there is no clear-cut point at which they can be logically excluded as explanations of events.

The importance of the second argument is not in any logical superiority it may have over the first one, but rather in its implication that psychotherapy is a more limited or less specific endeavor than one might otherwise guess it to be. The idea that insight facilitates control rather than removes symptoms reduces the responsibility of the therapist—he is no longer required to seek to cure the patient, but rather to put the patient in a position where, if he so wishes, he will now be able to cure himself!

In one sense, this position is more consistent with the actual techniques of Insight therapists than is the argument that success is defined by relief. Throughout the actual course of treatment, initiative is left to the patient and the responsibility for what is done in the sessions must be assumed by him. Then why not responsibility for the cure as well?

The scientific difficulty with this position is brought on, not by making the patient responsible for the removal of his own symptoms, but by exempting symptom-removal itself from the requirements of cure, for this removes the most clearly measurable means of assessing what psychotherapy has accomplished. When the connection between insight and symptoms is loosened, as it is here, it may be proper to "successfully" terminate treatment with symptoms still present, or conversely, to say that treatment is a failure even with all the symptoms gone unless insight has somehow been achieved. The first case is akin to saying that the treatment cured everything except what bothered the patient in the first place, while the second says that it does not matter if the patient is well unless he is also educated. Finally, since insight is itself applied to hidden motives whose precise quantity is made unsure by the very fact that they are hidden, how does one know how much insight is enough? The scientific status of the therapy depends upon its success or failure in terms of some measurable relationships between the insight it produces and the object towards which that insight is directed, and no object is more obvious than symptoms.

MORALS AND INSIGHT THERAPY

Despite these difficulties, the divorce of insight from such practical effects as symptom removal is not altogether senseless. It does not necessarily follow that, since the existence of symptoms is what starts the search for motives going in the first place, the discoveries which result will ipso facto satisfy the impetus for the search. The fact that Columbus failed to find a new route to India did not make the discovery of America less real or less important. The Insight therapist, by the same token, may propose to start on the motivational path suggested by the symptoms which confront him without prejudice as to where it will lead, with only the faith that it will lead somewhere worth going. But in so doing, he effectively abandons the elementary notions of treatment and cure that are common to patients and doctors alike for most ailments; for all practical purposes, he makes of insight an end unto itself, which, insofar as it does not relate to symptoms, forces a redefinition of his work; this new definition is one that casts him in the mold of a secular moralist. As long as the prescription of insight is rationalized in terms of its effect on some demonstrable set of symptoms, the therapist can claim that his is a technical operation, more or less scientifically conceived and directed at some measurable end. But the more the concrete ends are attenuated, the less is this possible, till even the idea that treatment is a preventive against some future chain of events which can act on a person to produce some specific symptoms is a weakened claim to practice. And when the justification of insight no longer bears on its effect upon some known distress, but on different ends, then the fitness of its dispensation is more a moral than a scientific matter.

The plainest moral problem in its dispensation is seen if we think of insight as having some moving effect upon one's life in every way except in its ability to cure symptoms, for the fact that the doctor is then trying to sell something other than what the patient intended to buy is morally questionable. The same question might apply almost as well, however, if insight cured symptoms too, for so long as it did more than that, it would do other than that; but in such events, it is usually easy to overlook the other effects. In any case, the point here is not so much one of establishing professional ethics, which are often no more than fair trade laws, as of assessing the very nature of the profession. It does not propose that Insight therapists, by doing something other than curing symptoms, are immoral rather than moral, but that they are thereby moralists rather than scientists. It is the generality of their efforts, not their efficacy, which forces this conclusion.

What is the morality they promote? By precept, it is the virtue of insight, or consciousness, or self-knowledge. By example, it is the necessity for each man to assume his own initiatives in the quest for insight and to be alone responsible for its achievement. By implication, it is the right of individuals above all else to live as they choose.

For the Freudian, the unknown self that needs knowing is ultimately one of violent and lustful impulses, denied as one's own, attributed only to the foulest parts of others, filled with the antitheses of the domestic or heroic virtues decreed by the culture and ordered to be exalted by the individual. For the Rogerian, it is a self of discrepancy, where exalted ideals and aspirations are masks for fear, and where deprecation of self is a false and unworthy treatment of an immeasurably acceptable, lovable person. For the existentialist, it is a self alone in a hostile universe who, to become capable of knowledge, must recognize its inevitable aloneness as the first step towards the imposition of meaning upon chaos. Regardless of the content to be exhumed, the supposition of all the Insight theorists is the same: that the self is valuable, that it is worthy of being known, and that its title to explication and intelligibility is its very existence rather than any behavior it undertakes or performance it sets in motion.

That one must in therapy assume initiative himself for the discovery of self is a technicality based partly on the assumption that he will refuse to hear or understand the meanings of self if they are delivered from outside. But it is also a means of reinforcing the moral doctrine of selfhood, by making the patient be alone even within the therapy sessions, by enforcing independence. And the moral goal this tactic finally serves— autonomy, freedom to experience the self, to enhance it, to gratify it, to unbind it, to give it rein to palpate itself and, so doing, to be fulfilled. What concrete acts subserve this end and constitute some therapeutic deeds? Exactly none, or any, or all—what serves the self, or fairly represents it to itself, can qualify.

The virtues of this moral are so popular among educated people in democratic countries that it would be redundant to recount them in any detail. It exonerates the individualism of the Protestant ethic in a more plausible context than could any believing Christian; it grounds the search for the justification of political autonomy in lawful biology; it poses man's right to independence in more elementary and final terms than could the best of eighteenth-century rationalists, offering in drive reduction theory a more "natural" order of things than Encyclopedists or natural theologians ever dreamed; it frees the artist from suspicion of perversity, both by assigning the same perversity to all mankind and by casting on conformism the shadow both of perversity and hypocrisy. It offers the ultimate justification of the individual, and so it has since its earliest, most conservative exposition at Freud's hand; his theory, for example, of the original bisexuality of man can be seen as an attempt to deny the biological sociality of humankind, and to assert the unique right of the individual to survive alone.

In its most modern and extreme form, culminating in existential analysis, Insight therapy strives to establish or restore meaning, not function, to life. This is as much as to say that the object of treatment here is not so much surcease of pain as the establishment of a context of meaning in life of which the pain is an intelligible part. This of course, is what religions have long since tried to do; and it is what, when they failed to maintain enough credibility for the intelligentsia of any age, philosophies tried to replace. Thus Stoicism and Epicureanism in the ancient world when the mystery religions gave up their strength. Now Zen Buddhism and such in the West, nonprofessional counterparts of existential analysis, all alike striving to replace the meanings that were lost with the loss of the extrinsic morality of Judaism and Christianity.

THE PROBLEMS OF INSIGHT MORALITY

The extent to which Insight therapy fails to restore function is the extent to which we must discount its scientific pretensions as an applied healing art, and any such scientific failure raises moral questions in its own right. But the evaluation of function is the bête noire of the Action therapists anyhow, so it is not necessary to look closely at it here. It is precisely to the meanings which are implicit in Insight therapy that the most significant moral questions must be addressed, and these questions, centering around the implications of hidden motives and the status of individualism, must be examined for more than their positive contributions to social philosophy. Insight therapies, particularly psychoanalysis, have become the psychological orthodoxies of our time, and like all orthodoxies, their moral orders have such a familiar ring that, at their worst, they may appear more comfortably familiar than repulsive.

The system proposes, for example, to operate by lending all initiatives to the patient. But does it really do so, or is the proposal itself part of a massive seduction that culminates when the patient voluntarily exercises the therapist's preferences? If the latter, then the seduction may become even more effective when the therapist shares the myth of his own psychological midwifery. By this idea, Insight therapists insulate themselves from all assaults—if they fail to relieve symptoms, they fail only passively, and are not much responsible for a condition whose cure resides within the patient alone to begin with; but if they succeed in changing him otherwise, and in ways that are opprobrious to the patient, or the therapist, or the society, they are not culpable there either—for all they have done is put him in contact with himself by catalyzing his own behavior, and the choices he makes are his, not theirs.

But are the choices really his either according to this system? The seeming endless chain of underlying motives, especially those unseen (and thus demanding *insight*), suggests that he is finally free of choice, or will, or all executive capacities. As Anna Balakian suggests, does not "the preoccupation with the subconscious . . . anesthetize the sensitivities of that faculty which used to be called 'conscience'?" That is, perhaps any moral sense must be attenuated beyond repair by introspection of a causal sequence that puts events so far in time and space from their inception that it makes the notion of responsibility absurd, literally *ab-surd*, rootless, unanchored in any recognizable self.

And if so, then the doctrine which espouses a search for some self hidden beneath the surface of behavior sustains this very rootlessness by claiming that there is a "real self" somehow different from what is seen. The assumption of massive complexity, the mental iceberg that Freud describes, by its denial of the relevance of parsimony and the possibility of measurement, will always witness in defense of nonresponsibility, leaving the individual free to see his self as unsullied and inviolable.

Perhaps the heart of the problem lies here, not in the question of whether the Insight therapist really can confer freedom of choice or even of whether he should want to, but rather that the outcome of his most successful efforts might be a person who, schooled in all the erstwhile hidden references to self, could be best described as a well-adjusted psychopath. This is not to say that such a person necessarily would be, except in the most conventional terms, amoral, but rather that his would be a moral order whose referents lay all within himself. If so, then the core question is whether the broad facilitation of this doctrine would

create individuals who could support a social order. If the methods of Insight therapy are effective in making a person cognizant of his self as an entity, then may he not see it ultimately in isolation? In this sense, the existentialists are quite correct in speaking of "the ultimate aloneness of man." Such a self is, at best, asocial, and its possessor could presumably be as antisocial as might serve his purposes at any time.

If sociality meant crude conformity to mindless automata or to the brutal dicta of aloof tyrannies, then nurturing the lonely self would preserve humanity. But this is not the usual case, and it is least so in societies where psychotherapies all flourish best and individuals are most secure from harm. For those individuals, C. P. Snow puts the problem clearly: "Most of our fellow human beings . . . are underfed and die before their time. In the crudest terms, *that* is the social condition. There is a moral trap which comes through the insight into man's loneliness: it tempts one to sit back, complacent in one's unique tragedy, and let the others go without a meal" (*The Two Cultures*, p. 7).

The asocial implications of Insight therapy have disturbed its adherents as well as its critics, and they have made many attempts, both formally and casually, to incorporate sociality within one or another rationale of Insight therapy. Arguments in this direction sometimes take the form that real selves are discovered finally in interpersonal relationships such as love, or that, since in the therapy situation the self is discovered through the medium of a social relation, a generalized need develops for fulfillment through relationships. Sophisticated theories, like those of H. S. Sullivan, offer these principles as more than articles of faith, and offer plausible descriptions of how the self comes into being in the first place in a social context, implying that its existence must be maintained in one. But none of these answers satisfy the question, for they say simply that the self can make use of sociality—we are asking whether it can be used for society.

In some ways, this question is tangential to the purposes of Insight therapy. For societies exploit people in terms of *functions*, and this system is ultimately directed at *meanings*. A man's social functions are things outside his self, but his existence is finally meaningful only with reference to his self. This argument is, I believe, common to all Insight therapies, and since they tend only to discuss self, not social functions, it commits all of them equally to a moral order in which individuals, pitted against societies, have prior right. But it is a right without mandatory commitment or responsibility, and in this, it differs not only from classical social theory, which, as Phillip Rieff so eloquently describes it, sees society as the true therapeutic agent and good citizenship as the final ·mental prophylactic. It differs too from classical definitions of virtue, both religious and secular, which hinge human dignity, or worthiness, or finally even meaning, to moral codes that lie outside the self, whether revealed in thunder and inscribed in stone, or elected into law by common counsel among peers.

If the latter have no more claim to truth than Insight, and surely age alone can give them none, they at least have the qualities of being represented in functions that are identifiable, and measurable, and—relative to insight doctrines—simple. And this suggests a final question of the moral force of Insight therapy.

The essence of this system is that it rationalizes behaviors in terms of the motives which precede or underlie them. But when the behaviors under study are weak or stupid or vile, representative of some *malfunction*, the distinction between explanation and excuse becomes

confused and arbitrary in fact, if not in theory. There is a danger then, since this system must in any case proceed this way, that the wholesale quest for insight into self which occupies so much of intellect in these times, is not so much a quest for truth at large, or even for control of self, as a grand apology for impotence in fact, which makes the search for meaning but a final desperate substitute for functions which were long since lost.

CONCLUSION

The earliest efforts of Insight therapists, as described here, were directed at the alleviation of symptoms. Later, more attention was paid to making it possible for the patient to increase control of his behavior, including control of some kinds of symptoms. Most recently, effort has been made to help people to discover meanings in their existence that would make life more worthwhile even if their symptoms were quite unchanged. In the first category, symptoms included things such as phobias and hysterical paralyses; the second class expanded the concept of symptoms, or at least of disorders amenable to psychotherapy, to things such as uncontrollable impulses, sexual perversions, and so-called disorders of character; and the third class expanded the scope of the Insight therapist to things such as a general concern with happiness, or death, or security. The last category clearly refers to matters of a traditionally moralistic rather than scientific nature, but it is the second category, with its obvious problems of perspective and of the social consequences of behavior, which requires that the finest distinctions be made between the roles of moralists and applied scientist. If Insight therapists have failed to concern themselves with this distinction, it is at least as much because they operate in a society basically sympathetic to individual liberty and rich and powerful enough to tolerate a great deal of deviation within it as because they have generally wished to reject the role of moralist. The latter is nonetheless true, as should be partly apparent from the very neutrality of their procedures. At all events, it seems plain that their theoretical positions are such that they would be thoroughly committed to a morality of individualism were they to specify their moral role. The single qualifier of importance currently popular among Insight therapists is that people, in doing what they please, should not hurt others. Adherents of Western religions and utopian social visions would, by and large, view this as an inadequate morality, however therapeutic for individuals. Opponents of Insight therapy among professional members of the therapeutic disciplines may see it as antitherapeutic for individuals, however moral.

The opponents of Insight therapy among psychotherapists are, if anything, even less concerned with morals than are Insight therapists. But they are, by their own lights, more concerned with science. Their indictment of Insight therapy has nothing to do with the category of problems of meaning, which they sometimes see as a meaningless concept, and not much more with the moral implications of the second category, problems of character. It is to the problem of symptom removal that they address themselves, proposing stridently that Insight therapy is, in the first place, generally incapable of relieving symptoms, that it is grossly uneconomical when it is successful, and that in those instances where successes are recorded, they have nothing to do with the achievement of insight, but are either accidental or the result of specific *actions* which can be identified and measured. Let us turn our attention now to these Action therapists to examine their origins, their indictments, their systems, and their prospects.

Critique and Reformation of "Learning Theory" Approaches to Psychotherapy and Neurosis

Louis Breger and James L. McGaugh

A careful look at the heterogeneous problems that are brought to psychotherapy points up the urgent need for new and varied theories and techniques. While some new methods have been developed in recent years, the field is still characterized by "schools"—groups who adhere to a particular set of ideas and techniques to the exclusion of others. Thus, there are dogmatic psychoanalysts, Adlerians,

Reprinted from *Psychological Bulletin*, 1965, vol. 63, pp. 338–358 with the permission of the American Psychological Association and the authors.

Rogerians, and, most recently, dogmatic behaviorists.

It is unfortunate that the techniques used by the behavior-therapy group (Bandura, 1961; Eysenck, 1960; Grossberg, 1964; Wolpe, 1958) have so quickly become encapsulated in a dogmatic "school," but this seems to be the case. Before examining the theory and practice of behavior therapy, let us first distinguish three different positions, all of which are associated with the behaviorism or "learning-theory" label. These are: (a) Dollard and Miller (1950) as represented in their book, (b) the Wolpe-Eysenck position as represented in Wolpe's work (1958; Wolpe, Salter, & Reyna, 1964) and in the volume edited by Eysenck (1960), and (c) the Skinnerian position as seen in Krasner (1961) and the work that appears in the *Journal of the Experimental Analysis of Behavior*.

Dollard and Miller present an attempt to translate psychoanalytic concepts into the terminology of Hullian learning theory. While many recent behavior therapists reject Dollard and Miller because of their identification with psychoanalysis and their failure to provide techniques distinct from psychoanalytic therapy, the Dollard-Miller explanation of neurotic symptoms in terms of conditioning and secondary anxiety drive is utilized extensively by Wolpe and his followers. Wolpe's position seems to be a combination of early Hullian learning theory and various active therapy techniques. He relies heavily on the idea of reciprocal inhibition, which is best exemplified by the technique of counterconditioning. In line with this Hullian background, Wolpe, Eysenck, and others in this group use explanations based on Pavlovian conditioning. They define neurosis as "persistent unadaptive habits that have been conditioned (that is, learned) [Wolpe *et al.*, 1964, p. 9]," and their explanation of neurosis stresses the persistence of "maladaptive habits" which are anxiety reducing.

The Skinnerian group (see Bachrach in Wolpe *et al.*, 1964) have no special theory of neurosis; in fact, following Skinner, they tend to disavow the necessity of theory. Their approach rests heavily on *techniques* of operant conditioning, on the use of "reinforcement" to control and shape behavior, and on the related notion that "symptoms," like all other "behaviors," are maintained by their effects.

Our discussion will be directed to the Wolpe-Eysenck group and the Skinner-

ians, keeping in mind that some of the points we will raise are not equally applicable to both. Insofar as the Skinnerians disavow a theory of neurosis, for example, they are not open to criticism in this area.

It is our opinion that the current arguments supporting a learning-theory approach to psychotherapy and neurosis are deficient on a number of grounds. First, we question whether the broad claims they make rest on a foundation of accurate and complete description of the basic data of neurosis and psychotherapy. The process of selecting among the data for those examples fitting the theory and techniques while ignoring a large amount of relevant data seriously undermines the strength and generality of the position. Second, claims for the efficacy of methods should be based on adequately controlled and accurately described evidence. And, finally, when overall claims for the superiority of behavioral therapies are based on alleged similarity to laboratory experiments and alleged derivation from "well-established laws of learning," the relevance of the laboratory experimental findings for psychotherapy data should be justified and the laws of learning should be shown to be both relevant and valid.

In what follows we will consider these issues in detail, beginning with the frequently voiced claim that behavior therapy rests on a solid "scientific" base. Next, we will examine the nature and adequacy of the learning-theory principles which they advocate. We will point out how their learning theory is unable to account for the evidence from laboratory studies of learning. That is to say, the laws or principles of conditioning and reinforcement which form the basis of their learning theory are insufficient explanations for the findings from laboratory experiments, let alone the complex learning phenomena that are encountered in psychotherapy. Then we will discuss how the inadequate conception of learning phenomena in terms of conditioned responses is paralleled by an equally in-adequate conception of neurosis in terms of discrete symptoms. Within learning theory, conceptions of habit and response have been shown to be inadequate and are giving way to conceptions empha-sizing "strategies," "plans," "programs," "schemata," or other complex central mediators. A central point of this paper is that conceptions of habit and response are also inadequate to account for neu-roses and the learning that goes on in psychotherapy and must here too be re-placed with conceptions analogous to strategies. Next we will turn our attention to an evaluation of the claims of success put forth by the proponents of behavior therapy. Regardless of the adequacy of their theory, the claims that the methods work are deserving of careful scrutiny. Here we shall raise a number of questions centering around the issue of adequate controls. Finally, we shall attempt a reformulation in terms of more recent developments within learning, emphasiz-ing the role of central processes.

Science Issue

Claims of scientific respectability are made with great frequency by the behav-ior therapists. Terms such as laboratory based, experimental, behavioral, system-atic, and control are continually used to support their position. The validity of a theory or method must rest on empirical evidence, however. Thus, their use of scientific sounding terminology does not make their approach scientific, but rather seems to obscure an examina-tion of the evidence on which their claims are based.

Let us examine some of this evidence. Bandura (1961) provides the following account of a typical behavior-therapy method (Wolpe's counterconditioning):

> On the basis of historical information, interview data, and psychological test responses, the therapist constructs an anxiety hierarchy, a ranked list of stimuli to which the patient reacts with anxiety. In the case of desensitization based on relaxation, the patient is hypnotized, and is given relaxation suggestions. He is then asked to imagine a scene represent-ing the weakest item on the anxiety hier-archy and, if the relaxation is unim-paired, this is followed by having the patient imagine the next item on the list, and so on. Thus, the anxiety cues are gradually increased from session to session until the last phobic stimulus can be presented without impairing the re-laxed state. Through this procedure, re-laxation responses eventually come to be attached to the anxiety evoking stimuli. [p. 144]

Without going into great detail, it should be clear from this example that the use of the terms stimulus and re-sponse are only remotely allegorical to the traditional use of these terms in psy-chology. The "imagination of a scene" is hardly an objectively defined stimulus, nor is something as general as "relaxa-tion" a specifiable or clearly observable response. What the example shows is that counterconditioning is no more ob-jective, no more controlled, and no more scientific than classical psychoanalysis, hypnotherapy, or treatment with tran-quilizers. The claim to scientific respect-ability rests on the misleading use of terms such as stimulus, response, and conditioning, which have become associ-ated with some of the methods of science because of their place in experimental psychology. But this implied association rests on the use of the same *words* and not on the use of the same *methods*.

We should stress that our quarrel is not with the techniques themselves but with the attempt to tie these techniques to principles and concepts from the field of learning. The techniques go back at least as far as Bagby (1928), indi-cating their independence from "modern learning theory." Although techniques such as these have received little atten-tion in recent years (except from the behavior therapists) they are certainly worth further consideration as potentially useful techniques.[1]

The use of the term conditioning brings us to a second point, that the claims to scientific respectability rest heavily on the attempts of these writers to associate their work with the prestigious field of learning. They speak of something called modern learning theory, implying that psychologists in the area of learning have generally agreed upon a large number of basic principles and laws which can be taken as the foundation for a "scientific" approach to psychotherapy. For example, Eysenck (1960) states:

> Behavior therapy . . . began with the thorough experimental study of the laws of learning and conditioning in normal people and in animals; these well-established principles were then applied to neurotic disorders. . . . It may be objected that learning theorists are not always in agreement with each other and that it is difficult to apply principles about which there is still so much argument. This is only very partially true; those points about which argument rages are usually of academic interest rather than of practical importance. . . . The 10% which is in dispute should not blind us to the 90% which is not—disagreements and disputes naturally attract more attention, but agreements on facts and principles are actually much more common. Greater familiarity with the large and rapidly growing literature will quickly substantiate this statement. [pp. 14–15]

As we shall show in the next section, this assertion is untenable. "Greater familiarity with the large and rapidly growing literature" shows that the very

core of "modern learning theory," as Eysenck describes it, has been seriously questioned or abandoned in favor of alternative conceptualizations. For example, the notion that the discrete response provides an adequate unit of analysis, or that reinforcement can be widely used as an explanation of both learning and performance, or that mediational processes can be ignored are being or have been rejected. Eysenck's picture of the field as one with 90% agreement about basic principles is quite simply untrue. The references that Eysenck himself give for this statement (Hilgard, 1956; Osgood, 1953) do not support the claim. Hilgard presented many theories, not one "modern learning theory," some of which (Gestalt, Tolman, Lewin) might just as easily be said to be in 90% disagreement with behavioristic conditioning approaches. In the same vein, Osgood's text was one of the first to give heavy emphasis to the role of mediation, in an attempt to compensate for the inadequacies of a simple conditioning or one-stage S-R approach. Eysenck seems largely unaware of the very problems within the field of learning which necessitated the introduction of mediational concepts, even by S-R theorists such as Osgood.

These inadequacies center, in part, around the problem of generalization. The problem of generalizing from the level of conditioning to the level of complex human behavior has been recognized for a long time (Lewin, 1951; Tolman, 1933). It is a problem that is crucial in simple laboratory phenomena such as maze learning where it has resulted in the introduction of a variety of mediational concepts, and it is certainly a problem when complex human behavior is being dealt with. For example, Dollard and Miller (1950) began their book with an attempt to explain neurosis with simple conditioning principles. A careful reading of the book reveals, however, that

---

[1] Another early application of behavioral techniques has recently been brought to our attention: Stevenson Smith's use of the Guthrie approach to learning in his work at the children's clinic at the University of Washington. Guthrie's interpretation of reinforcement avoids the pitfalls we discuss shortly, and contemporary behaviorists might learn something from a review of his work (see Guthrie, 1935).

as the behavior to be explained became more and more complex, their explanations relied more and more on mediational concepts, including language. The necessity for these mediators arises from the inadequacy of a simple *peripheral* S-R model to account for the generality of learning, the equivalence of responses, and the adaptive application of behavior in novel situations. We shall return to these points shortly; here we just wish to emphasize that the field of learning is not "one big happy family" whose problems have been solved by the widespread acceptance of a simple conditioning model. The claim to scientific respectability by reference back to established laws of learning is, thus, illusory.

Learning and Learning Theories

We have already noted the differences between the Wolpe-Eysenck and the Skinnerian approaches; let us now examine the similarities. Three things stand out: the focus on the overt response, the reliance on a conditioning model, and the notion of reinforcement. First, there is the belief that the response, consisting of some discrete aspect of overt behavior, is the most meaningful unit of human behavior. While this should ideally refer to a specific contraction of muscles or secretion of glands, with the possible exception of Guthrie (1935), traditional S-R theorists have tended to define response in terms of an effect on the environment rather than as a specific movement of the organism. The problems raised by the use of the response as a basic unit, both in traditional learning phenomena and in the areas of neuroses and psychotherapy will be discussed in the section entitled "What is Learned?" A second common assumption is that the concepts taken from conditioning, either as described by Pavlov or the operant conditioning of

Skinner, can be used as explanatory principles. The assumption in question here is that conditioning phenomena are the simplest kinds of learning and that all other behavior can be explained in terms of these "simple" principles. We shall deal with the problems that arise from this source in a second section. The third assumption is that rewards play an essential role in all learning phenomena. We shall consider the problems that stem from this assumption in a third section.

What is Learned?

Since its inception in the early twentieth century, behaviorism has taken overt stimuli and responses as its core units of analysis. Learning, as the behaviorist views it, is defined as the tendency to make a *particular response* in the presence of a *particular stimulus*; what is learned is a discrete response. Almost from its inception, however, this view has been plagued by a number of problems.

First, findings from studies of perception, particularly the fact of perceptual constancy, provide embarrassment for a peripheral S-R theory. Perceptual constancy findings show, for example, that the stimulus is much more than peripheral receptor stimulation. For example, once we have learned a song in a particular key (i.e., particular stimulus elements), we can readily recognize it or sing it in other keys. We are amazingly accurate in recognizing objects and events as being "the same" or equivalent, even though the particular stimulation they provide varies considerably on different occasions (Gibson, 1950). Although the bases of perceptual constancies (size, shapes, brightness, etc.) are not yet well understood, the facts of perceptual constancy—invariance in percept with variation in perceptual stimulation—are not in question. The related phenomenon of transposition has received considerable attention in animal experimentation. Animals, infrahuman as well as human, respond to relations among stimuli (Köhler, 1929). For a number of years, transposition was not considered to pose a serious problem for a peripheral S-R theory since it was thought that it could be adequately handled by principles of conditioning and stimulus generalization (Spence, 1937). This view has not been supported by later experiments, however (Lawrence & De Rivera, 1954; Riley, 1958). It now appears more likely that stimulus generalization is but a special case of the more general complex phenomenon of stimulus equivalence. The absolute theory of transposition was important and instructive because it revealed in clear relief the nature and limitations of a peripheral S-R approach to behavior. The effective stimulus is clearly more "central" than receptor excitation. The chapters on learning in the recent Koch series make it clear that workers in this area have seen the need for coming to terms with the facts of perception (Guttman, 1963; Lawrence, 1963; Leeper, 1963; Postman, 1963).

Second, the facts of response equivalence or response transfer posed the same kind of problem for a peripheral S-R view. A learned response does not consist merely of a stereotyped pattern of muscular contraction or glandular secretion. Even within the S-R tradition (e.g., Hull, Skinner) there has been a tendency to define responses in terms of environmental achievements. Anyone who has trained animals has recognized that animals can achieve the same general response, that is, make the same environmental change, in a variety of different ways once the response is learned. "What is learned," then, is not a mechanical sequence of responses but rather, *what needs to be done in order to achieve some final event*. This notion is not new; Tolman stressed it as early as 1932 when he wrote of "purposive behavior," and

it has been strongly supported by a variety of experimental findings (e.g., Beach, Hebb, Morgan, & Nissen, 1960; Ritchie, Aeschliman, & Peirce, 1950). As this work shows, animals somehow seem to be able to bypass the execution of specific responses in reaching an environmental achievement. They can learn to go to particular places in the environment in spite of the fact that to do so requires them to make different responses from trial to trial. The learning of relatively specific responses to specific stimuli appears to be a special case which might be called stereotyped learning (canalization) rather than a basic prototype on the basis of which all other learning may be explained.

It should be noted further that even the stereotyped learning that forms the basic model of S-R conditioning does not hold up under closer scrutiny. First, once a subject has learned a stereotyped movement or response, he is still capable of achieving a goal in other ways when the situation requires it. Thus, while we have all learned to write our names with a particular hand in a relatively stereotyped fashion, we can switch to the other hand, or even write our name with a pencil gripped in our teeth if we have to, in spite of the fact that we may not have made this specific response in this way before. Second, even a response that is grossly defined as constant, stable, or stereotyped does not appear as such a stereotyped pattern of muscular contractions when it is closely observed.[2] These findings in the area of response transfer indicate that a response seems to be highly variable and equipotential. This notion is, of course, quite old in the history of psychology, and it has been stressed repeatedly by numerous investigators including Lashley (see Beach *et al.*, 1960), Osgood (1953), Tolman (1932), and Woodworth (1958).

[2] G. Hoyle, personal communication, 1963.

The facts of both response transfer and stimulus equivalence seem much more adequately handled if we assume that what is learned is a *strategy* (alternatively called cognitive maps, programs, plans, schemata, hypotheses, e.g., Krechevsky, 1932) for obtaining environmental achievements. When we take this view, habits, in the traditional behaviorist sense, become a later stage of response learning rather than a basic explanation (building block) for later, more complex learning.

Perhaps this whole problem can be clarified if we look at a specific example such as language learning. As Chomsky (1959) has demonstrated in his excellent critique of Skinner's *Verbal Behavior* (1957), the basic facts of language learning and usage simply cannot be handled within an S-R approach. It seems clear that an adequate view of language must account for the fact that humans, at a rather early age, internalize a complex set of rules (grammar) which enable them to both recognize and generate meaningful sentences involving patterns of words that they may never have used before. Thus, in language learning, what is learned are not only sets of responses (words and sentences) but, in addition, some form of internal strategies or plans (grammar). We learn a grammar which enables us to generate a variety of English sentences. We do not merely learn specific English sentence habits. How this grammar or set of strategies is acquired, retained, and used in language comprehension and generation is a matter for serious research effort; but, it is clear that attempts to understand language learning on the basis of analogies from bar-pressing experiments are doomed before they start. To anticipate, we will argue shortly that if we are to make an attempt to understand the phenomena of neurosis, using analogies from the area of learning, it will be much more appropriate to take these analogies from the area of psycholinguistics and language learning rather

than, as has typically been done, from studies of classical and operant conditioning. That is, the focus will have to be on response transfer, equipotentiality, and the learning of plans and strategies rather than on stereotyped response learning or habituation.

Use of a Conditioning Model

As we indicated earlier, when writers in the behaviorist tradition say "learning theory," they probably mean a conditioning theory; most of the interpretations of clinical phenomena are reinterpretations in terms of the principles of conditioning. Thus, a phobic symptom is viewed as a conditioned response, maintained by the reinforcement of a secondary fear drive or by a Skinnerian as a single operant maintained by reinforcement. Two types of conditioning are involved in these explanations by reduction. The first is Pavlovian or classical conditioning, frequently used in conjunction with later Hullian concepts such as secondary drive; the second is operant conditioning of the kind proposed by Skinner. The use of both of these models to explain more complex phenomena such as transposition, response transfer, problem solving, language learning, or neurosis and psychotherapy poses a number of difficulties.

The basic assumption that underlies the use of either kind of conditioning as an explanation for more complex phenomena is that basic laws of behavior have been established in the highly controlled laboratory situation and may thus be applied to behavior of a more complex variety. When we look at the way conditioning principles are applied in the explanation of more complex phenomena, we see that only a rather flimsy analogy bridges the gap between such laboratory defined terms as stimulus, response, and reinforcement and their referents in the case of complex behavior. Thus, while a stimulus may be defined as an electric shock or a light of a certain intensity in a classical conditioning experiment, Bandura (1961) speaks of the "imagination of a scene"; or, while a response may consist of salivation or a barpress in a conditioning experiment, behavior therapists speak of anxiety as a response. As Chomsky (1959) puts it, with regard to this same problem in the area of langauge:

> He (Skinner in *Verbal Behavior*) utilizes the experimental results as evidence for the scientific character of his system of behavior, and analogic guesses (formulated in terms of a metaphoric extension of the technical vocabulary of the laboratory) as evidence for its scope. This creates the illusion of a rigorous scientific theory with a very broad scope, although in fact the terms used in the description of real-life and of laboratory behavior may be mere homonyms with at most a vague similarity of meaning. [p. 30]

A second and related problem stems from the fact that the behavior-therapy workers accept the findings of conditioning experiments as basic principles or laws of learning. Unfortunately, there is now good reason to believe that classical conditioning is no more simple or basic than other forms of learning. Rather, it seems to be a form of learning that is in itself in need of explanation in terms of more general principles. For example, a popular but naïve view of conditioning is that of stimulus substitution—the view that conditioning consists merely of the substitution of a conditioned stimulus for an unconditioned stimulus. Close examination of conditioning experiments reveals that this is not the case, however, for the conditioned response is typically *unlike* the unconditioned response (Zener, 1937). Apparently, in conditioning, a new response is learned. Most of the major learning theorists have taken this fact into account in abandoning the notion of conditioning as mere stimulus substitution.

More than this, the most important theoretical developments using essentially Pavlovian conditioning principles have not even stressed overt behavior (Osgood, 1953). Hull and the neo-Hullians, for example, have relied quite heavily on Tolman's (1932) distinction between learning and performance, performance being what is observed while learning (conditioning) is but one essential ingredient contributing to any instance of observed performance. The most important, and perhaps the most sophisticated, developments in Hullian and neo-Hullian theory concern the attempts to explain complicated goal-directed behavior in terms of the conditioning of fractional responses. Unobserved, fractional responses (already we see the drift away from the overt behavior criteria of response) are assumed to serve a mediating role in behavior. Once a fractional response is con ditioned in a particular situation, it is assumed to occur to the stimuli in that situation when those stimuli recur. The stimulus consequences of the fractional response referred to as the r_g are assumed to serve as guides to behavior either by serving as a cue or by activating responses or by serving to reinforce other responses by secondary reinforcement. The latterday proponents of a conditioning point of view (Bugelski, 1956; Osgood, 1953) have come to rely more and more heavily on concepts like the fractional response to bridge the gap between stimulus and overt behavior and to account for the facts of response transfer, environmental achievements, and equipotentiality. What this indicates is that a simple conditioning paradigm which rests solely on observable stimuli and responses has proved inadequate even to the task of encompassing simple conditioning and maze-learning phenomena, and the workers within this tradition have come to rely more and more heavily on mediational (central, cognitive, etc.) concepts, although they still attempt to clothe these concepts in traditional conditioning garb. To add to the problem, a number of recent papers (Deutsch, 1956; Gonzales & Diamond,

1960) have indicated that the r_g interpretations of complex behavior are neither simple nor adequate.

When we look again at the way conditioning principles have been applied to clinical phenomena, we see an amazing unawareness of these problems that have been so salient to experimental and animal psychologists working with conditioning.

While the above discussion has been oriented primarily to classical conditioning, the general argument would apply equally well to those attempts to make the principles of learning derived from operant conditioning the basis of an explanation of neurosis and psychotherapy (as in Krasner, 1961). The Skinnerians have been particularly oblivious to the wide variety of problems that are entailed when one attempts to apply concepts and findings from laboratory learning experiments to other, and particularly more complex, phenomena. While we will deal more directly with their point of view shortly, a few comments might be in order now concerning their use of the operant-conditioning paradigm as a basis for the handling of more complex data. When Skinnerians speak of laws of learning, they have reference to the curves representing rate of responding of rats pressing bars (Skinner, 1938), and pigeons pecking (Ferster & Skinner, 1957) which are, in fact, a function of certain highly controlled contingencies such as the schedule of reinforcement, the amount of deprivation, the experimental situation itself (there is very little else to do in a Skinner box), and the species of animals involved. These experiments are of some interest, both as exercises in animal training under highly restricted conditions, and for what light they may shed on the more general question of partial reinforcement. It is dubious that these findings constitute laws of learning that can be applied across species (see Breland & Breland, 1961) or even to situations that

differ in any significant way from the Skinner box.

Use of Reinforcement

Advocates of the application of learning theory to clinical phenomena have relied heavily on the "law of effect" as perhaps their foremost established principle of learning. We shall attempt to point out that a good deal of evidence from experimental animal studies argues strongly that, at the most, the law of effect is a weak law of performance.

Essentially, the controversy can be reduced to the question of whether or not reward is necessary for learning. The initial source of evidence indicating that it was not came from the findings of latent learning studies (Blodgett, 1929; Tolman & Honzik, 1930) in which it was found, for example, that rats who were allowed to explore a maze without reward made fewer errors when learning the maze than controls who had no opportunity for exploration. Thus, these early latent learning studies, as well as a variety of more recent ones (Thistlethwaite, 1951) indicate that learning can take place without reward but may not be revealed until a reward situation makes it appropriate to do so (or to put it another way, the reward elicits the performance but plays little role during learning). Other sources which point to learning without reward come from studies of perceptual learning (Hebb, 1949), imitation (Herbert & Harsh, 1944), language learning (Chomsky, 1959), and imprinting (Moltz, 1960).

Defenders of the point of view that reinforcement is necessary for learning have attempted to handle results such as these in a variety of ways. One has been by appealing to the concept of secondary reinforcement (e.g., a maze has secondary reinforcing properties which account for the learning during exploration). When this sort of thing is done, even with respect to experiments where attempts were made to minimize second-ary reinforcements (Thistlethwaite, 1951), it seems clear that this particular notion of reinforcement has become incapable of disproof. Another way of handling these potentially embarrassing results has been by the invention of a new set of drives (curiosity drive, exploratory drive, etc.) but this too has a post hoc flavor to it, and one wonders what kind of ex-planation is achieved by postulating an "exploratory drive" to account for the fact that animals and humans engage in exploration. In fact, the assumption that exploration reduces an exploratory drive makes it difficult to explain why a rat's tendency to enter an alley of a maze *decreases* after he has explored the alley (Watson, 1961). Finally, there are those (particularly the Skinnerians) who tend to define reinforcement so broadly that neither the findings from latent learning nor any other source can prove embarrass-ing, since whenever learning has taken place this "proves" that there has been reinforcement. To better understand this problem, however, we had best look for a moment at the general problem of de-fining reinforcement in a meaningful way.

Obviously, if the view that reinforce-ment is necessary for learning is to have any meaning, what constitutes a reinforce-ment must be defined independently from the learning situation itself. There has been a great deal of difficulty in getting around a circular definition of the law of effect, and it might be worthwhile to examine some of the attempts that have been made in the past.

One of the best known was the attempt to relate the reinforcing properties of stimuli to their drive reducing character-istics (Hull, 1951). The drive-reduction model has had to be abandoned, how-ever, because of evidence from a variety of areas including latent learning, sensory preconditioning (Brogden, 1939), and novelty and curiosity (Berlyne, 1960). Other evidence such as that of Olds and Milner (1954) on the effect of direct brain stimulation have strengthened the conviction that the drive-reduction in-terpretation of reinforcement is inade-quate; and, in fact, original adherents of this view have begun to abandon it (e.g., Miller, 1959).

The other most frequent solution to the circularity problem has been by way of the "empirical law of effect," an ap-proach typified by Skinner's definition of reinforcement as any stimulus that can be demonstrated to produce a change in response strength. Skinner argues that this is not circular since some stimuli are found to produce changes and others are not, and they can subsequently be classi-fied on that basis. This seems to be a reasonable position if it is adhered to; that is, if care is taken to define reinforce-ment in terms of class membership *inde-pendently* of the observations that show that learning has taken place. When we examine the actual use of the term rein-forcement by Skinner (see especially *Verbal Behavior*, 1957) and by other Skinnerians (Lundin, 1961), we find that care is only taken in this regard within the context of animal experiments, but that when the jumps are made to other phenomena, such as language and psy-chotherapy, care is usually *not* taken to define reinforcement independently from learning as indicated by response strength. This leads to a state of affairs where any observed change in behavior is said to occur *because of* reinforcement, when, in fact, the change in behavior is itself the only indicator of what the reinforcement has been. Chomsky (1959) reviews the use of the concept of reinforcement by Skinner with regard to language and reaches the following conclusion:

> From this sample, it can be seen that the notion of reinforcement has totally lost whatever objective meaning it may ever have had. Running through these ex-amples, we see that a person can be reinforced though he emits no response

at all, and the reinforcing "stimulus" need not impinge on the reinforced person or need not even exist (it is sufficient that it be imagined or hoped for). When we read that a person plays what music he likes (165), says what he likes (165), thinks what he likes (438–9), reads what books he likes (163), etc., *because* he finds it reinforcing to do so, or that we write books or inform others of facts *because* we are reinforced by what we hope will be the ultimate behavior of reader or listener, we can only conclude that the term "reinforcement" has a purely ritual function. The phrase "X is reinforced by Y (stimulus, state of affairs, event, etc.)" is being used as a cover term for "X wants Y," "X likes Y," "X wishes that Y were the case," etc. Invoking the term "reinforcement" has no explanatory force, and any idea that this paraphrase introduces any new clarity or objectivity into the description of wishing, liking, etc., is a serious delusion. [pp. 37–38]

This problem is exemplified in the area of psychotherapy by the attempts to use the studies of verbal conditioning (Krasner, 1958) as analogues to psychotherapy. First we should note that if these studies are taken at face value (i.e., if subjects are conditioned to increase the emission of certain responses because of reinforcement, without their awareness of this fact) it appears that a simple conditioning model is inadequate since subjects are presumably responding in terms of a class of responses (e.g., plural nouns, etc.) rather than in terms of a specific response (e.g., bar press), such classes implying response transfer and mediation. Second, and more to the point, a number of recent investigators (Eriksen, 1962) have begun to question whether verbal conditioning does occur without the subject's awareness. If it does not, the whole phenomenon begins to look like nothing more than a rather inefficient way to get subjects to figure out what the experimenter wants them to do (telling them directly to emit plural nouns would prob-

ably be much more efficient) after which they can decide whether they want to do it or not. In any case, there seems to be enough question about what goes on in verbal conditioning itself to indicate that it cannot be utilized as a more basic explanation for complex phenomena such as psychotherapy. Psychotherapists of many persuasions would agree that rewards of some kind are important in work with patients. Thus, the view that the psychotherapist is a "reinforcement machine" is trivial. The difficult problems are in specifying just what therapist activities are rewarding, in what ways, to what sorts of patients, and with what effects.

The above discussion should make clear that the use of the concept of reinforcement is only of explanatory usefulness when it is specified in some delimited fashion. As an empirical law of performance almost everyone in and out of psychology would accept it, including Lewin, Freud, Tolman, and others outside the traditional S-R movement. But this amounts to saying nothing more than that some events, when presented, tend to increase the probability of responses that they have followed. The hard job, but the only one that will lead to any meaningful use of the concept of reinforcement, is specifying what the various events called reinforcers have in common. Some have argued that since this is such a difficult task, we should restrict ourselves to listing and cataloging so-called reinforcers. But this is nearly impossible, in a general way, because reinforcers differ from individual to individual, from species to species, from situation to situation, and from time to time (the saying "one man's meat is another man's poison" is trite but true). Meaningful analysis must stem from a comprehensive study of the particular learning phenomena in question, whether it is language learning, the development of perceptual and perceptual-motor skills (Fitts, 1964; Hebb, 1949), the acquisition of particular species behavior patterns during critical periods of development (Scott, 1962), the learning of a neurosis, or the learning that takes place during psychotherapy. Experience with all of these phenomena has revealed that different kinds of events seem to be involved and that these can only be understood in the context of the phenomena in question. Lumping all these events together under the single term reinforcement serves to muddle rather than to clarify understanding.

The staunch reinforcement adherent might respond that all these complicated arguments may be true but we can ignore them, since all we are really interested in is predicting what the organism will do, and we can do this when we know the organism's reinforcement history. The answer to this is that the experimental literature does not support such a claim; rather, it shows that, in many instances, performance *cannot* be predicted on the basis of a knowledge of the history of reinforcement.

Latent learning studies indicate this quite clearly. Perhaps of more interest are the findings of discrimination-reversal learning studies (Goodwin & Lawrence, 1955; Mackintosh, 1963). Here we find that subjects that have been trained on a series of discrimination reversals learn to select the correct stimulus with very few errors even though they may have been rewarded *much more frequently and more recently for responding to another stimulus.* Similarly, in the double drive discrimination studies (Thistlethwaite, 1951) animals chose alleys leading to food when they were hungry and water when they were thirsty, even though they have been rewarded equally frequently on the alleys on previous trials. In other words, "what is learned" was not equivalent with "reinforcement history."

The law of effect is not disproved by these studies; it is merely shown to be irrelevant.

To summarize: The "law of effect," or reinforcement, conceived as a *"law of learning,"* occupies a very dubious status. Like the principles of conditioning, it appears to be an unlikely candidate as an explanatory principle of learning. As a strong law of learning it has already been rejected by many of the theorists who previously relied on it. As an empirical "law of *performance*" it is noncontroversial, but usually so generally stated as to be of little explanatory value.

Conception of Neurosis

In this section we will explicate the conception of neurosis that forms the basis of the behavior-therapy approach (particularly of the Wolpe-Eysenck group) and attempt to demonstrate its inadequacies both in terms of learning theory and as a way of accounting for the observed facts of neurosis. Our argument in the first instance will be that the conception of neurosis in terms of symptoms and anxiety parallels the general conception of learning in terms of overt responses, conditioning, and secondary drives, and suffers from the same inadequacies that we have outlined in the preceding section. With regard to the facts of neurosis, we will argue that the behavior-therapy position is inadequate at a descriptive level as well as being conceptually incorrect. It should be pointed out again that we are discussing the explanation or theory of neurosis here and not the techniques used by the behavior therapists. The strict Skinnerian may excuse himself at this point if he adheres to a "no-theory" position and is only concerned with the effects of environmental manipulation. Furthermore, certain techniques themselves may be useful and have some of the effects attributed to them regardless of the theory.

In its essence, the conception of neurosis put forth by the behavior therapists is that neuroses are conditioned responses or habits (including conditioned anxiety) and *nothing else*, though it should be noted that they do not adhere to this argument when they describe the success of their methods. Wolpe, for example, while ostensibly treating overt symptoms, describes his patients as becoming more productive, having improved adjustment and pleasure in sex, improved interpersonal relationships, and so forth. The argument that removal of a troublesome symptom somehow "generalizes" to all of these other areas begs the question. Their conception is typically put forth as an alternative to a psychodynamic viewpoint, which they characterize as resting on a distinction between symptoms and underlying causes (unconscious conflicts, impulses, defenses, etc.). They stress the point that inferences about underlying factors of this sort are unnecessary and misleading and that a more parsimonious explanation treats symptoms (which are typically equated with behavior or that which can be objectively observed) as the neurosis per se. They argue that by equating neurosis with symptoms, and symptoms, in turn, with habits (conditioned responses), they are able to bring "modern learning theory" with its "well-established laws" to bear on the understanding and treatment of neurosis.

As we have labored to show in the preceding section, the well-established laws of learning to which they refer have considerable difficulty within the area of simple animal behavior. More specifically, it seems clear that a wide variety of behaviors (from maze learning to more complex forms) cannot be adequately dealt with when the overt response and conditioned habit are the units of analysis. Furthermore, their learning position leads the behavior therapists into postulating an isomorphic relationship between antecedent learning and present behavior

in which observed differences are accounted for in terms of principles of generalization. This is a key issue, and we shall explore it a little further at this time.

Much of the behaviorist conception of neurosis rests on a rejection of the distinction between symptoms and underlying causes (Eysenck, 1960) as typified by Yates' (1958) argument against "symptom substitution." By focusing attention on overt symptoms and banishing all underlying causes, however, the behavior therapists are faced with the same problem that has long confronted behaviorism; namely, the difficulty of explaining how *generality* of behavior results from specific learning experiences. The problem of *generality* (i.e., as exemplified by the facts of transposition and response transfer) has, in fact, brought about the downfall of peripheral S-R learning, of the conditioned habit as a basic unit, and tangentially, is leading to the dethroning of the law of effect. With regard to neurosis, this view has led the behavior therapists into the position where they must posit a specific learning experience for each symptom of a neurosis. They have partly avoided this problem by focusing their attention on those neuroses that can be described in terms of specific symptoms (bed-wetting, if this is a neurosis, tics, specific phobias, etc.) and have tended to ignore those conditions which do not fit their model, such as neurotic depressions, general unhappiness, obsessional disorders, and the kinds of persistent interpersonal entanglements that characterize so many neurotics. This leaves them free to explain the specific symptom in terms of a specific learning experience, as, for example, when a fear of going outdoors is explained in terms of some previous experience in which the stimulus (outdoors) has been associated with (conditioned to) something unpleasant or painful and has now, through generalization, spread to any response of going outdoors. As our previous analysis should make clear, however, even a simple conceptualization such as this, in terms of stimuli, responses, and conditioning is extremely cumbersome and begs the important questions. Within an S-R framework, in which generalization occurs along the dimension of physical stimulus similarity, it is difficult, if not impossible, to show how a previous experience such as being frightened in the country as a child could generalize to the "stimulus" outdoors without a great deal of *mediation* in which the concept of "outdoors" carried most of the burden of generalization. As we have pointed out, most workers in the field of learning recognize this and rely heavily on mediational concepts in their explanations of complex behavior. Dollard and Miller (1950), for example, return again and again to mediational explanations once they move beyond the "combat neuroses" which lend themselves more readily to a simple isomorphic explanation.

A second important facet of the behavorist conception of neurosis is the use of the concept of anxiety as a secondary drive. Here, Wolpe and Eysenck and some others seem to follow the explanatory model laid down by Dollard and Miller. Anxiety is viewed as the main motivating force for symptoms and, in general, occupies a central place in their thinking. Briefly, it is worth pointing out that the concept of drive reduction, the distinction between primary drives and secondary drives, as well as the early thinking about the uniquely persistent qualities of fear-motivated behavior have had serious difficulty within learning theory (Watson, 1961; Solomon, 1964). The use of these concepts to explain clinical phenomena thus rests on an exceedingly shaky foundation.

Let us turn our attention now to the phenomena of neuroses. We shall try to point out that underlying the dispute over symptoms versus underlying causes is a real difference in definition that arises at the descriptive level, which, in a sense, antedates disagreements at the level of theory and explanation.

To keep the presentation simple, we will adopt the terms psychodynamic to refer to all those theorists and therapists, following Freud, whose view of neurosis and its treatment deals with motives (conscious and unconscious), conflict, etc. This covers a wide variety of workers, in addition to the more or less traditional followers of Freud, including Sullivan and his adherents (Fromm-Reichman, 1950), other neo-Freudians, and that broad group of psychiatrists and clinical psychologists who have been strongly influenced by the Freudian and neo-Freudian viewpoints even though they may not claim allegiance to any of the formal schools.

The point we wish to make here is that disagreement between the behaviorist and psychodynamic viewpoints seems to rest on a very real difference at the purely descriptive or observational level. The behaviorist looks at a neurotic and sees specific symptoms and anxiety. The psychodynamicist looks at the same individual and sees a complex intra- and interpersonal mode of functioning which may or may not contain certain observable fears[3] or certain behavioral symptoms such as compulsive motor acts. When the psychodynamicist describes a neurosis, his referent is a cohering component of the individual's functioning, including his characteristic ways of interacting with other people (e.g., sweet and self-effacing on the surface but hostile in covert ways), his characteristic modes of thinking and

[3] The term anxiety is frequently used as a theoretical inference, i.e., a patient deals with personal material in an overly intellectual fashion, and this is described as a defense mechanism—intellectualization—whose purpose is to ward off anxiety.

perceiving (e.g., the hysteric who never "remembers" anything unpleasant, the obsessive whose memories are overelaborated and circumstantial, etc.), characteristic modes of fantasy and dreaming, a variety of secondary gain features, and the like. Specific or isolatable symptoms may sometimes be a part of such an integrated neurotic pattern, but, even viewed descriptively, they in no sense constitute the neurosis per se.

So far, we have considered the behavior therapists' position at face value. In actuality, a good case can be made that they *behave* in a way which is quite inconsistent with their own position. A specific example, taken from one of Wolpe's own case descriptions, will illustrate this point, and, at the same time, show what the psychodynamicist sees when he looks at a neurotic. Wolpe (1960) presents the following case:

> Case 5—An attractive woman of 28 came for treatment because she was in acute distress as a result of her lovers' casual treatment of her. Every one of very numerous love affairs had followed a similar pattern—first she would attract the man, then she would offer herself on a platter. He would soon treat her with contempt and after a time leave her. In general she lacked assurance, was very dependent, and was practically never free from feelings of tensions and anxiety.

What is described here is a complex pattern of interpersonal relationships, psychological strategies and misunderstandings (such as the way she became involved with men, the way she communicated her availability to them, her dependency, etc.), expectations that she had (presumably that men would not react with contempt to her generosity, that being dependent might lead to being taken care of, etc.), and thoughts and feelings about herself (lack of assurance, acute distress, etc.). Many of the statements about her (e.g., the description of the course of

her love affairs) are abbreviations for very complex and involved processes involving two people interacting over a period of time. It is this, the psychodynamicist would argue, that *is* the neurosis. The tension and anxiety may be a part of it in this particular case (though there might be other cases in which there is no complaint of anxiety but, rather, its reverse—seeming inability to "feel" anything)—but it is secondary and can be understood only in relation to the other aspects of the patient's functioning. Wolpe's case histories are classic testaments to the fact that he cannot, and does not, apply the symptom approach when working with actual data. As a further example, consider the argument against a symptom-substitution point of view (Yates, 1958) in which it is implied that anything other than symptoms is some sort of metaphysical inference. While it may be true that theories such as psychoanalysis deal with a number of inferential and higher-order constructs in their attempts to integrate the complex mass of data that constitutes a neurosis, it is also true that much more than symptoms exist at the level of observation. Secondary-gain features of a neurosis, in which it is apparent that a variety of goals may be served by a set of interchangeable symptoms are the rule in most neurotic individuals. We are not defending the view (attributed to psychoanalysis by Yates) that if one symptom is removed another pops up to take its place; rather, we are arguing that the empirical phenomena of neurosis does not fit the symptom or response theory, but is much more compatible with a theory built around central mediators. Whether unconscious conflicts and defense mechanisms are adequate ways of conceptualizing the problem is an entirely separate question. What is clear is that a view stressing central mediators in which specific responses are seen as equipotential means of reaching certain goals is necessary to encompass the data of neurosis just as it has proven necessary to encompass the phenomena of animal learning.

To sum up, it would seem that the behaviorists have reached a position where an inadequate conceptual framework forces them to adopt an inadequate and superficial view of the very data that they are concerned with. They are then forced to slip many of the key facts in the back door, so to speak, for example, when all sorts of fantasy, imaginary, and thought processes are blithely called responses. This process is, of course, parallel to what has gone on within S-R learning theory where all sorts of central and mediational processes have been cumbersomely handled with S-R terminology (e.g., Deutsch, 1956). Thus, we have a situation where the behavior therapists argue strongly against a dynamic interpretation of neurosis at some points and at other points behave as if they had adopted such a point of view. This inconsistency should be kept in mind in reading the next section in which we evaluate the claims of success put forth by the behaviorist group. Insofar as there is disagreement as to what constitutes the descriptive facts of neurosis, it makes little sense to compare the effectiveness of different methods. However, since the behaviorist group adopts very broad (or psychodynamic, if you will) criteria for improvement, and since their *techniques* may have some effectiveness, in spite of theoretical and conceptual inadequacies, it is crucial that we look carefully at the empirical results that they lay claim to.

Claims of Success

While much of the writing of the behavior therapists consists of arguments and appeals to principles of science and learning, the claims that are made for the success of the methods seem open to empirical analysis. No doubt a great deal of the appeal of behavior therapy lies right here. Here seem to be methods whose application can be clearly described (unlike such messy psychodynamic methods as "handling countertransference" or "interpreting resistance"), whose course is relatively short, and which seem to achieve a large number of practical results in the form of removal of symptoms. Wolpe (1960), for example, presents the following data: of 122 cases treated with behavioral techniques, 44% were "apparently cured," 46% were "much improved," 7% were "slightly or moderately improved," and 3% were "unimproved." Combining categories, he claims 90% "apparently cured or much improved," and 10% "improvement moderate, slight or nil." (Criteria of improvement consists of "symptomatic improvement, increased productiveness, improved adjustment and pleasure in sex, improved interpersonal relationships and ability to handle ordinary psychological conflicts and reasonable reality stresses.")

He compares this with data from the Berlin Psychoanalytic Institute (Knight, 1941) which shows 62–40.5% in the first category and 38–59.5% in the second. Wolpe concludes, as have others (Bandura, 1961; Eysenck, 1960; Lazarus, 1963), that this demonstrates the superiority of the behavior therapy methods. The fact that the psychoanalytic methods showed as much as 62% improvement is explained as being due to whatever accidental "reciprocal inhibition" occurred during the therapy. (There is, however, no analysis or description of how this might have happened.) The behavioral methods achieve superior results presumably because of the more explicit application of these techniques.

It is fair to say that if these results can be substantiated they present a very strong argument in favor of behavioral *techniques*—even granting the theoretical and empirical inconsistencies we have discussed. However, we must ask if these claims are any better substantiated than those made by the practitioners of other methods of psychotherapy. Insofar as claims such as Wolpe's are based on uncontrolled case histories, they may reflect the enthusiasm of the practitioner as much as the effect of the method. History shows that new methods of therapy (ECS, tranquilizing drugs, as well as various schools of psychotherapy) have been oversold by their original proponents. Thus, a careful look at what lies behind the claims of the behavior-therapy group is in order.

The following does not purport to be a comprehensive review of the behavior-therapy literature. Rather, it is based on a survey of all the studies reported in the two reviews that have appeared (Bandura, 1961; Grossberg, 1964). The most striking thing about this large body of studies is that they are almost all case studies. A careful reading of the original sources reveals that only one study (Lang & Lazovik, 1963) is a controlled experiment, and here the subjects were not neurotics but normal college students. Thus, most of the claims (including those of Wolpe which have been widely quoted) must be regarded as no better substantiated than those of any other enthusiastic school of psychotherapy whose practitioners claim that their patients get better. Behavior therapy has appeared to differ on this score because of its identification with experimental psychology and with "well-established laws of learning." We have already dealt with this issue, so let us now turn to some problems in evaluating psychotherapy as a technique.

The problems here are essentially those of control, and they may be broken down into three areas: (*a*) sampling biases, (*b*) observer bias, and (*c*) prob-

lems of experimental control. While research in psychotherapy presents particular difficulties in controlling "experimental input," more sophisticated workers (Frank, 1959) have attempted to deal with at least the sampling and observer problems. It thus comes as somewhat of a surprise that the behavior-therapy workers, despite their identification with experimental psychology, base their claims on evidence which is almost totally lacking in any form of control. Let us examine these issues in greater detail.

Sampling biases. Obviously a claim such as Wolpe's of 90% success has meaning only when we know the population from which the sample of patients was drawn and the way in which they were selected. Ideally, a comparison of treatment techniques would involve the random assignment of patient from a common population pool to alternative treatments. Since, in practice, this is rarely feasible, it is essential for anyone making comparisons of different treatment methods to, at the very least, examine the comparability of the populations *and* of the methods used in selecting from these populations. Neither Wolpe's data nor that of Lazarus (1963) contains this evidence. Wolpe reports, for example, that:

Both series (70 patients reported on in 1952 and 52 patients reported on in 1954 on which the 90% figure is based) include only patients whose treatment has ceased after they have been afforded a reasonable opportunity for the application of the available methods; i.e., they have had as a minimum both a course of instruction on the changing of behavior in the life situation and a proper initiation of a course of relaxation-desensitization. This minimum takes up to about 15 interviews, including anamestic interviews and *no patient who has had 15 or more interviews has been omitted from the series.* [emphasis added]

We may conclude from this that some patients (how many we do not know) having up to 14 interviews have been excluded from the sample—a procedure highly favorable to the success of the method but which violates the simplest canons of sampling. Wolpe's final sample of 122 consists of those patients most likely to show improvement, since both they and he were satisfied enough with the first 14 (or less) interviews to warrant proceeding further. Those patients least likely to improve are those most likely to drop out early (14 sessions or less) and not be included in the computation of success rate. The fact that a large number of poor-prognosis patients would very likely be eliminated during these early sessions is supported by a variety of research findings (Strickland & Crowne, 1963), which show that most dropping-out of untreatable or unsuccessful cases occurs during the first 10 sessions. This serious sampling bias would be expected to spuriously inflate the percent showing improvement.

When we add this to whatever unknown factors operate to delimit the original population (presumably there is some self-selection of patients who seek out this form of treatment), it becomes apparent that little confidence can be given to the reports of success.

Observer bias. Psychologists have long been aware that human beings are fallible observers, particularly when they have predispositions or vested interests to protect. In controlled studies, we try to protect judges from their own biases by not acquainting them with the hypotheses, or with the nature of the groups they are judging, or by using blind and double-blind designs. This problem is particularly acute with regard to psychotherapy because both therapist and patient have investments of time, involvement, competence, and reputation to protect. For these reasons, workers in the area have become extremely skeptical of claims put forth for any method which rests on the uncontrolled observation of the person administering the treatment. At a minimum we expect some sort of external evidence. Beyond this minimum we hope for an independent judge who can compare differentially treated groups without knowing which is which.

In addition, there is the problem of the patient's freedom to report effects which may be seriously curtailed when all his reports go directly to the person who has treated him. It seems reasonable to assume that some patients are prevented from expressing dissatisfaction with treatment when they must report directly to the therapist, either because they do not want to hurt his feelings, or are afraid, or are just saying what they think is being demanded of them, or are being polite, or for some other reason. Again, it would be highly appropriate to provide the patients with the opportunity of reporting results in a situation as free from such pressure as possible.

Examination of the 26 studies reviewed by Bandura reveals a surprising lack of concern with these problems. Of the 26 studies sampled, only 12 report evaluation of results by persons other than the treating therapist; four of these use ratings of the hospital staff (who may be acquainted with the treatment), four use mothers or parents reporting on their children to the treating therapist, one is a wife reporting on her husband to the therapist, and three use a second observer. Obviously, whatever factors enter in to cause observer and reporter biases are allowed full reign in most of these cases. While we cannot conclude from this that the reported results are *due to* observer and reporter biases (as is clearly indicated with the sampling biases), it is impossible to rule them out. Furthermore, a great deal of evidence from many areas of psychology leads us to be very skeptical of claims in which biases of this sort go uncontrolled.

Experimental control. While control of sampling and observer effects are basic to a wide variety of research activities, including field and clinical research, more exacting control over experimental conditions has long been the sine qua non of the laboratory methods of experimental psychology. The power of the experimental method stems, in part, from keeping careful control over all but a few conditions, which are experimentally varied, with the subsequent effects of these variations being observed. Since psychotherapy is not a controlled experiment, it is probably unfair to expect this type of control. However, there are more and less accurate descriptions of what goes on during any form of therapy, and we can demand as accurate a description as possible in lieu of experimental control. Thus, while we are led to believe that methods, such as counterconditioning, extinction of maladaptive responses, methods of reward, and the like, are applied in a manner analogous to their laboratory counterparts—examination of what is *actually done* reveals that the application of the learning techniques is embedded in a wide variety of activities (including many of the traditional therapy and interview techniques) which make any attribution of effect to the specific learning techniques impossible. Let us consider a few examples. From Wolpe (1960):

Case 4—The patient had 65 therapeutic interviews, unevenly distributed over 27 months. The greater part of the time was devoted to discussions of how to gain control of her interpersonal relationships and stand up for herself. She had considerable difficulty with this at first, even though it had early become emotionally important to her to please the therapist. But she gradually mastered the assertive behavior required of her, overcame her anxieties and became ex-

ceedingly self-reliant in all interpersonal dealings, including those with her mother-in-law.

From Lazarus and Rachman (1957) on systematic desensitization:

Case 1—The patient was instructed in the use of assertive responses and deep (non-hypnotic) relaxation. The first anxiety hierarchy dealt with was that of dull weather. Starting from "a bright sunny day" it was possible for the subject to visualize "damp overcast weather" without anxiety after 21 desensitization sessions, and 10 days after the completion of this hierarchy, she was able to report that, "the weather is much better, it doesn't even bother me to look at the weather when I wake up in the morning" (previously depressing). . . . During the course of therapy, part of the reason for the development of the anxiety state in this patient was unearthed. When she was 17 years old she had become involved in a love affair with a married man 12 years her senior. This affair had been conducted in an extremely discreet manner for 4 years, during which time she had suffered from recurrent guilt feelings and shame—so much so, that on one occasion she had attempted suicide by throwing herself into a river. It was her custom to meet her lover after work *in the late afternoon.* The dull weather can be accounted for, as this affair took place in London.

From Rachman (1959):

Interview No. 12. The patient having received a jolt in her love relationship, this session was restricted to a sort of nondirective, cathartic discussion. No desensitizing was undertaken because of A.G.'s depressed mood and obvious desire to "just talk."

These excerpts have been presented because they seem representative of the practices of the behavioral therapists. As can be seen, the number and variety of activities that go on during these treatment sessions is great, including, in these few examples, discussions, explanations of techniques and principles, explanations of the unadaptiveness of anxiety and symptoms, hypnosis of various sorts, relaxation practice and training with and without hypnosis, "nondirective cathartic discussions," "obtaining an understanding of the patient's personality and background," and the "unearthing" of a 17-year-old memory of an illicit affair. The case reports are brief and presented anecdotally so that it is really impossible to know what else went on in addition to those things described. What should be abundantly clear from these examples is that there is no attempt to restrict what goes on to learning techniques. Since it seems clear that a great variety of things do go on, any attribution of behavior change to specific learning techniques is entirely unwarranted.

In summary, there are several important issues that must be differentiated. First, a review of both learning theory and of the empirical results of behavior therapy demonstrates that they can claim no special scientific status for their work on either ground. Second, there are important differences of opinion concerning the type of patient likely to be affected by behavior therapy. Grossberg (1964), for example, states that: "Behavior therapies have been most successful when applied to neurotic disorders with specific behavioral manifestations [p. 81]." He goes on to point out that the results with alcoholism and sexual disorders have been disappointing and that the best results are achieved with phobias and enuresis. He later states that "desensitization only alleviates those phobias that are being treated, but other coexisting phobias remain at high strength, indicating a specific treatment effect [p. 83]." Wolpe et al. (1964), on the other hand, argues that: "The conditioning therapist differs from his colleagues in that he seeks out the precise stimuli to anxiety, and finds himself able to break down

almost every neurosis into what are essentially *phobic systems* [p. 11]." The best controlled study (Lang & Lazovik, 1963) indicates that "desensitization is very effective in reducing the intense fear of snakes held by normal subjects, though it can be questioned whether this is a phobia in the clinical sense."

Thus, there seems to be some evidence that these *techniques* (as techniques and not as learning theory) are effective with certain conditions.[4] We feel that this bears stressing because psychotherapy has come to be narrowly defined in terms of dynamic, evocative, and nondirective methods, placing unnecessary limitations on the kind of patient suitable for psychotherapy. First, we must note that behavior techniques are not new (as Murray, 1964, points out in a recent article). Freud and Breuer used similar techniques prior to the development of psychoanalysis, Bagby described a number of these methods in 1928, and therapy based on techniques designed to eliminate undesirable responses was used for many years by Stevenson Smith at the University of Washington Clinic. While most of these techniques have been superseded by the various forms of dynamic psychotherapy, recent work (Frank, 1961) suggests that the time may be ripe for taking a fresh look at a variety of methods such as hypnosis, suggestion, relaxation, and other approaches of a more *structured nature* in which the therapist takes a *more active role*. Needless to say, this fresh look would best proceed unencumbered by an inadequate learning theory and with some minimal concern for control. As an example of a non-

---

[4] Just how many neurotics fit the phobia and/or specific symptom model is a complicated question, the answer to which depends in part on what one's own point of view leads one to look for. For example, an informal census of the first 81 admissions to the University of Oregon Psychology Clinic in 1964 revealed only 2 patients who could be so classified.

dynamic approach to patient management, we refer to the work of Fairweather (1964) and his colleagues.

REFORMULATION

Up to this point our analysis has been primarily critical. We have tried to show that many of the so-called principles of learning employed by workers with a behaviorist orientation are inadequate and are not likely to provide useful explanations for clinical phenomena. In this section we will examine the potential value of ideas from different learning conceptions. Before proceeding, however, we would like to discuss briefly the issue of the application of "laws," principles, and findings from one area (such as animal experimentation) to another (such as neurosis and psychotherapy). The behaviorists have traditionally assumed that principles established under highly controlled conditions, usually with animal subjects, form a scientific foundation for a psychology of learning. Yet when they come to apply these principles to human learning situations, the transition is typically bridged by rather flimsy analogies which ignore crucial differences between the situations, the species, etc. Recently, Underwood (1964) has made the following comments concerning this problem:

> Learning theories as developed in the animal-learning laboratory, have never seemed . . . to have relevance to the behavior of a subject in learning a list of paired associates. The emphasis upon the role of a pellet of food or a sip of water in the white rat's acquiring a response somehow never seemed to make contact with the human S learning to say VXK when the stimulus DOF was presented. [p. 74]

We would add that the relevance is at least equally obscure in applications of traditional S-R reinforcement theory to clinical phenomena.

We do *not* wish, however, to damn any and all attempts to conceptualize clinical phenomena in terms of principles of learning developed outside the clinic. On the contrary, recent work in learning may suggest certain theoretical models which may prove useful in conceptualizing the learning processes involved in psychotherapy and the development of neuroses. Whether these notions can form the basis for a useful learning conceptualization of clinical phenomena will depend upon the ingenuity with which they are subsequently developed and upon their adequacy in encompassing the facts of neurosis and psychotherapy. Further, we would like to stress that their association with experimental work in the field of learning does not give them any a priori scientific status. Their status as explanatory principles in the clinical area must be empirically established within that area. In what follows, then, we will outline some ideas about learning and make some suggestions concerning their relevance to clinical problems.

Our view of learning centers around the concepts of information storage and retrieval. Learning is viewed as the process by which information about the environment is acquired, stored, and categorized. This cognitive view is, of course, quite contrary to the view that learning consists of the acquisition of specific responses; responses, according to our view, are mediated by the nature of the stored information, which may consist of facts or of strategies or programs analogous to the grammar that is acquired in the learning of a language. Thus, "what is learned" may be a system for generating responses as a consequence of the specific information that is stored. This general point of view has been emphasized by Lashley (see Beach *et al.*, 1960), by Miller, Galanter, and Pribram (1960), in the form of the TOTE hypothesis, and by a number of workers in the cognitive learning tradition (Tolman, 1951; Woodworth, 1958). Recently it has even been suggested as a necessary formulation for dealing with that eminently S-R area, motor skills (Adams, 1964; Fitts, 1964).

This conception of learning may be useful in the clinical area in two ways: one, in formulating a theoretical explanation for the acquisition or development of neurosis, symptoms, behavior pathology, and the like, and, two, in conceptualizing psychotherapy as a learning process, and suggesting new methods stemming from this learning model.

A conceptualization of the problem of neurosis in terms of information storage and retrieval is based on the fundamental idea that what is learned in a neurosis is a set of central strategies (or a program) which guide the individual's adaptation to his environment. Neuroses are not symptoms (responses) but are strategies of a particular kind which lead to certain observable (tics, compulsive acts, etc.) and certain other less observable phenomena (fears, feelings of depression, etc.). The whole problem of symptom substitution is thus seen as an instance of response substitution or response equipotentiality, concepts which are supported by abundant laboratory evidence.

Similarly, the problem of a learning conceptualization of unconscious phenomena may be reopened. Traditional S-R approaches have equated the unconscious with some kind of avoidance of a verbalization response. From our point of view, there is no reason to assume that people can give accurate descriptions of the central strategies mediating much of their behavior any more than a child can give a description of the grammatical rules which govern the understanding and production of his language. As a matter of fact, consciousness may very well be a special or ex-

traordinary case—the rule being "unawareness" of the mediating strategies—which is in need of special explanation, rather than the reverse. This view avoids the cumbersome necessity of having to postulate specific fear experiences or the persistence of anxiety-motivated behavior, as has typically been done by S-R theorists with regard to unconscious phenomena. It also avoids equating the unconscious with the neurotic, which is a virtue since there is so much that goes on within "normal" individuals that they are unaware of. It further avoids the trap of attributing especially persistent and maladaptive consequences to painful experiences. As Solomon (1964) points out, the existing evidence does not support the view that punishment and pain lead unequivocally to anxiety and maladaptive consequences.

The view of learning we have outlined does not supply a set of ready-made answers to clinical problems that can be applied from the laboratory, but it indicates what sort of questions will have to be answered to achieve a meaningful learning conceptualization of neurosis and symptoms. Questions such as "What are the conditions under which strategies are acquired or developed?" stress the fact that these conditions may be quite different from the final observed behavior. That is to say, a particular symptom is not necessarily acquired because of some learning experience in which its stimulus components were associated with pain or fear-producing stimuli. Rather, a symptom may function as an equipotential response, mediated by a central strategy acquired under different circumstances. As an example, consider Harlow's (1958, 1962) monkeys who developed a number of symptoms, the most striking being sexual impotence (a much better animal analogue of human neurosis than those typically cited as experimental neuroses [Liddell, 1944]). Their longitudinal record, or "learning history," indicates that the development of this abnormal "affectional system," as Harlow terms it, is dependent on a variety of nonisomorphic experiences, including the lack of a mother-infant relationship and the lack of a variety of peer-play experiences.

These brief examples are only meant to give a flavor of where a learning conception of neurosis which stresses the acquisition of strategies will lead. A chief advantage of this view is that it has *generality* built in at the core, rather than imported secondarily, as is the case with S-R concepts of stimulus and response generalization.

Let us now turn our attention to the very difficult problem of applying learning concepts to psychotherapy. Basically, we would argue that the development of methods and techniques is largely a function of the empirical skill and ingenuity of the individual-craftsman-therapist. Even a carefully worked-out and well-established set of learning principles (which we do not have at this time) would not necessarily tell us how to modify acquired strategies in the individual case—just as the generally agreed-upon idea that rewards affect performance does not tell us what will be an effective reward in any specific instance.

Bearing these cautions in mind, we might still address ourselves to the question of what applications are suggested by the learning approach we have presented. As a first suggestion, we might consider the analogy of learning a new language. Here we see a process that parallels psychotherapy insofar as it involves modifying or developing a new set of strategies of a pervasive nature. A careful study of the most effective techniques for the learning of a new language might yield some interesting suggestions for psychotherapy. Learning a new language involves the development of a new

set of strategies for responding—new syntax as well as new vocabulary. Language learning *may or may not* be facilitated by an intensive attempt to make the individual *aware* of the strategies used, as is done in traditional language instruction which teaches old-fashioned grammar, and as is done, analogously, in those psychotherapies which stress insight. Alternatively, language learning sometimes seems most rapid when the individual is immersed in surroundings (such as a foreign country) where he hears nothing but the new language and where his old strategies and responses are totally ineffective.

Using this as a model for psychotherapy, we might suggest something like the following process: First, a careful study should be done to delineate the "neurotic language," both its vocabulary and its grammar, of the individual. Then a situation might be constructed (e.g., a group therapy situation) in which the individual's existing neurotic language is not understood and in which the individual must develop a new "language," a new set of central strategies, in order to be understood. The detailed working out of such a procedure might very well utilize a number of the techniques that have been found effective in existing therapies, both group and individual, and in addition draw on some new techniques from the fields of psycholinguistics and language learning.

These are, of course, but initial fragmentary guesses, and they may be wrong ones. But we believe that the conceptions on which these guesses are based are sufficiently supported by recent learning research to warrant serious attention. Although this reconceptualization may not lead immediately to the development of effective psychotherapeutic techniques, it may at least provide a first step in that direction.

Reply to a "Critique and Reformulation" of Behavior Therapy

S. Rachman and H. J. Eysenck

This reply to the recent paper by Breger and McGaugh (1965) will confine itself to a small number of crucial points; we will not discuss in detail, among others, two main contentions put forward by those authors. One of these is their "reformulation," according to which learning conceptions of neurosis should make use of the "acquisition of strategies." The suggestions made under this heading are so fragmentary, programmatic and elusive that we fail to see either their theoretical usefulness or any practical consequences which might follow from them; when Breger and McGaugh have some actual applications to report, or have at least succeeded in showing how the major facts of neurotic behavior can be accounted for in terms of their scheme, then may be the appropriate time to take issue with their "reformulation." The other contention relates to their preference for an "Expectancy $\times$ Value" type of theory, as compared to a "Drive $\times$ Habit" type of theory, to use Atkinson's (1964) phrase. They are, of course, free to make any preference choice they like, even without repeating at some length arguments presented many times before; here too, however, one would require some more direct evidence indicating that Expectancy $\times$ Value theories give rise to different and

Reprinted from *Psychological Bulletin*, 1966, vol. 65, pp. 165–169 with the permission of the American Psychological Association and the authors.

more efficient methods of treatment than Drive $\times$ Habit theories before entering into any formal argument. As this point is crucial to certain other assertions made by Breger and McGaugh, however, it will be referred to obliquely again below.

The first criticism made by Breger and McGaugh is labelled "science issue"; they feel that there is no such thing as "modern learning theory," that there is no agreement on sufficient points to make testable predictions and applications to the treatment of neurotics, and that behavior therapists are wrong in claiming that their procedures are based on scientific theories. Evaluation of this point may be aided by consideration of a quotation from Sir George Thompson, F.R.S. and Nobel-Laureate in physics. He points out that

> if differences of opinion . . . are still possible about space, time, and gravitation, this is an example of something common in physics. Very different points of view may lead to identical or nearly identical conclusions when translated into what can be observed. It is the observations that are closest to reality. The more one abstracts from them the more exciting indeed are the conclusions one draws and the more suggestive for further advances, but the less can one be certain that some widely different viewpoint would not do as well. [1961, p. 15]

Much the same is true in psychology. MacCorquodale and Meehl (1954), Atkinson (1964), and many others have pointed out that Expectancy $\times$ Value and Drive $\times$ Habit theories overlap in many ways, and give rise to similar predictions, although experimentalists may show a preference for one or the other of two ways of talking about phenomena. But both are agreed about most of these phenomena, and it is these which "are closest to reality," and which form the factual, scientific basis of behavior therapy. No learning theorists of any persuasion would deny statements of behavioral laws of this kind: "Reinforced pairings of CS and UCS under appropriate conditions produce conditioning"; "Intermittent reinforcement slows down extinction"; "Nonreinforcement produces extinction"; "Different schedules of reinforcement produce predictably different response rates." It is laws of this type that are made use of by behavior therapists, who may choose to talk about them in the language of Hull, Tolman, Skinner, or any other major learning theorist. As an example, consider the work of Lovibond (1962) who made detailed predictions on the basis of the known facts of learning theory for the behavior of enuretic patients, and showed how in doing so he could (a) accelerate recovery and (b) reduce relapses; Young and Turner (1965) may furnish another example in the same disorder. Many others are given in Eysenck (1959, 1964), Ullmann and Krasner (1965), Krasner and Ullmann (1965), Eysenck and Rachman (1965), Rachman (1965a), and others. The application of scientific principles to any area must be specific, and must be discussed in terms of specific results; Breger and McGaugh's failure to do so makes their ex cathedra condemnation meaningless.

This lack of specificity, unfortunately, runs throughout their paper.

On the critical side, their argument primarily consists of doubtful assertions presented as if they were self-evident truths. They often contradict themselves and also distort the nature of behavior therapy.

How, for instance, are they able to conclude that their quotations from three of the case histories mentioned are representative ("they seem representative of the practices of behavior therapists")? As two of the quotations were in fact taken from cases reported by one of the present writers, we take this opportunity to point out the following facts. The two sentences quoted from the treatment of patient A. G. (Rachman, 1959) describe *one* incident which occurred during the course of 22 interviews. At no time prior to the treatment of that patient, nor in the succeeding 6 years of work in this field, has a similar incident been encountered. Is this representative of behavior therapy as Breger and McGaugh claim, or is it a distortion caused by ignorance of therapeutic practice and of the literature on the subject? If Breger and McGaugh wish, in the other examples quoted, to indicate that behavior therapists actually speak to their patients and explain the rationale and nature of the treatment to them, then their point is taken even though it does lack novelty. Perhaps they are unaware that during the course of therapy, be it desensitization or any other method, the therapist also attempts to locate any sources of stress which may be provoking or maintaining the neurotic behavior. Where possible, these stresses are eliminated or at least ameliorated. The cases (of psychotic patients in these instances) described by Ayllon (1963) and Ayllon and Michael (1959) illustrate clearly how improvements can be obtained by breaking the links between stimulus and response patterns as they occur in the patient's environment (Eysenck & Rachman, 1965).

Breger and McGaugh's paper is also

self-contradictory. Immediately after deploring the emergence of a so-called dogmatic school of Behavior Therapy ("it is unfortunate that the techniques used by the Behavior Therapy group have so quickly become encapsulated in a dogmatic 'school' ") they proceed to distinguish between the "three different positions." They also imply that behavior therapy is oversimplified; in other parts of the paper, it is said to be cumbersome. Behavior therapists certainly pursue simplicity both in theory and in practice; this seems to us to be a desirable aim in itself and a welcome contrast to the convolutions of other psychotherapeutic theories. This contrast is neatly, if inaccurately, demonstrated by Breger and McGaugh themselves.

> The behaviorist looks at a neurotic and sees specific symptoms and anxiety. The psychodynamicist looks at the same individual and sees a complex intra- and interpersonal mode of functioning which may or may not contain certain observable fears or certain behavioral symptoms such as compulsive motor acts. When the psychodynamicist describes a neurotic, his referent is a cohering component of the individual's functioning . . . etc. [p. 349]

The doubtful assertions contained in the paper by Breger and McGaugh are numerous and cannot be reproduced in full. The following examples could be multiplied without effort. " 'What is learned,' then, is not a mechanical sequence of responses but rather, *what needs to be done in order to achieve some final event.*" Is all learning really an attempt at achievement? Have neurotic patients presumably also "learned what needs to be done" in order to achieve a neurosis? A conditioned PGR is, likewise, a doubtful achievement. The list is endless, but in any event who decides "what needs to be done," or what a "final event" is, or when it is achieved?

The phrase "some final event" is hardly a model of precise definition.

Another doubtful assertion is the statement that Harlow's experiments with monkeys provide a "much better animal analogue of human neuroses than those typically cited as experimental neuroses." This cavalier dismissal of the mass of work in the subject of experimental neuroses (see Broadhurst, 1960; Massermann, 1943; Wolpe, 1952; etc.) is neither explained nor justified by Breger and McGaugh. Their attitude to the evidence seems to stem from a belief that "saying so, makes it so."

Their assertion that the "attribution of behavior change to specific learning techniques is entirely unwarranted" is also misguided and appears to be based on ignorance of the relevant evidence. No mention is made of the experiments of Lazarus (1961), Wolpe (1952), Eysenck (1964), King, Armitage, & Tilton (1960), Lovibond (1962), or of the studies of Ayllon and his co-workers (1959, 1963). They will further be surprised by the accumulation of recent studies which bear on this point and which, with minor exceptions, corroborate the viewpoint of behavior therapists (see Eysenck, 1964; Eysenck & Rachman, 1965; Krasner & Ullmann, 1965; Rachman, 1965; Ullmann & Krasner, 1965, among others). The currently available evidence will, we feel certain, convince all but the most biased workers that the methods of behavior therapy are indeed effective in the modification of neurotic behavior. Not all the methods are successful; nor is it yet possible to treat all types of disturbances successfully. There is an immense amount of developmental work and experimentation which remains to be done, but a degree of optimism is not misplaced.

Breger and McGaugh are surely correct in drawing attention to the deficiencies of learning theory; most of their criticisms, however, have been stated by others before them. In any event, a detailed consideration of all their comments would be inappropriate here. Their arguments about the problem of perceptual constancy, for example, have been amply analyzed by Taylor and Papert (1956) and Taylor (1962), and the restating of their complex arguments and experiments would be out of place. The concept of reinforcement is of course replete with complexities and seems to us to be best regarded in terms of Mowrer's two-factor theory (1960). The difficulties which arise from a consideration of central activities such as thinking were discussed in an earlier review by Metzner (1961)—one which they appear to have missed—and again 2 years later (Metzner, 1964).

Certainly, it would be exceedingly foolish to regard "learning theory" as a complete, coherent, and final account of human behavior. This does not mean, however, that people engaged in therapy should ignore the established findings and the best available theories. Quite the contrary. We feel that they are obliged to use these findings and ideas wherever it is feasible to do so. Furthermore, four of the main techniques used in behavior therapy (desensitization, aversion treatment, operant retraining, and the "bell-and-pad" method) were derived solely or very largely from these findings and ideas. It is highly improbable that these methods would have been developed to their present stage and form sui generis.

Perhaps the most revealing reflection of the attitude of Breger and McGaugh to the entire subject of behavior modification is contained in their curiously unimaginative description of Skinner's work as "exercises in animal training." Some notion of the wider significance of the pecking of pigeons can easily be ascertained from the work of Staats and Staats

(1964) and Krasner and Ullmann (1965) among others.

Not merely doubtful, but definitely wrong, is the assertion that behavior therapists

> have partly avoided this problem [generality] by focusing their attention on those neuroses that can be described in terms of specific symptoms (bed-wetting, if this is a neurosis, tics, specific phobias, etc.) and have tended to ignore those conditions which do not fit their model, such as neurotic depressions, general unhappiness, obsessional disorders, and the kinds of persistent interpersonal entanglements that characterize so many neurotics. [p. 348]

This is wrong factually in two respects. Firstly, a large number of patients with interpersonal anxiety and a moderate number of obsessional patients have in fact been treated (e.g., Lazarus, 1963; Wolpe, 1958). Secondly, Wolpe (1958) and most other therapists did not focus their attention on anything in particular other than the symptoms presented by their patients, *who were not selected or chosen by the therapists.* Others, like Lovibond (1962), Lang and Lazowik (1963), Yates (1958), and the present writers (Eysenck & Rachman, 1965) have indeed experimented with specific symptoms, but not in order to avoid the theoretical problem of generality—the reason was simply that if specific predictions are to be tested, then responses must by preference be accurately measurable. It is possible to count the rate at which tics occur, the number of wet nights per week, or the strength of a snake phobia; therefore, it is possible to experiment with the effect of changing various independent variables on these dependent variables. This choice therefore permits the testing of quite precisely the sort of predictions which according to Breger and McGaugh cannot be made from learning theory principles; it would be interesting to hear their explanation of just how it is that verification has usually followed prediction!

Finally, we turn to criticisms of "claims of success." Breger and McGaugh state that "the most striking thing about this large body of studies is that they are almost all case studies. A careful reading of the original sources reveals that only one study (Lang & Lazowik, 1963) is a controlled experiment." This is simply not an accurate statement of the position as it obtained at the time of writing of the Breger and McGaugh review (June 1964 is the acceptance date). They do not refer to the work of Cooper (1963), Lazarus (1961), Ellis (1964), Anker and Walsh (1961), Lovibond (1962), and others, and their horizon is clearly bounded, as they themselves admit by the fact that theirs "does not purport to be a comprehensive review of the behavior-therapy literature. Rather, it is based on a survey of all the studies reported in the two reviews that have appeared (Bandura, 1961; Grossberg, 1964)." This seems to us an inexcusable defect. Behavior therapy may be said to have begun properly around 1958–59, with the publication of the Wolpe (1958) book and Eysenck's (1959) paper proposing the name "behavior therapy" and stating in some detail its nature and purpose. Given that controlled experiments take several years to execute, write up, and publish, it is clear why summaries of the field published in 1961 or even 1964 would not be adequate substantiation for such a far-reaching condemnation of a whole branch of study. Familiarity with *Behavior Research and Therapy* (Pergamon Press), a journal concerned entirely with research in behavior therapy and nowhere referred to by Breger and McGaugh, would have served adequately to bring them up to date in this field. (It may be added that several controlled trials of behavior therapy are in progress, to our knowledge; three of them prospective and one retrospective, Marks and Gelder, 1965, in the Maudsley Hospital alone.) Even the Eysenck and Rachman (1965) textbook, which went to press 6 months earlier than the Breger and McGaugh article, is very much more up to date than their account (additional evidence is discussed by Cooke, 1965; Davison, 1965; Paul, 1964; Rachman, 1965a, 1965b).

We must say, indeed, that we feel quite strongly that the burden of Breger and McGaugh's criticism is entirely misplaced. In half a dozen years a relatively small number of behavior therapists, with little official support and often against the most hostile opposition, have succeeded in carrying out more controlled (and better controlled) studies than have hundreds of psychiatrists and psychoanalysts in 60 years, with all the financial resources and the prestige so readily available to them. Even so, we do not consider our studies as in any way beyond criticism, nor do we feel that they go nearly far enough, or are sufficient to establish behavior therapy as superior to other types of therapy in any definitive way. We have concluded in our textbook (Eysenck & Rachman, 1965) that "the routine use of these methods is undoubtedly not yet feasible; it must await further improvement of techniques and definitive evidence of superiority over other available techniques." This is still our view, and nothing said by Breger and McGaugh would seem to contradict this summary or throw doubt on its accuracy. To call views of this kind "dogmatic" seems a curious misunderstanding of the meaning of the word.

Learning Theory and Behavior Therapy: A Reply to Rachman and Eysenck

Louis Breger and James L. McGaugh

As we pointed out in our analysis of current "learning theory" approaches to psychotherapy and neurosis (Breger & McGaugh, 1965), it is essential to distinguish clearly between learning theory, the practice of behavior therapy, and the effectiveness of treatment. Essentially we posed these three questions: "How adequate is the learning theory espoused by the behavior-therapy group?," "Do behavior therapists use techniques based on, or closely related to, learning theory?," and "Is treatment effective?" These are, of course, independent questions. Let us reconsider them in the light of Rachman and Eysenck's (1966) comments.

Learning Theory

First, we attempted to show that the kind of learning theory espoused by the behavior therapists is inadequate. While we need not repeat the arguments here, the fact that other writers have pointed out the deficiencies of learning theory does not make these deficiencies any less objectionable. Rachman and Eysenck's discussion of "Expectancy × Value" versus "Drive × Habit" theories completely ignores the issues we raised concerning the inability of peripheral S-R theory to account for the facts of perceptual constancy, language interpretation and generation, and response equipotentiality. It is no longer a question

Reprinted from *Psychological Bulletin*, 1966, vol. 65, pp. 170–173 with the permission of the American Psychological Association and the authors.

of being able to choose between an expectancy or a drive theory; the type of "Drive × Habit" theory to which Rachman and Eysenck refer, and that on which the behavior therapists continually rely, has been unable to handle the facts of learning. The reference to "laws of learning" that "no learning theorist of any persuasion would deny" further avoids the issue. What Rachman and Eysenck cite are *findings* from conditioning studies which are highly dependent on the conditions under which the observations are made. Although it may be that no learning theorist would deny that "reinforced pairings of CS and UCS under appropriate conditions produce conditioning," many would deny that this *finding* is a "law of learning" that can be generalized to situations which differ in significant ways from those obtaining in a conditioning experiment. The argument that these phenomena "are closest to reality" and that they "form the factual, scientific basis of behavior therapy" is doubly misleading. The phenomena (e.g., CS and UCS, extinction, effects of different schedules, etc.) are close to the "reality" of a highly artificial laboratory situation, but only contact other "realities" by what Chomsky (1959) has called "analogic guesses formulated in terms of a metaphoric extension of the technical vocabulary of the laboratory [p. 30]." This is starkly revealed when one sees how little the actual content of behavior therapy resembles any laboratory conditioning study. Behavior therapists utilize a learning theory which has great difficulty in dealing with behavior sequences and complex transfer phenomena, yet it is just such sequential behavior and complex transfer effects that are manifested by their patients. The neurotic presents a complex symptomatic picture, not a discrete "neurotic habit" that is analogous to a conditioned response. Furthermore, the behavior therapists claim rather widespread changes as a result of their treatment methods (e.g., improved interpersonal relations, increased productiveness), changes that are extremely difficult, if not impossible, to explain within their "learning theory" framework.

Behavior-Therapy Techniques

Although Rachman and Eysenck indicate that the techniques of behavior therapy were solely or very largely derived from learning-theory findings and ideas, it is clear that the techniques in question were in existence long before Rachman and Eysenck's learning theory. Pfaundler described an apparatus for treating enuresis in 1904 that greatly resembled Mowrer's conditioning technique, and Nye, a pediatrician, outlined a proposed method for treating enuresis in 1830 that included all of the elements of "conditioning" therapy (both cited in Lovibond, 1964). Circus animal trainers used "operant" and "shaping" techniques for centuries without the benefit of "learning theory." Thus, it is not true that learning theory has been necessary or even very important in *developing* the specific techniques in question. Rachman and Eysenck are also incorrect when they imply that the observable effects produced by some training technique (such as operant conditioning or desensitization) are support for the learning theory from which these techniques were "derived" in the sense that some very specific experiment supports the theory from which it was deduced. The prior existence of the techniques as well as the great *dissimilarity* between what goes on in behavior therapy and in most learning experiments indicates that the relationship between theory and technique is *nonspecific*.

In our previous paper, it was pointed out that many different activities go on during behavior therapy (few of them resembling conditioning and many of them resembling traditional psychotherapy), thus confounding any attempt to attribute effects to behavior therapy *per se*. Rachman and Eysenck argue that the present authors used an unrepresentative example of Rachman's work—a particular incident with one of his patients that he says never occurred again. Whether this particular incident occurred again or not is really irrelevant. The central point remains that behavior therapists do many things in the course of treatment other than so-called conditioning. Rachman and Eysenck, in the very article presently under consideration, admit that "the therapist also attempts to locate any sources of stress which may be provoking or maintaining the neurotic behavior. Where possible, these stresses are eliminated or at least ameliorated." Behavior-therapy case studies are replete with such examples, indicating that behavior therapists use a variety of techniques in addition to those they emphasize. In view of this, the task of assessing the relative effectiveness of the *specific* techniques of behavior therapy is indeed formidable. Our assertion that ". . . the attribution of behavior change to specific learning techniques is entirely unwarranted" remains justified.

Effectiveness of Treatment

In addition to their failure to control what goes on in behavior therapy, we originally cited observer and sampling biases as factors which mitigated against accepting the claims for success of behavior therapy at face value. Rachman and Eysenck responded to these criticisms by citing references which were not cited in our original paper.[1] After carefully reviewing these additional references, we must conclude that our original criticisms are still fully applicable. (Many of these references are not new, of course, since they consist of volumes of anthologised reprints.) Let us examine some of these sources cited by Rachman and Eysenck, beginning with Eysenck (1964).

This volume presents 42 separate articles; 19 are behavior-therapy case studies (9 of these report only a single case); 13 are case studies using operant techniques; and 2 describe other methods. All 34 of these case studies are fully subject to the sort of biases we pointed out previously. Six articles are attempts at theoretical treatment, and two, and only two, are studies with some sort of control. These are Lang and Lazovik (1963), originally cited in our review as the only example of a behavior-therapy study with some concern for control, and an article by Anker which re-reports the study (cited separately by Rachman and Eysenck) by Anker and Walsh (1961). Lang and Lazovik found that "desensitization is very effective in reducing the intense fear of snakes held by normal subjects, though it can be questioned whether this is a phobia in the clinical sense." Anker and Walsh demonstrated the superiority of activity groups (activity consisted of planning and putting on a play for other patients) over therapy groups in improving the ward behavior of schizophrenics. The relation of this study to "learning theory" eludes us, nor do Anker and Walsh make any mention of it. The study is a good example of

[1] It is not true, however, that the journal *Behavior Research and Therapy*, was ". . . nowhere referred to" by us. See Breger and McGaugh's (1965) reference to Lazarus (1963).

the kind of innovative approach to pation management that is closely allied to the work of Fairweather (1964) to which we referred in our original paper. Thus, this recent volume edited by Eysenck provides no additional unbiased data in support of behavior therapy.

Four other sources are specifically referred to by Rachman and Eysenck in response to our criticism of lack of control in behavior therapy case studies: Cooper (1963) which, unfortunately, was not available to us, Lazarus (1961), Ellis (1964), and Lovibond (1964). (Both Lazarus and Ellis also appear in Eysenck, 1964.) Lazarus reports that group desensitization is superior to interpretive group therapy in reducing symptoms. He was the therapist for both groups and also assessed the results. Need more be said concerning possible experimenter bias and lack of control? The article by Ellis contains a theoretical discussion of "rational psychotherapy," two uncontrolled case studies, and a report in which he compares his own notes on cases he has treated with various methods (psychoanalysis, psychoanalytic psychotherapy, and rational psychotherapy). The report shows that Ellis' patients, as assessed by him, do better when he administers his own brand of "rational psychotherapy." This report is fully subject to all three sorts of bias and, so far as we can tell, has little to do with any learning theory.

Finally, there is the book by Lovibond (1964) to which Rachman and Eysenck refer several times. This is a very interesting volume which nicely combines historical review, theoretical discussion, and a comparative evaluation of several methods for treating enuresis. Lovibond presents a rather convincing case that: (a) enuresis is *not* a neurosis (he presents evidence from several sources and concludes, "The enuertic population differs little from the general population of children in terms of psychological adjustment."); and (*b*) that the "conditioning" techniques utilizing immediate awakening are effective in bringing enuresis under control. His general discussion makes it clear that a simple conditioning model is inadequate in *conceptualizing* this condition, as exemplified by his references to: "consolidation of the trace [p. 133]," "central decision process in voluntary micturition [p. 149]," and the like. The following quote is taken from his concluding section:

> From this point of view an adequate general theory of behavior must be a centralist theory; one which gives appropriate emphasis to central integrating and regulatory processes. From their

neurophysiological aspect, these processes may be regarded as "autonomous" cerebral processes (Hebb, 1949), and from their psychological aspect they may be regarded as the processes of consciousness. [p. 152]

The detailed consideration of these references should make it clear that Rachman and Eysenck are as careless and misinformed about the references they cite as they are about the important issues in the field of learning. In sum, the case for behavior therapy appears as weak as before. The "new" references are as subject to bias as those previously cited, and the theoretical treatment of issues in the field of learning remains naive and misleading.

Behavior Therapy and Psychotherapy

Bernard Weitzman

A number of procedures which would, a decade ago, have claimed the status of "psychotherapies" (cf., e.g., Wolpe, 1958) have in the recent past characterized themselves as "behavior therapies." It is intended by its users that this nomenclature shall be pregnant with meaning (cf. Eysenck, 1960). Properly understood, it reflects the long-resisted penetration of clinical practice by that form of "scientism" which, earlier, had a hand in leading academic "psychologists" to their sea change into "behavioral scientists." While attempts to articulate the historical factors which underlie such transformations are always speculative, there seems little doubt that,

Reprinted from *Psychological Review*, 1967, vol. 74, pp. 300–317 with the permission of the American Psychological Association and the author.

in the case of clinical practice, the publication of Wolpe's psychotherapeutic manual is one causal nexus. The apparent effectiveness of the techniques devised by Wolpe, in particular the procedure called "systematic desensitization" (cf. Grossberg, 1964), has won him a following, and has invited the use of an argument of virtue by association in a bid to legitimize the host of procedures calling themselves "behavior therapies."

Many psychologists in clinical practice have found quite irresistible the promise of quick and effective results which Wolpe's procedure holds forth, despite a host of objections to it which arise from the various "dynamic" orientations. Others, feeling tempted, have resisted the demons of mechanization and dehumanization, and the danger of "loss of soul" which is understood to be implicit in the Weltanschauung of behaviorism. This resistance is buttressed by theoretical allegiances and made to seem necessary by a variety of therapeutic rubrics, for example, the expectation of symptom substitution, a problem which will be treated in some detail later.

The rejection, on grounds of principle, of behavior therapy by the clinical community, and the derogatory treatment of dynamic therapies by behavior therapists, have had the inevitable consequence of generating premature crystallizations of positions in both camps. The lines of battle have been most sharply and articulately drawn in the writings of Eysenck (1960), who asserts:

> . . . behavior therapy is an *alternative* type of treatment to psychotherapy [i.e., it is not ancillary]; . . . it is a *superior* type of treatment, both from the point of view of theoretical background and practical effectiveness; . . . in so far as psychotherapy is at all effective, it is so in virtue of certain principles which can be *derived from learning theory* . . . psychotherapy itself, when shorn of its inessential and irrelevant parts, can usefully be considered as a minor part of behavior therapy. [p. ix]

While the position taken by Eysenck is more extreme than other behavior therapists might prefer, its clarity makes it a useful target for analysis. Some comments on the contents of Eysenck's statement will clear the way for the major substance of this essay, that is, an examination of the grounds upon which clinicians have based their rejection of behavior therapy.

THE THEORETICAL BACKGROUND OF BEHAVIOR THERAPY

The evidence of the practical effectiveness of behavior therapy, while not conclusive, is indeed impressive. However, if one notes (as Eysenck does) that the term "behavior therapy" refers to a large and diverse group of treatment methods, clarity requires that the question of effectiveness must be put to each method. If one extracts from the mass of data the results of systematic desensitization therapy, one is left with an impression which is rather different from that intended by Eysenck. The residue, that is, the evidence of the practical effectiveness of behavior therapies other than systematic desensitization, while interesting, would excite the enthusiasm of few clinicians (cf. Grossberg, 1964). As a first step then, the accuracy of Eysenck's statement might be increased by appropriately reading "systematic desensitization" where he has written "behavior therapy." This sharpening of focus permits a more cogent appraisal of the evidence, and a more lucid analysis of the problems.

An issue of considerable importance is raised by Eysenck's claim of theoretical superiority for behavior therapy. It has been pointed out, from both camps, that analytic theory requires that symptom substitution or recurrence must attend a symptomatic treatment which, by defiinition, does not affect the dynamic sources of the symptoms. The evidence is rather impressive that neither substitution nor recurrence typically follows treatment by systematic desensitization. When occasional recurrences are reported, they are described as being of low intensity and, apparently, never catastrophic. Wolpe and Eysenck have both explicitly contended that this evidence constitutes a decisive empirical argument against psychoanalysis. A detailed analysis of the theoretical grounds upon which this contention is based will be undertaken later in this discussion. At this point, however, it must be noted that a crucial logical alternative, that is, that systematic desensitization does, as a technique, in some way affect the total psychological matrix, has not been given due theoretical consideration by behavior therapists or by psychotherapists. Attempts have been made to demonstrate, *empirically*, the specificity of the effects of systematic desensitization, that is, to demonstrate that desensitization is confined, in the locus of its effects, to the undoing of specific conditioned associations. The evidence, however, is not altogether convincing and certainly not conclusive. As long as the issue is empirically open, the *logical* analysis must be allowed.

When this analysis is undertaken it appears that there are implications of the data for Eysenck's theoretical model which have not been examined, and which seem to indicate that the Eysenckian position is vulnerable to criticisms similar to those leveled at psychoanalysis. Eysenck (1957) views neuroticism as a genetically determined constitutional predisposition. That is, all else being equal, there is a genetic determination of the likelihood that one individual will develop neurotic symptoms more readily than will another individual. Obviously, behavior therapy, in removing symptoms, cannot be expected to alter this genetic base. Thus, the likelihood of developing symptoms, insofar as this is genetically given, will remain constant. It would seem reasonable to assume that, in statistical mass, the number of patients treated as neurotics in any therapuetic setting will contain a disproportionately large number of individuals high in genetically determined neuroticism. If this reasoning is correct, Eysenck's model would seem to predict a high incidence of new symptom formations in patients who have already been treated for neurotic symptoms. Indeed, if one takes seriously the reports of almost total absence of new symptoms in patients treated by systematic desensitization, a problem of some difficulty arises for the

Eysenckian model. On the one hand there are difficulties in attempting to solve the problem by entertaining the speculation that a lasting transformation of learning processes has been achieved by this technique if one is determined to deny that there are any nonspecific characterological consequences attending its application. (An analysis of some of the conceptual difficulties for S-R theories in ". . . explaining how *generality* of behavior results from specific learning experiences" has been presented by Breger and McGaugh, 1965, p. 348.) On the other hand, if it is granted that there are such nonspecific consequences, the genetic hypothesis must be formulated in a manner which makes such consequences intelligible. The alternatives for Eysenck would seem to entail a surrender, both of the current conception of genetically determined neuroticism and of the insistence upon the specificity of the effects of desensitization.

Eysenck's intention, however, is not to burden his own theory with the support of his claim to theoretical superiority for behavior therapy. Rather, the burden falls more broadly on something called "learning theory." An issue which exists for many clinicians seems to pivot about the intrinsic relation which is claimed to exist between behavior therapy and this "learning theory." The clinician is asked to agree that if he accepts the method as therapeutically valid and gives credence to the data which support assertions of its effectiveness, he must "buy" some "S-R" model of man. But what model of man is, in fact, required? A number of comments on this relationship may be helpful.

In the foreword to a volume reporting the outcome of a summer symposium on learning theory (Estes, Koch, Mac-Corquodale, Meehl, Mueller, Schoenfeld & Verplanck, 1954), the editor writes:

It might be supposed that there would crystallize out from such a critical and unbiased analysis of theories and the experimental evidence on which they rest, some one basic theory of the learning process which all reasonable persons could accept. If there were any such expectations among the members of the group, they were soon dissipated. Each theory appeared to exist within its own closed system and to defy direct comparison and the pooling of data. Concepts, techniques, apparatus, units of measurement, and definitions of terms were peculiar to a given theory and could not safely be lifted out of their own frame of reference. Each theory, then, had to be examined and analyzed separately for internal consistency and the degree to which it satisfied the logic of science. [p. vii]

In the context of a discussion similar to the present one, Breger and McGaugh (1965, p. 341) conclude that "The claim to scientific respectability by reference back to established laws of learning is . . . illusory." In light of these reports it seems somewhat misleading to speak as if there were a monolithic system properly called "learning theory." Indeed, Eysenck (1960) concedes this point. To the objection that "learning theorists are not always in agreement with each other," he answers:

. . . those points about which argument rages are usually of academic [theoretical] interest rather than of practical importance. Thus, reinforcement theorists and contiguity theorists have strong differences of view about the necessity of reinforcement during learning and different reinforcement theorists have different theories about the nature of reinforcement. Yet there would be general agreement in any particular case about the optimum methods of achieving a quick rate of conditioning. . . . [p. 15]

In fact, only an eclectic learning theory which systematically avoids examination of the relations between its own assump-

tions—that is, a nontheoretical amalgamation of pragmatic principles—can hope to derive the effects of a behavioral setting as complex as the therapeutic interview. Whether or not the methodological consensus which Eysenck assumes really exists (the reader is referred once more to the quotation from Estes *et al.*, 1954), the theoretical limitation which is acknowledged must be as constraining for those procedures called "behavior therapy" as for psychotherapy. That is, if there is no "learning theory" competent to handle the data of behavior therapy, there is no "learning theory" competent to handle the data of psychotherapy. If, then, one accepts the data of behavior therapy, one is faced, not with a set of necessary theoretical conclusions, but with a set of theoretical problems.

THE METHOD OF SYSTEMATIC DESENSITIZATION: AN INQUIRY

Since the most impressive data have been produced by Wolpe's method, it will be worthwhile to turn now to a more detailed consideration of systematic desensitization, and the relation of its practical methodology to Wolpe's conception of it.

Wolpe (1962) has described the genesis of systematic desensitization in discussing his replication of Masserman's (1943) study. Masserman produced "neurotic" behavior in cats by directing blasts of air at the animals as they began to eat. Wolpe, in his replication, demonstrated that the confrontation of appetitive and avoidant drive states is not a necessary condition for eliciting this symptomatology; that is, he obtained apparently the same form of neurotic behavior by shocking cats in the absence of food. (It is worth noting, en passant, that Wolpe has claimed that this demonstration undermines the psychoanalytic theory of the relation of symptom and conflict.

While his study does seem to provide evidence concerning necessary conditions, it is not relevant to the premise that drive conflict is a *sufficient* condition for symptom formation.)

Wolpe then "deconditioned" the fear reaction by a procedure in which a gradual, stepwise approach was made to the feared stimuli (the experimental cage and room), each step accompanied by feedings. Feedings, sometimes repeated at a given step, led to extinction of the fear response at that level of approach and permitted feeding to be initiated at the next step. The animals were, finally, free of any signs of neurotic behavior. This result was rationalized by the assumption that the eating response inhibits the occurrence of anxiety and leads to the extinction of the anxiety response to the stimuli which are present at a given step.

Wolpe reasoned that eating is only one of a variety of behaviors which may be used to inhibit anxiety. This thinking led to the application of the procedure to human subjects. Relaxation was substituted for eating as the anxiety-inhibiting response, and the resulting method was called "systematic desensitization."

A description of this method sounds strikingly like the method used by Wolpe to cure his cats: The human subject is trained, by a short form of the Jacobson (1938) method, to develop high-strength relaxation responses. He is then, while in a relaxed condition, presented, one at a time, with preselected stimuli, known to produce anxiety and arranged in a series of intensity or approach steps. When, after one or a number of presentations, a given step elicits no anxiety response, the next stimuls in the intensity hierarchy is presented, until the most intense stimulus produces no anxiety.

In this description, however, is hidden a form of analogy-making which gives comfort to the behavior therapist but which obscures differences of profound significance between the systematic desensitizations of cats and men. The reaction of the clinician, that "they are treating patients the way they treat cats," fails to penetrate the flaws of the analogy. (It is not entirely beside the point to note that this reaction implicitly grants the legitimacy of the behavioristic interpretation of cat behavior. The necessity of that interpretation is, of course, open to question.) It is crucial that the above, stylized description of systematic desensitization be concretized and given a more detailed procedural analysis.

The human subject is trained in voluntary relaxation. The training directs the subject to careful observation of certain internal states, to the discrimination of tensions in the major muscle groups of the body, and to the voluntary cessation of muscular responding. When this highly complex "response" has been acquired, a stimulus is presented. That is to say, the patient is directed by the therapist to *imagine a stimulus* which he has previously described to the therapist and which he has placed, for the use of the therapist, among other anxiety-producing stimuli in a given hierarchical position. The patient is, in fact, required to produce a vivid visualization of a scene. It is this visualization which is the "stimulus" bandied about in discussions of systematic desensitization. As Breger and McGaugh (1965, p. 340) have put it, ". . . the use of the terms stimulus and response are only remotely allegorical to the traditional use of these terms in psychology." The importance of this characterization of the stimulus is underlined by the fact that *inability to produce such visualizations is grounds for rejecting a patient for treatment by this method.* Having "presented a stimulus," the therapist lapses into silence for periods of up to 1 minute. *Any stimulus present in this situation is produced by the patient's internal processes.*

The therapeutic effect of systematic desensitization thus seems to be produced in periods of silence. That is, the therapist describes a scene which, presumably, sets a process in motion. So long as this process continues neither therapist nor patient speaks, and neither acts. There is, thus, for the content of the therapeutic process itself, no response of record. In other words, the question of what transpires during these silences is not, and has not been, asked. In reaction to the formulation of this question, and to frequent spontaneous reports from patients who were concerned that their inability to maintain static visualizations of the scene described by the therapist might hamper therapy, the author undertook regular inquiry into the contents of these silences. Six patients being treated by the method of systematic desensitization were interviewed. An interview was conducted at the end of each session of desensitization, providing a sample of approximately 200 interviews. Without exception, when closely questioned, patients reported a flow of visual imagery. The initiating scene, once visualized, shifted and changed its form. Moreover, these transformations took place continuously and, when the imagining was terminated by the therapist, had produced images which were quite removed in their content from the intended stimulus. These contents, and the transformations they exhibit, compel a characterization as a form of spontaneous and apparently autonomous fantasy familiar to many dynamically oriented therapists and, in fact, a therapeutic focus for those analysts who use Jung's (1959) method of active imagination. (While there is one report in the literature—Weinberg & Zaslove, 1963—of " 'involuntary' manipulations of the imaginal process," during treatment by systematic desensitization, the observed shifts in the intended stimulus are understood by the authors as a form of "resistance" to the treatment.)

What emerges from this inquiry is the information that the initiating scene presented by the therapist undergoes a series of transformations and elaborations which are under the control of the patient's internal, psychological processes. With this information in hand, it is not surprising, to a dynamically oriented therapist, to find that a wealth of dynamically rich and exciting material results from desensitizations obtained with Wolpe's method. For example, in one case, immediately upon conclusion of a desensitization series dealing with the patient's fears about the eventual death of his mother, he spontaneously reported:

> It was as if my feelings about my mother were transformed. Whenever I thought about her dying what I really felt was a fear of my being deserted by her. Now if I think of her dying I feel sorry for *her* [patient's emphasis]. For the first time I feel sorry for her instead of for myself.

Such a reminder of the fact that one is engaging processes of profound depth and complexity is hardly unique in the writer's experience. Opportunities for similar observations will probably present themselves to any behavior therapist who is willing to listen, and might be expected to serve as a caution against the simplistic view that only a stimulus-response connection is being affected by the therapy.

To note that the stimulus of record in this procedure is a self-produced visualization, and then to observe that the period in which the therapeutic effect is produced is characterized by a flow of images and symbolic materials, stretches the analogy to Wolpe's procedure with the cats rather thin. The grounding of behavior therapy in the history of the past decade of experimental psychology, which behavior therapists hope has elevated them above the analytic schools and made a science of therapy, is placed in jeopardy by this finding. I am not aware of the existence, in the literature of experimental psychology generated by learning theories, of anything more than an unpaid promissory note in regard to conceptualizations of this form of cognitive activity.

When one notes, in addition, that in this procedure an internally produced, imagined representation of a stimulus has a reality in terms of its observable and specifiable behavioral consequences, equal to what one might expect of an externally produced stimulus, it is clear that the current conceptual horizons of S-R learning theories have been passed. What in fact seems to be demanded by these data is a conceptualization geared to understanding man as a cognitive being.

In all fairness to behavior therapists it should be noted that Wolpe has offered demonstrations of effectiveness for other procedures, including in vivo presentations of actual stimuli, based on his general principle of reciprocal inhibition, and using responses other than relaxation for the inhibition of anxiety. In addition, other behavior therapies have used therapeutic analogues which are, at least without closer scrutiny, better approximations of laboratory procedures with animals. The present critique, however, is justified by the status of systematic desensitization therapy, and does not require modification if its applicability to behavior therapies is not universal. In other words, the writer is not willing to prejudge the question of whether a single set of processes is responsible for the successes reported by every therapeutic school.

DEFENSE OF PSYCHOTHERAPY

Neither cognitive psychologists nor psychoanalysts have yet seized upon the data of systematic desensitization as providing an opportunity for theoretical growth. Nor have dynamically oriented therapists fulfilled their professional responsibility, which, or so it appears to me, requires the most careful investigation of a method which makes and supports claims to therapeutic efficacy. Here I am in full agreement with Eysenck (1960) when he says:

> . . . I have noted with some surprise that many psychotherapists have refused to use such methods [behavior therapies] . . . on a priori grounds, claiming that such mechanical methods simply could not work, and disregarding the large body of evidence available . . . only actual use can show the value of one method of treatment as opposed to another. [p. 14]

An attempt to weaken the claims of behavior therapists of the theoretical superiority of their position by a critical attack may be welcomed by analytically oriented psychologists but is not likely to prove constructive. It is, rather, necessary to turn attention to the attacks made upon psychotherapy and to seek out the legitimate sources of its defense. While this examination is cast in a theoretical context, it should be noted that there is also at issue, waiting offstage but providing a background of urgency, a question of therapeutic responsibility; that is, what degree of theoretical certainty justifies withholding an available therapeutic method from a client?

The Therapy-Theory Distinction

There are two issues, typically confounded in the literature, which need to be separated before an intelligible analysis can proceed. It is claimed by behavior therapists that the clinical successes of behavior therapy invalidate psychoanalysis. Statistics on rates of "cure" are adduced in support of the claim that behavior therapy is more effective than psychoanalysis. Whatever the persuasiveness of these statistics, final judgment is a complex matter. Definitions of therapeutic practice and diagnostic criteria remain inadequate. The uses of the word "cure" by behavior therapists and psychotherapists are often incommensurable. Regardless, however, of history's verdict on the value of psychoanalytic therapy as it is practiced today, the problem will remain that psychoanalysis as a theory requires evaluation by criteria different from those by which therapy is evaluated.

There appears in many places in the analytic literature the articulation of an awareness of Freud's intention to consider analytic theory and therapy as distinct endeavors. The metapsychology incorporates analytically derived data but goes, with full comprehension of this step, far beyond the data. On the other hand, the metapsychology requires, if it is to be properly implemented in practice, procedures which have not yet been invented. Thus Reich (1949) wrote:

> All problems of techniques converge in the one basic question whether and how an unequivocal technique of analytic therapy can be derived from the theory of the neuroses. . . . Ample experience[s] . . . have shown that we have hardly made a beginning at this task. [p. 3]

A responsible critique of psychoanalysis by behavior therapists would need to make this distinction clear. The adequate response from psychoanalysts would also make this distinction. If behavior therapy is indeed the more effective instrumentality, this fact should instigate a reexamination of the untapped technical resources of analytic

theory. One cannot expect progress to follow from defensive denials.

The Problem of Symptom Substitution

On other fronts, genuinely theoretical attacks have been leveled at psychoanalysis. The most potent of these is the claim that, according to analytic theory, symptom substitution or recurrence *must* follow a course of treatment which removes a symptom by treating it directly, that is, without altering the underlying source of the symptom. In fact, analysts have tended to the belief that symptomatic treatment may be worse than no treatment at all, that is, that it may be dangerous. Both Eysenck and Wolpe have stated that psychoanalytic theory is decisively undermined by the failure of this prediction. The expectation of symptom substitution is a clinical prejudice of long standing, but the data seem to require a reevaluation.

Freud (1936) considered the possibility that a symptom may be a behaviorally fixed pattern which has inherited the total cathectic energy of the impulse which existed at its time of origin:

> . . . of the repressed instinctual impulse itself we assumed that it persisted unchanged for an indefinite period in the unconscious. Now our interest shifts to the fate of the repressed, and we begin to feel that this persistence, unchanged and unchanging, is not a matter of course, is perhaps not even the rule. . . . Do there therefore still exist the old desires, of the earlier existence of which analysis informs us? The answer appears obvious and certain. The old repressed desires must still persist in the unconscious, since we find their lineal descendents, the symptoms, still alive. *But this answer is inadequate*; it does not make it possible to distinguish between the two possibilities that, on the one hand, *the old desire now operates only through its descendents*, the symptoms, *to which it has transformed all its cathectic energy*, or on

the other hand, that the desire itself per-
sists in addition. . . . There is much in
the phenomena of both the morbid and
the normal life of the psyche which
seems to demand the raising of such
questions. In my study of the breakdown
of the Oedipus complex, *I became mind-*
ful of the distinction between mere re-
pression and the true disappearance of
an old desire or impulse. [p. 83; italics
mine]

Successful symptomatic treatment may
be taken as evidence for this second
alternative, which might be extended and
elaborated in ways entirely compatible
with analytic theory.

On another level of analysis, Rapaport
(1959) has noted that psychoanalysis is,
essentially, a postdictive system. It can
rationalize events after their occurrence,
but cannot predict these events. This
assertion is, in part, based upon Freud's
conception of the energetic relations between the systems of the psychic economy. The originally unitary nature of the
psychic structure is conceived as remaining, in certain essential characteristics,
unalterable. Thus the energetics of those
psychic systems which emerge in the
course of the development of personality
remain highly interactive. This inter-
activity makes it extraordinarily difficult
to predict the consequences of alterations
of energy distributions in one psychic
system upon the other systems. Is it
possible, then, to state what follows of
theoretical necessity from the removal of
a symptom? Such an alteration of experience and behavior is, after all, likely
to involve a not inconsiderable redistri-
bution of cathectic processes. From this
vantage it would appear that predictions
of symptom substitution follow from a
clinical rubric, and not with strict necessity from the analytic theory of the
neuroses.

These considerations can be carried
still further. Another line of analysis

arises from the consequences of the
thesis that the ego depends, for its
development, on the greater efficiency of
the secondary, as compared to the primary, process. That is, because the operations of the secondary process lead to
increasing mastery of the relation of the
psychic structure to object reality, exercise of the secondary process results in
the binding of libidinal energies to the
service of the emerging ego. Among the
services to which energy is bound is that
termed "repression." If one now considers the consequences for the ego, in
its relations with object reality, of the
removal of a symptom, the strands of
the analysis come together. The removal
of a symptom typically involves an increased mastery of object relations; for
example, in the case of the person who
is freed to express love, or hostility, or
the person who is able, for the first
time in a decade, to climb a flight of
stairs without trembling. Such increased
mastery must lead to an increment in
the bound energy available to ego functioning. Even if one must insist that the
dynamic source of an original symptom
formation remains unaffected by the removal of that symptom, the consideration that an increase in bound energy
may well lead to an increase in the effectiveness of repressive cathexes should
prohibit any *certain* prediction that
symptom substitution must follow.

A final line of analysis of this problem is stimulated by a consideration of
Freud's conception of symptoms in their
relation to anxiety. It is useful to compare this conception with Wolpe's behavioristic formulation. Wolpe conceives
of anxiety as *the neurosis*. As such, it is
simply an acquired, that is, learned,
maladaptive response. In this formulation anxiety is not given a functional role
in the psychic system. Freud, on the
other hand, envisions symptoms, that is,
maladaptive responses, as means used by

the ego to protect itself from danger. Anxiety, in this context, serves as a signal to the ego that a dangerous instinctual demand is growing in strength. In response to this impending danger a symptomatic action is engaged which binds a portion of the energy available to the instinctual demand. This binding reduces the imperiousness of the instinctual demand and permits the ego to avoid engaging it. Thus conceived, the symptom is a behavior substituted for the behavior demanded by the instinctual arousal. It is a maladaptive substitute because the danger to the ego, which may, at the time of symptom formation, have been actual, no longer exists. The ego never discovers that the danger is past because every arousal of the instinct produces a signal of anxiety, which in turn produces a discharge of the instinctual energy through the substitutive action, that is, the symptom. Of immediate relevance to the problem in hand is that in order to bind, successfully, the energy of the instinct, the substitute formation must bear a certain meaningful relation to the original object of the instinct. That is, the symptom formation is governed by the same principles which govern every displacement from an original instinctual object. This is another way of saying that the symptom must contain, in some measure, a symbolically adequate representation of the original object. Thus, for example, an external, phobic stimulus must symbolically represent the meaning of the internal danger.

This analysis leads to another formulation of the belief that symptom substitution must follow symptom removal, but also contains a suggestion of the possible error of this belief. If a symptom is removed, it is argued, the instinctual demand is unaltered, but now the ego has been deprived of its safety valve, that is, of its means of binding the instinctual energy. Without a means of discharge

available the urgency of the impulse will increase, anxiety signals will come more and more frequently, and in the end the ego will either be inundated or a new substitute formation, that is, a new symptom, will appear to bind the energy which is pressing forward.

Among the many assumptions, both explicit and implicit, in the above argument, the postulated relations between an instinctual demand and its object underpins both psychoanalytic method and theory. Every displacement of cathexis from an existing object is determined by, and participates in, a system of associative and symbolic meaningfulness. It is this fact which permits the reading of dynamic messages in the overt behaviors of people. It is this premise which permits psychoanalytic theory a solution of the problem of joining an apparently limitless field of variations in human behavior to a limited number of motivational sources. Thus, when a therapist confronts a symptom as a substitute formation he is, by definition, confronting the inner dynamic as well, albeit at a remove. Insight is, after all, conceived as the grasping of this relationship in a particular instance. To speak analytically of treating a symptom is theoretically inexact, unless one envisions the psychic equivalent of a scalpel which can enter a body of tissue, excise a desired portion, and leave lower tissue layers unaffected.

The treatment of a symptom by the method of systematic desensitization has no sensible analogy to such an idealized surgical procedure. On the contrary, the entire ego system is engaged in an eidetic and introspective task. The patient confronts his fear and inhibits his flight reflex. His fear, then, decreases. This fact should not upset the analytic theorist. If, in treating a symptom, we are treating the symbolic carrier of a feared instinctual demand, it satisfies the "logic" of our understanding of unconscious processes to expect far-reaching effects. To the degree to which a substitute formation is an adequate binder of cathectic energy, we may expect that a reduction in the strength of the signal anxiety which sustains this formation will represent an increase in ego tolerance of the instinctual demand. Freedom from fear, theory leads us to expect, is characteristic of increased ego strength, and may signal the possibility of creating more adequate binding behaviors. Why then predict symptom substitution?

It would neither surprise nor distress the author if psychoanalytic theorists should find fault with the above arguments. If a critique leads to a more convincing and elegant penetration of the proper relationship between the data of behavior therapy and analytic theory, the intention of the present analysis will have been realized. What is of importance is that this relationship be examined. The considerations already outlined suggest the futility of the position taken by Wolpe and Eysenck. To maintain that the failure of symptom substitution to occur with any regularity following symptom removal by the interventions of behavioral therapists constitutes a decisive argument against the validity of psychoanalysis, is to seriously underestimate its theoretical resources. Similarly, the unexamined prediction that symptom substitution must occur, as the grounds for a refusal by clinicians to give the use of the technique of systematic desensitization due consideration, must be rejected.

SOME INTERACTIONS OF DESENSITIZATION WITH PSYCHOTHERAPY

The consequences, for a psychotherapist, of acknowledging the possible utility of systematic desensitization, bear illus-

tration. One may tentatively accept the data which report the effectiveness of this technique and which deny contraindicating consequences. One may use the technique to give relief to one's patients. When the use of this technique is allowed, and when its implications are permitted to interact with an existing analytic, or other, orientation, possibilities occur which, while quite foreign to the behavior therapists, may lead to technical and theoretical growth.

For example, the occurrence of resistance in analytic work lends itself to an analysis which suggests the use of systematic desensitization. Resistance, in general, is assumed to occur when a train of associative production approaches forbidden unconscious material. This approach produces anxiety signals which excite the defenses of the ego and which lead to renewed efforts at repression of the material in question. What would follow if a patient were presented with the associative content which energizes repressive cathexes as a stimulus for desensitization?

In order to explore this question, two patients in analytic therapy were given brief training in the relaxation method (Jacobson, 1938) used in preparation for systematic desensitization. (The author is aware of the concern which many therapists will feel in regard to the effects of this procedure upon the transference. While this is a problem of great theoretical importance, an adequate treatment would require at least as much space as is taken by the present article.) When these patients reported dreams for which they were able to produce only sparse associative material, the systematic desensitization procedure was used. Specifically, the patient was asked to relax and was then asked to imagine either the last image of the dream, or another image in the dream which seemed particularly significant or disturbing to him. (The procedure may be described as a marriage of the methods of active imagination as developed by Jung, and systematic desensitization.) When a scene produced no further anxiety reaction, the patient was again asked for associations to the dream. On the 12 occasions (10 with one patient and two with the other) when this procedure was attempted, the outcome was the production of a flood of associative material. Both patients developed spontaneous interpretations of their dreams in the course of this process during six of the sessions in which the method was used. A control for this observation is suggested by a history of unsuccessful efforts by these patients to engage the images in their dreams by the method of active imagination prior to relaxation training. Other explorations suggest themselves, in abundance, upon consideration of the possibilities involved.

A promising area of research which has been opened in the literature is the application of systematic desensitization to the treatment of psychosomatic complaints. Insofar as a conception is entertained in which the breakdown of an organ system is envisioned as a consequence of the repression of impulses to express significant affect, systematic desensitization offers the possibility of direct hypothesis testing. Among the most interesting desensitizations, from a dynamic point of view, are those which free a patient to express his feelings. For example, in two cases which the author has not yet reported in the literature, the desensitization of anxiety produced by impulses to express hostility led to the disappearance of migraine syndromes of extended duration. The time and energy which would be involved in a full-scale, controlled investigation of psychosomatic illness, using the method of systematic desensitization to test the hypothesis of its relation to affect suppression, seems

to this writer a small price to pay for the potential gains in understanding and therapeutic power. Applications to general medicine may also be envisioned in areas in which psychosomatic effects are apparent, for example, the postulated relations between preoperative emotional stress and postoperative prognoses. What gains would there be in desensitizing a patient's unrealistic fears about his impending surgery?

An Empirical Critique of Systematic Desensitization and a New Method of Treatment

Dynamic points of view also suggest possible technical innovations in the desensitization procedure itself which are not likely to present themselves to a behavior therapist of a learning theory persuasion. One such suggestion arises from the groundbreaking investigations of Gendlin (1962) undertaken from his Rogerian orientation. Gendlin has described the consequences of attending to internal, felt body-states associated with affective arousal. It is his observation that the decision to remain verbally quiet and passive while directing attention to feelings in the body results in the experience of an increase in the richness and complexity of these feelings and a sequence of transformations of the felt "meaning" of the sensations. There is typically reported a brief, sharp rise in the intensity of the feeling, followed by a decline in the intensity as the associative richness connected with the feeling is directly experienced.

Explorations of Gendlin's procedure, both by this writer and in the reports of patients who were asked to observe themselves in this way, produced descriptions bearing a marked resemblance to the reports of content flow which were obtained from the investigations of imagining during systematic desensitization which were reported earlier in this paper. The possibility presented itself that during systematic desensitization visualizations, time limitations placed on the imagining of a given scene do not permit the patient's feeling to pass the peak of anxiety. It thus appeared possible that the necessity of multiple, hierarchical presentations was an artifact of the technique itself.

Four patients were involved in an investigation of this possibility. Each of two of the patients who were already being treated by systematic desensitization was given a new set of instructions. The patient was told to relax as usual and to imagine the scene presented by the therapist; but as soon as a feeling arose he was to direct his attention to the way his body felt. He was to focus attention on the strongest locus of feeling and to keep watching it no matter what distracting thoughts or images came to mind, and no matter how intense the feeling might become. The patient was presented with scenes from his prepared hierarchies. The first presentation to each patient was made at the beginning of a session in which a new hierarchy was scheduled for treatment, and consisted of the most intensely disturbing scene in that series. A single presentation was limited to 15 minutes. The therapist repeated, every minute, one or another paraphrase of the following: "Attend to the way you feel. Don't talk! Don't think! If thoughts come, let them pass through your mind. Don't attach yourself to them. Keep watching your feelings." Each session consisted of two such presentations followed by half an hour of discussion of the contents which had been experienced. Both of the patients reported intensifications of anxiety, floods of associations, changes in their understanding of what they were feeling, and, finally, complete disappearance of any affect they were willing to call anxiety in

regard to the contents treated. (The interested reader is referred to Gendlin, since my description of the experienced process would add nothing to what he has already described in detail.) Both patients felt that, *in contrast to their experience with systematic desensitization,* they "made sense to themselves," felt good about themselves and "in touch with themselves" (cf. Gendlin, 1962) after each session. In addition, while the *effects* of desensitization were experienced as "real," the procedure seemed magical and mysterious. By contrast, in this new procedure, the patients felt that *they* had healed themselves.

Four such sessions were conducted with each patient. Each of the "Gendlin-like" sessions was followed by one session devoted to the standard systematic desensitization procedure in order to determine whether desensitization had, in fact, occurred. The first scene presented was, in each case, the same scene which had been treated by the "Gendlin-like" procedure. In the case of one of the patients, the systematic desensitization presentations of the scenes in *descending* hierarchical order produced no anxiety reactions whatever. In vivo behavior gave strong evidence that desensitization had taken place. In the case of the other patient, two of the four hierarchies followed the above pattern. The other two hierarchies showed an anxiety residue, although the patient felt that the anxiety was considerably less than he had anticipated when preparing the hierarchies. For each of these hierarchies, a second "Gendlin" session produced apparently complete desensitization.

Two additional patients were treated by the "Gendlin" procedure. In both cases the treatment was begun without prior relaxation training and, consequently, without experience of systematic desensitization. Each of these patients went through a standardized series of diagnostic sessions used in cases intended for treatment by systematic desensitization, which included the preparation of anxiety hierarchies. At the beginning of the first treatment session the patient was instructed to relax as well as he could and to attend to the way his body felt, that is, sensations of his clothing on his body, the chair against his back, the feeling in his "gut," etc. He was then given the instructions which have been described above and was presented with the most intense scene of his lowest hierarchy. One patient was flooded with anxiety and could not bear to continue on this first and two subsequent attempts. The procedure was, therefore, temporarily abandoned. The results with the second patient were identical with those which have been described for patients experienced with systematic desensitization. In this case, however, the "Gendlin sessions" were not alternated with systematic desensitization sessions. The evidence that desensitization occurred is, therefore, confined to self-reports and in vivo behavioral evidence.

The patient with whom the procedure had failed was subsequently trained in relaxation. Treatment by the "Gendlin procedure" was then resumed and, on this attempt, replicated the three cases which have been described. Relaxation training seemed to have had a striking effect. On the occasions of the initial attempts the patient reported poor visualization of the scenes described to him by the therapist. After relaxation training visualizations were vivid and feelings during sessions were sharp and distinct. The patient reported the, to him, fascinating observation that, while the anxiety was as strong during sessions following relaxation training as he remembered it having been before, he felt more in touch with his body and better able to tolerate the feeling. Relaxation training of the Jacobsen type may prove to be a

means of bringing patients into contact with their internal processes. Rather than fostering repression under the guise of relaxation, as one analyst has expressed his concern (Hillman, 1960), relaxation training may tend to induce an increased receptivity to unconscious contents.

It hardly seems necessary to point out the urgency of attempts to replicate these findings. These results, should they prove replicable, suggest that the use of intensity gradients and other means of controlling anxiety arousal may be unnecessary for desensitization, and call into question a crucial procedural and theoretical emphasis in systematic desensitization. Wolpe came upon this treatment procedure, in part, by analogy to his successful desensitization of conditioned phobic reactions in cats. It does not detract from the impressiveness of the successes this analogy has generated in the treatment of human subjects to suggest a modification and indeed a radical revision of his method. It may be that with human subjects a method which encourages an engagement of the dynamics of the anxiety reaction with a subject's cognitive processes will also produce desensitization.

In spite of the very preliminary nature of the data which have been described, they would seem to offer reason for optimism. Attempts to produce confrontations of the data and method of systematic desensitization with other perspectives and frames of reference may prove to be a source of enrichment of therapeutic practice and theory.

ANALYTIC INTERPRETATIONS OF BEHAVIOR THERAPY

Earlier in this discussion a challenge was made of Eysenck's assertion that the effects of psychotherapy can be understood in terms of principles derived from "learning theory." It remains, for the purposes of this paper, to show that the effects of behavior therapy (systematic desensitization) can be understood in terms of principles derived from analytic theories. In other words, it seems desirable to offer a preliminary demonstration that confrontations of analytic theories with the method of systematic desensitization may be undertaken with some degree of plausibility on theoretical grounds. In what follows an attempt will be made to show that psychotherapists can derive, from their theoretical perspective, means of understanding the effects of the technique of systematic desensitization. That is, some of the resources of analytic theories will be tapped in an effort to frame interpretations of the way in which the specific therapeutic interventions of this form of behavior therapy produce their effects. These interpretations should *not* do violence to dynamic points of view, and *should* lead to a rational expectation that desirable results will follow.

A Psychoanalytic Interpretation of Systematic Desensitization

A number of suggestions have already been made, for example, in the discussion of symptom substitution, which could lead to a rational derivation of the effects of systematic desensitization by psychoanalytic theory. There are, however, in the body of Freud's writings a number of formulations which lend themselves even more precisely to this purpose. For example, Freud (1936) considers that an analysis of anxiety yields three attributes: "(1) a specific unpleasurable quality, (2) efferent or discharge phenomena, and (3) the perception of these [p. 70]." This is true for symptomatic anxiety as well as for signal anxiety which leads to a mobilization of ego defenses and symptom formation. Were it possible to confront the ego with impulses which generate the signals of anxiety, by, for example,

asking the patient to imagine himself engaged in the expression of an impulse from which he normally flees, and, were it possible, at the same time, to prevent or inhibit the occurrence of anxiety signals by, for example, inducing deep relaxation and raising the threshold of the discharge phenomena, reality oriented binding of cathexes might be expected to follow. While aware of the oversimplifications in this analysis, the writer fails to see any urgent reason why the suggestions which it makes available should not be explored by the technique of systematic desensitization.

An Interpretation by Complex Psychology of Systematic Desensitization

Within the writings of Jung, as well, is contained abundant conceptual material for analyses similar to that which has been outlined for Freud. Strikingly suggestive parallels may be found in Jung's (1960) monograph on paranoid dementia. The terms of definition of the complex theory as they are presented in that paper lend themselves to our present purpose.

The psyche is conceived as consisting, in part, of an indefinite number of clusters of relatively autonomous associative complexes. Each complex is organized around an emotionally toned content which draws to it materials bearing similarities of meaning and materials which occur as stimulus input during periods of time in which that particular complex is behaviorally dominant. In ordinary circumstances the complex of greatest strength, stability, and clarity is called the "ego." The ego depends, for its stability, on the fact that it includes in its associative cluster the range of proprioceptive stimulation produced by normal bodily tone. Most stimuli which occur in the presence of this normal proprioceptive state are drawn into association with the ego complex and share its clarity and stability. When a stimulus, by its associative properties, excites a complex other than the ego, it also excites an alteration in body tone. This altered body tone is part of the ego-alien complex, and induces an alteration of proprioception. It is in such altered states of proprioception that we have emotions. The emotional state is characterized by a weakening of the ego complex, that is, a loss of its usual behavioral dominance, and a change of consciousness best described as a loss of apperceptive clarity. (For an extended theoretical discussion of the far-reaching conclusions as to the nature of consciousness to which Jung was led by these germinal considerations, the reader is referred to Jung, 1954.)

It seems to follow that if a content which ordinarily disturbs the ego complex could be made to occur without producing an alteration in proprioception, that is, without an emotional excitement, the consequence should be an integration of this content to the ego complex. The therapeutic gains would be considerable. If systematic desensitization produces effects which can be understood in this way, many interesting avenues of exploration will be opened to Jungian theorists.

An Interpretation of Systematic Desensitization from the Viewpoint of Interpersonal Psychiatry

From the vantage of interpersonal psychiatry a relatively straightforward interpretation can be formulated. Anxiety, in Sullivanian thinking, has a clearly articulated function in determining personality structure. Anxiety generates and is involved in maintaining a set of defensive processes, primary among which is the "self." Insofar as the habitual responses of the self are designed to avoid anxiety, they tend to have the character

of parataxic thinking, that is, thought processes in which association by contiguity rather than connection by rational structure is the guiding principle. An adult who is capable of syntactic or rational thought may, nonetheless, exhibit parataxic habits in the presence of anxiety. Anxiety typically produces this weakening of rational processes. While this set of concepts is already suggestive in the present context, its relationship to systematic desensitization is clarified by a further consideration. Sullivan (1940) supposed that the necessary precondition for emotional states is an increase in skeletal-muscular tension. This increase in tension, when it passes a threshold value, produces that clouding of consciousness which, when we perceive it, we call anxiety. It is this clouding of consciousness which results in the failure of rational thought mentioned above.

It follows that if the adequate stimulus for an increase in skeletal-muscular tension could be presented in such a fashion as to limit, or avoid, the increase in tension which is ordinarily contingent upon it, a clouding of consciousness might be avoided. The stimulus in question should, in these circumstances, come under the scrutiny of the syntactic process and might be expected to undergo rational integration. Systematic desensitization is "tailor-made" for testing this hypothesis, which, should it be validated, provides a possible rationale for the use of this technique by analysts of the interpersonal school.

An Interpretation of Desensitization Therapy by Decision Theory

Psychotherapists who are oriented toward decision-making models of cognitive functioning, and who prefer to avoid dynamic formulations of the analytic variety, should also find little difficulty in rationalizing the use of systematic desensitization. A single example, very loosely based upon the theory of signal detection and focused on the anxiety hysteric, will serve to illustrate this contention. (Another approach, from the point of view of "cognitive" learning theory, is outlined by Breger & McGaugh, 1965.)

Anxiety may be conceived as the adequate stimulus for an avoidance or flight response (signal anxiety in the Freudian sense). Anxiety, thus, reflects an organization of the utilities matrix which controls the decision-making process by which responses to certain stimulus classes are selected. Existing utilities may require that a stimulus class which has the demonstrated power of evoking the anxiety signal be avoided, so that no signal is generated. The situation will now be such that for a given class of stimuli, the threshold of the avoidance response has been lowered. In order to insure a high percentage of successes in the avoidance of danger the person is willing to make avoidance responses to a range of contents which include many innocuous stimuli. At the same time, avoidance of the anxiety signal will require that avoidance responses be initiated at the first signs of such proprioceptive alterations as might imply possible anxiety. Given a base level of proprioceptive stimuli which are not perceptually articulate, any given increase (as determined by the utilities) in the intensity of proprioceptive feedback, such as that produced by increased skeletal-muscular tension, may be an anxiety signal. We thus have a person who responds as if there were reason to be anxious to a wide range of stimuli, both external and proprioceptive. We say that such a person has unadaptive anxiety. If, in the therapeutic setting, we alter the a priori possibilities of stimulus input by decreasing the intensity of proprio-

ceptive feedback, we decrease the "false alarm" rate and raise the threshold of avoidance responses to signals of anxiety.

This can be accomplished by inducing a state of skeletal-muscular relaxation. If, at the same time, we decrease the chaos of perceptual inputs by directing a patient to close his eyes and, further, by asking that he produce a vivid visualization of particular stimuli, we once again reduce the a priori possibilities of "false alarms." The experience of specific stimuli which have, in the past, been the occasion for anxiety signals, in the presence of reduced intensity of proprioceptive feedback, might be expected to produce "therapeutic" alternations of utilities matrices. The task of rationalizing the effects of systematic desensitization should not present formidable difficulties for other cognitive theories.

CONCLUSION

This paper has attempted a form of relatively systematic desensitization, in regard to the use of a therapeutic technique, upon the dynamically oriented clinical-academic community. It must, however, be noted that many objections to the use of systematic desensitization which may be raised on analytic grounds have only been lightly touched upon in this paper, or not mentioned at all. The interpretation of the transference relationship, to select only one example, will require a formidable theoretical effort. It would miss the point, quite decisively, to proceed as if no problems remained.

On the other hand, exploratory arguments have been drawn with the intent of persuading psychotherapists of the urgency of examining the grounds of their resistance to the use of systematic desensitization and of reevaluating the theoretical necessity of these grounds. The primary motivation of this attempt is the conviction of the writer (qualified by the obvious need for better controls and further investigation) that systematic desensitization works, that is, that it produces behavioral change, reliably, sometimes dramatically, and therapeutically. Within the areas to which it has been applied it has demonstrated impressive effectiveness. It remains to determine the best theoretical formulation of the processes involved in producing its effects. The limit of its applicability and the best form for its application are empirical questions. However, as a source of data and as a source of therapeutic power, it demands exploitation.

The question of the form this exploitation *should* take has led to the theoretical exercises in this paper, and to the empirical investigations described. What shall be the field of investigation, and the theoretical attitude with which this tool will be applied? The stakes seem too high to settle for a battle between behavior therapists and psychoanalysts. That there is danger of this happening has been pointed out by Andrews (1966) in his appeal for more open scientific communication. Everyone, including the patient, is likely to lose in such warfare. There is room for each persuasion to increase its technical and theoretical sophistication. Preliminary considerations have been presented with the intention of demonstrating that proprietary rights to this technique cannot be established on theoretical grounds. In other words, there is nothing to fear, in the technique or in the data it generates, for psychoanalytic or cognitive theorists, provided they actively engage the problem. There is no reason to fear that the engagement will force them to "throw the psyche out of psychology." There is reason to think they may emerge from the combat with new strength. Freud (1936) put the alternative succinctly: "When the wayfarer whistles in the dark, he may be disavowing his timidity, but he does not see any the more clearly for doing so [p. 23]." There are theoretical grounds for the use of systematic desensitization, for hypothesis generation, and for experimental tests of its consequences from a variety of points of view.

So long as the relationship of theory to its data is sufficiently loose that logical arguments can take precedence over empirical arguments, and empirical decisions seem out of reach, we can, perhaps, justify uncritical loyalty to our preconceptions. When, however, a means presents itself of bringing our therapeutic concepts to an empirical confrontation we are obligated to do so. None of us can assume that we possess enough foresight to envision the theoretical consequences, the model of man which the data will require. Perhaps it helps to remember the words of the prophet, that the better is always the enemy of the good, and that the good must give way if the better is to be. In any case, whatever the outcome, to collect the data and to construct the model seem to this author to be our professional obligation.

9

The Effects of
Psychotherapy

In the last chapter, we found considerable disagreement about the nature of psychotherapy: How it works and, when it is successful, why it works. Some of this controversy comes from scientific questions about the nature of human learning and personality change. Some, however, is rooted in the more practical questions of how effective the traditional psychotherapies (the Insight therapies) have been. If the Insight therapies had been overwhelmingly successful, it is quite likely that scientists would have examined them for aspects that contributed to their success. But they have not been nearly as successful as one might have wished. Consequently, psychiatrists and psychologists have turned elsewhere for designs for psychotherapies.

In this section we examine some of the literature on the effectiveness of psychotherapy. There is, however, a sizable gap in the available literature. Although the varieties of Insight therapies are now nearly a century old (and some, who would include the therapy of wise men,

oracles, and priests throughout the centuries, would say much older), there is not one study that properly evaluates their effectiveness. It is undoubtedly true that such studies are difficult to conduct. The complexities of Insight therapies are enormous and overwhelming. A large variety of presenting problems with even more varied underlying dynamics are seen by therapists whose orientations and competencies are varied and difficult to assess. All of this constitutes understandable reason for the failure to evaluate these therapies. But while the failure can, perhaps, be condoned, it leaves the question of the effectiveness of Insight therapy unanswered. And indeed, as we noted earlier, there is at least a feeling among psychological scientists, supported by fragmentary data, that the Insight therapies have not lived up to their promise.

Because of the dearth of literature on the effectiveness of Insight therapies the papers in this chapter deal mainly with Action or Behavior therapies, which are applicable mainly to problems in which there is behavioral distress—a fear, an inhibition, an anxiety that has behavioral concomitants. True, Behavior therapies may very well lend themselves to problems of a more intrapsychic nature (see Weitzman's paper earlier), but their main thrust has been to the resolution of symptomatic problems. Their applicability to such widespread problems as the existential neurosis (see Maddi's paper earlier), to problems of feeling or of personal responsibility, is theoretically conceivable, but it has not yet been convincingly demonstrated. The reader, then, will want to bear this bias in mind, and with it the likelihood that therapies with broader applicability are likely to appear in the relatively near future.

One of the earliest attempts to apply the principles of conditioning and extinction to neurotic behavior is seen in Mary Cover Jones' early report on the elimination of fear in young children. By pairing an aversive response, fear, with a pleasurable one, eating, Jones demonstrated that the fear could be overcome. The following paper, by Geer and Turteltaub, indicates another way to reduce fear. These authors permitted a child to observe a fearless model. The same principles of observational learning that guide the acquisition, elicitation, and inhibition of a variety of social learnings appeared to operate successfully in this context also.

Gordon Paul's paper follows his earlier study in which he compared the effectiveness of Insight and Behavior therapy techniques in eliminating the fear of speaking before an audience. That study (Paul, 1964), which is among the best controlled comparative studies now available in the psychotherapeutic literature, generally supported the superiority of Behavior over Insight therapy for this kind of problem, at least over the short run. One is, however, entitled to ask whether the relative effectiveness of Behavior therapy is a lasting one. In the study presented here, Paul gives the long-term data for Insight and Behavior therapies.

While psychotherapy, as we have seen, is an enormously complex procedure, it is occasionally argued that simply having a relationship with a warm and benign person in the context of something called therapy is alone responsible for the improvement that occurs. If this is the case, then the effects of therapy, whether "real" or "pseudotherapy," should be greater for relatively suggestible people. Peter J. Lang, A. David Lazovik, and David J. Reynolds compare the effects of such a "pseudotherapy" with the desensitization procedures of Behavior therapy on people who are fearful of snakes. The comparison of real and placebo therapies with nontreatment yields data that are of considerable interest for assessing the effects of psychotherapy.

The Elimination of Children's Fears

Mary Cover Jones

The investigation of children's fears leads directly to a number of important problems in the genetic study of emotion. At the Johns Hopkins laboratory[1] Dr. John B. Watson has analyzed the process by which fears are acquired in infancy, and has shown that the conditioned reflex formula may apply to the transfer of emotional reactions from original stimuli (pain, loud noises, or loss of bodily support) to various substitute fear objects in the child's environment. This process has been further demonstrated by the author in the case of children from one to four years of age.[2] A study of how children's fears may be reduced or eradicated would seem to be the next point for an experimental attack. Such a study should include an attempt to evaluate, objectively, the various possible methods which laboratory experience has suggested.

The present research, an approach to this problem, was conducted with the advice of Dr. Watson, by means of a subvention granted by the Laura Spelman Rockefeller Memorial to the Institute of Educational Research of Teachers College.

The subjects, 70 children from 3 months to 7 years of age, were maintained in an institution for the temporary care of children. Admission to this institution depended as a rule upon conditions which made it difficult or impossible to keep the children at home: a case of illness in the family, the separation of father and mother, or an occupation which kept the mother away from home for a part of the day. As there was a charge for weekly care, those homes which were in actual poverty were not represented; the economic and social status of the parents, as well as the results of our intelligence tests (Kuhlmann and Terman) would indicate that this group of children was normal, and superior to the average for orphan asylums and similar institutions. As the danger of contagion is great in a group so constantly changing, a very thorough medical examination eliminated all those with symptoms of infection, and even those decidedly below normal in nutrition or general development. Our laboratory could not determine the admission and discharge of children, nor interfere in the prescribed routine of eating, sleeping and play. It was possible however for the experimenter to live in the building with the children in order to become acquainted with them in their usual environment, to observe them continuously for days at a time, and to take them daily, or oftener if desirable, to the laboratory where observations could be made under specifically controlled conditions.

In our selection of children from this group, we attempted to find those who would show a marked degree of fear under conditions normally evoking positive (pleasant) or mildly negative (unpleasant) responses. A wide range of situ-

Reprinted from the *Journal of Experimental Psychology*, 1924, vol. 7, pp. 382–390 with the permission of the author.

[1] Watson and Rayner, "Studies in Infant Psychology," *Scientific Monthly*, December, 1921.
[2] "Conditioned Fear in Children," 1924.

ations were presented in a fairly standardized way to all of the children: such as being left alone, being in a dark room, being with other children who showed fear, the sudden presentation of a snake, a white rat, a rabbit, a frog, false faces, loud sounds, etc. This procedure served to expose fear trends if they were already present; it was not designed as a conditioning process, but merely as a method of revealing prior conditionings. In the majority of the children tested, our standard situations failed to arouse observable negative responses. This survey of children's fears is reported in another article.

When specific fears were demonstrated, our next step was to attempt their removal. By what devices could we eliminate these harmful reactions, which in many cases were subject to diffusion, and were interfering with the formation of useful attitudes and necessary habits? Our method or combination of methods depended upon the type of case presented and the manner in which treatment was received, as well as upon such external circumstances as quarantines, and the length of time the child was likely to remain in the institution.

THE METHOD OF ELIMINATION
THROUGH DISUSE

A common assumption with regard to children's fears is that they will die out if left alone, i.e., if the child is carefully shielded from stimuli which would tend to re-arouse the fear. "Elimination through disuse" is the name given to this process. The following cases from our records provide suggestive material:

Case 1.—Rose D.
Age 21 months.

General situation: sitting in play-pen with other children, none of whom showed specific fears. A rabbit was introduced from behind a screen.

Jan. 19. At sight of the rabbit, Rose burst into tears, her crying lessened when the experimenter picked up the rabbit, but again increased when the rabbit was put back on the floor. At the removal of the rabbit she quieted down, accepted a cracker, and presently returned to her blocks.

Feb. 5. After 2 weeks the situation was repeated. She cried and trembled upon seeing the rabbit. E. (the experimenter) sat on the floor between Rose and the rabbit; she continued to cry for several minutes. E. tried to divert her attention with the peg-board; she finally stopped crying, but continued to watch the rabbit and would not attempt to play.

Case 8.—Bobby G.
Age 30 months.

Dec. 6. Bobby showed a slight fear response when a rat was presented in a box. He looked at it from a distance of several feet, drew back and cried. A 3-day period of training followed bringing Bobby to the point where he tolerated a rat in the open pen in which he was playing, and even touched it without overt fear indications. No further stimulation with the rat occurred until

Jan. 30. After nearly two months of no experience with the specific stimulus, Bobby was again brought into the laboratory. While he was playing in the pen, E. appeared, with a rat held in her hand. Bobby jumped up, ran outside the pen, and cried. The rat having been returned to its box, Bobby ran to E., held her hand, and showed marked disturbance.

Case 33.—Eleanor J.
Age 21 months.

Jan. 17. While playing in the pen, a frog was introduced from behind her. She watched, came nearer, and finally touched it. The frog jumped. She withdrew and when later presented with the frog, shook her head and pushed the experimenter's hand away violently.

March 26. After two months of no further experience with animals, Eleanor was taken to the laboratory and offered the frog. When the frog hopped she drew back, ran from the pen and cried.

These and similar cases show that an interval of "disuse," extending over a period of weeks or months, may not result in eliminating a fear response, and that when other conditions are approximately constant there may be no diminution in the degree of fear manifested. From our experience, it would appear to be an unsafe method to attempt the cure of a fear trend by ignoring it.

THE METHOD OF VERBAL APPEAL

As most of our subjects were under four years of age, the possibilities of verbal analysis and control were very limited. We attempted to find how much we could accomplish toward breaking down a negative reaction by merely talking about the fear-object, endeavoring to keep it in the child's attention, and connecting it verbally with pleasant experiences. This method showed no applicability except in the case of one subject, Jean E., a girl in her fifth year. At the initial presentation of the rabbit a marked fear response was registered. This was followed by ten minutes daily conversation about the rabbit; to hold her interest the experimenter introduced such devices as the picture book of "Peter Rabbit," toy rabbits, and rabbits drawn or modelled from plastocene. Brief stories were used, and there was always a reference to the "real" rabbit as well. On such occasions she would say, "Where is your rabbit?" or "Show me your rabbit," or once "I touched your rabbit, and

stroked it, and it never cried." (This latter was pure make-believe, and an interesting example of projection.) However, when the rabbit was actually presented again, at the end of a week, her reaction was practically the same as at the first encounter. She jumped up from her play and retreated; when coaxed, she reluctantly touched the rabbit while the experimenter held it; when the animal was put down on the floor she sobbed "Put it away," "Take it," and ran about the room frightened and distracted. She had learned to speak freely of rabbits, but this altered verbalization apparently was not accompanied by any change in her response to the rabbit itself. The experiment was interrupted after another three days of the same procedure, at the end of which time Jean left the institution with her initial fear patterns intact, so far as we could tell. It seems likely that many hours of training in the toleration of symbols may have little or no modifying effect on a mass reaction to the primary stimulus.

THE METHOD OF NEGATIVE ADAPTATION

This method is based on the theory that familiarity breeds indifference: if the stimulation is repeated often enough, monotonously, the subject finally becomes used to it and tempers his response accordingly.

Case 17.—Godfried W.
Age 3 years.

A white rat was introduced from behind a screen. Godfried sat quietly for a few minutes, watching the rat with close attention. He then began to cry, made avertive movements with his hands and feet, and finally withdrew as far as possible from the animal. At the next presentation of the rat, Godfried did not cry; he advanced cautiously, making quick startled withdrawals whenever the animal moved.

A few days later when the same situation was presented, Godfried smiled and said, "Put it down on the floor." After three hours the rat was again brought in and allowed to run free in the pen. It scurried about and occasionally came very near him, but Godfried made no attempt to withdraw even when the animal advanced and touched him.

In this case, with practically no reëducative measures except repeated stimulation, Godfried conquered his specific fear. The experiment was not carried to the point where he showed a distinct positive reaction to rats, but he had developed a socially satisfactory attitude. As a strictly non-verbal approach, the method of negative adaptation is undoubtedly useful with infants and animals. In actual practice, however, we find very few fears in children of the pre-language period, and with the older children it is inefficient to eliminate the degree of control, however slight, which language may afford.

Furthermore, with all but a few of our fear-objects the aim was not indifference, which negative adaptation implies, but something farther along the scale toward an acceptance reaction.

From our experience in general, it would appear that the repeated presentation of a feared object, with no auxiliary attempt to eliminate the fear, is more likely to produce a summation effect than an adaptation. With Godfried (the case just quoted) the loss of his resistance was possibly due to the fact that he had been afraid the animal would bite him. This fear, unrealized, was gradually overcome.

THE METHOD OF REPRESSION

In the home, as well as in the school and playground, social repression is per-haps the simplest and most common method of dealing with fear symptoms . . . a method, which, we may commonly note, often fails to remove the roots of the fear. As there are already too many examples of the maladaptive results of repression, we shall not attempt to add to their number. In our laboratory we used no repressive punishment, but within a group of children the familiar situations of ridicule, social teasing and scolding frequently appeared. Because of shame, a child might try to contain his fears without overt expression, but after a certain point had been reached, the reaction appeared notwithstanding.

Case 41.—Arthur G.
Age 4 years.

Arthur was shown the frogs in an aquarium, no other children being present. He cried, said "they bite," and ran out of the play-pen. Later, however, he was brought into the room with four other boys; he swaggered up to the aquarium, pressing ahead of the others who were with him. When one of his companions picked up a frog and turned to him with it, he screamed and fled; at this he was chased and made fun of, but with naturally no lessening of the fear on this particular occasion.

Three boys standing around the aquarium each cried "Give me one," holding out their hands for a frog. But when the frog was offered they all precipitously withdrew. When two girls (4 years old) sang out to Sidney (age 3) "Sidney is afraid, Sidney is afraid," Sidney nodded his head in assent . . . illustrating what often happens in the use of social ridicule: the emotion is re-suggested and entrenched, rather than stamped out.

THE METHOD OF DISTRACTION

A convenient method, used frequently and with fair results, involves offering the subject a substitute activity. In order to capture a safety pin from the baby's hand and still preserve peace, its attention may be distracted with another toy, while you steal away the pin. Such a device, known to every mother, may be applied to the problem of eliminating fear responses. Arthur, whose fear of frogs had received some attention from us, wished to play with a set of crayons kept in the laboratory. We placed the crayons close to a frog on the table. Arthur stepped forward cautiously; keeping his gaze on the frog, he grabbed paper and crayons and showed alacrity in darting out of the danger zone. The experience, however, seemed to reassure him. "I ran over there and got it," he told us, "He didn't bite me. Tomorrow I'll put it in a little box and bring it home." At one stage of his fear of the rabbit, Sidney would whine whenever the rabbit was brought near, but he could readily be diverted by conversation about the rabbit's name, or some innocuous detail. For verbal distraction the constant presence of a grown-up is of course necessary; this introduces factors which are not always advantageous (such as reliance upon adult protection). Essentially, distraction soothes a fear response by inducing the child temporarily to forget the fear-object. (Substitution of an alternate stimulus-response system.) This may fail to result in any permanent reduction of the fear trend. Where the situation is properly managed, however, distraction passes over into a method which we have found distinctly useful, and which will now be described.

THE METHOD OF
DIRECT CONDITIONING

It is probable that each of our methods involves conditioning in one form or another. Under this heading, however, we include all specific attempts to associate with the fear-object a definite stimulus, capable of arousing a positive (pleasant) reaction. The hunger motive appears to be the most effective for use in this connection. During a period of craving for food, the child is placed in a high chair and given something to eat. The fear-object is brought in, starting a negative response. It is then moved away gradually until it is at a sufficient distance not to interfere with the child's eating. The relative strength of the fear impulse and the hunger impulse may be gauged by the distance to which it is necessary to remove the fear-object. While the child is eating, the object is slowly brought nearer to the table, then placed upon the table, and finally as the tolerance increases it is brought close enough to be touched. Since we could not interfere with the regular schedule of meals, we chose the time of the mid-morning lunch for the experiment. This usually assured some degree of interest in the food, and corresponding success in our treatment. The effectiveness of this method increases greatly as the hunger grows, at least up to a certain point. The case of Peter (reported in detail elsewhere) illustrates our procedure; one of our most serious problem cases, he was treated by the method daily or twice daily for a period of two months. The laboratory notes for the first and the last days of the training period show an improvement which we were able to attribute specifically to the training measures used.

Case 30.—Peter.
Age 2 years, 10 months.

March 10, 10:15 A.M. Peter sitting in high chair, eating candy. Experimenter entered room with a rabbit in an open meshed wire cage. The rabbit was placed on the table 4 feet from Peter who immediately began to cry, insisting that the rabbit be taken away. Continued crying until the rabbit was put down 20 feet away. He then started again on the candy, but continued to fuss, "I want you to put Bunny outside." After three minutes he once more burst into tears; the rabbit was removed.

April 29, 9:55 A.M. Peter standing in high chair, looking out of the window. He inquired, "Where is the rabbit?" The rabbit was put down on the chair at Peter's feet. Peter patted him, tried to pick him up, but finding the rabbit too heavy asked the experimenter to help in lifting him to the window sill, where he played with him for several minutes.

This method obviously requires delicate handling. Two response systems are being dealt with: food leading to a positive reaction, and fear-object leading to a negative reaction. The desired conditioning should result in transforming the fear-object into a source of positive response (substitute stimulus). But a careless manipulator could readily produce the reverse result, attaching a fear reaction to the sight of food.

THE METHOD OF
SOCIAL IMITATION

We have used this method extensively, as it was one of the first to show signs of yielding results.

Case 8.—Bobby G.
Age 30 months.

Bobby was playing in the pen with Mary and Laurel. The rabbit was introduced in a basket. Bobby cried "No, no," and motioned for the experimenter to remove it. The two girls, however, ran up readily enough, looked in at the rabbit and talked excitedly. Bobby became promptly interested, said "What? Me see," and ran forward, his curiosity and assertiveness in the social situation over-mastering other impulses.

Case 54.—Vincent W.
Age 21 months.

Jan. 19. Vincent showed no fear of the rabbit, even when it was pushed against his hands or face. His only response was to laugh and reach for the rabbit's fur. On the same day he was taken into the pen with Rosey, who cried at the sight of the rabbit. Vincent immediately developed a fear response; in the ordinary playroom situation he would pay no attention to her crying, but in connection with the rabbit, her distress had a marked suggestion value. The fear transferred in this way persisted for over two weeks.

Feb. 6. Eli and Herbert were in the play-pen with the rabbit. When Vincent was brought in, he remained cautiously standing at some distance. Eli led Vincent over to the rabbit, and induced him to touch the animal. Vincent laughed.

The second case illustrated a fear socially induced (this is perhaps the most common source of maladjustive fear trends) and the later removal of the fear by social suggestion. Many of the fears we studied pointed to an origin in a specific traumatic experience; it would probably have been a valuable aid in our procedure, had we been able to trace the developmental history of each of these fears. It was usually impossible to do this, however, in view of the institutional life of our subjects, and the fact that parents, even when they could be reached and consulted, were as a rule ignorant of their children's emotional mishaps.

SUMMARY

In our study of methods for removing fear responses, we found unqualified success with only two. By the method of direct conditioning we associated the fear-object with a craving-object, and replaced the fear by a positive response. By the method of social imitation we allowed the subject to share, under controlled conditions, the social activity of a group of children especially chosen with a view to prestige effect. Verbal appeal, elimination through disuse, negative adaptation, 'repression,' and 'dis-traction' were methods which proved sometimes effective but were not to be relied upon unless used in combination with other methods. It should be remarked that apart from laboratory analysis we have rarely used any of the above procedures in pure form. Our aim has been to cure the fear, by the group of devices most appropriate at any given stage of treatment.

Fear Reduction
Following Observation of a Model[1]

James H. Geer and Alan Turteltaub

Fear or anxiety plays a central role in many theories that deal with human behavior, and the present study was designed to further knowledge concerning fear. Fear, for the purpose of this study, is conceived of as a negative emotional response to a specific stimulus. The study is one of a group (cf. Geer, 1965, 1966) that has attempted to investigate fear using objective behavioral measures. The fear-arousing situation used in most of the studies from this laboratory is analogous to animal investigations where variations in approach to a fear stimulus were taken as the measure of fear. A similar situation has been used as a criterion measure in some investigations of behavior therapy (cf. Lang, Lazovik, & Reynolds, 1965). Geer (1965), using approach to a fear stimulus as the dependent variable, reported that the sex of the experimenter and a time delay prior to approaching a fear stimulus were not effective in modifying fear behavior. An unpublished study by the same investigator reveals that different amounts of prior exposure to the fear stimulus do not affect subsequent approach behavior. The present study, also using approach to a fear object, reports the manipulation of fearful behavior where the independent variable was a social stimulus.

The effect of the presence of another person upon emotional behavior has been suggested by numerous investigators. Jones (1924) reported that the presence of a child who showed no fear of an object that was frightening to another child reduced the fear of the fearful child. She called this phenomenon fear reduction by social imitation. Freud (1955), using clinical evidence, noted that fear reduction sometimes occurred when phobic individuals were accompanied by "specially selected persons [p. 115]." Schachter (1959) studied affili-

Reprinted from the *Journal of Personality and Social Psychology*, 1967, vol. 6, pp. 327–331 with the permission of the American Psychological Association and the authors.

[1] The data for study were collected by the junior author as part of an undergraduate research project. The authors wish to thank Janice Mazer and Jeanne Salis who acted as confederates in this study.

ative behavior under conditions of anxiety arousal. In general, he found that subjects under conditions of anxiety arousal tend to affiliate. Schachter (1959) said, "People do serve an anxiety-reducing function for one another [p. 26]." Ring, Lipinski, and Braginsky (1965) reported a study in which the subject's moods were measured under conditions where confederates accompanying the subject behaved, depending upon experimental conditions, "extremely anxious," "moderately anxious," "somewhat anxious," or "low in anxiety." Ring *et al.* reported that the emotional state of the confederate has differential effects upon the subject's response to mood questionnaires, and that this effect varies with the subject's birth order.

In the present study an attempt was made to assess the effect of observing the behavior of others in a fear-arousing situation upon the subject's subsequent reaction in that situation. The hypothesis under examination was that observation by a fearful subject of either fearful or nonfearful behavior by a model would modify the observer's behavior in a direction to make the subject's behavior more like the model's behavior.

METHOD

Subjects. Subjects were 64 female undergraduates enrolled in introductory psychology at the University of Pennsylvania. About 1 month prior to the experiment, students in the course had been given the Fear Survey, Schedule-II (Geer, 1965). Class members were classified as high fear if their response to the item, "snakes," was either "terror" or "very much," and low fear if their response to the item was either "none" or "very little." From the pool of high-fear and low-fear students, 30 low fear and 35 high fear were selected for participation in the study. Four high-fear subjects were discarded from the study because they failed to meet a behavioral criterion; that is, when they were first asked to approach a snake they touched it. One high-fear subject could not be used because she refused to take the behavior test. The fear inventory was used to identify individuals who were likely to be, depending upon their response to the item, "snakes," either high or low fear; however, the criterion for high or low fear was the behavioral test.

Procedure. All subjects were met by a male undergraduate who acted as the experimenter in the study, and were told that they were to participate in a study that had two purposes. One purpose was to study people's reactions to a snake upon two occasions. The second purpose of the study was described as an evaluation of the accuracy of judging emotional reactions to a situation as a result of the rater's having had experience in that same situation. Subjects were told that they would be rating the reactions of another subject who was approaching the snake. Subjects were further told that their judgments would be compared with ratings made by observers who had not had the same experience as the individuals being rated. There were, however, no other raters for such a comparison.

Following this introduction, subjects were told that at the far end of the next room on the floor was a live nonpoisonous snake.[2] The subject was asked to accompany the experimenter into the room and to stand near the wall of the room opposite the snake. After the subject was properly located (approximately 17 feet from the snake), the experimenter walked up to the small 6-inch

[2] The snake was a 4-foot pine snake loaned to the investigators by the Academy of Natural Sciences, Philadelphia, Pennsylvania.

wire barrier behind which the snake was placed, stepped over the barrier, and bent down and touched the snake so that it moved. This procedure was employed to demonstrate that the snake was alive and not dangerous. After this demonstration, the experimenter moved back across the barrier and stopped about 12 feet from the barrier. The subject was then instructed to "Approach the snake as close as you comfortably can. Cross the barrier and bend down and touch the snake if you can." The experimenter pointed out that the task was not to be taken as a challenge in which the subject could show how much she could take, but she was to do what was comfortable. The subject began her approach on signal from the experimenter. If the subject did not touch the snake, the experimenter recorded the distance that she stopped from the snake. This was done by the experimenter noting the spot where the subject stopped. The actual distance was measured without the subject's knowledge, after the subject had left the room. The experimenter, using a stopwatch, also recorded the time from the start signal until the subject either touched the snake or was at the point of nearest proximity to the snake.

After the first behavior test, the subject was taken outside the room that contained the snake and conducted to a small room that had a one-way vision mirror looking into the room where the behavior tests were conducted. From this point the subject could see into the behavior test room; a stereo system was hooked up so that the subject could clearly hear all that occurred in the test room. The experimenter told the subject that he would get the next subject and would go through exactly the same procedure with the next subject that the subject had just experienced. The subject was then given a rating sheet that

she was to use in judging the reaction of the next subject. The items were:

1. Upon first viewing the snake, subject experienced the following amount of fear:
   None   Very Little   A Little   Some   Much   Very Much   Terror
2. How much tension or anxiety do you think subject felt when she was nearest the snake?
   None   Very Little   A Little   Some   Much   Very Much   Terror
3. Rate your impression of subject's overall fear level.
   None   Very Little   A Little   Some   Much   Very Much   Terror

The subject was also given a copy of Zuckerman's (1960) Affect Adjective Check List and instructed to check those items that described the emotional responses of the next subject. The subject was told to fill out the forms before the experimenter conducted an interview with the next subject. This interview, the subject was told, would be the criterion against which the subject's ratings would be compared. The rating sheet had two functions: (a) to make certain that the subject watched the next subject and (b) to have some means of assessing the effectiveness of the confederate. The subject was told that the one-way mirror was being used so that the next subject would not be aware of being observed. The subject was also told that during her second behavior test the observation room would be empty. The physical arrangement of the rooms was such that the subject could be fairly certain that she was not being observed during her second behavior test.

The next subject was one of two confederates who behaved in one of two manners. One manner was termed high fear, and in that condition the confederate appeared quite frightened. The confederate stopped 15 feet from the snake during the approach, and during the interview the high-fear confederate spoke of considerable discomfort and asked several times to be allowed to leave the room. The low-fear confederate acted in a manner such as to indicate very little fear. It may be noted that most of the verbal descriptions of their feelings used by the confederates during the interview were taken from the responses of several pilot subjects who were interviewed in order to obtain responses for this purpose. The confederate did not know whether the observer was a high-fear or a low-fear subject, and the one-way mirror prevented the confederate from gaining any cues as to the subject's reaction. Confederates acted either the high-fear or low-fear role on the basis of a prearranged random schedule.

Following the observation, the experimenter went to the observation room, collected the rating sheet, and conducted the subject back for the second behavior test. The second behavior test was identical to the first, with the exception that the experimenter did not redemonstrate that the snake was alive. The same behavior measures were obtained in the second behavior test that were obtained from the first. In addition to the high-fear and low-fear confederate conditions, a third control condition was employed. This consisted simply of two exposures to the snake with a time lapse of 5 minutes (the mean time elapsed when confederates were used) between behavior tests. The subject sat in a separate room during this time. The subject sat alone without books or reading material. She was told that the delay was to provide two separate exposures to the snake. This condition was used to control for the effects of two successive exposures to the fear stimulus. Thus there were three groups of subjects—high-fear confederate, low-fear confederate, and control condition with both high-fear and low-fear subjects.

RESULTS

The first set of results pertain to the ratings made by the subjects when observing the confederates. The first measure was the summed response to the three items on the rating scale with 0 being assigned to the rating of "none" and the numbers 1, 2, 3, 4, 5, and 6 being assigned to ratings of increasing fear. The maximum possible score for the confederate was 18. The mean summed rating of the high-fear confederates was 12.9; the mean summed rating of the low-fear confederates was 3.1. The difference between those means was highly significant ($t = 10.47$, $p < .001$) indicating that the high-fear confederates were rated as showing more fear. A similar analysis was performed on the Adjective Check List. Using Zuckerman's (1960) scoring formula, the mean score for high-fear confederates was 15.1 and the mean score for low-fear confederates was 7.1. The difference between those means also yielded a highly significant difference ($t = 10.32$, $p < .001$). In sum, it may be inferred that the confederates were successful in transmitting the desired impression. One final analysis of the ratings was made. It would have been of interest if high-fear subjects attributed more fear to the confederate than did low-fear subjects. The data were consistently in the direction of suggesting that high-fear subjects did rate confederate as being more frightened. However, this "projection" did not approach accepted levels of statistical significance when evaluated by t tests.

The data of primary interest are the results of the distance measure. Table 1

Table 1
Median Distance (Inches) from Snake for High-Fear Subjects and Number of Subjects that Moved Closer on Trial 2

	High-fear confed- erate	Control	Low-fear confed- erate	All high- fear subjects
Trial 1[a]	33	26.5	25	28
Trial 2	34	24.5	5	22.5
No. Ss moving closer on Trial 2	4	7	10	

[a] Mann-Whitney U test of differences between groups on Trial 1 did not approach statistical significance.

contains a summary of the results for high-fear subjects. The table contains the median distances for high-fear subjects on Trials 1 and 2, and also the number of high-fear subjects who moved nearer the snake on Trial 2. The dependent variable used to assess the effect of the various conditions was each subject's change in distance from the first to the second behavior test. The measure was obtained only for high-fear subjects since all low-fear subjects touched the snake on both behavior tests. A Kruskal-Wallis nonparametric analysis of the three conditions indicated that the three conditions differed significantly from each other ($H = 6.64$, $p < .05$). Figure 1 presents the median-distance change scores for high-fear subjects under the three conditions. Mann-Whitney U tests between the groups revealed that the subjects moved closer to the snake following observation of the low-fear confederates than after observing the high-fear confederates ($U = 22.5$, $p < .05$). The same test indicated that subjects moved closer to the snake following observation of the low-fear confederates than following the control condition ($U = 16.5$, $p < .02$). The same comparison

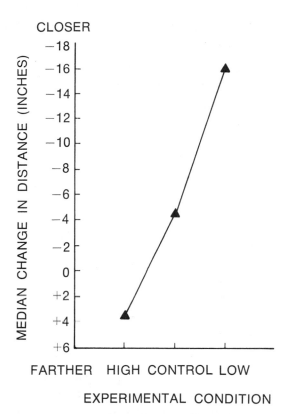

Figure 1 The median change in distance for the high-fear subjects as a function of experimental condition.

between the control conditions and the high-fear confederate condition did not reveal a significant difference.

It may be recalled that the snake was behind a low barrier. It appeared that crossing that barrier was a difficult task for high-fear subjects since only 4 of the usable 30 high-fear subjects crossed the barrier on the first behavior test. Taking the results of high-fear control-condition subjects as the base line, it would be expected that on Behavior Test 2 one high-fear subject would cross the barrier who had not done so on Behavior Test 1. One additional crossing did occur in the high-fear confederate group, while six additional crossings occurred for the low-fear confederate group. A chi-square test of those data yielded a significant difference $(x^2 = 27.8, \ p < .01)$ indicating that barrier crossings increased following observation of the low-fear confederate.

The trends of the latency data were all in the same direction as that of the distance data; however, there were no statistically significant differences. The reason for this appears to be in the nature of the task. Subjects were often noted to spend considerable time deciding whether or not to touch the snake, and this delay made the latency measure difficult to interpret and difficult to obtain accurately.

DISCUSSION

This study demonstrates that if an individual who displays fear of an object observes another person behaving unafraid of that object there is a tendency for the observer's fear behavior to be reduced. The obverse of this finding was not present in the data of this study; that is, subjects did not show significantly increased fearful behavior following observation of the high-fear confederate. Figure 1 reveals that there was a tendency for high-fear observers, having watched the high-fear confederate, to move further back on Behavior Test 2; however, the data did not attain accepted levels of statistical significance. This may be in part due to reverse psychology. Two high-fear subjects who observed the high-fear confederate reported that the other subject made them realize how "silly" their fear was, and thus on the second behavior test they showed much less fear than on the first test. It may also be that the subjects were quite frightened and only extreme measures would measurably increase the fear. Finally, it is possible that the confederates were unable to simulate fear accurately enough to affect the observer, while they could show low fear more effectively, since it was the con-

federates' normal response. Low-fear subjects could not move any closer to the snake upon viewing the low-fear model, since all low-fear subjects touched the snake on Trial 1. Viewing the high-fear model did not result in the low-fear subjects' moving away from the snake. Apparently the conditions of this study were not powerful enough to induce fear in low-fear subjects.

Several theoretical models may be employed to explain the results of this study. The most obvious to this writer is social learning theory such as discussed by Bandura and Walters (1963). They characterized one of the effects of a model's behavior upon an observer as a disinhibitory process. Disinhibition appears to be the major effect found in this study. Upon seeing a model behave in a nonfearful manner, the observer imitated the model and displayed behavior that had previously been inhibited, presumably because of fear. Social learning theory would further predict that the fearful models would have accentuated fearful behavior, however this did not occur. Several possible explanations of this failure were advanced above.

The present study does not indicate the mechanism by which behavior change occurs. A possible mechanism would involve self-instruction; that is, the observer, upon the occasion of the second behavior test, gave herself covert instructions such as, "If the other subject could do it, so can I." Indeed some subjects reported having such thoughts. It may be noted that such self-instruction could result in comfort responses which would function as competitors with (and thus reduce) fear. With fear thus reduced, approach behavior would continue. It is also possible that the subject's approach behavior was modified by self-instruction, but that other aspects of the fear response, such as autonomic components, were unmodified. Further studies are being conducted to investigate some of the possible mechanisms of the behavior change.

If it can be established that the changes in behavior that were reported in this study are relatively enduring, the results may have implications for the area of behavior modification. For example, the study suggests that fear reduction may be facilitated by the systematic and judicious use of models. Further, the effect of others upon fear may account for some of the results of group psychotherapy. This would seem to be particularly true if the members of the group had dissimilar fears.

Insight versus Desensitization in Psychotherapy Two Years after Termination[1]

Gordon L. Paul[2]

After a review of the difficulties of follow-up studies on psychotherapy, Sargent (1960) concluded that, "the importance of follow-up is equalled only by the magnitude of the methodological problems it presents." In the absence of a carefully designed outcome study on which to base follow-up investigations, the follow-up may be doomed from the start. Thus, in many studies, the methods of assessment at follow-up differ from those at pretreatment and posttreatment (e.g., Berle, Pinsky, Wolf, & Wolff, 1953;

Reprinted from the *Journal of Consulting Psychology*, 1967, vol. 31, pp. 333–348 with the permission of the American Psychological Association and the author.

[1] Appreciation is expressed to the Graduate College Research Board of the University of Illinois whose support made this study possible. The earlier data used in this paper were drawn from a study supported in part by Public Health Services Fellowship 1 F1 MH-19, 873, 01 from the National Institute of Mental Health, and in part by the Cooperative Research Program of the Office of Education, United States Department of Health, Education and Welfare, Contract No. 4-10-080, Project 006.

[2] Thanks are extended to Tom Brudenell for his aid in collating and analyzing FU₂ data. Correlational analyses were performed by the IBM-7090 computer of the University of Illinois Computer Science Laboratory.

Cowen & Combs, 1950; Sinett, Stimput, & Straight, 1965). Other studies, especially of a retrospective nature, have used assessment procedures of questionable reliability and validity (e.g., Cooper, Gelder, & Marks, 1965; Sager, Riess, & Gundlach, 1964; Schmidt, Castell, & Brown, 1965). Still others have neglected to include appropriate no-treatment control groups for assessing change in the absence of treatment (e.g., Bookbinder, 1962; Fiske & Goodman, 1965; Rogers & Dymond, 1954). The follow-up also suffers, inherently, from the uncontrolled nature of client experiences during the posttreatment period. This is especially important when the time between treatment termination and follow-up is considerably longer than the duration of treatment; environmental experiences during the posttreatment period may have more influence on Ss' status at follow-up than a brief program of treatment some months or years in the past. The greatest confounding comes from the fact that many Ss receive additional treatment of unknown nature during the posttreatment period, thus invalidating the design for determining cause-effect relationships for the specific treatment under investigation. This practical problem has limited the value of many follow-up studies (e.g., Braceland, 1966; Mc-Nair, Lorr, Young, Roth, & Boyd, 1964; Stone, Frank, Nash, & Imber, 1961).

Overshadowing all other problems of follow-up research is the practical difficulty of sample maintenance and attrition. Even adequately designed studies may not be able to obtain consistent follow-up data on treated Ss, let alone controls (e.g., Fairweather & Simon, 1963; Kogan, Hunt, & Bartelme, 1953; Lang & Lazovik, 1963). The problem of differential dropout and selective biasing of the sample cannot be ignored, since differences have been found between follow-up returnees and nonreturnees (Fiske & Goodman, 1965), and further, as May, Tuma, and Kraude (1965) point out, even if differences are not found, nonreturnees are clearly different in cooperation, mobility, or both. To highlight the magnitude of this problem, a thorough search of the literature failed to reveal a single study on individual treatment of noninstitutionalized adults which obtained data on all treated Ss 2 years or more after treatment termination, nor one which included an attempt to obtain such data on an appropriate group of control Ss.

The present study is a 2-year follow-up of an earlier investigation which was presented as a model design for the controlled evaluation of comparative therapeutic outcome (Paul, 1966). In the earlier study, a modified form of Wolpe's (1961) systematic desensitization was found to be significantly more effective in reducing maladaptive anxiety than insight-oriented psychotherapy or an attention-placebo treatment. Additionally, all three treated groups were found to show significant improvement over untreated controls. Although these effects

were found at termination of treatment, under stress-condition assessment, and were maintained at a 6-week follow-up, the differing theoretical models from which the treatment techniques are derived make a long-term follow-up even more desirable than is usually the case.

Specifically, the disease-analogy model underlying the insight-oriented approach to psychotherapy would interpret the results obtained by systematic desensitization and attention-placebo treatments as suggestion or positive transference—in either case, results which would be regarded as merely symptomatic and temporary (e.g., Hendrick, 1958). According to this model, not only would Ss treated by either systematic desensitization or attention placebo be expected to show "relapse" after the "supporting contact with the therapist fades [Sargent, 1960]," but possibly harmful results would also be expected because of the necessary occurrence of symptom substitution (see Ullmann & Krasner, 1965). In fact, the minimal symptom-substitution effect expected would be an increase in anxiety, introversion, rigidity, or dependency (Fenichel, 1945). Additionally, some unsuccessful cases treated by insight-oriented psychotherapy might be expected to realize benefits at some time after treatment termination when their "insights" have had time to "consolidate" (Sargent, 1960). On the other hand, the learning model underlying systematic desensitization would predict no greater relapse for one group than another after treatment termination, since relapse would be expected to occur only on the occasion of unusual stress or if conditions favoring the relearning of anxiety were encountered. Further, this model would expect to find no change in behaviors that were not the specific focus of treatment, except through generalization or an increase in behavior previously inhibited by target behaviors. Thus, from the learning framework, if any change in anxiety, introversion, rigidity, or dependency were to occur at all after treatment termination, it would be in the opposite direction of that expected from the symptom-substitution hypothesis (Paul, 1966). Although the findings at 6-week follow-up strongly favored the interpretation of the learning model, with none of the results expected on the basis of the disease model forthcoming, it is possible that the first follow-up period was too short to allow the expected processes to show their effects.

In the present study an attempt has been made to overcome the methodological and practical difficulties of follow-up research more adequately than previous attempts. By starting with a well-controlled outcome study, the same measures of assessment could be obtained from Ss at a consistent interval for long-term follow-up as were previously obtained at pretreatment and short-term follow-up. Persistent effort resulted in a greater return of data than has been reported before, not only for treated Ss, but for untreated controls as well. Additionally, specific frequency data were obtained to allow both the exclusion of Ss receiving additional treatment and the assessment of life stresses and possible symptom substitution during the post-treatment period. The major purpose of the present study was: (a) to determine the overall comparative effects of the different treatments from pretreatment to 2-year follow-up and (b) to examine the relative stability of improvement from the 6-week follow-up to the 2-year follow-up, particularly with regard to the questions of differential relapse and symptom substitution versus generalization, as predicted from the conflicting theories on which the treatments were based.

METHOD

Subjects

The Ss included in the present investigation consisted of three groups of 15 Ss each (10 males, 5 females) who received individual systematic desensitization, insight-oriented psychotherapy, or attention-placebo treatment and 44 Ss (32 males, 12 females) who composed an untreated control group. This included all Ss from the previous outcome study (Paul, 1966), except for a group of untreated controls who participated in a different therapy program in another context (Paul & Shannon, 1966). At pretreatment assessment all Ss were undergraduates ($Mdn =$ sophomore) enrolled in a required public speaking course at the University of Illinois, ranging in age from 17 to 24 years ($Mdn = 19$). Each S was selected on the basis of indicated motivation for treatment, high scores on performance anxiety scales, and low falsification from a population of 380 students who requested treatment for interpersonal performance anxiety, as described in detail in the earlier report (Paul, 1966). Although the public speaking situation was reported to be the most stressful condition imaginable, anxiety was also reported in almost any social, interpersonal, or evaluative situation. As a group, the Ss also differed from the normal student population by obtaining higher general anxiety and emotionality scores and lower extroversion scores. The Ss' degree of anxiety in performance situations was strong to severe, and was reported to be of 2–20 years duration.

Procedure

Pretreatment assessment consisted of the administration of a battery of personality and anxiety scales to the students enrolled in the speech course the week following their first classroom speech. The battery was constructed specifically to assess focal treatment effects and to show symptom substitution or generalization if such processes were operating. The battery thus included forms of (a) IPAT Anxiety Scale (Cattell, 1957); (b) Pittsburgh Social Extroversion-Introversion and Emotionality Scales (Bendig, 1962); (c) Interpersonal Anxiety Scales (speech before a large group, competitive contest, job interview, final course examination) of the S-R Inventory of Anxiousness (S-R; Endler, Hunt, & Rosenstein, 1962); (d) a scale of specific anxiety in a referenced speech performance (PRCS; Paul, 1966).[3] Following initial selection and prior to treatment assignment, Ss underwent stress-condition assessment in which they were required to give a 4-minute speech before an unfamiliar audience which included four psychologists recording the presence or absence of 20 observable manifestations of anxiety during each 30-second period on a timed behavioral checklist. In addition, the palmar sweat index and pulse rate were obtained immediately before the stress speech, as was the Anxiety Differential (see footnote 3). All Ss underwent stress evaluation except for an equated subgroup of controls initially used to evaluate the effects of the stress-condition assessment itself.

Following stress-condition evaluation the groups were formed, equating all groups on observable anxiety, with Ss randomly assigned to therapists. After a short screening interview, during which standard expectations were established, the treatments began—4 weeks after pretreatment assessment. Five experienced

psychotherapists (of Rogerian and Neo-freudian persuasion) worked individually with three Ss (two males, one female) in each of the three treatment groups for five sessions over a 6-week period. All three treatments were conducted concurrently, with missed sessions rescheduled during the same week. Within the week following treatment termination, a posttreatment stress-condition assessment was obtained on treated Ss and no-treatment controls, including the same measures used in the pretreatment stress condition. The first follow-up (FU_1) data were then obtained by a second administration of the test battery to all Ss 6 weeks after treatment termination. Attitudinal and improvement ratings were also obtained from treated Ss and therapists. The details of all aspects of procedure and results through FU_1 are reported in the earlier study (Paul, 1966).

The 2-year follow-up (FU_2) procedure required tracking down the Ss for a third administration of the test battery which had been administered at pretreatment and FU_1. For FU_2 the test battery was augmented to obtain specific frequency data regarding the occurrence of stress during the posttreatment period; the frequency of external behaviors which might reflect predicted symptom-substitution effects of increased dependency, anxiety, or introversion; and information concerning additional psychological treatment or use of drugs which might affect S's behavior or response to the anxiety scales.

Information on external stress was obtained by requesting Ss to indicate the number of times each of a number of events occurred since the last contact (FU_1). These events covered five major areas of stress: (a) illness or death of loved ones; (b) conflict (with fiancé or spouse, with persons in authority); (c) change in family structure (engagement, marriage, separation, divorce, pregnancy,

---

[3] The original battery also included a form of the Anxiety Differential (Husek & Alexander, 1963). This form was excluded from follow-up analysis since an additional stress administration was not obtained.

or birth); (*d*) personal illness or accident; (*e*) change in work or living arrangements (move to a different residence, move to a different city, take a new job, change vocational goals, leave college).

Behavioral frequencies regarding possible symptom substitution consisted of the following 13 items:

1. In the past *two weeks*, how many times did you seek advice, guidance or counsel from: friends?___; spouse/fiance? ___; instructor/supervisor?___; parents? ___; physician?___; others (please specify)?_____.
2. In the past *two weeks*, how many times was advice, guidance, or counsel *offered* which you did *not* seek from: (same as #1).
3. In the past *two weeks*, how many times did you *accept* advice, guidance, or counsel when it was provided from: (same as #1).
4. Of your close friends and relatives, with how many different people would you currently feel that you could discuss personal problems should the need arise?___
5. To how many clubs or organizations do you currently belong?___
6. How many dances, parties, or similar social events have you attended in the *past month?*___
7. In the *past month*, how many events have you attended as a "spectator" (such as concerts, meetings, sporting events, etc.)?___
8. How many times in the *past month* have other persons been to your home (or room) to visit you?___
9. In the *past month*, how many times have you visited or "gone-out" with another person?___
10. Of the *different people* you have visited, gone-out with socially, or who have visited you in the *past month*, how many were: males?___; females?___
11. How many times have you participated in group discussion in the past month?___
12. In the past *three months*, how many times have you spoken or appeared before a group?___

13. How many *different* groups have you appeared before in the past 3 *months?*___

Additional information was requested regarding the date and audience size of public appearances in order to appropriately analyze the PRCS and S-R speech scales. The same self-ratings of specific and general improvement which were obtained from treated Ss at FU_1 were also included at FU_2.

The procedure for FU_2 contact ran as follows: 24 months from the date of treatment termination a packet containing the test battery, behavioral questionnaires, and rating scales was mailed to the last known address of each S. The packet was accompanied by a cover letter explaining the importance of participation for one last time and was otherwise designed to enlist cooperation, including an offer to furnish the results of the investigation. This letter set a date 3 weeks in the future by which the completed forms were to be returned in a stamped, self-addressed envelope which was provided. Those Ss not returning forms by the first due date were sent a personal letter which further stated the importance of their specific participation, and a new due date was set 2 weeks hence. The Ss not responding to the second letter were then sent a complete new packet by registered mail, as were those Ss for whom new addresses were necessary. Those Ss not responding to the third letter were personally contacted by telephone and reminded of the importance of returning the data, and a promise was elicited to do so immediately. An arbitrary cut-off date was set exactly 27 months after treatment termination, for determining "nonreturnee" status of contacted Ss. Thus, although FU_2 was designated as a 2-year follow-up, the actual time from termination was 25–27 months, closer to 2 years from FU_1 than from treatment termination.

RESULTS

Return Rate

Of first concern was the adequacy of the follow-up procedure for locating Ss and eliciting their cooperation. Even though the sample was highly mobile (64% no longer in the local area, and 27% out of state or out of the country) all treated Ss and all but three control Ss were located. Complete data were returned by 100% of the treated Ss ($N = 45$), and 70% of the controls ($N = 31$). Of the 13 nonreturning controls (10 males, 3 females), 1 was deceased, 1 was in a mental hospital, 1 flatly refused, 7 failed to return after multiple contact, and 3 could not be located. Thus, the return rate was 79% for contacted controls who could return data, still significantly lower than the return rate for treated Ss ($p < .001$, Fisher exact probabilities test).

Since the purpose of the long-term follow-up was to determine the effects of the specific treatments included in the previous outcome study, Ss who received three or more sessions of psychological treatment during the posttreatment period were excluded from further analyses. On this basis, 3 Ss were excluded from the insight-oriented group, as were 1 each from systematic-desensitization and attention-placebo groups, and 12 returning controls; the difference between the proportion of treated Ss and controls receiving treatment during the follow-up period being highly significant ($\chi^2 = 9.87$, $df = 1$, $p < .01$). Additionally, one desensitization S was excluded because she was undergoing chemotherapy for a thyroid deficiency at FU_2, and one control was excluded on the basis of an extreme falsification score. While argument could be made either for including

Ss who received additional treatment or for counting all such Ss as relapses, the data available on such additional treatment is unclear. It appears that most of the treated controls, two of the treated insight Ss, and the attention-placebo S did seek treatment for anxiety-related difficulties, while the desensitization S and one insight S sought primarily vocational counseling.

Although data obtained at pretreatment and FU_1 revealed no significant differences between the treated Ss who obtained additional treatment and those who did not, there is no question that the retained controls constituted a biased subsample of the original control group. The nonreturning controls were found to differ from the retained controls in showing significantly greater increases from pretreatment to FU_1 (Pre–FU_1) on the general and examination anxiety scales, and a higher rate of academic failure over the follow-up period (78% versus 32%). Those controls excluded because they received treatment during the follow-up period also differed from retained controls by showing a greater Pre–FU_1 decrease in general anxiety, lower extroversion scores, and significantly greater increases on all specific anxiety scales. Even though there were no differences in demographic variables between retained controls and those lost or excluded, the retained controls appear to have improved more from pretreatment to FU_1, therefore raising the possibility that differences between treatment groups and controls at FU_2 may underestimate treatment effects. Likewise, if Ss excluded on the basis of additional treatment really were cases of relapse, the differential exclusion of these Ss would operate most in favor of the control group and, secondly, in favor of the insight-oriented group, while biasing results against systematic desensitization and attention-placebo treatments.

Comparative Treatment Effects from Pretreatment to FU₂ (Pre–FU₂)

The overall evaluation of treatment effectiveness is most reasonably made by a comparison of Pre–FU₂ changes between groups, since Pre–FU₁ changes had been subjected to detailed analysis earlier. Two scales of the battery (PRCS and S-R speech) focus specifically on performance anxiety in the speech situation, the specific treatment target. Unlike pretreatment and FU₁ assessments, however, there was no common reference speech for PRCS, and the size of audiences to which Ss had been exposed varied so widely that the separate consideration of S-R speech was no longer meaningful. Therefore, these two scales were converted to T scores and combined to form a Speech Composite score before analyses were undertaken. While the Speech Composite provides evaluation of specific treatment effects, the additional S-R scales report on performance anxiety

in three different interpersonal-evaluative situations, none of which were the specific focus of treatment. These latter scales, along with the general scales on Social Extroversion, Emotionality, and General Anxiety, provide information on generalization or, conversely, symptom substitution. Before carrying out the main analyses on the data, the possibility of systematic differences attributable to the five participating therapists was investigated. As was previously found on pretreatment and posttreatment stress-condition data and Pre–FU₁ analyses, in no instance for any measure were significant or suggestive Pre–FU₂ differences found among the overall (main) effects achieved by the five therapists or among the effects achieved by different therapists with the three different treatment procedures (interactions). Consequently, the Ss within treatment groups have been pooled in the following analyses.

The Speech Composite and each of the additional scales from the test bat-

Table 1

Mean Scores on Specific Anxiety Scales at Pretreatment, 6-Week Follow-up (FU₁), and 2-Year Follow-up (FU₂) for Subjects Retained at FU₂

Treatment	Testing	Composite Speech		S-R Interview		S-R Examination		S-R Contest	
		M	SD	M	SD	M	SD	M	SD
Desensitization (N = 13)	Pretreatment	115.5	9.74	43.2	11.01	46.8	10.32	35.6	7.92
	FU₁	85.0	16.10	37.4	8.82	43.2	10.81	35.5	7.28
	FU₂	82.5	16.07	31.5	8.79	36.5	9.28	30.5	6.68
Insight (N = 12)	Pretreatment	117.7	7.15	37.6	9.67	42.5	10.79	40.8	8.73
	FU₁	103.4	14.18	35.6	11.94	42.2	12.01	39.1	10.24
	FU₂	95.2	18.70	31.3	9.42	39.0	8.99	36.3	10.77
Attention-Placebo (N = 14)	Pretreatment	110.7	11.98	34.8	7.34	40.6	9.79	36.9	9.69
	FU₁	86.4	12.47	32.1	7.22	35.9	12.23	34.0	9.75
	FU₂	82.9	20.85	28.7	8.03	32.1	7.74	28.9	10.40
Control (N = 18)	Pretreatment	110.9	12.20	37.2	12.98	40.7	10.62	33.9	11.51
	FU₁	104.3	14.21	34.7	10.16	41.9	11.29	36.3	8.19
	FU₂	99.2	21.66	32.2	10.98	38.4	11.07	33.2	8.11

Table 2

Mean Scores on General Scales at Pretreatment, 6-Week Follow-up (FU₁), and 2-Year Follow-up (FU₂) for Subjects Retained at FU₂

Treatment	Testing	Extroversion-Introversion		Emotionality		IPAT Anxiety	
		M	SD	M	SD	M	SD
Desensitization	Pretreatment	14.1	7.58	19.8	6.03	40.7	10.69
($N = 13$)	FU_1	17.9	8.45	18.9	6.16	38.2	11.18
	FU_2	19.9	6.18	17.5	7.08	32.0	10.01
Insight	Pretreatment	16.4	6.57	17.2	5.59	33.7	10.09
($N = 12$)	FU_1	18.9	4.70	18.3	6.12	35.0	11.72
	FU_2	18.9	4.64	15.6	6.56	30.5	12.29
Attention-Placebo	Pretreatment	14.1	8.15	18.1	6.02	35.4	9.77
($N = 14$)	FU_1	17.1	7.68	16.8	7.01	30.7	11.74
	FU_2	16.1	7.01	17.1	6.75	28.2	12.12
Control	Pretreatment	17.9	5.53	17.9·	5.92	37.7	16.91
($N = 18$)	FU_1	20.2	6.30	18.4	6.31	37.7	11.48
	FU_2	19.4	6.56	17.2	7.97	33.6	14.34

tery were subjected to three-way analyses of variance (Treatments, Pre–FU₂, Subjects) on the scores of Ss retained at FU₂. Means and standard deviations for all assessment periods are presented in Table 1 for specific anxiety scales and in Table 2 for general scales.

These analyses indicate highly significant Pre–FU₂ changes ($p < .01$; $df = 1/53$), not only for the Speech Composite ($F = 82.70$), but for all other specific anxiety scales ($F = 35.94$, 26.93, 10.39 for S-R Interview, Examination, and Contest, respectively) and general scales ($F = 12.69$ and 15.21, respectively, for Extroversion and IPAT Anxiety Scale) except Emotionality, which only approached significance ($F = 3.05$, $p < .10$). More important, significant Treatment $\times$ Pre–FU₂ interactions ($df = 3/53$) were obtained for the Speech Composite ($F = 3.68$, $p < .05$) and for S-R Interview ($F = 5.14$, $p < .01$), S-R Examination ($F = 6.96$, $p < .01$), and IPAT Anxiety Scale ($F = 3.46$, $p < .05$), indicating differential changes among

groups from pretreatment to the 2-year follow-up. The nature of these changes may be seen in Figure 1, which presents the mean change for each group from pretreatment to FU₁ and FU₂ for all scales of the test battery. Unlike Pre–FU₁ changes, where significant overall effects were found only for speech anxiety and extroversion, the significant Pre–FU₂ main effects reported above reflect general trends in the improved direction for all scales at FU₂.

Of the significant Pre–FU₂ interactions, of most interest is the Speech Composite, which reflects change in the focal area of treatment. Inspection of Figure 1 reveals that all four groups maintained their relative positions from FU₁ to FU₂, with slight additional shifts in the direction of lower mean anxiety scores for all groups. As was the case with Pre–FU₁ comparisons, all three treatment groups were found to show significant improvement over controls ($t = 3.70$, 2.04, and 2.38 for desensitization, insight, and attention-placebo groups, respectively; $p < .05$), with no significant difference between the mean anxiety reduction achieved by the attention-placebo group and the insight group ($t < 1$). Also, like Pre–FU_1 comparisons, Ss treated by systematic desensitization showed significantly greater mean Pre–FU_2 reductions in anxiety on the Speech Composite than Ss who were treated by insight-oriented psychotherapy ($t = 2.09$, $p < .05$). However, even though the magnitude of the difference between mean anxiety-reduction scores of the desensitization group and the attention-placebo group for Pre–FU_2 comparisons was the same as that of Pre–FU_1 comparisons, these differences were no longer found to be significant at FU_2 ($t < 1$). This was the result of greater variability in the Pre–FU_2 change scores of the attention-placebo group, primarily due to a drop of 71 points for one attention-placebo S. The overall effects between these two groups may be seen better in the individual data presented below.

Having found essentially the same results to obtain for focal treatment effects at the 2-year follow-up as at the 6-week follow-up, the significant interactions between groups and Pre–FU_2 change scores on the other scales of the test battery become of interest. Of the additional specific anxiety scales and general scales, a significant interaction effect was found only for IPAT Anxiety in the earlier analysis of Pre–FU_1 data. The source of that interaction was found in significantly greater anxiety reduction for desensitization and attention-placebo groups than for controls. A significant overall increase in extroversion was also found on Pre-FU_1 analysis, but no significant interaction was obtained over that time period. As indicated above, significant Pre–FU_2 interactions were again found for IPAT Anxiety and, in addition, for S-R Interview and Examination anxiety scales. Inspection of the nature of these changes (Figure 1)

showed continued improvement over the follow-up period for the desensitization group on the S-R Interview scale, such that the Pre–FU_2 reduction for the desensitization group was significantly greater than that for controls ($t = 1.75$, $p < .05$) and approached significance when compared with insight and attention-placebo groups (respectively, $t = 1.39$, 1.61; $p < .10$). The source of the significant Pre–FU_2 interaction for S-R Examination was found in significantly greater reductions for both desensitization and attention-placebo Ss over controls ($t = 2.44$, 1.75; $p < .05$) and for desensitization over insight ($t = 1.72$, $p < .05$). Figure 1 shows that the significant interaction obtained on IPAT Anxiety at FU_2 is a result of the combined FU_2 reduction obtained by the desensitization and attention-placebo groups as compared to insight and control groups, although the latter two groups improved sufficiently from FU_1 to FU_2 that individual between-group comparisons alone were no longer significant. By the 2-year follow-up, the desensitization group had continued to show increased Social Extroversion scores to the point that the Pre–FU_2 increase in extroversion was significantly greater than that of the other three groups ($t = 2.06$, $df = 53$, $p < .05$). No other mean group comparisons approached significance from pretreatment to FU_2.

Although self-ratings of improvement by treated Ss had previously failed to discriminate between groups, direct ratings of perceived improvement were still included at FU_2 because of widespread usage in other follow-up studies. As before, in sharp contrast to the specific measures of anxiety reduction, no significant differences were found among groups on mean self-ratings of improvement. The Ss in all three treatment groups gave mean ratings ranging from "somewhat improved" to "much improved" for both specific reduction of

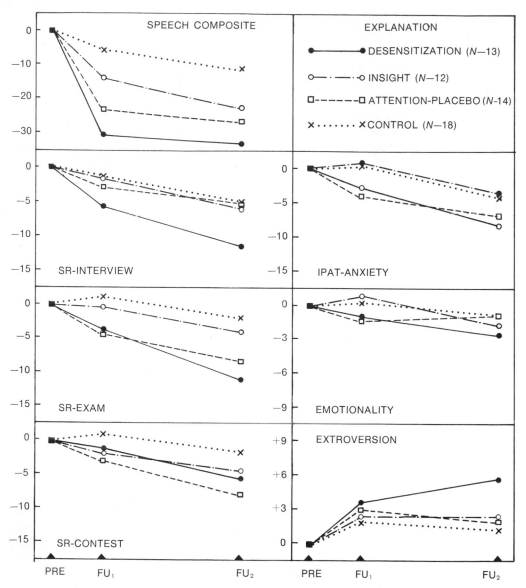

Figure 1   Mean change from pretreatment to 6-week follow-up (FU₁) and 2-year
follow-up (FU₂) for Ss retained at FU₂.

performance anxiety and improvement in other areas.

Individual S Improvement from Pretreatment to FU₂

Since clinical workers are more often concerned with percentage improvement in individual cases than with mean group differences, and since negative treatment effects or symptom substitution would be more easily identified from data on individuals, all test data were further evaluated on the basis of individually significant Pre–FU₂ change scores. An individual case was classified as "significantly improved" on each scale if the Pre–FU₂ reduction in anxiety score or increase in extroversion score exceeded

1.96 times the standard error of measurement for the instrument (two-tailed .05 level, as previously determined from a population of 523, Paul, 1966). Likewise, an individual case was classified as "significantly worse" on each scale if a Pre–FU_2 increase in anxiety score or decrease in extroversion score exceeded 1.96 times the standard error of measurement for the instrument.

Overall Pre–FU_2 improvement rates presented in Table 3 again disclosed sig-

Table 3
Percentage of Cases Showing Significant Change from Pretreatment to 2-Year Follow-up

Treatment	Significantly improved	No change	Significantly worse
Focal treatment (Speech Composite) [a]			
Desensitization	85%	15%	
Insight	50%	50%	
Attention-Placebo	50%	50%	
Control	22%	78%	
All other comparisons (six scales) [b]			
Desensitization	36%	64%	
Insight	25%	71%	4%
Attention-Placebo	25%	70%	5%
Control	18%	74%	8%

Note.—$N = 13, 12, 14,$ and 18, respectively, for desensitization, insight, attention-placebo, and control. Classifications derived by two-tailed .05 cut-offs on each individual change score (see text).
[a] $\chi^2 = 11.64, p < .01.$
[b] $\chi^2 = 8.11, p < .05.$

nificant differences between groups not only for focal treatment effects from the Speech Composite, but for all other comparisons as well. Particularly striking was the finding that not a single case retained at FU_2 in any group showed a significant increase in performance anxiety. Additionally, the percentage improvement of groups was remarkably

consistent with a similar classification made earlier on the basis of pre- to post-treatment change from stress-condition data. By comparing the percentage of improved Ss in the attention-placebo group with untreated controls, it was possible to estimate the percentage of Ss responding favorably to merely undergoing treatment, over and above the base-rate improvement from extratreatment experiences throughout the 2.5-year period—28%. Similarly, by comparing the percentage of Ss improved under attention-placebo with those improved under insight-oriented psychotherapy and systematic desensitization, it was possible to estimate the percentage of additional Ss receiving lasting benefit from either the achievement of "insight" or "emotional re-education," over and above the non-specific effects of undergoing treatment. For Ss receiving systematic desensitization, these comparisons revealed an additional lasting improvement of 35% for focal effects and 11% for generalized effects over that improvement expected from attention placebo. Again, no differences were found between the effects achieved by insight-oriented psychotherapy and attention-placebo treatment, although both produced better improvement rates than untreated controls. The "other comparisons" in Table 3 also favored a generalization interpretation of the effects of desensitization for changes found in areas which were not the specific focus of treatment, without the slightest suggestion of symptom substitution. Symptom substitution would be reflected in higher percentages in the "significantly worse" category for both attention-placebo and desensitization groups.

Comparative Relapse and Symptom Substitution over the Follow-up Period

While overall Pre–FU_2 evaluations gave no suggestive evidence to support the symptom-substitution hypothesis, nor any evidence that more Ss treated by desensitization and attention-placebo programs became significantly worse in any area, no information on relapse can be obtained from Pre–FU_2 comparisons. Rather, cases of relapse must be identified as those cases showing a significant increase in anxiety as reflected on the Speech Composite from FU_1 to FU_2. Similarly, if a symptom-substitution process were operating, a higher percentage of change in the "worse" direction should be obtained from FU_1 to FU_2 on nonfocal scales for desensitization and attention-placebo Ss who maintained improvement on the Speech Composite. As noted above, the data presented in Figure 1 show no evidence of relapse or symptom substitution for the groups as a whole from FU_1 to FU_2.

Before concluding that the symptom-substitution effects and differential relapse predicted by the disease model had not occurred, a more sensitive analysis was made of the individual data from FU_1 to FU_2. A case was classified as significantly worse on each scale if from FU_1 to FU_2 an increase in anxiety on the Speech Composite (relapse) or other anxiety score (symptom substitution) or a decrease in extroversion score (symptom substitution) exceeded 1.65 times the standard error of measurement for the instrument (one-tailed .05 level cut-offs). The percentage of Ss maintaining status versus the percentage "getting worse" from FU_1 to FU_2 for each group is presented in Table 4. No significant differences between groups were found on any measure. In fact, as the figures for the Speech Composite demonstrate, there was not a single case which could be considered a relapse in any of the retained Ss from the three treatment groups. Additionally, the percentage of scores in the significantly worse direction, which would reveal symptom substitu-

Table 4

Percentage of Cases Showing Relapse or Symptom Substitution from 6-Week Follow-up to 2-Year Follow-up

Treatment	Maintained FU_1 status	Significantly worse
Focal treatment (Speech Composite)		
Desensitization	100%	
Insight	100%	
Attention-Placebo	100%	
Control	89%	11%[a]
All other comparisons (six scales)		
Desensitization	97%	3%[b]
Insight	96%	4%[b]
Attention-Placebo	94%	6%[b]
Control	93%	7%[b]

Note.—$N = 13$, 12, 14, and 18, respectively, for desensitization, insight, attention-placebo, and controls. Classifications derived by one-tailed .05 cut-offs on each individual change score (see text).
[a] "Relapse."
[b] "Symptom substitution."

tion, did not differ from the .05 level for any group. If Ss who received additional treatment during the follow-up period were to be included as cases of relapse, the figures would be even less in favor of the predictions based on the disease model, with 93% maintaining status for both desensitization and attention-placebo groups, as compared to 80% for insight and less than 40% for controls.

The frequency data obtained from the 13-item behavioral questionnaire specifically constructed to reveal hypothesized symptom-substitution effects also failed to provide any support for the symptom-substitution hypothesis. Kruskal-Wallis one-way analyses of variance by ranks over the four groups on each item produced an $H \leq 3.66$ ($p > .30$) on all items but one. On that item—No. 9, frequency of social exchange—the value of H approached the .10 level of significance and was in favor of the desensitization group. In fact, a significant coefficient of concordance ($W = .47$, $p < .01$) over all items was obtained, with the desensitization Ss receiving an equal mean rank with the insight Ss, both in the direction opposite to symptom-substitution effects. Similarly, Kruskal-Wallis analyses over the four groups for frequencies of each of the five areas of stress reported over the follow-up period failed to reveal significant differences between groups (all $H < 3.66$, $p > .30$; except C, "Change in family structure," where $H = 5.08$, $p < .20$). Thus while the occurrence of stress might be considered as evidence of symptom substitution or an external influence on relapse (Stone, et al., 1961), these questions need not be of concern in the present study, since no differences in the reported occurrence of stress approached significance between groups.

Interrelationships among Variables

Since the earlier study assessed specific improvement through several different instruments, persons, and situations in addition to the instruments on which FU_2 data were obtained, information relating to both predictive and construct validity of improvement may be gained through the correlation of previous improvement scores with those obtained at FU_2. For systematic agreement across different instruments, positive correlations would be expected between all change scores for each measure of performance anxiety. FU_1 improvement ratings of Ss and therapists should be positively correlated with Ss' ratings at FU_2. Further, FU_1 ratings of improvement should be negatively correlated with Pre–FU_2 performance-anxiety change scores. Opposite relationships would be expected for therapist post-treatment ratings of prognosis, since these scales were reversed.

Table 5 presents the correlations of pre- to posttreatment stress-condition change scores, therapist posttreatment ratings, and FU_1 ratings of treated Ss with FU_2 ratings of treated Ss and Pre–FU_2 change on the Speech Composite and all other scales of the test battery. Specific FU_2 improvement data (Ss' ratings, Pre–FU_2 Speech Composite) were significantly correlated in the expected direction, with all indicants of specific improvement at posttreatment and FU_1, except for the relationship between the Physiological Composite and the Speech Composite. Previous analyses had also failed to find significant relationships between physiological and self-report data, although physiological change was significantly correlated with observable manifestations of anxiety under stress conditions as assessed by the behavioral checklist.

Of the correlations presented in Table 5, the relationship of the behavioral checklist with Pre–FU_2 assessments is of a special importance. The behavioral checklist was the most objective measure of all instruments used and was highly reliable (interrater reliability $= .96$). Additionally, checklist data were obtained in a situation where target behaviors were most likely to occur, and pre- to posttreatment checklist change was consistently related to all other prior indicants of specific anxiety reduction. The correlation of .61 between pre- to posttreatment change on the behavior checklist with Pre–FU_2 change on the Speech Composite is strong evidence for both the construct validity of focal improvement at FU_2 and for the predictive validity of observable posttreatment improvement.

Table 5 also reveals discriminative relationships in the correlations of therapist and subject ratings with Pre–FU_2 improvement. Therapist ratings of specific improvement and prognosis were significantly correlated with Pre–FU$_2$ Speech Composite change and with FU$_2$ ratings of improvement by treated Ss. Conversely, therapists' ratings of general improvement and prognosis were not significantly related to specific improvement, although "other prognosis" was related to Pre–FU$_2$ change in extroversion. Likewise, Ss' ratings at FU$_1$ were significantly related to Pre–FU$_2$ change in a discriminative way, although "method factors" predominate in improvement ratings of Ss as they had earlier.

The correlation of specific improvement data from the earlier time periods with Pre–FU$_2$ change on the scales of the test battery which were not directed towards focal treatment effects also showed several significant relationships. Inspection of the prime correlations among all variables presented in Table 5 found the source of covariation in every instance to result primarily from increased relationships at posttreatment and FU$_2$, with several of the prime correlations also reaching the .01 level of significance. The significant correlations presented in Table 5 may be interpreted as evidence for the stability of improvement and generalization effects, rather than as a result of relationships existing before treatment began. Further, when the specific posttreatment and FU$_1$ improvement variables from Table 5 were correlated with FU$_1$–FU$_2$ change for test

Table 5
Correlation of Prior Improvement Scores with all Change Scores from Pretreatment to 2-Year Follow-up

Prior improvement data	Subject FU$_2$ rating of improvement		Pre–FU$_2$ change						
	Specific	Other	Speech Composite	S-R Interview	S-R Exam	S-R Contest	IPAT Anxiety	Emotionality	Extroversion
Pre- to posttreatment stress-condition change									
Physiological composite	−.33*	−.31*	.11	.13	.32*	.22	.46**	.38**	−.09
Behavioral checklist	−.34*	−.13	.61**	.07	.20	.17	.20	.15	−.25*
Anxiety differential	−.33*	−.27*	.44**	.28*	.22	.26*	.46**	.23	−.34*
Standardized therapist posttreatment rating									
Specific improvement	.30*	.15	−.51**	−.18	−.24	−.31*	−.38**	.04	.12
Other improvement	.02	.03	.01	.07	.00	.02	.08	−.10	−.24
Specific prognosis	−.35*	−.31*	.50**	.13	.30*	.11	.24	.02	−.17
Other prognosis	−.19	−.19	.25	.05	.01	−.11	.16	−.09	−.32
Subject FU$_1$ rating									
Specific improvement	.68**	.47**	−.56**	−.04	−.30*	−.19	−.18	.03	.34*
Other improvement	.56**	.65**	−.24	−.15	−.03	−.19	−.11	.08	.20

Note.—N = 44 for stress condition; N = 39 for ratings.
* $p < .05$.
** $p < .01$.

battery scales, several low, but significant, coefficients were obtained ($Mdn|r| = .31$), all of which indicated that those Ss who showed greatest reduction in performance anxiety at posttreatment and FU_1 also showed greatest specific and generalized additional improvement over the period between FU_1 and FU_2. Since no significant correlations were obtained between pretreatment scores on the three general scales and change on the specific anxiety scales from Pre–FU_1, FU_1–FU_2, or Pre–FU_2, the slight additional improvement from FU_1 to FU_2 may be interpreted as the continuing effects of changes taking place during the treatment period, rather than as a function of pretreatment personality dimensions.

Further information concerning the stability of scores for each scale of the test battery over treatment and follow-up periods may be seen in the test-retest correlations from Pre–FU_1, Pre–FU_2, and FU_1–FU_2 (Table 6). The greater stability

Table 6
Intercorrelations of Each Test Battery Scale over the Three Testing Periods for Subjects Retained at FU_2

Scale	Stability coefficient[a]		
	Pre–FU_1	Pre–FU_2	FU_1–FU_2
Speech Composite	.27	.29	.68
S-R Interview	.57	.53	.63
S-R Examination	.50	.52	.51
S-R Contest	.47	.43	.64
IPAT Anxiety	.76	.44	.63
Emotionality	.80	.64	.72
Extroversion	.82	.59	.71

Note.—$N = 57$; $p = .05$, $r = .22$; $p = .01$, $r = .31$.
[a] Pearson r's.

of Speech Composite scores from FU_1 to FU_2, as compared to Pre–FU_1 and Pre–FU_2 relationships, again indicated the influence of treatment effects obtaining after pretreatment assessment, with Ss

holding relative positions in a reliable manner over the 2 years following FU_1. However, it appears that relatively greater position changes in Extroversion and IPAT Anxiety occurred over the follow-up period than over the treatment period.

Intercorrelations of FU_2 scores for all scales of the test battery revealed essentially the same relationships as those reported earlier for FU_1 scores. Significant intercorrelations were obtained among all scales (Mdn $r = .51$), except Extroversion which was significantly related only to the Speech Composite ($r = -.27$, $p < .05$). While the combined relationships reported above and in the earlier study support the assumption that FU_2 measures were internally consistent, the reliability of the Pre–FU_2 change for the primary measure can be directly estimated. The Pre–FU_2 changes for PRCS and S-R Speech (the scales which were converted to T scores and summed to obtain the Speech Composite) correlated .64, from which the reliability of the Speech Composite change can be estimated (by Spearman-Brown formula) at .78.

Although no differences between groups were found for the 13 items of the behavioral questionnaire, indirect support for the validity of the items was obtained through correlational analyses. Moderate but significant correlations were found among the items, which clustered in the following way: Nos. 1, 2, and 3, (Mdn $r = .53$); Nos. 6, 9, and 10 (Mdn $r = .43$); Nos. 3, 5, 8, 11, 12, 13 (Mdn $r = .35$). Only No. 7 was unrelated to other items. Numerous significant correlations (Mdn $r = .32$) were found between the items of the second and third clusters and all scales of the FU_2 test battery, indicating that Ss obtaining lower anxiety scores and higher extroversion scores also tended to report having more close friends, belonging to more organizations, attending more social events, entertaining more, "going out" more, and more frequent group discussions and public appearances. Similarly, of the five areas of stress on which frequency data were obtained, all but one (change in family structure) were significantly intercorrelated ($Mdn\ r = .35$). With one exception, no significant correlations were found between reported stress frequencies and items of the behavioral questionnaire, nor between either FU_1–FU_2 or Pre–FU_2 change for any scale of the test battery and stress frequencies. The exception was a significant relationship between the reported frequency of occurrence of change in family structure and FU_1–FU_2 change in extroversion ($r = -.42$, $p < .01$); that is, those Ss increasing in extroversion from FU_1 to FU_2 tended to report less change in family structure over the same time period.

One last check on the symptom-substitution hypothesis was carried out by correlating Pre–FU_2 change on the Speech Composite with all other data. Several significant correlations were obtained between Pre–FU_2 Speech Composite change and items from the behavioral questionnaire, but all were in the opposite direction predicted by the disease model and favored a generalization interpretation. Intercorrelations of Pre–FU_2 change scores among all seven scales of the test battery revealed positive correlations between change on the Speech Composite and change on all other anxiety scales ($Mdn\ r = .34$) and a negative correlation with change in Extroversion ($r = -.30$). Similar relationships were found among the other scales, with positive correlations among all anxiety and emotionality change scores and negative correlations between the latter and change in Extroversion. Of the 15 correlations, 10 achieved statistical significance ($Mdn\ r = .29$).

DISCUSSION

In general, the combined findings from individual and group data as well as correlational analyses showed the relative gains in focal treatment effects found earlier to be maintained over the 2-year follow-up period. Some additional relative improvement in related areas was found for Ss treated by systematic desensitization and, to a lesser extent, for those treated by attention placebo. Like the findings at 6-week follow-up, in no instance were the long-term effects achieved through insight-oriented psychotherapy significantly different from the effects achieved with attention-placebo treatment, although both groups showed significantly greater treatment effects than untreated controls. As a group, the systematic desensitization Ss continued to show greater positive treatment effects than any other group, with evidence of additional generalization, and no evidence even suggestive of symptom substitution. In fact, the comparative findings at 2-year follow-up are so similar to the findings at posttreatment and 6-week follow-up that the detailed discussion of results in relation to previous research, theoretical hypotheses concerning factors and effects within treatments, and methodological implications for research and clinical practice which were presented earlier (Paul, 1966, pp. 71–99) require no modification and need not be reiterated here.

The finding that effects of systematic desensitization are maintained over the follow-up period with evidence of additional improvement through generalization is consistent with the results of the only other controlled follow-up of systematic desensitization therapy (Lang & Lazovik, 1963) and with the suggestive findings from follow-up reports of accumulated case studies (Lazarus, 1963; Wolpe, 1961). Although all previous long-term follow-up studies have suffered considerably from the methodological problems described at the beginning of this report, the general trend of results for psychological treatment of noninstitutionalized adults has been for treatment effects to be maintained or slightly improved over the follow-up period (Stone *et al.*, 1961). Consistent with this trend, the present investigation found no relapse for any of the retained treated Ss, no matter what treatment they had received.

While these findings were somewhat surprising for systematic desensitization and insight-oriented psychotherapy, the stability of improvement resulting only from the nonspecific effects of attention-placebo treatment was almost completely unexpected. This was especially true since previous studies of placebo responsiveness had not only found relapse on 3–6-month follow-up (Gliedman, Nash, Imber, Stone, & Frank, 1958), but further, that Ss who improved most at the time of their initial placebo experience were more likely to relapse than those who improved least (Frank, Nash, Stone, & Imber, 1963). The difference between the latter effects of pure placebo (inert medication) and lasting effects of the attention-placebo treatment of the present investigation may lie in changes in attitudes and expectancies resulting from the interpersonal relationship with the therapist functioning as a "generalized reinforcer" (Krasner, 1955). Stone *et al.* (1961) point out that the long-term success of any form of treatment depends in large part on the extent to which changes that are accomplished are supported by the client's subsequent life experiences. This fact might be extended to suggest that no matter how change is brought about, it is likely to be maintained in a supportive environment which reinforces resulting behavior, and it is not likely to be maintained if the

resulting behavior is not reinforced or if new aversive consequences or extreme stress reinstitute negative emotional responses. While systematic desensitization produced a more direct modification of the emotional reactions associated with interpersonal performance situations, resulting in significantly higher improvement rates, the emergent behaviors of Ss experiencing anxiety reduction from all three treatments were likely to be regarded as socially appropriate and were likely to be rewarded, independently of the manner in which change initially came about.

The usual concern with "spontaneous remission" rates from other populations need not be considered in this investigation, since an untreated control group from the same population was assessed on the same instruments as were the treatment groups. Even though results were favorably biased towards the controls, due to differential loss of Ss, superior long-term effects for all treatment groups were still obtained. Additionally, the 22% "improved" without treatment at the 2-year follow-up for a favorably biased untreated subgroup seriously questions the "two-thirds spontaneous remission" rate so frequently quoted (e.g., Eysenck, 1966). Of course, Lesse (1964) notes:

> The concept of anything that is labeled as "spontaneous" must be considered in the light of the fact that it is spontaneous only because we do not understand the causes for the change or are at the present time unable to measure various factors that influence it. In all probability, therefore, so-called spontaneous remissions are probably not spontaneous at all [p. 111].

There is no reason to believe that factors other than the same environmental influences which maintained improvement for treated Ss were involved in the improvement and stability of untreated controls. In fact, processes similar to desensitization may take place through environmental interaction in the absence of formal treatment (Stevenson, 1961), and considerable nonspecific therapy may be expected without contacting a socially designated psychological helper (Goldstein, 1960).

While this investigation was able to overcome methodological difficulties more adequately than previous attempts, it still suffered from difficulties inherent in the nature of follow-up studies. The tight control procedures maintained during the earlier outcome study were not possible once Ss were "turned loose" after the 6-week follow-up. When control is not possible, attempts at assessment are a second-best choice. Although Ss were asked to indicate whether or not treatment had been received during the follow-up period, only 5 indicated that they had, when a total of 17 were actually identified as having received treatment through a survey of clinics and therapists. Considering the high return rate for this investigation, the problem of Ss not reporting additional treatment in other studies could be astronomical. Even though a higher return rate was obtained than in previous follow-up studies, total assessment of cause-effect relationships for treatment groups was not possible due to the necessity of S exclusion. Additionally, the untreated controls were known to be a favorably biased subgroup which may have underestimated treatment effects and overestimated (un)-spontaneous remission. Although the assessment instruments used possessed adequate reliability and validity for determining effects, the mobility of the sample precluded use of the instrument which was known to provide the most objective evaluation (i.e., the behavioral checklist).

These inherent difficulties have led

some investigators to question the value of long-term follow-ups. May et al. (1965) point out:

> formal, controlled studies are doomed to depreciate progressively with the passage of time from the end of the controlled treatment period with much of their discriminating power being eroded by contamination . . . it is inevitable that the longer the follow-up, the more all treatments approximate the same end result [p. 762].

On the basis of their own research, Stone et al. (1961) state further that, "evaluation of different forms of psychotherapy should be primarily in terms of their immediate results [p. 420]." In essential agreement, the stability of treatment effects over the 2-year follow-up period in the present study, combined with the failure to find a single case which could be considered evidence of relapse or symptom substitution for any treated S, suggests that the short-term follow-up provided adequate evaluation of comparative treatment effects. Thus, for the evaluation of psychological treatment with noninstitutionalized adults, more scientifically useful information is likely to be obtained if future efforts are directed towards short-term follow-ups, in which total sample assessment of treated Ss may be obtained, rather than longer follow-ups, which suffer from differential attrition and the effects of uncontrolled environmental influences. The number and timing of follow-ups should be determined by the nature of the population and problem, rather than preconceived theoretical notions (Paul, in press).

However, the methodological difficulties of follow-up studies should not overshadow the major findings of the present investigation. Namely, that modified systematic desensitization produced significant and lasting reductions in maladaptive anxiety, not only on an absolute level, but also in comparison with other treatment and control groups. None of the effects predicted on the basis of the traditional disease-analogy model were forthcoming, while considerable evidence was found for a learning model. Results as consistent as these are rare in the psychotherapy literature and require not only replication, but also an extension of evaluations across differing populations of clients, therapists, and problems, as well as parametric investigations of the mechanics involved.

Desensitization, Suggestibility, and Pseudotherapy[1]

Peter J. Lang, A. David Lazovik,
and David J. Reynolds

Positive change in psychotherapy has often been attributed to the relationship established between therapist and client, in the context of treatment. This phenomenon has been variously described as transference, suggestibility, the "hello-goodbye," or placebo effect. Lang and Lazovik (1963) demonstrated that phobic subjects who were briefly exposed to desensitization psychotherapy showed a significantly greater reduction in fear behavior than did untreated controls. The present experiment is an extension of this work, specifically to determine if the obtained change can be assigned to placebo effects.

A psychotherapeutic placebo is not as readily developed as the control medication of drug research. Psychological treatment is usually more prolonged; it involves a more complex interpersonal relationship, and the distinction between a placebo and the clinically effective agent can be less clearly delineated. Furthermore, the institution of a long pseudotreatment is generally impractical in the clinical situation. Not only is it wasteful of the patient's and therapist's time, but the necessary deception and delay of legitimate treatment can seldom be justified, and may be detrimental to the patient's future chances for cure.

These objections had considerably less validity in the experimental context considered here, which offered an opportunity to employ a stringent placebo control group. The subjects used in this research displayed phobic reactions to nonpoisonous snakes of considerable intensity. They systematically avoided snakes or places such as zoos or camping trips where they might be found. These individuals behaved so "unrealistically" as to react with anxiety not only to snakes themselves, but to pictures of snakes,

Reprinted from the *Journal of Abnormal Psychology*, 1965, vol. 70, pp. 395–402 with the permission of the American Psychological Association and the authors.

[1] This research was supported by Public Health Service Grant M-3880, from the National Institute of Mental Health. The authors would like to thank J. Geer, R. Miller, R. Romano, and Jean Wilkinson, who participated as therapists in this project. Appreciation is also expressed to Lynne Norris and R. Wiater, who assisted in organizing the data collection and analysing the results.

artifacts (a snakeskin belt), similar shapes, or the mere mention of the word. Nightmares concerning snakes were not uncommon in this group. Such statements, descriptive of their fear, as the following have been recorded: "There's nothing in the world that I'm more afraid of than snakes." "I'm just weak when I see one." "I don't even want to look at them in books." In nearly all respects, except the degree to which the phobia is an omnipresent source of concern, this fear resembled those that patients themselves bring to the attention of psychiatrists and psychologists.

However, these subjects were not drawn from a clinical population, but were selected from among normal college students by a classroom questionnaire and subsequent interview (their frequency is approximately one or two per hundred students surveyed). They volunteered to participate in an experiment on psychotherapy. They were instructed that the procedures used might reduce or eliminate their fear, but that the main purpose of the project was a scientific evaluation of different therapy methods.

The advantages of working with this population are obvious. Treatment can be specific. The number of sessions may be arbitrarily controlled. The moral responsibility to choose the best treatment is not involved. As this phobia is not a central life problem and these subjects were generally more stable than patients, extratherapeutic incidents less frequently interfere with the therapy process. Most important, the necessary rigor of experimental procedure can be closely respected.

As in all translations of natural events into a laboratory context, something is lost in vivacity. In this case, some of the subject characteristics mentioned above, the rigidity of procedure, are obviously different from what is characteristically found in the consulting room. However, much can be gained in the exactness and clarity with which natural events are elucidated. Thus, the present study does not constitute a clinical test of desensitization therapy (clinical statistics have already been reported by Wolpe, 1958), but it is rather an attempt to illuminate through experiment the mechanism by which fear reduction is achieved in this method. Specifically, this research is designed to determine if placebo effects account for the positive results achieved by systematic desensitization therapy, and also to evaluate the overall contribution of suggestibility, as a personality trait, to progress in desensitization and posttherapy fear reduction.

METHOD

Desensitization Therapy

The procedure has been described in detail elsewhere (Lang & Lazovik, 1963; Lazovik & Lang, 1960). Each subject first experienced 5 training sessions. At this time an *anxiety hierarchy* was constructed—a series of 20 phobic situations graded from least to most frightening. The subject was also trained in hypnosis and deep-muscle relaxation (Jacobson, 1938). Subsequently he participated in 11 desensitization sessions. During these meetings he was hypnotized and instructed to vividly imagine the scenes described in the hiararchy.[2] The scenes were presented one at a time, starting with the least frightening, and repeated until the subject no longer reported coincident anxiety. This desensitization occurred in the context of deep-muscle relaxation, which is held to counter condition or "reciprocally inhibit" (Wolpe, 1958) the fear response. Sessions lasted approximately 45 minutes at the rate of 1 or 2 per week.

[2] Six recently treated subjects experienced desensitization without hypnosis.

Pseudotherapy

An effort was made to involve the subject in a treatment procedure which was therapeutically neutral except for the therapist-client relationship. Because desensitization was to be evaluated, all procedures employed in that method were included in pseudotherapy. The subjects first experienced the same 5 training sessions as in desensitization, followed by 11 pseudotherapy sessions. The procedure for each of these latter sessions was the same. The subject was first hypnotized and then told to relax deeply. During the first 15 minutes of the therapy hour the subject was asked to imagine a series of scenes, which he had previously described as pleasant and relaxing. The last half hour was keyed to the hierarchy items. The items were taken in order during the course of therapy, and provided starting points for a discussion of nonanxiety evoking aspects of the subject's life. The therapist generally behaved in a nondirective manner. However, he did attempt to prevent phobic responses from being made in the context of the therapy hour. It was held that the occurrence of phobic verbal behavior could lead to positive change, for the same reason that theory predicts it in desensitization, that is, inhibition of anxiety by relaxation or comfort responses instigated by the therapist. Thus, the pseudotherapist gently steered the conversation away from phobic or other sensitive material—in the main, by reinforcing nonsensitive topics with nods and verbal signs of his attention, and failing to similarly reinforce comments directly pertinent to the subject's fear. For example, if the hierarchy item concerned a black snake at the farm of an uncle, the developing conversation might concern farms or farm animals, or experiences with the uncle, whatever the subject spontaneously brought up that did not directly refer to his anxieties.

The theoretical orientation given these subjects facilitated the pseudotherapist's task. In the first session the following explanation of procedure was offered:

> Perhaps if I impart a little bit of psychological theory to you, it will help you understand our next procedure. You have learned how to relax your muscles and this is going to be important in dealing with your fear. Previous research suggests that people with fears like yours have higher levels of autonomic tonus than others. What this means is that all the vegetative systems, digestive, circulatory, as well as the neural and muscular systems tend to overreact. They overreact mainly because they actually start from a higher level of tonus. Some psychologists hold that if this generally high tonus level could be reduced, the way would be paved for a general reduction in specific fears.
>
> What we hope to do in the rest of our sessions together is help you achieve a general lowering of the tonus levels. We will do this by first having you relax as you have learned to do. Then you will be hypnotized and even deeper relaxation will be achieved. To facilitate this process we will suggest pleasant scenes, from time to time, for you to concentrate on.
>
> As you probably know, fears such as yours are often related to situations which seem unimportant. After you are comfortable, that is deeply relaxed, we will want to begin a discussion with some of the items you used in the fear hierarchy. We will use these as starting points in our talks but plan to deviate from them. Our goal is to explore a number of areas of living, and produce a lowering of your overall tension levels. The theory holds that a person may overcome his fear if he obtains a better understanding of himself and learns to deeply relax.

The subjects participated eagerly. They came regularly and none discontinued treatment before the end of the experiment. Furthermore, no subject reported that he suspected he was involved in a nonviable treatment. The therapists reported consistently close, empathic relationships with these subjects, comparable or superior to those achieved during desensitization.[3]

Subjects

This research has been underway continuously since September 1960, and the present report describes the total sample of 44 subjects. Included are 23 desensitization subjects, 11 untreated controls, and 10 subjects who participated in pseudotherapy.[4]

All subjects were introductory psychology students at the University of Pittsburgh. They rated their fear of nonpoisonous snakes as "intense," on a fear questionnaire, and were included in this research only if a psychological interview corroborated this statement. The subjects who appeared to have impairing physical disabilities or latent psychosis (based on the psychotic scales of the MMPI or the clinical judgment of the interviewer) were excluded. None of the subjects in this study were being seen elsewhere because of psychological problems.

Assignment to groups was essentially random, although some pretreatment effort to balance control variables was made. A more elaborate description of

---

[3] Two factors probably helped considerably to insure that the pseudotherapist was not unmasked: (a) treatment was relatively brief, (b) metropolitan residents were being treated for a snake phobia. Therefore, subjects had little or no contact with the phobic object outside of the experimental situation. If subjects were treated for a more omnipresent fear over a longer time period, unfavorable feedback from the life situation might make the deception much more difficult to maintain.

[4] The untreated subjects and 13 desensitization subjects were described in a previous report (Lang & Lazovik, 1963). All desensitization subjects were combined as there was no significant difference between this 1963 group and subjects who have since participated, either in selection method or results on the major assessment variables. Change scores for the 1963 sample and all other subsequent desensitization subjects were, respectively: avoidance test, .23 and .32; fear thermometer, 2.47 and 2.38; FSS Number 38, 1.38 and 1.44.

the selection battery has already been reported (Lang & Lazovik, 1963).

Procedure

After the selection tests and interviews, all subjects were administered the Stanford Hypnotic Susceptibility Scale Form A (SHSS; Weitzenhoffer & Hilgard, 1959). Subsequently all subjects except the untreated controls participated in the five therapy training sessions, after which SHSS Form B was administered. Fear intensity was measured both before and after the subsequent 11 desensitization or pseudotherapy trials. Untreated subjects were not seen, except for evaluation sessions.

The measures employed (Lang & Lazovik, 1963) were: The Fear Survey Schedule (FSS), FSS Number 38, an avoidance test, and the "fear thermometer." The FSS is a list of 50 phobias that subjects rate on a 7-point scale. Item Number 38 is the snake item. In the avoidance test the subject was confronted with an alive, tame blacksnake. He was invited to approach the animal, in a controlled setting. The closest point of approach to the animal provided the basis for his test score. If the subject held the animal, he achieved a score of 1, refusal to go to the test room and observe the snake yielded a score of 19. Immediately after this experience the subject rated his situational anxiety during the avoidance test on a 10-point "fear theromometer" (Walk, 1956). An open-ended fear interview provided additional qualitative information.

The experimenters in this research were all experienced psychotherapists. Most of the subjects were seen by two psychologists who have a full time psychotherapy practice. The same experimenters who saw the pseudotherapy subjects also treated desensitization subjects. Fear evaluation was conducted by an experimenter who participated in no other aspect of the procedure.

RESULTS

Mean fear behavior change scores from pretest to posttest are presented in Table 1. The similarity of the pseudotherapy and no-treatment means is readily apparent. The t tests yielded no significant differences between these groups for any measure of fear change (see Table 2). Furthermore, the change score frequency distributions for the two groups were normal and overlapping. Pseudotherapy and no-treatment subjects were therefore combined into a single control group for subsequent analyses.

Mean change scores for the combined control group and the desensitization group are presented in Table 1. Desensitization subjects showed significantly greater fear reduction than controls as measured by all three indices of snake phobic behavior. The t's are presented in Table 2 and desensitization and control frequency distributions are illustrated in Figure 1. Except for the avoidance test the control sample yielded essentially normal distributions of fear change. The desensitization subjects have a primary modal score in the same interval as the controls, but the distributions are skewed positively or are frankly bimodal.

Progress in systematic desensitization is directly measured by the portion of the 20-item anxiety hierarchy completed in the 11 therapy sessions. Table 3 reveals that all measures of fear reduction are positively related to the number of hierarchy items successfully completed by each subject. No pretest measure of snake phobic behavior correlated significantly with the number of items subsequently completed, although the first presentation of the FSS and items completed yielded an r of $-.435$, ($p < .05$). Number of items completed was wholly unrelated to any of the SHSS measures (see Table 3).

A previous review of part of these data (Lang & Lazovik, 1963) suggested that while subjects who completed 15 items or more showed considerable positive change, subjects completing less than 15 showed no more change than untreated subjects. The current enlarged sample confirmed this trend. It may be noted in Table 1, that subjects completing more than 15 items have the highest average change scores for all fear measures. Furthermore, Figure 1 shows that

Table 1
Mean Pre- to Posttreatment Change Scores for all Fear Measures

Group	Avoidance test	Fear thermometer	FSS Number 38	Fear survey
Combined control ($N = 21$)	$-.03$	1.14	.48	12.14
Pseudotherapy ($N = 10$)	.14	1.30	.40	12.50
No treatment ($N = 11$)	$-.19$	1.00	.54	11.82
Desensitization ($N = 23$)[a] (hierarchy items completed)	.27	2.43	1.41	18.64
15 or more ($N = 13$)	.47	3.58	2.31	23.77
Less than 15 ($N = 10$)	.01	.89	.11	7.33

Note.—The avoidance test score is the percentage change statistic previously described (Lang & Lazovik, 1963). All other change scores were simply the difference between pre- and posttests. The correlations between initial performance and fear change for all measures were insignificant and inconsistent in direction.
[a] Data were incomplete for three Ss. The Fear Thermometer and FSS Ns are 22 and 21, respectively.

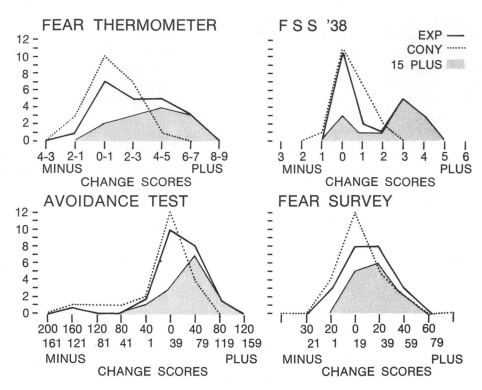

Figure 1   Fear change score frequency distributions for the combined control (CONT) and desensitization (EXP) samples. The shaded areas of the desensitization groups' distributions define the subjects who successfully completed 15 or more anxiety hierarchy items.

Table 2
T-Tests of Mean Fear Change Scores from Pre- to Posttreatment

Group	Avoidance test	Fear thermometer	FSS Number 38	Fear survey
Combined control versus desensitization	2.57*	2.12*	2.19*	1.25
Combined control versus 15 or more	3.26**	3.44**	3.99***	2.52*
Combined control versus less than 15	.14	.41	1.85	.41
Less than 15 versus 15 or more	2.33*	3.28**	5.00***	2.26*
Pseudotherapy versus no treatment	1.67	.48	.58	.12

Note.—The desensitization group was subdivided into two groups on the basis of performance in therapy. "15 or more" and "less than 15" refers to the number of anxiety hierarchy items successfully completed by the group during desensitization.
* $p < .05$.
** $p < .01$.
*** $p < .001$.

the 15 plus subjects clearly account for the positive skew of the distributions of experimental subjects. If the 15 plus group is eliminated, the remaining subjects are distributed normally around the control mode. These impressions were

Table 3

Pearson Correlations between the Number of Anxiety Hierarchy Items Successfully Completed During Desensitizaton and Measures of Fear Change and the Stanford Hypnotic Susceptibility Scale

Fear change	r	SHSS form	r
Avoidance test	.40*	A	−.06
Fear thermometer	.50*	B	−.03
FSS Number 38	.60**		
Fear survey	.50*	Change	−.05

Note.—SHSS change is the difference between Forms A and B.
* $p < .05.$
** $p < .01.$

Table 4

Pearson Correlations between the Stanford Hypnotic Susceptibility Scale and the Initial Measures of Fear and Fear Change Scores

Fear measure	SHSS Form		
	A	B	Change
Total sample ($N = 44$)			
(Initial score)			
Avoidance test	−.34*	−.47**	−.06
Fear thermometer	−.14	−.22	.04
FSS Number 38	.10	.19	.11
Fear survey	.00	−.10	−.13
Control group ($N = 21$)			
(Change score)			
Avoidance test	.00	.12	.06
Fear thermometer	.33	.46*	.15
FSS Number 38	.47*	.48*	−.02
Fear survey	.29	.36	−.23
Desensitization group			
($N = 23$)			
(Change score)			
Avoidance test	−.16	−.11	.28
Fear thermometer	−.16	.18	.39
FSS Number 38	.07	.02	−.19
Fear survey	.08	.07	.02

Note.—All correlational statistics were computed on the IBM 7090 at the University of Pittsburgh Data Processing Center.
* $p < .05.$
** $p < .01.$

assessed by the t test, and the results are reported in Table 2: 15 plus subjects show significantly more fear reduction than either controls or less than 15 subjects. The latter group was not superior to the control group on any change measure.

The correlations between the pretest fear measures and SHSS Forms A and B, and the difference score, are at the top of Table 4. Inspection of these coefficients reveals that only the avoidance test is significantly related to suggestibility. Correlations between fear reduction and the SHSS measures are listed in the bottom half of Table 4. It may be noted that avoidance test change is unrelated to suggestibility for either the desensitization or control subject. For control subjects both the fear thermometer and FSS 38 change are positively related to measures of suggestibility, and the Fear Survey shows a tendency in this direction. There is no significant relationship between the desensitization group's SHSS scores and any fear change measure.

DISCUSSION

Desensitization subjects clearly showed a significantly greater decrease in phobic behavior than did controls; subjects whose therapeutic experience was restricted to a placebo relationship yielded no more positive change than did the untreated group.

These results imply that the reduction in fear following desensitization does not stem from a suggestion to change implicit in being "in therapy." Both placebo and desensitization subjects were asked to participate in a procedure which had fear reduction as a goal, and both groups spent equal time at this task. The findings also indicate that hypnosis, training in muscle relaxation, hierarchy building, and their continued use in a therapeutic context, do not in themselves produce change in fear behavior. Finally, the results suggest that the relationship which developed between the experimenter and subject, with possible transference effects, was not in itself the vehicle of change.

The above inferences clearly depend on the extent to which the therapists kept their communications about goals the same for all subjects, and how well they succeeded in maintaining interpersonal relationships of comparable warmth and intensity with their client-subjects under both desensitization and placebo conditions. A number of factors argue that a high degree of comparability was achieved. The formal, experimental setting in which this research was carried out certainly assisted in this task. Each step of the procedure was defined, and a considerable portion of the therapists' communications with the subject were read from a mimeographed program. Furthermore, it is unlikely that the therapists who saw most of the subjects in this study were personally committed to any outcome. They were paid for their participation, at the same rate per therapy hour regardless of the procedure administered, and they were involved in no other aspect of the experiment. It must also be mentioned that all subjects were seen by clinicians with considerable experience in interviewing and traditional psychotherapy, who would be well above average in their ability to meet the relationship requirements of the experiment. Finally, the posttherapy interviews with the subjects, and discussions with the therapists, did not suggest that placebo subjects were less closely involved, nor did they yield subjects who doubted the fact that a true therapeutic procedure was being undertaken.

On the other hand, the possibility of error in procedure can never be completely discounted, and is best detected by independent attempts at replication. Furthermore, despite the fact that many of the same procedures were used in both placebo therapy and desensitization, the way they were used undoubtedly influenced the character of the experimenter-subject relationship. Unlike the pseudo-therapy group, desensitization subjects received regular feedback concerning progress through the hierarchy. Clearcut success experiences (as well as failures) were part of the therapeutic interaction. In this context, a good therapeutic relationship may be one in which the therapist has gained the properties of a reinforcer, and this capacity is in the service of a specific program of behavior change. Desensitization would then progress more rapidly if approval is given for the completion of items. The better the relationship, the more effective such reinforcement is likely to be. On the other hand, it should be pointed out that the completion of an item is in itself reinforcing and many subjects compliment themselves on their own progress. Thus, the quality of the relationship may be less relevant to a well-motivated subject's performance. These variables merit the continued attention of researchers.

While the desensitization subjects as a group showed considerable fear reduction, the change score distributions are skewed and some individual members changed no more than controls. The current experiment was limited to a brief 11 desensitization sessions, and it is, of course, possible that all subjects would have improved with a sufficient exposure. It is also possible that there are personality differences between those who profit and those who do not. As the sample size increases this contingency will be explored. In any event, suggestibility is clearly not one of the potential distinguishing traits. While a significant part of the control subject's fear change is attributable to the SHSS, no similar relationship between this scale and fear reduction was found for the experimental group. For desensitization subjects the positive effects of treatment were so overriding as to render undetectable any variance assignable to suggestibility.

All measures of fear change yielded high positive correlations with number of hierarchy items completed. Furthermore, subjects who completed at least 15 items showed significantly less fear than controls at the end of the experiment; subjects who failed to move this far along in the hierarchy were no different from pseudotherapy or untreated subjects. The correlations indicate that a general relationship exists between fear change and a measurable aspect of therapy process. It is unlikely that Item 15 represents a "critical point" in this process. However, given the measures used here, the data suggest that the therapeutic task must be well advanced before effects clearly greater than those achieved by control subjects are observed.

As would be predicted by an S-R theoretical model, fears other than the phobia treated showed less marked reduction. The desensitization group as a whole yielded significantly greater change than controls on FSS Number 38; an analogous result was not obtained for the entire FSS. Nevertheless, 15 plus subjects did show a significant reduction on the FSS when compared either to control subjects or to the less than 15 group. These findings suggest that the treatment was specific, as intended, and when it was successful that fear reduction generalized positively.

These findings are inconsistent with some predictions from psychoanalytic theory. Fear reduction occurred without exploration of the phobia's dynamic background. Posttreatment interviews revealed no examples of symptom substitution. Positive generalization of fear reduction was indicated, rather than an increase in other fears. Furthermore, a transference cure interpretation of the fear change is weakened by the failure to find marked placebo effects.

Although the relationship by itself was shown to be less effective therapy than client-centered theorists have sometimes argued, this experiment does not constitute a test of that treatment method. A quasi-non-directive technique was employed as part of the pseudotherapy procedure, but its object was the opposite of client-centered therapy, to avert affect-laden statements rather than to encourage them. As was already suggested, theory would predict positive change in true client-centered treatment for the same reasons as for desensitization. Advocates of the latter treatment hold, of course, that behavior therapy is more specific and systematic, and therefore faster and more thorough. The present experimental design offers an excellent setting for a test of this assumption. Now that the level of placebo changes is known the way is open for meaningful, comparative evaluation of psychotherapies.

Both the limitations and the advantages of the subject population used in this experiment were mentioned at the outset, and they must be continually held in mind. However, the course of laboratory desensitization very closely followed the treatment process reported by clinical workers. Considerable success was achieved in 11 desensitization sessions, which compares favorably with the 11.6 average sessions per hierarchy reported by Wolpe (1958) for neurotic patients. Furthermore, many of the phenomena observed by the authors in clinical cases, and reported by others, were found with these experimental subjects. The systematic weakening of anxiety with repeated presentation of a hierarchy item was of course the typical result. However, subjects occasionally showed a perseveration of anxiety, and apparent summation with repetition, that presented all the difficulties that this situation creates when it occurs in a clinical case. Similarly, problems with visualization were frequently observed, as well as avoidance behavior when individual items were particularly upsetting. While these problems were undoubtedly fewer and less intense than would occur in clinical practice, they did not appear to differ in quality or kind.

Despite this apparent verisimilitude, generalization to the clinic must be cautiously undertaken. Many issues are raised that need more intensive investigation. Nevertheless, the results obtained here encourage four important conclusions: (*a*) simply being in a therapeutic context and relating to a therapist (even when all the trappings of desensitiza-tion—hypnosis, hierarchy building, relaxation—are included) does not in itself effect the important changes in phobic behavior achieved by systematic desensitization; (*b*) successful desensitization is relatively independent of the subject's suggestibility; (*c*) change in verbal and motor indices of fear behavior may be directly predicted from measurable events that occur during desensitization therapy; (*d*) the systematic desensitization of a specific fear generalizes positively to other fears. These findings are further presumptive evidence that desensitization therapy process conforms to its theoretical model, that it is an adapting out or systematic counter-conditioning of fear responses to specific stimuli.

Positive Social Behaviors

10

Genius
and
Creativity

Before beginning this chapter, we need to recall the perspective expressed in the introduction to this book. Note that this section is titled "Positive Social Behaviors." We distinguish between negative abnormalities, ordinarily called the psychopathologies, and positive ones, but we include both because we view them as equally abnormal: abnormal in that they are rare, abnormal in that they attract attention from the surrounding society, abnormal in that they reflect special kinds of social judgments. Of course positive and negative abnormalities are different from each other in many important ways. Just as one would rather be a genius than a schizophrenic, one would rather be positively than negatively valued in one's society. But here we want to stress their similarity, the notions of rareness and of social salience that seem common to both. It is the underlying statistical principle and the underlying principle of social judgment that unite these abnormalities. If we are geniuses it is, in part, because

society through its "Knowers" deems us so, much as we are schizophrenic because we have been so labeled by our society.

Note that the statistical view of abnormality does not deny other views. Any view of abnormality may have dynamics that have nothing to do with statistical distributions. The roles of anxiety, guilt, and conflict are not less important in psychopathology because we take a statistical view, nor are the roles of intellectual stimulation and emotional support for the encouragement of genius minimized. Indeed, the evidence for these factors can be seen throughout the book. The possibility that similar social processes underlie positive and negative abnormalities is, however, underscored by the normative view.

The first paper in this section, by Francis Galton, illustrates the particular meaning of abnormality that we have in mind. Galton's genius ranged over a wide variety of topics that were central to the development of psychology: from genetics to psychophysics, from the assessment of emotion and character type through the uncovering of genius. His demonstration of the inherited nature of intellectual eminence revealed some of his greatest talents. In the excerpts presented here, Galton arrives at the view that certain talents are distributed in such a manner that it is a rare man who possesses them in the extreme and an equally rare man who possesses none at all. His analyses, whether of physical strength, height, or intelligence, lend themselves easily to the familiar bell-shaped curve, indicating that most people have something of a particular talent and that very few have either none at all or a great deal. What Galton wrote of intelligence and physical prowess can probably also be said of adjustment, postive character traits, psychopathology, and the like: some people have very little, some a lot, and most are in the middle.

In fact, elements of Galton's argument were subsequently found wrong, or at least lacking in reliable evidence. This is particularly true for his arguments about race. For the most part, however, the thesis described in these selections was subsequently verified, and it stimulated extensive examinations of the nature of intelligence, its distribution, and the statistical properties of various talents.

Arthur Koestler's concern is for the processes involved in the creative act, be it in arts, sciences, or literature, or simply in lesser creative arts that are testimony to inventive intelligence. He begins, as Freud in similar studies began, with little matters: jokes and puns. What makes a joke funny? Are there parallels between the novelty involved in the joke and the novelty of other creative work? Koestler finds that there are striking parallels, that the *bisociative* process involved in humor

pervades the creative endeavor, from wit to scientific creativity.

Koestler is concerned with the formation of the creative product, the thought matrices which, when joined, result in the original contribution. Frank Barron and Donald MacKinnon are concerned with the creative person. Creativity, they hold, is not an isolated phenomenon, occurring in mind alone. It is also the product of the person. It is rarely performed once and then never again. Rather, it pervades the person. Some people are thoroughly original, others less so, and some few not at all. Barron, in the next paper, demonstrates the presence of a surprising degree of unity in performance on a variety of tests that purport to measure originality. The tendency to think with originality, as it were, is not content or situation bound, but rather appears to occur in a variety of contexts. Moreover, a wide variety of personality dispositions distinguish the original from the relatively less original mind, supporting the view that the creative act involves more than thought alone, that it includes generalized affective and personal dispositions.

Some readers will be less than fully satisfied with relatively artificial test measures of originality when our society seems to abound in the "real thing": men and women who have contributed genuinely creative products to society. Fortunately, studies of creative people have been conducted by Donald MacKinnon and members of the Institute for Personality Assessment at the University of California at Berkeley. These intensive "depth" analyses of creative individuals are landmarks for this kind of research, and the findings suggest that creative people differ from relatively less creative ones in a variety of ways, both personal and cognitive.

Classification of Men
According to Their Reputation

Francis Galton

The arguments by which I endeavour to prove that genius is hereditary, consist in showing how large is the number of instances in which men who are more or less illustrious have eminent kinsfolk. It is necessary to have clear ideas on the two following matters before my arguments can be rightly appreciated. The first is the degree of selection implied by the words "eminent" and "illustrious." Does "eminent" mean the foremost in a hundred, in a thousand, or in what other number of men? The second is the degree to which reputation may be accepted as a test of ability.

It is essential that I, who write, should have a minimum qualification distinctly before my eyes whenever I employ the phrases "eminent" and the like, and that the reader should understand as clearly as myself the value I attach to those qualifications. An explanation of these words will be the subject of the present chapter. A subsequent chapter will be given to the discussion of how far "eminence" may be accepted as a criterion of natural gifts. It is almost needless for me to insist that the subjects of these two chapters are entirely distinct.

I look upon social and professional life as a continuous examination. All are candidates for the good opinions of others, and for success in their several professions, and they achieve success in proportion as the general estimate is large of their aggregate merits. In ordinary scholastic examinations marks are allotted in stated proportions to various specified subjects—so many for Latin, so many for Greek, so many for English history, and the rest. The world, in the same way, but almost unconsciously, allots marks to men. It gives them for originality of conception, for enterprise, for activity and energy, for administrative skill, for various acquirements, for power of literary expression, for oratory, and much besides of general value, as well as for more specially professional merits. It does not allot these marks according to a proportion that can easily be stated in words, but there is a rough commonsense that governs its practice with a fair approximation to constancy. Those who have gained most of these tacit marks are ranked, by the common judgment of the leaders of opinion, as the foremost men of their day.

The metaphor of an examination may be stretched much further. As there are alternative groups in any one of which a candidate may obtain honours, so it is with reputations—they may be made in law, literature, science, art, and in a host of other pursuits. Again: as the mere attainment of a general fair level will obtain no honours in an examination, no more will it do so in the struggle for eminence. A man must show conspicuous power in at least one subject in order to achieve a high reputation.

Let us see how the world classifies people, after examining each of them, in her patient, persistent manner, during the

Reprinted from *Hereditary Genius: An Inquiry into Its Laws and Consequences* (New York: Appleton and Co., 1880), pp. 6–13.

years of their manhood. How many men of "eminence" are there, and what proportion do they bear to the whole community?

I will begin by analysing a very painstaking biographical handbook, lately published by Routledge and Co., called *Men of the Time*. Its intention, which is very fairly and honestly carried out, is to include none but those whom the world honours for their ability. The catalogue of names is 2,500, and a full half of it consists of American and Continental celebrities. It is well I should give in a footnote[1] an analysis of its contents, in order to show the exhaustive character of its range. The numbers I have prefixed to each class are not strictly accurate, for I measured them off rather than counted them, but they are quite close enough. The same name often appears under more than one head.

On looking over the book, I am surprised to find how large a proportion of the "Men of the Time" are past middle age. It appears that in the cases of high (but by no means in that of the highest) merit, a man must outlive the age of fifty to be sure of being widely appreciated. It takes time for an able man, born in the humbler ranks of life, to emerge from

them and to take his natural position. It would not, therefore, be just to compare the numbers of Englishmen in the book with that of the whole adult male population of the British isles; but it is necessary to confine our examination to those of the celebrities who are past fifty years of age, and to compare their number with that of the whole male population who are also above fifty years. I estimate, from examining a large part of the book, that there are about 850 of these men, and that 500 of them are decidedly well known to persons familiar with literary and scientific society. Now, there are about two millions of adult males in the British isles above fifty years of age; consequently, the total number of the "Men of the Time" are as 425 to a million, and the more select part of them as 250 to a million.

The qualifications for belonging to what I call the more select part are, in my mind, that a man should have distinguished himself pretty frequently either by purely original work, or as a leader of opinion. I wholly exclude notoriety obtained by a single act. This is a fairly well-defined line, because there is not room for many men to be eminent. Each interest or idea has its mouthpiece, and a man who has attained and can maintain his position as the representative of a party or an idea, naturally becomes much more conspicuous than his coadjutors who are nearly equal but inferior in ability. This is eminently the case in positions where eminence may be won by official acts. The balance may be turned by a grain that decides whether A, B, or C shall be promoted to a vacant post. The man who obtains it has opportunities of distinction denied to the others. I do not, however, take much note of official rank. People who have left very great names behind them have mostly done so through non-professional labours. I certainly should not include mere officials, except of the

---

[1] Contents of the *Dictionary of Men of the Time*, (1865):—62 actors, singers, dancers, etc.; 7 agriculturists; 71 antiquaries, archaeologists, numismatists, etc.; 20 architects; 120 artists (painters and designers); 950 authors; 400 divines; 43 engineers and mechanicians; 10 engravers; 140 lawyers, judges, barristers, and legists; 94 medical practitioners, physicians, surgeons, and physiologists; 39 merchants, capitalists, manufacturers, and traders; 168 military officers; 12 miscellaneous; 7 moral and metaphysical philosophers, logicians; 32 musicians and composers; 67 naturalists, botanists, zoologists, etc.; 36 naval officers; 40 philologists and ethnologists; 60 poets (but also included in authors); 60 political and social economists and philanthropists; 154 men of science, astronomers, chemists, geologists, mathematicians, etc.; 29 sculptors; 64 sovereigns, members of royal families, etc.; 376 statesmen, diplomatists, colonial governors, etc.; 76 travellers and geographers.

highest ranks, and in open professions, among my select list of eminent men.

Another estimate of the proportion of eminent men to the whole population was made on a different basis, and gave much the same result. I took the obituary of the year 1868, published in the *Times* on January 1, 1869, and found in it about fifty names of men of the more select class. This was in one sense a broader, and in another a more rigorous selection than that which I have just described. It was broader, because I included the names of many whose abilities were high, but who died too young to have earned the wide reputation they deserved; and it was more rigorous, because I excluded old men who had earned distinction in years gone by, but had not shown themselves capable in later times to come again to the front. On the first ground, it was necessary to lower the limit of the age of the population with whom they should be compared. Forty-five years of age seemed to me a fair limit, including, as it was supposed to do, a year or two of broken health preceding decease. Now, 210,000 males die annually in the British isles above the age of forty-five; therefore, the ratio of the more select portion of the "Men of the Time" on these data is as 50 to 210,000, or as 238 to a million.

Thirdly, I consulted obituaries of many years back, when the population of these islands was much smaller and they appeared to me to lead to similar conclusions, viz. that 250 to a million is an ample estimate.

There would be no difficulty in making a further selection out of these, to any degree of rigour. We could select the 200, the 100, or the 50 best out of the 250, without much uncertainty. But I do not see my way to work downwards. If I were asked to choose the thousand per million best men, I should feel we had descended to a level where there existed no sure data for guidance, where accident and opportunity had undue influence, and where it was impossible to distinguish general eminence from local reputation, or from mere notoriety.

These considerations define the sense in which I propose to employ the word "eminent." When I speak of an eminent man, I mean one who has achieved a position that is attained by only 250 persons in each million of men, or by one person in each 4,000. 4,000 is a very large number—difficult for persons to realize who are not accustomed to deal with great assemblages. On the most brilliant of starlight nights there are never so many as 4,000 stars visible to the naked eye at the same time; yet we feel it to be an extraordinary distinction to a star to be accounted as the brightest in the sky. This, be it remembered, is my narrowest area of selection. I propose to introduce no name whatever into my lists of kinsmen (unless it be marked off from the rest by brackets) that is less distinguished.

The mass of those with whom I deal are far more rigidly selected—many are as one in a million, and not a few as one of many millions. I use the term "illustrious" when speaking of these. They are men whom the whole intelligent part of the nation mourns when they die; who have, or deserve to have, a public funeral; and who rank in future ages as historical characters.

Permit me to add a word upon the meaning of a million, being a number so enormous as to be difficult to conceive. It is well to have a standard by which to realize it. Mine will be understood by many Londoners; it is as follows. One summer day I passed the afternoon in Bushey Park to see the magnificent spectacle of its avenue of horse-chestnut trees, a mile long, in full flower. As the hours passed by, it occurred to me to try to count the number of spikes of flowers facing the drive on one side of the long avenue—I mean all the spikes that were visible in full sunshine on one side of the road. Accordingly, I fixed upon a tree of average bulk and flower, and drew imaginary lines—first halving the tree, then quartering, and so on, until I arrived at a subdivision that was not too large to allow of my counting the spikes of flowers it included. I did this with three different trees, and arrived at pretty much the same result; as well as I recollect, the three estimates were as nine, ten, and eleven. Then I counted the trees in the avenue, and, multiplying all together, I found the spikes to be just about 100,000 in number. Ever since then, whenever a million is mentioned, I recall the long perspective of the avenue of Bushey Park, with its stately chestnuts clothed from top to bottom with spikes of flowers, bright in the sunshine, and I imagine a similarly continuous floral band, of ten miles in length.

In illustration of the value of the extreme rigour implied by a selection of one in a million, I will take the following instance. The Oxford and Cambridge boat race excites almost a national enthusiasm, and the men who represent their Universities as competing crews have good reason to be proud of being the selected champions of such large bodies. The crew of each boat consists of eight men, selected out of about 800 students; namely, the available undergraduates of about two successive years. In other words, the selection that is popularly felt to be so strict, is only as one in a hundred. Now, suppose there had been so vast a number of universities that it would have been possible to bring together 800 men, each of whom had pulled in a University crew, and that from this body the eight best were selected to form a special crew of comparatively rare merit: the selection of each of these would be as 1 to 10,000 ordinary men. Let this process be repeated, and then, and not till then, do you arrive at a superlative crew, representing selections of one in a million. This is a perfectly fair deduction, because the youths at the Universities are a haphazard collection of men, so far as regards their thews and sinews. No one is sent to a University on account of his powerful muscle. Or, to put the same facts into another form:—it would require a period of no less than 200 years, before either University could furnish eight men, each of whom would have sufficient boating eminence to rank as one of the medium crew. Twenty thousand years must elapse before eight men could be furnished, each of whom would have the rank of the superlative crew.

It is, however, quite another matter with respect to brain power, for, as I shall have occasion to show, the Universities attract to themselves a large proportion of the eminent scholastic talent of all England. There are nearly a quarter of a million males in Great Britain who arrive each year at the proper age for going to the University: therefore, if Cambridge, for example, received only one in every five of the ablest scholastic intellects, she would be able, in every period of 20 years, to boast of the fresh arrival of an undergraduate, the rank of whose scholastic eminence was that of one in a million.

Classification of Men According to Their Natural Gifts

Francis Galton

I have no patience with the hypothesis occasionally expressed, and often implied, especially in tales written to teach children to be good, that babies are born pretty much alike, and that the sole agencies in creating differences between boy and boy, and man and man, are steady application and moral effort. It is in the most unqualified manner that I object to pretensions of natural equality. The experiences of the nursery, the school, the University, and of professional careers, are a chain of proofs to the contrary. I acknowledge freely the great power of education and social influences in developing the active powers of the mind, just as I acknowledge the effect of use in developing the muscles of a blacksmith's arm, and no further. Let the blacksmith labour as he will, he will find there are certain feats beyond his power that are well within the strength of a man of herculean make, even although the latter may have led a sedentary life. Some years ago, the Highlanders held a grand gathering in Holland Park, where they challenged all England to compete with them in their games of strength. The challenge was accepted, and the well-trained men of the hills were beaten in the foot-race by a youth who was stated to be a pure Cockney, the clerk of a London banker.

Everybody who has trained himself to physical exercises discovers the extent of his muscular powers to a nicety. When he begins to walk, to row, to use the dumb bells, or to run, he finds to his great delight that his thews strengthen, and his endurance of fatigue increases day after day. So long as he is a novice, he perhaps flatters himself there is hardly an assignable limit to the education of his muscles; but the daily gain is soon discovered to diminish, and at last it vanishes altogether. His maximum performance becomes a rigidly determinate quantity. He learns to an inch, how high or how far he can jump, when he has attained the highest state of training. He learns to half a pound, the force he can exert on the dynamometer, by compressing it. He can strike a blow against the machine used to measure impact, and drive its index to a certain graduation, but no further. So it is in running, in rowing, in walking, and in every other form of physical exertion. There is a definite limit to the muscular powers of every man, which he cannot by any education or exertion overpass.

This is precisely analogous to the experience that every student has had of the working of his mental powers. The eager boy, when he first goes to school and confronts intellectual difficulties, is astonished at his progress. He glories in his newly-developed mental grip and growing capacity for application, and, it may be, fondly believes it to be within his reach to become one of the heroes who have left their mark upon the history of the world. The years go by; he competes in the examinations of school and college,

Reprinted from *Hereditary Genius: An Inquiry into Its Laws and Consequences* (New York: Appleton and Co., 1880), pp. 14–36.

over and over again with his fellows, and soon finds his place among them. He knows he can beat such and such of his competitors; that there are some with whom he runs on equal terms, and others whose intellectual feats he cannot even approach. Probably his vanity still continues to tempt him, by whispering in a new strain. It tells him that classics, mathematics, and other subjects taught in universities, are mere scholastic specialties, and no test of the more valuable intellectual powers. It reminds him of numerous instances of persons who had been unsuccessful in the competitions of youth, but who had shown powers in after-life that made them the foremost men of their age. Accordingly, with newly furbished hopes, and with all the ambition of twenty-two years of age, he leaves his University and enters a larger field of competition. The same kind of experience awaits him here that he has already gone through. Opportunities occur—they occur to every man—and he finds himself incapable of grasping them. He tries, and is tried in many things. In a few years more, unless he is incurably blinded by self-conceit, he learns precisely of what performances he is capable, and what other enterprises lie beyond his compass. When he reaches mature life, he is confident only within certain limits, and knows, or ought to know, himself just as he is probably judged of by the world, with all his unmistakable weakness and all his undeniable strength. He is no longer tormented into hopeless efforts by the fallacious promptings of overweening vanity, but he limits his undertakings to matters below the level of his reach, and finds true moral repose in an honest conviction that he is engaged in as much good work as his nature has rendered him capable of performing.

There can hardly be a surer evidence of the enormous difference between the intellectual capacity of men, than the prodigious differences in the numbers of marks obtained by those who gained mathematical honours at Cambridge. I therefore crave permission to speak at some length upon this subject, although the details are dry and of little general interest. There are between 400 and 450 students who take their degrees in each year, and of these, about 100 succeed in gaining honours in mathematics, and are ranged by the examiners in strict order of merit. About the first forty of those who take mathematical honours are distinguished by the title of wranglers, and it is a decidedly creditable thing to be even a low wrangler; it will secure a fellowship in a small college. It must be carefully borne in mind that the distinction of being the first in this list of honours, or what is called the senior wrangler of the year, means a vast deal more than being the foremost mathematician of 400 or 450 men taken at haphazard. No doubt the large bulk of Cambridge men are taken almost at haphazard. A boy is intended by his parents for some profession; if that profession be either the Church or the Bar, it used to be almost requisite, and it is still important, that he should be sent to Cambridge or Oxford. These youths may justly be considered as having been taken at haphazard. But there are many others who have fairly won their way to the Universities, and are therefore selected from an enormous area. Fully one-half of the wranglers have been boys of note at their respective schools, and, conversely, almost all boys of note at schools find their way to the Universities. Hence it is that among their comparatively small number of students, the Universities include the highest youthful scholastic ability of all England. The senior wrangler, in each successive year, is the chief of these as regards mathematics, and this, the highest distinction, is, or was, continually won by youths who had no mathematical training of importance before they went to Cambridge. All their instruction had been received during the three years of their residence at the University. Now, I do not say anything here about the merits or demerits of Cambridge mathematical studies having been directed along a too narrow groove, or about the presumed disadvantages of ranging candidates in strict order of merit, instead of grouping them, as at Oxford, in classes, where their names appear alphabetically arranged. All I am concerned with here are the results; and these are most appropriate to my argument. The youths start on their three years' race as fairly as possible. They are then stimulated to run by the most powerful inducements, namely, those of competition, of honour, and of future wealth (for a good fellowship *is wealth*); and at the end of the three years they are examined most rigorously according to a system that they all understand and are equally well prepared for. The examination lasts five and a half hours a day for eight days. All the answers are carefully marked by the examiners, who add up the marks at the end and range the candidates in strict order of merit. The fairness and thoroughness of Cambridge examinations have never had a breath of suspicion cast upon them.

Unfortunately for my purposes, the marks are not published. They are not even assigned on a uniform system, since each examiner is permitted to employ his own scale of marks; but whatever scale he uses, the results as to proportional merit are the same. I am indebted to a Cambridge examiner for a copy of his marks in respect to two examinations, in which the scales of marks were so alike as to make it easy, by a slight proportional adjustment, to compare the two together (Table 1). This was, to a certain degree, a confidential communication, so that it would be improper for me to publish anything that would identify the years to

which these marks refer. I simply give them as groups of figures, sufficient to show the enormous differences of merit. The lowest man in the list of honours gains less than 300 marks; the lowest wrangler gains about 1,500 marks; and the senior wrangler, in one of the lists now before me, gained more than 7,500 marks. Consequently, the lowest wrangler has more than five times the merit of the lowest junior optime, and less than one-fifth the merit of the senior wrangler.

Table 1

Scale of Merit among the Men Who Obtain Mathematical Honours at Cambridge[a]

Number of marks obtained by candidates	Number of candidates in the two years, taken together, who obtained those marks
Under 500	24[b]
500 to 1,000	74
1,000 to 1,500	38
1,500 to 2,000	21
2,000 to 2,500	11
2,500 to 3,000	8
3,000 to 3,500	11
3,500 to 4,000	5
4,000 to 4,500	2
4,500 to 5,000	1
5,000 to 5,500	3
5,500 to 6,000	1
6,000 to 6,500	0
6,500 to 7,000	0
7,000 to 7,500	0
7,500 to 8,000	1
	200

[a] The results of two years are put into a single table. The total number of marks obtainable in each year was 17,000.

[b] I have included in this table only the first 100 men in each year. The omitted residue is too small to be important. I have omitted it lest, if the precise number of honour men were stated, those numbers would have served to identify the years. For reasons already given, I desire to afford no data to serve that purpose.

The precise number of marks obtained by the senior wrangler in the more remarkable of these two years was 7,634;

by the second wrangler in the same year, 4,123; and by the lowest man in the list of honours, only 237. Consequently, the senior wrangler obtained nearly twice as many marks as the second wrangler, and more than thirty-two times as many as the lowest man. I have received from another examiner the marks of a year in which the senior wrangler was conspicuously eminent. He obtained 9,422 marks, whilst the second in the same year—whose merits were by no means inferior to those of second wranglers in general—obtained only 5,642. The man at the bottom of the same honour list had only 309 marks, or one-thirtieth the number of the senior wrangler. I have some particulars of a fourth very remarkable year, in which the senior wrangler obtained no less than ten times as many marks as the second wrangler, in the "problem paper." Now, I have discussed with practised examiners the question of how far the numbers of marks may be considered as proportionate to the mathematical power of the candidate, and am assured they are strictly proportionate as regards the lower places, but do not afford full justice to the highest. In other words, the senior wranglers above mentioned had more than thirty, or thirty-two times the ability of the lowest men on the lists of honours. They would be able to grapple with problems more than thirty-two times as difficult; or when dealing with subjects of the same difficulty, but intelligible to all, would comprehend them more rapidly in perhaps the square root of that proportion. It is reasonable to expect that marks would do some injustice to the very best men, because a very large part of the time of the examination is taken up by the mechanical labour of writing. Whenever the thought of the candidate outruns his pen, he gains no advantage from his excess of promptitude in conception. I should, however, mention that some of

the ablest men have shown their superiority by comparatively little writing. They find their way at once to the root of the difficulty in the problems that are set, and, with a few clean, apposite, powerful strokes, succeed in proving they can overthrow it, and then they go on to another question. Every word they write tells. Thus, the late Mr. H. Leslie Ellis, who was a brilliant senior wrangler in 1840, and whose name is familiar to many generations of Cambridge men as a prodigy of universal genius, did not even remain during the full period in the examination room: his health was weak, and he had to husband his strength.

The mathematical powers of the last man on the list of honours, which are so low when compared with those of a senior wrangler, are mediocre, or even above mediocrity, when compared with the gifts of Englishmen generally. Though the examination places 100 honour men above him, it puts no less than 300 "poll men" below him. Even if we go so far as to allow that 200 out of the 300 refuse to work hard enough to get honours, there will remain 100 who, even if they worked hard, could not get them. Every tutor knows how difficult it is to drive abstract conceptions, even of the simplest kind, into the brains of most people—how feeble and hesitating is their mental grasp—how easily their brains are mazed—how incapable they are of precision and soundness of knowledge. It often occurs to persons familiar with some scientific subject to hear men and women of mediocre gifts relate to one another what they have picked up about it from some lecture— say at the Royal Institution, where they have sat for an hour listening with delighted attention to an admirably lucid account, illustrated by experiments of the most perfect and beautiful character, in all of which they expressed themselves intensely gratified and highly instructed. It is positively painful to hear what they say. Their recollections seem to be a mere chaos of mist and misapprehension, to which some sort of shape and organization has been given by the action of their own pure fancy, altogether alien to what the lecturer intended to convey. The average mental grasp even of what is called a well-educated audience, will be found to be ludicrously small when rigorously tested.

In stating the differences between man and man, let it not be supposed for a moment that mathematicians are necessarily one-sided in their natural gifts. There are numerous instances of the reverse, of whom the following will be found, as instances of hereditary genius, in the appendix to my chapter on "Science." I would especially name Leibnitz, as being universally gifted; but Ampère, Arago, Condorcet, and D'Alembert, were all of them very far more than mere mathematicians. Nay, since the range of examination at Cambridge is so extended as to include other subjects besides mathematics, the differences of ability between the highest and lowest of the successful candidates, is yet more glaring than what I have already described. We still find, on the one hand, mediocre men, whose whole energies are absorbed in getting their 237 marks for mathematics; and, on the other hand, some few senior wranglers who are at the same time high classical scholars and much more besides. Cambridge has afforded such instances. Its lists of classical honours are comparatively of recent date, but other evidence is obtainable from earlier times of their occurrence. Thus, Dr. George Butler, the Head Master of Harrow for very many years, including the period when Byron was a schoolboy (father of the present Head Master, and of other sons, two of whom are also head masters of great public schools,) must

have obtained that classical office on account of his eminent classical ability; but Dr. Butler was also senior wrangler in 1794, the year when Lord Chancellor Lyndhurst was second. Both Dr. Kaye, the late Bishop of Lincoln, and Sir E. Alderson, the late judge, were the senior wranglers and the first classical prizemen of their respective years. Since 1824, when the classical tripos was first established, the late Mr. Goulburn (brother of Dr. Goulburn, Dean of Norwich, and son of the well-known Serjeant Goulburn[1]) was second wrangler in 1835, and senior classic of the same year. But in more recent times, the necessary labour of preparation, in order to acquire the highest mathematical places, has become so enormous that there has been a wider differentiation of studies. There is no longer *time* for a man to acquire the necessary knowledge to succeed to the first place in more than one subject. There are, therefore, no instances of a man being absolutely first in both examinations, but a few can be found of high eminence in both classics and mathematics, as a reference to the lists published in the "Cambridge Calendar" will show. The best of these more recent degrees appears to be that of Dr. Barry, late Principal of Cheltenham, and now Principal of King's College, London (the son of the eminent architect, Sir Charles Barry, and brother of Mr. Edward Barry, who succeeded his father as architect). He was fourth wrangler and seventh classic of his year.

In whatever way we may test ability, we arrive at equally enormous intellectual differences. Lord Macaulay (*see* under "Literature" for his remarkable kinships) had one of the most tenacious of memories. He was able to recall many pages of hundreds of volumes by various

[1] Erroneous; corrected at p. 301. [i.e. nephew of Serjeant Goulburn—Eds.]

authors, which he had acquired by simply reading them over. An average man could not certainly carry in his memory one thirty-second—ay, or one hundredth —part as much as Lord Macaulay. The father of Seneca had one of the greatest memories on record in ancient times (*see* under "Literature" for his kinships). Porson, the Greek scholar, was remarkable for this gift, and, I may add, the "Porson memory" was hereditary in that family. In statesmanship, generalship, literature, science, poetry, art, just the same enormous differences are found between man and man; and numerous instances recorded in this book, will show in how small degree, eminence, either in these or any other class of intellectual powers, can be considered as due to purely special powers. They are rather to be considered in those instances as the result of concentrated efforts, made by men who are widely gifted. People lay too much stress on apparent specialities, thinking over-rashly that, because a man is devoted to some particular pursuit, he could not possibly have succeeded in anything else. They might just as well say that, because a youth had fallen desperately in love with a brunette, he could not possibly have fallen in love with a blonde. He may or may not have more natural liking for the former type of beauty than the latter, but it is as probable as not that the affair was mainly or wholly due to a general amorousness of disposition. It is just the same with special pursuits. A gifted man is often capricious and fickle before he selects his occupation, but when it has been chosen, he devotes himself to it with a truly passionate ardour. After a man of genius has selected his hobby, and so adapted himself to it as to seem unfitted for any other occupation in life, and to be possessed of but one special aptitude, I often notice, with admiration, how well he bears himself when circumstances sud-

denly thrust him into a strange position. He will display an insight into new conditions, and a power of dealing with them, with which even his most intimate friends were unprepared to accredit him. Many a presumptuous fool has mistaken indifference and neglect for incapacity; and in trying to throw a man of genius on ground where he was unprepared for attack, has himself received a most severe and unexpected fall. I am sure that no one who has had the privilege of mixing in the society of the abler men of any great capital, or who is acquainted with the biographies of the heroes of history, can doubt the existence of grand human animals, of natures pre-eminently noble, of individuals born to be kings of men. I have been conscious of no slight misgiving that I was committing a kind of sacrilege whenever, in the preparation of materials for this book, I had occasion to take the measurement of modern intellects vastly superior to my own, or to criticise the genius of the most magnificent historical specimens of our race. It was a process that constantly recalled to me a once familiar sentiment in bygone days of African travel, when I used to take altitudes of the huge cliffs that domineered above me as I travelled along their bases, or to map the mountainous landmarks of unvisited tribes, that loomed in faint grandeur beyond my actual horizon.

I have not cared to occupy myself much with people whose gifts are below the average, but they would be an interesting study. The number of idiots and imbeciles among the twenty million inhabitants of England and Wales is approximately estimated at 50,000, or as 1 in 400. Dr. Seguin, a great French authority on these matters, states that more than thirty per cent. of idiots and imbeciles, put under suitable instruction, have been taught to conform to social and moral law, and rendered capable of order, of good feeling, and of working like *the third* of an average man. He says that more than forty per cent. have become capable of the ordinary transactions of life, under friendly control; of understanding moral and social abstractions, and of working like *two-thirds* of a man. And, lastly, that from twenty-five to thirty per cent. come nearer and nearer to the standard of manhood, till some of them will defy the scrutiny of good judges, when compared with ordinary young men and women. In the order next above idiots and imbeciles are a large number of milder cases scattered among private families and kept out of sight, the existence of whom is, however, well known to relatives and friends; they are too silly to take a part in general society, but are easily amused with some trivial, harmless occupation. Then comes a class of whom the Lord Dundreary of the famous play may be considered a representative; and so, proceeding through successive grades, we gradually ascend to mediocrity. I know two good instances of hereditary silliness short of imbecility and have reason to believe I could easily obtain a large number of similar facts.

To conclude, the range of mental power between—I will not say the highest Caucasian and the lowest savage—but between the greatest and least of English intellects, is enormous. There is a continuity of natural ability reaching from one knows not what height, and descending to one can hardly say what depth. I propose in this chapter to range men according to their natural abilities, putting them into classes separated by equal degrees of merit, and to show the relative number of individuals included in the several classes. Perhaps some persons might be inclined to make an off-hand guess that the number of men included in the several classes would be pretty equal. If he thinks so, I can assure him he is most egregiously mistaken.

The method I shall employ for discovering all this, is an application of the very curious theoretical law of "deviation from an average." First, I will explain the law, and then I will show that the production of natural intellectual gifts comes justly within its scope.

The law is an exceedingly general one. M. Quetelet, the Astronomer-Royal of Belgium, and the greatest authority on vital and social statistics, has largely used it in his inquiries. He has also constructed numerical tables, by which the necessary calculations can be easily made, whenever it is desired to have recourse to the law. Those who wish to learn more than I have space to relate, should consult his work, which is a very readable octavo volume, and deserves to be far better known to statisticians than it appears to be. Its title is "Letters on Probabilities," translated by Downes. Layton and Co. London: 1849.

So much has been published in recent years about statistical deductions, that I am sure the reader will be prepared to assent freely to the following hypothetical case:—Suppose a large island inhabited by a single race, who intermarried freely, and who had lived for many generations under constant conditions; then the average *height* of the male adults of that population would undoubtedly be the same year after year. Also—still arguing from the experience of modern statistics, which are found to give constant results in far less carefully-guarded examples—we should undoubtedly find, year after year, the same proportion maintained between the number of men of different heights. I mean, if the average stature was found to be sixty-six inches, and if it was also found in any one year that 100 per million exceeded seventy-eight inches, the same proportion of 100 per million would be closely maintained in all other years. An equal constancy of proportion would be maintained between any other limits of height we pleased to specify, as between seventy-one and seventy-two inches; between seventy-two and seventy-three inches; and so on. Statistical experiences are so invariably confirmatory of what I have stated would probably be the case, as to make it unnecessary to describe analogous instances. Now, at this point, the law of deviation from an average steps in. It shows that the number per million whose heights range between seventy-one and seventy-two inches (or between any other limits we please to name) can be *predicted* from the previous datum of the average, and of any one other fact, such as that of 100 per million exceeding seventy-eight inches.

A diagram will make this more intelligible. Suppose a million of the men to stand in turns, with their backs against a vertical board of sufficient height, and their heights to be dotted off upon it. The board would then present the appearance shown in the diagram. The line of average height is that which divides the dots into two equal parts, and stands, in the case we have assumed, at the height of sixty-six inches. The dots will be found to be ranged so symmetrically on either side of the line of average, that the lower half of the diagram will be almost a precise reflection of the upper. Next, let a hundred dots be counted from above downwards, and let a line be drawn below them. According to the conditions, this line will stand at the height of seventy-eight inches. Using the data afforded by these two lines, it is possible, by the help of the law of deviation from an average, to reproduce, with extraordinary closeness, the entire system of dots on the board.

M. Quetelet gives tables in which the uppermost line, instead of cutting off 100 in a million, cuts off only one in a million. He divides the intervals between that line and the line of average, into

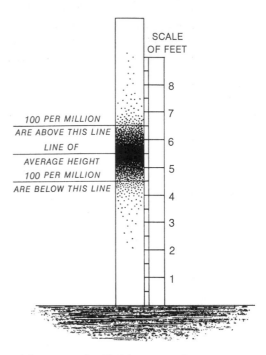

eighty equal divisions, and gives the number of dots that fall within each of those divisions. It is easy, by the help of his tables, to calculate what would occur under any other system of classification we pleased to adopt.

This law of deviation from an average is perfectly general in its application. Thus, if the marks had been made by bullets fired at a horizontal line stretched in front of the target, they would have been distributed according to the same law. Wherever there is a large number of similar events, each due to the resultant influences of the same variable conditions, two effects will follow. First, the average value of those events will be constant; and secondly, the deviations of the several events from the average, will be governed by this law (which is, in principle, the same as that which governs runs of luck at a gaming-table).

The nature of the conditions affecting the several events must, I say, be the same. It clearly would not be proper to combine the heights of men belonging to two dissimilar races, in the expectation that the compound results would be governed by the same constants. A union of two dissimilar systems of dots would produce the same kind of confusion as if half the bullets fired at a target had been directed to one mark, and the other half to another mark. Nay, an examination of the dots would show to a person, ignorant of what had occurred, that such had been the case, and it would be possible, by aid of the law, to disentangle two or any moderate number of superimposed series of marks. The law may, therefore, be used as a most trustworthy criterion, whether or no the events of which an average has been taken, are due to the same or to dissimilar classes of conditions.

I selected the hypothetical case of a race of men living on an island and freely intermarrying, to ensure the conditions under which they were all supposed to live, being uniform in character. It will now be my aim to show there is sufficient uniformity in the inhabitants of the British Isles to bring them fairly within the grasp of this law.

For this purpose, I first call attention to an example given in Quetelet's book. It is of the measurements of the circumferences of the chests of a large number of Scotch soldiers. The Scotch are by no means a strictly uniform race, nor are they exposed to identical conditions. They are a mixture of Celts, Danes, Anglo-Saxons, and others, in various proportions, the Highlanders being almost purely Celts. On the other hand, these races, though diverse in origin, are not very dissimilar in character. Consequently, it will be found that their deviations from the average, follow theoretical computations with remarkable accuracy. The instance is as follows. M. Quetelet obtained his facts from the thirteenth volume of the *Edinburgh Medical Journal*, where the measurements are given in respect to 5,738 soldiers, the results being grouped in order of magnitude, proceeding by differences of one inch. Professor Quetelet compares these results with those that his tables give, and here is the result. The marvellous accordance between fact and theory must strike the most unpractised eye. I should say that, for the sake of convenience, both the measurements and calculations have been reduced to per thousandths.

I will now take a case where there is a greater dissimilarity in the elements of which the average has been taken. It is the height of 100,000 French conscripts. There is fully as much variety in the French as in the English, for it is not very many generations since France was

Table 2

Measures of the chest in inches	Number of men per 1,000 by experience	Number of men per 1,000 by calculation	Measures of the chest in inches	Number of men per 1,000 by experience	Number of men per 1,000 by calculation
33	5	7	41	1,628	1,675
34	31	29	42	1,148	1,096
35	141	110	43	645	560
36	322	323	44	160	221
37	732	732	45	87	69
38	1,305	1,333	46	38	16
39	1,867	1,838	47	7	3
40	1,882	1,987	48	2	1

divided into completely independent kingdoms. Among its peculiar races are those of Normandy, Brittany, Alsatia, Provence, Bearne, Auvergne—each with their special characteristics; yet the following table shows a most striking agreement between the results of experience compared with those derived by calculation, from a purely theoretical hypothesis.

Table 3

Height of Men	Number of Men	
	Measured	Calculated
Inches		
Under 61.8	28,620	26,345
61.8 to 62.9	11,580	13,182
62.9 to 63.9	13,990	14,502
63.9 to 65.0	14,410	13,982
65.0 to 66.1	11,410	11,803
66.1 to 67.1	8,780	8,725
67.1 to 68.2	5,530	5,527
68.2 to 69.3	3,190	3,187
Above 69.3	2,490	2,645

The greatest differences are in the lowest ranks. They include the men who were rejected from being too short for the army. M. Quetelet boldly ascribes these differences to the effect of fraudulent returns. It certainly seems that men have been improperly taken out of the second rank and put into the first, in order to exempt them from service. Be this as it may, the coincidence of fact with theory is, in this instance also, quite close enough to serve my purpose.

I argue from the results obtained from Frenchmen and from Scotchmen, that, if we had measurements of the adult males in the British Isles, we should find those measurements to range in close accordance with the law of deviation from an average, although our population is as much mingled as I described that of Scotland to have been, and although Ireland is mainly peopled with Celts. Now, if this be the case with stature, then it will be true as regards every other physical feature—as circumference of head, size of brain, weight of grey matter, number of brain fibres, etc.; and thence, by a step on which no physiologist will hesitate, as regards mental capacity.

This is what I am driving at—that analogy clearly shows there must be a fairly constant average mental capacity in the inhabitants of the British Isles, and that the deviations from that average—upwards towards genius, and downwards towards stupidity—must follow the law that governs deviations from all true averages.

I have, however, done somewhat more than rely on analogy. I have tried the results of those examinations in which the candidates had been derived from the same classes. Most persons have noticed the lists of successful competitors for various public appointments that are published from time to time in the newspapers, with the marks gained by each candidate attached to his name. These lists contain far too few names to fall into such beautiful accordance with theory, as was the case with the Scotch soldiers. There are rarely more than 100 names in any one of these examinations, while the chests of no less than 5,700 Scotchmen were measured. I cannot justly combine the marks of several independent examinations into one fagot, for I understand that different examiners are apt to have different figures of merit; so I have analysed each examination separately. I give a calculation I made on the examination last before me; it will do as well as any other. It was for admission into the Royal Military College at Sandhurst, December 1868. The marks obtained were clustered most thickly about 3,000, so I take that number as representing the average ability of the candidates. From this datum, and from the fact that no candidate obtained more than 6,500 marks, I computed the column B in the following table, by the help of Quetelet's numbers. It will be seen that column B accords with column A quite as closely as the small number of persons examined could have led us to expect.

The symmetry of the descending branch has been rudely spoilt by the conditions stated at the foot of column A. There is, therefore, little room for doubt, if everybody in England had to work up some subject and then to pass before examiners who employed similar figures of merit, that their marks would be found to range, according to the law of deviation from an average, just as rigorously as the heights of French conscripts, or the circumferences of the chests of Scotch soldiers.

The number of grades into which we may divide ability is purely a matter of option. We may consult our convenience by sorting Englishmen into a few large classes, or into many small ones. I will select a system of classification that shall be easily comparable with the numbers of eminent men, as determined in the previous chapter. We have seen that 250 men per million become eminent; accordingly, I have so contrived the classes in the following table that the two highest, F and G, together with X (which includes all cases beyond G, and which are unclassed), shall amount to about that number—namely, to 248 per million.

It will, I trust, be clearly understood that the numbers of men in the several classes in my table depend on no uncertain hypothesis. They are determined by the assured law of deviations from an average. It is an absolute fact that if we pick out of each million the one man who is naturally the ablest, and also the one man who is the most stupid, and divide the remaining 999,998 men into fourteen classes, the average ability in each being separated from that of its neighbours by *equal grades*, then the numbers in each of these classes will, on the average of many millions, be as is stated in the table. The table may be applied to special, just as truly as to general ability. It would be true for every examination that brought out natural gifts, whether it be in painting, in music,

Table 4

Number of marks obtained by the Candidates	Number of Candidates who obtained those marks	
	A According to fact	B According to theory
6,500 and above	0	0
5,800 to 6,500	1	1
5,100 to 5,800	3	5
4,400 to 5,100	6	8
3,700 to 4,400	11 } 73	13 } 72
3,000 to 3,700	22	16
2,300 to 3,000	22	16
1,600 to 2,300	8	13
1,100 to 1,600	Either did not venture to compete, or were plucked.	8
400 to 1,100		5
below 400		1

Table 5
Classification of Men According to Their Natural Gifts

Grades of natural ability, separated by equal intervals		Numbers of men comprised in the several grades of natural ability, whether in respect to their general powers, or to special aptitudes								
		Proportionate, viz. one in	In each million of the same age	In total male population of the United Kingdom, viz. 15 millions, of the undermentioned ages:						
Below average	Above average			20–30	30–40	40–50	50–60	60–70	70–80
a	A	4	256,791	651,000	495,000	391,000	268,000	171,000	77,000
b	B	6	162,279	409,000	312,000	246,000	168,000	107,000	48,000
c	C	16	63,563	161,000	123,000	97,000	66,000	42,000	19,000
d	D	64	15,696	39,800	30,300	23,900	16,400	10,400	4,700
e	E	413	2,423	6,100	4,700	3,700	2,520	1,600	729
f	F	4,300	233	590	450	355	243	155	70
g	G	79,000	14	35	27	21	15	9	4
x	X								
All grades below g	All grades above G	1,000,000	1	3	2	2	2		
On either side of average			500,000	1,268,000	964,000	761,000	521,000	332,000	149,000
Total, both sides			1,000,000	2,536,000	1,928,000	1,522,000	1,042,000	664,000	298,000

The proportions of men living at different ages are calculated from the proportions that are true for England and Wales. (Census 1861, Appendix, p. 107.)

Example—The class F contains 1 in every 4,300 men. In other words, there are 233 of that class in each million men. The same is true of class f. In the whole United Kingdom there are 590 men of class F (and the same number of f) between the ages of 20 and 30; 450 between the ages of 30 and 40; and so on.

or in statesmanship. The proportions between the different classes would be identical in all these cases, although the classes would be made up of different individuals, according as the examination differed in its purport.

It will be seen that more than half of each million is contained in the two mediocre classes a and A; the four mediocre classes a, b, A, B, contain more than four-fifths, and the six mediocre classes more than nineteen-twentieths of the entire population. Thus, the rarity of commanding ability, and the vast abundance of mediocrity, is no accident, but follows of necessity, from the very nature of these things.

The meaning of the word "mediocrity" admits of little doubt. It defines the standard of intellectual power found in most provincial gatherings, because the attractions of a more stirring life in the metropolis and elsewhere, are apt to draw away the abler classes of men, and the silly and the imbecile do not take a part in the gatherings. Hence, the residuum that forms the bulk of the general society of small provincial places, is commonly very pure in its mediocrity.

The class C possesses abilities a trifle higher than those commonly possessed by the foreman of an ordinary jury. D includes the mass of men who obtain the ordinary prizes of life. E is a stage lower. Then we reach F, the lowest of those yet superior on bases of intellect, with which this volume is chiefly concerned.

On descending the scale, we find by the time we have reached f, that we are already among the idiots and imbeciles. We have seen in p. 25, that there are

400 idiots and imbeciles, to every million of persons living in this country; but that 30 per cent. of their number, appear to be light cases, to whom the name of idiot is inappropriate. There will remain 280 true idiots and imbeciles, to every million of our population. This ratio coincides very closely with the requirements of class f. No doubt a certain proportion of them are idiotic owing to some fortuitous cause, which may interfere with the working of a naturally good brain, much as a bit of dirt may cause a first-rate chronometer to keep worse time than an ordinary watch. But I presume, from the usual smallness of head and absence of disease among these persons, that the proportion of accidental idiots cannot be very large.

Hence we arrive at the undeniable, but unexpected conclusion, that eminently gifted men are raised as much above mediocrity as idiots are depressed below it; a fact that is calculated to considerably enlarge our ideas of the enormous differences of intellectual gifts between man and man.

I presume the class F of dogs, and others of the more intelligent sort of animals, is nearly commensurate with the f of the human race, in respect to memory and powers of reason. Certainly the class G of such animals is far superior to the g of humankind.

Comparison of the Two Classifications

Francis Galton

Is reputation a fair test of natural ability? It is the only one I can employ—am I justified in using it? How much of a man's success is due to his opportunities, how much to his natural power of intellect?

This is a very old question, on which a great many commonplaces have been uttered that need not be repeated here. I will confine myself to a few considerations, such as seem to me amply adequate to prove what is wanted for my argument.

Let it clearly be borne in mind, what I mean by reputation and ability. By reputation, I mean the opinion of contemporaries, revised by posterity—the favourable result of a critical analysis of each man's character, by many biographers. I do not mean high social or official position, nor such as is implied by being the mere lion of a London season; but I speak of the reputation of a leader of opinion, of an originator, of a man to whom the world deliberately acknowledges itself largely indebted.

By natural ability, I mean those qualities of intellect and disposition, which urge and qualify a man to perform acts that lead to reputation. I do not mean capacity without zeal, nor zeal without capacity, nor even a combination of both of them, without an adequate power of doing a great deal of very laborious work. But I mean a nature which, when left to itself, will, urged by an inherent stimulus, climb the path that leads to eminence, and has strength to reach the summit— one which, if hindered or thwarted, will fret and strive until the hindrance is overcome, and it is again free to follow its labour-loving instinct. It is almost a contradiction in terms, to doubt that such

Reprinted from *Hereditary Genius: An Inquiry into Its Laws and Consequences* (New York: Appleton and Co., 1880), pp. 37–49.

men will generally become eminent. On the other hand, there is plenty of evidence in this volume, to show that few have won high reputations, without possessing these peculiar gifts. It follows that the men who achieve eminence, and those who are naturally capable, are, to a large extent, identical.

The particular meaning in which I employ the word ability, does not restrict my argument from a wider application; for, if I succeed in showing—as I undoubtedly shall do—that the concrete triple event, of ability combined with zeal and with capacity for hard labour, is inherited, much more will there be justification for believing that any one of its three elements, whether it be ability, or zeal, or capacity for labour, is similarly a gift of inheritance.

I believe, and shall do my best to show, that, if the "eminent" men of any period, had been changelings when babies, a very fair proportion of those who survived and retained their health up to fifty years of age, would, notwithstanding their altered circumstances, have equally risen to eminence. Thus—to take a strong case—it is incredible that any combination of circumstances, could have repressed Lord Brougham to the level of undistinguished mediocrity.

The arguments on which I rely, are as follow. I will limit their application for the present, to men of the pen and to artists. First, it is a fact, that numbers of men rise, before they are middle-aged, from the humbler ranks of life to that worldly position, in which it is of no importance to their future career, how their youth has been passed. They have overcome their hindrances, and thus start fair with others more fortunately reared, in the subsequent race of life. A boy who is to be carefully educated is sent to a good school, where he confessedly acquires little useful information, but where he is taught the art of learning. The man of whom I have been speaking, has contrived to acquire the same art in a school of adversity. Both stand on equal terms, when they have reached mature life. They compete for the same prizes, measure their strength by efforts in the same direction, and their relative successes are thenceforward due to their relative natural gifts. There are many such men in the "eminent" class, as biographies abundantly show. Now, if the hindrances to success were very great, we should expect all who surmounted them, to be prodigies of genius. The hindrances would form a system of natural selection, by repressing all whose gifts were below a certain very high level. But what is the case? We find very many who have risen from the ranks, who are by no means prodigies of genius; many who have no claim to "eminence," who have risen easily in spite of all obstacles. The hindrances undoubtedly form a system of natural selection that represses mediocre men, and even men of pretty fair powers—in short, the classes below D; but many of D succeed, a great many of E, and I believe a very large majority of those above.

If a man is gifted with vast intellectual ability, eagerness to work, and power of working, I cannot comprehend how such a man should be repressed. The world is always tormented with difficulties waiting to be solved—struggling with ideas and feelings, to which it can give no adequate expression. If, then, there exists a man capable of solving those difficulties, or of giving a voice to those pent-up feelings, he is sure to be welcomed with universal acclamation. We may almost say that he has only to put his pen to paper, and the thing is done. I am here speaking of the very first-class men—prodigies—one in a million, or one in ten millions, of whom numbers will be found described in this volume, as specimens of hereditary genius.

Another argument to prove, that the hindrances of English social life, are not effectual in repressing high ability is, that the number of eminent men in England, is as great as in other countries where fewer hindrances exist. Culture is far more widely spread in America, than with us, and the education of their middle and lower classes far more advanced; but, for all that, America most certainly does not beat us in first-class works of literature, philosophy, or art. The higher kind of books, even of the most modern date, read in America, are principally the work of Englishmen. The Americans have an immense amount of the newspaper-article-writer, or of the member-of-congress stamp of ability; but the number of their really eminent authors is more limited even than with us. I argue that, if the hindrances to the rise of genius, were removed from English society as completely as they have been removed from that of America, we should not become materially richer in highly eminent men.

People seem to have the idea that the way to eminence is one of great self-denial, from which there are hourly temptations to diverge: in which a man can be kept in his boyhood, only by a schoolmaster's severity or a parent's incessant watchfulness, and in after life by the attractions of fortunate friendships and other favourable circumstances. This is true enough of the great majority of men, but it is simply not true of the generality of those who have gained great reputations. Such men, biographies show to be haunted and driven by an incessant instinctive craving for intellectual work. If forcibly withdrawn from the path that leads toward eminence, they will find their way back to it, as surely as a lover to his mistress. They do not work for the sake of eminence, but to satisfy a natural craving for brain work, just as athletes cannot endure repose on account of their muscular irritability, which insists upon exercise. It is very unlikely that any conjunction of circumstances, should supply a stimulus to brain work, commensurate with what these men carry in their own constitutions. The action of external stimuli must be uncertain and intermittent, owing to their very nature; the disposition abides. It keeps a man ever employed—now wrestling with his difficulties, now brooding over his immature ideas—and renders him a quick and eager listener to innumerable, almost inaudible teachings, that others less keenly on the watch, are sure to miss.

These considerations lead to my third argument. I have shown that social hindrances cannot impede men of high ability, from becoming eminent. I shall now maintain that social advantages are incompetent to give that status, to a man of moderate ability. It would be easy to point out several men of fair capacity, who have been pushed forward by all kinds of help, who are ambitious, and exert themselves to the utmost, but who completely fail in attaining eminence. If great peers, they may be lord-lieutenants of counties; if they belong to great county families, they may become influential members of parliament and local notabilities. When they die, they leave a blank for awhile in a large circle, but there is no Westminster Abbey and no public mourning for them—perhaps barely a biographical notice in the columns of the daily papers.

It is difficult to specify two large classes of men, with equal social advantages, in one of which they have high hereditary gifts, while in the other they have not. I must not compare the sons of eminent men with those of non-eminent, because much which I should ascribe to breed, others might ascribe to parental encouragement and example. Therefore, I will compare the sons of eminent men with the adopted sons of Popes and other dignitaries of the Roman Catholic Church. The practice of nepotism among ecclesiastics is universal. It consists in their giving those social helps to a nephew, or other more distant relative, that ordinary people give to their children. Now, I shall show abundantly in the course of this book, that the nephew of an eminent man has far less chance of becoming eminent than a son, and that a more remote kinsman has far less chance than a nephew. We may therefore make a very fair comparison, for the purposes of my argument, between the success of the sons of eminent men and that of the nephews or more distant relatives, who stand in the place of sons to the high unmarried ecclesiastics of the Romish Church. If social help is really of the highest importance, the nephews of the Popes will attain eminence as frequently, or nearly so, as the sons of other eminent men; otherwise, they will not.

Are, then, the nephews, etc. of the Popes, on the whole, as highly distinguished as are the sons of other equally eminent men? I answer, decidedly not. There have been a few Popes who were offshoots of illustrious races, such as that of the Medici, but in the enormous majority of cases the Pope is the ablest member of his family. I do not profess to have worked up the kinships of the Italians with any especial care, but I have seen amply enough of them, to justify me in saying that the individuals whose advancement has been due to nepotism, are curiously undistinguished. The very common combination of an able son and an eminent parent, is not matched, in the case of high Romish ecclesiastics, by an eminent nephew and an eminent uncle. The social helps are the same, but hereditary gifts are wanting in the latter case.

To recapitulate: I have endeavoured to show in respect to literary and artistic eminence—

1. That men who are gifted with high abilities—even men of class E—easily rise through all the obstacles caused by inferiority of social rank.

2. Countries where there are fewer hindrances than in England, to a poor man rising in life, produce a much larger proportion of persons of culture, but not of what I call eminent men.

3. Men who are largely aided by social advantages, are unable to achieve eminence, unless they are endowed with high natural gifts.

It may be well to add a few supplementary remarks on the small effects of a good education on a mind of the highest order. A youth of abilities G, and X, is almost independent of ordinary school education. He does not want a master continually at his elbow to explain difficulties and select suitable lessons. On the contrary, he is receptive at every pore. He learns from passing hints, with a quickness and thoroughness that others cannot comprehend. He is omnivorous of intellectual work, devouring in a vast deal more than he can utilize, but extracting a small percentage of nutriment, that makes, in the aggregate, an enormous supply. The best care that a master can take of such a boy is to leave him alone, just directing a little here and there, and checking desultory tendencies.

It is a mere accident if a man is placed in his youth in the profession for which he has the most special vocation. It will consequently be remarked in my short biographical notices, that the most illustrious men have frequently broken loose from the life prescribed by their parents, and followed, careless of cost, the paramount dictation of their own natures: in short, they educate themselves. D'Alembert is a striking instance of this kind of self-reliance. He was a foundling (afterwards shown to be well bred as respects ability), and put out to nurse as a pauper baby, to the wife of a poor glazier. The child's indomitable tendency to the higher studies, could not be repressed by his foster-mother's ridicule and dissuasion, nor by the taunts of his school-fellows, nor by the discouragements of his schoolmaster, who was incapable of appreciating him, nor even by the reiterated deep disappointment of finding that his ideas, which he knew to be original, were not novel, but long previously discovered by others. Of course, we should expect a boy of this kind, to undergo ten or more years of apparently hopeless strife, but we should equally expect him to succeed at last; and D'Alembert did succeed in attaining the first rank of celebrity, by the time he was twenty-four. The reader has only to turn over the pages of my book, to find abundant instances of this emergence from obscurity, in spite of the utmost discouragement in early youth.

A prodigal nature commonly so prolongs the period when a man's receptive faculties are at their keenest, that a faulty education in youth, is readily repaired in after life. The education of Watt, the great mechanician, was of a merely elementary character. During his youth and manhood he was engrossed with mechanical specialities. It was not till he became advanced in years, that he had leisure to educate himself, and yet by the time he was an old man, he had become singularly well-read and widely and accurately informed. The scholar who, in the eyes of his contemporaries and immediate successors, made one of the greatest reputations, as such, that any man has ever made, was Julius Caesar Scaliger. His youth was, I believe, entirely unlettered. He was in the army until he was twenty-nine, and then he led a vagrant professional life, trying everything and sticking to nothing. At length he fixed himself upon Greek. His first publications were at the age of forty-seven, and between that time and the period of a somewhat early death, he earned his remarkable reputation, only exceeded by that of his son. Boyhood and youth—the period between fifteen and twenty-two years of age, which afford

to the vast majority of men, the only period for the acquirement of intellectual facts and habits—are just seven years—neither more nor less important than other years—in the lives of men of the highest order. People are too apt to complain of their imperfect education, insinuating that they would have done great things if they had been more fortunately circumstanced in youth. But if their power of learning is materially diminished by the time they have discovered their want of knowledge, it is very probable that their abilities are not of a very high description, and that, however well they might have been educated, they would have succeeded but little better.

Even if a man be long unconscious of his powers, an opportunity is sure to occur—they occur over and over again to every man—that will discover them. He will then soon make up for past arrears, and outstrip competitors with very many years' start, in the race of life. There is an obvious analogy between the man of brains and the man of muscle, in the unmistakable way in which they may discover and assert their claims to superiority over less gifted, but far better educated, competitors. An average sailor climbs rigging, and an average Alpine guide scrambles along cliffs, with a facility that seems like magic to a man who has been reared away from ships and mountains. But if he have extraordinary gifts, a very little trial will reveal them, and he will rapidly make up for his arrears of education. A born gymnast would soon, in his turn, astonish the sailors by his feats. Before the voyage was half over, he would outrun them like an escaped monkey. I have witnessed an instance of this myself. Every summer, it happens that some young English tourist who had never previously planted his foot on crag or ice, succeeds in Alpine work to a marvellous degree.

Thus far, I have spoken only of literary

men and artists, who, however, form the bulk of the 250 per million, that attain to eminence. The reasoning that is true for them, requires large qualifications when applied to statesmen and commanders. Unquestionably, the most illustrious statesmen and commanders belong, to say the least, to the classes F and G of ability; but it does not at all follow that an English cabinet minister, if he be a great territorial lord, should belong to those classes, or even to the two or three below them. Social advantages have enormous power in bringing a man into so prominent a position as a statesman, that it is impossible to refuse him the title of "eminent," though it may be more than probable that if he had been changed in his cradle, and reared in obscurity, he would have lived and died without emerging from humble life. Again, we have seen that a union of three separate qualities—intellect, zeal, and power of work—are necessary to raise men from the ranks. Only two of these qualities, in a remarkable degree, namely intellect and power of work, are required by a man who is pushed into public life; because when he is once there, the interest is so absorbing, and the competition so keen, as to supply the necessary stimulus to an ordinary mind. Therefore, many men who have succeeded as statesmen, would have been nobodies had they been born in a lower rank of life: they would have needed zeal to rise. Talleyrand would have passed his life in the same way as other grand seigneurs, if he had not been ejected from his birth right, by a family council on account of his deformity, and thrown into the vortex of the French Revolution. The furious excitement of the game overcame his inveterate indolence, and he developed into the foremost man of the period, after Napoleon and Mirabeau. As for sovereigns, they belong to a peculiar category. The qualities most suitable to the ruler of a great nation, are not such as lead to eminence in private life. Devotion to particular studies, obstinate perseverance, geniality and frankness in social relations, are important qualities to make a man rise in the world, but they are unsuitable to a sovereign. He has to view many interests and opinions with an equal eye; to know how to yield his favourite ideas to popular pressure, to be reserved in his friendships and able to stand alone. On the other hand, a sovereign does not greatly need the intellectual powers that are essential to the rise of a common man, because the best brains of the country are at his service. Consequently, I do not busy myself in this volume with the families of merely able sovereigns; only with those few whose military and administrative capacity is acknowledged to have been of the very highest order.

As regards commanders, the qualities that raise a man to a peerage, may be of a peculiar kind, such as would not have raised him to eminence in ordinary times. Strategy is as much a speciality as chess playing, and large practice is required to develop it. It is difficult to see how strategical gifts, combined with a hardy constitution, dashing courage, and a restless disposition, can achieve eminence in times of peace. These qualities are more likely to attract a man to the hunting-field, if he have enough money; or if not, to make him an unsuccessful speculator. It consequently happens that generals of high, but not the very highest order, such as Napoleon's marshals and Cromwell's generals, are rarely found to have eminent kinsfolk. Very different is the case, with the most illustrious commanders. They are far more than strategists and men of restless dispositions; they would have distinguished themselves under any circumstances. Their kinships are most remarkable, as will be seen in my chapter on commanders, which includes the names of Alexander, Scipio, Hannibal, Caesar,

Marlborough, Cromwell, the Princes of Nassau, Wellington, and Napoleon.

Precisely the same remarks are applicable to demagogues. Those who rise to the surface and play a prominent part in the transactions of a troubled period, must have courage and force of character, but they need not have high intellectual powers. Nay, it is more appropriate that the intellects of such men should be narrow and one-sided, and their dispositions moody and embittered. These are not qualities that lead to eminence in ordinary times. Consequently, the families of such men, are mostly unknown to fame. But the kinships of popular leaders of the highest order, as of the two Gracchi, of the two Arteveldes, and of Mirabeau, are illustrious.

I may mention a class of cases that strikes me forcibly as a proof, that a sufficient power of command to lead to eminence in troublous times, is much less unusual than is commonly supposed, and that it lies neglected in the course of ordinary life. In beleaguered towns, as for example during the great Indian mutiny, a certain type of character very frequently made its appearance: People rose into notice who had never previously distinguished themselves, and subsided into their former way of life, after the occasion for exertion was over; while during the continuance of danger and misery, they were the heroes of their situation. They were cool in danger, sensible in council, cheerful under prolonged suffering, humane to the wounded and sick, encouragers of the faint-hearted. Such people were formed to shine only under exceptional circumstances. They had the advantage of possessing too tough a fibre to be crushed by anxiety and physical misery, and perhaps in consequence of that very toughness, they required a stimulus of the sharpest kind, to goad them to all the exertions of which they were capable.

The result of what I have said, is to show that in statesmen and commanders, mere "eminence" is by no means a satisfactory criterion of such natural gifts as would make a man distinguished under whatever circumstances he had been reared. On the other hand, statesmen of a high order, and commanders of the very highest, who overthrow all opponents, must be prodigiously gifted. The reader must judge the cases I quote, in proof of hereditary gifts, by their several merits. I have endeavoured to speak of none but the most illustrious names. It would have led to false conclusions, had I taken a larger number, and thus descended to a lower level of merit.

In conclusion, I see no reason to be dissatisfied with the conditions under which I am bound, of accepting high reputation as a very fair test of high ability. The nature of the test would not have been altered, if I had attempted to readjust each man's reputation according to his merits, because this is what every biographer does. If I had possessed the critical power of a St. Beuve, I should have merely thrown into literature another of those numerous expressions of opinion, by the aggregate of which, all reputations are built.

To conclude: I feel convinced that no man can achieve a very high reputation without being gifted with very high abilities; and I trust I have shown reason to believe, that few who possess these very high abilities can fail in achieving eminence.

The Logic of Laughter

Arthur Koestler

The three panels of the rounded triptych (Figure 1) indicate three domains of creativity which shade into each other without sharp boundaries: Humour, Discovery, and Art. The reason for this seemingly perverse order of arrangement—the Sage flanked by the Jester and the Artist on opposite sides—will become apparent as the argument unfolds.

Each horizontal line across the triptych stands for a pattern of creative activity which is represented on all three panels; for instance: comic comparison—objective analogy—poetic image. The first is intended to make us laugh; the second to make us understand; the third to make us marvel. The logical pattern of the creative process is the same in all three cases; it consists in the discovery of hidden similarities. But the emotional climate is different in the three panels: the comic simile has a touch of aggressiveness; the scientist's reasoning by analogy is emotionally detached, i.e. neutral; the poetic image is sympathetic or admiring, inspired by a positive kind of emotion. I shall try to show that all patterns of creative activity are tri-valent: they can enter the service of humour, discovery, or art; and also, that as we travel across the triptych from left to right, the emotional climate changes by gradual transitions from aggressive to neutral to sympathetic and identificatory—or, to put it another way, from an absurd through an abstract to a tragic or lyric view of existence. This may

Reprinted from *The Act of Creation* (New York: Macmillan Co., 1964) Chap. 1, with the permission of the Macmillan Company and the author.

look like a basketful of wild generalizations but is meant only as a first indication of the direction in which the inquiry will move.

The panels on the diagram meet in curves to indicate that there are no clear dividing lines between them. The fluidity of the boundaries between Science and Art is evident, whether we consider Architecture, Cooking, Psychotherapy, or the writing of History. The mathematician talks of 'elegant' solutions, the surgeon of a 'beautiful' operation, the literary critic of 'two-dimensional' characters. Science is said to aim at Truth, Art at Beauty; but the criteria of Truth (such as verifiability and refutability) are not as clean and hard as we tend to believe, and the criteria of Beauty are, of course, even less so. A glance at Figure 2 will indicate that we can arrange neighbouring provinces of science and art in series which show a continuous gradient from 'objective' to 'subjective', from 'verifiable truth' to 'aesthetic experience'. One gradient, for instance, leads from the so-called exact sciences like chemistry through biochemistry to biology, then through medicine—which is, alas, a much less exact science—to psychology, through anthropology to history, through biography to the biographical novel, and so on into the abyss of pure fiction. As we move along the sloping curve, the dimension of 'objective verifiability' is seen to diminish steadily, and the intuitive or aesthetic dimension to increase. Similar graded series lead from construction engineering through architecture and interior design to the hybrid 'arts and crafts' and finally

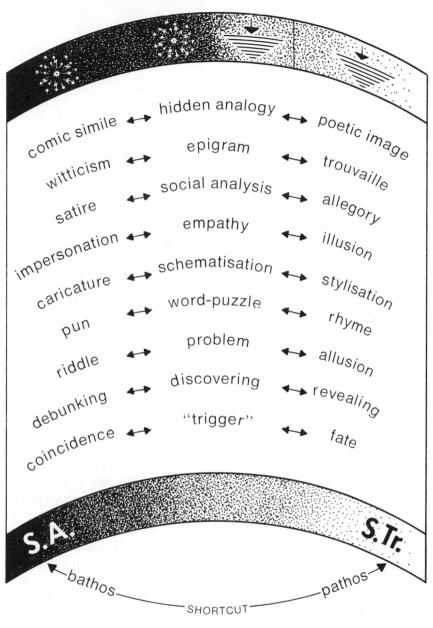

Figure 1

to the representative arts; here one variable of the curve could be called 'utility', the second 'beauty'. The point of this game is to show that regardless of what scale of values you choose to apply, you will move across a continuum without sharp breaks; there are no frontiers where the realm of science ends and that of art begins, and the *uomo universale* of the Renaissance was a citizen of both.

On the other side of the triptych the boundaries between discovery and comic invention are equally fluid—as the present chapter will show—although at first sight

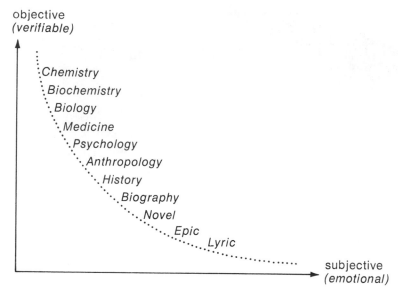

Figure 2

this is less obvious to see. That the Jester should be brother to the Sage may sound like blasphemy, yet our language reflects the close relationship: the word 'witticism' is derived from 'wit' in its original sense of ingenuity, inventiveness.[1] Jester and savant must both 'live on their wits'; and we shall see that the Jester's riddles provide a useful back-door entry, as it were, into the inner workshop of creative originality.

---

[1] 'Wit' stems from *witan*, understanding, whose roots go back (via *videre* and εἰδω) to the sanskrit *veda*, knowledge. The German *Witz* means both joke and acumen; it comes from *wissen*, to know; *Wissenschaft*—science, is a close kin to *Fürwitz* and *Aberwitz*—presumption, cheek, and jest. French teaches the same lesson. *Spirituel* may either mean witty or spiritually profound; to amuse comes from to muse (*à-muser*), and a witty remark is a *jeu d'esprit*—a playful, mischievous form of discovery.

The word 'jester', too, has a respectable ancestry. The *chansons de geste* played a prominent part in medieval literature from the eleventh to the fifteenth centuries. They were epics centred on heroic events; their name is derived from the Latin *gesta*: deeds, exploits. With the coming of the Renaissance, satire tended to replace the epics of chivalry, and in the sixteenth century the heroic 'geste' turned into 'jest'.

THE LAUGHTER REFLEX

Laughter is a reflex. The word reflex, as Sir Charles Sherrington said, is a useful fiction. However much its definitions and connotations differ according to various schools—it has in fact been the central battleground of psychology for the last fifty years—no one is likely to quarrel with the statement that we are the more justified to call an organism's behaviour 'reflex' the more it resembles the action of a mechanical slot-machine; that is to say, the more instantaneous, predictable, and stereotyped it is. We may also use the synonyms 'automatic', 'involuntary', etc., which some psychologists dislike; they are in fact implied in the previous sentence.

Spontaneous laughter is produced by the co-ordinated contraction of fifteen facial muscles in a stereotyped pattern and accompanied by altered breathing. The following is a description abridged from Sully's classic essay on the subject.

Smiling involves a complex group of facial movements. It may suffice to remind the reader of such characteristic changes as the drawing back and slight lifting of the corners of the mouth, the raising of the upper lip, which partially uncovers the teeth, and the curving of the furrows betwixt the corners of the mouth and the nostrils (the naso-labial furrows). To these must be added the formation of wrinkles under the eye, which is a further result of the first movement . . . and the increased brightness of the eyes.

These facial changes are common to the smile and the laugh, though in the more violent forms of laughter the eyes are apt to lose under their lachrymal suffusion the sparkle which the smile brings.

We may now pass to the larger experience of the audible laugh. That this action is physiologically continuous with the smile has already been suggested. . . . How closely connected are smiling and moderate laughing may be seen by the tendency we experience when we reach the broad smile and the fully open mouth to start the respiratory movements of laughter. As Darwin and others have pointed out, there is a series of gradations from the faintest and most decorous smile up to the full explosion of the laugh.

. . . The series of gradations here indicated is gone through, more or less rapidly, in an ordinary laugh. . . . The recognition of this identity of the two actions is evidenced by the usages of speech. We see in the classical languages a tendency to employ the same word for the two. . . . This is particularly clear in the case of the Latin *ridere*, which means to smile as well as to laugh, the form *subridere* being rare (Italian, *ridere* and *sorridere*; French *rire* and *sourire*; German *lachen* and *lächeln*).

We may now turn to the distinguishing characteristics of laughing; that is, the production of the familiar series of sounds. . . . (Sully, 1902).

But these do not concern us yet. The point to retain is the continuity of the scale leading from the faint smile to Homeric laughter, confirmed by laboratory experiments. Electrical stimulation of the *zygomatic major*, the main lifting muscle of the upper lip, with currents of varying intensity, produces expressions ranging from smile to broad grin to the facial contortions typical of loud laughter (Duchenne de Boulogne, 1862). Other researchers made films of tickled babies and of hysterics to whom tickling was conveyed by suggestion. They again showed the reflex swiftly increasing from the first faint facial contraction to paroxysms of shaking and choking—as the quicksilver in a thermometer, dipped into hot water, rapidly mounts to the red mark.

These gradations of intensity not only demonstrate the reflex character of laughter but at the same time provide an explanation for the rich variety of its forms—from Rabelaisian laughter at a spicy joke to the rarefied smile of courtesy. But there are additional reasons to account for this confusing variety. Reflexes do not operate in a vacuum; they are to a greater or lesser extent interfered with by higher nervous centres; thus civilized laughter is rarely quite spontaneous. Amusement can be feigned or suppressed; to a faint involuntary response we may add at will a discreet chuckle or a leonine roar; and habit-formation soon crystallizes these reflex-plus-pretence amalgams into characteristic properties of a person.

Furthermore, the same muscle contractions produce different effects according to whether they expose a set of pearly teeth or a toothless gap—producing a smile, a simper, or smirk. Mood also superimposes its own facial pattern—hence gay laughter, melancholy smile, lascivious grin. Lastly, contrived laughter and smiling can be used as a conventional signal-language to convey pleasure or embarrassment, friendliness or derision. We are concerned, however, only with spontaneous laughter as a specific response to the comic; regarding which we can conclude with Dr. Johnson that 'men have been wise in very different modes; but they have always laughed in the same way'.

THE PARADOX OF LAUGHTER

I have taken pains to show that laughter is, in the sense indicated above, a true reflex, because here a paradox arises which is the starting point of our inquiry. Motor reflexes, usually exemplified in textbooks by knee-jerk or pupillary contraction, are relatively simple, direct responses to equally simple stimuli which, under normal circumstances, function autonomously, without requiring the intervention of higher mental processes; by enabling the organism to counter disturbances of a frequently met type with standardized reactions, they represent eminently practical arrangements in the service of survival. But what is the survival value of the involuntary, simultaneous contraction of fifteen facial muscles associated with certain noises which are often irrepressible? Laughter is a reflex, but unique in that it serves no apparent biological purpose; one might call it a luxury reflex. Its only utilitarian function, as far as one can see, is to provide temporary relief from utilitarian pressures. On the evolutionary level where laughter arises, an element of frivolity seems to creep into a humourless universe governed by the laws of thermodynamics and the survival of the fittest.

The paradox can be put in a different way. It strikes us as a reasonable arrangement that a sharp light shone into the eye makes the pupil contract, or that a pin stuck into one's foot causes its instant withdrawal—because both the 'stimulus' and the 'response' are on the same physiological level. But that a complicated mental activity like the reading of a page by Thurber should cause a specific motor response on the reflex level is a lopsided

phenomenon which has puzzled philosophers since antiquity.

There are, of course, other complex intellectual and emotional activities which also provoke bodily reactions—frowning, yawning, sweating, shivering, what have you. But the effects on the nervous system of reading a Shakespeare sonnet, working on a mathematical problem, or listening to Mozart are diffuse and indefinable. There is no clearcut predictable response to tell me whether a picture in the art gallery strikes another visitor as 'beautiful'; but there is a predictable facial contraction which tells me whether a caricature strikes him as 'comic'.

Humour is the only domain of creative activity where a stimulus on a high level of complexity produces a massive and sharply defined response on the level of physiological reflexes. This paradox enables us to use the response as an indicator for the presence of that elusive quality, the comic, which we are seeking to define—as the tell-tale clicking of the geiger-counter indicates the presence of radioactivity. And since the comic is related to other, more exalted, forms of creativity, the backdoor approach promises to yield some positive results. We all know that there is only one step from the sublime to the ridiculous; the more surprising that Psychology has not considered the possible gains which could result from the reversal of that step.

The bibliography of Greig's *Psychology of Laughter and Comedy*, published in 1923, mentioned three hundred and sixty-three titles of works bearing partly or entirely on the subject—from Plato and Aristotle to Kant, Bergson, and Freud. At the turn of the century T. A. Ribot summed up these attempts at formulating a theory of the comic: 'Laughter manifests itself in such varied and heterogeneous conditions . . . that the reduction of all these causes to a single one remains a vary problematical undertaking. After so much work spent on such a trivial phenomenon, the problem is still far from being completely explained' (Ribot). This was written in 1896; since then only two new theories of importance have been added to the list: Bergson's *Le Rire* and Freud's *Wit and its Relations to the Unconscious*. I shall have occasion to refer to them.[2]

The difficulty lies evidently in the enormous range of laughter-producing situations—from physical tickling to mental titillation of the most varied kinds. I shall try to show that there is unity in this variety; that the common denominator is of a specific and specifiable pattern which is of central importance not only in humour but *in all domains of creative activity*. The bacillus of laughter is a bug difficult to isolate; once brought under the microscope, it will turn out to be a yeast-like, universal ferment, equally useful in making wine or vinegar, and raising bread.

THE LOGIC OF LAUGHTER: A FIRST APPROACH

Some of the stories that follow, including the first, I owe to my late friend John von Neumann, who had all the makings of a humorist: he was a mathematical genius and he came from Budapest.

> Two women meet while shopping at the supermarket in the Bronx. One looks cheerful, the other depressed. The cheerful one inquires:
> 'What's eating you?'
> 'Nothing's eating me.'
> 'Death in the family?'
> 'No, God forbid!'
> 'Worried about money?'
> 'No . . . nothing like that.'
> 'Trouble with the kids?'
> 'Well, if you must know, it's my little Jimmy.'

[2] A critical discussion of both theories can be found in Appendix I of *Insight and Outlook*.

> 'What's wrong with him, then?'
> 'Nothing is wrong. His teacher said he must see a psychiatrist.'
> Pause. 'Well, well, what's wrong with seeing a psychiatrist?'
> 'Nothing is wrong. The psychiatrist said he's got an Oedipus complex.'
> Pause. 'Well, well, Oedipus or Shmoedipus, I wouldn't worry so long as he's a good boy and loves his mamma.'

The next one is quoted in Freud's essay on the comic.

> Chamfort tells a story of a Marquis at the court of Louis XIV who, on entering his wife's boudoir and finding her in the arms of a Bishop, walked calmly to the window and went through the motions of blessing the people in the street.
> 'What are you doing?' cried the anguished wife.
> 'Monseigneur is performing my functions,' replied the Marquis, 'so I am performing his.'

Both stories, though apparently quite different and in their origin more than a century apart, follow in fact the same pattern. The Chamfort anecdote concerns adultery; let us compare it with a tragic treatment of that subject—say, in the Moor of Venice. In the tragedy the tension increases until the climax is reached: Othello smothers Desdemona; then it ebbs away in a gradual catharsis, as (to quote Aristotle) 'horror and pity accomplish the purgation of the emotions' (see Figure 3–a).

In the Chamfort anecdote, too, the tension mounts as the story progresses, but it never reaches its expected climax. The ascending curve is brought to an abrupt end by the Marquis' unexpected reaction, which debunks our dramatic expectations; it comes like a bolt out of the blue, which, so to speak, decapitates the logical development of the situation. The narrative acted as a channel directing the flow of emotion; when the channel is punctured the emotion gushes out like a

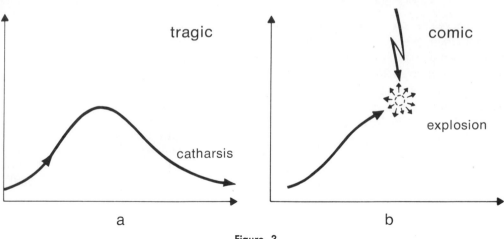

Figure 3

liquid through a burst pipe; the tension is suddenly relieved and exploded in laughter (Figure 3–b).

I said that this effect was brought about by the Marquis' unexpected reaction. However, unexpectedness alone is not enough to produce a comic effect. The crucial point about the Marquis' behaviour is that it is both unexpected and perfectly logical—but of a logic not usually applied to this type of situation. It is the logic of the division of labour, the *quid pro quo*, the give and take; but our expectation was that the Marquis' actions would be governed by a different logic or code of behaviour. It is the clash of the two mutually incompatible codes, or associative contexts, which explodes the tension.

In the Oedipus story we find a similar clash. The cheerful woman's statement is ruled by the logic of common sense: if Jimmy is a good boy and loves his mamma there can't be much wrong. But in the context of Freudian psychiatry the relationship to the mother carries entirely different associations.

The pattern underlying both stories is *the perceiving of a situation or idea, L, in two self-consistent but habitually incompatible frames of reference, M₁ and M₂* (Figure 4). The event L, in which

the two intersect, is made to vibrate simultaneously on two different wavelengths, as it were. While this unusual situation lasts, L is not merely linked to one associative context, but *bisociated* with two.

I have coined the term 'bisociation' in order to make a distinction between the routine skills of thinking on a single 'plane', as it were, and the creative act, which, as I shall try to show, always operates on more than one plane. The former may be called single-minded, the latter a double-minded, transitory state of unstable equilibrium where the balance of both emotion and thought is disturbed. The forms which this creative instability takes in science and art will be discussed later; first we must test the validity of these generalizations in other fields of the comic.

At the time when John Wilkes was the hero of the poor and lonely, an ill-wisher informed him gleefully: 'It seems that some of your faithful supporters have turned their coats.' 'Impossible,' Wilkes answered. 'Not one of them has a coat to turn.'

In the happy days of *La Ronde*, a dashing but penniless young Austrian officer tried to obtain the favours of a fashionable courtesan. To shake off this unwanted suitor, she explained to him that her heart was, alas, no longer free. He replied politely: 'Mademoiselle, I never aimed as high as that.'

'High' is bisociated with a metaphorical and with a topographical context. The coat is turned first metaphorically, then literally. In both stories the literal context evokes visual images which sharpen the clash.

> A convict was playing cards with his gaolers. On discovering that he cheated they kicked him out of gaol.

This venerable chestnut was first quoted by Schopenhauer and has since been roasted over and again in the literature of the comic. It can be analysed in a single sentence: two conventional rules ('offenders are punished by being locked up' and 'cheats are punished by being kicked out'), each of them self-consistent, collide in a given situation—as the ethics of the *quid pro quo* and of matrimony collide in the Chamfort story. But let us note that the conflicting rules were merely *implied* in the text; by making them explicit I have destroyed the story's comic effect.

Shortly after the end of the war a memorable statement appeared in a fashion article in the magazine *Vogue*:

> Belsen and Buchenwald have put a stop to the too-thin woman age, to the cult of undernourishment ('This England,' January, 1964).

It makes one shudder, yet it is funny in a ghastly way, foreshadowing the 'sick jokes' of a later decade. The idea of starvation is bisociated with one tragic, and another, utterly trivial context. The following quotation from *Time* magazine (1946) strikes a related chord:

> REVISED VERSION
> Across the first page of the Christmas issue of the *Catholic Universe Bulletin*, Cleveland's official Catholic diocesan newspaper, ran this eight-column banner head:
> 'It's a boy in Bethlehem.
> Congratulations God—congratulations Mary—congratulations Joseph.'

Here the frames of reference are the sacred and the vulgarly profane. A technically neater version—if we have to dwell on blasphemy—is the riposte which

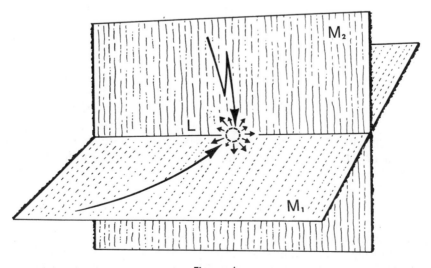

Figure 4

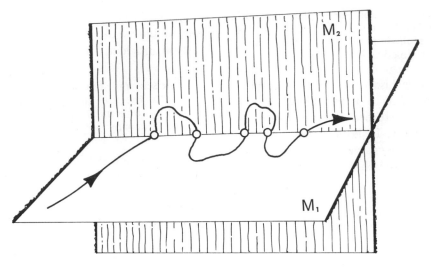

Figure 5

appeared, if I remember rightly, in the *New Yorker*: 'We wanted a girl.'

The samples discussed so far all belong to the class of jokes and anecdotes with a single point of culmination. The higher forms of sustained humour, such as the satire or comic poem, do not rely on a single effect but on a series of minor explosions or a continuous state of mild amusement. Figure 5 is meant to indicate what happens when a humorous narrative oscillates between two frames of reference—say, the romantic fantasy world of Don Quixote, and Sancho's cunning horse-sense.

MATRICES AND CODES

I must now try the reader's patience with a few pages (seven, to be exact) of psychological speculation in order to introduce a pair of related concepts which play a central role in this book and are indispensable to all that follows. I have variously referred to the two planes in Figures 4 and 5 as 'frames of reference', 'associative contexts', 'types of logic', 'codes of behaviour', and 'universes of discourse'. Henceforth I shall use the expression 'matrices of thought' (and 'matrices of behaviour') as a unifying formula. I shall use the word '*matrix*' to denote any ability, habit, or skill, any pattern of ordered behaviour governed by a '*code*' of fixed rules. Let me illustrate this by a few examples on different levels.

The common spider will suspend its web on three, four, and up to twelve handy points of attachment, depending on the lie of the land, but the radial threads will always intersect the laterals at equal angles, according to a fixed *code of rules* built into the spider's nervous system; and the centre of the web will always be at its centre of gravity. The *matrix*—the web-building skill—is flexible: it can be adapted to environmental conditions; but the rules of the code must be observed and set a limit to flexibility. The spider's choice of suitable points of attachment for the web are a matter of *strategy*, depending on the environment, but the form of the completed web will always be polygonal, determined by the code. The exercise of a skill is always under the dual control (a) of a fixed code of rules (which may be innate or acquired by learning) and

(b) of a flexible strategy, guided by environmental pointers—the 'lie of the land'.

As the next example let me take, for the sake of contrast, a matrix on the lofty level of verbal thought. There is a parlour game where each contestant must write down on a piece of paper the names of all towns he can think of starting with a given letter—say, the letter 'L'. Here the code of the matrix is defined by the rule of the game; and the *members* of the matrix are the names of all towns beginning with 'L' which the participant in question has ever learned, regardless whether at the moment he remembers them or not. The task before him is to fish these names out of his memory. There are various strategies for doing this. One person will imagine a geographical map, and then scan this imaginary map for towns with 'L', proceeding in a given direction—say west to east. Another person will repeat sub-vocally the syllables Li, La, Lo, as if striking a tuning fork, hoping that his memory circuits (Lincoln, Lisbon, etc.) will start to 'vibrate' in response. His strategy determines which member of the matrix will be called on to perform, and in which order. In the spider's case the 'members' of the matrix were the various sub-skills which enter into the web-building skill: the operations of secreting the thread, attaching its ends, judging the angles. Again, the order and manner in which these enter into action is determined by strategy, subject to the 'rules of the game' laid down by the web-building code.

All coherent thinking is equivalent to playing a game according to a set of rules. It may, of course, happen that in the course of the parlour game I have arrived via Lagos in Lisbon, and feel suddenly tempted to dwell on the pleasant memories of an evening spent at the night-club La Cucaracha in that town. But that would be 'not playing the game', and I must regretfully proceed to Leeds. Drifting from one matrix to another characterizes the dream and related states; in the routines of disciplined thinking only one matrix is active at a time.

In word-association tests the code consists of a single command, for instance 'name opposites'. The subject is then given a stimulus word—say, 'large'—and out pops the answer: 'small'. If the code had been 'synonyms', the response would have been 'big' or 'tall', etc. Association tests are artificial simplifications of the thinking process; in actual reasoning the codes consist of more or less complex sets of rules and sub-rules. In mathematical thinking, for instance, there is a great array of special codes, which govern different types of operations; some of these are hierarchically ordered, e.g. addition—multiplication—exponential function. Yet the rules of these very complex games can be represented in 'coded' symbols: $x + y$, or $x.y$ or x^y or $x\sqrt{y}$, the sight of which will 'trigger off' the appropriate operation—as reading a line in a piano score will trigger off a whole series of very complicated finger-movements. Mental skills such as arithmetical operations, motor skills such as piano-playing or touch-typing, tend to become with practice more or less automatized, pre-set routines, which are triggered off by 'coded signals' in the nervous system—as the trainer's whistle puts a performing animal through its paces.

This is perhaps the place to explain why I have chosen the ambiguous word 'code' for a key-concept in the present theory. The reason is precisely its nice ambiguity. It signifies on the one hand a set of rules which must be obeyed—like the Highway Code or Penal Code; and it indicates at the same time that it operates in the nervous system through 'coded signals'—like the Morse alphabet —which transmit orders in a kind of compressed 'secret language'. We know that not only the nervous system but all controls in the organism operate in this fashion (starting with the fertilized egg, whose 'genetic code' contains the blue-print of the future individual. But that blue-print in the cell nucleus does not show the microscopic image of a little man; it is 'coded' in a kind of four-letter alphabet, where each letter is represented by a different type of chemical molecule in a long chain; see Book Two, I).[3]

Let us return to reasoning skills. Mathematical reasoning is governed by specific rules of the game—multiplica-

[3] The choice of the term 'matrix' is less easy to explain. In an earlier version I used 'field' and 'framework', but 'field' is too vague, and 'frame' too rigid. 'Matrix' is derived from the Latin for womb and is figuratively used for any pattern or mould in which things are shaped and developed, or type is cast. Thus the exercise of a habit or skill is 'moulded' by its matrix. In mathematics, matrices are rectangular arrays of numbers capable of all sorts of magic; they can be subjected to various transformations without losing their identity—i.e. they are both 'flexible' and 'stable.' Also, matrices have a constant attached to them, called their 'determinant', which remains un-affected by any of these transformations. But the analogy between 'determinant' and 'code' is extremely loose and in more than one re-spect misleading.

tion, differentiation, integration, etc. Verbal reasoning, too, is subject to a variety of specific codes: we can discuss Napoleon's defeat at Waterloo 'in terms of' (a) historic significance, (b) military strategy, (c) the condition of his liver, (d) the constellation of the planets. We can call these 'frames of reference' or 'universes of discourse' or 'associative contexts'—expressions which I shall frequently use to avoid monotonous repetitions of the word 'matrix'. The jokes in the previous section can all be described as universes of discourse colliding, frames getting entangled, or contexts getting confused. But we must remember that each of these expressions refers to specific patterns of activity which, though flexible, are governed by sets of fixed rules.

A chess player looking at an empty board with a single bishop on it does not see the board as a uniform mosaic of black and white squares, but as a kind of magnetic field with lines of force indicating the bishop's possible moves: the board has become patterned, as in Figure 6–a; Figure 6–b shows the pattern of the rook.

When one thinks of 'matrices' and

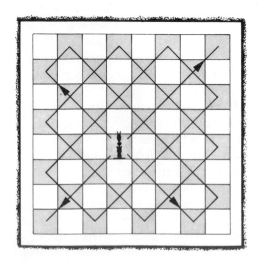 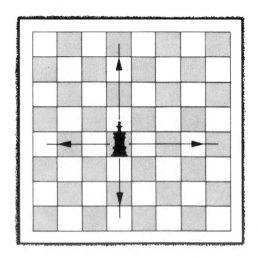

Figure 6

'codes' it is sometimes helpful to bear these figures in mind. The *matrix* is the pattern before you, representing the ensemble of permissible moves. The *code* which governs the matrix can be put into simple mathematical equations which contain the essence of the pattern in a compressed, 'coded' form; or it can be expressed by the word 'diagonals'. The code is the fixed, invariable factor in a skill or habit; the matrix its variable aspect. The two words do not refer to different entities, they refer to different *aspects* of the same activity. When you sit in front of the chessboard your *code* is the rule of the game determining which moves are permitted, your *matrix* is the total of possible choices before you. Lastly, the choice of the actual move among the variety of permissible moves is a matter of *strategy*, guided by the lie of the land—the *'environment'* of other chessmen on the board. We have seen that comic effects are produced by the sudden clash of incompatible matrices: to the experienced chess player a rook moving bishopwise is decidedly 'funny'.

Consider a pianist playing a set-piece which he has learned by heart. He has incomparably more scope for 'strategy' (tempo, rhythm, phrasing) than the spider spinning its web. A musician transposing a tune into a different key, or improvising variations of it, enjoys even greater freedom; but he too is still bound by the codes of the diatonic or chromatic scale. Matrices vary in flexibility from reflexes and more or less automatized routines which allow but a few strategic choices, to skills of almost unlimited variety; but all coherent thinking and behaviour is subject to some specifiable code of rules to which its character of coherence is due—even though the code functions partly or entirely on unconscious levels of the mind, as it generally does. A bar-pianist can perform in his sleep or while conversing with the barmaid; he has handed over control to the automatic pilot, as it were.

HIDDEN PERSUADERS

Everybody can ride a bicycle, but nobody knows how it is done. Not even engineers and bicycle manufacturers know the formula for the correct method of counteracting the tendency to fall by turning the handlebars so that 'for a given angle of unbalance the curvature of each winding is inversely proportional to the square of the speed at which the cyclist is proceeding' (Polànyi, 1958, p. 50). The cyclist obeys a code of rules which is specifiable, but which he cannot specify; he could write on his number-plate Pascal's motto: *'Le cœur a ses raisons que la raison ne connaît point.'* Or, to put it in a more abstract way:

The controls of a skilled activity generally function below the level of consciousness on which that activity takes place. The code is a hidden persuader.

This applies not only to our visceral activities and muscular skills, but also to the skill of perceiving the world around us in a coherent and meaningful manner. Hold your left hand six inches, the other twelve inches, away from your eyes; they will look about the same size, although the retinal image of the left is twice the size of the right. Trace the contours of your face with a soapy finger on the bathroom mirror (it is easily done by closing one eye). There is a shock waiting: the image which looked life-size has shrunk to half-size, like a headhunter's trophy. A person walking away does not seem to become a dwarf—as he should; a black glove looks just as black in the sunlight as in shadow—though it should not; when a coin is held before the eyes in a tilted position its retinal projection will be a more or less flattened ellipse; yet we see it as a circle, because we *know* it to be a circle; and it takes some effort to see it actually as a squashed oval shape. Seeing is believing, as the saying goes, but the reverse is also true: knowing is seeing. 'Even the most elementary perceptions', wrote Bartlett (1958), 'have the character of inferential constructions.' But the inferential process, which controls perception, again works unconsciously. Seeing is a skill, part innate, part acquired in early infancy.[4] The selective codes in this case operate on the input, not on the output. The stimuli impinging on the senses provide only the raw material of our conscious experience—the 'booming, buzzing confusion' of William James; before reaching awareness the input is filtered, processed, distorted, interpreted, and reorganized in a series of relay-stations at various levels of the nervous system; but the processing itself is not experienced by the person, and the rules of the game according to which the controls work are unknown to him.

The examples I mentioned refer to the so-called 'visual constancies' which enable us to recognize that the size, brightness, shape of objects remain the same even though their retinal image changes all the time; and to 'make sense' out of our sensations. They are shared by all people with normal vision, and provide the basic structure on which more personal 'frames of perception' can be built. An apple looks different to Picasso and to the greengrocer because their visual matrices are different.

Let me return once more to verbal thinking. When a person discusses, say, the problem of capital punishment he may do so 'in terms of' social utility or religious morality or psychopathology.

Each of these universes of discourse is governed by a complex set of rules, some of which operate on conscious, others on unconscious levels. The latter are axiomatic beliefs and prejudices which are taken for granted and implied in the code. Further implied, hidden in the space between the words, are the rules of grammar and syntax. These have mostly been learned not from textbooks but 'by ear', as a young gypsy learns to fiddle without knowing musical notation. Thus when one is engaged in ordinary conversation, not only do the codes of grammar and syntax, of courtesy and common-or-garden logic function unconsciously, but even if consciously bent on doing so we would find it extremely difficult to define these rules which define our thinking. For doing that we need the services of specialists—the semanticists and logicians of language. In other words, there is less difference between the routines of thinking and bicycle-riding than our self-esteem would make us believe. Both are governed by implicit codes of which we are only dimly aware, and which we are unable to specify.[5]

HABIT AND ORIGINALITY

Without these indispensable codes we would fall off the bicycle, and thought would lose its coherence—as it does when the codes of normal reasoning are sus-

[4] Congenitally blind patients, who acquire vision after surgical operations at a mature age, have great difficulties in recognizing patterns and faces, and in orienting themselves in space. Cf. Senden (1932), quoted by Hebb (1949).

[5] The dual concepts of matrices and codes were designed with one eye on psychology, the other on physiology. Their theoretical implications in this wider context are discussed in Book Two.

The reader versed in experimental psychology will have been reminded by now of such old friends from the Würzburg School as *Aufgabe, Einstellung, Bewusstseinslage*; and of their Anglo-Saxon relatives: 'determining tendency', 'expectancy', 'task', 'schema' and 'set'. He will probably also remember that J. J. Gibson in a famous article (quoted by Humphrey, 1951, p. 105) listed some forty different meanings in which the word 'set' was used. I hope to show that 'matrices' and 'codes' are concepts at the same time more precise, and of more general validity, than *Aufgaben* or 'sets'.

pended while we dream. On the other hand, thinking which remains confined to a single matrix has its obvious limitations. It is the exercise of a more or less flexible skill, which can perform tasks only of a kind already encountered in past experience; it is not capable of original, creative achievement.

We learn by assimilating experiences and grouping them into ordered schemata, into stable patterns of unity in variety. They enable us to cope with events and situations by applying the rules of the game appropriate to them. The matrices which pattern our perceptions, thoughts, and activities are condensations of learning into habit. The process starts in infancy and continues to senility; the hierarchy of flexible matrices with fixed codes—from those which govern the breathing of his cells, to those which determine the pattern of his signature, constitute that creature of many-layered habits whom we call John Brown. When the Duke of Wellington was asked whether he agreed that habit was man's second nature he exclaimed: 'Second nature? It's ten times nature!'

Habits have varying degrees of flexibility; if often repeated under unchanging conditions, in a monotonous environment, they tend to become rigid and automatized. But even an elastic strait-jacket is still a strait-jacket if the patient has no possibility of getting out of it. Behaviourism, the dominant school in contemporary psychology, is inclined to take a view of man which reduces him to the station of that patient, and the human condition to that of a conditioned automaton. I believe that view to be depressingly true up to a point. The argument of this book starts at the point where, I believe, it ceases to be true.

There are two ways of escaping our more or less automatized routines of thinking and behaving. The first, of course, is the plunge into dreaming or dream-like states, when the codes of rational thinking are suspended. The other way is also an escape—from boredom, stagnation, intellectual predicaments, and emotional frustration—but an escape in the opposite direction; it is signalled by the spontaneous flash of insight which shows a familiar situation or event in a new light, and elicits a new response to it. The bisociative act connects previously unconnected matrices of experience; it makes us 'understand what it is to be awake, to be living on several planes at once' (to quote T. S. Eliot, somewhat out of context).

The first way of escape is a regression to earlier, more primitive levels of ideation, exemplified in the language of the dream; the second an ascent to a new, more complex level of mental evolution. Though seemingly opposed, the two processes will turn out to be intimately related.

MAN AND MACHINE

When two independent matrices of perception or reasoning interact with each other the result (as I hope to show) is either a *collision* ending in laughter, or their *fusion* in a new intellectual synthesis, or their *confrontation* in an aesthetic experience. The bisociative patterns found in any domain of creative activity are tri-valent: that is to say, the same pair of matrices can produce comic, tragic, or intellectually challenging effects.

Let me take as a first example 'man' and 'machine'. A favourite trick of the coarser type of humour is to exploit the contrast between these two frames of reference (or between the related pair 'mind' and 'matter'). The dignified schoolmaster lowering himself into a rickety chair and crashing to the floor is perceived simultaneously in two incompatible contexts: authority is de-bunked by gravity. The savage, wistfully addressing the carved totem figure— 'Don't be so proud, I know you from a plum-tree'—expresses the same idea: hubris of mind, earthy materiality of body. The variations on this theme are inexhaustible: the person slipping on a banana skin; the sergeant-major attacked by diarrhoea; Hamlet getting the hic-coughs; soldiers marching like automata; the pedant behaving like a mechanical robot; the absent-minded don boiling his watch while clutching the egg, like a machine obeying the wrong switch. Fate keeps playing practical jokes to deflate the victim's dignity, intellect, or conceit by demonstrating his dependence on coarse bodily functions and physical laws—by degrading him to an automaton. The same purpose is served by the reverse technique of making artefacts behave like humans: Punch and Judy, Jack-in-the-Box, gadgets playing tricks on their masters, hats in a gust of wind escaping the pursuer as if with calculated malice.

In Henri Bergson's book on the prob-lem of laughter this dualism of subtle mind and inert matter ('the mechanical encrusted on the living') is made to serve as an explanation of *all* forms of the comic; whereas in the present theory it applies to only one variant of it among many others. Surprisingly, Bergson failed to see that each of the examples just mentioned can be converted from a comic into a tragic or purely intellectual experience, based on the same logical pattern—i.e. on the same pair of bisoci-ated matrices—by a simple change of emotional climate. The fat man slipping and crashing on the icy pavement will be either a comic or a tragic figure ac-cording to whether the spectator's atti-tude is dominated by malice or pity: a callous schoolboy will laugh at the spec-tacle, a sentimental old lady may be inclined to weep. But in between these two there is the emotionally balanced

attitude of the physician who happens to pass the scene of the mishap, who may feel both amusement and compas-sion, but whose primary concern is to find out the nature of the injury. Thus the victim of the crash may be seated in any of the three panels of the triptych. Don Quixote gradually changes from a comic into a puzzling figure if, instead of relishing his delusions with arrogant condescension, I become interested in their psychological causes; and he changes into a tragic figure as detached curiosity turns into sympathetic identification—as I recognize in the sad knight my brother-in-arms in the fight against windmills. The stock characters in the farce—the cuckold, the miser, the stutterer, the hunchback, the foreigner—appear as comic, intellectually challenging, or tragic figures according to the different emo-tional attitudes which they arouse in spectators of different mental age, cul-ture, or mood.

The 'mechanical encrusted on the living' symbolizes the contrast between man's spiritual aspirations and his all-too-solid flesh subject to the laws of physics and chemistry. The practical joker and the clown specialize in tricks which exploit the mechanical forces of gravity and inertia to deflate his human-ity. But Icarus, too, like the dinner guest whose chair collapsed, is the victim of a practical joke—the gods, instead of break-ing the legs of his chair, have melted away his wings. The second appeals to loftier emotions than the first, but the logical structure of the two situations and their message is the same: whatever you fancy yourself to be you are subject to the inverse square law like any other lump of clay. In one case it is a comic, in the other a tragic message. The dif-ference is due to the different character of the emotions involved (malice in the first case, compassionate admiration in the second); but also to the fact that in the first case the two frames of reference collide, exploding the tension, while in the second they remain juxtaposed in a tragic confrontation, and the tension ebbs away in a slow catharsis. The third alternative is the reconciliation and synthesis of the two matrices; its effect is neither laughter, nor tears, but the arousal of curiosity: just *how* is the mechanical encrusted on the living? How much acceleration can the organism stand, and how does zero gravity affect it?

According to Bergson, the main sources of the comic are the mechanical attributes of inertia, rigidity, and repetitiveness impinging on life; among his favourite examples are the man-automaton, the puppet on strings, Jack-in-the-Box, etc. However, if rigidity contrasted with organic suppleness were laughable in itself, Egyptian statues and Byzantine mosaics would be the best jokes ever invented. If automatic repetitiveness in human behaviour were a necessary and sufficient condition of the comic there would be no more amusing spectacle than an epileptic fit; and if we wanted a good laugh we would merely have to feel a person's pulse or listen to his heart-beat, with its monotonous ticktack. If 'we laugh each time a person gives us the impression of being a thing' (Bergson, 1916) there would be nothing more funny than a corpse.

In fact, every one of Bergson's examples of the comic can be transposed, along a horizontal line as it were, across the triptych, into the panels of science and art. His *homme-automate*, man and artefact at the same time, has its lyric counterpart in Galatea—the ivory statue which Pygmalion made, Aphrodite brought to life, and Shaw returned to the comic domain. It has its tragic counterpart in the legends of Faust's Homunculus, the Golem of Prague, the monsters of Frankenstein; its origins reach back to Jehovah manufacturing Adam out of *adamāh*, the Hebrew word

for earth. The reverse transformation—life into mechanism—has equally rich varieties: the pedant whom ensalvement to habit has reduced to an automaton is comic because we despise him; the compulsion-neurotic is not, because we are puzzled and try to understand him; the catatonic patient, frozen into a statute, is tragic because we pity him. And so again back to mythology: Lot's wife turned into a pillar of salt, Narcissus into a flower, the poor nymph Echo wasting away until nothing is left but her voice, and her bones changed into rocks.

In the middle-panel of the triptych the *homme-automate* is the focal, or rather bi-focal, concept of all sciences of life. From their inception they treated, as the practical joker does, man as both mind and machine. The Pythagoreans regarded the body as a musical instrument whose soul-strings must have the right tension, and we still unwittingly refer to our mortal frame as a kind of stringed guitar when we speak of 'muscle *tone*', or describe John as 'good tempered'. The same bifocal view is reflected in the four Hippocratic 'humours'—which were both liquids of the body and moods of the spirit; and *spiritus* itself is, like *pneuma*, ambiguous, meaning also breath. The concept of *catharsis* applied, and still does, to the purgation of either the mind or the bowels. Yet if I were to speak earnestly of halitosis of the soul, or of laxatives to the mind, or call an outburst of temper a humourrhage, it would sound ludicrous, because I would make the implicit ambiguities explicit for the purpose of maliciously contrasting them; I would tear asunder two frames of reference that our Greek forbears had managed to integrate, however tentatively, into a unified, psychosomatic view which our language still reflects.

In modern science it has become accepted usage to speak of the 'mechanisms' of digestion, perception, learning, and cognition, etc., and to lay increasing or exclusive stress on the automaton aspect of the *homme-automate*. The mechanistic trend in physiology reached its symbolic culmination at the beginning of the century in the slogan 'Man a machine'—the programmatic title of a once famous book by Jacques Loeb; it was taken over by behaviouristic psychology, which has been prominent in the Anglo-Saxon countries for half a century. Even a genial naturalist like Konrad Lorenz, whose *King Solomon's Ring* has delighted millions, felt impelled to proclaim that to regard Newton and Darwin as automata was the only permissible view for 'the inductive research worker who does not believe in miracles' (1951). It all depends, of course, on what one's definition of a miracle is: Galileo, the ideal of all 'inductive research workers', rejected Kepler's theory that the tides were due to the moon's attraction as an 'occult fancy'. (Santillana, ed., 1953, p. 469). The intellectual climate created by these attitudes has been summed up by Cyril Burt, writing about 'The Concept of Consciousness' (which behaviourists have banned, as another 'occult fancy', from the vocabulary of science): 'The result, as a cynical onlooker might be tempted to say, is that psychology, having first bargained away its soul and then gone out of its mind, seems now, as it faces an untimely end, to have lost all consciousness' (British Journal of Psychology, 1962).

I have dwelt at some length on Bergson's favourite example of the comic, because of its relevance to one of the leitmotifs of this book. The man-machine duality has been epitomized in a laconic sentence—'man consists of ninety per cent water and ten per cent minerals'— which one can regard, according to taste, as comic, intellectually challenging, or tragic. In the first case one has only to think of a caricature showing a fat man under the African sun melting away into a puddle; in the second, of the 'inductive research worker' bent over his test-tube; in the third, of a handful of dust.

Other examples of Bergson's man-automaton need be mentioned only briefly. The puppet play in its naïve Punch and Judy version is *comic*; the sophisticated marionette theatre is a traditional form of *art*; life-imitating contraptions are used in various branches of *science* and technology: from the dummy figures of dressmakers to the anatomical models in medical schools; from the artificial limbs of the orthopaedist to robots imitating the working of the nervous system (such as Grey Walter's electronic tortoises). In the *metaphorical* sense the puppet on strings is a timeless symbol, either comic or tragic, of man as a plaything of destiny—whether he is jerked about by the gods or suspended on his own chromosomes and glands. In the neutral zone between comedy and tragedy philosophers have been tireless in their efforts to reconcile the two conflicting aspects of the human puppet: his experience of free will and moral responsibility on the one hand; the strings of determinism, religious or scientific, on the other.

An extreme variant of the puppet motif is Jack-in-the-Box, symbol of the stubborn, mechanical repetitiveness, but also of the indestructibility, of life. Its opposite number is the legendary monster who instantly grows a new tentacle or head when the hero has cut it off; or the old woman in Raskolnikof's dream who, after each stroke of the axe on her skull, turns round and laughs in his face. In the biological sciences Jack-in-the-Box is a familiar figure, represented in all processes of the trigger-release type—the muscle-twitch, the epileptic fit, the 'sign-releasers' of the animal kingdom, whose symbolic message activates the springs of hopping mad or tenderly amorous, innate behaviour patterns.

The Disposition toward Originality [1,2]

Frank Barron

There has been a marked tendency in psychological research on originality to focus attention upon the single original act in itself, rather than upon the total personality of the originator. This is understandable, for the birth and development of the original idea is usually more immediately interesting and dramatically vivid than the birth and history of the man who had the idea. Newton's apple and Archimedes' tub and the well of Eratosthenes are thus naturally the circumstances with which we associate the remarkable insights of these original geniuses; we do not often ask ourselves whether these men were for the most part disposed to express or to suppress erotic impulses, or whether their emotions were fluent or turgid, or how subject to intense anxiety they were, or how much given to violent action. We tend

Reprinted from the *Journal of Abnormal and Social Psychology*, 1955, vol. 51, pp. 478–485 with the permission of the American Psychological Association and the author.

[1] Acknowledgment is made to the Rockefeller Foundation for its generous financial support of the program of research being carried on by the Institute of Personality Assessment and Research, of which this study is a part.
[2] This research is supported in part by the United States Air Force under Contract No. AF 18 (600) -8, monitored by Technical Director, Detachment #7, (Officer Education Research Laboratory), Air Force Personnel and Training Research Center, Maxwell Air Force Base, Alabama. Permission is granted for reproduction, translation, publications, use, and disposal in whole and in part by or for the United States Government. Personal views or opinions expressed or implied in this publication are not to be construed as necessarily carrying the official sanction of the Department of the Air Force or of the Air Research and Development Command.

to disembody the creative act and the creative process by limiting our inquiry to the creator's mental content at the moment of insight, forgetting that it is a highly organized system of responding that lies behind the particular original response which, because of its validity, becomes an historical event.

There is good reason for believing, however, that originality is almost habitual with persons who produce a really singular insight. The biography of the inventive genius commonly records a lifetime of original thinking, though only a few ideas survive and are remembered to fame. Voluminous productivity is the rule and not the exception among individuals who have made some noteworthy contribution. Original responses, it would seem, recur regularly in some persons, while there are other individuals who do not ever depart from the stereotyped and the conventional in their thinking.

If, then, some persons are regularly original, while others are regularly unoriginal, it must be the case that certain patterns of relatively enduring traits either facilitate or impede the production of original acts. Rather than focusing on the immediate conditions which have triggered the original response, the present study was concerned with the underlying disposition toward originality which it may be presumed exists in those persons who are regularly original. The research was directed first of all toward identifying individuals who performed consistently in a relatively more or relatively less original way; when this had been done, the more original were compared with the less original in terms of personality organization. Independent evidence concerning the personalities of the Ss was obtained both through the use of standardized paper-and-pencil tests and through employment of the living-in assessment method, with its emphasis upon observation of the Ss through several days of informal social interaction, situational tests, group discussions, psychodrama, and the like. The observers were of course kept in ignorance of the scores earned by the Ss on tests of originality.

THE RELATIVITY OF ORIGINALITY

It is a basic assumption of this study that acts are original only in relation to some specified commonality. The original must be defined relative to the usual, and the degree of originality must be specified statistically in terms of incidence of occurrence. Thus the first criterion of an original response is that it should have a certain stated uncommonness in the particular group being studied. A familiar example of this in psychological practice is the definition of an original response to the Rorschach inkblots, the requirement there being that the response should, in the examiner's experience, occur no more often than once in 100 examinations.

In the present study, we propose to deal with a relatively low order of originality, its limits being set by the nature of the sampling of Ss. The Ss are 100 captains in the United States Air Force, and originality as discerned here is originality in relation to the usual responses of only 100 persons. Furthermore, these 100 persons are not themselves especially selected for originality in relation to the population in general. Nevertheless, as we shall show later, some of the 100 captains are regularly original in comparison with the remainder, while

others are regularly unoriginal in relation to the entire group. Apart from their military status, the sample may be described as a group of normal, healthy young men, of average intelligence, socioeconomically of the lower middle class in their pre-army background, and similar to young men in general in terms of the usualness and the unusualness of their responses to the tests of originality employed in this experiment.

A second criterion that must be met if a response is to be called original is that it must be to some extent adaptive to reality. The intent of this requirement is to exclude uncommon responses which are merely random, or which proceed from ignorance or delusion. An example of the application of this second criterion may be taken from the scoring of one of the measures of originality used in this experiment: the measure is a count of the number of uncommon *and correct* anagram solutions to the test word "generation." Many Ss did not hesitate to offer solutions that were incorrect, and that were usually unique. In such instances, the application of the second criterion of originality was straightforward and decisive. Not all of the tests called for such purely cognitive responses with unambiguous denotative meaning, however: in the case of inkblot tests, e.g., we come closer to the problems involved in evaluating fantasy or works of art, and verification cannot be had by recourse to a dictionary. Instead, when E himself cannot "see" the form pointed to by S, he must have recourse to other psychologists who have given many Rorschachs and who can be considered fairly open to suggestions as to what the blots might reasonably look like. Consensual verification is thus sought for such imaginings. Poor forms, or uncommon responses that did not sufficiently respect the inkblot reality, were not credited as original in this study.

THE MEASUREMENT OF ORIGINALITY

Eight test measures were accepted here as indicative of originality. They are described below. The first three of these measures are taken from the creativity battery developed by Guilford and his associates (5, 6) in the Project on Aptitudes of High-Level Personnel at the University of Southern California. These three tests had significant loadings on the Originality factor in the Guilford researches.[3] Of the remaining five measures, two are derived from commonly used projective techniques, the Rorschach Psychodiagnostic (10) and the Thematic Apperception Test (9); another is a commonly used anagram test, and the remaining two tests were devised by the writer.

1. Unusual uses. This test calls upon the subject to list six uses to which each of several common objects can be put. It is scored for infrequency, in the sample under study, of the uses proposed. Odd-even reliability in this sample is .77.

2. Consequences B. In this test, S is asked to write down what would happen if certain changes were suddenly to take place. The task for him is to list as many consequences or results of these changes as he can. The responses are scored according to how obvious the imagined consequences are, the less obvious responses receiving the higher scores. Interrater agreement is .71.

3. Plot titles B. Two story plots are presented, and S is asked to write as many titles as he can think of for each plot. The titles are rated on a scale of cleverness from 0 to 5. The number of titles rated 2, 3, 4, or 5 constitutes the cleverness score. Interrater agreement in this study was .43.

[3] The present writer is indebted to Dr. Guilford and the personnel of the Project not only for permission to use the tests, but also for the actual scoring of the protocols.

4. Rorschach O +. This is a count of the number of original responses given by S to the 10 Rorschach blots and adjudged by two scorers, working separately, to be good rather than poor forms. Standard Rorschach administrative procedure was followed. Interrater agreement was .72, and only those responses scored by both scorers as 0+ were credited.

5. Thematic apperception test: originality rating. Two raters, working independently of one another, rated the TAT protocols of the 100 Ss on a 9-point scale, using approximate normal curve frequencies for each point along the scale. Interrater agreement was .70. The S's score was the average of the two ratings.

6. Anagrams. The test word "generation" was used, and the anagram solutions were scored for infrequency of occurrence in the sample under study. If S offered a solution that was correct and that was offered by no more than two other Ss, he received one point for originality. Total score is therefore the number of such uncommon but correct solutions.

7. Word rearrangement test: originality rating. In this test, S is given 50 words which were selected at random from a list of common nouns, adjectives, and adverbs. He is told to make up a story which will enable him to use as many as possible of the listed words. His composition is rated for originality on a 9-point scale, just as the TAT was. Interrater agreement in this instance was .67.

8. Achromatic inkblots. This is a set of 10 achromatic inkblots constructed locally. The S is asked to give only one response to each blot. Responses were weighted according to their frequency of occurrence in the sample under study, the more infrequent responses receiving the higher weights. Score is the sum of the weights assigned to S's responses on all 10 blots. Odd-even reliability was .43.

It is worth noting that all eight of these tests are free-response tests; the respondent is not presented with alternatives devised by the test maker, but must instead summon from within himself his own way of solving problems, seeing the blots, interpreting the pictures, putting together the words or letters, and so on. There is considerable latitude allowed for self-expression and for idiosyncratic interpretation.

Furthermore, diverse media are presented for the respondent to express himself through. The two inkblot tests allow for original visualization or original perceptual organization of visual forms. The TAT and the Word Rearrangement Test permit originality of verbal composition to show itself. Consequences and Unusual Uses call for bright ideas in more or less discrete form. Plot Titles evokes epigrammatic or sloganistic originality, while Anagrams requires a combination of word fluency and ease of perceptual reorganization.

If originality is indeed a dimension, and if some persons are regularly original while others are regularly unoriginal, we should expect the intercorrelations of these measures to be positive and to be statistically significant; we should not, however, expect the coefficients to be very high, for it is reasonable that the dimension of originality would have its variance

apportioned to several media of expression. Even regularly original persons can be expected to be outstandingly original in only one or two ways. The extent to which these expectations are confirmed in the present study may be seen from Table 1, in which the Pearsonian correlation coefficients of all eight test measures with one another are given. (With an N of 100, a Pearsonian r is significant at the .05 level if it is .20 or greater; an r of .26 is significant at the .01 level.)

As Table 1 shows, the correlations of the eight measures with one another tend to be positive and to be significantly different from zero. The inkblot tests alone appear to bear little relationship to the other measures; indeed, they do not even correlate significantly with one another. If the two inkblot tests are excluded, however, two-thirds of the intercorrelations of the remaining six measures are significant at the .05 level, and all are positive. Table 1 thus provides satisfactory evidence of the expected coherence or regularity of the manifestations of originality, with considerable reservations, however, concerning the relevance of inkblot originality to the dimension here being measured.

Since it is quite possible that originality is simply a multifactorial dimension in which certain factors bear little relationship to other factors but yet are positively related to the underlying dimension as a whole, it would probably be premature to

Table 1
Interrelations of Eight Originality Measures

Test Measures	1.	2.	3.	4.	5.	6.	7.	8.
1. Unusual Uses		.42	.37	.08	.17	.29	.06	.17
2. Consequences B	.42		.46	−.02	.21	.21	.16	.09
3. Plot Titles B	.37	.46		.17	.26	.17	.16	.07
4. Rorschach O+	.08	−.02	.17		.21	.03	−.05	.17
5. TAT Originality	.17	.21	.26	.21		.36	.41	.02
6. Anagrams	.29	.21	.17	.03	.36		.33	.38
7. Word Synthesis Orig.	.06	.16	.16	−.05	.41	.33		.09
8. Inkblot Originality	.17	.09	.07	.17	.02	.38	.09	

exclude the inkblot measures from this battery of tests of originality. Considerable doubt must be entertained concerning their validity, however, and there is another piece of evidence which reinforces the doubt. The staff psychologists who conducted the three-day living-in assessments were particularly interested in two theoretically central variables which they sought to rate on the basis of their observations: one of these variables was Originality (the other was Personal Stability). The correlations between this final over-all rating on Originality and the eight test measures of originality are shown in Table 2. Also given in Table 2 are the correlations of the eight measures individually with a variable which is the sum of the standard scores earned by each S on each of the eight tests; in other words, each test measure is correlated with a composite of which it is itself a part. The correlations thus show the relative contributions of each test to the total score on the battery of tests.

Table 2 provides evidence that the test

Table 2

Relationship of Eight Test Measures to Rated Originality and to Composite Test Originality

Test Measures	9.	10.
1. Unusual uses	.30	.60
2. Consequences B	.36	.59
3. Plot Titles B	.32	.62
4. Rorschach O+	.18	.38
5. TAT: Originality	.45	.59
6. Anagrams	.22	.62
7. Word Synthesis Originality	.45	.51
8. Inkblot Originality	.07	.46
9. Staff Rating: Originality		.55
10. Composite Test Originality	.55	

battery is in substantial agreement with the staff psychologists who gave ratings on Originality without knowledge of the test scores. The correlation of .55 between the test composite and the observers'

ratings is encouraging evidence that inexpensive, objective, and efficient measurement of originality is possible.

Again, however, the inkblot measures have relatively little relationship to these composite variables. The staff rating of Originality correlates significantly with six of the eight measures (well beyond the .01 level of significance with five of them); but neither Rorschach Originality nor Inkblot Originality is significantly related to the staff rating. As would be expected, these measures also have the least contribution to make to the test composite.

In spite of this situation, both inkblot measures were retained in the battery for purposes of identifying regularly original and regularly unoriginal Ss. The reasoning was as follows: On the face of it, uncommon responses to inkblots are original acts within the definition of originality being employed here. Tendencies toward uncommon visual perceptions are of course not readily recognized in ordinary social situations, since they have to be verbalized to be socially visible. Hence the failure of inkblot tests to correlate with the staff rating of Originality, based on observations of social behavior alone, should be discounted. The lack of a verbal component in perceptual originality, and its conspicuous presence in the other originality tests, may also account for the relative independence of the inkblot tests in the test composite. Finally, if the inkblot measures contribute only error variance to the composite, their retention will result in failure of some true relationships to appear, but this will be an error on the conservative side; and if they do in fact contribute true variance not contributed by any other test, they may add appreciable validity to the picture of the personality correlates of originality. They were therefore retained for the purpose of identifying regularly original and regularly unoriginal subjects.

A dual criterion was now established for calling a given subject regularly original: (*a*) he had to be at least one standard deviation above the mean on the test composite; (*b*) he had to be at least two standard deviations above the mean on at least one of the eight measures. Fifteen regularly original Ss were thus identified; more than half of them were at least two standard deviations above the mean on two or more of the eight tests.

For comparison purposes, the 15 lowest scorers on the final distribution of summed standard scores were selected; all of these Ss also met the criterion of being at least two standard deviations below the mean on at least one of the eight measures. They will be referred to as the regularly unoriginal subjects.

SOME HYPOTHESES SUGGESTED BY PREVIOUS WORK

The existence of a very general attitude toward experience, of a sort which disposes toward complexity of outlook, independence of judgment, and originality, has been suggested by the results of studies reported earlier by the present writer. It was found, e.g., that individuals who refused to yield to strong pressure from their peers to concur in a false group opinion described themselves, on an adjective check list, as "original" and "artistic" much more frequently than did subjects who yielded to such group pressure (1). In addition, the independent (nonyielding) Ss showed a marked preference for complex and asymmetrical line drawings, as opposed to simple and symmetrical drawings. This preference for the complex and asymmetrical had been shown previously to be highly correlated both with the choice of art as a vocation (3) and with rated artistic ability among art students. Furthermore, in a sample of Ph.D. candidates in the sciences, preference for the complex and asymmetrical

figures proved to be significantly related to rated originality in graduate work (2). This same relationship was found among graduating medical school seniors who were rated for originality by the medical school faculty. Other evidence indicated that the opposed preferences, for complexity or for simplicity, were related to a generalized experiential disposition: the preference for complexity is associated with a perceptual attitude which seeks to allow into the perceptual system the greatest possible richness of experience, even though discord and disorder result, while the preference for simplicity is associated with a perceptual attitude which allows into the system only as much as can be integrated without great discomfort and disorder, even though this means excluding some aspects of reality.

From all of these considerations, certain hypotheses as to the characteristics of original persons were derived and put to the test in the present study. The hypotheses, and the ways in which they were tested, or partially tested, are described below.

Hypothesis 1

That original persons prefer complexity and some degree of apparent imbalance in phenomena.

Test 1a. The Barron-Welsh Art Scale of the Figure Preference Test. Preference for complex-asymmetrical figures earns the subject a high score.

Hypothesis 2

That original persons are more complex psychodynamically and have greater personal scope.

Test 2a. Psychiatric interviewer rating on "Complexity and Scope as a Person." The Ss receiving high ratings are those who were diagnosed by a psychiatric interviewer, on the basis of a two-hour interview, as having a "more complex personality structure and greater potential for complex ego-synthesis." Ratings were on a 9-point scale with approximate normal curve frequencies being assigned to each point along the scale.

Hypothesis 3

That original persons are more independent in their judgments.

Test 3a. The Independence of Judgment Scale. On this inventory scale, which was developed against the criterion of actual behavior in the Asch group pressure experiment in previous studies, high scores indicate similarity to persons who manifest independence.

Test 3b. A modification of the Asch group pressure experiment.[4] This is a situational test in which Ss are put under pressure from their peers to agree to certain apparent group judgments. High scores indicate yielding to such pressures; regularly original persons should therefore have lower scores.

Hypothesis 4

That original persons are more self-assertive and dominant.

Test 4a. Dominance-submission ratings in a psychodramatic situation especially designed to elicit such tendencies in the subjects. Ratings were on a 9-point scale.

Test 4b. The Social Dominance scale of the California Psychological Inventory (4). This is a thoroughly studied and validated scale for the measurement of dominance in real-life social situations.

[4] This version of the group pressure experiment retains the prototypical psychological situation used by Asch, but introduces novel methods of experimental control and greatly expands the kinds of judgments on which group pressure is brought to bear. The new technique was devised by Richard S. Crutchfield, who has reported its details in his presidential address, "Conformity and Character," before the Division of Personality and Social Psychology, American Psychological Association, New York City, September 4, 1954. (*Amer. Psychologist*, 1955, 10, 191–198.)

Test 4c. Staff rating on Dominance, based on three days of observation of social behavior. Dominance was defined for the raters as follows: "Self-assurance, ascendance, and self-confidence in dealing with others; forceful, authoritative, resolute, not easily intimidated." A 5-point rating scale was used.

Test 4d. The Self-assertiveness scale of the California Psychological Inventory.

Test 4e. The Phallicism scale of the Personal Preference Scale (8). This scale is intended as a measure of the derivatives and residuals in the adult personality of propensities which were highly cathected in the phallic stage of psychosexual development. High scores indicate an emphasis on personal power and desire for recognition.

Hypothesis 5

That original persons reject suppression as a mechanism for the control of impulse. This would imply that they forbid themselves fewer thoughts, that they dislike to police themselves or others, that they are disposed to entertain impulses and ideas that are commonly taboo, and in general that they express in their persons the sort of indiscipline which psychoanalytic theory would ascribe to a libidinal organization in which derivatives of the early anal rather than of the late anal stage in psychosexual development predominate.

Test 5a. An index of suppression-expression on the Minnesota Multiphasic Personality Inventory (7) is obtained by adding the T scores on the Lie, Hysteria, and K scales and subtracting from that sum the sum of T scores on Psychopathic Deviation and Hypomania. On this index, regularly original Ss should obtain lower scores.

Test 5b. The Policeman Interest scale of the Strong Vocational Interest Blank (11). While this is bound to be a somewhat derivative measure of the personality tendency toward suppression of outlawed impulse, it does at least reflect the similarity of the subject's interests to those of persons who are regularly employed at maintaining law, order, and civil discipline—who, in short, seem vocationally suited to policing. Regularly original Ss should earn low scores.

Test 5c. The Early Anal and the Late Anal scales of the Personal Preference Scale (Grygier revision).[5] If the scales are valid and the hypothesis is correct, regularly original Ss should score higher on Early Anal and lower on Late Anal than do regularly unoriginal Ss.

Test 5d. The Impulsivity Scale of the California Psychological Inventory. Since high scorers are those who express impulse readily, the regularly original Ss should earn higher scores than the regularly unoriginal Ss.

Test 5e. Staff rating: Impulsivity. Again, regularly original Ss should receive higher ratings.

The group comparisons specified in these predictions are presented in detail in Table 3. As that table shows, 12 of the 15 predictions proved correct. A fairly conservative criterion of confirmation was adopted: significance at the .05 level when the two-tailed test was applied. The theoretical formulation suggested by the previous work on complexity-simplicity and on independence of judgment is substantially confirmed by these results.

DISCUSSION

The five major hypotheses in this study have been stated in terms derived directly from previous observations. There is another way of looking at them, however,

[5] The form of the Personal Preference Scale used in this study is a revision made by Tadeusz Grygier. The revision consisted chiefly of the addition of items to certain scales, including the Early and Late Anal scales.

which permits the results to be considered in somewhat other terms, and in a broader context. Since the hypotheses have already been stated and to some extent justified, it may be appropriate in discussing these results to venture somewhat beyond the literal meaning of the findings to date.

We have spoken here of the disposition toward originality, with originality being so measured as to be equivalent to the capacity for producing adaptive responses which are unusual. But unusualness of response may be considered a function as well of the objective freedom of an organism, where this is defined as the range of possible adaptive responses available in all situations. As the response repertoire of any given organism increases, the number of statistically infrequent responses, considered relative to the population of like organisms, will also increase. Thus the ability to respond in an unusual or original manner will be greatest when freedom is greatest.

Now freedom is related in a very special manner to degree and kind of organization. In general, organization, in company with complexity, generates freedom; the more complex the level of integration, the greater is the repertoire of adaptive responses. The tendency toward organization may, however, operate in such a fashion as to maintain a maladaptive simplicity. We are familiar in the political sphere with totalitarian states which depend upon suppression to achieve unity; such states are psychodynamically similar to the neurotic individual who suppresses his own impulses and emotions in order to maintain a semblance of stability. There are at hand enough case histories of both such organizations, political and private, to make it clear that the sort of unity and balance that depends upon total suppression of the claims of minority affects and opinions is maladaptive in the long run.

Table 3
Tests of Hypotheses

Hypotheses	Originals (N = 15)		Unoriginals (N = 15)			
	M	SD	M	SD	t	P
1. Preference for complexity						
Test 1a. Barron-Welsh Art Scale	19.40	12.28	12.67	10.69	2.16	.02
2. Complexity as a person						
Test 2a. Psychiatric rating: "Complexity as a person"	6.40	1.82	4.00	1.67	3.58	.001
3. Independence of judgment						
Test 3a. Independence of Judgment Scale	9.60	1.67	8.00	2.94	1.74	.05
Test 3b. Group pressure situation*	5.00	1.87	8.60	1.80	3.93	.001
4. Self-assertion and Dominance						
Test 4a. Psychodrama: Dominance rating	41.13	11.70	38.40	7.78	0.72	.23
Test 4b. CPI: Social Dominance Scale	36.60	3.74	28.87	4.75	4.74	.001
Test 4c. Staff rating: Dominance	34.40	7.10	25.40	4.06	4.05	.001
Test 4d. SCPI: Self-Assertiveness Scale	15.73	1.44	15.07	2.74	0.78	.22
Test 4e. PPS: Phallicism Scale (VIK)	13.20	2.37	9.13	4.27	3.08	.01
5. Rejection of suppression; tendency towards expression of impulse						
Test 5a. MMPI: (L + Hy + K)— (Pd + Ma)	43.47	26.24	58.87	12.30	1.78	.045
Test 5b. SVIB: Policeman Interest Scale	44.67	9.87	55.00	10.81	−2.61	.01
Test 5c. PPS: Early Anal Scale (IVB)	20.33	4.57	17.87	2.90	1.66	.06
Late Anal Scale (VB)	23.53	4.59	26.80	4.85	−1.81	.05
Test 5d. CPI: Impulsivity Scale	23.13	7.86	16.60	6.08	1.98	.03
Test 5e. Staff rating: Impulsivity	32.27	6.41	27.80	5.42	4.74	.001

* For the test of this hypothesis, only eight Ss in each group (eight Originals and eight Unoriginals) were available. This occurred because half of the subjects in the study were used as controls in the Crutchfield experiment, and hence made the judgments without being under pressure to conform to group opinion.

Suppression is a common way of achieving unity, however, because in the short run it often seems to work. Increasing complexity puts a strain upon an organism's ability to integrate phenomena; one solution of the difficulty is to inhibit the development of the greater level of complexity, and thus to avoid the temporary disintegration that would otherwise have resulted.

Originality, then, flourishes where suppression is at a minimum and where some measure of disintegration is tolerable in the interests of a final higher level of integration.

If we consider the case of a human being who develops strongly the disposition toward originality, we must posit certain personal characteristics and personal history which facilitated the development of such a disposition. In our hypotheses, the term "dominance" was used to describe one trait of the regularly original individual. This may be translated as a strong need for personal mastery, not merely over other persons, but over all experience. It initially involves self-centeredness, which in its socialized form may come to be known as self-realization. One aspect of it is the insistence on self-regulation, and a rejection of regulation by others.

For such a person, the most crucial developmental crisis in relation to control of impulse comes at the anal stage of socialization. What our hypotheses have suggested is that there is a positive rebellion against the prohibition of unregulated anal production, and a carrying of the derivatives of anal indiscipline into adult life. The original person, in adulthood, thus often likes things messy, at least at first; the tendency is toward a final order, but the necessary preliminary is as big a mess as possible. Viewed developmentally, the rejection of externally imposed control at the anal stage is later generalized to all external control of impulse, with the tendency toward socially unlicensed phallic activity, or phallic exhibitionism in its more derivative forms, being simply another expression of the general rejection of regulation of impulse by others, in favor of regulation of impulse by oneself.

The disposition toward originality may thus be seen as a highly organized mode of responding to experience, including other persons, society, and oneself. The socially disrated traits which may go along with it include rebelliousness, disorderliness, and exhibitionism, while the socially valued traits which accompany it include independence of judgment, freedom of expression, and novelty of construction and insight.

SUMMARY

This research was directed first of all toward identifying individuals who performed consistently in a relatively more or relatively less original way. The Ss were 100 captains in the United States Air Force, who took part in three days of living-in assessment at the house of the Institute of Personality Assessment and Research. Originality was defined in terms of uncommonness of response to eight tests which could be scored objectively or rated reliably. To be called original, a response had to be uncommon in the sample under study, and at the same time be adequate to the realistic demands of the problem situations. For the most part, the eight tests proved to be significantly correlated with one another and with an over-all staff rating of Originality based on observation of the Ss through three days of social interaction. Two groups of Ss, the regularly original and the regularly unoriginal, were then defined, and were used to test a set of five major hypotheses which generated 15 predictions concerning originality and which were suggested by previous findings from studies of independence of judgment and of the preference for complexity as opposed to simplicity. Twelve of the predictions were confirmed. Originality was found to be related to independence of judgment, to personal complexity, and to the preference for complexity in phenomena, to self-assertion and dominance, and finally to the rejection of suppression as a mechanism for the control of impulse.

Personality and the Realization of Creative Potential[1]

Donald W. MacKinnon

In the late 1920s at the Harvard Psychological Clinic, I first came across the writings of Otto Rank. There it was that I read *The Myth of the Birth of the Hero* (1914) and *The Trauma of Birth* (1929); and later in the '30s when they appeared in English I read his *Art and Artist* (1932), and *Truth and Reality* and *Will Therapy*, later published as a single book, *Will Therapy and Truth and Reality* (1945).

In view of this earlier exposure to Rank, it is hard to realize that when a few years ago I turned my attention to the problem of creativity I did so without once thinking of the implications of Rankian theory for the work I was about to undertake. Insofar as I thought about what psychoanalytic theory or the theories of derivative schools of psychoanalysis had to say about creativity, my thoughts turned to Freud's theory of primary and secondary process and his concept of sublimation, to Kris's notions concerning regression in the service of the ego, and to Kubie's emphasis on the role of preconscious processes in creative thought and action. I recalled vividly Jung's ideas on the reconciliation of the opposites: the dichotomies of conscious-unconscious, rational-irrational, sensation-intuition, thinking-

Reprinted from *American Psychologist*, 1965, vol. 20, pp. 273–281 with the permission of the American Psychological Association and the author.

[1] Presidential Address presented at Western Psychological Association, Portland, Oregon, April 1964. The research associated with this Address was supported by a grant from the Carnegie Corporation of New York.

feeling, extraversion-introversion, persona-anima, the individual versus the collective, and the archetypal images and the processes of individuation. And, of course, I thought of Maslow's notion of the self-actualizing person, of Rogers' concept of the fully functioning individual, and of Allport's description of becoming. I was aware of the influence of all these ideas on my own thought as I planned and undertook my research on creativity. I even vaguely recalled Adler's concept of a creative instinct, but found not much help in that. But not once did I consciously think of Rank's theories.

It was only after all of the data had been collected and I had spent long hours pondering their meaning that suddenly I was struck by a congruence between what I had actually done in designing the experiment and in selecting the samples for study and what I would have done had I recalled at the time what Rank had written about the development of creative potential and individuality.

Since becoming aware of my own strange oversight of Rank, I have searched the current extensive psychological literature on creativity without finding a single reference to his work. This present neglect of Rank is the more striking since it was he among all the early psychoanalysts who was most concerned with the problem of creativity. His first book, published in 1907, which was written before he joined Freud's circle in Vienna, and which was indeed the book which brought Rank to Freud's attention and led to his becoming an analyst, was entitled *Der*

Künstler (The Artist). *Art and Artist* published in 1932 was an extension and modification of many of the ideas first developed in the earlier work. During the intervening years his publications were devoted almost entirely to the application of psychoanalytic concepts to a better understanding of art, literature, and the humanities. And even after his break with Freud he continued to concern himself with the artist in his attempt to understand the factors that make it possible for a person to create out of his own life a work of art.

When one considers other contemporary trends in the psychology of personality it is even more difficult to understand why references to Rank's work are so lacking, not only in the literature on creativity, but in the psychological literature more generally. In making *will* a central concept in his psychology, and in defining it as the integrative power of the self, and in explicating its role in the development of personality, Rank was a pioneer in the field of ego psychology. In being the first to set a time limit upon the duration of analytic therapy, he stimulated later widespread efforts to achieve briefer forms of psychotherapy. He described the therapeutic process in terms of relationship and wrote of interpersonal relations before Sullivan defined psychiatry as the study of interpersonal relations. He was the first analyst to reject the narrower concept of psychoanalysis in favor of the broader and more widely employed term of psychotherapy, and he was the innovator of a new form of therapy which led to the conception of "helping a client" instead of "curing a patient." Rogers (1939) in his early work acknowledged the influence which Rank had had upon his thinking, but I suspect that there are many psychologists today who do not know how much there is of Rank in Rogers, or how much in other ways his thought foreshadowed present-day emphases in the psychology of personality, most notably in the writings of Fromm and Maslow. Perhaps that is the way it should be in psychology. At least it is the way Boring thinks it ought to be in psychology as in all science: It is the contributions to theory and method that are important, not the persons who make them. Read Boring's (1964) address to the XVIIth International Congress of Psychology, "Eponym as Placebo." But I am enough of a historian, as well as a psychologist, to be interested in knowing from whom my ideas come, even though my knowledge of the sources as well as of their ideas may at times be, as I have confessed today, preconscious rather than conscious.

The major relevance of Rank's theories for our study of creative persons is to be found in his conceptualization of three stages or phases in man's winning his own individuality and in realizing his own creative potential. Rank writes of these sometimes as stages or phases of development, sometimes as three types of persons which like all typological descriptions presuppose that the types are never fully actualized. When formulated as types they were labeled by Rank as the adapted type, the neurotic type, and the creative type. He also referred to them as the average or normal man, the conflicted or neurotic person, and the artist or man of will and deed.

The first unconscious—or should I say preconscious?—congruence between Rank's typology and the study which I shall report was the decision in studying creativity in architects to draw three samples from the profession, hopefully differing in the degree to which they had maximized and realized their creative potential.

But first, why should architects be chosen as the profession to be studied? It seemed to me, and to my collaborator in this research, Wallace B. Hall, that architects might as a group reveal that which is most characteristic of the creative person. If an architect's designs are to give delight, the architect must be an artist; if they are to be technologically sound and efficiently planned he must also be something of a scientist, at least an applied scientist or engineer. Yet clearly if one has any knowledge of architects and their practice, one realizes that it does not suffice that an architect be at one and the same time artist and scientist if he is to be highly creative in the practice of his profession. He must also to some extent be businessman, lawyer, advertiser, author-journalist, psychiatrist, educator, and psychologist (MacKinnon, 1962b).

To obtain our first sample of highly creative architects we asked five professors of architecture at the University of California, Berkeley, each working independently, to nominate the 40 most outstandingly creative architects in the country.

Had there been perfect agreement among the nominators, each would have mentioned the same 40. All told they gave us 86 names. Of these 86, 13 were nominated by all five panel members, 9 were nominated by four, 11 were nominated by three, 13 by two, while 40 were individual nominations by a single panel member. Subsequently, each panel member rated the creativity of those not nominated by him originally, provided he knew them well enough to do so.

On the basis of the mean rating of their creativeness and the summary statements as to why each had been nominated, which the panel members had also given us, the architects were listed in the order in which we would invite them to participate in the study. Our hope had been to win the cooperation of the first 40 whom we invited, but to get 40 acceptances we had to write 64 architects.

The 40 who accepted our invitation came to Berkeley in groups of 10, where they were subjects of an intensive assessment. But what of the 24 who declined our invitation to be studied? Are they more or less creative than the 40 who were willing to be assessed, or indistinguishable from them in their level of creativeness? When the nominating panel's mean ratings of creativity of each of the 64 architects were converted to standard scores, and the means for the 24 versus the 40 were compared, they were found to be identical: 50.0 ($SD = $ 9.9) for the 24 not assessed as against 50.1 ($SD = 9.5$) for the 40 assessed architects.

We can make no claim to have studied the most creative architects in the country. We are assured, however, that the 40 whom we did assess, and to whom I shall hereafter refer as Architects I, are as a group indistinguishable in the level of their creativeness from the 24 who declined to be studied.

But to have limited our study to the assessment of 40 architects, each of whom was recognized as highly creative, would not have permitted us to say anything with confidence about the personality correlates of creativity. For the distinguishing characteristics of this sample—and there were many that we found —might well have nothing to do with their creativeness. Obviously the design of our study required that the profession of architecture be widely sampled beyond the assessed 40 Architects I, in order to discover whether and to what extent the traits of creative architects are characteristic of architects in general or peculiar to those who are highly creative.

To this end the *Directory of Architects* published in 1955 was searched in order to select two additional samples of architects both of which would match with respect to age and geographic location of practice the assessed sample of 40. The first of the supplementary samples, which I shall call Architects II, is composed of 43 architects, each of whom met the additional requirement that he had had at least 2 years of work experience and association with one of the 64 originally nominated and invited creative architects. The other additional sample, which I shall label Architects III, is composed of 41 architects, none of whom had ever worked with any of the nominated creative architects.

Architects I, II, and III were selected in this manner in hopes of tapping a range of creative talent sufficiently wide to be fairly representative of the profession as a whole. To determine whether or not we had succeeded, ratings on a 7-point scale of the creativity of all 124 architects were obtained from six groups of architects and architectural experts: the 5 members of the original nominating panel at the University of California, 19 professors of architecture distributed nationwide, 6 editors of the major American architectural journals, 32 Architects I, 36 Architects II, and 28 Architects III. The mean ratings of creativity for the three groups are: for Architects I, 5.46; Architects II, 4.25; and for Architects III, 3.54. The differences are in the expected direction and are statistically highly significant ($p < .001$). In other words, the three groups do indeed represent significantly different levels of creativeness (MacKinnon, 1962b). At the same time, however, it must be noted that the three samples show an overlap in their judged creativity; they are not discontinuous groups, but, combined, approximate a normal distribution of judged creativeness ranging from a low of 1.9 to a high of 6.5 on a 7-point rating scale (MacKinnon, 1963).

In view of the approximately normal distribution of the rated creativity for the total sample of 124 architects, and with the further evidence that Architects I, II, and III do indeed represent significantly different levels of creativity, we

have examined our data by two major means: (a) computing the correlations between the external judgments of the creativeness of our 124 architects and their scores on a multiplicity of traits, and (b) comparing differences of mean scores among Architects I, II, and III on these same assessed variables.

I must first point out, however, that our data are not so extensive for Architects II and III as for Architects I. Where the latter experienced a 3-day-long assessment, the former groups, working independently and at home, spent about 6 or 7 hours completing a selection of tests, questionnaires, and inventories from our total assessment battery. Under these conditions some tests, notably tests of intelligence and timed tests, could not be administered to Architects II and III.

Having recruited for study three groups of architects which, as it turned out, are discriminably different with respect to their mean level of actualized and manifest creativeness, the question I wish now to raise is whether and to what extent the traits and characteristics of Architects, I, II, and III correspond to, and in that sense confirm, the qualities attributed by Rank to his three stages or types of personality structure and creative development or, on the other hand, fail to do so.

This is neither the time nor the place to attempt a full explication of Rank's theories. Instead I shall limit myself to a brief discussion of those aspects of his thought about which one must be reasonably clear if one is to understand his ideas about the constructive formation of personality and creative development.

Rank sees man as moving through life from the trauma of birth to the trauma of death. The character of this journey and the nature of the personality which develops en route are shaped and determined in large measure by the interaction and varying strengths of man's two basic and opposed fears: the fear of life and the fear of death.

The fear of life is basically the fear of separation, experienced first as the primal anxiety of the birth trauma which separates the infant from the mother, the womb, the wholeness of which it was formerly a part. The fear of life drives a person backward to earlier states of symbiotic union, symbolized as union with the mother, as well as to later stages of dependence on other persons and groups of persons more powerful than the self. The fear of life is the fear of having to stand alone and be alone, the fear of partialization and differentiation of oneself from the collectivity, the fear of standing out from the mass, the fear of all that living one's own life entails, the fear of true independence, the fear of becoming oneself and of being oneself.

But the life fear, the fear of separation and independence, is opposed by the fear of death, the fear of union and dependence, which makes one afraid of all that the life fear drives one toward—for symbolic union is experienced as a sort of death, a regression, a return to the womb, a loss of individuality, indeed a loss of life itself.

Thus, Rank sees man as characterized by a basic ambitendency: driven by life fear to union with others, to relationships of symbiosis and dependence, to losing oneself and one's identity in the collectivity—and, on the other hand, driven by death fear to an assertion of oneself and one's individuality, to a separation of oneself from others, to independence and uniqueness. And Rank takes as a measure of the development of a person the extent to which he achieves a constructive integration of these conflicting trends.

Central to his theory of development of the person are Rank's concepts of will and guilt. Will is, for him, the integrative power of the personality as a whole, "a positive guiding organization and integration of the self which utilizes creatively, as well as inhibits and controls the instinctual drives [1945, p. 112]." It is first experienced by the child negatively as counterwill—as resistance to the restraints, demands, frustrations which he experiences from the parents because of his very dependence upon them. But the assertion of his counterwill against their will causes him to experience feelings of guilt, since he is still bound to them by dependence upon them, identification with them, love and gratitude for them.

If, in this process of separation in which the will of the parents is opposed by the child's counterwill and self-assertion, the parents accept the child as a more or less separate individual, granting him autonomy and opportunity to assert his own will, the child moves healthily toward the attainment of a secure sense of self and the expression of positive will in selecting, organizing, modifying, and recreating his own experiences. Being accepted by the parents as separate and different from them, the child does not feel separated from them in the sense of being rejected by them but has the experience of separating himself from them through exercising his own will, and consequently he wins for himself some measure of individuality.

Not all children in the expression of their counterwill experience so fortunate a fate. Not accepted by their parents as separate and different, they experience their will as a source of continuing guilt rather than of growing ego strength. They feel rejected, and thus are not able through an exercise of positive will to achieve for themselves that measure of separation which is the prerequisite for individuality.

Though every child experiences some measure of counterwill, there are many,

Rank believes, who quite early are able so to identify their will with that of their parents as to be spared the pain of developing their own will further, and of developing the guilt which comes from striving for separation. Those who thus easily adapt to the will of their parents may later also find it easy to adapt to the will of society and to incorporate within themselves its dictates and its norms. Such a person, who now wills what he was earlier compelled to will, represents what Rank calls the adapted type. Rank sees this as a type of adjustment which often is established relatively early in the life of an individual, and one beyond which Rank's "normal, average man" never goes.

For such a person there is no strong drive toward individuation and also no conflict over conformance to the social norms. Such an adjustment guarantees a relatively harmonious working of the personality. Rank does not think of such a person as consciously conforming for the sake of expediency, but as naturally conforming to society because he never seriously thought of doing anything else. He is largely one with his surroundings and feels himself to be a part of them. Munroe (1955) has suggested that the adapted type's

> relations with his society are reminiscent of the symbiotic relationship between person and environment which prevailed in the womb. They represent the first and easiest solution of the problem set by birth. [p. 585][2]

The adapted type's form of adjustment, according to Rank (1945),

> permits fewer possibilities of conflict but also fewer creative possibilities of any kind. . . . He has the consciousness of in-

dividuality but at the same time the feeling of likeness, of unity, which makes the relation to the outer world pleasant. [p. 264][3]

The next step or phase on the road to the development of individuality and the realization of creative potential is characterized, as Rank (1945) sees it,

> by the feeling of division in the personality, through the disunity of will and counter-will which means a struggle (moral) against the compulsion of the outer world as well as an inner conflict between the two wills. [p. 264; see Footnote 3]

At this level of development the person strikes out on his own and attempts to form goals, ideals, and moral and ethical standards other than the socially sanctioned ones. He begins to take new attitudes towards himself and towards the world. There are here possibilities of development not achieved at the first level. If they are realized the person moves to the third level of creative and productive functioning, becoming the creative type. But if they are not realized, due to the inability of the person on this second level to resolve his conflicts, he remains stuck there plagued by self-criticism and feelings of guilt and inferiority.

Unlike the first type who "accepts reality with its demands and so adjusts his own individuality that he perceives and can accept himself as part of reality [Rank, 1945, p. 266]," the second type is conflicted in the sense that his own separateness is great enough to preclude his complete union with society, yet not sufficiently developed to permit him to win through to a creative expression of his own individuality. He is, in Rank's phrase, "a conflicted and neurotic man" whose creative potential is, however, greater than that of the average man.

[2] From Ruth L. Munroe, *Schools of Psychoanalytic Thought*, copyright 1955 by Holt, Rinehart and Winston, Inc.

[3] Reprinted by permission of Alfred A. Knopf, Inc.

Rank (1945) describes the third and highest level of development as

> characterized by a unified working together of the three fully developed powers, the will, the counter-will, and the ideal formation born from the conflict between them which itself has become a goal-setting, goal-seeking force. Here the human being . . . is again at one with himself; what he does, he does fully and completely in harmony with all his powers and his ideals. [p. 264; see Footnote 3]

Rank calls him variously the artist, the man of will and deed, the creative type.

The correspondences, if any are to be found, between our three samples of architects and Rank's three stages of the development of individuality would, I think we would agree, be expected to be found between Architects I and the creative type, the artist or man of will and deed; between Architects II and the conflicted or neurotic type; and between Architects III and the adapted type, the normal or average man.

The areas or domains in which we might search for differences between our three samples, and correspondences between them and the Rankian types, are several. I shall limit myself, however, to a discussion of three: (*a*) the nature of the individual's socialization and his interpersonal behavior, (*b*) the level of richness or complexity of his psychological development, and (*c*) the degree of personal soundness or psychological health which he manifests.

The presentation of such a complex body of data as we have collected poses a difficult problem of communication in a lecture like this. In the interest of obtaining as much simplicity and clarity as possible I shall, in reporting differences between groups, not present any actual mean scores. I shall instead merely indicate the nature of the differences, discussing, however, unless otherwise indi-

cated, only differences that are significant at or beyond the .05 level of confidence.

The first domain in which one might expect to find differences between our three samples and the Rankian types is, as I have suggested, the area of socialization and interpersonal behavior. The most socialized, and consequently the least individualized, of Rank's three types is the adapted man. His adjustment to society, his incorporation of its norms within himself, and his identification with his surroundings is the most complete.

On the Heilbrun keys (Gough & Heilbrun, 1965) of the Adjective Check List (Gough, 1961), which measure several of the needs first conceptualized by Murray (1938), Architects III (the least creative group) score higher than Architects I (the most creative) on abasement, affiliation, deference, endurance, intraception, and nurturance—and on all of these dimensions the mean scores of Architects II are intermediate between the higher scores of Architects III and the lower scores of Architects I.

It is the other way around, though, on the scales measuring aggression and autonomy. On these dimensions the most creative group scores significantly higher than Architects II, who, in turn, score higher than Architects III.

Since the California Psychological Inventory (CPI; Gough, 1957a) was expressly developed to measure significant dimensions of interpersonal behavior, one would also expect the three groups of architects to reveal differences on this instrument congruent with the Rankian differentiations, and indeed they do. On every one of the Class II scales of the Inventory, scales designed to measure various aspects of socialization, Architects III earn higher mean scores than the highly creative Architects I. That is, they score higher on Socialization (So), Responsibility (Re), Self-Control (Sc),

Tolerance (To), Good Impression (Gi), and Communality (Cm). And it is of interest to note that the mean scores of Architects II on all of these scales are intermediate between the higher scores of Architects III and the lower scores of Architects I, though the differences between the mean scores of Architects II and Architects III, and of Architects II and Architects I, are not significant.

On the Fundamental Interpersonal Relations Orientations-Behavior questionnaire (FIRO-B; Schutz, 1958), the greater socialization of the least creative Architects III is further demonstrated. On scales which measure the expressed desire to include others in one's activities (E^I), the expressed desire to be included in others' activities (W^I), as well as the expressed desire to be controlled by others, Architects III score higher than Architects I. The order is reversed, however, on the scale that measures the expressed desire to control others (E^c): There the most creative Architects I score higher than Architects II, and Architects II in turn higher than Architects III.

Something of the intermediate, ambitendent, conflicted nature of Architects II, congruent with the Rankian description of the second type, is likewise revealed by their scores on the FIRO-B. While they differ from Architects III in revealing less desire to include others in their activities, they are not distinguishable from them in the desire to be, themselves, included in others' activities. Similarly, while Architects II do not differ from Architects III in their desire to be controlled by others, they do differ from them in showing more desire to control others.

With respect to the number of organizations to which they belong, Architects I differ from both Architects II and Architects III in belonging to fewer so-cial groups. Though on this measure of social belongingness Architects II do differ from Architects I, they do not differ from Architects I on an Institute of Personality Assessment and Research (IPAR) scale which measures independence (Barron, 1953c). On this scale, however, Architects I score as significantly more independent than Architects III. The obverse is revealed on the Vassar scale of social integration (Webster, Freedman, & Heist, 1962), with Architects III showing, in accordance with expectation, a greater measure of social integration than do Architects I.

An examination of the Q values of items, sorted first to describe themselves in their architectural practice and second to describe the ideal architect, reveals differences among the three groups that confirm and elaborate the picture already obtained.

Architects I see, as most characteristic of themselves and of the ideal architect, some inner artistic standard of excellence and a sensitive appreciation of the fittingness of architectural solutions to that standard.

Architects II apparently place more stress upon the efficient execution of architecture, seeing as most saliently characteristic of the ideal the possession of that intellective ability, "strong powers of spatial visualization," which clearly is so crucial to the effective practice of architecture.

Architects III, unlike both Architects I and Architects II, choose as most characteristic of the ideal architect not the meeting of one's own standard but rather the standard of the profession. Once again they show that strong sense of responsibility to the group, rather than to themselves or to some inner ideal of perfection which is uniquely theirs (MacKinnon, 1963).

In summary, in the domains of socialization and interpersonal behavior we do indeed find a congruence between the differences revealed by our three samples of architects and the differences attributed by Rank to his three stages of the development of individuality.

With respect to the second domain on which I propose to compare our samples with Rank's types, namely, the level of richness or complexity of psychological development, we should be prepared to find increasing richness and complexity as we move from Architects III to Architects II to Architects I. At the same time if our data match or confirm Rank's descriptions, we should not expect to find such clear and sharp distinctions between Architects I and II as between Architects I and III, for, with respect to many traits and attributes, Rank considers the conflicted neurotic type to be close to the creative type since it is only out of such richness, and complexity, and conflict as the former experiences that the creative integrations of the latter are achieved.

On nine scales, each of which in its own way measures some aspect of psychological richness and complexity, Architects I do indeed score significantly higher than Architects III, yet despite the general tendency for Architects II to score slightly lower on these scales than Architects I, on only three of them do they score significantly lower. These measures of psychological richness and complexity are: the Psychological-Mindedness scale (Py), the Flexibility scale (Fx), and the Femininity scale (Fe) of the CPI; the Feminine Interests scale (Mf) of the Minnesota Multiphasic Personality Inventory (MMPI; Hathaway & McKinley, 1945); the Barron-Welsh Art scale (Barron & Welsh, 1952) of the Welsh Figure Preference Test (Welsh, 1959); the IPAR Preference for Complexity scale (CS; Barron, 1953a), and the IPAR (0–4) esthetic sensitivity scale

(Gough, 1957b); and the perceptiveness and intuitiveness scales of the Myers-Briggs Type Indicator (Myers, 1962).

The next question to which I wish to direct our attention is whether there is any evidence in our data that the psychological richness and complexity, which both Architects II and I experience, is more effectively managed by Architects I than by Architects II. This is what we should expect to find if Architects I exemplify the creative type and Architects II the conflicted neurotic type, and if the characteristics attributed to these types by Rank are valid.

First we may note that Architects II give evidence of less emotional stability or personal soundness and at the same time manifest more anxiety than either of the other two groups. On the IPAR scale of Personal Soundness (S) they score lower, and on the Taylor (1953) Manifest Anxiety scale they score higher than both Architects I and Architects III. Although the following differences do not reach statistical significance, they all point in the same direction: Architects II score higher than either Architects I or Architects III on the mean of the eight clinical scales of the MMPI, higher on the Welsh Anxiety factor scale of the MMPI, and higher on two IPAR scales developed by Block: Bimodal Ego Control scale (indicative of vacillation between under- and over-control of impulse) and the scale designed to measure psychoneurotic tendencies (PN). On the latter scale Architects II score significantly higher than Architects III.

There is, then, unequivocal evidence as well as some suggestive data that Architects II are more conflicted and more psychologically disturbed than either Architects I or III. We must note, however, that on several of these measures of tension, conflict, and anxiety, Architects I stand very close to Architects

II. That being the case, what is it that gives them a greater capacity to handle the psychic turbulence which they also experience? On the two tests in our assessment battery which come closest to being measures of will, as Rank conceives of it as the integrative power of the person as a whole, Architects I earn the highest mean score. These are the Ego Strength (*Es*) scale of the MMPI developed by Barron (1953b), and the IPAR scale of Self-Assertiveness (Hb) developed by Gough, though I am certain that neither of my colleagues in developing these measures had any thought that their scales had anything to do with the Rankian concept of will.

Just as we have found in our test data a considerable degree of confirmation of the Rankian descriptions of the stages of development of individuality and the realization of creative potential, so also in the life-history protocols of our subjects we have obtained supportive evidence for many of the kinds of early interpersonal experiences which Rank would have thought most strengthening of positive will and most conducive to the fullest development of the individual. They may be briefly summarized as follows: an extraordinary respect by the parent for the child, and an early granting to him of an unusual freedom in exploring his universe and in making decisions for himself; an expectation that the child would act independently but reasonably and responsibly; a lack of intense closeness between parent and child so that neither overdependence was fostered nor a feeling of rejection experienced, in other words, the sort of interpersonal relationship between parent and child which had a liberating effect upon the child; a plentiful supply in the child's extended social environment of models for identification and the promotion of ego ideals; the presence within the family

of clear standards of conduct and ideas as to what was right and wrong; but at the same time an expectation, if not requirement, of active exploration and internalization of a framework of personal conduct; an emphasis upon the development of one's own ethical code; the experience of frequent moving within single communities, or from community to community, or from country to country which provided an enrichment of experience, both cultural and personal, but which at the same time contributed to experiences of aloneness, shyness, isolation, and solitariness during childhood and adolescence; the possession of skills and abilities which, though encouraged and rewarded, were nevertheless allowed to develop at their own pace; and finally the absence of pressures to establish prematurely one's professional identity (MacKinnon, 1962a).

Though it is clear that I have found Rank's writings a hive of great suggestiveness, and have been impressed by the degree of match of our samples with his types, I would in many instances wish to use a language different from his. I am thinking not only of his frequent use of philosophical and religious terms where the language of psychology would have served him much better in his discussion of psychological problems, but more specifically and concretely of his use of the word "neurotic" to describe his second type.

If I were to apply to Architects II any of the words which Rank used in describing his second stage of psychological development it would be his term, "conflicted," for this at least carries connotations of differentiation, of opposition of forces, of richness and complexity, of psychic turbulence, of possibilities of synthesis and resolution, and of potentiality for further development. These, indeed, were stressed in Rank's discussion of the second stage, for it is clear that Rank thought of it not so much as a state of illness as a condition carrying within it the possibilities of further development.

In my judgment it would be grossly unfair to label Architects II as neurotic, though there is evidence that the neurotic process is more pronounced in them than in either of the other two samples. And I would reject any inference, which might be drawn from my remarks, that one must first be neurotic if one is to become creative. Rather, in agreement with Lawrence Kubie (1961), I believe that both neurotic and creative potential are inherent in the structure of the human psyche. It is a question of which gets emphasized and most developed in any given person.

If I were to draw a summary picture of each of our three groups of architects, I would say that what is most impressive about Architects I is the degree to which they have actualized their creative potentialities. They have become in large measure the persons they were capable of becoming. Since they are not preoccupied with the impression they make on others or the demands that others make on them, they are freer than the other two groups to set their own standards and to achieve them in their own fashion. It is not that they are socially irresponsible, but that their behavior is guided by esthetic values and ethical standards which they have set for themselves and which have been effectively integrated into their images of themselves and of their ideals. They are perhaps the prototype of the person of strong ego, the man of will and deed. Confident of themselves and basically self-accepting, they are to an unusual degree able to recognize and give expression to most aspects of inner experience and character, and thus are able more fully to be themselves and to realize their own ideals.

Architects III, on the other hand, appear to have incorporated into their egos, and into their images of the persons they are and the persons they would like to be, the more conventional standards of society and of their profession. More dependent upon the good opinion of others for their own good opinion of themselves, their goals and ideals are to an important degree those of the group rather than uniquely their own.

If I may, for the moment, lapse into the Freudian vernacular, where the egos of Architects I are on more intimate terms with the id, the egos of Architects III are more at home with their superegos. It is as though Architects I have decided that where id was ego shall be, while Architects III have determined that superego shall be where ego might have been. The egos of Architects I are characterized by effective integration of the id and the development of positive will, while the egos of Architects III are distinguished by a more marked integration of superego and conscience (MacKinnon, 1963).

Architects II, by and large less creative than Architects I but more creative than Architects III, show an overlapping of traits with both of the other groups and consequently appear to experience more conflict than do either of the others.

Finally, I would observe that Rank, a pioneer in the field of ego psychology, was one of the first to note the role of the self-image in determining an individual's behavior and the exercise of his will. Let us look then at the one adjective out of 300 on the Gough Adjective Check List which each of our three groups most often checked as descriptive of the self.

Rank described the adapted man as

one who most fully incorporates within himself the norms and dictates of society; 98% of our least creative Architects III check the adjective *conscientious*. He described the creative man, the artist, as one who in large measure creates his own reality; 98% of creative Architects I say they are *imaginative*. In describing the conflicted neurotic type, Rank observed, as many others also have, the relation of neurosis to civilization; the adjective checked most often, by 95% of our intermediate Architects II, is the adjective *civilized*.

I I

Socially
Constructive
Character Traits

There are possibly as many positive as negative abnormalities. Genius and creativity, as we have seen, are among them. So, too, are managerial success, high mechanical aptitude, and financial wizardry. Among the many positive abnormalities that might have been chosen, good character offers considerable excitement because it is both socially and theoretically important.

There was once considerable interest in the matter of good character. Hartshorne, May, and their associates, for example, were concerned with the nature of moral behavior in the 1920s. Their researches into the ubiquity and personal generality of such traits as stealing, cheating, honesty, and service to others resulted in three voluminous treatises—and that, for quite a while, was the end of the matter. It is conceivable that with the publication of their exhaustive work, it was felt that all that needs to be known was known: to wit, that there is no such thing as character, that honesty is situation bound, and that notions of the good man must give way to notions of the stimulus-bound man. Man was honest, it came to be felt, not because he was principled but rather because he was scared. And fright being what it is, one could hardly predict its occurrence from one situation to the next.

Other themes may have led to the abandonment of interest in moral behavior. The brutalities of the second World War, needless to say, shattered many a myth about the extent of human decency and replaced them with equally false notions of human selfishness and bestiality. And the dimness of the prospect of an enduring and honorable peace may very well have left men cool to the ideas of honor and character that earlier generations had held in esteem. In any event, research in this area was nearly completely abandoned until the middle 1950s, when it was revived in various laboratories throughout the country.

Roger Burton, in the first selection

offered here, brought new methodologies to old data, and arrived at an optimistic conclusion regarding character. Examining the works of Hartshorne and May with the techniques of factor analysis, he found the situation not as dismal as those authors had portrayed it. There are some common characteristics among the honesty behaviors assessed in that study, Burton held, and though the unity is by no means immense, neither is there reason to believe that matters of honesty reduce entirely to situational factors.

Although concerns for moral behavior in the sense of avoiding sin have increased, interest in the pursuit of virtue has been even more recent. In part, disinterest in these matters has been rooted in conceptual problems. One can conceptualize the *avoidance* of certain behaviors in terms of anxiety and fearfulness, in terms of fantasied punishment or situational considerations. Aronfreed's paper in Chapter 3 illustrated this. Prosocial behavior, particularly the kinds of behavior that require personal sacrifice, are not so apparently amenable to such interpretations. However, the phenomena of prosocial behavior have fortunately remained with us, adequate conceptualizations notwithstanding. And indeed, it may be asked, if man seeks to increment pleasure and avoid pain, how does one account for his willingness to give up pleasure for the sake of another? The paper by David Rosenhan summarizes a variety of naturalistic and experimental studies. It reports that children and adults are altruistic for no better reason than that they have been influenced by a model who was altruistic. Such evidence constitutes support for the role of identification in the acquisition of prosocial (as well as other kinds of) behavior, a role upon which we have remarked earlier (Chapter 1). With regard to prosocial behavior, however, observation of a model may be augmented by the opportunity to rehearse with the model. But regardless of process, the paper indicates that the quest for personal reward constitutes only one aspect of human functioning. Pleasure in giving rewards to others may very well be another.

Generality of Honesty Reconsidered

Roger V. Burton[1]

In the 1920s there was a substantial amount of research dealing with the complex domain of honesty, or moral behavior. This research reached a culmi-

Reprinted from *Psychological Review*, 1963, vol. 70, pp. 481–499 with the permission of the American Psychological Association and the author.

[1] I am especially indebted to John D. Campbell and to two anonymous reviewers for their constructive comments on this paper.

nation in the classic studies of Hartshorne and May (1928) and their collaborators (Hartshorne, May, & Maller, 1929; Hartshorne, May, & Shuttleworth, 1930). After their efforts, investigation into this area of human behavior concentrated on exploring the cognitive structure and development of morality, while studies of overt choice behavior in test situations declined until relatively recently. The loss of enthusiasm for this area of research may have been due to the very thorough, excellent job done by Hartshorne and May. Another reason for the turning away from honesty as a subject for study may have been the conclusion from their study that conflict between honest or deceitful behavior is quite specific to each situation, that one could not generalize about a subject's honesty from a few samples of his behavior.

In the 1950s there was a renewed interest in the area of morality, especially in the developmental aspects of such behavior. Those working in this area must take into account the generality of their findings, especially when they utilize only a single behavioral test of honesty. It is the purpose of this paper to reconsider the specificity conclusion by looking again at the Hartshorne and May data and other evidence relevant to this question.

GENERALITY VERSUS SPECIFICITY

The two extreme points of view about honest behavior can be quickly sketched. The unidimensional approach holds that a person is, or strongly tends to be, consistent in his behavior over many different kinds of situations. Thus a person who lies in one situation is not only likely to lie in other situations, but is also highly likely to cheat, steal, not feel guilty, and so on. This conception of the generality of character has been more fully presented by MacKinnon (1938) in a study supplying empirical support for such an interpretation. The graduate student subjects in his study who cheated on a problem solving task by copying also tended to lie about their behavior, to report that they rarely felt guilty, and to perceive the task as being unfair. The students who did not cheat reported that they often felt guilty even when they were not aware of having transgressed, and that they perceived themselves as

inadequate to solve the task rather than that the task was unfair. The conclusion is that these findings demonstrate a consistency in personality, and that one is justified in drawing conclusions from relationships between one sample of honest behavior and other measures relevant to one's investigation. MacKinnon recognized that he did not test over different kinds of situations, but he argued that the consistency he found was sufficient to support his interpretation. In general, this interpretation is consonant with most psychoanalytic formulations of superego behavior based on an identification hypothesis. As Maccoby (1959) has pointed out, theoretical formulations stemming from Piaget's (1932) schema also conform to this "unitary process" conceptualization of morality.

The doctrine of specificity of moral behavior holds that a person acts in each situation according to the way he has been taught to act under these particular conditions. The predictability of one's moral behavior from one situation to another depends on the number of identical elements which the two settings share. This formulation does not accept the abstract concept of "honesty" as a valid character trait, but instead argues that there are many different kinds of specific behaviors which tend to be independent even though they may be included under the same rubric. Therefore, knowing that a person has cheated in a final examination in no way permits one to predict what the same person would do if tempted to cheat in a different setting such as a competitive game or business venture. Furthermore, there is little if any association between the extent to which a person will experience anxiety following a deviation in one moral area with the intensity of guilt following deviation in a different area. The study reported by Allinsmith (1960) reflects to some extent this interpretation. Utilizing a story completion method for his measures of moral behavior, he found there was little consistency in the intensity of guilt expressed in junior high school students over different transgressions. He also found a noticeable lack of correlation between the measures of guilt and the measures of resistance to temptation. He concludes, therefore, that there are specific "guilts" which tend to be unrelated to resistance to temptation rather than a unified character trait representing an individual's morality.

The reader may note that the two studies cited have measured both the tendency to deviate in a temptation situation and the reaction to having already deviated. This simultaneous consideration of resistance to temptation and of guilt is customary in studies addressed to the development of moral behavior, of the superego, or conscience. However, there seems good reason, both theoretically and empirically (Burton, 1959; Burton, Maccoby, & Allinsmith, 1961), to consider these aspects of morality separately and then to investigate the extent of the correspondence between them. This paper is addressed primarily to a consideration of the generality of resistance to temptation as measured by behavior in lifelike temptation settings, and also by questionnaires and projective techniques.

STUDIES IN DECEIT

Hartshorne and May's *Studies in Deceit* (1928) is undoubtedly the most comprehensive and well-known study of temptation and cheating behavior. One of the most important conclusions from this study was that there was no general trait of honesty. Consistency of behavior from one situation to another was due to similarities in the situations and not to a consistent personality trait in people.

However, these authors did recognize that there seemed to be some similar overlapping elements in all the test situations:

> It may be contended of course that as a matter of fact we rarely reach a zero correlation, no matter how different may be our techniques, and that this implies some such common factor in the individual as might properly be called a trait. We would not wish to quarrel over the use of a term and are quite ready to recognize the existence of some common factors which tend to make individuals differ from one another on any one test or on any group of tests. Our contention, however, is that this common factor is not an inner entity operating independently of the situations in which the individuals are placed but is a function of the situation in the sense that an individual behaves similarly in different situations in proportion as these situations are alike, have been experienced as common occasions for honest or dishonest behavior, and are comprehended as opportunities for deception or honesty. [p. 385]

The emphasis, then, was on the specificity of each test situation which involved different motives, different values in conflict, and—most importantly—different learned responses for that particular setting. The basis for their conclusion was that the correlations between the cheating tests were too low to produce evidence of a unified character trait of honesty or deceitfulness.

Table 1 gives the intercorrelations as reported in *Studies in Deceit*. The upper half (summed scores) presents the intercorrelations of the types of deceptive behavior in which each person's score on a particular kind of test is summed with his scores on the same kind of test to give a single, composite score for that type of cheating. The top diagonals are the reliabilities for these summed scores. The lower half (average correlations) of the table gives the average cross-correlations between single tests of different techniques. The diagonals of this half of the table are the average correlation of one kind and type of test with the other tests of the same kind and type. Thus, .871 is the reliability of the summed score for the three copying tests, .450 is the correlation between the summed scores for the three copying and the six speed tests, .696 represents the average correlation for the three copying tests, and the average correlation among these three copying tests with the six speed tests is .292.

Table 1
Intercorrelations of Hartshorne and May

	A	B	C	D	E	F	G	H	I
A. Copying (3 tests)	(.871)(.696)	.450	.400	.400	.172	.288	.118	.143	.350
B. Speed (6 tests)	.292	(.825)(.440)	.374	.425	.193	.345	.169	.173	.248
C. Peeping (3 tests)	.285	.219	(.721)(.462)	.300	.234	.100	.250	.200	.108
D. Faking (3 tests)	.291	.255	.196	(.750)(.500)		.300	.122	.346	.256
E. Home (1 test)	.154	.141	.187		(.240)(.240)	.142	−.015	−.010	.400
F. Athletic (4 tests)	.198	.194	.062	.184	.087	(.772)(.458)	.118	.283	.230
G. Parties (3 tests)								.210	−.004
H. Stealing (1 test)	.127	.128	.160	.283	−.010	.162			.132
I. Lying (1 test)	.312	.254	.161	.208	.400	−.003		.132	(.836)(.836)

Note.—Hartshorne and May, 1928, Book II, pp. 122, 123, 212.
The upper half is based on summed scores for each type of test. The lower half was computed by averaging the correlations for each type of test. Reliabilities for each method of computing these scores are in the diagonal.

The individual's score for each test contributing to these correlations was determined as follows. First, a distribution of performance scores under carefully supervised (i.e., enforced honesty) conditions was obtained, and the mean and standard deviation of this distribution were computed. The scores for some tests (e.g., Copying, Speed, and Athletic) were the differences between performance at Time 1 and performance at Time 2. For the other tests (e.g., Peeping, Puzzle, and Lying), the scores were based on a single performance. The mean as thus determined for each test became the reference point for honest behavior, and the standard deviation became the unit of measurement. When a subject was then tested for deception, his raw test score was converted into the number of standard deviation units it was away from this previously established mean of honest behavior. For example, the mean for the changes on the Arithmetic Copying test was a gain of 1.06 with a standard deviation of 3.10. If a person obtained a change in score of a loss of 10, his converted score would become −3.57, which is the score used in computing the correlations with the other tests.[2]

[2] Hartshorne and May also used a "fact" score as well as this "amount" score. They arbitrarily decided that any score which was three or more standard deviations from the honest mean was labeled a "cheat." The fact score was used in reporting the percentages of cheaters on independent variables such as age, sex, ethnicity, etc.

Looking at the intercorrelation table, it is seen, as Hartshorne and May pointed out, that the sizes of the correlations tend to decrease as the similarities of the situations decrease. This certainly supports their argument that there are factors in the temptation situation which influence the behavior of the child irrespective of any proclivity for cheating or resistance he brings with him. They also had evidence showing that variables external to the individual, such as ease of cheating, extent of the risk involved, and magnitude of the deviation required for success, effect the probability that one will cheat and also the extent to which one will deviate.

However, it is striking that almost all of the correlations are positive and that most of the very low correlations are contributed by tests with very low or unknown reliabilities. Furthermore, with the low reliabilities of some of the tests, the intercorrelations (especially in the upper half) are relatively high. Consideration of these facts suggest that a reexamination of the authors' rejection of an underlying character trait of honesty in temptation situations is warranted.[3]

PRINCIPAL COMPONENT ANALYSIS

Hartshorne and May (1928) state in a footnote when discussing the data on specificity of conduct that "Spearman's criterion of the presence of a common factor was not applied to these inter-*r*'s, as they were not obtained from the same cases throughout [Book II, p. 215]." Unfortunately, they do not report the size of the samples for the correlations. But

[3] J. Merrill Carlsmith and David G. Beswich also considered this issue and carried out an analysis using Thurstone's centroid method. Their results are essentially the same as those reported in this paper. By coincidence their analysis was made simultaneously with that reported here. I am most appreciative to them for making their results available for this paper.

from their tables giving the numbers of students in each school who were given each test, it seems safe to estimate that the sample sizes ranged from at least 75 to over 6,000, with most of the reported correlations being based on samples between 200 and 350 in size (Hartshorne & May, 1928, Book I, pp. 107–108). With these samples drawn from similar populations without apparent systematic bias, it would seem that the correlations reported are fairly good approximations to the true population values. If this assumption is accepted, there is no problem in performing a principal component analysis on these matrices. To be more confident of the stability of the results, only tests with at least .70 reliabilities for the summed scores were included. Therefore, only the Copying (A), Speed (B), Peeping (C), Faking (D), Athletic (F), and Lying (I) tests were chosen.

DESCRIPTIONS OF THE TESTS

The *copying* tests were intelligence tests which involved the child's writing answers to questions, having the papers collected and copies of each paper made, returning the papers to the pupils, and having them correct their own papers. Their cheating score consisted of any changes they made on their papers.

The *speed* tests consisted of simple tasks such as number and digit cancellation. Three short forms of these tests were given, two under honest conditions called "practice" sessions, and the last was the test. The pupil was permitted to score his own test on the last administration. The score was the amount of increase on the last relative to the second trial.

Peeping tests involved tracing mazes or marking "x's" in circles while keeping one's eyes closed. Deception was determined by comparing the child's performance against a norm established under honest conditions.

The puzzles used in the *faking* solutions tests were either impossible to solve or extremely difficult. To achieve a satisfactory solution in the time given, a child would have to cheat. His deception score consisted of how closely he approached a perfect solution.

The *athletic* tests were a dynamometer test for measuring strength of hand grip, a spirometer test for measuring lung capacity, a chinning test, and a standard broad jump. Each student was tested privately. Three "warm-up" trials were given in the presence of the tester who recorded the student's best performance. The child was then left alone to record his own score on the next five trials. Previous standardization of performance on the tests permitted scoring improbable achievement during the test trials compared with the best score on the first three trials.

The *lying* test consisted of questions about the child's personal conformity to socially approved morality. After failing to standardize the test on school classes, the test was standardized on a class of graduate students who attempted to answer truthfully about their own childhood. This standard was then used to determine the deception score for the school pupils.[4]

Lawley's (1910) test of significance (also see Maxwell, 1961) was applied to these matrices and indicated that the sample size would have to be at least *n* of 26 for all the matrices to be significant at the .001 level. Since all these correlations are based on at least 200 pupils, these matrices are statistically significant and justify the extraction of common variance.

[4] A complete description of these tests and the procedures for scoring is given in Hartshorne and May (1928), along with the other tests which we have not used in our factor analysis and therefore have not described.

The hypothesis was that a significant amount of variance would be extracted by the first component and that all the tests would have high loadings on this component. The standards for determining the statistical significance of the factor loadings and extracted variance are not yet agreed on by statisticians so that the decision as to evidence required to reject the null hypothesis is arbitrary. It seemed reasonable to set the criterion at a minimum of 30% of the total variance in the matrix for the component to have a "g" characteristic and for the loadings on all tests to be a minimum of .40. Furthermore, components extracted after the first should account for much less of the variance relative to the first and should tend to be specific to individual tests.

RESULTS

The results for the principal component analyses of the two matrices are presented in Table 2. The matrix based on the average intercorrelations (bottom half of Table 1) yields a component structure which barely meets our arbitrary criterion. As this matrix was computed in a conservative manner, that is, contains what is probably the lowest estimates of the true correlations, these results can be considered to represent the minimum magnitude of common variance and loadings for each component. The results for the other matrix (upper half of Table 1 based on summed scores) show that the magnitude of the variance accounted for by the first component is larger as are the loadings of each test on this component. These results are based on matrices having unities in the diagonal and with the correlations being those given in Table 1 whose reliabilities were at least .70. These correlations were not corrected for attenuation. Analyses using reliabilities in the diagonal produce

Table 2
Principal Components

	Based on summed scores						Based on average intercorrelations					
	I	II	III	IV	V	VI	I	II	III	IV	V	VI
A. Copying	.764	.092	.207	−.166	−.116	.570	.718	−.054	.013	−.046	−.444	.530
B. Speed	.754	.106	−.195	−.047	.614	−.056	.651	.065	−.134	−.403	.607	.151
C. Peeping	.581	.660	.084	−.233	−.239	−.329	.540	−.237	.768	−.060	−.002	−.244
D. Faking	.703	.017	−.139	.677	−.168	−.029	.619	.140	.088	.736	.217	−.028
F. Athletic	.555	−.504	−.537	−.293	−.234	−.095	.387	.825	.041	−.177	−.240	−.282
I. Lying	.526	−.504	.638	−.030	.023	−.245	.561	−.501	−.474	−.105	−.207	−.394
% of Variance	42.8	16.1	13.4	10.5	8.9	8.4	34.6	17.0	14.0	12.5	11.8	10.0

similar results and are not reported here. The main change is that the amount of variance extracted by the first component is much greater using the reliabilities.[5]

These analyses conform in the main to our hypothesis and lend support to the generality position. In all cases, the first component accounts for at least twice as much variance as the second

component. Also, the loadings on this component are all positive and exceed .50, with the exception of the athletic tests for the matrix of averaged intercorrelations.

There appeared to be more than one factor to be extracted, however, which would indicate that there may be some other common variance. The second component rather consistently accounts for about 17% of the variance in the total matrix and is related (before rotation) to three of the tests. A weak third component, common to the two out-of-classroom tests, also was extracted and accounted for about 14% of the total variance.

Several criteria were considered in deciding when to end the extraction of components. First, the percentage of variance for each component was plotted. The curve flattened out after the third component suggesting that the analysis should be stopped regardless of the size of the sample. It is also seen that Components IV, V, and VI are specific to single tests. Tests of significance of the residual matrices (Lawley, 1940; Maxwell, 1961) indicated that *n*s of under 200 would have justified the extraction of the second and third components. These criteria encouraged the extraction

[5] I have also done analyses of these matrices corrected for attenuation. Again the results were approximately the same but show a consistent increase in the magnitudes of the loadings and amount of variance extracted by the first component as the size of the original correlations increased due to their respective methods of calculation. The results of these analyses even more strongly indicate a generality conclusion. For example, the amount of variance in the first component for the matrix of average correlations corrected for attenuation increases from 48% to 69%. The second component accounted for 19% of the variance and the third factor tended to vanish. However, the greater magnitude of the first component produced by using matrices having reliabilities in the diagonals and/or correlations corrected for attenuation may be spurious. It seems possible that the additional variance extracted by the first of these component matrices results from the common "correction" for measurement error injected by the reliability coefficients. Therefore, only the results based on the uncorrected matrices with unities in the diagonals are reported as these are the most conservative estimates of the common variance for these tests and the most likely to reject the generality hypothesis.

of at least two components and perhaps three. However, a theoretical limitation on the extraction of variance is that the communality (h^2) for any one test cannot be greater than the reliability of that test. This theoretical restriction makes even the second factor suspect. The communality for the third test (Peeping) exceeds its reliability by a small amount. With the extraction of the third component, three tests (Peeping, Athletic, and Lying) exceed their reliabilities.

To help clarify these results, we have proceeded to obtain a unique solution using Lawley's method of maximum likelihood in order to test for the sample size required to extract more than the first factor. The solution is given in Table 3 and shows that samples of at least 333 for the summed scores and 608 for the averaged scores would be required to reject the null hypothesis of the adequacy of a single factor.[6]

We see that these analyses are the most conservative in testing our hypothesis but still produce results very similar to those of the principal component model. The athletic tests contribute very little to this general factor for the averaged correlations, with 92% specific variance for these tests. But the analysis based on the summed scores meets our original arbitrary criterion for factor loadings of at least .40 for all tests.

If a conservative judgment is made from all our analyses, only the first component is permitted. Such a conclusion would clearly support a single factor hypothesis with some consideration that the athletic tests are independent of the other types of tests. For those readers who agree with this conclusion, the following rotations of components will be superfluous. Since others may feel that these considerations are too severe with a principal component model which achieves a unique solution accounting for all the variance in the matrix, we have rotated the first three factors extracted in our analyses.

Rotated Factor Structure

Three factors were orthogonally rotated by Kaiser's (1958) analytic varimax model. The rotated factors indicate that there seems to be a difference between those tests administered inside the classroom and the athletic tests which are given in an out-of-class setting. Factor I' for the summed scores seems to clearly indicate a classroom cheating factor which involves actual behavior. The second factor (II') is mainly a performance cheating factor with the main loading from the athletic tests and rather substantial loadings from the speed and faking tests, all of which involve some kind of physical performance. The third factor (III') is defined primarily by the questionnaire test on acceptance of the general moral code. The classroom copying tests also contribute to this factor.

Table 3

Lawley's Solution for a Single Factor

Tests	Based on summed scores	Based on averaged correlations
	Factor loadings	Factor loadings
A. Copying	.697	.642
B. Speed	.686	.516
C. Peeping	.497	.412
D. Faking	.607	.481
F. Athletic	.443	.275
I. Lying	.415	.442
	N > 333*	N > 608*
	N > 500**	N > 914**

* $p = .05$, $df = 15$.
** $p = .001$, $df = 15$.

[6] The estimated factor loadings and communalities for beginning this analysis were taken from the principal axis solutions. I would like to acknowledge the advice and direct assistance of Donald F. Morrison of the National Institutes of Health in performing these analyses.

The rotated factors for the averaged cross correlations indicate a somewhat similar structure. The main difference is in the exchange of places by the peeping and lying tests, and by the greater degree of specificity of the second and third factors. Factor I' is again a classroom test factor but is defined more by the lying test than the actual behavioral tests. The second factor (II') is again an athletic dimension. The peeping tests are specific to the last factor (III').

Table 4
Orthogonal Rotation of Factors

Tests	Summed scores				Average cross −r			
	I'	II'ᵃ	III'	h^2	I'	II'	III'	h^2
A. Copying	.633	.223	.428	.634	.600	.205	.343	.519
B. Speed	.611	.479	.120	.617	.581	.288	.161	.447
C. Peeping	.878	−.085	−.037	.780	.142	−.013	.957	.937
D. Faking	.516	.460	.187	.513	.509	.349	.173	.411
F. Athletic	.030	.916	.101	.851	.090	.907	−.020	.831
I. Lying	.081	.113	.959	.939	.841	−.280	−.068	.791

	Transformation matrices						
		T				T	
	.731	−.535	.424		.821	.355	.447
	.680	.514	−.523		−.300	.935	−.191
	.061	.670	.740		−.485	.022	.874

ᵃ This factor has been reflected.

These results are what we might have expected from our Lawley solutions. We see that the athletic tests tend to have specific variance in the Lawley solution and to define the second factor in the rotational analyses. Also the copying, speed, and faking tests tend to be more "general" in that their loadings are all positive on the rotated factors, contribute to more than one of the factors, and have the largest communalities in the Lawley solutions. It is not clear whether the peeping and lying tests should be included in the general factor of class-room honesty tests or should be considered as specific tests. From Brogden's (1940) analysis to be discussed below, it seems the inclusion of the peeping tests with the first factor with the lying factor tending to be independent is the more stable structure.

SIMPLE ANALYSIS

Guttman (1955) has developed an alternative model to factor analysis as a way of investigating the single-common-factor hypothesis.[7] He proposes that if a matrix of intercorrelations can be ordered in a hierarchical gradient conforming to certain criteria the tests can be considered to be in the same universe and to vary along a single dimension, an ordering he has called a simplex.

These criteria are that "the largest correlations are all next to the main diagonal, and taper off as one goes to the upper right and lower left of the table," and that the totals of the columns will be curvilinear with the lowest totals

[7] I would like to thank Morris Rosenberg for bringing this alternative method to my attention after I had already completed the factor analyses.

Table 5
Guttman Simplex of Summed Scores

Tests	Summed scores								
	E	I	C	A	B	D	F	H	G
E. Home (1 test)	(.240)	.400	.234	.172	.193		.142	−.010	−.015
I. Lying (1 test)	.400	(.836)	.108	.350	.248	.256	.230	.132	−.004
C. Peeping (3 tests)	.234	.108	(.721)	.400	.374	.300	.100	.200	.250
A. Copying (3 tests)	.172	.350	.400	(.871)	.450	.400	.288	.143	.118
B. Speed (6 tests)	.193	.248	.374	.450	(.825)	.425	.345	.173	.169
D. Faking (3 tests)		.256	.300	.400	.425	(.750)	.300	.346	.122
F. Athletic (4 tests)	.142	.230	.100	.288	.345	.300	(.772)	.283	.118
H. Stealing (1 test)	−.010	.132	.200	.143	.173	.346	.283		.210
G. Parties (3 tests)	−.015	.004	.250	.118	.169	.122	.118	.210	
Total	1.116[a]	1.720	1.966	2.321	2.377	2.149[a]	1.806	1.477	.968

[a] These totals are minus any contributions from r_{DE}.

at the right and left extremes and the largest total in the middle. Tables 5 and 6 present an ordering of the Hartshorne and May intercorrelation matrix into quasi-simplexes. The preponderance of "errors" in the ordering are contributed by the Home (E), Stealing (H), and Parties (G) tests. These tests either have very low or unreported reliabilities which would itself tend to introduce errors into the ordering. It will be seen that the matrix within the heavy lines approaches a perfect simplex. These are the same tests we have chosen for the principal component analyses on the basis of acceptable reliabilities. Our results again support the generality hypothesis.

A comparison of the ordering of the same tests utilized in the factor analysis shows that only the tests in the center of the simplex—copying, speed, and faking—contribute positively to all the rotated factors. The lying, peeping, and athletic tests contribute only to one factor and are seen to be at the extremes of the simplex. It is interesting that the positions of the two extreme tests in the two simplex orderings correspond to the two specific, rotated factors; i.e., the athletic tests define Factor II' for both the rotational analyses and are also at the far right in both simplexes, and the lying tests define the specific Factor III' for the summed scores and are at the ex-

Table 6
Guttman Simplex of Average Cross-Correlations

Tests	Average cross −r							
	E	C	I	A	B	D	F	H
E. Home	(.240)	.187	.400	.154	.141		.087	−.010
C. Peeping	.187	(.462)	.161	.285	.219	.196	.062	.160
I. Lying	.400	.161	(.836)	.312	.254	.208	−.003	.132
A. Copying	.154	.285	.312	(.696)	.292	.291	.198	.127
B. Speed	.141	.219	.254	.292	(.440)	.255	.194	.128
D. Faking		.196	.208	.291	.255	(.500)	.184	.283
F. Athletic	.087	.062	−.003	.198	.194	.184	(.458)	.162
H. Stealing	−.010	.100	.132	.127	.128	.283	.162	
Total	.959[a]	1.270	1.464	1.659	1.483	1.417[a]	.884	.982

[a] These totals are minus any contributions from r_{DE}.

treme left for this simplex, whereas the peeping tests have these characteristics for the averaged cross-correlation matrix. It is also notable that these extreme tests contribute the only errors in the simplex.

RELATED STUDIES

Other investigators have come to similar conclusions regarding the generality of honest behavior. One of the first after Hartshorne and May's final volume was a short paper published by Maller (1934) who had been a co-author in *Studies in Service and Self-Control* (Hartshorne *et al.*, 1929). Maller analyzed the correlations of the summary scores for the character tests of Honesty, Cooperation, Inhibition, and Persistence as reported in *Studies in the Organization of Character* (Hartshorne *et al.*, 1930). He utilized Spearman's tetrad difference technique and concluded that there was evidence for a common factor in all three matrices which were based on quite different populations. He interpreted the common factor as being delay of gratification: "the readiness to forego an immediate gain for the sake of a remote but greater gain." He pointed out, however, that one should be cautious in accepting his analysis as proof of a general factor due to the very low magnitude of the original intercorrelations. On the other hand, he predicted that higher correlations would be forthcoming when character tests were constructed with greater reliability and validity.

Brogden (1940) also utilized the factor analytic model in his analysis of 40 character tests. The intercorrelations were based on a sample of 100 middle-class boys with average or above IQ. Four of the tests were the same or similar to the Hartshorne and May (1928) tests of deceit and six were the same paper-and-pencil character tests used in *Studies in the Organization of Character* (Hart-

shorne *et al.*, 1930). The most clearly defined factor obtained in this analysis was an honesty factor. All the behavioral tests of cheating had high loadings on this factor, and two of the paper-and-pencil tests contributed to a small extent. Brogden suggested, as did Maller, that the paper-and-pencil tests could be refined to correlate more highly with the honesty factor by doing an item analysis on two groups of subjects with extreme scores on the factor; but this analysis is not reported. Brogden also found an "acceptance of the moral code" factor. It is interesting that these two factors are orthogonal to one another in this analysis. The honesty factor consists mainly of the behavioral tests whereas the "moral code" factor is defined by paper-and-pencil tests and story completions which measured how much the child would express the socially acceptable (desirable) response. These results indicate that even though there are some paper-and-pencil tests which contribute to a behavioral factor of honesty the elements in them are not well determined and that the cognitive aspect of morality seems for the most part to be independent of the behavioral choice situation.

Barbu (1951) reports a program of research dealing with honesty in children which he conducted in Roumania between 1935 and 1940. In one study of 250 14-year-old boys tested with nine behavioral tests and one questionnaire test of honesty, he found an average intercorrelation of .456 and concluded there was strong evidence for a general trait of honesty. He also analyzed his data using Thurstone's multiple factor model and found evidence of a general factor. To some extent, however, the consistency of Barbu's results may be due to his choice of tests which are all similar to the Hartshorne and May classroom tests which had the high loadings on the general factor in our analysis.

DISCUSSION

The results of our analyses, and those of Maller, Brogden, and Barbu, lead us to reconsider the specificity hypothesis regarding behavioral honesty in favor of a more general position.

Previous writers have also given theoretical consideration to this question and decided in favor of a generality of behavior. Allport (1937) presented challenging arguments against the specificity position pointing out the difficulties involved in predicting the important "identical elements" in different situations. Eysenck's (1953) review of Hartshorne and May points out the intercorrelations of these types of measures, each based on from one to six behavioral tests, should not be expected to reach the magnitudes of intercorrelations based on intelligence tests composed of 50 or more items. This consideration does make Hartshorne and May's criterion of a theoretical predictive reliability of .90 for acceptable evidence of a generality of honesty behavior quite stringent. The obtained theoretical predictive reliability for their tests was .725 based on an average intercorrelation for the nine types of tests of .227, which included the tests with the very low reliabilities. A battery of 31 such honesty tests would be required to obtain the theoretical criterion of .90, assuming that the average inter-r remains the same. By eliminating the tests with low reliabilities, the average inter-r increases to .305, which still gives just a .725 as the theoretical predictive reliability for the remaining 6 tests. However, only 21 tests would be necessary to reach the criterion of .90 reliability with another battery of 21 similar honesty tests.[8]

The conclusion to draw from these analyses is not greatly different from that made by Hartshorne and May, but the strong emphasis on lack of relation between tests is removed. Our analyses indicate that one may conclude there is an underlying trait of honesty which a person brings with him to a resistance to temptation situation. However, these results strongly agree with Hartshorne and May's rejection of an "all or none" formulation regarding a person's character. I feel the results can best be incorporated by a learning model which would predict a generalization gradient over the different types of tests. Since all the cheating tests have much face validity of being in the area of resistance to temptation, one would expect that the generalization gradient would extend to all the tests. This expectation is supported by the evidence of a general factor underlying the intercorrelations of the tests. However, the model would also predict that as the tests become less similar the probability of the same response in both situations would become less and less. This prediction would account for the decrement in the magnitude of the correlations as the situations become more dissimilar.

This model would make some additional predictions about consistency in responses over the different tests contingent on different learning conditions of the subjects. It would predict that the parent who consistently defines all temptation situations the same way as interpreted in the honesty tests and also consistently administers positive reinforcement for honest behavior and punishment for dishonest behavior would facilitate for his child the discrimination of the critical cues in situations which call for an honest response. With these critical cues discriminated, the child should show much generality in his behavior across the different types of honesty tests. On the other hand, parents

[8] For fuller discussions of the measurement problems and theory on which these computations are based, see Hartshorne and May (1928) and Eysenck (1953).

who define cheating in one situation as being unacceptable, e.g., stealing money, but do not censure cheating in another situation in which a highly valued gain may be obtained, .e.g., cheating on a college entrance examination, would produce children who are not consistent on these honesty tests.[9] These children may learn to be honest in particular situations but would not learn to discriminate the critical elements calling for an honest response in any situation which involves a moral choice. But I must emphasize I mean here consistency in *defining* the situation for the child as calling for an honest response and in *administering* positive or negative reinforcement contingent on his response. For we would expect from the experimental literature that once a particular response is well established, a kind of inconsistency in the *predictability* of the reinforcer will flatten out the generalization gradient (Humphreys, 1939; Wickens, Schroder, & Snide, 1954). Such a variable reinforcement schedule will also increase the resistance of the response to extinction, i.e., conditions of no longer being reinforced. Thus parental consistency in interpreting the moral elements of a situation and in the positive or negative characteristics of the reinforcement they dispense depending on the child's behavior, combined with a gradual inconsistency in their dispensing of such reinforcement are the conditions maximizing the learning, generalization, and persistence of a moral response.

An important aspect of this generalization model in predicting and explaining

moral behavior is the part played by cognitive mediation. In addition to the generalization gradient in which only the elements of the original stimulus complex and response are concerned, there is another gradient involving cognitively mediated generalization. This part of our model would predict that the greater the cognitive, especially verbal, association between two kinds of temptation situations, the greater will be the probability of the same response being performed in both settings. It would be possible, therefore, to place an individual in a test situation appearing to be totally new in his experience but yet having some elements which he would *define* as a temptation conflict. That is, there may be very little similarity as far as the immediate stimulus complex is concerned, but there are elements of a cognitive nature by which mediational generalization may occur. When both specific stimulus generalization and cognitive mediation are combined, the probability of predicting behavior from one situation to another should be some additive function of these two generalization gradients.[10]

Theoretically, it seems these two generalization gradients may be quite independent. The child rearing practices of some parents may be very appropriate for the learning of honest behavior in particular settings and for the broad generalization of such behavior to other similar stimulus complexes. But these same parents may not apply verbal labels to such situations. Their children are learning to be honest in specific situ-

---

[9] There is the assumption made in this area of research that the "average" parent in our American culture agrees on what is honest and dishonest behavior in the test situations. There may be some cases in which parents are slightly psychopathic and would not consider it wrong to cheat; but in sampling a large group of subjects, these deviant cases should not contribute too much "noise" to the analyses.

[10] MacRae (1954) postulated "two distinct processes of moral development" which are analogous to the two generalization gradients proposed here. Although his data were all based on what we have called the "cognitive" type of measure, he hypothesized a " 'cognitive' moral development, involving the learning of what behavior patterns are approved and disapproved, and 'emotional' moral development, including the association of anxiety with one's own deviance and moral indignation with that of others" [p. 17].

ations, and any generalization of their behavior will come through similarity of new situations to these specific learning conditions. Other parents may emphasize the verbal labeling of situational conditions so that their children learn to discriminate certain cognitive elements in quite different kinds of stimulus situations.[11] These children are learning that under certain abstract conditions one should act in some ways and not in others. However, some of these same parents may not be efficient in teaching their children to perform the desirable response under these conditions. These children would know the acceptable moral code in many temptation situations, but such knowledge would not necessarily determine their overt choice behavior.[12] In actual practice it seems from our analyses that the majority of parents, especially of the middle class on which most research in honesty has been done, attempt to achieve both kinds of generalization in their children.

Experimental results also indicate the influence of these two kinds of generalization on behavior. The generalization of specific stimulus situations is well demonstrated in the literature (e.g., Osgood, 1953). But experiments in which both the specific, external stimuli and cognitive elements can be simultaneously assessed for their relative contributions to generalization are somewhat rare. Hull (1920) demonstrated that a concept can be learned even though the critical cues might not be subject to conscious awareness, indicating the discrimination and generalization of very specific cues em-

bedded in a conceptual task without the need of verbal mediation. Bugelski and Scharlock (1952) extended this finding to show that actual verbal mediation can also occur without awareness. Other experiments indicate, however, that conscious verbal mediation facilitates discriminations in new situations where the verbal labels are still relevant (Goodwin & Lawrence, 1955; Kendler & Kendler, 1959; Kuenne, 1946). Such discrimination would increase the probability of generalizing to different situations in which these labels continue to be appropriate. The differences in types of discrimination and generalization associated with age and intelligence further demonstrate the distinction between the dimensions of purely external stimulus elements and cognitive labeling (Kendler, Kendler, & Wells, 1960; Kuenne, 1946; Luria, 1957).

Relating this experimental evidence to the honesty data, the analyses of Maller (1934) and Brogden (1940) indicate that to some extent most parents are inculcating both generalization of a specific, situational sort and also of a more cognitive kind. The ordering of the Hartshorne and May tests into a quasi-simplex also indicates that the students were defining these different tests as being in the same realm. The further fact that those tests which could be ordered into a nearly perfect simplex clearly had stimulus elements in common shows that both kinds of generalization appear to be influencing these results. Brogden's finding two factors which seem to measure these kinds of generalization, and the rotational analysis of the summed scores, provide some empirical support for the behavioral and cognitive dimensions contributing separate variance to these honesty tests. More recent investigations also indicate that behavioral measures and cognitive indices of morality are not necessarily correlated (Burton, 1959;

---

[11] Although this notion seems to be popular now, I believe John W. M. Whiting first suggested this hypothesis regarding the importance of verbal labeling in learning moral standards.

[12] More extended discussions of the child rearing practices considered conducive for learning resistance to temptation and honest behavior are in Burton (1959), and Burton, Maccoby, and Allinsmith (1961).

Burton et al., 1961; Unger, 1960). This consideration follows the point made by Maccoby (1959) that comparisons between different studies of morality involve the problem of reliability across measures, i.e., their intercorrelations, even though they may be highly reliable tests themselves. Thus, if one study employs Hartshorne and May's peeping test and another uses the lying questionnaire, there will probably not be great agreement in the results as there is so little overlap in the tests. The model we have presented indicates that the tests may differ on at least two dimensions: they may test different environmental settings (e.g., in-classroom versus out-of-classroom, in-school versus out-of-school), and they may differ in the extent to which they test actual choice behavior in a conflict situation versus cognitive structuring of hypothetical conditions as in a paper-pencil questionnaire or Piaget-type interview. Campbell and Fiske (1959) have suggested a procedure which appears relevant for these issues. Their recommendation is to use several methods to measure a number of different traits in order to assess the convergent and discriminant validity of the tests and of the constructs they are purported to measure. The last book in the Character Education Inquiry of Hartshorne and May (1930) *Studies in the Organization of Character* comes close to considering this same procedure. The four traits of honesty, cooperation, inhibition, and persistence were measured by different tests ultizing different methods. Furthermore, they employed the behavioral tests in different settings. Unfortunately, the original intercorrelations between all the individual tests are not reported so that the evaluations recommended by Campbell and Fiske are not possible. Hopefully, a study based on a multitrait-multi-method-multisetting design employing reliable tests on an adequate sampling

of subjects will be done making possible the different analytic approaches used in this paper as well as those recommended by Campbell and Fiske in order to elucidate more directly the questions we are considering. Other traits which would seem relevant for a multitrait design are guilt, achievement motivation, rigidity, conformity-compliance, and social desirability. But these are considerations for the future.

Let us look now at some implications of this double-generalization model and relate them to some research findings.

Intelligence

Hartshorne and May found that IQ was positively correlated with honesty ($r = .344$). Shuttleworth's analysis (Hartshorne et al., 1930) in the last volume showed a strong relationship ($r = .776$) between honesty and consistency in behavior, i.e., honest persons tended to be consistent in behavior and dishonest persons tended to be inconsistent. As might be expected from these relationships, intelligence and consistency of honest behavior were also related ($r = .226$). These results are consonant with speculations from our model that the generality of honesty would be positively related to intelligence. The temptation is to end presenting the data from their analyses at this point. But all the evidence is not so strongly in this direction. When honesty is partialed out, the relation between consistency and intelligence tends to disappear. The relation between IQ and honesty remains significant at .216 even when controlling on consistency. As the authors noted, they may have partialed out too much when they controlled on honesty and consistency so that there is probably some real association between IQ and consistency. But the results suggest that intelligence is more strongly related to behavioral honesty than to consistency. Our model would indicate that IQ should be especially relevant for tests of knowledge of a consensual moral code. This assumes that conceptual generalization will be positively related to IQ. We would expect greater verbal mediation from persons with higher IQ as they should be more capable of abstracting the moral implications of the different test situations. Thus, at least part of the greater consistency of honest persons who tend also to have higher IQs may be accounted for by the cognitive generalization gradient of our model. As we are unable to separate the cognitive tests from the behavioral tests used by Hartshorne and May, we are also unable to test our speculations regarding these differences between behavioral and cognitive measures.

Age

In line with this interpretation would be the expectation that generality should increase with age. Cognitive moral development has consistently been positively related to age in studies involving children's conceptions of morality (Boehm, 1957; Bronfenbrenner, 1962; Durkin, 1959; Harrower, 1935; Hoffman, 1961; Kohlberg, 1958, 1963; Lerner, 1937; MacRae, 1954; Medinnus, 1959; Morris, 1958; Peel, 1959; Piaget, 1932). Experimental results also indicate that with age, verbal mediation, and the control such verbalizations have on overt choice behavior increase (Kendler *et al.*, 1960; Kuenne, 1946; Luria, 1957). However, in *Studies in Deceit* (Hartshorne & May, 1928) age was slightly negatively correlated with honesty. The tendency for a negative correlation of age with honesty when honesty is positively correlated with consistency is not in harmony with our model. In this case the further analysis in Volume 3 (Hartshorne *et al.*, 1930) reveals data supporting our predictions. For the two groups of children studied intensively in this volume it was found

that both groups became more consistent with age but the high social class children became more honest and those from the lower-class school became more dishonest.

Social Class

Kohn (1959) has found that there are different value systems characteristic of the working class and the middle class. The working-class parents stress the immediate implications of a child's act and want the child to stay out of trouble by not doing the "wrong" thing, whereas the middle-class parents want their child to understand the implications of his behavior so that he chooses to do the "right" thing. If these interpretations are correct, one would expect that the child rearing practices of middle-class parents would be more conducive to their children's discriminating the moral implications of different settings and performing an honest response than would be the child rearing practices of the working-class parents. These different value systems and presumably related child rearing practices should produce both greater situational generalization and greater cognitive generalization in the middle-class children than in the working-class children. We should expect these differences to be reflected in greater generality on tests of morality of both a behavioral response type and a cognitive knowledge kind. The findings that behavioral honesty was positively correlated with social class and that the consistency for the upper social class group was significantly greater than that for the lower-class group strongly support this expectation. Their analysis showing age related to consistency with the upper social class group increasing in consistency faster than the lower-class group is also directly in line with our model. Researchers using cognitive measures of morality have consistently found their measures related to social class (Aronfreed, 1961;

Boehm, 1957; Bronfenbrenner, 1962; Durkin, 1959; Hoffman, 1961; Kohlberg, 1958, 1959, 1963; Lerner, 1937; MacRae, 1954), but in general have not analyzed their data to test for differences in consistency between classes.

Sex

Of the eight types of tests used by Hartshorne and May (1928), three showed significant, and three more nearly significant, differences in girls cheating more than boys. They attributed these differences to the possibility that girls were more motivated to succeed on a school task and to conform to accepted standards than were boys. One of these tests was the lying test which measured the student's tendency to score himself as conforming to acceptable standards. The other tests were more directly behavioral in a temptation situation. Generally, girls tend to be more verbally developed than boys (Goodenough, 1954) on intelligence and achievement tests, although there are exceptions (Bayley, 1957). Girls are also rated as being more honest than boys (Hartshorne & May, 1928) and as developing a conscience earlier than boys (Sears, Maccoby, & Levin, 1957). In light of these findings, we might predict from our verbal generalization model that girls would be more consistent than boys. But there is also the evidence that girls tended actually to cheat more and also that girls tended to make up the "pure" (i.e., consistently) deceptive group, and boys the pure honest group in Hartshorne and May (1928). It would seem that the prediction would have to be limited to verbal or cognitive measures of morality, what Brogden (1940) called "acceptance of the moral code" factor, so that girls

would evidence greater generality of morality only on verbal measures. Barbu (1951) reports sex differences for areas involved in a questionnaire lying test. Boys lied more than girls about power and courage, whereas girls lied more about being morally good. One interpretation for these differences is that they reflect real differences in behavior, i.e., boys' behavior is more courageous and assertive than girls,' whereas girls' behavior does conform to "goodness" more than boys' behavior. But it is also possible that the cognitive measures of acceptance of the moral code are mainly addressed to the areas of morality which are more salient to girls who therefore are more motivated than boys to distort their responses. If this were so, girls would tend to appear more moral than boys on such tests which are not measuring lying or distortion but only cognitive acceptance of morality. Aronfreed (1961) has shown that girls appear to be much more concerned with display of being "good" than are boys. Be this as it may, why is it that boys should tend to be more honest and more consistent on the Hartshorne and May temptation tests but girls tend to appear more conforming to the general moral code as measured by verbal tests or ratings by parents or teachers? The model we are proposing would lead us to investigate the possibility of differential child rearing practices contingent on the sex of the child and of differential role modeling by the parents.[13]

[13] It is suggested here that direct methods of observation or experimental designs in the home or in natural situations be used to obtain measures of child rearing. It seems that the important differences in child rearing for boys and girls, especially at very young ages, may be too subtle to be measured by interview techniques.

Some Origins of Concern for Others[1]

David Rosenhan

I take it that the central message of American experimental psychology over the past fifty years has been that if man seeks anything, he seeks to avoid pain and to gain his own rewards. I take it also that a similar message seems to emerge from psychoanalytic psychology over the same period: man is a drive-reducing organism that seeks to satisfy its instinctual concerns.

Both of these psychologies have become more differentiated during these fifty years than the above statements imply. Yet this central concept has undergone little change. Man is integumented (Allport, 1960), these psychologies would hold, concerned with his own skin and little else.

There have always been phenomena that challenge this concept of man's concerns, phenomena for which there are few experimental data. An insistent one is that man sometimes seems much more concerned with the rewards and sufferings of *others*. Indeed, concern for others occurs throughout the animal kingdom (see, for example, Hebb & Thompson, 1954; Lorenz, 1952). These theoretically troublesome phenomena include the abiding concern of parents for children, attachment to mates and lovers, courage in war and other circumstances when the actor's life is at stake, rescue behavior, devotion to altruistic causes, principled behaviors that involve enormous sacrifices, charitability, generosity to the unknown and unthanking poor. All of these are altruistic acts in the sense in which Comte intended that term: they reflect concern for others. And none of them are immediately reconcilable with current theory.

Of course, it is possible to fit altruistic behaviors into the current theoretical frameworks. Mowrer (1960, p. 435), for example, raises the possibility that what we call courage may simply be the absence of fear where fear is ordinarily expected. Glover (1925), Freud (1937), and Fenichel (1945), in the psychoanalytic tradition, suggest that the dynamics of guilt and self-destruction and conflicts about masculinity may variously account for these acts. Theoretical possibility is not a substitute for evidence, however, and we need to begin to assemble hard data to determine whether altruistic phenomena support or injure current psychological conceptions.

This essay summarizes some of the evidence concerning the origins and dy-

[1] It is a pleasure to acknowledge the efforts of assistants and students who have energetically facilitated the research reported here, among them Anne Burrowes Bloxom, Janet Cuca, Michael Davenport, Fred Hipp, Jr., Irene Kostin, David Mantell, Edward Nystrom, Barry Ranieri, Anita F. Thompson and Patricia Warren. Henrietta Gallagher performed the statistical computations. Professor Glenn M. White joined me in the design and conduct of several of these studies and was a major contributor to the development of the research. A considerable debt is owed Professors James Bryan, Perry London, and Silvan S. Tomkins, all of whom contributed generously of their ideas and critique to these studies. The studies were supported in part by Grant # 1 PO 1 HD 01762 from the National Institute of Child Health and Human Development to the Educational Testing Service, and by Grant # MH-HD 13893 from the National Institute of Mental Health to the writer.

This paper is adapted from a colloquium given to the Department of Psychology, University of California at Berkeley, January 11, 1968.

namics of concern for others. It begins with a study of committed altruistic independence as it occurs in the everyday environment, a study that was intended to provide theoretical clues to an understanding of this phenomenon. It then examines some laboratory experiments designed to test aspects of a theory and to more clearly elucidate the phenomenon.

CHILDREN OF ANAK:
THE ALTRUISM OF COMMITTED
CIVIL RIGHTS WORKERS

Several years ago, as part of a project that sought to discover the relations between cognition and behavior, I and my laboratory associates assembled field data on people who were associated with, or sympathetic to, the civil rights movement. Three concerns of that study are relevant to this discussion. First, in our study we wanted to examine whether the theories of altruistic behavior were reflected in the altruism that was apparently involved in civil rights activity. Second, we hoped to compile a detailed oral history of altruistic behavior which might be valuable to scholars in many disciplines, particularly when combined with other such histories (a hope, it might be mentioned, that was not quite fulfilled). Finally, we hoped that the data emerging from this study might yield hypotheses that could be subjected to experimental scrutiny. With regard to this last intention, it is clear that field studies have the singular virtue of coming close to what is going on in the "real" world and therefore of directing one's attention to hypotheses that are maximally relevant to that world. But field studies also suffer a liability; they provide too many data whose interrelations can rarely be made clear. Nevertheless, our hope was to illuminate the matrix of variables associated with altruistic behavior and to examine, separately and together, the relative impact of these variables.

Interviewing began early in 1963 and continued through 1964. It concentrated on the events leading up to the spring and summer of 1961, when activity on behalf of civil rights appeared to reach a peak; marches and freedom rides occurred throughout the South and in Washington, D. C. With the cooperation of the Student Nonviolent Coordinating Committee and the Congress of Racial Equality we were able to obtain the names and addresses of those who had taken part in these efforts or had supported them financially. We interviewed most of the respondents in the North and also made two trips to the South. When we explained the nature of our study, nearly all who were approached consented to be interviewed. Agreeing was no small matter; the interviews often lasted as long as twelve hours, in two- and three-hour sessions. We are grateful for the cooperation that was given.

Generally speaking, the interview was conic in structure; it began with general questions and ended with specific ones. It was concerned with three areas:

1. Facts of involvement. How the respondents became involved in the movement (precipitating circumstances), the course and nature of their involvement, the dates, the people worked with, the perceived and actual risks (where relevant), the degree to which missions were accomplished, and the material and psychological gains and losses were discussed. We "trained" the respondents to give us as much information as possible by letting them know that everything they had to say was of interest to us.

2. Personal history. Relationships with parents, siblings, peers, teachers, authorities, vocational and educational history, family vocation and social history, estimates of perceived and actual social class, health and "cosmetic" history were elicited.

3. *Perceptions of motivations for participating.* We elicited the respondents' views of their own behaviors, of the behaviors of others who were like them or different from them, and of the opposition.

Black respondents were interviewed by a black, and white respondents by a white. Both interviewers were well experienced. Nearly 90 people were interviewed, and we obtained 68 usable interviews—36 from people who participated in civil rights work and 32 from those who sympathized with and gave financial support to it. (In the main, the other interviews were pilot studies in which we attempted to structure the interview schedule and make it fairly constant, to train the interviewers, and to begin to sense what would be the most profitable and theoretically the most interesting direction for the interview to take.)

After we examined and coded the interviews, and compared those who physically participated in civil rights work with those who only supported the movement —and this was to be the major comparison in the study—we did not feel much scientific compensation. There were some findings regarding the role and nature of conformity pressures that were of interest and that require further examination. But on the whole, the comparisons were disappointing, and I shall not have much more to say about them here. Rather, I want to focus on some rich and thoroughly accidental findings that emerged from the interviews of the active respondents.

On reading and rereading these interviews, we noticed that we had two subsamples among those who were committed to civil rights. The first group had been involved in civil rights only to the extent of having participated in one or two freedom rides. The second had been active for at least a year, often longer, mainly in the South, in such projects as voter registration and education of the underprivileged. The numbers of respondents in each of these subsamples is shown in Table 1.

Table 1

1961 Sample: Current (1964) Activity Status of Civil Rights Workers

1	Fully Committed	Partially Committed
Negro	3	5
White	12	16

Because we have yet to find nonpejorative labels for these two groups, we have accepted the convenient labels of "partially committed" for the first group and "fully committed" for the second.

The Role and Function of the Altruistic Socializer

It was not difficult to obtain reliable retrospective reports from the respondents regarding who they felt was the main socializing parent during their childhood. Moreover, one could confirm from the content of the interviews whether the respondent's conscious report was accurate. We found two important differences between the fully and the partially committed with regard to the function of this socializer.

Table 2 summarizes our judgment regarding the quality of relationship between the socializing parent and the respondent during the latter's formative years, and also, as it turns out, until the time of the interview. Fully committed respondents seem to have maintained a positive, cordial, warm, and respecting relationship with their parent. True, there were disagreements. True also, these disagreements often extended to matters of considerable substance and importance to both the respondent and his parent, including the matter of whether the respondent should be a participant in civil rights activities. Despite all this, one easily sensed considerable fondness between parent and child.

Table 2

1961 Sample: Affective Valence Towards the Primary Socializing Parent

	Fully Committed	Partially Committed
Positive	12	3
Negative or distinctly ambivalent	3	18

The partially committed described the parent in negative or ambivalent terms. A substantial proportion described their relations with the socializing parent as actually hostile during their formative years, and at best cool and avoidant at the time they were interviewed. One sensed discomfort, often anxiety and hostility, and sometimes guilt of an unspecified nature flowing from child to parent, and perhaps vice versa.

More striking than the quality of relationship, however, was the cognitive substance of the relationship. Both sets of socializers were concerned with moral issues; indeed, during the first coding when we examined "moral concerns in the socializing agent" we could locate no differences. But one or both of the parents of the fully committed were themselves fully committed to an altruistic cause during some extended period of the respondents' formative years, while the parents of the partially committed reportedly evidenced considerable ambivalence and confusion about the nature of particular moralities. At least it seemed so to the respondents, so much so that we had occasion to call their moral confrontation with their parents a "crisis of

hypocrisy." Table 3 summarizes the coarse grain of these findings.

Table 3

1961 Sample: Evidence for Discrepancy between Teaching and Practice by a Socializing Parent

	Fully Committed	Partially Committed
Discrepancy present	2	13
Discrepancy absent	11	3
Evidence unclear or absent	2	5

Some of the respondents' actual remarks may be illuminating in this regard. One of the fully committed reported that "my father carried me on his shoulders during the Sacco-Vanzetti parades"; another described how his father fought on the side of the Loyalists in the Spanish Civil War; a third described how his mother "felt close to Jesus and was warmed by His teachings. She devoted her entire life to Christian education." Finally, another respondent's father was outraged by the Nazi atrocities and, though overage and apparently disqualified on grounds of health, was finally accepted into the military during the Second World War. In short, we seemed to have found the presence of altruistic models in the backgrounds of the committed altruists, models whose behavior apparently influenced the course of their children's activities. The matter may not be so simple, as we shall see when we examine the laboratory studies of altruistic behavior. But this was our working hypothesis after we analyzed the interview data from this project.

Among parental socializers of the partially committed, there was evidence of a discrepancy between what was preached and what was practiced. A number of the respondents indicated that their parents told them one thing, but practiced another. Often these discrepancies reflected inconsistencies in culturally stereotyped principles of conduct, but regardless of source, it was clear that the respondents had noted them and responded angrily. One respondent literally railed against his father, who had often preached a stern honesty but vigorously condoned dishonesty toward members of a cultural outgroup. The respondent was startled by the vigor of his own expressed anger, remarking that he had not even thought about these incidents in more than a decade.

Although I am not yet committed to a theoretical view of the relevance of the "crisis of hypocrisy" to partial altruistic commitment, I am tempted by the following speculation: the child who is morally polarized by his socializers and is thereby angered will be severe in his judgment of his elder if, and only if, he is able to see himself as "good" and the elder as "bad" or "hypocritical" on the moral dimension in question. Avowed sinners, as we know, are quite gentle in their judgments of others; only those who believe themselves without sin can afford to throw stones. But the child, and subsequently the adult, has little basis for internalizing or believing in his moral purity, since he has been exposed to moral models who, insofar as their deeds are concerned, are ambiguous at best and repellent at worst. In order to retain his judgment of bad others, he needs to reassure himself that he is morally good. Going on a freedom ride is sufficient to that need, and having gone on one, there is no real need to engage in another. The self, as it were, is already convinced of its worthiness.

Those who grew up in an altruistic environment, on the other hand, respond to the social need for civil rights from an entirely different matrix. They have learned, by loving precept and percept, to respond easily to the needs of others.

Such a response is called forth by the structure of their perceptions of the environment. This is the meaning of identification: an intense emotional experience, rich in behavioral and cognitive contents, that imprints a relatively enduring attitudinal and behavioral matrix, a matrix that proves relatively resistant to the pressures and temptations of the immediate surroundings.

In short, these data lead us to believe that the differences between the fully and the partially committed are greater than might simply appear from the behavioral differences in involvement in civil rights activity. For the partially committed, the act of participation is concomitantly an act of personal reassurance. For the fully committed, commitment is very much a matter of concern for others. The altruist in psychoanalytic literature (Coles, 1963; Fishman & Solomon, 1964; Solomon & Fishman, 1964), who is beset by one or another conflict, is probably our partially committed. Indeed, we find support for this belief from the fact that half of our partially committed respondents had spent some time in psychotherapy, while none of the fully committed had. In short, there is more to full altruistic commitment than the reduction of tension and the dynamics of guilt.

In closing this section, I cannot resist one further observation on the difference between the partially and the fully committed, this one dealing with the length of the interviews. The average interview with the partially committed was one hour longer than with the fully committed. That difference was totally unexpected, indeed quite surprising, since the nature of the interview gave the partially committed less to say. The first section of the interview was a detailed description of the involvement. Those who had been on one or two freedom rides surely had less to tell than those whose involvement had extended over a

considerable period. And indeed, this was
true. But the partially committed more
than made up for their shortcoming here
in the third section of the interview,
which dealt with self-perception and perception of others and which rapidly
drifted into a discussion of the philosophy of civil rights. Here, the partially
committed were brilliant and compelling,
offering insight after insight in inexhaustible profusion. The fully committed,
on the other hand, had considerably less
to say. It was not that they were not as
bright: on the dimensions of education
and verbal intelligence (the latter assessed
from the interview), there were no significant differences between the groups.
Rather, the fully committed came to the
point directly and simply. Perhaps they
had exhausted themselves during the earlier parts of the interview. It is also possible that the relationship between
cognition and behavior was affected by
the length of the interview: when one
of them is amplified, the other may be
constricted. Amplified cognition and in-
cisive speech may have served the partially committed as a substitute for
behavioral involvement, perhaps in the
manner described by sensory tonic theory
(Werner & Wapner, 1952). On the other
hand, having acted, the fully committed
had less need to speak at great length.

THE CONSTRUCTIVE REBEL AND
THE OBEDIENT LAMB:
AN EXPERIMENT ON
CONSTRUCTIVE REBELLION

The field studies were designed to provide hypotheses about the nature and
development of prosocial behaviors that
might be further investigated under con-
'trolled laboratory conditions. For example, one observation was that exposure
to prosocial models facilitated prosocial
behavior in the observer—a finding that

can be subjected to experimental verification.

Our first experiment[2] was concerned, in
part, with the effects of disobedient models on obedience. The experimental paradigm was similar to that used by Milgram
(1963) in a series of brilliant experiments
that examined the extent to which people obey a legitimate authority. Milgram's
basic experimental paradigm is straightforward. Two subjects come to a psychological laboratory and are told that the
scientist is investigating the effects of
punishment on learning. In this experiment, the punishment, electric shocks, is
administered in increasingly severe doses
each time the learner makes a mistake on
a paired associates test. After having been
fully instructed, the subjects draw straws
to determine who will be the learner and
who the teacher. The teacher then straps
the learner to a chair, tapes the electrodes
on his hands, and returns to a large and
enormously impressive instrument panel,
on which are clearly marked shock dos-
ages that range from 15 to 450 volts in
steps of 15 volts. Above each dosage is
a lever, and the teacher's task is to press
one of these levers each time the learner
makes a mistake. To convince the teacher
that the shock levers actually give shocks,
the experimenter gives him a sample
shock of 45 volts. The "learner," however,
is a stooge; he only pretends to receive
the shock and to feel pain.

The experiment then begins. The
teacher reads a long list of paired associates to the learner. He then reads a
second list in which the second element
of each pair is embedded in four alterna-

[2] A more elaborate description of this study, including its rationale, method, precautions taken
to insure the welfare of the subjects, and the
methods used to determine the degree of insight
the subjects had into the experimental procedures, will be found in D. Rosenhan, "Obedience
and rebellion: Observations on the Milgram
three-party paradigm," in preparation.

tives and requires the learner to produce the correct alternative to the first member of the pair. Each time the learner fails to answer correctly he is given a shock; first 15 volts, then 30 volts, then 45, and so on. The learner protests, at first weakly then more vigorously as the shock increases. The teacher turns to the experimenter to ask advice. The experimenter responds, "Please continue the experiment." And the experiment continues. The critical question is: At what point will the teacher refuse to continue to administer shock?

Milgram's findings were as distressing as they were unexpected: nearly 70 percent of his subjects continued to shock the learner through the entire shock series. The teachers protested vigorously to the experimenter and some of them were emotionally upset, but they nevertheless continued to participate in the experiment simply because the experimenter told them to continue.

In our experiment, four conditions were used. The first was quite similar to that used by Milgram and described above. For the remaining three, the subject who was subsequently to be the teacher arrived in the experimental room and was asked to wait until another subject finished "teaching." He thus could watch another subject—a model—perform in one of three ways:

(1) The humane model. In this condition, the model teacher continued to protest but nevertheless to obey the experimenter until he had passed 210 volts and the learner's protests seemed unbearable. He then turned to the experimenter and courteously informed him that he simply could not continue the experiment because the learner was in great pain. The interchange between model and experimenter stressed the plight of the learner and resulted in the teacher's refusal to continue and his leaving the room.

(2) The illegitimizing model. The model continued to protest but to deliver shock, as in the first condition. When he passed 210 volts, he turned to the experimenter and asked if the experimenter was a member of the faculty. The experimenter shook his head. The model then asked with some surprise if he was a graduate student. The experimenter looked away in some embarrassment. Model then asked with indignation whether the experimenter was an undergraduate. Again, no answer. Model: "Is your professor in town?" Again, no answer. "You mean you're just a college freshman and you're conducting an experiment like this? Asking me to fry someone? . . ." In evident outrage, the model refuses to continue and stomps out of the room.

(3) The obedient model. In this condition, the model protested as had the others, but unlike them, continued to administer the full 450 volts.

The results of this experiment are shown in Table 4. Nearly 80 percent of

Table 4

Obedience and Disobedience According to Experimental Condition among Subjects Who Believed the Experiment Was "Real"

Experimental Condition	Obedient	Dis-obedient	Total
Base rate	17 (85%)	3	20
Obedient model	15 (88%)	2	17
Humane model	11 (58%)	8	19
Illegitimizing model	10 (53%)	9	19
	52	22	75

$\chi^2 = 8.99$; df $= 3$; $.05 > p < .025$

the subjects (as teachers) in the no-model condition obeyed the experimenter and administered the full complement of voltage. A similar proportion of the subjects who had observed an obedient model obeyed the experimenter. There was no difference between subjects who had observed either of the two disobedient models: more than 50 percent of these subjects obeyed the experimenter.

Even after observing a disobedient model, a majority of the subjects continued to obey the experimenter, despite the fact that nearly all subjects protested in the course of their effort that the shock was terribly painful, if not downright dangerous, to the learner. On a subsequent interview, the "teachers" showed that they were aware of the averseness of the procedure; almost all of them refused to participate in the experiment again, this time as learners.

While we had verified our hypothesis that observation of a prosocial model, whether humane or illegitimizing, facilitates prosocial disobedience in the observer, when one considers the painfulness of the procedure and the elaborateness of our disobedient model conditions, the effects obtained were weak indeed. Such weak effects will be found throughout the series of experiments described here, and they are also found in other studies relevant to these issues (see Bryan & Test, 1967; Darley & Latané, 1968). The reader will note that similar weak effects are found in the natural environment, and he may want to speculate on that matter.

We tested two areas of hypotheses from the civil rights study on children. First, we examined the hypotheses about hypocrisy in a series of experiments (see Rosenhan, Frederick & Burrowes, 1968; Rosenhan & Hilmo, in preparation[3]) that I shall not discuss here. Second, we began a series of studies designed to assess what impact prior social relationships and observation of altruistic models had on the

[3] Rosenhan, D., & Hilmo, J. "Maintenance of an imposed behavior standard as a function of method of socialization." In preparation.

acquisition and elicitation of charitable behavior.

EXPERIMENTS ON CHILDREN'S CHARITABILITY

In an early study (Rosenhan & White, 1967), we attempted to simulate positive and negative relationships with children during brief interaction periods. Establishing a positive relationship was, for that experiment, a matter of positively reinforcing a variety of the child's behaviors, while the negative relationship was established by negatively reinforcing his behaviors. The child and the adult then took turns playing with an attractive miniature bowling game. Each time the adult won, he took two gift certificates and ceremoniously reached past the child in order to contribute one of his gift certificates to the Trenton Orphans' Fund, a fund we had established for our own experimental purposes. The gift certificates were, in fact, money surrogates, redeemable at a well-known neighborhood toy and candy store (with parental signature), and used in these experiments because we wanted to be certain that the children were really giving up something prized if they decided to contribute anything to the orphans' fund. While the child played, the experimenter looked the other way, jumping up and down and pounding his hands as if waiting impatiently for his turn. This was an attempt to minimize the degree of tacit approval or disapproval that the child might feel was warranted by his donation behavior.

When this game was completed, the experimenter pretended he had to leave and asked the child if he would like to play the game by himself. Each child agreed, and the experimenter told him to "lock the door so that no one bothers you" and to return to class when he had finished. It was made clear that he would not see the experimenter again. He was left alone with several hundred dollars' worth of gift certificates and allowed to play until the game's buzzer went off.

In this experiment, some of our hypotheses were put to a difficult test. Note that there was a minimal prior relationship with the experimenter. Note also that the child's donation behavior was not reinforced. And note finally, that we encouraged the child to believe that he was alone when the experimenter left. The concern was with the child's internalized behavior, not with his ability to conform or comply. We were successful in the formal aspects of the experiment. Each child was interviewed after the game-playing by an experimenter (not the one with whom he had played) who was ostensibly signing up volunteers for extracurricular activities. Since one of these activities was bowling, she was able to indicate that she had heard that there had been a bowling game in the school, and to ask the children what their perceptions of it had been. Even when the interviewer encouraged the child to give expression to his experimental insights ("You mean you were left there alone with all that money and no one was watching you?"), no child realized that he had been observed, though several said that there might have been "some trick."

Our first concern was whether the observation of a charitable model elicited internalized charitability in the children. As Table 4 shows, this was true. None of the control children who had not observed a model contributed to the charity, while nearly half of the experimental children did. Altruistic models, even in a narrow laboratory situation, serve to facilitate altruism in children.

Our second concern turned on the question of the relationship between conformity in the model's presence and internalization in his absence. As Table 5 indicates, 51 of the 57 children who internalized the charitable behavior—nearly

Table 5

Altruistic Responses of Ss Who Were or Were Not Exposed to Models

		Exposed to Model		
		Yes	No	Totals
Gave in model's absence	Yes	57	0	57
	No	63	10	73
Totals		120	10	130

90 percent—had conformed in the presence of the model. (This is to be considered a state phenomenon, not a trait; by statistical test, these 51 children differed also from the 10 controls.) Thus, it was both observing an altruistic model and the opportunity to corehearse with that model that elicited altruistic behavior in the child.

We felt that this finding added a new dimension of meaning to our interviews with the civil rights' workers. When a respondent says, "My father carried me on his shoulders during the Sacco-Vanzetti parades," he may be describing not only an observational phenomenon but also one of rehearsal—that is, "I was with him during those parades." Similarly, respondents whose parents sought military duty in the Second World War may very well have vicariously experienced something of that war with the parent. Although we did not think to obtain this material explicitly during these interviews, it is just possible that on some level, they corehearsed the altruistic behavior with the parent.

In the matter of demonstrating the effects of prior relationship with the model on altruistic behavior, we were not at all successful, as Figure 1 indicates. No real differences obtained between the positive and negative relationships. Some interesting sex differences in conformity and internalization seemed to emerge as

Table 6

Relationship between Giving in the Presence and the Absence of a Model

| | | Gave in model's presence (conformity) | | | | | | |
| | | Yes | | | No | | | |
		Boys	Girls	Total	Boys	Girls	Total	All Ss
Gave in model's absence	Yes	28	23	51	3	3	6	57
(internalization)	No	9	16	25	20	18	38	63
Totals		37	39	76	23	21	44	120

a function of prior contact with the model, but in the matter that was of central concern to us—the effects of prior positive and negative relationships—there were no significant findings. Of course, this may be due to the briefness of the period of prior relationship to which the children were exposed, and we intend to examine this matter in greater detail in subsequent experiments.

OBSERVATION, REHEARSAL, OR BOTH?

As a result of this experiment, we became interested in understanding more about the nature of the observation-

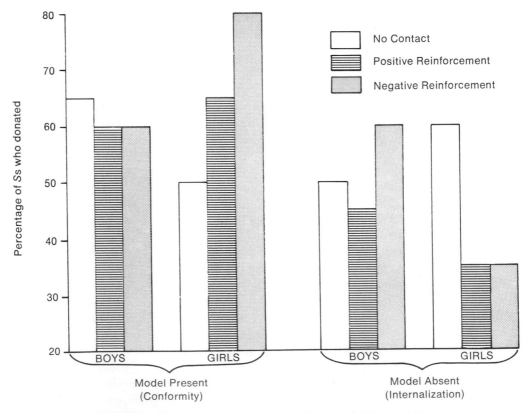

Figure 1   Conformity and internalization as a function of prior relationship with the model. (From Rosenhan & White, 1967).

rehearsal sequence and its effect on internalization. If you look carefully again at Table 5, you will notice that nearly 90 percent of the children who donated in the absence of the model, donated also in his presence. This finding raises an interesting question: Was it the observation of the model that was most influential for the subsequent internalization, or was it the rehearsal? Or was it the combination? This experiment could not possibly answer these questions, since observation and rehearsal were purposely confounded. The next experiment, however, performed by Glenn White (1967), seemed a first step towards understanding this matter.

Three experimental treatments were employed. In the first, called *enforced rehearsal*, the child was required to contribute to the charity in the presence of the experimenter without, however, having observed a model do so. This situation was designed to assess the impact of giving in the presence of an adult (rehearsal), on subsequent internalization. The second condition was identical to the one we examined earlier in the section, *observation and voluntary rehearsal*. The third condition examined the effects of observation alone. In it, the child observed a model play the game and donate to the charity, but did not play or rehearse in the presence of the model. In a third situation, a control condition was imposed. The child was simply asked to play the game, and, if he wanted to, to contribute to the orphans. As in the earlier experiment, the experimenter or model departed after describing the treatment and the children played the game again while alone.

We had no doubt that the enforced rehearsal condition would have the greatest immediate impact on the child's private behavior because any instructional condition gives a child a fixed structure within which to play the game. But we expected that a second exposure to the game would loosen the structure consid-

erably and that children in this condition would be more variable after a few days had elapsed than they had been immediately. The experiment was therefore designed in such a way that children in all of the experimental conditions could play twice: once immediately after they had been trained, and again several days later.

As Figure 2 indicates, we were not disappointed. When children in the enforced rehearsal condition were tested immediately after training (Session 1), they contributed an enormous amount to the Trenton Orphans' Fund, much more than did children in the other conditions. However, when tested again several days later, their performance fell considerably: to or below the level of performance provided by children in the observation and voluntary rehearsal condition. We had similar findings when we examined the *number* of children who internalized (as opposed to the average amount they gave) in the first and second sessions (Figure 3). While nearly all of the enforced rehearsal children gave in the first session, slightly more than half gave during the second session. Their performance was clearly less stable than those in the observation and voluntary rehearsal condition.

One might argue that the variable behavior demonstrated by the children in the enforced rehearsal condition was due to the fact that, having given in the first session, they experienced no need to give in the second. They had already satisfied their obligation, whereas children in the observation and voluntary rehearsal simply had not. Internal analyses, however, indicate that this position is untenable. Correlations between contributions during Sessions I and II for subjects in the observation and voluntary rehearsal condition was .67. Further analyses indicate that this figure was not inflated by the number of nongivers in both sessions. Correlations between Sessions I and II for the other conditions were substantially

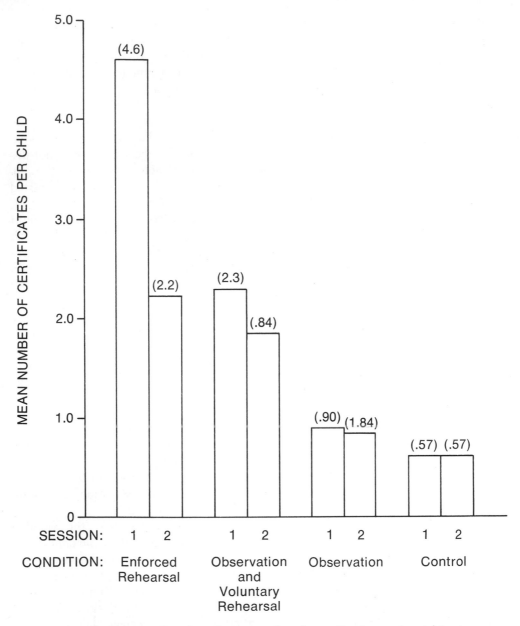

Figure 2   Mean number of certificates contributed according to experimental treatment and session. (Modified from White, 1967).

lower (enforced rehearsal, .38; observation, .40).

We have two further reasons for believing that the dynamics associated with enforced rehearsal are quite different in kind from those involved in observation and rehearsal. The first has to do with the rigidity of the child's performance during the first session. In each experimental condition, there were six opportunities to contribute gift certificates to the orphans. If, during the first game, a child in the enforced rehearsal condition contributed on each and every oppor-

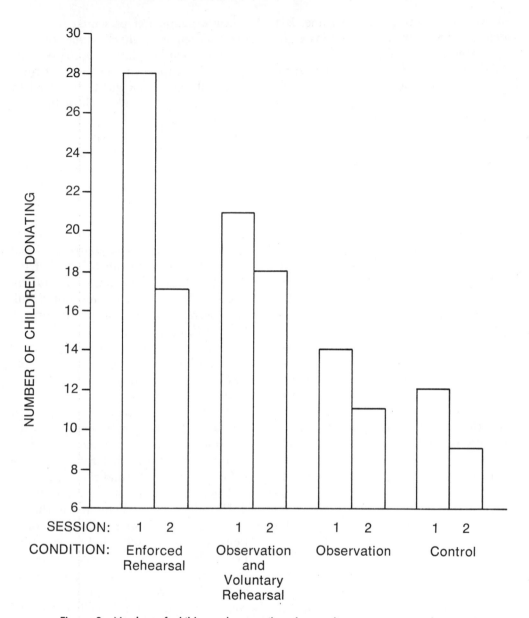

Figure 3 Number of children who contributed according to experimental treatment and session. (Modified from White, 1967).

tunity, it was extremely likely that he would contribute at least one certificate during the second session. If, on the other hand, he failed to contribute during the first game on *every* trial, it was extremely *unlikely* that he would contribute at all during the second session. In short, if the child had broken the rule at all during the first game, he broke it with impunity during the second. Such rigidity did not mark children in the observation and voluntary rehearsal conditions. Although they observed a model donate on every trial, they commonly did not give on every trial during the first game. But such rule flexibility did not eliminate giving during the second game.

The second reason has to do with stealing behavior during the experiment. You will recall that during the internalization trials, the children were left alone with several hundred dollars worth of gift certificates, strewn about the table in such a way that it was clear that no one would miss a few if they were taken. Stealing was, thus, a salient alternative to giving. As might be expected from the rigidity argument, children in the enforced rehearsal condition did not steal at all—during the first session. During the second session, however, 25 percent of them stole. Compare this to stealing among the children exposed to observation and voluntary rehearsal, where less than five percent stole in either session. We hold, therefore, that effects of enforced rehearsal on charitability during the first session were marked because the instructions established rigid rules for the task. But they are not enduring because as subjects begin to test the rules and fail to suffer consequences, they make up more convenient rules. For children in the observation and voluntary contribution conditions the central focus is on the Orphans' Fund and on their freedom to give or not to give to the orphans. For these children the structure is considerably less rigid: Such rules as exist are voluntary and reasonable, and attention is more easily centered on the plight of the orphans. Consequently, greater consistency and less cheating is found. Similar findings in the context of adult helpfulness have been reported by Horowitz (1968).

All of this, of course, is speculative, but the reader may be interested in one further bit of evidence that is consistent with this formulation. Three weeks after a subsequent experiment that involved some of these conditions and several new ones,

a new experimenter presented herself to the children in each class and thanked them for their help in testing the bowling game. It so happened, she said, that there were still quite a few gift certificates left, and she wanted to give each of the children some additional gift certificates in appreciation of their assistance. She did this, and then mentioned that there was another envelope in the envelope that contained the gift certificates. This envelope contained empty contribution envelopes. If any child so desired, he could put some of his gift certificates in this unmarked envelope and contribute them to charity. For approximately half of the children, the charity was the Trenton Orphans' Fund, while the remaining children were permitted to contribute to UNICEF. Contributions were, of course, relatively anonymous, since the contribution envelopes were unmarked, and the children left their donations in a basket as they were leaving class.

We had, of course, recorded the gift certificate numbers, and could trace the contributions to the donors. And it shortly became clear that children in the enforced rehearsal condition gave less, and generalized in voluntary giving less to UNICEF than did children in the observation and voluntary rehearsal conditions. This is precisely what we expected. For children in the enforced rehearsal conditions, donating was rigidly associated with the game context, so they gave considerably less outside of that context.

COGNITIVE DEVELOPMENT AND CONCERN FOR OTHERS

Observation of an altruistic model the child liked and voluntary corehearsal with him may be necessary to the promotion of altruism in the observer (the child in these experiments) but, according to our current thinking, they are by no means sufficient. Also necessary is a well-prepared *cognitive-affective* matrix in the observer.

There is a lot of evidence that norms of social responsibility (Berkowitz, 1968; Berkowitz & Connor, 1966; Berkowitz & Daniels, 1963, 1964; Daniels & Berkowitz, 1963; Goranson & Berkowitz, 1966) and reciprocity (Gouldner, 1960) are necessary in the performance of altruistic acts. The bases for these norms presumably lie in the altruist's capacity to relinquish his personal perspectives and to perceive and experience the universe from the perspective of another, in this instance, a person

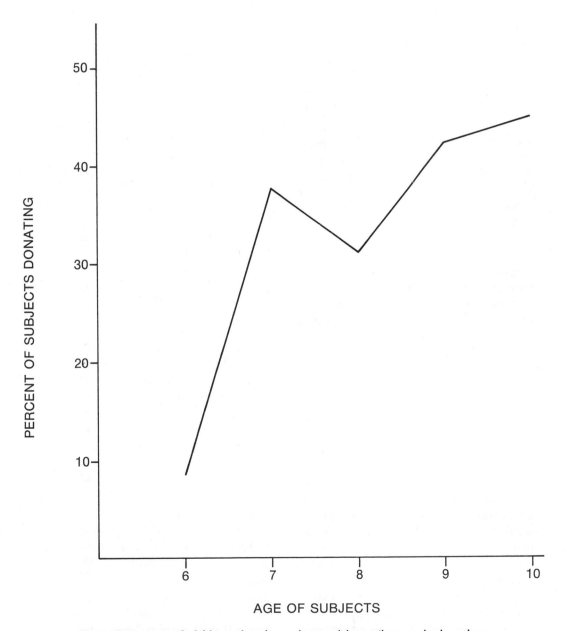

Figure 4 Percent of children who observed a model contribute and who subsequently internalized, by age.

in need. To the extent that this capacity is developed, we hold, is the observation of an altruistic model meaningfully internalized.

The results of experiments with children appear to be consistent with this view. Six-year-old children are still relatively egocentric, unable to take easily the role of another (Piaget, 1926; Flavell, 1966). And, as Figure 4 indicates, fewer six-year-olds than older children (who have observed a model contribute to charity and have had the opportunity to corehearse with him) contribute to the Trenton Orphans' Fund when alone. The lower incidence of contributors among six-year-olds is clearly *not* a matter of their failure to *acquire* the necessary behaviors from the model, since the behaviors involved are neither mentally nor physically complex. Rather we would urge that young children's feelings for others and their capacity to understand the needs of others are relatively muted compared to their capacity to experience their own desires for as many rewards as they can earn. And because the behavior of the model is only vaguely relevant to their own understandings, they do not implement it when alone.

If this is the case, then an experimental treatment that heightens momentarily the neediness of others, should also increase the incidence of donors among young children. That this is true is seen in Figure 5. The model elaborates on the needs of orphans ("They don't have parents . . . no one to buy them toys or candy or even shoes or clothing . . . And when you and I have Christmas they just won't have any because there's no one to care for them . . . If you want to give some of your pennies to the orphans you can, but you don't have to"). Because the model then makes a donation, many six-year-old children internalize his behaviors and contribute in his absence. Their number remains far below the number of contributing eleven-year-olds, since for the latter the model's elaboration mobilizes elements of a cognitive-affective structure that is already well-formed and quite salient.

SUMMARY

We have made some headway in dealing with the problem posed in the first pages of this paper. Some forms of altruism, particularly that of the partially committed, seem clearly compatible with the descriptions emerging from psychoanalytic literature. Others do not. Nor do these others fit the reward-seeking, punishment-avoiding conceptions of man that arise from experimental psychology. As further evidence is accumulated, the match and fit between these theories and particular kinds of altruistic behavior ought to become clearer.

We know from these studies that observation of a positively regarded altruistic model facilitates altruism in some observers. Moreover, voluntary rehearsal of altruistic behavior with the model greatly increases the likelihood that altruism will be internalized in the observer. Finally, we speculate that certain cognitive and affective structures need to be relatively well-formed if the model's altruistic behavior is to result in altruism on the part of the observer.

When a child observes a model's performance, it is by no means automatic that he will imitate the performance. Even experimenters who utilize "salient" models, which is to say, models who engage in a variety of "outlandish" tactics designed to capture the observer's attention (Bandura & Walters, 1963), find that some children do not imitate the demonstrated behavior. One can imagine some children saying "that looks like fun, I think I'll try it," and others saying "what a silly thing to do. Not me!" The model's behavior is cognitively processed, and whether or not the child imitates it depends on the linkages that exist between the observed behavior and other structures in the knowledge assembly— the cognitive and affective components that are organized around a particular dimension. With regard to the altruism dimension, we speculate that among the elements in such an assembly are abilities: To experience the role of a needy other; to share a social responsibility norm; and

to experience joy because the receiver will be happy (Aronfreed & Paskal, 1965; Midlarsky & Bryan, 1967). When these elements are present, an altruistic model's behavior is easily incorporated and integrated. When, on the other hand, they are either absent or muted, or when a nonaltruistic knowledge assembly is salient ("Why should I help orphans. I want all I can get."), observation of an altruistic model is not likely to give rise to internalized altruism.

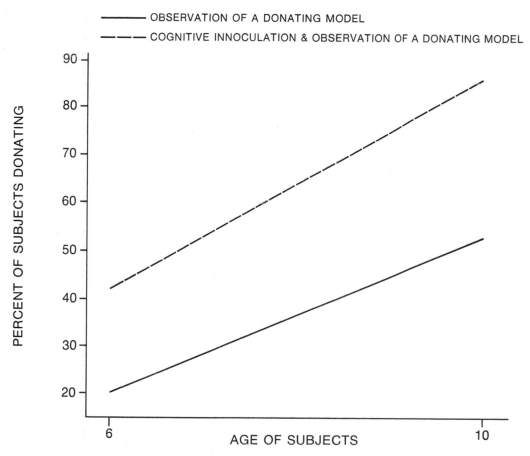

Figure 5 Percent of children who observed a model contribute and who subsequently internalized, by age and experimental treatment.

References Cited

Acker, C. W. An investigation of the variability in repeated psycho-physiological measurements in tranquilized mental patients. *American Psychologist*, 1963, *18*, 454. (Abstract.) Lang & Buss

Adams, J. A. Motor skills. In P. R. Farnsworth (Ed.), *Annual Review of Psychology*, 1964, *15*, 181–202. Breger & McGaugh, p. 316

Adler, N., & Hogan, J. A. Classical conditioning and punishment of an instinctive response in *Bettal splendens*. *Animal Behavior*, 1963, *11*, 351–354. Solomon

Adorno, T. W., Frenkel-Brunswik, E., Levinson, D., & Sanford, N. *The authoritarian personality*. New York: Harper & Row, 1950. Smith

Allinsmith, W. The learning of moral standards. In D. R. Miller, G. E. Swanson, *et al.*, *Inner conflict and defense*. New York: Holt, Rinehart and Winston, 1960. Pp. 141–176. Aronfreed; Burton

Allinsmith, W., & Greening, T. C. Guilt over anger as predicted from parental discipline: A study of superego development. *American Psychologist*, 1955, *10*, 320. (Abstract.) Hoffman & Saltzstein

Allport, G. W. *Personality, a psychological interpretation*. New York: Holt, Rinehart and Winston, 1937. Burton

Allport, G. W. The open system in personality theory. *Journal of Abnormal and Social Psychology*, 1960, *61*, 301–310. Rosenhan

Allport, G. W. Personality: Normal and abnormal. In *Personality and social encounter*. Boston: Beacon, 1960. Pp. 155–168. Smith

Altschule, M. D., & Sulzbach, W. M. Effect of carbon dioxide on acrocyanosis in schizophrenia. *Archives of Neurology and Psychiatry*, 1949, *61*, 44–55. Lang & Buss

Alvarez, R. R. A comparison of the preferences of schizophrenic and normal subjects for rewarded and punished stimuli. Unpublished doctoral dissertation, Duke University, 1957. Buss & Lang

American Psychiatric Association, Committee on Relations between Psychiatry and Psychology. Resolution on relations of medicine and psychology. *American Psychiatric Association Mail Pouch*, October 1954. Mowrer

American Psychological Association, Ad Hoc Planning Group on the Role of the APA in Mental Health Programs and Research. Mental health and the American Psychological Association. *American Psychologist*, 1959, *14*, 820–825. Smith

Andrews, J. D. W. Psychotherapy of phobias. *Psychological Bulletin*, 1966, *66*, 455–480. Weitzman

Angyal, A. The perceptual basis of somatic delusions in a case of schizophrenia. *Archives of Neurology and Psychiatry*, 1935, *34*, 270–279. Lang & Buss

Angyal, A. The experience of the body-self in schizophrenia. *Archives of Neurology and Psychiatry*, 1936, *35*, 1029–1053. Lang & Buss

Angyal, A., & Blackman, N. Vestibular reactivity in schizophrenia. *Archives of Neurology and Psychiatry*, 1940, *44*, 611–620. Lang & Buss

After each entry are the names of authors of the articles in which the reference is cited.

Angyal, A., & Blackman, N. Paradoxical vestibular reactivity in schizophrenia under influence of alcohol, of hyperpnea and CO_2 inhalation. *American Journal of Psychiatry*, 1941, 97, 894–903. Lang & Buss

Angyal, A., & Sherman, N. A. Postural reactions to vestibular stimulation in schizophrenics and normal subjects. *American Journal of Psychiatry*, 1942, 98, 857–862. Lang & Buss

Anker, J., & Walsh, R. Group psychotherapy, a special activity program and group structure in the treatment of chronic schizophrenics. *Journal of Consulting Psychology*, 1961, 25, 476–481. Rachman & Eysenck; Breger & McGaugh, p. 344

Appel, J. B. Punishment and shock intensity. *Science*, 1963, 141, 528–529. Solomon

Arendt, H. *Eichmann in Jerusalem—a report on the banality of evil.* New York: Viking, 1964. Maddi

Arey, L. B. The indirect representation of sexual stimuli by schizophrenic and normal subjects. *Journal of Abnormal and Social Psychology*, 1960, 61, 424–431. Buss & Lang

Arieti, S. *Interpretation of schizophrenia.* New York: Bruner, 1955. Buss & Lang; Lang & Buss

Arieti, S. *American handbook of psychiatry.* New York: Basic Books, 1959. Braginsky and Braginsky

Aronfreed, J. Moral behavior and sex identity. In D. R. Miller, G. E. Swanson, *et al., Inner conflict and defense.* New York: Holt, Rinehart and Winston, 1960. Pp. 177–193. Aronfreed

Aronfreed, J. The nature, variety, and social patterning of moral responses to transgression. *Journal of Abnormal and Social Psychology*, 1961, 63, 223–240. Aronfreed; Hoffman & Saltzstein; Burton

Aronfreed, J. The effects of experimental socialization paradigms upon two moral responses to transgression. *Journal of Abnormal and Social Psychology*, 1963, 66, 437–448. Aronfreed

Aronfreed, J. The origin of self-criticism. *Psychological Review*, 1964, 71, 193–218. Aronfreed.

Aronfreed, J., Cutick, R. A., & Fagan, S. A. Cognitive structure, punishment, and nurturance in the experimental induction of self-criticism. *Child Development*, 1963, 34, 281–294. Aronfreed

Aronfreed, J., & Paskal, V. Altruism, empathy, and the conditioning of positive affect. Unpublished manuscript, University of Pennsylvania, 1965. Rosenhan

Artiss, K. L. *The symptom as communication in schizophrenia.* New York: Grune & Stratton, 1959. Braginsky & Braginsky

Astrup, C. *Schizophrenia: Conditional reflex studies.* Springfield, Ill.: Charles C. Thomas, 1962. Lang & Buss

Atkinson, B. (Ed.) *The selected writings of Ralph Waldo Emerson.* New York: Modern Library, 1940. Maddi

Atkinson, J. W. *An introduction to motivation.* New York: Van Nostrand, 1964. Rachman & Eysenck

Atkinson, R. L., & Robinson, N. M. Paired-associate learning by schizophrenic and normal subjects under conditions of personal and impersonal reward and punishment. *Journal of Abnormal and Social Psychology*, 1961, 62, 322–326. Buss & Lang

Auersperg, A. P. Vom Werden der Angst. *Nervenarzt*, 1958, 29, 193–201. Kessen & Mandler

Ausubel, D. P. *Ego development and the personality disorders.* New York: Grune & Stratton, 1952. Ausubel

Ausubel, D. P. Relationships between psychology and psychiatry: The hidden issues. *American Psychologist*, 1956, 11, 99–105. Ausubel

Ausubel, D. P. Personality disorder is disease. *American Psychologist*, 1961, 16, 69–74. Ausubel

Ax, A. F. Psychological differentiation of emotional states. *Psychosomatic Medicine*, 1953, 15, 433–442. Schachter & Singer

Ayllon, T. Intensive treatment of psychotic behavior by stimulus satiation and food reinforcement. *Behavior Research and Therapy*, 1963, 1, 47–58. Rachman & Eysenck

Ayllon, T., & Michael, J. The psychiatric nurse as a behavioral engineer. *Journal of the Experimental Analysis of Behavior*, 1959, 2, 323–334. Rachman & Eysenck

Azrin, N. H. Some effects of two intermittent schedules of immediate and non-immediate punishment. *Journal of Psychology*, 1956, 42, 8–21. Solomon

Azrin, N. H. Punishment and recovery during fixed-ratio performance. *Journal of Experimental Analysis of Behavior*, 1959, 2, 301–305. Solomon

Azrin, N. H., & Holz, W. C. Punishment during fixed-interval reinforcement. *Journal of Experimental Analysis of Behavior*, 1961, 4, 343–347. Solomon

Bagby, E. *The psychology of personality.* New York: Holt, Rinehart and Winston, 1928. Breger & McGaugh, p. 316

Bandura, A. Psychotherapy as a learning process. *Psychological Bulletin*, 1961, 58, 143–159. Breger & McGaugh, p. 316

Bandura, A., & Huston, A. C. Identification as a process of incidental learning. *Journal of Abnormal and Social Psychology*, 1961, 63, 311–318. Aronfreed

Bandura, A., & Walters, R. H. *Adolescent aggression.* New York: Ronald, 1959. Aronfreed

Bandura, A., & Walters, R. H. *Social learning and personality development.* New York: Holt, Rinehart and Winston, 1963. Geer & Turteltaub; Rosenhan

Barber, T. X. Toward a theory of pain: Relief of chronic pain by prefrontal leucotomy, opiates, placebos, and hypnosis. *Psychological Bulletin*, 1959, 56, 430–460. Kessen & Mandler

Barbu, Z. Studies in children's honesty. *Quar-*

terly Bulletin of the British Psychological Society, 1951, 2, 53–57. Burton

Barratt, E. S. CNS correlates of intra-individual variability of ANS activity. Paper read at American Psychological Association, St. Louis, September 1962. Lang & Buss

Barrett-Lennard, G. T. Dimensions of therapist response as causal factors in therapeutic change. *Psychological Monographs: General and Applied*, 1962, 76 (43, Whole No. 562). Rogers

Barron, F. Complexity-simplicity as a personality dimension. *Journal of Abnormal and Social Psychology*, 1953, (a) 48, 163–172. Barron; MacKinnon

Barron, F. An ego-strength scale which predicts response to psychotherapy. *Journal of Consulting Psychology*, 1953, (b) 17, 327–333. Mac-Kinnon

Barron, F. Some personality correlates of independence of judgment. *Journal of Personality*, 1953, (c) 21, 287–297. Barron; MacKinnon

Barron, F. The disposition toward originality. *Journal of Abnormal and Social Psychology*, 1955, 51, 478–485. Barron

Barron, F., & Welsh, G. S. Artistic perception as a factor in personality style: Its measurement by a figure-preference test. *Journal of Psychology*, 1952, 33, 199–203. Barron; Mac-Kinnon

Bartlett, Sir Frederick. *Thinking*. London: G. Allen, 1958. Koestler

Baxter, J. C., & Becker, J. Anxiety and avoidance behavior in schizophrenics in response to parental figures. *Journal of Abnormal and Social Psychology*, 1962, 64, 432–437. Buss & Lang

Bayley, N. Data on the growth of intelligence between 16 and 21 years as measured by the Wechsler-Bellevue scale. *Journal of Genetic Psychology*, 1957, 90, 3–15. Burton

Beach, F. A., Conovitz, M. W., Steinberg, F., & Goldstein, A. C. Experimental inhibition and restoration of mating behavior in male rats. *Journal of Genetic Psychology*, 1956, 89, 165–181. Solomon

Beach, F. A., Hebb, D. O., Morgan, C. T., & Nissen, H. W. *The neuropsychology of Lashley*. New York: McGraw-Hill, 1960. Breger & McGaugh, p. 316

Beach, F. A., & Jaynes, J. Effects of early experience upon the behavior of animals. *Psychological Bulletin*, 1954, 51, 239–263. Campbell & Jaynes

Beck, R. C. On secondary reinforcement and shock termination. *Psychological Bulletin*, 1961, 58, 28–45. Aronfreed

Becker, E. *The revolution in psychiatry*. London: Collier-Macmillan, 1964. Braginsky & Braginsky

Becker, W. Consequences of different kinds of parent discipline. In M. L. & L. W. Hoffman (Eds.), *Review of child development research*. Vol. 1, New York: Russell Sage Foundation, 1964. Pp. 169–208. Hoffman & Saltzstein

Bellak, C. *Schizophrenia: A review of the syndome*. New York: Logos Press, 1958. Braginsky & Braginsky

Bender, L., & Schilder, P. Unconditioned and conditioned reactions to pain in schizophrenia. *American Journal of Psychiatry*, 1930, 87, 365–384. Lang & Buss

Bendig, A. W. Pittsburgh scale of social extroversion-introversion and emotionality. *Journal of Psychology*, 1962, 53, 199–210. Paul

Benton, A. L., Jentsch, R. C., & Wahler, H. J. Effects of motivating instructions on reaction time in schizophrenia. *Journal of Nervous and Mental Disease*, 1960, 130, 26–29. Buss & Lang

Bergson, H. L., *Le Rire*. Paris: Alcan, 1916. (15th ed.) Koestler

Berkowitz, L. Responsibility, reciprocity, and social distance in help-giving: An experimental investigation of English social class differences. *Journal of Experimental Social Psychology*, 1968, 4, 46–63. Rosenhan

Berkowitz, L., & Connor, W. H. Success, failure and social responsibility. *Journal of Personality and Social Psychology*, 1966, 4, 664–669. Rosenhan

Berkowitz, L., & Daniels, L. R. Responsibility and dependency. *Journal of Abnormal and Social Psychology*, 1963, 66, 429–436. Rosenhan

Berkowitz, L., & Daniels, L. R. Affecting the salience of the social responsibility norm: Effects of past help on the response to dependency relationships. *Journal of Abnormal and Social Psychology*, 1964, 68, 275–281. Rosenhan

Berle, B. B., Pinsky, R. H., Wolf, S., & Wolff, H. E. Appraisal of the results of treatment of stress disorders. *Research Publications Association for Research in Nervous and Mental Disease*, 1953, 31, 167–177. Paul

Berlyne, D. E. *Conflict, arousal, and curiosity*. New York: McGraw-Hill, 1960. Breger & McGaugh, p. 316

Bettelheim, B. Individual and mass behavior in extreme situations. *Journal of Abnormal and Social Psychology*, 1943, 38, 417–452. Aronfreed

Bitterman, M. E., & Holtzman, W. H. Conditioning and extinction of the galvanic skin response as a function of anxiety. *Journal of Abnormal and Social Psychology*, 1952, 47, 615–623. Aronfreed

Blackburn, H. L. Effects of motivating instructions on reaction time in cerebral disease. *Journal of Abnormal and Social Psychology*, 1958, 56, 359–366. Buss & Lang

Blaufarb, H. A demonstration of verbal abstracting ability in chronic schizophrenics under enriched stimulus and instructional conditions. *Journal of Consulting Psychology*, 1962, 26, 471–475. Lang & Buss

Bleke, R. C. Reward and punishment as determiners of reminiscence effects in schizophrenic and normal subjects. *Journal of*

Personality, 1955, *23*, 479–498. Buss & Lang; Lang & Buss

Bleuler, E. *Dementia praecox of the group of schizophrenias.* New York: International Universities Press, 1950. Lang & Buss

Blodgett, H. C. The effect of introduction of reward upon the maze performance of rats. *University of California Publications in Psychology*, 1929, *4*, 113–134. Breger & McGaugh, p. 316

Blum, G. S. A study of the psychoanalytic theory of psychosexual development. *Genetic Psychology Monographs*, 1949, *39*, 3–99. Rabin

Blum, G. S. *The Blacky pictures* (manual of instructions). New York: Psychological Corporation, 1950. Rabin

Boehm, L. The development of independence: A comparative study. *Child Development*, 1957, *28*, 85–92. Burton

Bolles, M., & Goldstein, K. A study of schizophrenic patients. *Psychiatric Quarterly*, 1938, *12*, 42–65. Buss & Lang

Bookbinder, L. J. Follow-up versus discharge status of psychiatric in-patients. *Journal of Clinical Psychology*, 1962, *18*, 501–503. Paul

Boring, E. G. Eponym as placebo. In *Proceedings of the XVIIth International Congress of Psychology.* Amsterdam: North-Holland, 1964. Pp. 9–23. MacKinnon

Braceland, F. J. (Ed.) Special section: Follow-up studies. *American Journal of Psychiatry*, 1966, *122*, 1088–1124. Paul

Brady, J. V. Ulcers in "executive monkeys." *Scientific American*, 1958, *199*, 95–103. Aronfreed

Brady, J. V., Schreiner, L., Geller, I., & Kling, A. Subcortical mechanisms in emotional behavior: The effect of rhinencephalic injury upon the acquisition and retention of a conditioned avoidance response in cats. *Journal of Comparative and Physiological Psychology*, 1954, *47*, 179–186. Aronfreed

Braginsky, B. M., & Braginsky, D. D. Schizophrenic patients in the psychiatric interview: An experimental study of their effectiveness at manipulation. *Journal of Consulting Psychology*, 1967, *31*, 543–547. Braginsky & Braginsky

Braginsky, B., Grosse, M., & Ring, K. Controlling outcomes through impression management: An experimental study of the manipulative tactics of mental patients. *Journal of Consulting Psychology*, 1966, *30*, 295–300. Braginsky & Braginsky

Braginsky, B., Holzberg, J., Finison, L., & Ring, K. Correlates of the mental patient's acquisition of hospital information. *Journal of Personality*, 1967, *35*, 323–342. Braginsky & Braginsky

Breger, L., & McGaugh, J. L. Critique and reformulation of "learning-theory" approaches to psychotherapy and neurosis. *Psychological Bulletin*, 1965, *63*, 338–358. Breger & McGaugh, p. 316; Rachman & Eysenck; Breger & McGaugh, p. 344; Weitzman

Breger, L., & McGaugh, J. L. Learning theory and behavior therapy: A reply to Rachman and Eysenck. *Psychological Bulletin*, 1966, *65*, 170–173. Breger & McGaugh, p. 344

Breland, K., & Breland, M. The misbehavior of organisms. *American Psychologist*, 1961, *16*, 681–684. Breger & McGaugh, p. 316

British Journal of Psychology (1962), *53*, 3, 229. Koestler

Broadhurst, P. Abnormal animal behavior. In H. J. Eysenck (Ed.), *Handbook of abnormal psychology.* London: Sir Isaac Pitman & Sons, 1960. Pp. 726–763. Rachman & Eysenck

Brodsky, M. J. Interpersonal stimuli as interference in a sorting task. *Dissertation Abstracts*, 1961, *22*, 2068. Buss & Lang

Brogden, H. E. A factor analysis of 40 character traits. *Psychological Monographs: General and Applied*, 1940, *52* (3, Whole No. 234), 39–55. Burton

Brogden, W. J. Sensory preconditioning. *Journal of Experimental Psychology*, 1939, *25*, 323–332. Breger & McGaugh, p. 316

Brogden, W. J. Acquisition and extinction of conditioned avoidance response in dogs. *Journal of Comparative and Physiological Psychology*, 1949, *42*, 296–302. Solomon

Bronfenbrenner, U. Socialization and social class through time and space. In E. E. Maccoby, T. M. Newcomb, & E. L. Hartley (Eds.), *Readings in social psychology.* (3d ed.) New York: Holt, Rinehart & Winston, 1958. Pp. 400–425. Aronfreed; Hoffman & Saltzstein

Bronfenbrenner, U. Freudian theories of identification and their derivatives. *Child Development*, 1960, *31*, 15–40. Aronfreed

Bronfenbrenner, U. Some familial antecedents of responsibility and leadership in adolescents. In L. Petrullo & B. L. Bass (Eds.), *Leadership and interpersonal behavior.* New York: Holt, Rinehart, & Winston, 1961. Pp. 239–272. Aronfreed

Bronfenbrenner, U. The role of age, sex, class, and culture in studies of moral development. *Religious Education*, 1962, *57* (4, Research Supplement), S3–S17. Burton

Brooker, H. The effects of differential verbal reinforcement on schizophrenic and non-schizophrenic hospital patients. Unpublished doctoral dissertation, Indiana University, 1962. Buss & Lang

Brown, J. S. Gradients of approach and avoidance responses and their relation to level of motivation. *Journal of Comparative and Physiological Psychology*, 1948, *41*, 450–465. Solomon

Brown, R. L. The effects of aversive stimulation on certain conceptual error responses of schizophrenics. *Dissertation Abstracts*, 1961, *22*, 629. Buss & Lang

Brush, F. R., Brush, E. S., & Solomon, R. L. Traumatic avoidance learning: The effects of CS-US interval with a delayed-conditioning procedure. *Journal of Comparative and Physi-*

ological Psychology, 1955, *48*, 285–293. Aronfreed

Bryan, J. H., & Test, M. A. Models and helping: Naturalistic studies in aiding behavior. *Journal of Personality and Social Psychology*, 1967, *6*, 400–407. Rosenhan

Buchanan, G. The effects of various punishment-escape events upon subsequent choice behavior of rats. *Journal of Comparative and Physiological Psychology*, 1958, *51*, 355–362. Aronfreed

Buck, C. W., Carscallen, H. B., & Hobbs, G. E. Temperature regulation in schizophrenia: I. Comparison of schizophrenic and normal subjects. II. Analysis by duration of psychosis. *Archives of Neurology and Psychiatry*, 1950, *64*, 828–842. Lang & Buss

Bugelski, B. R. *The psychology of learning.* New York: Holt, Rinehart & Winston, 1956. Solomon; Breger & McGaugh, p. 316

Bugelski, B., & Scharlock, D. An experimental demonstration of unconscious mediated association. *Journal of Experimental Psychology*, 1952, *44*, 334–338. Burton

Bühler, K. *The mental development of the child.* New York: Harcourt, 1930. Kessen & Mandler

Burday, G. The performance of schizophrenic, brain-damaged and nonpsychiatric patients on a modified matching concept formation test and the effects of positive motivation on concept formation performance. Unpublished doctoral dissertation, Temple University, 1962. Buss & Lang

Burstein, A. G. Primary process in children as a function of age. *Journal of Abnormal and Social Psychology*, 1959, *59*, 284–286. Buss & Lang

Burstein, A. G. Some verbal aspects of primary process thought in schizophrenia. *Journal of Abnormal and Social Psychology*, 1961, *62*, 155–157. Buss & Lang

Burton, R. V. Some factors related to resistance to temptation in four-year-old children. Unpublished doctoral dissertation, Harvard University, 1959. Burton

Burton, R. V. Generality of honesty reconsidered. *Psychological Review*, 1963, *70*, 481–499. Burton

Burton, R. V., Maccoby, E. E., & Allinsmith, W. Antecedents of resistance to temptation in four-year-old children. *Child Development*, 1961, *32*, 689–710. Burton

Buss, A. H., Braden, W., Orgel, A., & Buss, E. H. Acquisition and extinction with different verbal reinforcement combinations. *Journal of Experimental Psychology*, 1956, *52*, 288–295. Buss & Lang

Buss, A. H., & Buss, E. H. The effect of verbal reinforcement combinations on conceptual learning. *Journal of Experimental Psychology*, 1956, *52*, 283–287. Buss & Lang

Buss, A. H., & Lang, P. J. Psychological deficit in schizophrenia: I. Affect, reinforcement, and concept attainment. *Journal of Abnormal Psychology*, 1965, *70*, 2–24. Buss & Lang; Lang & Buss

Buss, A. H., Weiner, M., & Buss, E. H. Stimulus generalization as a function of verbal reinforcement combinations. *Journal of Experimental Psychology*, 1954, *48*, 433–436. Buss & Lang

Calloway, E., III, & Dembo, D. Narrowed attention. *Archives of Neurology and Psychiatry*, 1958, *79*, 74–90. Lang & Buss

Cameron, N. S. Reasoning, regression and communication in schizophrenics. *Psychological Monographs: General and Applied*, 1938, *50*, (1, Whole No. 221). Buss & Lang

Cameron, N. S. Experimental analysis of schizophrenic thinking. In J. S. Kasanin (Ed.), *Language and thought in schizophrenia.* Berkeley: University of California Press, 1946. Pp. 50–64. Buss & Lang

Cameron, N., & Magaret, A. *Behavior pathology.* Boston: Houghton Mifflin, 1951. Buss & Lang

Campbell, B. A., & Campbell, E. H. Retention and extinction of learned fear in infant and adult rats. *Journal of Comparative and Physiological Psychology*, 1962, *55*, 1–8. Campbell & Jaynes

Campbell, B., & Jaynes, J. Reinstatement. *Psychological Review*, 1966, *73*, 478–480. Campbell & Jaynes

Campbell, D. A study of some sensorimotor functions in psychiatric patients. Unpublished doctoral dissertation, University of London, 1957. Lang & Buss

Campbell, D. T., & Fiske, D. W. Convergent and discriminant validation by the multitrait-multimethod matrix. *Psychological Bulletin*, 1959, *56*, 81–105. Burton

Camus, A. *The stranger.* New York: Knopf, 1946. Maddi

Camus, A. *The myth of Sisyphus and other essays.* (Trans. by J. O'Brien) New York: Knopf, 1955. Maddi

Cannon, W. B. The James-Lange theory of emotions: A critical examination and an alternative theory. *American Journal of Psychology*, 1927, *39*, 106–124. Kessen & Mandler

Cannon, W. B. *Bodily changes in pain, hunger, fear and rage.* (2d ed.) New York: Appleton, 1929. Schachter & Singer

Cantril, H., & Hunt, W. A. Emotional effects produced by the injection of adrenalin. *American Journal of Psychology*, 1932, *44*, 300–307. Schachter & Singer

Carlsmith, J. M. The effect of punishment on avoidance responses: The use of different stimuli for training and punishment. Paper read at Eastern Psychological Association, Philadelphia, April 1961. Solomon

Carrigan, P. M. Selective variability in schizophrenia. *American Psychologist*, 1963, *18*, 427. (Abstract.) Lang & Buss

Cattell, R. B. *The IPAT Anxiety Scale.* Champaign, Ill.: Institute for Personality and Ability Testing, 1957. Paul

Cavanaugh, D. Improvement in the performance of schizophrenics on concept formation tasks as a function of motivational change. *Journal of Abnormal and Social Psychology*, 1958, 57, 8–12. Buss & Lang

Cavanaugh, D., Cohen, W., & Lang, P. J. The effect of "social censure" and "social approval" on the psychomotor performance of schizophrenics. *Journal of Abnormal and Social Psychology*, 1960, 60, 213–218. Buss & Lang

Chapman, J., & McGhie, A. A comparative study of disordered attention in schizophrenia. *Journal of Mental Science*, 1962, 108, 487–500. Lang & Buss

Chapman, L. J. Distractibility in the conceptual performance of schizophrenics. *Journal of Abnormal and Social Psychology*, 1956, (a) 53, 286–291. Lang & Buss

Chapman, L. J. The role of type of distracter in the "concrete" performance of schizophrenics. *Journal of Personality*, 1956, (b) 25, 130–141. Buss & Lang

Chapman, L. J. Intrusion of associative responses into schizophrenic conceptual performance. *Journal of Abnormal and Social Psychology*, 1958, 56, 374–379. Lang & Buss

Chapman, L. J. A reinterpretation of some pathological disturbances in conceptual breadth. *Journal of Abnormal and Social Psychology*, 1961, 62, 514–519. Buss & Lang

Chapman, L. J. Stimulus generalization and verbal behavior in schizophrenia. Paper read at Midwestern Psychological Association, Detroit, May 1962. Lang & Buss

Chapman, L. J., Burstein, A. G., Day, D., & Verdone, P. Regression and disorders of thought. *Journal of Abnormal and Social Psychology*, 1961, 63, 540–545. Buss & Lang

Chapman, L. J., & Taylor, J. A. The breadth of deviate concepts used by schizophrenics. *Journal of Abnormal and Social Psychology*, 1957, 54, 118–123. Buss & Lang

Choderkoff, B., & Mussen, P. Qualitative aspects of the vocabulary responses of normals and schizophrenics. *Journal of Consulting Psychology*, 1952, 16, 43–48. Buss & Lang

Chomsky, N. Review of B. F. Skinner, *Verbal behavior*. *Language*, 1959, 35, 26–58. Breger & McGaugh, p. 316; Breger & McGaugh, p. 344

Church, R. M. Transmission of learned behavior between rats. *Journal of Abnormal and Social Psychology*, 1957, 54, 163–165. Aronfreed

Church, R. M. The varied effects of punishment on behavior. *Psychological Review*, 1963, 70, 369–402. Solomon

Church, R. M., Brush, F. R., & Solomon, R. L. Traumatic avoidance learning: The effects of CS-US interval with a delayed-conditioning procedure in a free-responding situation. *Journal of Comparative and Physiological Psychology*, 1956, 49, 301–308. Aronfreed

Claridge, G. The excitation-inhibition balance in neurotics. In H. J. Eysenck (Ed.), *Experiments in Personality*. Vol. 2. London: Routledge, 1960. Pp. 107–154. Lang & Buss

Clausen, J. A. *Sociology and the field of mental health*. New York: Russell Sage Foundation, 1956. Smith

Cohen, B. D. Motivation and performance in schizophrenia. *Journal of Abnormal and Social Psychology*, 1956, 52, 186–190. Buss & Lang

Cohen, B. D., Ludy, E. E., Rosenbaum, G., & Gottlieb, J. S. Combined sernyl and sensory deprivation. *Comprehensive Psychiatry*, 1960, 1, 345–348. Lang & Buss

Cohen, B. D., Rosenbaum, G., Dobe, S. I., & Gottlieb, J. S. Sensory isolation: Hallucinogenic effects of a brief procedure. *Journal of Nervous and Mental Diseases*, 1959, 129, 486–491. Lang & Buss

Cohen, B. D., Rosenbaum, G., Luby, E. D., & Gottlieb, J. S. Comparison of phencyclidine hydrochloride (sernyl) with other drugs. *Archives of General Psychiatry*, 1962, 6, 395–401. Lang & Buss

Cohen, B. D., Senf, R., & Huston, P. E. Perceptual accuracy in schizophrenia, depression, and neurosis, and effects of amytal. *Journal of Abnormal and Social Psychology*, 1956, 52, 363–367. Lang & Buss

Cohen, M. Ocular findings in 323 patients with schizophrenia: Preliminary report. *Archives of Opthalmology*, 1949, (a) 41, 697–700. Lang & Buss

Cohen, M. Preliminary report on ocular findings in 323 schizophrenic patients. *Psychiatric Quarterly*, 1949, (b) 23, 667–671. Lang & Buss

Colbert, E. C., Koegler, R. R., & Markham, C. H. Vestibular dysfunction in childhood schizophrenia. *Archives of General Psychiatry*, 1959, 1, 600–617. Lang & Buss

Coles, R. Serpents and doves: Non-violent youth in the South. In E. Erikson (Ed.), *The challenge of youth*. New York: Basic Books, 1967. Rosenhan

Cooke, G. The efficacy of two desensitization procedures: An analogue study. *Behavior Research and Therapy*, 1966, 4, 17–24. Rachman & Eysenck

Cooper, J. E. A study of behavior therapy in 30 psychiatric patients. *The Lancet*, 1963, 1, 411–415. Rachman & Eysenck; Breger & McGaugh, p. 344

Cooper, J. E., Gelder, M. G., & Marks, I. M. Results of behavior therapy in 77 psychiatric patients. *British Medical Journal*, 1965, 1, 1222–1225. Paul

Cooper, R. Objective measures of perception in schizophrenics and normals. *Journal of Consulting Psychology*, 1960, 24, 209–214. Lang & Buss

Cowen, E. L., & Combs, A. W. Follow-up study of 32 cases treated by non-directive psychotherapy. *Journal of Abnormal and Social Psychology*, 1950, 45, 232–258. Paul

Crookes, T. G. Size constancy and literalness in

the Rorschach test. *British Journal of Medical Psychology*, 1957, 30, 99–106. Lang & Buss

Crumpton, E. Persistence of maladaptive responses in schizophrenia. *Journal of Abnormal and Social Psychology*, 1963, 66, 615–618. Lang & Buss

Culver, C. M. The effect of cue value on size estimation in schizophrenic subjects. Unpublished doctoral dissertation, Duke University, 1961. Buss & Lang

D'Alessio, G. R., & Spence, J. T. Schizophrenic deficit and its relation to social motivation. *Journal of Abnormal and Social Psychology*, 1963, 66, 390–393. Buss & Lang

D'Amato, M. R., & Gumenik, W. E. Some effects of immediate versus randomly delayed shock on an instrumental response and cognitive processes. *Journal of Abnormal and Social Psychology*, 1960, 60, 64–67. Aronfreed

Daniels, L. R., & Berkowitz, L. Liking and response to dependency relations. *Human Relations*, 1963, 16, 141–148. Rosenhan

Darby, C. L., & Riopelle, A. J. Observational learning in the rhesus monkey. *Journal of Comparative and Physiological Psychology*, 1959, 52, 94–98. Aronfreed

Darley, J. M., & Latané, B. Bystander intervention in emergencies: Diffusion of responsibility. *Journal of Personality and Social Psychology*, 1968, 8, 377–383. Rosenhan

Davis, R. H., & Harrington, R. W. The effect of stimulus class on the problem-solving behavior of schizophrenics and normals. *Journal of Abnormal and Social Psychology*, 1957, 54, 126–128. Buss & Lang

Davison, G. The influence of systematic desensitization, relaxation, and graded exposure to imaginal stimuli in the modification of phobic behaviour. Unpublished doctoral dissertation, Stanford University, 1965. Rachman & Eysenck

Davitz, J. R., Mason, D. J., Mowrer, O. H., & Viek, P. Conditioning of fear: A function of the delay of reinforcement. *American Journal of Psychology*, 1957, 70, 69–74. Aronfreed

Deering, G. Affective stimuli and disturbance of thought processes. *Journal of Consulting Psychology*, 1963, 27, 338–343. Buss & Lang

Deese, J. *The psychology of learning.* New York: McGraw-Hill, 1958. Solomon

Della, M. P. *Oration on the dignity of man.* (Trans. by A. R. Caponigri) Chicago: Gateway, 1956. Maddi

de Santillana, G., ed., *Galileo Gallilei Dialogue on the Great World Systems.* Chicago: Chicago University Press, 1953. Koestler

Deutsch, J. A. The inadequacy of Hullian derivations of reasoning and latent learning. *Psychological Review*, 1956, 63, 389–399. Breger & McGaugh, p. 316.

Deutsch, J. A. *The structural basis of behavior.* Chicago: University of Chicago Press, 1960. Kessen & Mandler

DeVault, S. Psychological responsiveness in reactive and process schizophrenia. *Dissertation Abstracts*, 1957, 17, 1387. Lang & Buss

DeWolfe, A. S. The effect of affective tone on the verbal behavior of process and reactive schizophrenics. *Journal of Abnormal and Social Psychology*, 1962, 64, 450–455. Buss & Lang

Dillon, D. Differences between ascending and descending flicker-fusion thresholds among groups of hospitalized psychiatric patients and a group of normal control persons. *Journal of Psychology*, 1959, 48, 255–262. Lang & Buss

Dinsmoor, J. A. Punishment: I. The avoidance hypothesis. *Psychological Review*, 1954, 61, 34–46. Aronfreed

Dinsmoor, J. A. Punishment: II. An interpretation of empirical findings. *Psychological Review*, 1955, 62, 96–105. Solomon

Dobzhansky, T. Of flies and men. *American Psychologist*, 1967, 22, 41–48. Dobzhansky

Dobzhansky, T., & Spassky, B. Selection for geotaxis in monomorphic and polymorphic populations of *Drosophila pseudoobscura. Proceedings of the National Academy of Science*, 1962, 48, 1704–1712. Dobzhansky

Dollard, J., Doob, W., Miller, N. E., Mowrer, O. H., & Sears, R. R. *Frustration and aggression.* New Haven: Yale University Press, 1939. Mussen & Rutherford

Dollard, J., & Miller, N. E. *Personality and psychotherapy.* New York: McGraw-Hill, 1950. Kessen & Mandler; Breger & McGaugh, p. 316

Donahoe, J. W., Curtin, M. E., & Lipton, L. Interference effects with schizophrenic subjects in the acquisition and retention of verbal material. *Journal of Abnormal and Social Psychology*, 1961, 62, 553–558. Lang & Buss

Downing, R. W., Ebert, J. N., & Shubrooks, S. J. Effects of three types of verbal distractors on thinking in acute schizophrenia. *Perceptual and Motor Skills*, 1963, 17, 881–882. Lang & Buss

Draguns, J. G. Responses to cognitive and perceptual ambiguity in chronic and acute schizophrenics. *Journal of Abnormal and Social Psychology*, 1963, 66, 24–30. Lang & Buss

Dreyfuss, F., & Czaczkes, J. W. Blood cholesterol and uric acid of healthy medical students under the stress of an examination. *AMA Archives of Internal Medicine*, 1959, 103, 708. Ausubel

DuBois, C. *The people of Alor.* Minneapolis: University of Minnesota Press, 1944. Smith

Duchenne (de Boulogne), G., *Le Méchanisme de la Physionomie Humaine.* Paris: P. Asselin, 1862. Koestler

Duffy, E. *Activation and behavior.* New York: Wiley, 1962. Lang & Buss

Dunham, R. M. Sensitivity of schizophrenics to parental censure. Unpublished doctoral dissertation, Duke University, 1959. Buss & Lang

Dunn, W. L. Visual discrimination of schizophrenic subjects as a function of stimulus meaning. *Journal of Personality*, 1954, 23, 48–64. Buss & Lang; Lang & Buss

Durkheim, E. *Suicide*. New York: Free Press, 1951. Maddi

Durkin, D. Children's concepts of justice: A comparison with the Piaget data. *Child Development*, 1959, 30, 59–67. Burton

Edwards, A. L. *Statistical analysis*. New York: Holt, Rinehart & Winston, 1948. Rabin

Edwards, A. S., & Harris, A. C. Laboratory measurements of deterioration and improvement among schizophrenics. *Journal of General Psychology*, 1953, 49, 153–156. Lang & Buss

Ehrenworth, J. The differential responses to effective and neutral stimuli in the visual-motor performance of schizophrenics and normals. Unpublished doctoral dissertation, Boston University, 1960. Buss & Lang

Ellingson, R. J. Incidence of EEG abnormality among patients with mental disorders of apparently non-organic origin: Critical review. *American Journal of Psychiatry*, 1954, 111, 263–275. Lang & Buss

Ellis, A. Rational psychotherapy. In H. J. Eysenck (Ed.), *Experiments in behaviour therapy*. New York: Pergamon Press, 1964. Pp. 287–323. Rachman & Eysenck; Breger & McGaugh, p. 344

Ellsworth, R. B. The regression of schizophrenic language. *Journal of Consulting Psychology*, 1951, 15, 378–391. Buss & Lang

Endler, N. S., Hunt, J. McV., & Rosenstein, A. J. An S-R inventory of anxiousness. *Psychological Monographs: General and Applied*, 1962, 76 (17, Whole No. 536). Paul

Epstein, S. Overinclusive thinking in a schizophrenic and a control group. *Journal of Consulting Psychology*, 1953, 17, 384–388. Buss & Lang

Eriksen, C. W. (Ed.) *Behavior and awareness*. Durham, N.C.: Duke University Press, 1962. Breger & McGaugh, p. 316

Erlenmeyer-Kimling, L., Hirsch, J., & Weiss, J. M. Studies in experimental behavior genetics. III. Selection and hybridization analyses of individual differences in the sign of geotaxis. *Journal of Comparative and Physiological Psychology*, 1962, 55, 722–731. Dobzhansky

Estes, W. K. An experimental study of punishment. *Psychological Monographs: General and Applied*, 1944, 57 (3, Whole No. 263). Solomon; Aronfreed

Estes, W. K., & Johns, M. D. Probability learning with ambiguity in the reinforcing stimulus. *American Journal of Psychology*, 1958, 71, 219–228. Kagan

Estes, W. K., Koch, S., MacCorquodale, K., Meehl, P. E., Mueller, C. G., Jr., Schoenfeld, W. N., & Verplanck, W. S. *Modern learning theory*. New York: Appleton, 1954. Weitzman

Eysenck, H. J. *The structure of human personality*. New York: Wiley, 1953. Burton

Eysenck, H. J. *The dynamics of anxiety and hysteria*. New York: Praeger, 1957. Weitzman

Eysenck, H. J. Learning theory and behaviour therapy. *Journal of Mental Science*, 1959, 105, 61–74. Rachman & Eysenck

Eysenck, H. J. (Ed.) *Behaviour therapy and the neuroses*. New York: Pergamon Press, 1960. Breger & McGaugh, p. 316; Weitzman

Eysenck, H. J. Psychosis, drive, and inhibition: A theoretical and experimental account. *American Journal of Psychiatry*, 1961, 118, 198–204. Lang & Buss

Eysenck, H. J. (Ed.) *Experiments in behaviour therapy*. New York: Pergamon Press, 1964. Rachman & Eysenck; Breger & McGaugh, p. 344

Eysenck, H. J. *The effects of psychotherapy*. New York: International Science Press, 1966. Paul

Eysenck, H. J., Granger, G. W., & Brengelmann, J. C. *Perceptual processes and mental illness*. New York: Basic Books, 1957. Lang & Buss

Eysenck, H. J., & Rachman, S. *The causes and cures of neurosis*. San Diego: Knapp, 1965. Rachman & Eysenck

Faibish, G. M. Schizophrenic response to words of multiple meaning. *Journal of Personality*, 1961, 29, 414–427. Lang & Buss

Fairweather, G. W. *Social psychology in treating mental illness: An experimental approach*. New York: Wiley, 1964. Breger & McGaugh, p. 316; Breger & McGaugh, p. 344

Fairweather, G. W., & Simon, R. A further follow-up of psychotherapeutic programs. *Journal of Consulting Psychology*, 1963, 27, 186. Paul

Fanconi, G., & Ferrazzini, F. Kongenitale Analgie: Kongenitale generalisierte Schmerzindifferenz. *Helvetica paediatrica Acta*, 1957, 12, 79–115. Kessen & Mandler

Farber, I. E. Response fixation under anxiety and non-anxiety conditions. *Journal of Experimental Psychology*, 1948, 38, 111–131. Aronfreed

Feffer, M. H. The influence of affective factors on conceptualization in schizophrenia. *Journal of Abnormal and Social Psychology*, 1961, 63, 588–596. Buss & Lang

Feifel, H. Qualitative differences in the vocabulary response of normals and abnormals. *Genetic Psychology Monographs*, 1949, 39, 151–204. Buss & Lang

Feldman, M. J., & Drasgow, J. A visual-verbal test for schizophrenia. *Psychiatric Quarterly Supplement*, 1951, Part I, 1–10. Lang & Buss

Feldstein, S. The realtionship of interpersonal involvement and affectiveness of content to the verbal communication of schizophrenic patients. *Journal of Abnormal and Social Psychology*, 1962, 64, 39–45. Buss & Lang

Felice, A. Some effects of subject-examiner interaction on the task performance of schizophrenics. Unpublished doctoral dissertation, Temple University, 1961. Buss & Lang

Fenichel, O. *The psychoanalytic theory of neurosis*. New York: Norton, 1945. Rabin; Lang & Buss; Paul; Rosenhan

Ferster, C. B., & Skinner, B. F. *Schedules of*

reinforcement. New York: Appleton, 1957. Breger & McGaugh, p. 316

Feshbach, S. The drive-reducing function of fantasy behavior. *Journal of Abnormal and Social Psychology,* 1955, *50,* 3–11. Mussen & Rutherford

Feshbach, S. The catharsis hypothesis and some consequences of interaction with aggressive and neutral play objects. *Journal of Personality,* 1956, *24,* 449–462. Mussen & Rutherford

Festinger, L. A theory of social comparison processes. *Human Relations,* 1954, *7,* 114–140. Schachter & Singer

Fey, E. T. The performance of young schizophrenics on the Wisconsin Card Sorting Test. *Journal of Consulting Psychology,* 1951, *15,* 311–319. Buss & Lang

Fischer, E. H. Task performance of chronic schizophrenics as a function of verbal evaluation and social proximity. *Journal of Clinical Psychology,* 1963, *19,* 176–178. Buss & Lang

Fisher, S. Patterns of personality rigidity and some of their determinants. *Psychological Monographs: General and Applied,* 1950, *64* (1, Whole No. 307). Buss & Lang

Fishman, J. R., & Solomon, F. Youth and social action. *The Journal of Social Issues,* 1964, *20,* 1–28. Rosenhan

Fiske, D. W., & Goodman, G. The posttherapy period. *Journal of Abnormal Psychology,* 1965, *70,* 169–179. Paul

Fitts, P. M. Perceptual-motor skill learning. In A. W. Melton (Ed.), *Categories of human learning.* New York: Academic Press, 1964. Pp. 244–285. Breger & McGaugh, p. 316

Flavell, J. H. Abstract thinking and social behavior in schizophrenia. *Journal of Abnormal and Social Psychology,* 1956, *52,* 208–211. Buss & Lang

Flavell, J. H. Role-taking and communication skills in children. *Young Children,* 1966, *21,* 164–177. Rosenhan

Foote, N. N., & Cottrell, L. S., Jr. *Identity and interpersonal competence.* Chicago: University of Chicago Press, 1955. Smith

Frank, J. D. Problems of controls in psychotherapy as exemplified by the psychotherapy research project of the Phipps Psychiatric Clinic. In E. A. Rubenstein & M. B. Parloff (Eds.), *Research in psychotherapy.* Washington, D.C.: American Psychological Association, 1959. Breger & McGaugh, p. 316

Frank, J. D. *Persuasion and healing: A comparative study of psychotherapy.* Baltimore: Johns Hopkins Press, 1961. Breger & McGaugh, p. 316

Frank, J. D., Nash, E. H., Stone, A. R., & Imber, S. D. Immediate and long-term symptomatic course of psychiatric outpatients. *American Journal of Psychiatry,* 1963, *120,* 429–439. Paul

Frankl, V. *The doctor and the soul.* (Trans. by R. Winston & C. Winston) New York: Knopf, 1955. Maddi

Franks, C. M. An experimental study of conditioning as related to mental abnormality. Unpublished doctoral dissertation, University of London, 1954. Lang & Buss

Freeman, G. L. *The energetics of human behavior.* Ithaca: Cornell University Press, 1948. Lang & Buss

Freeman, G. L., & Pathman, J. H. Physiological reactions of psychotics to experimentally induced displacement. *American Journal of Psychiatry,* 1943, *100,* 406–412. Lang & Buss

Freeman, H., & Rodnick, E. H. Autonomic and respiratory responses of schizophrenics and normal subjects to changes of intrapulmonary atmosphere. *Psychosomatic Medicine,* 1940, *2,* 101–109. Lang & Buss

Freeman, H., & Rodnick, E. H. Effect of rotation on postural steadiness in normal and schizophrenic subjects. *Archives of Neurology and Psychiatry,* 1942, *48,* 47–53. Lang & Buss

Freud, A. *The ego and the mechanisms of defense.* London: Hogarth, 1937. Kagan; Rosenhan

Freud, A. *The ego and the mechanisms of defense.* New York: International Universities Press, 1946. Aronfreed

Freud, S. *The problem of lay analysis.* New York: Brentano, 1927. Mowrer

Freud, S. *New introductory lectures in psychoanalysis.* New York: Norton, 1933. Kagan; Mowrer

Freud, S. *Autobiography.* New York: Norton, 1935. Mowrer

Freud, S. *The ego and the id.* London: Hogarth, 1935. Kagan

Freud, S. *The problem of anxiety.* New York: Norton, 1936. Kessen & Mandler; Aronfreed; Weitzman

Freud, S. *Group psychology and the analysis of the ego.* London: Hogarth, 1949. Freud

Freud, S. *Group psychology and the analysis of the ego.* New York: Liveright Publishing Corporation, 1951. Pp. 60–70; 75–76. Freud

Freud, S. *The standard edition of the complete psychological works of . . . .* (Trans. by J. Strachey) Toronto: Clarke, Irwin, 1955. Geer & Turteltaub

Fromm, E. *The sane society.* New York: Holt, Rinehart and Winston, 1955. Maddi

Fromm-Reichmann, F. *Principles of intensive psychotherapy.* Chicago: University of Chicago Press, 1950. Breger & McGaugh, p. 316

Funkenstein, D. H., Greenblatt, M., & Solomon, H. C. Autonomic changes paralleling psychological changes in mentally ill patients. *Journal of Nervous and Mental Diseases,* 1951, *114,* 1–18. Lang & Buss

Galton, F. *Hereditary genius: An inquiry into its laws and consequences.* New York: Appleton, 1880. Pp. 6–49. Galton

Gantt, W. H. *Experimental basis for neurotic behavior.* New York: Hoeber, 1944. Solomon

Garmezy, N. Stimulus differentiation by schizophrenic and normal subjects under conditions of reward and punishment. *Journal of Per-*

sonality, 1952, *21*, 253–276. Buss & Lang; Lang & Buss

Garmezy, N., & Rodnick, E. H. Premorbid adjustment and performance in schizophrenia: Implications for interpreting heterogeneity in schizophrenia. *Journal of Nervous and Mental Diseases*, 1959, *129*, 450–466. Buss & Lang

Geer, J. H. Development of a scale to measure fear. *Behavior Research and Therapy*, 1965, *3*, 45–53. Geer & Turteltaub

Geer, J. H. Effect of fear arousal upon task performance and verbal behavior. *Journal of Abnormal Psychology*, 1966, *71*, 119–123. Geer & Turteltaub

Geer, J., & Turteltaub, A. Fear reduction following observation of a model. *Journal of Personality and Social Psychology*, 1967, *6*, 327–331. Geer & Turteltaub

Gellhorn, E. *Physiological foundations of neurology and psychiatry*. Minneapolis: University of Minnesota Press, 1953. Lang & Buss

Gellhorn, E. *Autonomic imbalance and the hypothalamus*. Minneapolis: University of Minnesota Press, 1957. Lang & Buss

Gendlin, E. T. Experiencing: A variable in the process of therapeutic change. *American Journal of Psychotherapy*, 1961, *15*, 233–245. Rogers

Gendlin, E. T. *Experiencing and the creation of meaning*. New York: Free Press, 1962. Rogers; Weitzman

Gibson, J. J. *The perception of the visual world*. Boston: Houghton Mifflin, 1950. Breger & McGaugh, p. 316

Gindis, I. Z. The pathological changes in higher nervous activity in the various forms of schizophrenia. *Pavlow Journal of Higher Nervous Activity*, 1960, *10*, 434–439. Lang & Buss

Ginsburg, S. W. The mental health movement: Its theoretical assumptions. In R. Kotinsky & H. Witmer (Eds.), *Community programs for mental health*. Cambridge: Harvard University Press, 1955. Pp. 1–29. Smith

Gleitman, H. Place learning without prior performance. *Journal of Comparative and Physiological Psychology*, 1955, *48*, 77–79. Aronfreed

Gliedman, L. H., Nash, E. H., Imber, S. D., Stone, A. R., & Frank, J. D. Reduction of symptoms by pharmacologically inert substances and short-term psychotherapy. *AMA Archives of Neurology and Psychiatry*, 1958, *79*, 345–351. Paul

Glover, E. Notes on oral character formation. *International Journal of Psycho-analysis*, 1925, *6*, 131–154. Rosenhan

Glueck, S., & Glueck, E. *Unraveling juvenile delinquency*. New York: Commonwealth Fund, 1950. Hoffman & Saltzstein

Goffman, E. *The presentation of self in everyday life*. New York: Doubleday, 1959. Braginsky & Braginsky

Goffman, E. *Asylums*. New York: Doubleday, 1961. Braginsky & Braginsky

Goldman, A. E. A comparative-developmental approach to schizophrenia. *Psychological Bulletin*, 1962, *59*, 57–69. Buss & Lang

Goldstein, A. P. Patient's expectancies and nonspecific therapy as a basis for (un)spontaneous remission. *Journal of Clinical Psychology*, 1960, *16*, 399–403. Paul

Goldstein, K. *The organism*. New York: American Book, 1939. Kagan

Goldstein, K. Methodological approach to the study of schizophrenic thought disorder. In J. S. Kasanin (Ed.), *Language and thought in schizophrenia*. Berkeley: University of California Press, 1946, Pp. 17–40. Buss & Lang

Goldstein, K. Concerning the concreteness in schizophrenia. *Journal of Abnormal and Social Psychology*, 1959, *59*, 146–148. Buss & Lang

Goldstein, K., & Scheerer, M. Abstract and concrete behavior: An experimental study with special tests. *Psychological Monographs: General and Applied*, 1941, *53* (2, Whole No. 239). Buss & Lang

Gonzales, R. C., & Diamond, L. A test of Spence's theory of incentive motivation. *American Journal of Psychology*, 1960, *73*, 396–403. Breger & McGaugh, p. 316

Goodenough, F. L. The measurement of mental growth in childhood. In L. Carmichael (Ed.), *Manual of child psychology*. (2d ed.) New York: Wiley, 1954. Pp. 459–491. Burton

Goodson, F., & Brownstein, A. Secondary reinforcing and motivating properties of stimuli contiguous with shock onset and termination. *Journal of Comparative and Physiological Psychology*, 1955, *48*, 381–386. Aronfreed

Goodstein, L. D., Guertin, W. H., & Blackburn, H. L. Effects of social motivational variables on choice reaction time in schizophrenics. *Journal of Abnormal and Social Psychology*, 1961, *62*, 24–27. Buss & Lang

Goodwin, W. R., & Lawrence, D. H. The functional independence of two discrimination habits associated with a constant stimulus situation. *Journal of Comparative and Physiological Psychology*, 1955, *48*, 437–443. Breger & McGaugh, p. 316; Burton

Goranson, R. E., & Berkowitz, L. Reciprocity and responsibility reactions to prior help. *Journal of Personality and Social Psychology*, 1966, *3*, 227–232. Rosenhan

Gordon, J. E., & Cohn, F. Effect of fantasy arousal of affiliation drive on doll play aggression. *Journal of Abnormal and Social Psychology*, 1963, *66*, 301–307. Hoffman & Saltzstein

Gough, H. G. *A preliminary guide for the use and interpretation of the California Psychological Inventory*. Berkeley: Research Bulletin of the Institute of Personality Assessment and Research, 1954. Barron

Gough, H. G. *California Psychological Inventory manual*. Palo Alto, Calif.: Consulting Psychologists Press, 1957 (a). MacKinnon

Gough, H. G. Imagination—undeveloped resource. In *Proceedings, First Conference in Research and Development in Personnel Man-*

agement. Los Angeles: University of California, Institute of Industrial Relations, 1957 (b). Pp. 4–10. MacKinnon

Gough, H. G. *The Adjective Check List*. Palo Alto, Calif.: Consulting Psychologists Press, 1961. MacKinnon

Gough, H. G., & Heilbrun, A. B., Jr. *The Adjective Check List manual*. Palo Alto, Calif.: Consulting Psychologists Press, 1965. MacKinnon

Gould, L. N. Verbal hallucinations as automatic speech. The reactivation of dormant speech habits. *American Journal of Psychiatry*, 1950, *107*, 110–119. Lang & Buss

Gouldner, A. W. The norm of reciprocity: A preliminary statement. *American Sociological Review*, 1960, *25*, 161–178. Rosenhan

Gray, S. W., & Klaus, R. The assessment of parental identification. *Genetic Psychology Monographs*, 1956, *54*, 87–114. Kagan

Greenberg, A. Directed and undirected learning in chronic schizophrenia. *Dissertation Abstracts*, 1954, *14*, 1457–1458. Buss & Lang

Grisell, J. L., & Rosenbaum, G. Effects of auditory intensity on schizophrenic reaction time. *American Psychologist*, 1963, *18*, 394. (Abstract.) Lang & Buss

Gromoll, H. F., Jr. The process-reactive dimension of schizophrenia in relation to cortical activation and arousal. Unpublished doctoral dissertation, University of Illinois, 1961. Lang & Buss

Grossberg, J. M. Behavior therapy: A review. *Psychological Bulletin*, 1964, *62*, 73–88. Breger & McGaugh, p. 316; Weitzman

Guilford, J. P., Wilson, R. C., Christensen, P. R., & Lewis, D. J. *A factor-analytic study of creative thinking: I. Hypotheses and description of tests*. Los Angeles: University of Southern California, Psychological Laboratory, No. 3, 1951. Barron

Guilford, J. P., Wilson, R. C., & Christensen, P. R. *A factor-analytic study of creative thinking: II. Administration of tests and analysis of results*. Los Angeles: University of Southern California, Psychological Laboratory, No. 8, 1952. Barron

Gunderson, E. K. Autonomic balance in schizophrenia. Unpublished doctoral dissertation, University of California, Los Angeles, 1953. Lang & Buss

Guthrie, E. R. *The psychology of learning*. New York: Harper & Row, 1935. (Rev. ed., 1952.) Solomon; Breger & McGaugh, p. 316

Guttman, L. A new approach to factor analysis: The radex. In P. F. Lazarsfeld (Ed.), *Mathematical thinking in the social sciences*. New York: Free Press, 1955. Pp. 258–348. Burton

Guttman, N. Laws of behavior and facts of perception. In S. Koch (Ed.), *Psychology: A study of a science*. Vol. 5. New York: McGraw-Hill, 1963. Pp. 114–179. Breger & McGaugh, p. 316

Gwinn, G. T. The effects of punishment on acts motivated by fear. *Journal of Experimental Psychology*, 1949, *39*, 260–269. Aronfreed

Hadler, N. Genetic influence on phototaxis in *Drosophila melanogaster*. *Biological Bulletin*, 1964, (a) *126*, 264–273. Dobzhansky

Hadler, N. Heritability and phototaxis in *Drosophila melanogaster*. *Genetics*, 1964, (b) *50*, 1269–1277. Dobzhansky

Hall, J. C. Some conditions of anxiety extinction. *Journal of Abnormal and Social Psychology*, 1955, *51*, 126–132. Lang & Buss

Hall, K., & Stride, E. The varying responses to pain in psychiatric disorders: A study in abnormal psychology. *British Journal of Medical Psychology*, 1954, *27*, 48–60. Lang & Buss

Hanfmann, E., & Kasanin, J. A method for the study of concept formation. *Journal of Psychology*, 1937, *3*, 521–540. Buss & Lang

Hanfmann, E., & Kasanin, J. S. Conceptual thinking in schizophrenia. *Nervous and Mental Disease Monographs*, 1942, No. 67. Buss & Lang

Harlow, H. F. The nature of love. *American Psychologist*, 1958, *13*, 673–685. Kessen & Mandler; Breger & McGaugh, p. 316

Harlow, H. F. The heterosexual affectional system in monkeys. *American Psychologist*, 1962, *17*, 1–9. Breger & McGaugh, p. 316

Harrington, R., & Ehrmann, J. C. Complexity of response as a factor in the vocabulary performance of schizophrenics. *Journal of Abnormal and Social Psychology*, 1954, *49*, 362–364. Buss & Lang

Harris, A. Sensory deprivation and schizophrenia. *Journal of Mental Science*, 1959, *105*, 235–237. Lang & Buss

Harris, J. G., Jr. Size estimation of pictures as a function of thematic content for schizophrenic and normal subjects. *Journal of Personality*, 1957, *25*, 651–671. Buss & Lang

Harrower, M. R. Social status and moral development. *British Journal of Educational Psychology*, 1935, *4*, 75–95. Burton

Hartshorne, H., & May, M. A. *Studies in the nature of character*. Vol. 1. *Studies in deceit*. New York: Macmillan, 1928. Aronfreed; Burton

Hartshorne, H., May, M. A., & Maller, J. B. *Studies in the nature of character*. Vol. 2. *Studies in service and self-control*. New York: Macmillan, 1929. Burton

Hartshorne, H., May, M. A., & Shuttleworth, F. K. *Studies in the nature of character*. Vol. 3. *Studies in the organization of character*. New York: Macmillan, 1930. Burton

Hathaway, S. R., & McKinley, J. C. *Manual for the Minnesota Multiphasic Personality Inventory*. Minneapolis: University of Minnesota Press, 1943. Barron

Hathaway, S. R., & McKinley, J. C. *Minnesota Multiphasic Personality Inventory*. New York: Psychological Corporation, 1945. MacKinnon

Heath, R. (Ed.) *Studies in schizophrenia*. Cambridge: Harvard University Press, 1954. Lang & Buss

Hebb, D. O. On the nature of fear *Psychological*

Review, 1946, *53*, 259–276. Kessen & Mandler

Hebb, D. O. *The organization of behavior: A neurophysiological theory.* New York: Wiley, 1949. Breger & McGaugh, p. 316

Hebb, D. O. Drives and the CNS (conceptual nervous system). *Psychological Review*, 1955, *62*, 243–254. Lang & Buss

Hebb, D. O. The American revolution. *American Psychologist*, 1960, *15*, 735–745. Solomon

Hebb, D. O., & Thompson, W. R. The social significance of animal studies. In G. Lindzey (Ed.), *Handbook of social psychology*, Vol. I. Reading, Mass.: Addison-Wesley, 1954. Pp. 532–561. Rosenhan

Heinecke, C. M. Some antecedents and correlates of guilt and fear in young boys. Unpublished doctoral dissertation, Harvard University, 1953. Aronfreed

Hendrick, I. *Facts and theories of psychoanalysis.* New York: Knopf, 1958. Paul

Henschel, A., Brozek, J., & Keys, A. Indirect vasodilation in normal man and in schizophrenic patients. *Journal of Applied Psychology*, 1951, *4*, 340–344. Lang & Buss

Herbert, M. J., & Harsh, C. M. Observational learning by cats. *Journal of Comparative Psychology*, 1944, *37*, 81–95. Breger and McGaugh, p. 316

Hernandez-Péon, R., Scherrer, H., & Jouvet, M. Modification of electrical activity in cochlear nucleus during "attention" in unanesthetized cats. *Science*, 1956, *123*, 331–332. Lang & Buss

Hess, E. H. Imprinting. *Science*, 1959, *130*, (a) 133–141. Solomon

Hess, E. H. Two conditions limiting critical age for imprinting. *Journal of Comparative and Physiological Psychology*, 1959, (b) *52*, 515–518. Solomon

Higgins, J., & Mednick, S. A. Reminiscence and stage of illness in schizophrenia. *Journal of Abnormal and Social Psychology*, 1963, *66*, 314–317. Lang & Buss

Hilgard, E. R. *Theories of learning.* New York: Appleton, 1956. Breger & McGaugh, p. 316

Hill, W. F. Learning theory and the acquisition of values. *Psychological Review*, 1960, *67*, 317–331. Aronfreed; Hoffman & Saltzstein

Hillman, J. *Emotion.* London: Routledge, 1960. Weitzman

Hinde, R. A. Changes in responsiveness to a constant stimulus. *British Journal of Animal Behaviour*, 1954, *2*, 41–55. Kessen & Mandler

Hirsch, J. Individual differences in behavior and their genetic basis. In E. L. Bliss, *Roots of behavior.* New York: Harper & Row, 1962. Pp. 3–23. Dobzhansky

Hirsch, J., & Erlenmeyer-Kimling, L. Studies in experimental behavior genetics. IV. Chromosome analyses for geotaxis. *Journal of Comparative and Physiological Psychology*, 1962, *55*, 732–739. Dobzhansky

Hock, P., Kubis, J. F., & Rouke, F. L. Psychogalvanometric investigations in psychoses and other abnormal states. *Psychosomatic Medicine*, 1944, *6*, 237–243. Lang & Buss

Hoffman, M. L. Power assertion by the parent and its impact on the child. *Child Development*, 1960, *31*, 129–143. Hoffman & Saltzstein

Hoffman, M. L. Childrearing practices and moral development: Generalizations from empirical research. *Child Development*, 1963, (a) *34*, 295–318. Hoffman & Saltzstein; Burton

Hoffman, M. L. Parent discipline and the child's consideration for others. *Child Development*, 1963, (b) *34*, 573–588. Hoffman & Saltzstein

Hoffman, M. L. Personality, family structure, and social class as antecedents of parental power assertion. *Child Development*, 1963, (c) *34*, 869–884. Hoffman & Saltzstein

Hoffman, M. L. Socialization practices and the development of moral character. In M. L. Hoffman (Ed.), *Character development in the child.* Chicago: Aldine, in press. Hoffman & Saltzstein

Hoffman, M. L., & Saltzstein, H. D. Parent practices and the development of children's moral orientations. In W. E. Martin (Chm.), Parent behavior and children's personality development: Current project research. Symposium presented at American Psychological Association, Chicago, September 1, 1960. Hoffman & Saltzstein

Hoffman, M. L., & Saltzstein, H. D. Parent discipline and the child's moral development. *Journal of Personality and Social Psychology*, 1967, *5*, 45–57. Hoffman & Saltzstein

Hollingshead, A. B., & Redlich, F. C. *Social class and mental illness.* New York: Wiley, 1958. Szasz

Holz, W., & Azrin, N. H. Discriminative properties of punishment. *Journal of Experimental Analysis of Behavior*, 1961, *4*, 225–232. Solomon

Holz, W. C., & Azrin, N. H. Interactions between the discriminative and aversive properties of punishment. *Journal of Experimental Analysis of Behavior*, 1962, *5*, 229–234. Solomon

Horowitz, I. A. Effect of choice and locus of dependence on helping behavior. *Journal of Personality and Social Psychology*, 1968, *8*, 373–376. Rosenhan

Hoskins, R. G. *The biology of schizophrenia.* New York: Norton, 1946. Lang & Buss

Howe, E. S. GSR conditioning in anxiety states, normals, and chronic functional schizophrenic subjects. *Journal of Abnormal and Social Psychology*, 1958, *56*, 183–189. Lang & Buss

Hull, C. L. Quantitative aspects of the evolution of concepts: An experimental study. *Psychological Monographs: General and Applied*, 1920, *28* (1, Whole No. 123). Burton

Hull, C. L. *Principles of behavior.* New York: Appleton, 1943. Kagan

Hull, C. L. *Essentials of behavior.* New Haven: Yale University Press, 1951. Breger & McGaugh, p. 316

Humphreys, L. G. Generalization as a function

of method of reinforcement. *Journal of Experimental Psychology*, 1939, 25, 361–372. Burton

Hunt, J. McV., & Cofer, C. Psychological deficit in schizophrenia. In J. McV. Hunt (Ed.), *Personality and the behavior disorders*. Vol. 2. New York: Ronald Press, 1944. Pp. 971–1032. Buss & Lang; Lang & Buss

Hunt, J. McV., Cole, M. W., & Reis, E. E. Situational cues distinguishing anger, fear, and sorrow. *American Journal of Psychology*, 1958, 71, 136–151. Schachter & Singer

Hunt, J. McV., & Schlosberg, H. Behavior of rats in continuous conflict. *Journal of Comparative and Physiological Psychology*, 1950, 43, 351–357. Solomon

Hunter, W. S. Conditioning and extinction in the rat. *British Journal of Psychology*, 1935, 26, 135–148. Solomon

Husek, T. R., & Alexander, S. The effectiveness of the Anxiety Differential in examination situations. *Educational and Psychological Measurement*, 1963, 23, 309–318. Paul

Huston, P. E., & Shakow, D. Learning in schizophrenia: I. Pursuit learning. *Journal of Personality*, 1948, 17, 52–74. Lang & Buss

Huston, P. E., & Shakow, D. Learning capacity in schizophrenia. *American Journal of Psychiatry*, 1949, 105, 881–888. Lang & Buss

Huston, P. E., Shakow, D., & Riggs, L. A. Studies of motor function in schizophrenia: II. Reaction time. *Journal of General Psychology*, 1937, 16, 39–82. Lang & Buss

Imada, M. The effects of punishment on avoidance behavior. *Japanese Psychological Research*, 1959, 1, 27–38. Solomon

Irvine, E. R. Observations on the aims and methods of child-rearing in communal settlements in Israel. *Human Relations*, 1952, 247–275. Rabin

Isaacs, W., Thomas, J., & Goldiamond, I. Application of operant conditioning to reinstate verbal behavior in psychotics. *Journal of Speech and Hearing Disorders*, 1960, 25, 8–12. Buss & Lang

Jacobson, E. *Progressive relaxation*. Chicago: University of Chicago Press, 1938. Weitzman; Lang, Lazovik, & Reynolds

Jahoda, M. Toward a social psychology of mental health. In R. Kotinsky & H. Witmer (Eds.), *Community programs for mental health*. Cambridge: Harvard University Press, 1955. Pp. 296–322. Smith

Jahoda, M. *Current conceptions of positive mental health*. New York: Basic Books, 1958. Smith

James, W. *The principles of psychology*. New York: Holt, Rinehart and Winston, 1890. Schachter & Singer; Kessen & Mandler

Jaynes, J. Imprinting: The interaction of learned and innate behavior: II. The critical period. *Journal of Comparative and Physiological Psychology*, 1957, 50, 6–7. Campbell and Jaynes

Jenkins, W. O. A temporal gradient of derived

reinforcement. *American Journal of Psychology*, 1950, 63, 237–243. Aronfreed.

Johannsen, W. J. Responsiveness of chronic schizophrenics and normals to social and nonsocial feedback. *Journal of Abnormal and Social Psychology*, 1961, 62, 106–113. Buss & Lang

Johannsen, W. J. Effect of reward and punishment on motor learning by chronic schizophrenics and normals. *Journal of Clinical Psychology*, 1962, 18, 204–207. Buss & Lang

Johannsen, W. J., Friedman, S. H., Leitschuh, T. H., & Ammons, H. A study of certain schizophrenic dimensions and their relationship to double alternation learning. *Journal of Consulting Psychology*, 1963, (a) 27, 375–382. Lang & Buss

Johannsen, W. J., Friedman, S. H., & Liccione, J. V. Visual perception as a function of chronicity in schizophrenia. *American Psychologist*, 1963, (b) 18, 364–365. (Abstract). Lang & Buss

Johnson, R. C., Weiss, R. L., & Zelhart, P. F. Similarities and differences between normal and psychotic subjects in response to verbal stimuli. *Journal of Abnormal and Social Psychology*, 1964, 68, 221–226. Lang & Buss

Joint Commission on Mental Illness and Health. *Action for mental health: Final report of the joint commission*. New York: Basic Books, 1961. Smith; Braginsky & Braginsky

Jones, E. *The life and work of Sigmund Freud*. Vol. 3, New York: Basic Books, 1957. Mowrer; Szasz

Jones, M. C. The elimination of children's fears. *Journal of Experimental Psychology*, 1924, 7, 382–390. Jones; Geer & Turteltaub

Josephson, E., & Josephson, M. (Eds.) *Man alone*. New York: Dell, 1962. Maddi

Jung, C. G. The spirit of psychology. In J. Campbell (Ed.), *Spirit and nature*. New York: Pantheon, 1954. Pp. 371–444. Weitzman

Jung, C. G. *The archetypes and the collective unconscious*. New York: Pantheon, 1959. Weitzman

Jung, C. G. *The psychogenesis of mental disease*. New York: Pantheon, 1960. Weitzman

Jurko, M., Jost, H., & Hill, T. S. Pathology of the energy system: An experimental clinical study of physiological adaptiveness capacities in a nonpatient, a psychoneurotic, and an early paranoid schizophrenic group. *Journal of Psychology*, 1952, 33, 183–189. Lang & Buss

Kagan, J. The child's perception of the parent. *Journal of Abnormal and Social Psychology*, 1956, 53, 257–258. Kagan

Kagan, J. The concept of identification. *Psychological Review*, 1958, (a) 65, 296–305. Kagan; Aronfreed

Kagan, J. Socialization of aggression and the perception of parents in fantasy. *Child Development*, 1958, (b) 29, 311–320. Kagan

Kaiser, H. F. Varimax criterion for analytic

rotation in factor analysis. *Psychometrika*, 1958, *23* (3), 187–200. Burton

Kamin, L. J. The delay-of-punishment gradient. *Journal of Comparative and Physiological Psychology*, 1959, *52*, 434–437. Solomon; Aronfreed

Karras, A. The effects of reinforcement and arousal on the psychomotor performance of chronic schizophrenics. *Journal of Abnormal and Social Psychology*, 1962, *65*, 104–111. Lang & Buss

Karsh, E. B. Effects of number of rewarded trials and intensity of punishment on running speed. *Journal of Comparative and Physiological Psychology*, 1962, *55*, 44–51. Solomon

Karsh, E. B. Changes in intensity of punishment: Effect on runway behavior of rats. *Science*, 1963, *140*, 1084–1085. Solomon

Kasanin, J. S. The disturbance of conceptual thinking in schizophrenia. In J. S. Kasanin (Ed.), *Language and thought in schizophrenia*. Berkeley: University of California Press, 1946. Pp. 41–49. Buss & Lang

Kendler, T. S., & Kendler, H. H. Reversal and nonreversal shifts in kindergarten children. *Journal of Experimental Psychology*, 1959, *58*, 56–60. Burton

Kendler, T. S., Kendler, H. H., & Wells, D. Reversal and nonreversal shifts in nursery school children. *Journal of Comparative and Physiological Psychology*, 1960, *53*, 83–88. Burton

Kessen, W., & Mandler, G. Anxiety, pain, and the inhibition of distress. *Psychological Review*, 1961, *68*, 396–404. Kessen & Mandler

Kety, S. S. Biochemical theories of schizophrenia: Part I. *Science*, 1959, *129*, 1528–1532. Part II. *Science*, 1959, *129*, 1590–1596. Kety

Kidd, A. H. Monocular distance perception in schizophrenics. *Journal of Abnormal and Social Psychology*, 1964, *68*, 100–103. Lang & Buss

Kierkegaard, S. *The sickness unto death*. (Trans. by W. Lowrie) New York: Doubleday, 1954. Maddi

Killberg, J. The differentiating effects of nonverbal and verbal rewards in the modification of verbal behavior of schizophrenic and normal subjects. Unpublished doctoral dissertation, Columbia University, 1962. Buss & Lang

King, G. F. Differential autonomic responsiveness in the process-reactive classification of schizophrenia. *Journal of Abnormal and Social Psychology*, 1958, *56*, 160–164. Lang & Buss

King, G. F., Armitage, S., & Tilton, J. A therapeutic approach to schizophrenics of extreme pathology. *Journal of Abnormal and Social Psychology*, 1960, *61*, 276–286. Rachman & Eysenck

King, G., David, M., & Lovinger, E. Operant motor behavior in acute schizophrenics. *Journal of Personality*, 1957, *25*, 317–326. Buss & Lang

King, H. E. *Psychomotor aspects of mental disease*. Cambridge: Harvard University Press, 1954. Lang & Buss

King, H. E. Some explorations in psychomotility. *Psychiatric Research Reports*, 1961, *14*, 62–86. Lang & Buss

King, H. E. Anticipatory behavior: Temporal matching by normal and psychotic subjects. *Journal of Psychology*, 1962, (a) *53*, 425–440. Lang & Buss

King, H. E. Reaction-time as a function of stimulus intensity among normal and psychotic subjects. *Journal of Psychology*, 1962 (b) *54*, 299–307. Lang & Buss

King, H. E. Two flash and flicker fusion thresholds for normal and schizophrenic subjects. *Perceptual and Motor Skills*, 1962, (c) *14*, 517–518. Lang & Buss

Klein, D. C. Some concepts concerning the mental health of the individual. *Journal of Consulting Psychology*, 1960, *24*, 288–293. Smith

Knight, R. P. Introjection, projection and identification. *Psychoanalytic Quarterly*, 1940, *9*, 334–341. Kagan

Knight, R. P. Evaluation of the results of psychoanalytic therapy. *American Journal of Psychiatry*, 1941, *98*, 434. Breger & McGaugh, p. 316

Koch, H. L. Attitudes of young children toward their peers as related to certain characteristics of their siblings. *Psychological Monographs: General and Applied*, 1956, *70*, No. 19 (Whole No. 426). Kagan

Koestler, A. The logic of laughter. In *The act of creation*. New York: Macmillan, 1964. Koestler

Kogan, L. S., Hunt, J. McV., & Bartelme, P. *A follow-up study of the results of social casework*. New York: Family Service Association of America, 1953. Paul

Kohlberg, L. Moral judgment in the years ten to sixteen. Unpublished doctoral dissertation, University of Chicago, 1958. Burton

Kohlberg, L. Status as perspective in society: An interpretation of class differences in children's moral judgment. Paper read at Society for Research in Child Development, Bethesda, Maryland, March 1959. Burton

Kohlberg, L. The development of children's orientations toward a moral order. *Vita Humana*, 1963, (a) *6*, 11–33. Hoffman & Saltzstein

Kohlberg, L. Moral development and identification. In H. W. Stevenson (Ed.), *The Yearbook of the National Society for Studies in Education*. Chicago: The University of Chicago Press, 1963. Burton

Kohlberg, L. Development of moral character and moral ideology. In M. L. Hoffman & L. W. Hoffman (Eds.), *Review of Child Development Research*: Vol. I, New York: Russell Sage Foundation, 1964. Aronfreed

Köhler, W. *Gestalt psychology*. New York: Liveright, 1929. Breger & McGaugh, p. 316

Kohn, M. L. Social class and the exercise of

parental authority. *American Sociological Review*, 1959, 24, 352–366. Burton

Koppenhaver, N. D. The effects of verbal and nonverbal reinforcement on the performance of schizophrenic subjects. Unpublished doctoral dissertation, Purdue University, 1961. Buss & Lang

Kovach, J. K., & Hess, E. H. Imprinting: Effects of painful stimulation upon the following response. *Journal of Comparative and Physiological Psychology*, 1963, 56, 461–464. Solomon

Krasner, L. The use of generalized reinforcers in psychotherapy research. *Psychological Reports*, 1955, 1, 19–25. Paul

Krasner, L. Studies of the conditioning of verbal behavior. *Psychological Bulletin*, 1958, 55, 148–170. Breger & McGaugh, p. 316

Krasner, L. The therapist as a social reinforcement machine. In H. H. Strupp (Ed.), *Second research conference on psychotherapy*. Chapel Hill, N.C.: American Psychological Association, 1961. Breger & McGaugh, p. 316

Krasner, L., & Ullman, L. *Research in behavior modification*. New York: Holt, Rinehart & Winston, 1965. Rachman & Eysenck

Krechevsky, I. The genesis of "hypotheses" in rats. *University of California Publications in Psychology*, 1932, 6, 45–64. Breger & McGaugh, p. 316

Kreinik, P. S. Parent-child themas and concept attainment in schizophrenia. Unpublished doctoral dissertation, Duke University, 1959. Buss & Lang

Krout, M. H., & Tabin, J. K. Measuring personality in developmental terms. *Genetic Psychology Monographs*, 1954, 50, 289–335. Barron

Kubie, L. S. *The neurotic distortion of the creative process*. New York: Noonday Press, 1961. MacKinnon

Kuenne, M. K. Experimental investigation of the relation of language to transposition behavior in young children. *Journal of Experimental Psychology*, 1946, 36, 471–490. Burton

Kugelmass, S., & Foundeur, M. P. Zaslow's test of concept formation: Reliability and validity. *Journal of Consulting Psychology*, 1955, 19, 227–229. Buss & Lang

Lacey, J. I. The evaluation of autonomic responses: Toward a general solution. *Annals of the New York Academy of Sciences*, 1956, 67, 123–164. Lang & Buss

Lacey, J. I., & Lacey, B. C. The relationship of testing autonomic activity to motor impulsivity. *Research Publications of the Association for the Study of Nervous and Mental Diseases*, 1958, (a) 36, 144–209. Lang & Buss

Lacey, J. I., & Lacey, B. C. Verification and extension of the principle of autonomic response stereotypy. *American Journal of Psychology*, 1958, (b) 71, 50–73. Lang & Buss

Ladd, C. E. The digit symbol performance of schizophrenic and non-psychiatric patients as a function of motivational instructions and task difficulty. Unpublished doctoral dissertation, University of Iowa, 1960. Buss & Lang

Landis, C., & Hunt, W. A. Adrenalin and emotion. *Psychological Review*, 1932, 39, 467–485. Schachter & Singer

Lang, P. J. The effect of aversive stimuli on reaction time in schizophrenia. *Journal of Abnormal and Social Psychology*, 1959, 59, 263–268. Buss & Lang; Lang & Buss

Lang, P. J., & Buss, A. H. Psychological deficit in schizophrenia: II. Inference and activation. *Journal of Abnormal Psychology*, 1965, 70, 77–106. Lang & Buss

Lang, P. J., & Lazovik, A. D. Experimental desensitization of a phobia. *Journal of Abnormal and Social Psychology*, 1963, 66, 519–525. Paul; Lang, Lazovik, & Reynolds; Rachman & Eysenck

Lang, P. J., Lazovik, A. D., & Reynolds, D. J. Desensitization, suggestibility, and pseudotherapy. *Journal of Abnormal Psychology*, 1965, 70, 395–402. Geer & Turteltaub; Lang, Lazovik, & Reynolds.

Lang, P. J., & Luoto, K. Mediation and associative facilitation in neurotic, psychotic, and normal subjects. *Journal of Abnormal and Social Psychology*, 1962, 64, 113–120. Lang & Buss

Langer, S. K. *Philosophy in a new key*. New York: Mentor Books, 1953. Szasz

Latané, B., & Schachter, S. Adrenalin and avoidance learning. *Journal of Comparative and Physiological Psychology*, 1962, 65, 369–372. Schachter & Singer

Lauro, L. P. Recall of nouns varying in clustering tendency by normals and schizophrenics. Unpublished doctoral dissertation, New York University, 1962. Lang & Buss

Lawes, T. C. G. Schizophrenia, "sernyl" and sensory deprivation. *British Journal of Psychiatry*, 1963, 109, 243–250. Lang & Buss

Lawley, D. N. The estimation of factor loadings by the method of maximum likelihood. *Proceedings of the Royal Society of Edinburgh, Series A*, 1940, 40, 64–82. Burton

Lawrence, D. H. The nature of a stimulus: Some relationships between learning and perception. In S. Koch (Ed.), *Psychology: A study of a science*. Vol. 5. New York: McGraw-Hill, 1963. Pp. 179–212. Breger & McGaugh, p. 316

Lawrence, D. H., & DeRivera, J. Evidence for rational transposition. *Journal of Comparative and Physiological Psychology*, 1954, 47, 465–471. Breger & McGaugh, p. 316

Lazarus, A. A. Group therapy of phobic disorders. *Journal of Abnormal and Social Psychology*, 1961, 63, 504–512. Rachman & Eysenck; Breger & McGaugh, p. 344

Lazarus, A. A. The results of behaviour therapy in 126 cases of severe neuroses. *Behaviour Research and Therapy*, 1963, 1, 69–79. Breger & McGaugh, p. 316; Rachman & Eysenck; Paul

Lazarus, A. A., & Rachman, S. The use of systematic desensitization in psychotherapy.

South African Medical Journal, 1957, *32*, 934–937. Breger & McGaugh, p. 316

Lazovik, A. D., & Lang, P. J. A laboratory demonstration of systematic desensitization psychotherapy. *Journal of Psychological Studies*, 1960, *11*, 238–247. Lang, Lazovik, & Reynolds

Lazowick, L. M. On the nature of identification. *Journal of Abnormal and Social Psychology*, 1955, *51*, 175–183. Kagan

Leach, W. W. Nystagmus: An integrative neural deficit in schizophrenia. *Journal of Abnormal and Social Psychology*, 1960, *60*, 305–309. Lang & Buss

Lebow, K. E., & Epstein, S. Thematic and cognitive responses ,of good premorbid schizophrenics to cues of nurturance and rejection. *Journal of Consulting Psychology*, 1963, *27*, 24–33. Buss & Lang

Leeper, R. L. Learning and the fields of perception, motivation, and personality. In S. Koch (Ed.), *Psychology: A study of a science*. Vol. 5. New York: McGraw-Hill, 1963. Pp. 365–487. Breger & McGaugh, p. 316

Leibowitz, H. W., & Pishkin, V. Perceptual size constancy in chronic schizophrenia. *Journal of Consulting Psychology*, 1961, *25*, 196–199. Lang & Buss

Lerner, E. The problem of perspective in moral reasoning. *American Journal of Sociology*, 1937, *43*, 248–269. Burton

Lerner, I. M. *Genetic homeostasis*. Edinburgh & London: Oliver & Boyd, 1954. Dobzhansky

Lesse, S. Placebo reactions and spontaneous rhythms: Their effects on the results of psychotherapy. *American Journal of Psychotherapy*, 1964, *18* (Monogr. Suppl. No. 1), 99–115. Paul

Lester, J. R. Production of associative sequences in schizophrenia and chronic grain syndrome. *Journal of Abnormal and Social Psychology*, 1960, *60*, 225–233. Lang & Buss

Leventhal, A. M. The effects of diagnostic category and reinforcer on learning without awareness. *Journal of Abnormal and Social Psychology*, 1959, *59*, 162–166. Buss & Lang

Levin, H., & Sears, R. R. Identification with parents as a determinant of doll play aggression. *Child Development*, 1956, *27*, 135–153. Mussen & Rutherford

Levine, L. S., & Kantor, R. E. Psychological effectiveness and imposed social position: A descriptive framework. Paper presented at the symposium, Positive conceptions of mental health: Implications for research and service, American Psychological Association, Chicago, September 5, 1960. Smith

Levinson, D. S., & Gallagher, E. B. *Patienthood in the mental hospital*. Boston: Houghton Mifflin, 1964. Braginsky & Braginsky.

Lewin, K. *A dynamic theory of personality*. New York: McGraw-Hill, 1935. Kessen & Mandler

Lewin, K. *Field theory in social science*. New York: Harper & Row, 1951. Breger & McGaugh, p. 316

Lewontin, R. C., & Hubby, J. L. A molecular approach to the study of genic heterozygosity in natural populations. *Genetics*, 1966, *54*, 595–609. Dobzhansky

Lhamon, W. T., & Goldstone, S. The time sense. *Archives of Neurology and Psychiatry*, 1956, *76*, 625–629. Lang & Buss

Lichtenstein, F. E. Studies of anxiety: I. The production of a feeding inhibition in dogs. *Journal of Comparative and Physiological Psychology*, 1950, *43*, 16–29. Solomon

Liddell, H. S. Conditioned reflex method and experimental neuroses. In J. McV. Hunt (Ed.), *Personality and the behavior disorders*. New York: Ronald Press, 1944. Ch. 12. Breger & McGaugh, p. 316

Lindsley, D. B. Emotion. In S. S. Stevens (Ed.), *Handbook of experimental psychology*. New York: Wiley, 1951. Pp. 473–516. Schachter & Singer; Lang & Buss

Lindsley, O. Characteristics of the behavior of chronic psychotics as revealed by free-operant conditioning methods. *Diseases of the Nervous System Monograph Supplement*, 1960, *21*. Buss & Lang

Lindsley, O., & Skinner, B. F. A method for the experimental analysis of the behavior of psychotic patients. *American Psychologist*, 1954, *9*, 419–420. Buss & Lang

Littman, R., & Wade, E. A. A negative test of the drive-reduction hypothesis. *Quarterly Journal of Experimental Psychology*, 1955, *7*, 56–66. Aronfreed

London, P. The secrets of the heart: Insight therapy. In *The modes and morals of psychotherapy*. New York: Holt, Rinehart and Winston, Inc., 1964. London

Lorenz, K. *King Solomon's ring* London: Methuen, 1952. Rosenhan

Lorenz, K. L. In L. L. Whyte (Ed.), *Aspects of form*. London: Lund Humphries, 1951. Pp. 176–178. Koestler

Lorr, M. Multidimensional scale for rating psychiatric patients. *Veterans Administration Technical Bulletin*, 1953, *51*, 119–127. Braginsky & Braginsky

Losen, S. M. The differential effect of censure on the problem solving behavior of schizophrenics and normal subjects. *Journal of Personality*, 1961, *29*, 258–272. Buss & Lang

Lothrop, W. W. Psychological test covariates of conceptual deficit in schizophrenia. *Journal of Consulting Psychology*, 1960, *24*, 496–499. Buss & Lang

Lovibond, S. H. The Object Sorting Test and conceptual deficit in schizophrenia. *Australian Journal of Psychology*, 1954, *6*, 52–70. Buss & Lang

Lovibond, S. H. *Conditioning and enuresis*. New York: Pergamon Press, 1964. Rachman & Eysenck; Breger & McGaugh, p. 344

Lovinger, E. Perceptual contact with reality. *Journal of Abnormal and Social Psychology*, 1956, *52*, 87–91. Lang & Buss

Luby, E. D., Gottlieb, J. S., Cohen, B. D.,

Rosenbaum, G., & Domino, E. F. Model psychoses and schizophrenia. *American Journal of Psychiatry*, 1962, *119*, 61–67. Lang & Buss

Ludwig, A. M., Wood, B. S., & Downs, M. P. Auditory studies in schizophrenia. *American Journal of Psychiatry*, 1962, *119*, 122–127. Lang & Buss

Lundin, R. W. *Personality: An experimental approach.* New York: Macmillan, 1961. Breger and McGaugh, p. 316

Luria, A. R. *The nature of human conflicts.* New York: Liveright, 1932. Lang & Buss

Luria, A. R. The role of language in the formation of temporary connections. In B. Simon (Ed.), *Psychology in the Soviet Union.* Stanford: Stanford University Press, 1957. Burton

Maccoby, E. E. The generality of moral behavior. *American Psychologist*, 1959, (a) *14*, 358. Burton

Maccoby, E. E. Role-taking in childhood and its consequences for social learning. *Child Development*, 1959, (b) *30*, 239–252. Aronfreed

Maccoby, E. E., & Wilson, W. C. Identification and observational learning from films. *Journal of Abnormal and Social Psychology*, 1957, *55*, 76–87. Kagan

MacCorquodale, R., & Meehl, P. G. Edward C. Tolman. In *Modern learning theory.* New York: Appleton, 1954. Pp. 177–266. Rachman & Eysenck

MacGregor, G. *Warriors without weapons.* Chicago: Chicago University Press, 1946. Smith

MacKinnon, D. W. Violation of prohibitions. In H. A. Murray *et al.* (Eds.), *Explorations in personality.* New York: Oxford University Press, 1938. Pp. 491–501. Aronfreed; Burton

MacKinnon, D. W. The nature and nurture of creative talent. *American Psychologist*, 1962, (a) *17*, 484–495. MacKinnon

MacKinnon, D. W. The personality correlates of creativity: A study of American architects. In G. S. Nielsen (Ed.), *Proceedings of the XIV International Congress of Applied Psychology, Copenhagen, 1961.* Copenhagen: Munksgaard, 1962. (b) Vol. 2. Pp. 11–39. MacKinnon

MacKinnon, D. W. Creativity and images of the self. In R. W. White (Ed.), *The study of lives.* New York: Atherton Press, 1963. Pp. 251–278. MacKinnon

MacKinnon, D. W. Personality and the realization of creative potential. *American Psychologist*, 1965, *20*, 273–281. MacKinnon

Mackintosh, N. J. Extinction of a discrimination habit as a function of overtraining. *Journal of Comparative and Physiological Psychology*, 1963, *56*, 842–847. Breger & McGaugh, p. 316

MacRae, D., Jr. A test of Piaget's theories of moral development. *Journal of Abnormal and Social Psychology*, 1954, *49*, 14–18. Burton

Maddi, S. The existential neurosis. *Journal of Abnormal Psychology*, 1967, *72*, 311–325. Maddi

Maginley, H. J. The effect of "threats" of failure upon the conceptual learning performance of hospitalized mental patients. Unpublished doctoral dissertation, University of Pittsburgh, 1956. Buss & Lang

Maier, N. R. F. *Frustration: The study of behavior without a goal.* Ann Arbor: University of Michigan Press, 1949. Solomon; Aronfreed

Maller, J. B. General and specific factors in character. *Journal of Social Psychology*, 1934, *5*, 97–102. Burton

Malmo, R. B. Experimental studies of mental patients under stress. In M. L. Reymert (Ed.), *Feelings and emotions.* New York: McGraw-Hill, 1950. Pp. 229–265. Lang & Buss

Malmo, R. B. Measurement of drive: An unsolved problem of psychology. In M. R. Jones (Ed.), *Nebraska symposium on motivation.* Lincoln: University of Nebraska Press, 1958. Pp. 44–105. Lang & Buss

Malmo, R. B., & Shagass, C. Physiological studies of reaction to stress in anxiety states and early schizophrenia. *Psychosomatic Medicine*, 1949, *11*, 9–24. Lang & Buss

Malmo, R. B., & Shagass, C. Studies of blood pressure in psychiatric patients under stress. *Psychosomatic Medicine*, 1952, *14*, 82–93. Lang & Buss

Malmo, R. B., Shagass, C., & Smith, A. A. Responsiveness in chronic schizophrenia. *Journal of Personality*, 1951, *19*, 359–375. Lang & Buss

Maltzman, I., Cohen, S., & Belloni, M. Associative behavior in normal and schizophrenic children. Technical report No. 11, 1963, University of California, Los Angeles, Contract Nonr 233(50), Office of Naval Research. Lang & Buss

Maltzman, I., Seymore, S., & Licht, L. Verbal conditioning of common and uncommon word associations. *Psychological Reports*, 1962, *10*, 363–369. Lang & Buss

Mandl, B. S. T. An investigation of rigidity in paranoid schizophrenics as manifested in a perceptual task. *Dissertation Abstracts*, 1954, *14*, 2401–2402. Lang & Buss.

Mandler, G., & Kessen, W. *The language of psychology.* New York: Wiley, 1959. Kessen & Mandler

Mandler, G., & Kremen, I. Autonomic feedback: A correlational study. *Journal of Personality*, 1958, *26*, 388–399. (Erratum, 1960, *28*, 545) Kessen & Mandler

Mandler, G., & Sarason, S. B. A study of anxiety and learning. *Journal of Abnormal and Social Psychology*, 1952, *47*, 166–173. Kessen & Mandler

Marañon, G. Contribution à l'étude de l'action émotive de l'adrénaline. *Revue Française Endocrinologie*, 1924, *2*, 301–325. Schachter & Singer

Marks, I., & Gelder, M. A controlled retrospective study of behaviour therapy in phobic patients. *British Journal of Psychiatry*, 1965, *111*, 561–573. Rachman & Eysenck

Marquis, D. P. A study of frustration in newborn

infants. *Journal of Experimental Psychology*, 1943, *32*, 123–138. Kessen & Mandler

Martin, I. Levels of muscle activity in psychiatric patients. *Acta Psychologia*, Amsterdam, 1956, *12*, 326–341. Lang & Buss

Martin, W. E. Learning theory and identification: III. The development of value in children. *Journal of Genetic Psychology*, 1954, *84*, 211–217. Kagan

Marx, A. The effect of interpersonal content on conceptual task performance of schizophrenics. Unpublished doctoral dissertation, University of Oklahoma, 1962. Buss & Lang

Marx, M. H. Some relations between frustration and drive. In M. R. Jones (Ed.), *Nebraska symposium on motivation: 1956*. Lincoln: University of Nebraska Press, 1956. Kessen & Mandler

Maslow, A. H. *Motivation and personality*. New York: Harper & Row, 1954. Smith

Masserman, J. H. *Behavior and neuroses*. Chicago: Chicago University Press, 1943. Solomon; Rachman & Eysenck; Weitzman

Masserman, J. M., & Pechtel, C. Neurosis in monkeys: A preliminary report of experimental observations. *Annals of the New York Academy of Science*, 1953, *56*, 253–265. Solomon

Maxwell, A. E. Recent trends in factor analysis. *Journal of the Royal Statistical Society, Series A*, 1961, *124* (Pt. 1), 49–59. Burton

May, P. R. Pupillary abnormalities in schizophrenia and during muscular effort. *Journal of Mental Science*, 1948, *94*, 89–98. Lang & Buss

May, P. R. A., Tuma, A. H., & Kraude, W. Community follow-up of treatment of schizophrenia—issues and problems. *American Journal of Orthopsychiatry*, 1965, *35*, 754–763. Paul

May, R., Angel, E., & Ellenberger, H. F. (Eds.) *Existence: A new dimension in psychiatry and psychology*. New York: Basic Books, 1958. Kessen and Mandler; Maddi

Mayr, E. *Animal species and evolution*. Cambridge: Harvard University Press, 1963. Dobzhansky

McCann, R. V. *Delinquency: Sickness or sin?* New York: Harper & Row, 1957. Mowrer

McClelland, D. C. *Personality*. New York: Sloane, 1951. Kagan

McCord, J., & McCord, W. The effect of parental role model on criminality. *Journal of Social Issues*, 1958, *14*, 66–75. Hoffman & Saltzstein

McDonough, J. M. Critical flicker frequency and the spiral aftereffect with process and reactive schizophrenia. *Journal of Consulting Psychology*, 1960, *24*, 150–155. Lang & Buss

McGaughran, L. S. Predicting language behavior from object sorting. *Journal of Abnormal and Social Psychology*, 1954, *49*, 183–195. Buss & Lang

McGaughran, L. S., & Moran, L. J. "Conceptual level" vs. "conceptual area" analysis of object sorting behavior of schizophrenic and non-

psychiatric groups. *Journal of Abnormal and Social Psychology*, 1956, *52*, 43–50. Buss & Lang

McGaughran, L. S., & Moran, L. J. Differences between schizophrenic and brain-damaged groups in conceptual aspects of object sorting. *Journal of Abnormal and Social Psychology*, 1957, *54*, 44–49. Buss & Lang

McGhie, A., & Chapman, J. Disorders of attention and perception in early schizophrenia. *British Journal of Medical Psychology*, 1961, *34*, 103–116. Lang & Buss

McGinnies, E., & Adornetto, J. Perceptual defense in normal and schizophrenic observers. *Journal of Abnormal and Social Psychology*, 1952, *47*, 833–837. Lang & Buss

McNair, D. M., Lorr, M., Young, H. H., Roth, I., & Boyd, R. W. A three-year follow-up of psychotherapy patients. *Journal of Clinical Psychology*, 1964, *20*, 258–263. Paul

Medinnus, G. R. Immanent justice in children: A review of the literature and additional data. *Journal of Genetic Psychology*, 1959, *94*, 253–262. Burton

Mednick, S. A. Distortions in the gradient of stimulus generalization related to cortical brain damage and schizophrenia. *Journal of Abnormal and Social Psychology*, 1955, *51*, 536–542. Lang & Buss

Mednick, S. A. Generalization as a function of manifest anxiety and adaptation to psychological experiments. *Journal of Consulting Psychology*, 1957, *21*, 491–494. Lang & Buss

Mednick, S. A. A learning theory approach to research in schizophrenia. *Psychological Bulletin*, 1958, *55*, 316–327. Kessen & Mandler; Lang & Buss

Melzack, R., & Scott, T. H. The effects of early experience on the response to pain. *Journal of Comparative and Physiological Psychology*, 1957, *50*, 155–161. Kessen & Mandler

Metzner, R. Learning theory and the therapy of the neuroses. *British Journal of Psychology Monograph Supplement*, 1961, *33*. Rachman & Eysenck

Metzner, R. Re-evaluation of Wolpe and Dollard/Miller. *Behavior Research and Therapy*, 1964, *1*, 213–217. Rachman & Eysenck

Meyer, J. S., Griefenstein, F., & Devault, M. A new drug causing symptoms of sensory deprivation. *Journal of Nervous and Mental Disease*, 1959, *129*, 54–61. Lang & Buss

Meyer, W. J., & Offenbach, S. I. Effectiveness of reward and punishment as a function of task complexity. *Journal of Comparative and Physiological Psychology*, 1962, *55*, 532–534. Buss & Lang

Michalson, C. *Faith for personal crises*. London: Epworth, 1958. Mowrer

Michaux, W. Schizophrenic apperception as a function of hunger. *Journal of Abnormal and Social Psychology*, 1955, *50*, 53–58. Buss & Lang

Midlarsky, E., & Bryan, J. H. Training charity in

children. *Journal of Personality and Social Psychology*, 1967, *5*, 408–415. Rosenhan

Milgram, S. Behavioral study of obedience. *Journal of Abnormal and Social Psychology*, 1963, *67*, 371–378. Rosenhan

Miller, A. *After the fall.* New York: Viking, 1964. Maddi

Miller, G. A., Galanter, E. H., & Pribram, K. H. *Plans and the structure of behavior.* New York: Holt, Rinehart & Winston, 1960. Breger & McGaugh, p. 316

Miller, N. E. Learnable drives and rewards. In S. S. Stevens (Ed.), *Handbook of experimental psychology.* New York: Wiley, 1951. Kessen & Mandler

Miller, N. E. Liberalization of basic S-R concepts: Extensions to conflict behavior, motivation, and social learning. In S. Koch (Ed.), *Psychology: A study of a science.* Vol. 2. *General systematic formulations, learning, and special processes.* New York: McGraw-Hill, 1959. Pp. 196–292. Solomon; Aronfreed; Breger & McGaugh, p. 316

Miller, N. E. Learning resistance to pain and fear: Effects of over-learning, exposure, and rewarded exposure in context. *Journal of Experimental Psychology*, 1960, *60*, 137–145. Solomon

Miller, N. E., & Dollard, J. *Social learning and imitation.* New Haven: Yale University Press, 1941. Kagan; Aronfreed

Miller, N. E., & Murray, E. J. Displacement and conflict-learnable drive as a basis for the steeper gradient of approach than of avoidance. *Journal of Experimental Psychology*, 1952, *43*, 227–231. Solomon

Miller, R. D., & Swanson, G. E. *Inner conflict and defense.* New York: Holt, Rinehart and Winston, 1960. Aronfreed

Miller, W. Lower class culture as a generating milieu of gang delinquency. *Journal of Social Issues*, 1958, *14*, 5–19. Hoffman & Saltzstein

Moltz, H. Imprinting, empirical basis, and theoretical significance. *Psychological Bulletin*, 1960, *57*, 291–314. Breger & McGaugh, p. 316

Moltz, H., Rosenblum, L., & Halikas, N. Imprinting and level of anxiety. *Journal of Comparative and Physiological Psychology*, 1959, *52*, 240–244. Solomon

Montgomery, K. C., & Galton, B. B. A test of the drive-reduction explanation of learned fear. Paper read at Eastern Psychological Association, Philadelphia, April 1955. Aronfreed

Moran, L. J. Vocabulary knowledge and usage among normal and schizophrenic subjects. *Psychological Monographs: General and Applied*, 1953, *67* (20, Whole No. 370). Buss & Lang; Lang & Buss

Moriarty, D., & Kates, S. L. Concept attainment on materials involving social approval and disapproval. *Journal of Abnormal and Social Psychology*, 1962, *65*, 355–364. Buss & Lang

Morris, C. W. *Varieties of human value.* Chicago: University of Chicago Press, 1956. Rogers

Morris, J. F. The development of adolescent value-judgments. *British Journal of Educational Psychology*, 1958, *28*, 1–14. Burton

Mowrer, O. H. A stimulus-response analysis of anxiety and its role as a reinforcing agent. *Psychological Review*, 1939, *46*, 553–566. Kessen & Mandler

Mowrer, O. H. *Learning theory and personality dynamics.* New York: Ronald, 1950. Kagan; Aronfreed

Mowrer, O. H. Changing conceptions of the unconscious. *Journal of Nervous and Mental Disease*, 1959, *129*, 222–234. Mowrer

Mowrer, O. H. *Learning theory and behavior.* New York: Wiley, 1960. (a) Solomon; Aronfreed; Rachman & Eysenck; Weitzman

Mowrer, O. H. *Learning theory and the symbolic processes.* New York: Wiley, 1960. (b) Aronfreed

Mowrer, O. H. "Sin," the lesser of two evils. *American Psychologist*, 1960, (c) *15*, 301–304. Mowrer; Ausubel

Mowrer, O. H., & Aiken, E. G. Contiguity vs. drive-reduction in conditioned fear: Temporal variations in conditioned and unconditioned stimulus. *American Journal of Psychology*, 1954, *67*, 26–38. Aronfreed

Mowrer, O. H., & Lamoreaux, R. R. Avoidance conditioning and signal duration—a study of secondary motivation and reward. *Psychological Monographs: General and Applied*, 1942, *54* (5, Whole No. 247). Aronfreed

Mowrer, O. H., & Viek, P. An experimental analogue of fear from a sense of helplessness. *Journal of Abnormal and Social Psychology*, 1948, *43*, 193–200. Aronfreed

Munroe, R. L. *Schools of psychoanalytic thought.* New York: Dryden Press, 1955. MacKinnon

Murphy, L. B. *Social behavior and child personality.* New York: Columbia University Press, 1937. Hoffman & Saltzstein

Murray, E. J. Sociotropic learning approach to psychotherapy. In P. Worchel & D. Byrne. (Eds.), *Personality change.* New York: Wiley, 1964. Pp. 249–288. Breger & McGaugh, p. 316

Murray, E. J., & Berkun, M. M. Displacement as a function of conflict. *Journal of Abnormal and Social Psychology*, 1955, *51*, 47–56. Solomon

Murray, H. A. *Explorations in personality.* New York: Oxford University Press, 1938. MacKinnon

Murray, H. A. *Thematic Apperception Test manual.* Cambridge, Mass.: Harvard University Printing Office, 1943. Barron

Murray, H. A. Toward a classification of interaction. In T. Parsons & E. A. Shils (Eds.), *Toward a general theory of action.* Cambridge, Mass.: Harvard University Press, 1954. Pp. 435 ff. Maddi

Mussen, P., & Distler, L. M. Masculinity, identification, and father-son relationships. *Journal of Abnormal and Social Psychology*, 1959, 59, 350–356. Aronfreed

Mussen, P., & Rutherford, E. Effects of aggressive cartoons on children's aggressive play. *Journal of Abnormal and Social Psychology*, 1961, 62, 461–464. Mussen & Rutherford

Myers, I. B. *The Myers-Briggs Type Indicator manual.* Princeton, N.J.: Educational Testing Service, 1962. MacKinnon

Myrdal, G. *An American dilemma.* New York: Harper & Row, 1944. Smith

Nathan, P. A comparative investigation of conceptual ability in relation to frustration tolerance. Unpublished doctoral dissertation, Washington University, 1962. Buss & Lang

National Assembly on Mental Health Education. *Mental health education: A critique.* Philadelphia: Pennsylvania Mental Health, Inc., 1960. Smith

Nefzger, W. D. The properties of stimuli associated with shock reduction. *Journal of Experimental Psychology*, 1957, 53, 184–188. Aronfreed

Neiditch, S. J. Differential response to failure in hospital and non-hospital groups. *Journal of Abnormal and Social Psychology*, 1963, 66, 449–453. Buss & Lang

Nelson, S., & Caldwell, W. E. Perception of affective stimuli by normal and schizophrenic subjects in a depth perception task. *Journal of General Psychology*, 1962, 67, 323–335. Buss & Lang

Nowlis, V., & Nowlis, H. H. The description and analysis of mood. *Annals of the New York Academy of Science*, 1956, 65, 345–355. Schachter & Singer

Nye, I. F. *Family relationships and delinquent behavior.* New York: Wiley, 1958. Aronfreed

O'Connor, N. Reminiscence and work decrement in catatonic and paranoid schizophrenics. *British Journal of Medical Psychology*, 1957, 30, 188–193. Lang & Buss

O'Connor, N., & Rawnsley, K. Two types of conditioning in psychotics and normals. *Journal of Abnormal and Social Psychology*, 1959, 58, 157–161. Lang & Buss

Olds, J., & Milner, P. Positive reinforcement produced by electrical stimulation of septal area and other regions of rat brain. *Journal of Comparative and Physiological Psychology*, 1954, 47, 419–427. Breger & McGaugh, p. 316

Olson, G. W. Failure and subsequent performance of schizophrenics. *Journal of Abnormal and Social Psychology*, 1958, 57, 310–314. Buss & Lang

Orne, M. On the social psychology of the psychological experiment: With particular reference to demand characteristics and their implications. *American Psychologist*, 1962, 17, 776–783. Buss & Lang

Osgood, C. E. *Method and theory in experimental psychology.* New York: Oxford University Press, 1953. Breger & McGaugh, p. 316; Burton

Paintal, A. S. A comparison of the GSR in normals and psychotics. *Journal of Experimental Psychology*, 1951, 41, 425–428. Lang & Buss

Pascal, C., & Swensen, G. Learning in mentally ill patients under unusual motivation. *Journal of Personality*, 1952, 21, 240–249. Buss & Lang

Paul, G. L. Effects of insight, desensitization and attention-placebo treatment of anxiety. Unpublished doctoral dissertation, University of Illinois, 1964. Rachman & Eysenck

Paul, G. L. *Insight vs. desensitization in psychotherapy: An experiment in anxiety reduction.* Stanford: Stanford University Press, 1966. Paul

Paul, G. L. Insight versus desensitization in psychotherapy two years after termination. *Journal of Consulting Psychology*, 1967, 31, 333–348. Paul

Paul, G. L. Behavior modification research: Design and tactics. In C. M. Franks (Ed.), *Behavior therapy: Appraisal and status.* New York: McGraw-Hill, in press. Paul

Paul, G. L., & Shannon, D. T. Treatment of anxiety through systematic desensitization in therapy groups. *Journal of Abnormal Psychology*, 1966, 71, 124–135. Paul

Pavlov, I. P. *Conditioned reflexes and psychiatry.* New York: Oxford University Press, 1941. Lang & Buss

Payne, D. E., & Mussen, P. H. Parent-child relations and father identification among adolescent boys. *Journal of Abnormal and Social Psychology*, 1956, 52, 358–362. Kagan

Payne, R. W., & Hewlett, J. H. G. Thought disorder in psychotic patients. In H. J. Eysenck (Ed.), *Experiments in personality.* Vol. II. London: Routledge, 1960, Pp. 3–104. Buss & Lang; Lang & Buss

Payne, R. W., Mattussek, P., & George, E. I. An experimental study of schizophrenic thought disorder. *Journal of Mental Science*, 1959, 105, 627–652. Buss & Lang; Lang & Buss

Pearl, D., & Berg, P. S. D. Time perception and conflict arousal in schizophrenia. *Journal of Abnormal and Social Psychology*, 1963, 66, 332–338. Lang & Buss

Peel, E. A. Experimental examination of some of Piaget's schemata concerning children's perception and thinking, and a discussion of their educational significance. *British Journal of Educational Psychology*, 1959, 29, 89–103. Burton

Peiper, A. *Die Eigenart der kindlichen Hirntätigkeit.* (2d ed.) Stuttgart: Thieme, 1956. Kessen & Mandler

Peters, H. N. Multiple choice learning in the chronic schizophrenic. *Journal of Clinical Psychology*, 1953, 9, 328–333. Buss & Lang

Peters, H. N., & Jenkins, R. L. Improvement of chronic schizophrenic patients with guided problem-solving motivated by hunger. *Psychiatric Quarterly*, 1954, 28, 84–101. Buss & Lang

Peters, H. N., & Murphree, O. D. The conditioned reflex in the chronic schizophrenic.

Journal of Clinical Psychology, 1954, *10*, 126–130. Lang & Buss

Peters, R. S. *The concept of motivation*. London: Routledge, 1958. Szasz

Peters, R. S. Private wants and public tradition. *Listener*, 1960, July 14, 46–47. Smith

Petursson, E. Electromyographic studies of muscular tension in psychiatric patients. *Comprehensive Psychiatry*, 1962, *3*, 29–36. Lang & Buss

Pfaffman, C., & Schlosberg, H. The conditioned knee jerk in psychotic and normal individuals. *Journal of Psychology*, 1936, *1*, 201–206. Lang & Buss

Phillips, L. Case history data and prognosis in schizophrenia. *Journal of Nervous and Mental Disease*. 1953, *117*, 515–525. Buss & Lang

Piaget, J. *The language and thought of the child*. New York: Harcourt, 1926. Rosenhan

Piaget, J. *The moral judgment of the child*. New York: Harcourt, 1932. Burton

Piaget, J. *The moral judgment of the child*. New York: Free Press, 1948. Aronfreed; Hoffman & Saltzstein

Pishkin, V., & Hershiser, D. Respiration and GSR as functions of white sound in schizophrenia. *Journal of Consulting Psychology*, 1963, *27*, 330–337. Lang & Buss

Pishkin, V., Smith, T. E., & Leibowitz, H. W. The influence of symbolic stimulus value on perceived size in chronic schizophrenia. *Journal of Consulting Psychology*, 1962, *26*, 323–330. Buss & Lang; Lang & Buss

Polànyi, M., *Personal Knowledge*. London: Routledge, 1958. Koestler

Postman, L. Perception and learning. In S. Koch (Ed.), *Psychology: A study of a science*. Vol. 5. New York: McGraw-Hill, 1963. Pp. 30–113. Breger & McGaugh, p. 316

Purpura, D. P., Pool, J. L., Ransohoff, J., Freeman, H. J., & Housepian, E. M. Observations of evoked dendritic potentials of the human cortex. *EEG and Clinical Neurophysiology*, 1957, *9*, 453–459. Lang & Buss

Rabin, A. I. Infants and children under conditions of "intermittent" mothering in the Kibbutz (Israeli collective settlement). Paper read at American Orthopsychiatry Association, Chicago, March 1957. (a) Rabin

Rabin, A. I. Time estimation of schizophrenics and non-psychotics. *Journal of Clinical Psychology*, 1957, (b) *13*, 88–90. Lang & Buss

Rabin, A. I. Some psychosexual differences between kibbutz and nonkibbutz Israeli boys. *Journal of Projective Techniques*, 1958, *22*, 328–332. Rabin

Rachman, S. The treatment of anxiety and phobic reactions by systematic desensitization psychotherapy. *Journal of Abnormal and Social Psychology*, 1959, *58*, 259–263. Breger & McGaugh, p. 316; Rachman & Eysenck

Rachman, S. Disinhibition and the reminiscence effect in a motor learning task. *British Journal of Psychology*, 1962, *53*, 149–157. Lang & Buss

Rachman, S. Inhibition and disinhibition in schizophrenics. *Archives of General Psychiatry*, 1963, *8*, 91–98. Lang & Buss

Rachman, S. The current status of behavior therapy. *Archives of General Psychiatry*, 1965, (a) *13*, 418–423. Rachman & Eysenck

Rachman, S. Studies in desensitization: I. The separate effects of relaxation and desensitization. *Behaviour Research and Therapy*, 1965, (b) *3*, 245–252. Rachman & Eysenck

Rachman, S., & Eysenck, H. J. Reply to a "critique and reformation" of behavior therapy. *Psychological Bulletin*, 1966, *65*, 165–169. Rachman & Eysenck; Breger & McGaugh, p. 344

Rakusin, J. M., & Fierman, L. B. Five assumptions for treating chronic psychotics. *Mental Hospitals*, 1963, *14*, 140–148. Braginsky & Braginsky

Rank, O. *Der Künstler*. Vienna: Heller, 1907. MacKinnon

Rank, O. *The myth of the birth of the hero: A psychological interpretation of mythology*. (Trans. by F. Robbins & S. E. Jelliffe) New York: Journal of Nervous and Mental Disease Publishing Company, 1914. MacKinnon

Rank, O. *The trauma of birth*. New York: Harcourt, 1929. Kessen & Mandler; MacKinnon

Rank, O. Art and artist: *Creative urge and personality development*. (Trans. by C. F. Atkinson) New York: Knopf, 1932. MacKinnon

Rank, O. *Will therapy and truth and reality*. (Trans. by J. Taft) New York: Knopf, 1945. MacKinnon

Rapaport, D. The structure of psychoanalytic theory: A systematizing attempt. In S. Koch (Ed.), *Psychology: A study of a science*. Vol. 1. New York: McGraw-Hill, 1959. Pp. 55–183. Weitzman

Rashkis, H. A. Three types of thinking disorder. *Journal of Nervous and Mental Disease*, 1947, *106*, 650–670. Buss & Lang

Raush, H. L. Perceptual constancy in schizophrenia. 1. Size constancy. *Journal of Personality*, 1952, *21*, 176–187. Lang & Buss

Raush, H. L. Object constancy in schizophrenia: The enchancement of symbolic objects and conceptual stability. *Journal of Abnormal and Social Psychology*, 1956, *52*, 231–234. Buss & Lang; Lang & Buss

Ray, T. S. Electrodermal indications of levels of psychological disturbance in chronic schizophrenia. *American Psychologist*, 1963, *18*, 393. (Abstract) Lang & Buss

Redlich, F. C., & Freedman, D. T. *The theory and practice of psychiatry*. New York: Basic Books, 1966, *29*, 67–77. Braginsky & Braginsky

Reich, W. *Character-analysis*. New York: Noonday, 1949. Braginsky & Braginsky

Reisman, M. N. Size constancy in schizophrenics and normals. Unpublished doctoral dissertation, University of Buffalo, 1961. Lang & Buss

Reitman, E. E., & Cleveland, S. E. Changes in body image following sensory deprivation in schizophrenic and control groups. *Journal of Abnormal and Social Psychology*, 1964, 68, 168–176. Lang & Buss

Reynolds, D. J. An investigation of the somatic response system in chronic schizophrenia. Unpublished doctoral dissertation, University of Pittsburgh, 1962. Lang & Buss

Reynolds, G. A. Perceptual constancy in schizophrenics and "normals." *Dissertation Abstracts*, 1954, *14*, 1000–1001. Lang & Buss

·Ribot, T. A., *La psychologie des sentiments*. Paris: Alcan, 1896. Koestler

Riesman, D. *The lonely crowd*. New Haven: Yale University Press, 1950. Smith

Riley, D. A. The nature of the effective stimulus in animal discrimination learning: Transposition reconsidered. *Psychological Review*, 1958, *65*, 1–7. Breger & McGaugh, p. 316

Ring, K., Lipinski, C. E., & Braginsky, D. The relationship of birth order to self-evaluation, anxiety reduction, and susceptibility to emotional contagion. *Psychological Monographs: General and Applied*, 1965, 79 (10, Whole No. 603), 1–24. Geer & Turteltaub

Ritchie, B. F., Aeschliman, B., & Peirce, P. Studies in spatial learning. VIII. Place performance and the acquisition of place dispositions. *Journal of Comparative and Physiological Psychology*, 1950, *43*, 73–85. Breger & McGaugh, p. 316

Rodnick, E. H., & Garmezy, N. An experimental approach to the study of motivation in schizophrenia. In M. R. Jones (Ed.), *Nebraska symposium on motivation: 1957*. Lincoln: University of Nebraska Press, 1957. Pp. 109–184. Buss & Lang

Rodnick, E. H., & Shakow, D. Set in the schizophrenic as measured by a composite reaction time index. *American Journal of Psychiatry*, 1940, 97, 214–225. Lang & Buss

Rogers, C. R. *The clinical treatment of the problem child*. Boston: Houghton Mifflin, 1939. MacKinnon

Rogers, C. R. *Client-centered therapy*. Boston: Houghton Mifflin, 1951. Rogers

Rogers, C. R. A theory of therapy, personality and interpersonal relationships. In S. Koch (Ed.), *Psychology: A study of a science*. Vol. 3. *Formulations of the person and the social context*. New York: McGraw-Hill, 1959. Pp. 184–256. Rogers; Maddi

Rogers, C. R. *On becoming a person*. Boston: Houghton Mifflin, 1961. Maddi

Rogers, C. R. Toward a modern approach to values: The valuing process in the mature person. *Journal of Abnormal and Social Psychology*, 1964, 68, 160–167. Rogers

Rogers, C. R., & Dymond, R. F. (Eds.) *Psychotherapy and personality change*. Chicago: University of Chicago Press, 1954. Paul

Rorschach, H. *Psychodiagnostics*. Bern: Huber, New York: Grune and Stratton, Distributors, 1942. Barron

Rosenbaum, G., Cohen, B. D., Luby, E. D., Gottleib, J. S., & Yelen, D. Comparison of

sernyl with other drugs. *Archives of General Psychiatry*, 1959, *1*, 651–656. Lang & Buss

Rosenbaum, G., Grisell, J. L., & Mackavey, W. R. The relationship of age and privilege status to reaction time indices of schizophrenic motivation.· *Journal of Abnormal and Social Psychology*, 1957, (a) *55*, 202–207. Buss & Lang

Rosenbaum, G., Mackavey, W. R., & Grisell, J. L. Effects of biological and social motivation on schizophrenic reaction time. *Journal of Abnormal and Social Psychology*, 1957, (b) *54*, 364–368. Buss & Lang

Rosenhan, D. Some origins of concern for others. In P. Mussen (Ed.), *New directions in developmental psychology*. New York: Holt, Rinehart and Winston, 1969. Rosenhan

Rosenhan, D., Frederick, F., & Burrowes, A. Preaching and practicing: Effects of channel discrepancy on norm internalization. *Child Development*, 1968, 39, 291–301. Rosenhan

Rosenhan, D., & Hilmo, J. Maintenance of an imposed behavior standard as a function of method of socialization. In preparation. Rosenhan

Rosenhan, D., & White, G. M. Observation and rehearsal as determinants of prosocial behavior. *Journal of Personality and Social Psychology*, 1967, *5*, 424–431. Rosenhan

Rosenthal, D., Lawlor, W. G., Zahn, T. P., & Shakow, D. The relationship of some aspects of mental set to degree of schizophrenic disorganization. *Journal of Personality*, 1960, 28, 26–38. Lang & Buss

Rotter, J. B. *Social learning and clinical psychology*. Englewood Cliffs, N.J.: Prentice-Hall, 1954. Breger & McGaugh, p. 316

Rubin, L. Patterns of adrenergic-cholinergic imbalance in the functional psychoses. *Psychological Review*, 1962, 69, 501–519. Lang & Buss

Ruckmick, C. A. *The psychology of feeling and emotion*. New York: McGraw-Hill, 1936. Schachter & Singer

Sager, C. J., Riess, B. F., & Gundlach, R. Follow-up study of the results of extramural analytic psychotherapy. *American Journal of Psychotherapy*, 1964, *18* (Monogr. Suppl. No. 1), 161–173. Paul

Salzinger, K. Shift in judgment of weights as a function of anchoring stimuli and instructions in early schizophrenics and normals. *Journal of Abnormal and Social Psychology*, 1957, *55*, 43–49. Lang & Buss

Sanders, R., & Pacht, A. R. Perceptual size constancy in known clinical groups. *Journal of Consulting Psychology*, 1952, *16*, 440–444. Lang & Buss

Sanford, R. N. The dynamics of identification. *Psychological Review*, 1955, 62, 106–118. Kagan

Sargent, H. D. Methodological problems of follow-up studies in psychotherapy research. *American Journal of Psychotherapy*, 1960, 30, 495–506. Paul

Sartre, J. P. *Being and nothingness*. (Trans. by

H. Barnes) New York: Philosophical Library, 1956. Maddi

Schachter, J. Pain, fear, and anger in hypertensives and normotensives: A psychophysiologic study. *Psychosomatic Medicine*, 1957, *19*, 17–29. Schachter & Singer

Schachter, S. *The psychology of affiliation*. Stanford, Calif.: Stanford University Press, 1959. Schachter & Singer; Maddi

Schachter, S., & Singer, J. E. Cognitive, social, and physiological determinants of emotional state. *Psychological Review*, 1962, *69*, 379–399. Schachter & Singer

Schachter, S., & Wheeler, L. Epinephrine, chlorpromazine, and amusement. *Journal of Abnormal and Social Psychology*, 1962, *65*, 121–128. Schachter & Singer

Schlosberg, H. Conditioned responses in the white rat. *Journal of Genetic Psychology*, 1934, *45*, 303–335. Solomon

Schmidt, E., Castell, D., & Brown, P. A retrospective study of 42 cases of behavior therapy. *Behaviour Research and Therapy*, 1965, *3*, 9–19. Paul

Schneirla, T. R. An evolutionary and developmental theory of biphasic processes underlying approach and withdrawal. In M. R. Jones (Ed.), *Nebraska symposium on motivation: 1959*. Lincoln: University of Nebraska Press, 1959. Kessen

Schoenfeld, W. N., Antonitis, J. J., & Bersh, P. J. A preliminary study of training conditions necessary for secondary reinforcement. *Journal of Experimental Psychology*, 1950, *40*, 40–45. Aronfreed

Schooler, C. Affiliation among schizophrenics: Preferred characteristics of the other. *Journal of Nervous and Mental Disease*, 1963, *137*, 438–446. Lang & Buss

Schooler, C., & Parkel, D. The overt behavior of chronic schizophrenics and its relationship to their internal state and personal history. *Psychiatry*, 1966, *29*, 67–77. Braginsky & Braginsky

Schooler, C., & Spohn, H. E. The susceptibility of chronic schizophrenics to social influence in the formation of perceptual judgments. *Journal of Abnormal and Social Psychology*, 1960, *61*, 348–354. Buss & Lang

Schutz, W. C. *FIRO: A three-dimensional theory of interpersonal behavior*. New York: Holt, Rinehart and Winston, 1958. MacKinnon

Scott, J. P. Critical periods in behavioral development. *Science*, 1962, *138*, 949–958. Campbell & Jaynes; Breger & McGaugh, p. 316

Searles, H. F. *Collected papers on schizophrenia and related subjects*. New York: International Universities Press, 1965. Braginsky & Braginsky

Sears, P. S. Doll play aggression in normal young children: Influence of sex, age, sibling status, father's absence. *Psychological Monographs: General and Applied*, 1951, *65* (6, Whole No. 323). Kagan

Sears, P. S. Child rearing factors related to playing sex-typed roles. *American Psychologist*, 1953, *8*, 431. (Abstract) Kagan; Aronfreed

Sears, R. R. *Survey of objective studies of psychoanalytic concepts*. New York: Social Science Research Council, 1943. Rabin

Sears, R. R., Maccoby, E. E., & Levin, H. *Patterns of child rearing*. New York: Harper & Row, 1957. Kagan; Hoffman & Saltzstein; Burton; Aronfreed

Sears, R. R., Pintler, M. H., & Sears, P. S. Effect of father separation on pre-school children's doll play aggression. *Child Development*, 1946, *17*, 219–243. Kagan

Selye, H. *The stress of life*. New York: McGraw-Hill, 1956. Kessen & Mandler

Seth, G., & Beloff, H. Language impairment in a group of schizophrenics. *British Journal of Medical Psychology*, 1959, *32*, 288–293. Buss & Lang

Seward, J. P. Learning theory and identification: II. The role of punishment. *Journal of Genetic Psychology*, 1954, *84*, 201–210. Kagan

Shagass, C., & Schwartz, M. Reactivity cycle of somatosensory cortex in humans with and without psychiatric disorder. *Science*, 1961, *134*, 1757–1759. Lang & Buss

Shagass, C., & Schwartz, M. Some drug effects on evoked cerebral potentials in man. *Journal of Neuropsychiatry*, 1962, *3*, 49–58. Lang & Buss

Shagass, C., & Schwartz, M. Cerebral responsiveness in psychiatric patients. *Archives of General Psychiatry*, 1963, *8*, 177–189. Lang & Buss

Shakow, D. Some psychological features of schizophrenia. In M. L. Reymert (Ed.), *Feelings and emotions*. New York: McGraw-Hill, 1950. Pp. 383–390. Lang & Buss

Shakow, D. Segmental set: A theory of the formal psychological deficit in schizophrenia. *Archives of General Psychiatry*, 1962, *6*, 17–33. Lang & Buss

Shakow, D. Psychological deficit in schizophrenia. *Behavioral Science*, 1963, *8*, 275–305. Lang & Buss

Shankweiler, D. P. Effects of success and failure instructions on reaction time in brain-injured patients. *Journal of Comparative and Physiological Psychology*, 1959, *52*, 546–549. Buss & Lang

Shipley, W. C. Studies of catatonia: VI. Further investigation of the perseverative tendency. *Psychiatric Quarterly*, 1934, *8*, 736–744. Lang & Buss

Shoben, E. J., Jr. Toward a concept of the normal personality. *American Psychologist*, 1957, *12*, 183–189. Smith

Sidman, M., & Boren, J. The relative aversiveness of warning signal and shock in an avoidance situation. *Journal of Abnormal and Social Psychology*, 1957, *55*, 339–344. Aronfreed

Sidman, M., Herrnstein, R. J., & Conrad, D. G. Maintenance of avoidance behavior by unavoidable shocks. *Journal of Comparative and Physiological Psychology*, 1957, *50*, 553–557. Aronfreed

Siegel, A. E. Film-mediated fantasy aggression and strength of aggressive drive. *Child Development*, 1956, 27, 365–378. Mussen & Rutherford

Siegel, A. E., & Koun, L. G. Permissiveness, permission, and aggression: The effect of adult presence or absence on aggression in children's play. *Child Development*, 1959, 30, 131–141. Mussen & Rutherford

Silverman, J. Noxious cue sensitivity in schizophrenia. Paper read at American Psychological Association, Philadelphia, August 1963. (a) Buss & Lang

Silverman, J. Psychological deficit reduction in schizophrenia through response contingent noxious reinforcement. *Psychological Reports*, (b) 1963, 13, 187–210. Lang & Buss

Simpson, G. G. *Principles of animal taxonomy.* New York: Columbia University Press, 1961. Dobzhansky

Sinett, E. R., Stimput, W. E., & Straight, E. A five-year follow-up study of psychiatric patients. *American Journal of Orthopsychiatry*, 1965, 35, 573–580. Paul

Singer, J. E. The effects of epinephrine, chlorpromazine and dibenzyline upon the fright responses of rats under stress and non-stress conditions. Unpublished doctoral dissertation, University of Minnesota, 1961. Schachter & Singer

Skinner, B. F. *The behavior of organisms.* New York: Appleton, 1938. Solomon; Breger & McGaugh, p. 316

Skinner, B. F. *Walden Two.* New York: Macmillan, 1948. Solomon

Skinner, B. F. *Science and human behavior.* New York: Macmillan, 1953. Solomon

Skinner, B. F. *Verbal behavior.* New York: Appleton, 1957. Breger & McGaugh, p. 316

Skinner, B. F. *Cumulative record.* New York: Appleton, 1961. Solomon

Slechta, J., Gwynn, W., & Peoples, C. Verbal conditioning of schizophrenics and normals in a situation resembling psychotherapy. *Journal of Consulting Psychology*, 1963, 27, 223–227. Buss & Lang

Smith, M. B. Research strategies toward a conception of positive mental health. *American Psychologist*, 1959, 14, 673–681. Smith

Smith, M. B. "Mental health" reconsidered: A special case of the problem of values in psychology. *American Psychologist*, 1961, 16, 299–306. Smith

Smith, S., Thakurdis, H., & Lawes, T. G. G. Perceptual isolation and schizophrenia. *Journal of Mental Science*, 1961, 107, 839–844. Lang & Buss

Smith, W. O. Rotary pursuit performance in reactive and process schizophrenics. Unpublished doctoral dissertation, Michigan State University, 1959. Lang & Buss

Smock, C. D., & Vancini, J. Dissipation rate of the effects of social censure in schizophrenics. *Psychological Reports*, 1962, 10, 531–536. Buss & Lang; Lang & Buss

Snow, C. P. *The two cultures and the scientific revolution.* New York: Cambridge University Press, 1959. Smith

Snyder, S. Perceptual closure in acute paranoid schizophrenics. *Archives of General Psychiatry*, 1961, 5, 406–410. Lang & Buss

Snyder, S., Rosenthal, D., & Taylor, I. A. Perceptual closure in schizophrenia. *Journal of Abnormal and Social Psychology*, 1961, 63, 131–136. Lang & Buss

Solomon, A. P., Darrow, C. W., & Blaurock, M. Blood pressure and palmer sweat (galvanic) responses of psychotic patients before and after insulin and metrazol therapy. *Psychosomatic Medicine*, 1939, 1, 118–137. Lang & Buss

Solomon, F., & Fishman, J. R. Youth and peace: A psycho-social study of student peace demonstrators in Washington, D.C. *The Journal of Social Issues*, 1964, 20, 54–73. Rosenhan

Solomon, R. L. Punishment. *American Psychologist*, 1964, 19, 239–253. Solomon; Breger & McGaugh, p. 316

Solomon, R. L., & Brush, E. S. Experimentally derived conceptions of anxiety and aversion. In M. R. Jones (Ed.), *Nebraska symposium on motivation: 1956.* Lincoln: University of Nebraska Press, 1956. Pp. 212–305. Kessen & Mandler; Soloman; Aronfreed

Solomon, R. L., & Turner, L. H. Discriminative classical conditioning in dogs paralyzed by curare can later control discriminative avoidance responses in the normal state. *Psychological Review*, 1962, 69, 202–219. Aronfreed

Solomon, R. L., & Wynne, L. C. Traumatic avoidance learning: The principle of anxiety conservation and partial irreversibility. *Psychological Review*, 1954, 61, 353–385. Kessen & Mandler; Aronfreed

Sommer, R., Dewar, R., & Osmond, H. Is there a schizophrenic language? *Archives of General Psychiatry*, 1960, 3, 665–673. Lang & Buss

Sommer, R., Witney, G., Osmond, H. Teaching common associations to schizophrenics. *Journal of Abnormal and Social Psychology*, 1962, 65, 58–61. Lang & Buss

Spence, J. T., & Lair, C. V. Associative interference in the verbal learning performance of schizophrenics and normals. *Journal of Abnormal and Social Psychology*, 1964, 68, 204–209. Lang & Buss

Spence, K. W. The differential response in animals to stimuli varying within a single dimension. *Psychological Review*, 1937, 44, 430–440. Breger & McGaugh, p. 316

Spence, K. W., & Taylor, J. A. The relation of conditioned response strength to anxiety in normal, neurotic, and psychotic subjects. *Journal of Experimental Psychology*, 1953, 45, 265–277. Lang & Buss

Spiro, M. *Kibbutz-venture in utopia.* Cambridge, Mass.: Harvard University Press, 1956. Rabin

Spohn, H. E., & Wolk, W. Effect of group problem solving experience upon social withdrawal in chronic schizophrenics. *Journal of*

Abnormal and Social Psychology, 1963, *66*, 187–190. Buss & Lang

Staats, A., & Staats, C. *Complex human behavior*. New York: Wiley, 1964. Rachman & Eysenck

Stevenson, I. Processes of "spontaneous" recovery from the psychoneuroses. *American Journal of Psychiatry*, 1961, *117*, 1057–1064. Paul

Stoke, S. M. An inquiry into the concept of identification. *Journal of Genetic Psychology*, 1950, *76*, 163–189. Kagan

Stone, A. R., Frank, J. D., Nash, E. H., & Imber, S. D. An intensive five-year follow-up study of treated psychiatric outpatients. *Journal of Nervous and Mental Disease*, 1961, *133*, 410–422. Paul

Stone, L. J. Aggression and destruction games: Balloons. In L. B. Murphy (Ed.), *Personality in young children*. New York: Basic Books, 1956. Ch. 10. Mussen & Rutherford

Storms, L. H., Boroczi, C., & Broen, W. E. Punishment inhibits on instrumental response in hooded rats. *Science*, 1962, *135*, 1133–1134. Solomon

Storms, L. H., Boroczi, C., & Broen, W. E. Effects of punishment as a function of strain of rat and duration of shock. *Journal of Comparative and Physiological Psychology*, 1963, *56*, 1022–1026. Solomon

Stotsky, B. Motivation and task complexity as factors in the psychomotor responses of schizophrenics. *Journal of Personality*, 1957, *25*, 327–343. Buss & Lang

Strickland, B. R., & Crowne, D. P. The need for approval and the premature termination of psychotherapy. *Journal of Consulting Psychology*, 1963, *27*, 95–101. Breger & McGaugh, p. 316

Strong, E. K., Jr. *Vocational Interest Blank for Men*. Palo Alto: Stanford University Press, 1938. Barron

Sullivan, H. S. *Conceptions of modern psychiatry*. New York: Norton, 1940. Weitzman

Sullivan, H. S. The language of schizophrenia. In J. S. Kasanin (Ed.), *Language and thought in schizophrenia*. Berkeley: University of California Press, 1946. Pp. 4–16. Buss & Lang

Sully, J., *An essay on laughter*. London: Longmans, 1902. Koestler

Sutton, S., Hakerem, G., Zubin, J., & Portnoy, M. The effect of shift of sensory modality on serial reaction-time: A comparison of schizophrenics and normals. *American Journal of Psychology*, 1961, *74*, 224–232. Lang & Buss

Sykes, G. (Ed.) *Alienation*. New York: Braziller, 1964. Maddi

Syz, H. C. Psychogalvanic studies in schizophrenia. *Archives of Neurology and Psychiatry*, 1926, *16*, 747–760. Lang & Buss

Syz, H. C., & Kinder, E. F. Electrical skin resistance in normal and in psychotic subjects. *Archives of Neurology and Psychiatry*, 1928, *19*, 1026–1035. Lang & Buss

Szasz, T. S. Malingering: "Diagnosis" or social condemnation? *AMA Archives of Neurology and Psychiatry*, 1956, *76*, 432–443. Szasz

Szasz, T. S. *Pain and pleasure: A study of bodily feelings*. New York: Basic Books, 1957. (a) Szasz

Szasz, T. S. The problem of psychiatric nosology: A contribution to a situational analysis of psychiatric operations. *American Journal of Psychiatry*, 1957, (b) *114*, 405–413. Szasz

Szasz, T. S. On the theory of psychoanalytic treatment. *International Journal of Psycho-Analysis*, 1957, (c) *38*, 166–182. Szasz

Szasz, T. S. Psychiatry, ethics and the criminal law. *Columbia Law Review*, 1958, *58*, 183–198. Szasz

Szasz, T. S. Moral conflict and psychiatry. *Yale Review*, 1959. Szasz

Szasz, T. S. The myth of mental illness. *American Psychologist*, 1960, *15*, 113–118. Mowrer; Szasz; Ausubel; Smith

Szasz, T. S. *The myth of mental illness*. New York: Hoeber, 1961. Braginsky & Braginsky

Szasz, T. S. *Psychiatric justice*. New York: Macmillan, 1965. Braginsky & Braginsky

Taylor, J. A. A personality scale of manifest anxiety. *Journal of Abnormal and Social Psychology*, 1953, *48*, 285–290. Kessen & Mandler; MacKinnon

Taylor, J. A., & Spence, K. W. Conditioning level in the behavior disorders. *Journal of Abnormal and Social Psychology*, 1954, *49*, 497–502. Lang & Buss

Taylor, J. G. *The behavioral basis of perception*. New Haven: Yale University Press, 1962. Rachman & Eysenck

Taylor, J. G., & Papert, S. A theory of perceptual constancy. *British Journal of Psychology*, 1956, *47*, 216–224. Rachman & Eysenck

Thistlethwaite, D. A critical review of latent learning and related experiments. *Psychological Bulletin*, 1951, *48*, 97–129. Breger & McGaugh, p. 316

Thomson, G. *The inspiration of science*. Oxford: University Press, 1961. Rachman & Eysenck

Thorndike, E. L. *Human learning*. New York: Appleton, 1931. Solomon

Tillich, P. *The courage to be*. New Haven: Yale University Press, 1952. Maddi

Tilton, J. R. The use of instrumental motor and verbal learning techniques in the treatment of chronic schizophrenics. *Dissertation Abstracts*, 1956, *16*, 1180–1181. Buss & Lang

Tizard, J., & Venables, P. H. Reaction time responses by schizophrenics, mental defectives, and normal adults. *American Journal of Psychiatry*, 1956, *112*, 803–807. Lang & Buss

Tizard, J., & Venables, P. H. The influence of extraneous stimulation on the reaction time of schizophrenics. *British Journal of Psychology*, 1957, *48*, 299–305. Lang & Buss

Tolman, E. C. *Purposive behavior in animals and men*. New York: Appleton, 1932. Breger & McGaugh, p. 316

Tolman, E. C. Sign gestalt or conditioned reflex.

Psychological Review, 1933, *40*, 391–411. Breger & McGaugh, p. 316

Tolman, E. C. *Collected papers in psychology.* Berkeley: University of California Press, 1951. Breger & McGaugh, p. 316

Tolman, E. C., Hall, C. S., & Bretnall, E. P. A disproof of the law of effect and a substitution of the laws of emphasis, motivation, and disruption. *Journal of Experimental Psychology*, 1932, *15*, 601–614. Solomon

Tolman, E. C., & Honzik, C. H. Introduction and removal of reward and maze performance in rats. *University of California Publications in Psychology*, 1930, *4*, 257–275. Breger & McGaugh, p. 316

Tolstoi, L. *The death of Ivan Illych.* New York: Signet, 1960. Maddi

Tomkins, S. S. The psychology of commitment: I. The constructive role of violence and suffering for the individual and for his society. In S. S. Tomkins, & C. E. Izard (Eds.), *Affect, cognition, and personality.* New York: Springer, 1965. Tomkins

Topping, G., & O'Connor, N. The response of chronic schizophrenics to incentives. *British Journal of Medical Psychology*, 1960, *33*, 211–214. Buss & Lang

Tourney, G., Frohman, C. E., Beckett, P. G. S., & Gottlieb, J. S. Biochemical mechanisms in schizophrenia. In R. Roessler and N. S. Greenfield (Eds.), *Psychological correlates of psychological disorder.* Madison: University of Wisconsin Press, 1962. Lang & Buss

Towbin, A. P. Understanding the mentally deranged. *Journal of Existentialism*, 1966, *7*, 63–83. Braginsky & Braginsky

Turbiner, M. Choice discrimination in schizophrenic and normal subjects for positive, negative, and neutral affective stimuli. *Journal of Consulting Psychology*, 1961, *25*, 92. Buss & Lang

Turner, L. H., & Solomon, R. L. Human traumatic avoidance learning: Theory and experiments on the operant-respondent distinction and failures to learn. *Psychological Monographs: General and Applied*, 1962, *76* (40, Whole No. 559). Solomon

Ullmann, L., & Krasner, L. *Case studies in behavior modification.* New York: Holt, Rinehart & Winston, 1965. Rachman & Eysenck; Paul

Underwood, B. J. The representativeness of rote verbal learning. In A. W. Melton (Ed.), *Categories of human learning.* New York: Academic Press, 1964. Pp. 47–78. Breger & McGaugh, p. 316

Unger, S. M. On the development of the guilt response systems. Unpublished doctoral dissertation, Cornell University, 1960. Burton

Venables, P. H. Factors in the motor behavior of functional psychotics. *Journal of Abnormal and Social Psychology*, 1959, *58*, 153–156. Lang & Buss

Venables, P. H. The effect of auditory and visual stimulation on the skin potential response of schizophrenics. *Brain*, 1960, *83*, 77–92. Lang & Buss

Venables, P. H. Changes due to noise in the threshold of fusion of paired light flashes in schizophrenics and normals. *British Journal of Social and Clinical Psychology*, 1963, (a) *2*, 94–99. Lang & Buss

Venables, P. H. Selectivity of attention, withdrawal, and cortical activation. *Archives of General Psychiatry*, 1963, (b) *9*, 74–78. Lang & Buss

Venables, P. H., & O'Connor, N. Reaction times to auditory and visual stimulation in schizophrenic and normal subjects. *Quarterly Journal of Experimental Psychology*, 1959, *11*, 175–179. Lang & Buss

Venables, P. H., & Tizard, J. The effects of stimulus light intensity on the reaction time of schizophrenics. *British Journal of Psychology*, 1956, (a) *47*, 144–145. Lang & Buss

Venables, P. H., & Tizard, J. Paradoxical effects in the reaction time of schizophrenics. *Journal of Abnormal and Social Psychology*, 1956, (b) *53*, 220–224. Lang & Buss

Venables, P. H., & Tizard, J. Performance of functional psychotics on a repetitive task. *Journal of Abnormal and Social Psychology*, 1956, (c) *53*, 23–26. Lang & Buss

Venables, P. H., & Tizard, J. The effect of auditory stimulus intensity on the reaction time of schizophrenics. *Journal of Mental Science*, 1958, *104*, 1160–1164. Lang & Buss

Venables, P. H., & Wing, J. K. Level of arousal and the subclassification of schizophrenia. *Archives of General Psychiatry*, 1962, *7*, 114–119. Lang & Buss

Walk, R. D. Self-ratings of fear in a fear-invoking situation. *Journal of Abnormal and Social Psychology*, 1956, *52*, 171–178. Lang, Lazovik, & Reynolds

Walters, G. C., & Rogers, J. V. Aversive stimulation of the rat: Long term effects on subsequent behavior. *Science*, 1963, *142*, 70–71. Solomon

Warden, C. J., & Aylesworth, M. The relative value of reward and punishment in the formation of a visual discrimination habit in the white rat. *Journal of Comparative Psychology*, 1927, *7*, 117–127. Solomon

Waters, T. J. Censure reinforcement, cue conditions and the acute-chronic schizophrenia distinction. Unpublished doctoral dissertation. University of Missouri, 1962. Buss & Lang

Watson, A. J. The place of reinforcement in the explanation of behavior. In W. H. Thorpe & O. L. Zangwill, (Eds.) *Current problems in animal behavior.* Cambridge: Cambridge University Press, 1961. Breger & McGaugh, p. 316

Watson, J. B. *Psychology from the standpoint of a behaviorist.* Philadelphia: Lippincott, 1919. Kessen & Mandler

Webb, W. W. Conceptual ability of schizophrenics as a function of threat of failure.

Journal of Abnormal and Social Psychology, 1955, 50, 221–224. Buss & Lang

Webster, H., Freedman, M., & Heist, P. Personality changes in college students. In N. Sanford (Ed.), *The American college*. New York: Wiley, 1962. Pp. 805–846. MacKinnon

Weckowicz, T. E. Size constancy in schizophrenic patients. *Journal of Mental Science*, 1957, 103, 475–486. Lang & Buss

Weckowicz, T. E. Autonomic activity as measured by the Mecholyl test and size constancy in schizophrenic patients. *Psychosomatic Medicine*, 1958, 20, 66–71. Lang & Buss

Weckowicz, T. E. Perception of hidden pictures by schizophrenic patients. *Archives of General Psychiatry*, 1960, 2, 521–527. Lang & Buss

Weckowicz, T. E. Shape constancy in schizophrenic patients. *Journal of Abnormal and Social Psychology*, 1964, 68, 177–183. Lang & Buss

Weckowicz, T. E., & Blewitt, D. B. Size constancy and abstract thinking in schizophrenic patients. *Journal of Mental Science*, 1959, 105, 909–934. Buss & Lang; Lang & Buss

Weckowicz, T. E., & Hall, R. Distance constancy in schizophrenics and non-schizophrenic mental patients. *Journal of Clinical Psychology*, 1960, 16, 272–276. Lang & Buss

Weckowicz, T. E., Sommer, R., & Hall, R. Distance constancy in schizophrenic patients. *Journal of Mental Science*, 1958, 104, 1174–1182. Lang & Buss

Weinberg, N. H., & Zaslove, M. "Resistance" to systematic desensitization of phobias. *Journal of Clinical Psychology*, 1963, 19, 179–181. Weitzman

Weitzenhoffer, A. M., & Hilgard, E. R. *Stanford Hypnotic Susceptibility Scale*. Palo Alto, Calif.: Consulting Psychologists Press, 1959. Lang, Lazovik, & Reynolds

Weitzman, B. Behavior therapy and psychotherapy. *Psychological Review*, 1967, 74, 300–317. Weitzman

Welsh, G. S. *Welsh Figure Preference Test: Preliminary manual*. Palo Alto, Calif.: Consulting Psychologists Press, 1959. MacKinnon

Wendt, G. R. An interpretation of inhibition of conditioned reflexes as competition between reaction systems. *Psychological Review*, 1936, 43, 258–281. Solomon

Wenger, M. A. *Evaluation of project 6, summary of proceedings: Second cooperative psychological research conference*. Cincinnati: Veterans Administration Hospital, 1959. Lang & Buss

Wenger, M. A., Jones, N. F., & Jones, M. H. *Physiological psychology*. New York: Holt, Rinehart and Winston, 1956. Lang & Buss

Werner, H. *Comparative psychology of mental development*. Chicago: Follett, 1948. Buss & Lang

Werner, H., & Wapner, S. Toward a general theory of perception. *Psychological Review*, 1952, 59, 324–338. Rosenhan

Wertham, F. *Seduction of the innocent*. New York: Holt, Rinehart and Winston, 1953. Mussen & Rutherford

West, L. J., & Farber, I. E. The role of pain in emotional development. University of Oklahoma Medical School, 1960. (Mimeo). Kessen & Mandler

Whatmore, C. B., & Ellis, R. M., Jr. Some motor aspects of schizophrenia: An EMG study. *American Journal of Psychiatry*, 1958, 114, 882–889. Lang & Buss

White, G. M. The elicitation and durability of altruistic behavior in children. Unpublished doctoral dissertation, Princeton University, and ETS Research Bulletin 67-27. Princeton, N.J.: Educational Testing Service, 1967. Rosenhan

White, M. A. A study of schizophrenic language. *Journal of Abnormal and Social Psychology*, 1949, 44, 61–74. Buss & Lang

White, R. W. *The abnormal personality*. (2d ed.) New York: Ronald Press, 1956. Campbell & Jaynes

White, R. W. Motivation reconsidered: The concept of competence. *Psychological Review*, 1959, 66, 297–333. Kessen & Mandler; Smith

Whiteman, M. The performance of schizophrenics on social concepts. *Journal of Abnormal and Social Psychology*, 1954, 49, 266–271. Buss & Lang

Whiting, J. W. M. Sorcery, sin, and the superego: Some cross-cultural mechanisms of social control. In M. R. Jones (Ed.), *Nebraska symposium on motivation: 1959*. Lincoln: University of Nebraska Press, 1959. Pp. 174–195. Aronfreed

Whiting, J. W. M. Resource mediation and learning by identification. In I. Iscoe & H. W. Stevenson (Eds.), *Personality development in children*. Austin, Tex.: University of Texas Press, 1960. Pp. 112–126. Aronfreed

Whiting, J. W. M., & Child, I. L. *Child training and personality*. New Haven: Yale University Press, 1953. Aronfreed

Whiting, J. W. M., & Mowrer, O. H. Habit progression and regression—a laboratory study of some factors relevant to human socialization. *Journal of Comparative Psychology*, 1943, 36, 229–253. Solomon

Whyte, L. L. *The next development in man*. New York: Mentor Books, 1950. Rogers

Wickens, D. D., Schroder, H. M., & Snide, J. D. Primary stimulus generalization of the GSR under two conditions. *Journal of Experimental Psychology*, 1954, 47, 52–56. Burton

Wienckowski, L. A. Stimulus factors influencing the disjunctive reaction time of schizophrenic and "normal" subjects. Unpublished doctoral dissertation, University of Buffalo, 1959. Lang & Buss

Wilcoxon, F. *Some rapid approximate statistical procedures*. New York: American Cyanamid Company, 1949. Rabin

Wilder, J. The law of initial values. *Psychosomatic Medicine*, 1950, 12, 392–401. Lang & Buss

Williams, E. B. Deductive reasoning in schizophrenia. Unpublished doctoral dissertation, Columbia University, 1962. Buss & Lang

Williams, M. Psychophysiological responsiveness to psychological stress in early chronic schizophrenic reactions. *Psychosomatic Medicine*, 1953, *15*, 456–462. Lang & Buss

Winer, H. R. Incidental learning in schizophrenics. *Dissertation Abstracts*, 1954, *14*, 1002–1003. Buss & Lang

Wing, J. K., & Freudenberg, R. K. The responses of severely ill chronic schizophrenics to social stimulation. *American Journal of Psychiatry*, 1961, *118*, 311–322. Buss & Lang

Name Index

Acker, C. W., 279
Adams, J. A., 337
Adler, N., 80 fn., 297
Adornetto, J., 268
Adorno, T. W., 206
Aeschliman, B., 321
Agarwal, P. S., 158
Aiken, E. G., 100
Akerfeldt, S., 153
Alexander, S., 382 fn.
Allinsmith, Wesley, 9 fn., 97, 117, 127, 475, 476, 487
Allport, G. W., 202, 485, 491
Altschule, M. D., 278
Alvarez, R. R., 247
Alzheimer, 142
Amin, A. H., 156
Amsel, 88
Andrews, J. D. W., 364
Angel, E., 74, 225
Angyal, A., 280, 282
Anker, J., 346
Antonitis, J. J., 102
Appel, J. B., 77 fn.
Arendt, Hannah, 234
Arey, L. B., 245
Arieti, S., 256, 261, 273, 292
Armitage, S., 341
Armstrong, M. D., 148
Aronfreed, Justin, 67, 95–119, 127, 474, 489, 490, 507
Artiss, K. L., 292, 293
Astrup, C., 280
Atkinson, B., 231, 233
Atkinson, J. W., 339

Atkinson, Rita L., 250, 251, 252
Auersperg, A. P. Vom Werden der Angst, 71 fn.
Ausubel, David P., 180–201
Ax, A. F., 45
Axelrod, J., 148, 149
Aylesworth, M., 87
Ayllon, T., 340, 341
Azrin, N. H., 77, 79

Bachrach, A. J., 317
Bagby, E., 318, 335
Balakian, Anna, 313
Bandura, A., 116, 316, 318, 322, 331, 332, 333, 343, 378, 506
Banerjee, S., 158
Barber, T. X., 69, 70
Barbu, Z., 484, 485, 490
Barratt, E. S., 277
Barrett-Lennard, G. T., 218
Barron, Frank, 410, 451–460, 468, 469, 470
Bartelme, P., 380
Bartlett, Sir Frederick, 37, 39, 446
Barton, Walter, 210
Baxter, J. C., 243, 244
Bayley, Nancy, 490
Beach, F. A., 78, 92, 321, 336
Beck, R. C., 100
Becker, E., 292
Becker, J., 243, 244
Becker, W., 138

Beers, Clifford, 203
Bellak, C., 292
Belloni, Marigold, 271
Beloff, Halla, 258
Bender, Lauretta, 274
Bendig, A. W., 382
Benton, A. L., 246
Berg, P. S. D., 269
Bergson, 449, 450
Berkowitz, L., 505
Berkun, M. M., 85
Berle, B. B., 379
Berlyne, D. E., 325
Bernheim, 221
Bersh, P. J., 102
Beswich, David G., 478 fn.
Bettelheim, B., 116
Birney, James, 32–41
Bitterman, M. E., 111
Blackburn, H. L., 246, 247
Blackman, N., 280, 282
Blaufarb, H., 270
Blaurock, M., 279
Bleke, R. C., 241, 276
Bleuler, E., 142, 270
Blew, Maryly, 18 fn.
Blewitt, D. B., 258, 267
Blodgett, H. C., 324
Blum, G. S., 121, 123, 308 fn.
Boehm, Leonore, 489, 490
Bolles, Marjorie, 254
Bookbinder, L. J., 379
Boren, J., 114
Boring, E. G., 462
Boroczi, C., 77

Boyd, R. W., 380
Braceland, F. J., 380
Braden, W., 250
Brady, J. V., 89, 98
Braginsky, Benjamin M., 222, 292–298
Braginsky, Dorothea D., 222, 292–298, 374
Breger, Louis, 298, 316–347, 349, 350, 351, 363
Breland, K., 324
Breland, M., 324
Brengelmann, J. C., 267
Bretnall, E. P., 86
Breuer, 309, 335
Broadhurst, P., 341
Brodsky, M. J., 244
Broen, W. E., 77
Brogden, H. E., 484, 485, 487, 490
Brogden, W. J., 83, 325
Bronfrenbrenner, U., 10 fn. 102, 116, 117, 136, 489, 490
Brooker, H., 252
Brown, J. S., 77, 84
Brown, P. A., 379
Brown, R. L., 250
Brownstein, A., 100
Brozek, J., 278
Brush, Elinor S., 70, 87, 98, 99, 110, 111
Brush, F. R., 98, 101, 111
Bryan, J. H., 498, 507
Buchanan, G., 100
Buck, C. W., 280
Bugelski, B. R., 87, 323, 487
Bühler, K., 74 fn.
Burday, G., 248
Burrowes, A., 498
Burstein, A. G., 256
Burt, Cyril, 450
Burton, Roger V., 473, 474–490
Buss, Arnold H., 221, 239–291
Buss, Edith H., 250

Caldwell, W. E., 245
Calloway, E., III, 284
Cameron, N. S., 255, 256–257
Campbell, Byron A., 67, 92–95
Campbell, D., 276, 488
Campbell, E. H., 93, 94
Camus, A., 234
Cannon, W. B., 24, 45, 47 fn., 71, 72
Cantril, H., 46
Carlin, Jean, 44 fn.
Carlsmith, J. M., 80, 478 fn.
Carrigan, P. M., 279
Carscallen, H. B., 280
Castell, D., 379
Cattell, R. B., 382
Cavanaugh, D., 249, 250, 251

Chapman, A. H., 159
Chapman, J., 266, 267, 269
Chapman, L. J., 254, 256, 257, 258, 271, 275
Charcot, J. M., 221
Child, I. L., 96, 102, 116, 117
Choderkoff, B., 256
Chomsky, N., 322, 324, 325, 344
Church, R. M., 88, 99, 101, 111
Claridge, G., 276, 277
Clausen, J. A., 160, 210
Cleveland, S. E., 283
Cofer, C., 239, 260, 277
Cohen, B. D., 249, 267, 276, 280, 283
Cohen, M., 265
Cohen, S., 271
Cohen, W., 250
Cohn, F., 140 fn.
Colbert, E. C., 280, 282
Cole, M. W., 45, 46 fn.
Coles, R., 495
Combs, A. W., 379
Connor, W. H., 505
Conovitz, M. W., 78
Conrad, D. G., 111
Cooke, G., 343
Cooper, J. E., 343, 346, 379
Cooper, R., 267
Cottrell, L. S., Jr., 202
Cowen, E. L., 379
Crandall, Vaughn J., 9 fn.
Crawford, T. B. B., 156
Crookes, T. G., 267
Crowne, D. P., 333
Crumpton, Evelyn, 270
Crutchfield, Richard S., 457 fn., 459
Culver, C. M., 244
Curtin, Mary E., 271
Cutick, R. A., 98
Czaczkes, J. W., 197

D'Alessio, G. R., 246
D'Amato, M. R., 114
Daniels, L. R., 505
Darby, C. L., 99
Darley, J. M., 498
Darrow, C. W., 279
Darwin, Charles, 238
David, M., 248
Davis, R. H., 244
Davison, G., 343
Davitz, J. R., 101
Deering, Gayle, 245, 262
Deese, J., 87
Della Mirandola, Pico, 236
Dembo, D., 284
De Rivera, J., 320
Deutsch, J. A., 73 fn., 323, 331
Devault, M., 283
DeVault, S., 278, 281

Dewar, R., 271
Dewey, John, 175
DeWolfe, A. S., 244
Diamond, L., 323
Dillon, D., 267
Dinsmoor, J. A., 81–82, 83, 84, 114
Distler, L. M., 116
Dobe, Shirley I., 283
Dobzhansky, Theodosius, 141, 165–175
Dollard, J., 9, 10, 18, 68, 99, 316, 319, 329
Domino, E. F., 283
Donahoe, J. W., 271
Doob, W., 18
Downing, R. W., 271
Downs, M. P., 288
Draguns, J. G., 266
Drasgow, J., 270
Dreyfuss, F., 197
DuBois, Cora, 206
Duffy, Elizabeth, 287
Dunham, R. M., 242, 244
Dunn, W. L., 242, 244, 275
Durkheim, E., 230, 235
Durkin, Dolores, 489, 490
Dymond, R. F., 379

Ebert, J. N., 271
Edisen, C. B., 153
Edwards, A. L., 125
Edwards, A. S., 278
Ehrenworth, J., 244
Ehrmann, J. C., 256
Ellenberger, H. F., 74, 225
Ellingson, R. J., 284
Ellis, A., 346
Ellis, R. M., Jr., 278
Ellsworth, R. B., 256
Endler, N. S., 382
Engel, Edward, 26
Epstein, S., 243, 257
Eriksen, C. W., 308 fn. 326
Erlenmeyer-Kimling, L., 167
Estes, W. K., 13 fn. 86, 114, 349, 350
Eysenck, Hans J., 267, 276, 298, 316, 317, 319, 320, 327, 328, 329, 331, 339–347, 395, 485

Fagan, S. A., 98
Faibish, G. M., 272
Fairweather, G. W., 336, 346, 380
Fanconi, G., 69
Farber, I. E., 69, 114
Feffer, M. H., 245
Feifel, H., 256
Feigley, C. A., 163
Feldman, M. J., 270
Feldstein, S., 244
Felice, A., 247

Fenichel, O., 121, 122, 273, 380, 491
Ferrazzini, F., 69
Ferster, C. B., 324
Feshbach, S., 18, 19, 21
Festinger, L., 46
Fey, Elizabeth T., 254
Fiedler, 302
Fierman, L. B., 292
Finison, L., 293
Fischer, E. H., 252
Fisher, S., 254
Fishman, J. R., 495
Fiske, D. W., 379, 380, 488
Fitts, P. M., 327, 337
Flataker, L., 154
Fladeland, 37, 39, 40, 41
Flavell, J. H., 256, 506
Fondeur, M. P., 257
Foote, N. N., 202
Frank, J. D., 332, 335, 380, 395
Frankl, V., 234
Franks, C. M., 274
Frazier, 86
Frederick, F., 498
Freedman, A. M., 154
Freedman, D. T., 292
Freedman, M., 468
Freeman, G. L., 277, 280, 287
Freeman, H. J., 284
Frenkel-Brunswik, Else, 206
Freud, Anna, 10, 11, 14, 114, 491
Freud, Sigmund, 4–8, 10, 11, 13, 16, 66, 67, 94, 96, 102, 114, 120, 122, 182–183, 186, 192 fn., 221, 238, 239, 261, 297, 300, 302, 309, 314, 326, 329, 335, 354, 355, 361, 364, 373, 461–462
Freudenberg, R. K., 246
Friedman, S. H., 267
Fromm, E., 225, 226, 228, 329, 462
Fromm-Reichman, Frieda, 329
Funkenstein, D. H., 281

Gaddum, J. H., 156, 158
Galanter, E. H., 336
Gallagher, E. B., 292
Galton, B. B., 99, 100
Galton, Francis, 409–410, 411–433
Gantt, W. H., 78, 89
Garmezy, N., 240, 241, 242, 248, 250, 252, 274
Garrison, William Floyd, 32–42
Geer, James H., 366, 373–379
Geer, J., 373, 374, 397 fn.
Gelder, M. G., 343, 379
Geller, I., 98
Gellhorn, E., 277, 281

Gendlin, E. T., 216, 217, 358–360
George, E. I., 257, 290
Gerty, F. J., 146
Gestalt, 319
Ghent, L., 154
Gibbs, E., 154
Gibson, J. J., 320, 446 fn.
Gindis, I. Z., 279
Ginsberg, S. W., 202
Gjessing, L., 147
Gjessing, R., 147
Gleitman, H., 99
Gliedman, L. H., 395
Glover, E., 491
Glueck, E., 136
Glueck, S., 136
Goffman, E., 292
Goldiamond, I., 248
Goldman, A. E., 255–256, 261
Goldstein, A. C., 78
Goldstein, A. P., 396
Goldstein, H., 143
Goldstein, K., 254, 255, 261
Goldstone, S., 269
Gonzales, R. C., 323
Goodenough, Florence L., 490
Goodman, G., 379, 380
Goodson, F., 100
Goodstein, L. D., 247
Goodwin, W. R., 327, 487
Goranson, R. E., 505
Gordan, G. S., 146
Gordon, J. E., 140 fn.
Gottlieb, J. S., 276–277, 283
Gough, H. G., 467, 469, 470, 471
Gould, L. N., 280
Gouldner, A. W., 505
Granger, G. W., 267
Gray, Susan W., 10
Greenberg, A., 251
Greening, T. C., 127
Greifenstein, F., 283
Grisell, J. L., 249, 264
Gromoll, H. F., Jr., 284
Grossberg, J. M., 316, 332, 335, 343, 347, 348
Grosse, M., 292
Grygier, Tadeusz, 458
Guertin, W. H., 247
Guilford, J. P., 453
Gullock, A. H., 143
Gumenik, W. E., 114
Gunderson, E. K., 278, 281
Gundlach, R., 379
Guthrie, E. R., 88, 318 fn. 320
Guttman, L., 482
Guttman, N., 321
Gwinn, G. T., 111, 114
Gwynn, W., 246

Hadler, N., 168
Hakerem, 266

Halikas, N., 80
Hall, C. S., 86
Hall, Julia C., 113
Hall, K., 280
Hall, R., 267
Hall, Wallace B., 462
Hanfmann, Eugenia, 254
Harlow, H. F., 72, 75, 337–338, 341
Harrington, R. W., 244, 256
Harris, A., 278, 283
Harris, J. G., Jr., 243, 244
Harris, M. M., 146
Harrower, M. R., 489
Harsh, C. M., 324
Hart, 41
Hartshorne, H., 96, 473, 474–478, 479 fn., 484, 485, 487, 488, 489, 490
Hase, Ruth, 44 fn.
Hathaway, S. R., 469
Heath, R. G., 148, 152, 291
Hebb, D. O., 69, 91 fn., 282, 286, 321, 324, 327, 347, 446 fn., 491
Heilbrun, A. B., Jr., 467
Heinecke, C. M., 116
Heist, P., 468
Hendrick, I., 380
Henschel, A., 278
Herbert, M. J., 324
Hernandez-Péon, R., 282, 288
Herrnstein, R. J., 111
Hershiser, D., 274, 278
Hess, E. H., 80
Hewlitt, J. H. G., 255, 257, 289, 290
Higgins, J., 276
Hilgard, E. R., 319, 400
Hill, T. S., 278
Hill, W. F., 99, 127
Hillman, J., 360
Hilmo, J., 498
Hinde, R. A., 68
Hirsch, J., 167, 168, 173
Hitler, Adolf, 234
Hobbs, G. E., 280
Hock, P., 278, 280, 281
Hoffer, A., 148
Hoffman, Lois W., 126 fn.
Hoffman, Martin L., 120, 126–140, 489, 490
Hogan, J. A., 80 fn.
Hollingshead, A. B., 191
Holmberg, C. G., 148, 152
Holtzman, W. H., 111
Holz, W. C., 77, 79
Holzberg, J., 293
Honzik, C. H., 324
Horowitz, I. A., 504
Horwitt, M. K., 143, 146, 163
Hoskins, R. G., 277
Houspian, E. M., 284
Howe, E. S., 274
Hoyle, G., 321 fn.

Hubby, J. L., 166
Hull, C. L., 87, 88, 273, 316, 317, 321, 323, 325, 340, 487
Humphrey, 446 fn.
Humphreys, L. G., 486
Hunt, J. McV., 45, 46 fn., 78, 239, 260, 277, 380, 382
Hunt, W. A., 46
Hunter, W. S., 83
Husek, T. R., 382 fn.
Huston, Aletha C., 116
Huston, P. E., 267, 269, 276

Imada, M., 81
Imber, S. D., 380, 395
Irvine, Elizabeth R., 122
Irwin, F. W., 95 fn.
Isaacs, W., 248

Jackson, D. D., 160
Jacobson, E., 351, 357, 360, 398
Jahoda, Marie, 202, 209, 210
James, W., 24, 44, 45, 47 fn., 71, 72
Jaynes, Julian, 67, 92–95
Jenkins, W. O., 102
Jenkins, R. L., 247
Jentsch, R. C., 246
Johannsen, W. J., 247, 251, 267, 268, 289
Johns, Marcia D., 13 fn.
Johnson, R. C., 271
Jones, E., 183, 192 fn.
Jones, M. H., 279
Jones, Mary Cover, 366, 367–373
Jones, N. F., 279
Josephson, E., 225
Josephson, M., 225
Jost, H., 278
Jung, C. G., 352, 361, 362
Jurko, M., 278, 279, 280

Kagan, Jerome, 4, 9–17, 115
Kaiser, H. F., 481
Kallmann, F. J., 160, 162, 162 fn.
Kamin, L. J., 77, 101
Kantor, R. E., 207, 209
Karras, A., 265
Karsh, E. B., 77, 77 fn.
Kasanin, J., 254, 255, 256
Kates, S. L., 243
Kelman, H., 15 fn.
Kelsey, F. E., 143
Kelsey, F. O., 143
Kendler, H. H., 487
Kendler, Tracy S., 487, 489
Kenyon, M., 148
Kessen, William, 66, 67–75
Kety, Seymour S., 141, 142–164
Keup, W., 143, 153

Keys, A., 278
Kidd, Aline H., 268
Kierkegaard, S., 226
Killberg, J., 248
Kimble, 87
Kinder, E. F., 278
King, G., 248, 280, 341
King, H. E., 264, 269, 279, 281, 282
Klaus, R., 10
Klein, D. C., 209
Kling, A., 98
Knight, R. P., 10, 331
Koch, Helen, 16
Koch, S., 349
Koegler, R. R., 280, 282
Koestler, Arthur, 410, 434–450
Kogan, L. S., 380
Kohlberg, L., 97, 98 fn., 119 fn., 138, 489, 490
Köhler, W., 320
Kohn, L. G., 21, 22
Kohn, M. L., 489
Koppenhaver, N. D., 250
Kornetsky, C., 163
Kovach, J. K., 80
Krasner, L., 316, 324, 326, 340, 341, 342, 380, 395
Kraude, W., 380
Kraepelin, 142
Krechevsky, I., 321
Kreinik, Phyllis S., 242, 244
Kremen, I., 71
Kris, 461
Kubie, L. S., 461, 471
Kubis, J. F., 278, 280
Kuenne, Margaret K., 487, 489
Kugelmass, S., 257

Labrosse, E. H., 147
Lacey, Beatrice C., 277, 278, 288, 290
Lacey, J. I., 277, 278, 280, 287, 288, 290
Ladd, C. E., 247
Lader, 41
Lair, C. V., 272
Lamoreaux, R. R., 101
Landis, C., 46
Lang, Peter J., 222, 239–291, 332, 335, 342, 343, 346, 366, 373, 380, 394, 397–406
Lange, 45, 47 fn. 71
Langer, Susanne, 193
Lansky, Leonard M., 9 fn.
Lashley, 321, 336
Latané, Bibb, 44 fn., 63, 498
Laurell, C. B., 148, 152
Lauro, L. P., 272
Lawes, T. C. G., 283
Lawley, D. N., 479, 480, 482
Lawlor, W. G., 278

Lawrence, D. H., 320, 321, 327, 487
Lazarus, A. A., 331, 334, 341, 342, 343, 346, 346 fn., 394
Lazovik, A. David, 332, 335, 346, 366, 373, 380, 394, 397–406
Lazowick, L. M., 10
Lazowik, R. D., 342, 343, 346
Leach, B. E., 148, 152
Leach, W. W., 280, 282
Lebow, K. E., 243
Lee, Katie, 185
Leeper, R. L., 321
Leibowitz, H. W., 244, 268
Lerner, E., 489, 490
Lerner, I. M., 170
Lesse, S., 395
Lester, J. R., 272
Leventhal, A. M., 250, 252
Levin, H., 10, 21, 96, 127, 490
Levine, L. S., 207, 209
Levinson, D., 206, 292, 293
Lewin, K., 69, 319, 326
Lewontin, R. C., 166
Liccione, J. V., 267
Licht, L., 271
Lichtenstein, F. E., 78, 79
Liddell, H. S., 337
Lindsley, D. B., 65, 287
Lindsley, O., 248
Lipinski, C. E., 374
Lipton, L., 271
Littman, R., 100
London, Perry, 299–316
Lorenz, Konrad, 450, 491
Lorr, M., 294, 380
Losen, S. M., 250, 251, 253
Lothrop, W. W., 254
Lovibond, S. H., 257, 340, 341, 342, 343, 345, 346
Lovinger, E., 248, 267, 268
Lowe, I. P., 154
Luby, E. D., 276, 283
Ludwig, A. M., 288
Lundin, R. W., 325
Luoto, 272
Luria, A. R., 280, 487, 489
Luxenburger, H., 162

Maccoby, Eleanor E., 10, 16, 96, 115, 127, 475, 476, 487, 488, 490
MacCorquodale, R., 339, 349
MacGregor, G., 206
Mackavey, W. R., 249
MacKinnon, Donald W., 117, 410, 461–472, 475
Mackintosh, N. J., 327
MacRae, D., Jr., 486 fn., 489, 490
Maddi, Salvatore R., 221, 222–239
Margaret, Ann, 257

Maginley, H. J., 251, 252
Maier, N. R. F., 76, 89, 90, 114
Maller, J. B., 474, 484, 485, 487
Malmo, R. B., 277, 278, 279, 280, 282, 287
Maltzman, I., 271
Mandl, Billie Sue T., 270
Mandler, George, 66–75
Mann, J. D., 147
Marañon, G., 46
Marcuszewicz, 7 fn.
Markham, C. H., 280, 282
Marks, I., 343, 379
Marquis, Dorothy P., 69
Martin, W. E., 10
Marx, A., 244
Marx, M. H., 69
Maslow, A. H., 202, 204, 461, 462
Mason, D. J., 101
Masserman, J., 76, 78, 79, 89, 90, 341, 350
Matussek, P., 257, 290
Maxwell, A. E., 479, 480
May, M. A., 96, 473, 474–478, 479 fn., 484, 485, 487, 488, 489, 490
May, P. R., 280, 380, 396
May, R., 74, 225, 226, 233, 234
Mayr, E., 172
McCann, Richard V., 184
McClelland, D. C., 11 fn.
McCord, J., 136
McCord, W., 136
McDonald, R. K., 149, 152
McDonough, J. M., 267
McFarland, R. A., 143
McGaugh, James L., 298, 316–347, 349, 350, 351, 363
McGaughran, L. S., 254, 255
McGhie, A., 266, 267, 269
McGinnies, E., 268
McKinley, J. C., 469
McNair, D. M., 380
Medinnus, G. R., 489
Mednick, S. A., 71, 272, 273, 274, 275, 276, 286
Meduna, L. J., 146
Meehl, P. G., 339, 349
Melzack, R., 70
Mendel, Gregor, 165
Merril, 40
Metzner, R., 342
Meyer, J. S., 283
Meyer, W. J., 251
Michael, J., 340
Michalson, Carl, 185
Michaux, W., 248
Midlarsky, E., 507
Milgram, S., 496–497
Miller, Arthur, 185, 230, 236

Miller, G. A., 336
Miller, George, 87
Miller, N. E., 9, 10, 18, 64, 67, 68, 77, 85, 99, 110, 114, 316, 319, 325, 329
Miller, Neal, 84
Miller, Perry, 34
Miller, R., 397 fn.
Miller, R. D., 96, 102
Miller, W., 136
Milner, P., 325
Moltz, H., 80, 324
Montgomery, K. C., 99, 100
Moran, L. J., 254, 255, 257, 271
Morgan, C. T., 321
Moriarty, D., 243
Morris, Charles, 212
Morris, J. F., 489
Morrison, Donald F., 481 fn.
Moss, Howard A., 9 fn.
Mowrer, O. Hobart, 9, 10, 11, 14, 18, 64, 66, 67, 78, 82, 83, 84, 90, 91, 97, 99, 100, 101, 114, 116, 180, 181–186, 194–196, 199, 342, 345, 491
Moya, F., 146
Mueller, C. G., Jr., 349
Munroe, Ruth L., 466
Murphree, O. D., 274
Murphy, L. B., 139
Murray, E. J., 85, 335
Murray, H. A., 238, 467
Mussen, Paul, 4, 15, 18–22, 116, 256
Myers, Isabel B., 469
Myrdal, G., 206

Nash, E. H., 380, 395
Nathan, P., 255
Nefzger, W. D., 100
Neiditch, S. J., 241
Nelson, Sandra, 245
Nissen, H. W., 321
Norris, Lynne, 397 fn.
Nowlis, H. H., 64
Nowlis, V., 64
Nye, I. F., 116, 345

O'Connor, N., 248, 264 fn., 274, 277, 281
Offenbach, S. I., 251
Olds, J., 157, 325
Olds, M. E., 157
Olson, G. W., 246
Orgel, A., 250
Orne, M., 246
Osgood, C. E., 319, 321, 323, 487
Osmond, H., 271

Pacht, A. R., 268
Paintal, A. S., 281
Papert, S., 342

Parkel, D., 292
Pascal, C., 248
Paskal, V., 507
Pathman, J. H., 277
Paul, Gordon, L., 343, 366, 379–397
Pavlov, Ivan, 66, 276, 286
Payne, D. E., 15
Payne, R. W., 255, 257, 289, 290
Pearl, D., 269
Pechtel, C., 76, 79, 90
Peel, E. A., 489
Peiper, A., 68, 70
Peirce, P., 321
Peoples, C., 246
Perlin, S., 149
Peters, H. N., 247, 274
Peters, R. S., 190, 203–204, 205
Petursson, E., 278
Pfaffman, C., 274
Pfaundler, 345
Phillips, L., 259
Phillips, Wendell, 32–42
Piaget, J., 96, 138, 475, 489, 506
Pinsky, R. H., 379
Pintler, Margaret H., 17
Pishkin, V., 244, 268, 274, 278
Polànyi, M., 445
Pool, J. L., 284
Portnoy, M., 266
Postman, L., 321
Pribram, K. H., 336
Purpura, D. P., 284

Rabin, Albert, 120, 121–126, 269
Rachman, S., 276, 277, 298, 334, 339–347
Rakusin, J. M., 292
Rank, O., 68, 461–462, 464–467, 469, 470–471
Ransohoff, J., 284
Rapaport, D., 355
Rashkis, H. A., 254
Rausch, H. L., 244, 245, 267, 268
Rawnsley, K., 274
Ray, T. S., 278, 279, 281
Rayner, 367 fn.
Razran, 308 fn.
Redlich, F. C., 191, 292
Reich, W., 354
Reichman, 329
Reis, E. E., 45, 46 fn.
Reisman, M. N., 267
Reitman, E. E., 283
Reyna, L. J., 316
Reynolds, D. J., 278, 279, 280, 281, 290, 366, 373, 397–406
Reynolds, G. A., 267

Richter, D., 143, 146
Riesman, D., 202
Riess, B. F., 379
Riggs, L. A., 269
Riley, D. A., 320
Ring, K., 292, 293, 374
Riopelle, A. J., 99
Ritchie, B. F., 321
Robins, E., 154, 155
Robinson, Nancy M., 250, 251, 252
Rodnick, E. H., 240, 241, 242, 248, 250, 269, 280
Rogers, Carl R., 181, 211–220, 233, 237, 297, 300, 302, 379, 461, 462
Rogers, J. V., 77 fn.
Romano, R., 397 fn.
Rorschach, H., 452, 453
Rosanoff, A. J., 162
Rosenbaum, G., 249, 269, 276, 282, 283
Rosenberg, Morris, 482 fn.
Rosenblum, L., 80
Rosenhan, David, 474, 491–507
Rosenstein, A. J., 382
Rosenthal, D., 160, 267, 278
Roth, I., 380
Rouke, F. L., 278, 280
Rubin, L., 279
Ruchames, 37, 38
Ruckmick, C. A., 45
Russell, Anna, 182, 185
Rutherford, Eldred, 4, 18–22

Sager, C. J. 379
Salter, A., 316
Saltzstein, Herbert D., 120, 126–140
Salzinger, K., 268
Sanders, R., 268
Sanford, N., 206
Sanford, R. N., 9, 10, 11
Santillana, 450
Sarason, S. B., 68 fn.
Sargent, H. D., 379, 380
Sartre, J. P., 226, 228
Schachter, J., 45
Schachter, Stanley, 24, 44–65, 373, 374
Scharlock, D., 487
Scheerer, M., 254
Scheinberg, P., 146
Schieve, J. F., 146
Schilder, P., 274
Schlosberg, H., 65, 78, 81, 82, 83, 274
Schmidt, E., 379
Schneirla, T. R., 71
Schoenfeld, W. N., 102, 349
Schooler, C., 247, 289, 292
Schreiner, L., 98
Schroder, H. M., 485
Schutz, W. C., 468

Schwartz, M., 284
Scott, J. P., 92, 327
Scott, T. H., 70
Searles, H. F., 292
Sears, P. S., 15, 16, 17
Sears, R. R., 10, 14, 17, 18, 21, 96, 102, 116, 117, 121, 127, 130, 140, 490
Selye, H., 68
Senden, 446 fn.
Senf, Rita, 267
Seth, G., 258
Seward, J. P., 10
Seymore, S., 271
Shagass, C., 278, 280, 284
Shakow, D., 246, 251, 260, 269, 270, 272, 276, 280
Shankweiler, D. P., 247
Shannon, D. T., 381
Shaw, E., 156, 158
Sheffield, F. D., 74
Sherman, N. A., 280
Shipley, W. C., 274
Shoben, E. J., Jr., 202
Shubrooks, S. J., 271
Shuttleworth, F. K., 474, 488
Sidman, M., 111, 114
Siegel, Alberta E., 18, 19, 21, 22
Silverman, J., 245, 265 fn.
Simon, R., 380
Simpson, G. G., 172
Sinett, E. R., 379
Singer, Jerome E., 24, 44–65
Skinner, B. F., 76, 86–87, 89, 248, 316, 317, 320, 321, 322, 323, 324, 325, 340
Slater, E., 160, 162
Slechta, Joan, 246
Smith, A. A., 278
Smith, K., 154
Smith, M. Brewster, 181, 201–211
Smith, S., 283
Smith, Stevenson, 318 fn., 335
Smith, T., 244, 268
Smith, W. O., 270
Smock, C. D., 241, 276
Snide, J. D., 485
Snow, C. P., 211, 314
Snyder, S., 267
Sokoloff, L., 146
Solomon, A. P., 279, 280, 281
Solomon, F., 495
Solomon, Richard L., 66, 70, 71 fn., 75–92, 95 fn., 97, 98, 99, 101, 110, 111, 113, 114, 329, 337
Sommer, R., 267, 271
Spassky, B., 167, 168, 169
Spence, Janet T., 87, 88, 246, 272, 273, 275
Spence, K. W., 275, 320
Spiro, M., 122
Spohn, H. E., 246, 247

Staats, A., 342
Staats, C., 342
Steinberg, F., 78
Stevenson, I., 396
Stimput, W. E., 379
Stoke, S. M., 10
Stone, A. R., 380, 395, 396
Stone, L. J., 19
Storms, L. H., 77
Stotsky, B., 247
Strachey, Mrs. Alix, 4 fn.
Straight, E., 379
Strickland, Bonnie R., 333
Stride, E., 280
Sullivan, Harry Stack, 191, 255, 297, 300, 314, 329, 362
Sully, J., 437
Sulzbach, W. M., 278
Sutton, S., 266
Swenson, G., 248
Sykes, G., 225
Syz, H. C., 278
Szara, S., 149
Szasz, Thomas S., 180, 184 fn., 186–201, 209, 292

Taylor, I. A., 267
Taylor, J. G., 342
Taylor, Janet A., 68 fn., 254, 257, 275, 469
Test, M. A., 498
Thakurdas, H., 283
Thistlethwaite, D., 324, 327
Thomas, J., 248
Thomas, 37, 40
Thompson, Sir George, 339
Thompson, W. R., 491
Thorndike, E. L., 88
Thudichum, J. W. L., 142
Thurstone, 478 fn., 484
Tillich, P., 234
Tilton, J. R., 248, 341
Tizard, J., 264, 265, 269, 276, 282
Tolman, E. C., 86, 319, 321, 323, 324, 326, 337, 340
Tolstoi, L., 229
Tomkins, Silvan S., 23, 24–44
Topping, Gillian, 248
Tourney, G., 281 fn.
Towbin, A. P., 292
Tuma, A. H., 380
Turbiner, M., 242, 244
Turner, L. H., 82, 99
Turner, R. K., 340
Turteltaub, Alan, 366, 373–379

Ullmann, L., 340, 341, 342, 380
Underwood, B. J., 336
Unger, S. M., 488
Urse, V. G., 146

Vancini, J., 241, 276
Venables, P. H., 264, 264 fn., 265, 269, 276, 277, 281, 282
Vercors, 173
Verdone, 256
Verplanck, W. S., 349
Viek, P., 101, 114

Wade, E. A., 100
Wahler, H. J., 246
Walk, R. D., 400
Walsh, R., 346
Walters, G. C., 77 fn.
Walters, H., 378
Walters, R. H., 116, 506
Wapner, S., 496
Warden, C. J., 87
Waters, T. J., 252
Watson, A. J., 325, 329
Watson, J. B., 68, 78, 367
Webb, W. W., 240
Weber, 238
Webster, H., 468
Weckowicz, T. E., 258, 267, 268, 281
Weinberg, N. H., 352
Weiss, J. M., 167
Weiss, R. L., 271
Weitzenhoffer, A. M., 400
Weitzman, Bernard, 298, 347–364
Weld, Theodore, 32–41
Weller, Leonard, 44 fn.
Wells, Doris, 487

Welsh, G. S., 469
Wendt, G. R., 88
Wenger, M. A., 279
Werner, H., 255, 261, 496
Wertham, F., 18
West, L. J., 69
Whatmore, C. B., 278
Wheeler, L., 63
White, G. M., 498, 501
White, Mary A., 254
White, R. W., 74 fn., 94, 202
Whiteman, M., 244
Whiting, J. W. M., 78, 91, 96, 97, 102, 115, 116, 117, 487
Whyte, Lancelot, 217
Wiater, R., 397 fn.
Wickens, D. D., 486
Wienckowski, L. A., 265, 267
Wiener, M., 250
Wilcoxon, F., 125
Wilder, J., 280, 287
Wilkinson, Jean, 397 fn.
Williams, E. B., 254
Williams, M., 278, 280
Wilson, W. C., 10, 16
Wilson, P. T., 162 fn.
Wilson, W. P., 146
Winer, H. R., 251
Wing, J. K., 246, 281
Winter, C. A., 154
Wishner, J., 280, 287
Witney, Gwynneth, 271
Wittman, Phyllis, 246

Wolf, S., 45, 379
Wolff, H., 45, 379
Wolk, W., 246
Wolpe, J., 316–317, 318, 320, 327, 329, 330, 331, 332, 333, 335, 341, 342, 347, 348, 350–355, 357, 360, 380, 394, 398, 405
Wood, B. S., 288
Woodworth, R. S., 65, 81, 82, 321, 337
Woolley, D. W., 156, 158
Wrightsman, L. S., 49
Wynne, L. C., 71 fn., 99, 111, 113, 114, 271
Wynne, R. D., 271

Yarrow, L. J., 19
Yates, A. J., 89–90, 328, 330, 342
Yelen, D., 277
Young, G., 340
Young, H. H., 380

Zahn, T. P., 241, 243, 244, 269, 278
Zaslove, M., 352
Zaslow, R. W., 257
Zelhart, P. F., 271
Zener, K., 323
Zigler, E., 259
Zubin, J., 266
Zuckerman, M., 375, 376

Subject Index

Abstractness, loss of, 254
Acquisition, 97–110
  procedure for the study of, 104–108
  results and discussion of the study of, 108–110
  socialization, naturalistic and experimental, 100–102
  socialization paradigms, 102–104
  subjects for the study, 104
Adaptation, negative, elimination of children's fears through, 369–370
Addiction, psychological, 28–30
Affect, 23–24
Affect, Imagery and Consciousness (Tomkin), 23
Affect and reinforcement, psychological deficit in schizophrenia, 240–253
  motivation, insufficient, 246–253, 260–261
    cooperation, urging and, 246–247
    nonverbal reward and punishment, 247–250
    verbal reward and punishment, 250–253
  social censure, 240–242, 259–260
  stimuli, affective, 242–246
    censure stimuli, 242–244
    in general, 244–246
    sensitivity to, 260
Affection, parental, child moral indexes and, 136, 137
After the Fall (Miller), 230
Aggression, aggressive cartoons, effect on aggressive play, 18–22
  interpersonal, 21
  test of, 19
Aggression-test data, group means for, 20
  variance for, analysis of, 20
Aggressor, identification with, 10

Altruism of committed civil rights workers, 492–496
American Medical Association, 183
American Psychiatric Association, 183
American Psychoanalytic Association, 183
American Psychologist, 194
American Scholar, The (Emerson), 231
Amines, schizophrenia and, 147–148
Amino acids, schizophrenia and, 147–148
Anxiety, 66
  associational deficit and, 273–276
  inhibition of, 72–74
Arousal, somatic, *see* Somatic arousal
Art and Artist (Rank), 463
Associational deficit, anxiety and, 273–276
Associations, intrusive, of schizophrenia, 271–272
  of schizophrenics, uncommoness of, 271
Associative interference, 270–273
Attention, 264–269
  interference theory, 257–258
Autobiography (Freud), 182–183

Behavior, acquisition of, similar to a model, 14–15
  genetics of, 167–168, 172
  motives of, insight therapy and, 305–308
  social, *see* Positive social behavior; Social behavior
Behavior Research and Therapy, 343
Behavior therapy, analytic interpretations of, 360–363
  background of, theoretical, 348–350
  critique and reformulation of, 339–343

desensitization, systematic, interactions of, with psychotherapy, 357–360
  method of, 350–353
  learning theory and, 344–347
  psychotherapy, defense of, 353–357
    symptom substitution, problem of, 354–357
    therapy-theory distinction, 353–354
  psychotherapy and, 347–364
  techniques of, 345
Biochemical theories of schizophrenia, 142–149, 151–163
  amines, 147–148
  amino acids, 147–148
  carbohydrate, 145–147
  ceruloplasmin, 152–156
  energetics, 145–147
  epinephrine hypothesis, 148–149
  error, sources of, 143–145
  oxygen, 145–147
  program of the Laboratory of Clinical Science, 145
  serotonin, 156–158
  taraxein, 152–156
Brain disease, mental illness as sign of, 187–188
Brain pathology, mental symptoms and, 196–197

Carbohydrates, schizophrenia and, 145–147
Cardiovascular system, respiration and, somatic arousal and, 278
Cartoons, aggressive, effect on aggressive play, 18–22
Censure stimuli, 242–244
Ceruloplasmin, schizophrenia and, 152–156
Character traits, socially constructive, 473–507
  concern for others, origins of, 491–507
    charitability of children, experiments on, 498–500
    civil rights workers, committed, altruism of, 492–496
    cognitive development and, 504–506
    constructive rebellion, experiment on, 496–498
    observation-rehearsal sequence, experiment on, 500–504
  honesty, generality of, 474–490
    deceit, studies in, 476–478
    discussion, 485–491
    principal component analysis, 478
    related studies, 484
    results, 479–483
    simple analysis, 482–483
    specificity versus, 475–476
    tests, description of, 478–479
Charitability of children, experiments on, 498–500
Children, charitability of, experiments on, 498–500
  consideration for others, 130
  fears of, elimination of, 367–373
    direct conditioning, method of, 371–372
    distraction, method of, 370–371
    disuse, through, method of, 368–369
    negative adaptation, method of, 369–370

      repression, method of, 370
      social imitation, method of, 372
      verbal appeal, method of, 369
Civil rights workers, committed, altruism of, 492–496
Client-centered therapy, 302–305
Clinical depression, 4
Cognitive determinants of emotional state, 44–65
Cognitive development, concern for others and, 504–506
Commitment, psychology of, 24–44
  violence and suffering, constructive role of, 24–44
    high density end of continuum, 27–28
    ideo-affective density, 25
    low density end of continuum, 26–27
    positive high density ideo-affective organization, 28–32
    reformers, committed, 32–42
Communication, loss of, 254–255
Conceived values, 212
Concept attainment, psychological deficit in schizophrenia, 254–259
  abstractness, loss of, 254
  communication, loss of, 254–255
  interference theory, 256–258, 262, 287–289
    attention, 257–258
    overinclusion, 256–257
  regression to childish thinking, 255–256, 261–262
Concern for others, origins of, 491–507
  charitability of children, experiments on, 498–500
  civil rights workers, committed, altruism of, 492–496
  cognitive development and, 504–506
  constructive rebellion, experiments on, 496–498
  observation-rehearsal sequence, experiment on, 500–504
Conditioned emotional reaction (CER), 84, 85, 86
Conditioning, direct, elimination of children's fears through, 371–372
Consciousness, uses of, insight therapy and, 308–309
Constructive rebellion, experiment on, 496–498
Cooperation, urging and, 246–247
Creative potential, realization of, personality and, 461–472
Creativity, see Genius, creativity and

Death of a Salesman (Miller), 185
Death of Ivan Ilych, The (Tolstoi), 229
Deceit, studies in, 476–478
Decision theory, interpretation of desensitization therapy by, 362–363
Delinquency—Sickness or Sin? (McCann), 184
Depression, analysis of, 7–8
  clinical, 4
Desensitization, systematic, complex psychology of, interpretation by, 361–362
  empirical critique of, 358–360

interpretation of, from viewpoint of interpersonal psychiatry, 362
method of, 350–353
psychoanalytic interpretation of, 361
Desensitization therapy, insight versus, effects of,
  379–396
  interpretation of, by decision theory, 362–363
  suggestibility, pseudotherapy and, 397–406
Development, cognitive, concern for others and,
  504–506
  ideal and deviant, 236–237
Deviant development, ideal and, 236–237
Dictionary of Men of the Time, 412
Direct conditioning, elimination of children's
  fears through, 371–372
Discharge induction, psychiatric interview, 293–
  294
Discipline, middle-class, 133–136
  nonpower assertive, 127–128
  parental, 120–121
    moral development of the child and, 126–
    140
Disease, personality disorder as, 194–201
  Szasz-Mowrer position, 195–200
Distraction, elimination of children's fears
  through, 370–371
Distress, fundamental, nature of, 70–72
  inhibition of, anxiety, pain and, 67–75
Drive, 273–277, 286
  anxiety, associational deficit and, 273–276
  reactive inhibition, reminiscence and, 276–
  277
Drosophila fly, men and, genetics of, 164–175

Effects of psychotherapy, 365–406
  children's fears, elimination of, 367–373
    direct conditioning, method of, 371–372
    disuse, through, method of, 368–369
    distraction, method of, 370–371
    negative adaptation, method of, 369–370
    repression, method of, 370
    social imitation, method of, 372
    verbal appeal, method of, 369
  fear reduction following observation of a
    model, 373–379
  insight therapy, desensitization versus, 379–
    396
  pseudotherapy, desensitization, suggestibility
    and, 397–406
Ego, the, 8
  analysis of, 4–8
Ego ideal, 8
Emotion, determinants of, 44–65
Empathy, 6, 128, 139, 305
End of continuum, high density, 27–28
  low density, 26–27
Energetics, schizophrenia and, 145–147
Environment, schizophrenia in twins, factors of,
  162
Epinephrine hypothesis, schizophrenia and, 148–
  149
Ethics in psychiatry, role of, 190–192
Existential neurosis, 222–239
  development, ideal and deviant, 236–237

ideal personality, 231–235
  precipitating stress and, 235–236
  model for, 222–224
precipitating stress, 229–231
  ideal personality and, 235–237
premorbid personality, 226–229
symptoms called, 224–226
Experience, vicarious affective, 10–11
Extinction paradigms, 112–113

Faith for Personal Crises (Michalson), 185
Father, disciplinary role of, 136–137
Fear, children's, elimination of, 367–373
  direct conditioning, method of, 371–372
  distraction, method of, 370–371
  disuse, through, method of, 368–369
  negative adaptation, method of, 369–370
  repression, method of, 370
  social imitation, method of, 372
  verbal appeal, method of, 369
  reduction of, following observation of a
    model, 373–379
Fraternal twins, schizophrenia in, environmental
  factors in, 162
Frustration and Conflict (Yates), 89
Frustration groups, 19
Fundamental distress, nature of, 70–72

Genetics, schizophrenic disorders and, 158–161
  science of, 165–175
Genius, creativity and, 409–472
  creative potential, realization of, personality
    and, 461–472
  laughter, logic of, 434–450
    first approach, 439–442
    habit and originality, 446–447
    hidden persuaders, 445–446
    laughter reflex, 436–438
    man and machine, 447–450
    matrices and codes, 442–445
    paradox of, 438–439
  natural gifts, men classified according to, 415–
    427, 427–433
  orginality, disposition toward, 451–460
    discussion, 458–460
    hypotheses suggested by previous work, 456–
    458
    measurement of, 453–456
    relativity of, 452
  reputation, men classified according to, 411–
    414, 427–433
Group psychology, analysis of the ego and, 4–8
Guilt, sense of, 5, 6, 129

Hallucinations, 180
Heredity, 165–175
High density end of continuum, 27–28
Homosexuality, male, genesis of, 7
Honesty, generality of, 474–490
  deceit, studies in, 476–478
  discussion, 485–491
    age, 489

intelligence, 488–489
  sex, 490
  social class, 489–490
  principal component analysis, 478
  related studies, 484
  results, 479–483
  simple analysis, 482–483
  specificity versus, 475–476
  tests, description of, 478–479
Human Learning (Thorndike), 88

Ideal development, deviant and, 236–237
Ideal personality, 231–235
  precipitating stress and, 235–236
Ideation, 25
Identical twins, schizophrenia in, environmental
      factors in, 162
Identification, 4–8, 130–131
  acquisition of, 11–14
  concept of, 9–17
  definitions of, 11
  goals motivating, 15–16
  imitation learning, 9–10
    motives for, 14–15
  maintenance of, 11–14
  motives for, 14–15
  primary, 11
  prohibition learning, 10
    motives for, 14–15
  secondary, 11
  strength of, factors influencing, 16–17
  vicarious affective experience, 10–11
  with aggressor, 10
Ideo-affective density, 25
Ideo-affective organization, positive high density,
      28–32
  addition, psychological, 28–30
  commitment, 30–32
Illness, concept of, 188
Imitation, social, elimination of children's fears
      through, 372
Imitation learning, 9–10
  motives for, 14–15
Immorality, 182
Individuality, genetic, theory of, 165–166
Induction, 128
  conditions of, psychiatric interview, 293–294
    discharge induction, 293–294
    mental status induction, 294
    open ward induction, 294
  regarding parents disciplinary practice, 131
Inference and activation, psychological deficit in
      schizophrenia, 263–291
  associative interference, 270–273, 287–289
  attention, 264–269
  discussion, 285–291
  drive, 273–277, 286
    anxiety, associational deficit and, 273–276
    reactive inhibition, reminiscence and, 276–
      277
  methodological considerations, 289–291
  set, 269–270
  somatic arousal, 277–285, 286–287
    activity, habitual level of, 277–284
Inhibition, reactive, reminiscence, and 276–277

Insight therapy, 299–316
  behavior, motives of, 305–308
  client-centered therapy, 302–305
  consciousness, uses of, 308–309
  desensitization versus, effects of, 379–396
  morals and, 311–313
  problems of, 313–315
  psychoanalysis, 302–305
  science and, 309–311
  technical equivalence of, 300–302
Interference, associative, 270–273
Interference theory, 256–258, 262, 287–289
  attention, 257–258
  overinclusion, 256–257
Internationale Zeitschrift für Psychoanalyse, 7
Internalization, 97
Interpersonal aggression, 21
Interview, psychiatric, schizophrenic patients in,
      292–298
  induction conditions, 293–294
  method, 293–295
  predictions, 294–295
  results and discussion, 295–298
  subjects, 295
Irresponsibility, 182

James-Lange theory, 45, 47 n., 71
Journal of the Experimental Analysis of Behavior,
      316

Kibbutz and nonkibbutz boys, psychosexual dif-
      ferences between, 121–126
Künstler, Der (Rank), 462

Laboratory of Clinical Science, schizophrenia
      program of, 145
Laughter, logic of, 434–450
  first approach, 439–442
  habit and originality, 446–447
  hidden persuaders, 445–446
  laughter reflex, 436–438
  man and machine, 447–450
  matrices and codes, 442–445
  paradox of, 438–439
Laughter reflex, 436–438
Learning, imitation, 9–10
    motives for, 14–15
  learning theories and, 320
  prohibition, 10
    motives for, 14–15
Learning theory, 344–345
  behavior therapy and, 344–347
  critique and reformulation of, 316–338, 339–
      343
    conditioning model, use of, 322–324
    learned material, 320–322
    learning and, 320
    neurosis, conception of, 327–331
    reformulation, 336–338
    reinforcement, use of, 324–327
    science issue, 318–320
    success, claims of, 331–336

List problem, 207–208
Logic of laughter, *see* Laughter, logic of
Love, goal motivating identification, 15–16
Love-withdrawal punishment, 127, 131, 139
Low-density end of continuum, 26–27

Maintenance, 110–113
  extinction paradigms, 112–113
Manipulation by schizophrenic patients, effectiveness at, 292–298
Mastery, goal motivating identification, 15–16
Measurement of originality, 453–456
Mental health, 179–220
  as a rubric, 208–210
  conception of, 210
  list problem, 207–208
  positive, value-laden conception of, search for, 203–205
  religion and, 184–185
  value problem, 201–211
    modern approach to, 211–220
Mental illness, 179–220
  moral responsibility and, 199–200
  myth of, 184 n., 186–194
    brain disease, mental illness as sign of, 187–188
    choice, responsibility, psychiatry and, 192–193
    ethics in psychiatry, role of, 190–192
    problems in living, as a name for, 188–190
  personality disorder as disease, 194–201
    Szasz-Mowrer position, 195–200
  problems of living and, 198–199
    name for mental illness, 188–190
  religion and, 184–185
  sin, concept of, 181–186
Mental status induction, psychiatric interview, 294
Mental symptoms, brain pathology and, 196–197
  physical symptoms versus, 197–198
Middle-class discipline, 133–136
Model, conditioning, use of, 322–324
  fear reduction following observation of, 373–379
Monopolism, negative, 27–28
Moral development, parent discipline and, 126–140
  method of the study, 128–132
  results and discussion of the study, 132–140
Moral judgments, internalized, 129–130
Moral responsibility, mental illness and, 199–200
Morals, insight therapy and, 311–313
Mortality indexes, child, 128–131
Motivation, insufficient, 246–253, 260–261
  cooperation, urging and, 246–247
  nonverbal reward and punishment, 247–250
  verbal reward and punishment, 250–253
  social, 285–286
Motives, behavior, insight therapy and, 305–308
Muscle activity, somatic arousal and, 278–280
Myth of mental illness, 184 n., 186–194
  brain disease, as sign of, 187–188
  choice, responsibility, psychiatry and, 192–193

  ethics in psychiatry, role of, 190–192
  problems in living, as a name for, 188–190
Myth of the Birth of the Hero (Rank), 461

Narcissism, 8
Natural gifts, men classified according to, 415–427, 427–433
Nature of psychotherapy, 299–364
  behavior therapy and, 347–364
    analytic interpretations of, 360–363
    background of, theoretical, 348–350
    critique and reformulation of, 339–343
    desensitization, systematic, method of, 350–353
    desensitization with psychotherapy, interactions of, 357–360
    learning theory and, 344–347
  insight therapy, 299–316
    behavior, motives of, 305–308
    client-centered therapy, 302–305
    consciousness, uses of, 308–309
    morals and, 311–313
    problems of, 313–315
    psychoanalysis, 302–305
    science and, 309–311
    technical equivalence of, 300–302
  learning theory approaches to, critique and reformulation of, 316–338, 339–343
  behavior therapy and, 344–347
    conditioning model, uses of, 322–324
    learned materials, 320–322
    learning and, 320
    neuroses, conception of, 327–331
    reformulation, 336–338
    reinforcement, use of, 324–327
    science issue, 318–320
    success, claims of, 331–336
  psychoanalysis, insight therapy and, 302–305
Negative adaptation, elimination of children's fears through, 369–370
Negative monopolism, 27–28
Neurosis, conception of, 183, 185–186, 327–331
  existential, 222–239
    development, ideal and deviant, 236–237
    ideal personality, 231–236
    model for, 222–224
    precipitating stress, 229–231, 235–236
    premorbid personality, 226–229
    symptoms called, 224–226
  learning theory approaches to, critique and reformulation of, 316–338, 339–343
  conception of neurosis, 327–331
    conditioning model, use of, 322–324
    learned materials, 320–322
    learning and, 320
    reformulation, 336–338
    reinforcement, use of, 324–327
    science issues, 318–320
    success, claims of, 331–336
New Introductory Lectures on Psychoanalysis (Freud), 186
Nonverbal reward and punishment, 247–250
Nurturance, internalized consequences of punishment and, 115–118

Objective values, 212
Observation-rehearsal sequence, experiment on, 500–504
Oedipus complex, 4, 5, 7, 120, 121–122, 125
Open ward induction, psychiatric interview, 294
Operative values, 212
Oration on the Dignity of Man (Mirandola), 236
Originality, disposition toward, 451–460
    discussion of, 458–460
    habit and, logic of laughter, 446–447
    hypotheses suggested by previous work, 456–458
    measurement of, 453–456
    relativity of, 452
Overinclusion, interference theory, 256–257
Oxygen, schizophrenia and, 145–147

Pain, death of, 68–70
    inhibition of distress and, 67–75
Parental discipline, 120–121
    moral development of child and, 126–140
        method of the study, 128–132
        results and discussion of the study, 132–140
    practices of parent, measures of, 131–132
Patients, schizophrenic, see Schizophrenic patients
Personality, ideal, 231–235
    precipitating stress and, 235–236
    premorbid, 226–229
    realization of the creative potential and, 461–472
Personality disorder as disease, 194–201
    Szasz-Mowrer position, 195–200
        mental symptoms, brain pathology and, 196–197
        moral responsibility, mental illness and, 199–200
        physical symptoms, mental symptoms versus, 197–198
        problems of living, mental illness and, 198–199
Personality dysfunction, mental health and illness, 179–220
    myth of, 184 n., 186–194
    personality disorder as disease, 194–201
    sin, concept of, 181–186
    values, problem of, 201–211
    valuing process in the mature person, 211–220
    psychopathology, 221–298
        existential neurosis, 222–239
        schizophrenia, psychological deficit in, 239–262, 263–291
        schizophrenic patients in psychiatric interview, 292–298
    psychotherapy, effects of, 365–406
        children's fears, elimination of, 367–373
        fear reduction following observation of a model, 373–379
        insight therapy, desensitization versus, 379–396
        pseudotherapy, desensitization and, 397–406
    psychotherapy, nature of, 299–364

behavior therapy and, 347–364
insight therapy, 299–316
learning theory approaches to, critique and reformulation of, 316–338
Phobias, 180
Phobic systems, 335
Physical symptoms, mental symptoms versus, 197–198
Positive high density, ideo-affective organization, 28–32
Positive social behaviors, 409–507
    character traits, socially constructive, 473–507
        concern for others, origins of, 491–507
        honesty, generality of, 474–490
    genius, creativity and, 409–472
        creative potential, realization of, personality and, 461–472
        laughter, logic of, 434–450
        originality, disposition toward, 451–460
        reputation, men classified according to, 411–414, 427–433
        social gifts, men classified according to, 415–427, 427–433
Power assertion, disciplinary practice, 131
Precipitating stress, 229–231
    ideal personality and, 235–236
Premorbid personality, 226–229
Problem of Lay Analysis, The (Freud), 183
Problems of living, mental illness and, 188–190, 198–199
Prohibition learning, 10
    motives for, 14–15
Pseudotherapy, 398–400
    desensitization, suggestibility and, 397–406
"Psychiatric Folksong" (Russell), 182, 185
Psychiatry, choice and, 192–193
    ethics in, role of, 190–192
    interpersonal, interpretation of systematic desensitization from viewpoint of, 362
    responsibility and, 192–193
Psychoanalysis, 302–305
Psychological deficit in schizophrenia, 239–262, 263–291
    affect and reinforcement, 240–253
        motivation, insufficient, 246–253
        social censure, 240–242, 259–260
        stimuli, affective, 242–246, 253
    concept attainment, 254–259
        abstractness, loss of, 254
        communication, loss of, 254–255
        interference theory, 256–258, 262, 287–289
        regression to childish thinking, 255–256
    inference and activation, 263–291
        associative interference, 270–273
        attention, 264–269
        discussion, 285–291
        drive, 273–277, 286
        methodological considerations, 289–291
        set, 269–270
        somatic arousal, 277–285, 286–287
        theory, 285
Psychological determinants of emotional state, 44–65
Psychology, group, see Group psychology
    values in, see Values

Psychology, the Science of Mental Life (Miller), 87
Psychology of Laughter and Comedy (Grieg), 438
Psychopathology, 185, 221–298
  existential neurosis, 222–239
    development, ideal and deviant, 236–237
    ideal personality, 231–236
    model for, 222–224
    precipitating stress, 229–231, 235–236
    premorbid personality, 226–229
    symptoms called, 224–226
  reactivity and, 280–281
  schizophrenia, psychological deficit in, 239–262, 263–291
    affect and reinforcement, 240–253
    concept attainment, 254–259
    inference and activation, 263–291
  schizophrenic patients in psychiatric interview, 292–298
Psychosexual differences between kibbutz and nonkibbutz boys, 121–126
Psychosis, example of, 3–4
Psychotherapy, 179
  defense of, 353–357
    symptom substitution, problem of, 354–357
    therapy-theory distinction, 353–354
  effects of, *see* Effects of psychotherapy
  nature of, *see* Nature of psychotherapy
  sin in, concept of, 181–186
Punishment, 75–92
  consequences of, internalized, nurturance and, 115–118
  experiments, sample, 75–81
  legends, 86–91
  love-withdrawal, 127, 131, 139
  nonverbal, 247–250
  reproduction of, 114–115
  theory, 81–83
    applications of, 83–86
  verbal, 250–253

Reactive inhibition, reminiscence and, 276–277
Reactivity, pathology and, 280–281
  properties of the stimulus and, 281–284
Reflex, laughter, 436–438
Reformers, committed, 32–42
  commitment of society, engaging, 40–42
  increased commitment, 37–40
  resonance, original, 34–36
  risk is ventured, 36
  romances, deepened, 37–40
  suffering in consequence of risk taking, 36–37
Reformulation, behavior therapy, 336–338
Regression to childish thinking, 255–256, 261–262
Reinforcement, psychological deficit in schizophrenia, *see* Affect and reinforcement
  use of, 324–327
Reinstatement, 92–95
Relativity of originality, 452
Religion, mental health and, 184–185
Reminiscence, reactive inhibition and, 276–277

Repression, 182
  elimination of children's fears through, 370
Reputation, men classified according to, 411–414, 427–433
Respiration, cardiovascular system and, somatic arousal and, 278
Responsibility, moral, mental illness and, 199–200
  psychiatry and, 192–193
Reward, nonverbal, 247–250
  verbal, 250–253

Schizophrenia, biological theories of, 142–149, 151–163
  amines, 147–148
  amino acids, 147–148
  carbohydrate, 145–147
  ceruloplasmin, 152–156
  energetics, 145–147
  epinephrine hypothesis, 148–149
  error, sources of, 143–145
  oxygen, 145–147
  program of the Laboratory of Clinical Science, 145
  serotonin, 156–158
  taraxein, 152–156
  genetics and disorders of, 158–161
  psychological deficit in, 239–262, 263–291
    affect and reinforcement, 240–253
    concept attainment, 254–259
    inference and activation, 263–291
  twins, environmental factors in, 162
Schizophrenic patients, associations of, uncommonness of, 271
  interview of, psychiatric, 292–298
    induction conditions, 293–294
    method, 293–295
    predictions, 294–295
    results and discussion, 295–298
    subjects, 295
  manipulation by, effectiveness at, 292–298
Science, insight therapy and, 309–311
Self-criticism, acquisition, 97–110
    procedure for the study of, 104–108
    results and discussion of the study of, 108–110
    socialization, naturalistic and experimental, 100–102
    socialization paradigms, 102–104
    subject for the study of, 104
  learning of, 98–99
  maintenance, 110–113
    extinction paradigms, 112–113
  origin of, 95–119
  theoretical implications, further, 114–119
    internalized consequences of punishment, nurturance and, 115–118
    reproduction of punishment, 114–115
    self-evaluation, cognitive processes in, 118–119
Self-evaluation, cognitive processes in, 118–119
Serotonin, schizophrenia and, 156–158
Set, 269–270
Sex role acquisition, 4

Sin, concept of, in psychotherapy, 181–186
Skin color, 167
Skin resistance, basal, somatic arousal and, 278
Social behavior, positive, *see* Positive social behaviors
Social censure, 240–242, 259–260
Social determinants of emotional state, 44–65
Social imitation, elimination of children's fears through, 372
Socialization, experimental, 100–102
  naturalistic, 100–102
  paradigms, 102–104
Social motivation, 285–286
Somatic arousal, 277–285, 286–287
  activity, habitual level of, 277–284
    cardiovascular system, respiration and, 278
    muscle activity, 278–280
    skin resistance, basal, 278
  reactivity, pathology and, 280–281
  properties of the stimulus and, 281–284
Stimuli, "affective," 242–246, 253
  sensitivity to, 260
  censure, 242–244
  properties of, reactivity and, 281–284
Strategy, 321
Stress, precipitating, 229–231
  ideal personality and, 235–236
Studies in Deceit (Hartshorne and May), 489
Studies in Service and Self-Control (Hartshorne et al.), 484
Studies in the Organization of Character (Hartshorne et al.), 484, 488
Suffering, violence and, *see* Violence and suffering
Suggestibility, desensitization, pseudotherapy and, 397–406
Symptom formation, 5–6
Symptoms, existential neurosis, 224–226
  mental, brain pathology and, 196–197
    physical symptoms versus, 197–198
  physical, mental symptoms versus, 197–198
Symptom substitution, problem of, 354–357
Szasz-Mowrer position on mental illness, 195–200
  mental symptoms, brain pathology and, 196–197
  moral responsibility, mental illness and, 199–200
  physical symptoms, mental symptoms versus, 197–198
  problems of living, mental illness and, 198–199

Taraxein, schizophrenia and, 152–156
Therapy-theory distinction, 353–354
Thinking, childish, regression to, 255–256, 261–262
Transgression, overt reactions to, 130
Trauma of Birth, The (Rank), 461

Value problem, 205–207
Values, conceived, 212
  definition of, 212
  introjected, in station of experiencing, 216
  mental health and illness, meanings of, 179–220
    modern approach to, 211–220
    myth of, 184 n., 186–194
    personality disorder is disease, 194–201
    problem of, 201–211
    sin, concept of, 181–186
    valuing process in the mature person, 211–220
  objective, 212
  operative, 212
Valuing, characteristics of adult, 214–215
  contact with experience, restoring, 215–216
  discrepancy in, fundamental, 215
  infant's war of, 212–213
  introjected patterns of, 214
  process of, change in, 213–214
    mature person, 211–220
    outcomes of, propositions regarding, 218–220
    propositions regarding, 217–218
Verbal appeal, elimination of children's fears through, 369
Verbal Behavior (Skinner), 322, 323, 325
Verbal reward and punishment, 250–253
Vicarious affective experience, 10–11
Violence and suffering, constructive role of, 24–44
  high density end of continuum, 27–28
  ideo-affective density, 25
  low density end of continuum, 26–27
  reformers, committed, 32–42

Walden Two (Skinner), 86–87
Wrong doing, 182